T0230102

Lecture Notes in Computer Science 575

Edited by G. Goos and J. Hartmanis

Advisory Board: W. Brauer D. Gries J. Stoer

K. G. Larsen, A. Skou (Eds.)

Computer Aided Verification

3rd International Workshop, CAV '91
Aalborg, Denmark, July 1-4, 1991
Proceedings

Springer-Verlag
Berlin Heidelberg New York
London Paris Tokyo
Hong Kong Barcelona
Budapest

K. G. Larsen   A. Skou (Eds.)

Computer Aided Verification

3rd Intenational Workshop, CAV '91
Aalborg, Denmark, July 1-4, 1991
Proceedings

Springer-Verlag

Berlin Heidelberg New York
London Paris Tokyo
Hong Kong Barcelona
Budapest

Series Editors

Gerhard Goos
GMD Forschungsstelle
Universität Karlsruhe
Vincenz-Priessnitz-Straße 1
W-7500 Karlsruhe, FRG

Juris Hartmanis
Department of Computer Science
Cornell University
Upson Hall
Ithaca, NY 14853, USA

Volume Editors

Kim G. Larsen
Arne Skou
Institute for Electronic Systems
Dept. of Mathematics and Computer Science, Aalborg University
Frederik Bajers Vej 7, DK-9220 Aalborg, Denmark

CR Subject Classification (1991): C.2.2, C.3, F.3–4

ISBN 3-540-55179-4 Springer-Verlag Berlin Heidelberg New York
ISBN 0-387-55179-4 Springer-Verlag New York Berlin Heidelberg

Typesetting: Camera ready by author
Printing and binding: Druckhaus Beltz, Hemsbach/Bergstr.
45/3140-543210 - Printed on acid-free paper

Preface

This volume contains the proceedings of the *Third International Workshop on Computer Aided Verification*, CAV'91, held in Aalborg, Denmark, July 1–4, 1991. The objective of this series of workshops is to bring together researchers and practitioners interested in the development and use of methods, tools and theories for automatic verification of (finite) state systems. In particular, the workshop provides a unique opportunity for comparing the numerous verification methods and associated verification tools, and the extent to which they may be utilized in application design. The emphasis is not only on new research results but also on the applications of existing results to real verification problems.

The workshop was attended by 110 researchers and practitioners, and the presentations included 42 refereed papers plus 2 invited talks by Joseph Sifakis, IMAG Grenoble, France, and Colin Stirling, University of Edinburgh, Scotland. The papers cover the following topics, though the list is not exhaustive: verification and validation tools for hardware and software (hardware controllers, communication protocols, real–time systems, etc.); verification methods by theorem proving, model checking, automata based methods; and verification theories and their applicability. Special sessions for demonstration of 12 verification tools were scheduled. The material included in the proceedings was revised by the lecturers after the workshop took place.

The workshop was sponsored by the Danish National Research Council and by Aalborg University through the basic research project Programming Environments in Theory and Practice. The workshop series has official recognition from IFIP WG10.2 (Hardware Description Languages).

The overall planning of CAV'91 was carried out by the following Steering Committee: E.M. Clarke (Carnegie Mellon University), R.P. Kurshan (AT&T Bell Laboratories), K.G. Larsen (Aalborg University), A. Pnueli (Weizmann Institute), J. Sifakis (LGI–IMAG).

The following Program Committee was responsible for the reviewing and selection of papers: Gregor Bochmann (U. Montreal), Robert Brayton (U. California, Berkeley), Ed Brinksma (Twente U.), Randy Bryant (Carnegie Mellon), Rance Cleaveland (N.C. State), Olivier Coudert (Bull), Costas Courcoubetis (U. Crete), David Cohen (Bell Core), Werner Damm (U. Oldenburg), David Dill (Stanford U.), Allen Emerson (U. Texas, Austin), Masahiro Fujita (Fujitsu), Orna Grumberg (Technion), Hiromi Hiraishi (Kyoto U.), Gerard Holtzmann (AT&T Bell Labs), Bengt Jonsson (SICS), Kurt Keutzer (AT&T Bell Labs), Harry Lewis (Harvard), Michael Lightner (U.Colorado), George Milne (U. Strathclyde), Willem de Roever (Kiel U.), Prasad Sistla (GTE Labs), Colin Stirling (Edinburgh U.), P.A. Subrahmanyam (AT&T Bell Labs), Pierre Wolper (U. Liege), Michael Yoeli (Technion).

The local organizers wish to thank all the members of the Program Committee for their meritorious work in evaluating the submitted papers. We would also like to thank all referees who assisted the members of the Program Committee: P. Abdulla (U. Uppsala), F. Andersen (TFL–DK), A. Bailey (U. Strathclyde), M. Barbeau (U. Montreal), P. Berlioux (LGI–IMAG), J. Bradfield (U. Edinburgh), P. Broekroelofs (AT&T Bell Labs), G. Bruns (U. Edinburgh), J. Burch (Carnegie Mellon), H. Caravel (LGI–IMAG), M. Dam (U. Edinburgh), P. Ernberg (SICS), J. Feigenbaum (AT&T Bell Labs), J-C.Fernandez (LGI–IMAG), L. Fredlund (SICS), G. Gopalakrishnan (U. Montreal), S. Graf (LGI–IMAG), H. Hansson (SICS), H. Hüttel (U. Edinburgh), A. Ingolfsdottir (U. Aalborg), W.T.M. Kars (U. Twente), R. Langerak (U. Twente), M. Leightner (U. Colorado), L. Logrippo (U. Ottawa), D. Long (Carnegie Mellon), K.L. McMillan (Carnegie Mellon), F. Moller (U. Edinburgh), L. Mounier (LGI–IMAG), X. Nicollin (LGI–IMAG), M. Nielsen (U. Aarhus), J. Parrow (SICS), D. Probst (Concordia), C. Ratel (LGI–IMAG), A. Rensink (U. Twente), P. de Saqui-Sannes (U. Montreal), H. Schlingloff (Carnegie Mellon), R. Sharp (ID–DTH), G. Sjödin (SICS), J. Staunstrup (ID–DTH), R.J. Waldinger (Stanford U.), H. Wang-Toi (Stanford U.),

Aalborg, January 1992

Kim Guldstrand Larsen

Arne Skou

Contents

Session 1: Equivalence Checking

Taming Infinite State Spaces 1
C. Stirling (Edinburgh U.), (Invited Speaker)

Silence is Golden: Branching Bisimilarity is Decidable for Context–Free Processes 2
H. Hüttel (Edinburgh U.)

Computing Distinguishing Formulas for Branching Bisimulation 13
H. Korver (CWI, Amsterdam)

Session 2: Model Checking

Compositional Checking of Satisfaction 24
H. Andersen, G. Winskel (Aarhus U.)

An Action Based Framework for Verifying Logical and Behavioural Properties of
Concurrent Systems 37
R. De Nicola, A. Fantechi, S. Gnesi, G. Ristori (Pisa)

A Linear-Time Model-Checking Algorithm for the Alternation-Free Modal Mu-Calculus. 48
R. Cleaveland (North Carolina U.), B. Steffen (Aachen U.)

Session 3: Applications 1

Automatic Temporal Verification of Buffer Systems 59
A. P. Sistla (Illinois U.), L. D. Zuck (Yale U.)

Mechanically Checked Proofs of Kernel Specifications 70
W. Bevier (Comp. Logic, Austin), J. Søgaard-Andersen (ID-DTH, Copenhagen)

A Top Down Approach to the Formal Specification of SCI Cache Coherence 83
S. Gjessing, S. Krogdahl, E. Munthe–Kaas (Oslo U.)

Session 4: Applications 2

Integer Programming in the Analysis of Concurrent Systems 92
G. S. Avrunin, J. C. Corbett (Massachusetts U.), U. A. Buy (Illinois U.)

The Lotos Model of a Fault Protected System and its Verification Using a Petri Net
Based Approach 103
M. Barbeau, G. v Bochmann (Montreal U.)

Error Diagnosis in Finite Communicating Systems 114
A. Rasse (LGI-IMAG, Grenoble)

Temporal Precondition Verification of Design Transformations 125
R. Vemuri, A. Sridhar (Cincinnati U.)

Session 5: Tools for Process Algebras

Pam: A Process Algebra Manipulator 136
H. Lin (Sussex U.)

The Concurrency Workbench with Priorities 147
C. T. Jensen (Aarhus U.)

A Proof Assistant for PSF 158
S. Mauw, G. Veltink (Amsterdam U.)

Session 6: The State Explosion Problem

Avoiding State Explosion by Composition of Minimal Covering Graphs 169
A. Finkel (Cachan U.), L. Petrucci (CEDRIC-IIE, Evry)

"On the fly" Verification of Behavioural Equivalences and Preorders 181
J.-C. Fernanadez, L. Mounier (IMAG-LGI, Grenoble)

Bounded-memory Algorithms for Verification On-the-fly 192
C. Jard, Th. Jeron (IRISA, Rennes)

Session 7: Symbolic Model Checking

Generating BDDs for Symbolic Model Checking in CCS 203
R. Enders, T. Filkorn, D. Taubner (Siemens, Munich)

Vectorized Symbolic Model Checking of Computation Tree Logic for Sequential
Machine Verification 214
H. Hiraishi, K. Hamaguchi, H. Ochi, S. Yajima (Kyoto U.)

Functional Extension of Symbolic Model Checking 225
T. Filkorn (Siemens, Munich)

Session 8: Verification and Transformation Techniques

An Automated Proof Technique for Finite–State Machine Equivalence 233
W. Mao, G. Milne (Strathclyde U.)

From Data Structures to Process Structure 244
E. Brinksma (Twente U.)

Checking for Language Inclusion Using Simulation Relations 255
D. L. Dill, A. J. Hu, H. Wong-Toi (Stanford U.)

A Semantic Driven Method to Check the Finiteness of CCS Processes 266
N. de Francesco, P. Inverardi (Pisa)

Session 9: Higher Order Logic

Using the HOL Prove Assistant for Proving the Correctness of Term Rewriting
Rules reducing Terms of Sequential Behaviour.. 277
M. Mutz (Passau U.)

Mechanizing a Proof by Induction of Process Algebra Specifications in Higher Order Logic   288
M. Nesi (Cambridge U.)

A Two-Level Formal Verification Methodology using HOL and COSMOS................ 299
C.-J. Seger, J. J. Joyce (British Columbia U.)

Efficient Algorithms for Verification of Equivalences for Probabilistic Processes 310
L. Christoff, I. Christoff (Uppsala U.)

Session 10: Partial Order Approaches

Partial-Order Model Checking: A Guide for the Perplexed............................. 322
D. K. Probst, H. F. Li (Concordia U.)

Using Partial Orders for the Efficient Verification of Deadlock Freedom and Safety
Properties 332
P. Godefroid, P. Wolper (Liège U.)

Complexity Results for POMSET Languages.. 343
J. Feigenbaum, C. Lund (AT&T), J. A. Kahn (Harvard)

Session 11: Hardware Verification

Mechanically Verifying Safety and Liveness Properties of Delay Insensitive Circuits 354
D. M. Goldschlag (Comp. Logic, Austin)

Automating Most Parts of Hardware Tools in HOL.................................... 365
K. Schneider, R. Kumar, T. Kropf (Karlsruhe U.)

Session 13: Timed Specification and Verification 1

An Overview and Synthesis on Timed Process Algebras 376
J. Sifakis (IMAG-LGI, Grenoble), (Invited Speaker)

Minimum and Maximum Delay Problems In Real-Time Systems....................... 399
C. Courcoubetis (Crete U.), M. Yannakakis (AT&T)

Formal Verification of Speed-Dependent Asynchronous Circuits Using Symbolic
Model Checking of Branching Time Regular Temporal Logic 410
K. Hamaguchi, H. Hiraishi, S. Yajima (Kyoto U.)

Session 14: Timed Specification and Verification 2

Verifying Properties of HMS Machine Specifications of Real-Time Systems.............. 421
A. Gabrielian, R. Iyer (Thomson-CSF, Palo Alto)

A Linear Time Process Algebra.. 432
A. Jeffrey (Chalmers U.)

Deciding Properties of Regular Real Timed Processes 443
U. Holmer, W. Yi (Chalmers U.), K. Larsen (Aalborg U.)

Session 15: Automata

An Algebra of Boolean Processes... 454
C. Corcoubetis (Crete U.), S. Graf, J. Sifakis (LGI-IMAG, Grenoble)

Comparing Generic State Machines 466
M. Langevin, E. Cerny (Montreal U.)

An Automata Theoretic Approach to Temporal Logic 477
G. G. de Jong (Eindhoven U.)

Taming Infinite State Spaces

Colin Sterling
Department of Computer Science
University of Edinburgh
Edinburgh EH9 3JZ, U.K.

Abstract

We present a sound and complete tableau proof system for establishing whether a set of elements of an arbitrary transition system model has a property expressed in (a slight extension of) the modal mu-calculus. The proof system, we belcive, offers a very general verification method applicable to a wide range of computational systems.

Silence is Golden:
Branching Bisimilarity is Decidable for Context-Free Processes

Hans Hüttel *

Laboratory for the Foundations of Computer Science, JCMB
University of Edinburgh, Edinburgh EH9 3JZ
SCOTLAND

Abstract

We show that the branching bisimulation equivalence introduced by Rob
van Glabbeek is decidable for the class of normed, recursively defined BPA
processes with silent actions, thus generalizing the decidability result for
strong bisimilarity by Baeten, Bergstra, and Klop.

1 Introduction

In their paper [BBK87] Baeten, Bergstra, and Klop showed that strong bisimulation equivalence is
decidable for normed recursively defined BPA processes [BK88], a class of processes corresponding to
that of irredundant context-free grammars without empty productions. In this paper we generalize
this result by showing that the branching bisimilation equivalence introduced by van Glabbeek and
Weijland in [vGW89] is decidable for the class of normed recursively defined BPA processes with
silent actions. The proof generalizes that of the decidability of strong bisimulation equivalence given
by Colin Stirling and the present author in [HS91], relying as it does on a similar tableau-based
decision method. This tableau method is related to the equivalence algorithms for certain classes
of context-free grammars introduced by Korenjak and Hopcroft [KH66], and it directly reflects
usual intuitions about determining the equivalence of processes by means of successive matchings
of transitions.

Since the class of processes considered allows infinite state spaces, the present result further under-
pins the fact that the decidability of behavioural equivalences can extend beyond the finite-state
case, and that decidability should be seen as a criterion for determining the relative merits and
deficiencies of behavioural equivalences.

Section 2 introduces the notion of branching bisimilarity and the class of normed BPA^τ_{rec} processes.
In Section 3 we describe the tableau system, prove its soundness and completeness, give a complexity
measure and establish the decidability result of branching bisimilarity. Section 4 sums up conclusions
and gives suggestions for further work.

---

*Present address: Department of Mathematics and Computer Science, Aalborg University Centre, Fredrik Bajer-
svej 7E, 9220 Aalborg Ø, Denmark. E-mail: hans@iesd.auc.dk

2 Preliminaries

2.1 Branching bisimilarity

The processes that we will be looking at have their behavioural semantics given by transition graphs with silent actions. For comparison we first describe the notion of weak bisimulation equivalence, introduced by Milner [Mil80, Mil89], which is essentially bisimulation equivalence defined on the derived *weak* transition relations that disregard silent actions.

Definition 2.1 *For a transition graph* $\mathcal{G} = (Pr, Act \cup \{\tau\}, \rightarrow)$ *with silent action* τ, *the weak transition relations* $\{ \stackrel{s}{\Longrightarrow} \mid s \in Act \cup \{\epsilon\} \}$ *are given by* $\stackrel{a}{\Longrightarrow} = \stackrel{\tau}{\rightarrow}{}^* \stackrel{a}{\rightarrow} \stackrel{\tau}{\rightarrow}{}^*$ *for* $a \in Act$ *and* $\stackrel{\epsilon}{\Longrightarrow} = \stackrel{\tau}{\rightarrow}{}^*$

In the definition below, we use the 'observational' mapping $\phi : (Act \cup \{\tau\})^* \rightarrow Act^*$ which is the homomorphic extension of the function defined by $\phi(a) = a$ for $a \in Act$ and $\phi(\tau) = \epsilon$.

Definition 2.2 [Mil89] *A weak bisimulation on* $\mathcal{G}$ *is a symmetric relation* $R \subseteq Pr \times Pr$ *such that whenever* pRq *for any* $a \in Act \cup \{\tau\}$ *we have that* $p \stackrel{a}{\rightarrow} p'$ *implies that there exists a* q' *such that* $q \stackrel{\phi(a)}{\Longrightarrow} q'$ *with* $p'Rq'$. *We define* $\approx$ *by*

$$\approx = \{(p,q) \mid pRq \text{ for some weak bisimulation } R\}$$

If $p \approx q$ *we say that* p *and* q *are* weakly bisimilar.

The notion of branching bisimilarity was put forward by van Glabbeek and Weijland in [vGW89] as an alternative to weak bisimulation.

Definition 2.3 [vGW89] *A branching bisimulation (bb) on* $\mathcal{G}$ *is a symmetric relation* $R \subseteq Pr \times Pr$ *such that whenever* pRq *for any* $a \in Act \cup \{\tau\}$ *we have that* $p \stackrel{a}{\rightarrow} p'$ *implies*

- $a = \tau$ *and* $p'Rq$ *or*
- *there exist* q'_1, q' *such that* $q \stackrel{\epsilon}{\Longrightarrow} q'_1 \stackrel{a}{\rightarrow} q'$ *with* $pRq'_1, p'Rq'$

We define $\approx_b$ *by*

$$\approx_b = \{(p,q) \mid pRq \text{ for some bb } R\}$$

If $p \approx_b q$ *we say that* p *and* q *are* branching bisimilar.

Unlike weak bisimulation equivalence, changes in branching properties caused by individual τ-transitions must always be taken into account in branching bisimulation. (Example 2.2 provides an example of the importance of this, namely two processes that are weakly bisimilar but not branching bisimilar). An equivalent definition which reflects this *stuttering property* better is the one below which we will be using in the tableau system presented in Section 3.

Proposition 2.1 *A branching bisimulation on* $\mathcal{G}$ *is a symmetric relation* $R \subseteq Pr \times Pr$ *such that whenever* pRq *for any* $a \in Act \cup \{\tau\}$ *we have that if* $p \stackrel{a}{\rightarrow} p'$ *then either*

- $a = \tau$ *and* $p'Rq$ *or*
- *there exist* $q'_0, \ldots, q'_n, q'$ *such that* $q = q'_0 \stackrel{\tau}{\rightarrow} q'_1 \stackrel{\tau}{\rightarrow} \cdots \stackrel{\tau}{\rightarrow} q'_n \stackrel{a}{\rightarrow} q'$ *with* pRq'_i *for* $0 \leq i \leq n$ *and* $p'Rq'$.

2.2 Normed BPA$^\tau_{rec}$

Recursive Basic Process Algebra (BPA) with silent actions, the class BPA$^\tau_{rec}$ [BK88], consists of processes given by systems of defining equations $\Delta = \{X_i \stackrel{\text{def}}{=} E_i \mid 1 \leq i \leq m\}$. The process expressions E_i are given by the syntax

$$E ::= a \mid \tau \mid E_1 + E_2 \mid E_1 E_2 \mid X$$

where τ is a new, silent action not in Act. In the following, elements of Var^* will be denoted by Greek letters: $\alpha, \beta, \ldots$ and BPA expressions in general by $E, F \ldots$. The operational semantics given by the transition relations $\{\stackrel{a}{\rightarrow} \mid a \in Act \cup \{\tau\}\}$ is as given below.

Definition 2.4 *Any system of BPA process equations Δ defines a labelled transition graph. The transition relations are given as the least relations satisfying the following rules:*

$$\frac{E \stackrel{a}{\rightarrow} E'}{E + F \stackrel{a}{\rightarrow} E'} \qquad\qquad \frac{F \stackrel{a}{\rightarrow} F'}{E + F \stackrel{a}{\rightarrow} F'}$$

$$\frac{E \stackrel{a}{\rightarrow} E'}{EF \stackrel{a}{\rightarrow} E'F} \qquad\qquad a \stackrel{a}{\rightarrow} \epsilon \quad a \in Act \cup \{\tau\}$$

$$\frac{E \stackrel{a}{\rightarrow} E'}{X \stackrel{a}{\rightarrow} E'} \quad X \stackrel{\text{def}}{=} E \in \Delta$$

We restrict our attention to *weakly normed* systems of process equations.

Definition 2.5 *The* weak norm *of any $X \in Var$ is given by*

$$\|X\| = \min\{length(w) \mid X \stackrel{w}{\Longrightarrow} \epsilon, w \in Act^*\}$$

A system of defining equations Δ is weakly normed if for any $X \in Var$ $0 < \|X\| < \infty$. The maximal norm of any variable in Δ is defined by $M_\Delta = \max\{\|X\| \mid X \in Var\}$.

Since norms must be strictly positive, all variables must eventually perform an observable action and processes can therefore *not* terminate silently.

In Section 3 we shall also need the notion of a strong norm (cf. [HS91]).

Definition 2.6 *The* strong norm *of a BPA$^\tau_{rec}$ expression E is defined as*

$$|E| = \min\{length(w) \mid E \stackrel{w}{\rightarrow} \epsilon, w \in Act^+\}$$

A system of defining equations Δ is strongly normed if for any variable $X \in Var$ $|X| < \infty$. The maximal strong norm of any variable in Δ is $m_\Delta = \max\{|X| \mid X \in Var\}$.

Clearly, if Δ is weakly normed it is also strongly normed.

Finally, we restrict our attention to systems of defining equations given in 3-Greibach Normal Form (3-GNF).

Definition 2.7 *A system of BPA equations* Δ *is said to be in* Greibach Normal Form (GNF) *if all equations are of the form*

$$\{X_i \stackrel{\text{def}}{=} \sum_{j=1}^{n_i} a_{ij}\alpha_{ij} \mid 1 \leq i \leq m\}$$

If for each i, j *the variable sequence* α_{ij} *has* $length(\alpha_{ij}) < k$, Δ *is said to be in* k-GNF.

The normal form is called Greibach Normal Form by analogy with context-free grammars (without the empty production) in Greibach Normal Form (see e.g. [HU79]). There is an obvious correspondence with grammars in GNF: process variables correspond to non-terminals, the root is the start symbol, actions correspond to terminals, and each equation $X_i \stackrel{\text{def}}{=} \sum_{j=1}^{n_i} a_{ij}\alpha_{ij}$ can be viewed as the family of productions $\{X_i \rightarrow a_{ij}\alpha_{ij} \mid 1 \leq j \leq n_i\}$. The notion of normedness says that the grammar must not have useless productions. The requirement of norms being positive is in analogy with the requirement that a grammar has no empty productions.

It is well-known that any context-free language (without the empty string) is generated by a grammar in 3-GNF [HU79]. One can show that actually is not a real restriction, since any system of process equations Δ in $\text{BPA}^{\tau}_{\text{rec}}$ can effectively be rewritten to a Δ' which is *strongly* bisimilar to Δ and therefore weakly normed iff Δ is [BBK87]. This leaves us with transition graphs whose states are strings of process variables; the further restriction to variable sequences of length at most 2 guarantees limited growth when determining single transitions:

Proposition 2.2 *Suppose* Δ *is in 3-GNF. Then, for any* $\alpha \in Var^*$, *whenever* $\alpha \stackrel{a}{\rightarrow} \alpha'$ *we have* $length(\alpha') \leq length(\alpha) + 1$.

Because weak norms are assumed strictly positive, we have a simple relationship between lengths and norms:

Proposition 2.3 *For* $\alpha \in Var^*$ $length(\alpha) \leq ||\alpha||$ *and* $||\alpha|| \leq M_\Delta length(\alpha)$.

The weak norm is additive under sequential composition:

Proposition 2.4 *For* $\alpha, \beta \in Var^*$ $||\alpha\beta|| = ||\alpha|| + ||\beta||$.

Note that for weakly normed systems we have

Proposition 2.5 $\alpha \approx_b \beta$ *implies that* $||\alpha|| = ||\beta||$.

Example 2.1 Consider $\Delta_1 = \{A \stackrel{\text{def}}{=} a + bBC; B \stackrel{\text{def}}{=} \tau A; C \stackrel{\text{def}}{=} c\}$ and $\Delta_2 = \{X \stackrel{\text{def}}{=} a + bXY; Y \stackrel{\text{def}}{=} c\}$. The transition graphs are shown in Figure 1. For Δ_1 we have $L_{obs}(A) = \{b^n ac^n \mid n \geq 0\}$, $L_{obs}(B) = L_{obs}(A)$ and $L_{obs}(C) = \{c\}$. $X \approx_b A$ because of the branching bisimulation

$$\{(XY^n, AC^n) \mid n \geq 0\} \cup \{(XY^n, BC^n) \mid n \geq 1\} \cup \{(Y^n, C^n) \mid n \geq 1\} \cup \{(\epsilon, \epsilon)\}$$

$\square$

For the tableau system we need the following results - firstly, $\approx_b$ is a congruence w.r.t. sequential composition:

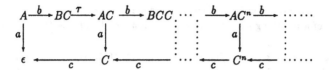

Figure 1: Transition graph for $A \stackrel{\text{def}}{=} a + bBC$; $B \stackrel{\text{def}}{=} \tau A$; $C \stackrel{\text{def}}{=} c$

Proposition 2.6 *If $\alpha_1 \approx_b \beta_1$ and $\alpha_2 \approx_b \beta_2$ then $\alpha_1 \alpha_2 \approx_b \beta_1 \beta_2$*

The other result is a 'split' lemma that allows us to discard identical tails:

Lemma 2.1 *If $\alpha_1 \alpha \approx_b \alpha_2 \alpha$ then $\alpha_1 \approx_b \alpha_2$.*

It is important to note that this does *not* hold for weak bisimulation. The following counterexample arose in a discussion with Kim Larsen and is due to him.

Example 2.2 Consider $\Delta = \{X = aY, Y = a + \tau X, A = a + aB, B = a\}$. As $\|X\| = 2, \|Y\| = 1, \|A\| = 1$ and $\|B\| = 1$, Δ clearly obeys all requirements stated above. It is easily seen that $X \approx BY$ and that $A \not\approx B$. However, we have $AY \approx BY$, since $\{(AY, BY), (BY, X), (Y, Y), (\epsilon, \epsilon), (X, X)\}$ is a weak bisimulation. The problem lies in the fact that weak bisimilarity does not require the results of intermediate steps in weak transitions to be related. In particular, $AY \stackrel{a}{\to} Y$ is matched by $BY \Longrightarrow X$. The latter is due to $BY \stackrel{a}{\to} Y \stackrel{\tau}{\to} X$, where we clearly have that $AY \not\approx Y$. □

3 A tableau system for branching bisimulation

3.1 Building tableaux

A tableau for determining branching bisimilarity is a maximal proof tree built using the proof rules in Table 1. Tableaux consist of a number of subtableaux. These are built from successive applications of the STEP rule.

STEP is applicable iff there is a possibility of matching transitions. A *possible match* is any set of equations whose sides are the results of successful matching transitions according to the definition of branching bisimilarity in Proposition 2.1:

Definition 3.1 *A set of equations M is a possible match for $\alpha = \beta$ if for any $a \in Act$ we have that if $\alpha \stackrel{a}{\to} \alpha'$ then either*

- *$a = \tau$ and $\alpha' = \beta \in M$ or*

- *there exist $\beta_0' = \beta, \ldots, \beta_n', \beta'$ such that $\beta_0 \stackrel{\tau}{\to} \beta_1' \stackrel{\tau}{\to} \cdots \stackrel{\tau}{\to} \beta_n' \stackrel{a}{\to} \beta'$ with $\alpha = \beta_i' \in M$ for $0 \le i \le n$ and $\alpha' = \beta' \in M$.*

and similarly for any $\beta \stackrel{a}{\to} \beta'$.

This definition appears to allow *infinitely* many possible matches, since there seems to be no bound on the length n of a matching transition sequence. However, this is not the case. Firstly, we have

Proposition 3.1 *If $\alpha \approx_b \beta$ we can find a possible match M for $\alpha = \beta$ such that whenever $\alpha \xrightarrow{a} \alpha'$ is matched by $\beta'_0 = \beta, \ldots, \beta'_n, \beta'$ such that $\beta_0 \xrightarrow{\tau} \beta'_1 \xrightarrow{\tau} \cdots \xrightarrow{\tau} \beta'_n \xrightarrow{a} \beta'$ with $\alpha = \beta'_i \in M$ for $0 \leq i \leq n$ and $\alpha' = \beta' \in M$ all β'_i $(0 \leq i \leq n)$ are distinct.*

Secondly, we have

Proposition 3.2 *If $X\alpha \approx_b Y\beta$ and $X\alpha \xrightarrow{a} \alpha'\alpha$ is matched by $Y\beta \stackrel{\epsilon}{\Longrightarrow} \beta'_1\beta \xrightarrow{a} \beta'\beta$ any intermediate state β'' in $Y\beta \stackrel{\epsilon}{\Longrightarrow} \beta'_1\beta$ has $length(\beta'') \leq M_\Delta + length(\beta)$. Furthermore, $length(\beta') \leq M_\Delta + length(\beta) + 1$*

The outbranching is a multiple of the bound $B_{X,Y}$ on the number of single transition steps for $X\alpha = Y\beta$; this factor only depends on the leftmost variables and is given by

$$B_{X,Y} = \{\alpha' \mid X \xrightarrow{a} \alpha', a \in Act \cup \{\tau\}\} \cup \{\beta' \mid Y\beta \xrightarrow{a} \beta', a \in Act \cup \{\tau\}\}$$

Proposition 3.3 *Let v be the cardinality of Var. If $X\alpha \approx_b Y\beta$, there is a possible match for $X\alpha = Y\beta$ with at most $B_{X,Y} \sum_{j=2}^{2K} (j-1)v^j$ equations, where $K = M_\Delta + 1 + \max(length(\alpha), length(\beta))$.*

Clearly, STEP is forwards sound in the following sense:

Proposition 3.4 (Forwards soundness of STEP) *If $\alpha \approx_b \beta$, then there is a possible match M such that whenever $\alpha' = \beta' \in M$ we have $\alpha' \approx_b \beta'$.*

An eliminating subtableau for $X\alpha = Y\beta$ consists of attempted matches to the depth where an equation of the form $\alpha = \gamma\beta$ is reached. When $|X| \leq |Y|$ each non-residual leaf of an eliminating subtableau for $X\alpha = Y\beta$ is either labelled $\alpha = \gamma\beta$ (a *residual* of the subtableau), or $\alpha_i\alpha = \beta_i\beta$. Because the number of successive attempted matches is $|X|$ there is at least one residual and since all norms are strictly positive, α and β must persist as suffixes throughout the subtableau. For any such subtableau we pick one residual node and call it *the* residual. If instead $|Y| < |X|$ the same holds, only now the residual is $\gamma\alpha = \beta$. Unless a subtableau leaf is a successful terminal (Definition 3.3 below) it is used as the basis of a new subtableau. However, before a new subtableau is constructed, for every leaf one of the SUB rules is used to trim the length of the expressions in the new subtableau root. From Propositions 2.6 and 2.1 we see that the SUB rules are forwards sound in the following sense:

Proposition 3.5 (Soundness of SUBL and SUBR) *If $\alpha_i\alpha \approx_b \beta_i\beta$ and $\alpha \approx_b \gamma\beta$ then $\alpha_i\gamma \approx_b \beta_i$. If $\gamma\alpha_i \approx_b \beta_i$ then $\alpha_i \approx_b \beta_i\gamma$*

The rules are only applied to nodes that are not *terminal*. Terminal nodes can either be *successful* or *unsuccessful*.

Definition 3.2 *A tableau node is an* unsuccessful terminal *if it has one of the forms*

    1. $\alpha = \beta$ *with* $\|\alpha\| \neq \|\beta\|$

    2. $\alpha = \beta$ *with* $\alpha \neq \epsilon, \beta \neq \epsilon$ *and no possible match exists (i.e. STEP is inapplicable).*

Rule within a subtableau

STEP $\quad \dfrac{\alpha = \beta}{\alpha_1 = \beta_1 \dots \alpha_k = \beta_k} \qquad$ where $\{\alpha_1 = \beta_1 \dots \alpha_k = \beta_k\}$

$\qquad\qquad\qquad\qquad\qquad\qquad\qquad$ is a possible match for $\alpha = \beta$

Rules for new subtableaux

SUBL $\quad \dfrac{\alpha_i \alpha = \beta_i \beta}{\alpha_i \gamma = \beta_i} \qquad$ where $\alpha = \gamma\beta$ is the residual

SUBR $\quad \dfrac{\alpha_i \alpha = \beta_i \beta}{\alpha_i = \beta_i \gamma} \qquad$ where $\gamma\alpha = \beta$ is the residual

Table 1: The tableau rules

In both of these cases it is obvious that the expressions compared are not branching bisimilar. Thus, whenever we see an unsuccessful terminal the whole tableau construction aborts.

The nodes that can be successful terminals are those that are potential roots of eliminating subtableaux:

Definition 3.3 *A residual or consequent of an application of a SUB rule is a successful terminal if it has one of the forms*

1. $\alpha = \beta$ *where there is another subtableau root above it on the path from the root also labelled* $\alpha = \beta$

2. $\alpha = \alpha$

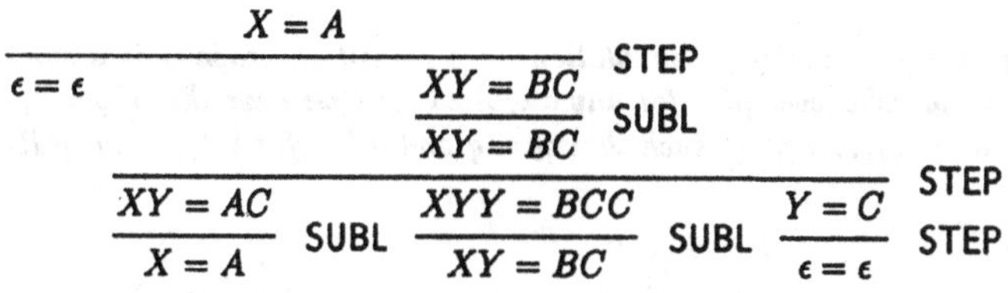

$$\dfrac{\quad \dfrac{\quad \dfrac{\quad \dfrac{X = A}{XY = BC}\ \text{STEP}}{XY = BC}\ \text{SUBL} \quad}{\dfrac{XY = AC}{X = A}\ \text{SUBL} \quad \dfrac{XYY = BCC}{XY = BC}\ \text{SUBL} \quad \dfrac{Y = C}{\epsilon = \epsilon}\ \begin{array}{l}\text{STEP}\\\text{STEP}\end{array}}}{\epsilon = \epsilon}$$

Figure 2: A successful tableau for $X = A$

Example 3.1 (Example 2.1 cont.) The tableau in Figure 2 is a successful tableau for $X = A$. $\quad\square$

3.2 Termination, completeness, and soundness

It is important for our decidability result that all tableaux are finite. Since our tableaux are finitely branching by Proposition 3.3, by König's Lemma an infinite tableau would have an infinite path. This would then be caused by the combined absence of unsuccessful termination and the successful termination condition 1 along that path. Since we have assumed 3-GNF and normedness, there is a uniform bound on the total length of the consequent of a SUB rule. Assume wlog that we have a subtableau with root $X\alpha = Y\beta$ and that a SUBL rule was applied to a subtableau leaf:

$$\frac{\alpha_1\alpha = \beta_1\beta}{\alpha_1\gamma = \beta_1} \quad \text{SUBL}$$

Because the depth of the subtableau is at most m_Δ, repeated applications of Proposition 3.2 tell us that $length(\alpha_1) \leq m_\Delta(M_\Delta + 1)$, $length(\beta_1) \leq m_\Delta(M_\Delta + 1)$ and $length(\gamma) \leq m_\Delta(M_\Delta + 1)$. This implies a uniform bound on the length of SUB consequents of $3m_\Delta(M_\Delta + 1)$, so there can be no infinite path through infinitely many SUB applications since there are of course only finitely many different equations of any given length. Nor can an infinite path pass through infinitely many residuals. For if a residual $\alpha_0 = \beta_0$ is above the residual $\alpha_1 = \beta_1$ we have that $||\alpha_0|| = ||\beta_0|| < ||\alpha_1|| = ||\beta_1||$. By Proposition 2.3, any subsequence of residuals therefore has a uniform bound on the total lengths of expressions compared, again ensuring termination.

Theorem 3.1 *For any equation $\alpha = \beta$ all tableaux are finite.*

By the forwards soundness of the STEP and SUB rules (Propositions 3.4 and 3.5) we can use the tableau rules in such a way that only valid consequents arise. It is therefore easily seen that the tableau system is complete:

Theorem 3.2 *If $\alpha \approx_b \beta$, $\alpha = \beta$ has a successful tableau.*

Finally we must show soundness of the tableau system, namely that the existence of a successful tableau for $\alpha = \beta$ indicates that $\alpha \approx_b \beta$. This follows from the fact that the tableau system tries to construct a 'bisimulation up to a sequential congruence', which, if a successful tableau is reached, consists of the symmetric closure of the set of nodes in the successful tableau. This notion is the counterpart of the notion of a self-bisimulation used in the tableau system of [HS91] and in [Cau90]. In order to define the corresponding notion for branching bisimulation, we need a simple rephrasing of Proposition 2.1:

Proposition 3.6 *A branching bisimulation on a transition graph $\mathcal{G}$ is a symmetric relation $R \subseteq Pr \times Pr$ such that whenever pRq for any $a \in Act \cup \{\tau\}$ we have that if $p = p_0 \xrightarrow{\tau} p_1 \xrightarrow{\tau} \cdots p_m \xrightarrow{a} p'$ then there exist $q_0, q_1, \ldots, q_m, q'$ such that $q_0 = q$ and p_iRq_i for $1 \leq i \leq m$, $p'Rq'$ and for $i < m$*

-
  - $q_i = q_{i+1}$ *or*
  - *there exist $q_{i_1}, \ldots, q_{i_{n(i)}}$ such that $q_i \xrightarrow{\tau} q_{i_1} \xrightarrow{\tau} \cdots q_{i_{n(i)}} \xrightarrow{\tau} q_{i+1}$ with p_iRq_{ij} for $1 \leq j \leq n(i)$*

and either

- $a = \tau$ *and* $q_m = q'$ *or*

- there exist $q_{m_1}, \ldots, q_{m_{n(m)}}$ such that $q_m \xrightarrow{\tau} q_{m_1} \xrightarrow{\tau} \cdots q_{m_{n(m)}} \xrightarrow{a} q'$

Definition 3.4 *For any binary relation R on Var^*, $\xrightarrow[R]{}$ is the least precongruence w.r.t. sequential composition that contains R, $\underset{R}{\longleftrightarrow}$ the symmetric congruence of $\xrightarrow[R]{}$ and $\underset{R}{\longleftrightarrow^*}$ the transitive closure of $\underset{R}{\longleftrightarrow}$ and thus the least congruence w.r.t. sequential composition containing R.*

Definition 3.5 *A branching bisimulation up to sequential congruence (sbb) is a symmetric relation $R \subseteq Var \times Var$ such that whenever $\alpha R \beta$ $\alpha = \epsilon$ iff $\beta = \epsilon$ and for any $a \in Act \cup \{\tau\}$ we have that if $\alpha = \alpha_0 \xrightarrow{\tau} \alpha_1 \xrightarrow{\tau} \cdots \alpha_m \xrightarrow{a} \alpha'$ then there exist $\beta_0, \beta_1, \ldots, \beta_m, \beta'$ such that $\beta_0 = \beta$ and $\alpha_i \underset{R}{\longleftrightarrow^*} \beta_i$ for $1 \le i \le m$, $\alpha' \underset{R}{\longleftrightarrow^*} \beta'$ and for $i < m$*

- $\quad - \ \beta_i = \beta_{i+1}$ or
  $\quad -$ there exist $\beta_{i_1}, \ldots, \beta_{i_{n(i)}}$ s.t. $\beta_i \xrightarrow{\tau} \beta_{i_1} \xrightarrow{\tau} \cdots \beta_{i_{n(i)}} \xrightarrow{\tau} \beta_{i+1}$ with $\alpha_i \underset{R}{\longleftrightarrow^*} \beta_{ij}$
  $\quad \ \ $ for $1 \le j \le n(i)$

and either

- $a = \tau$ and $\beta_m = \beta'$ or

- there exist $\beta_{m_1}, \ldots, \beta_{m_{n(i)}}$ s.t. $\beta_m \xrightarrow{\tau} \beta_{m_1} \xrightarrow{\tau} \cdots \beta_{m_{n(m)}} \xrightarrow{a} \beta'$ with $\alpha_m \underset{R}{\longleftrightarrow^*} \beta_{mj}$ for $1 \le j \le n(m)$.

The reason why a bisimulation up to sequential congruence can be said to be an essential part of a bisimulation lies in the following result.

Lemma 3.1 *If R is an sbb then $\underset{R}{\longleftrightarrow^*}$ is a bb.*

Corollary 3.1 *$\alpha \approx_b \beta$ iff there is an sbb R such that $\alpha R \beta$.*

We then have

Theorem 3.3 *If $\alpha = \beta$ has a successful tableau $\mathbf{T}$ then*

$$R_{\mathbf{T}} = \{(\alpha', \beta') \mid \alpha' = \beta' \text{ or } \beta' = \alpha' \text{ is an equation in } \mathbf{T}\}$$

is an sbb.

So we now get the soundness of the tableau system as

Corollary 3.2 *If $\alpha = \beta$ has a successful tableau then $\alpha \approx_b \beta$.*

3.3 Complexity of the tableau system and decidability

The complexity of the tableau system can be measured in terms of the maximal depth of a tableau, i.e. the length w.r.t. STEP applications of the longest possible path in a successful tableau for an equation $X\alpha = Y\beta$. Let v be the cardinality of Var. By the discussion preceding Theorem 3.1 we have that any SUB consequent has a length of at most $3m_\Delta(M_\Delta + 1)$, so an upper bound on the number of distinct SUB consequents along any tableau path is $\sum_{j=2}^{3m_\Delta(M_\Delta+1)}(j-1)v^j$. Between any two SUB consequents there can be at most $\lceil\frac{3m_\Delta(M_\Delta+1)}{2}\rceil$ residuals, so any path that contains SUB consequents can have at most $\lceil\frac{3m_\Delta(M_\Delta+1)}{2}\rceil\sum_{j=2}^{3m_\Delta M_\Delta+3}(j-1)v^j$ subtableau roots. As for the leftmost path, all of whose subtableau roots are residuals, there can be at most $\max(||\alpha||, ||\beta||)$ residuals, since the norm of the residuals is strictly decreasing. So, since a subtableau can have a depth w.r.t. STEP applications of at most m_Δ, any path can have a length of at most

$$m_\Delta \max(||\alpha||, ||\beta||, \lceil\frac{3m_\Delta(M_\Delta + 1)}{2}\rceil \sum_{j=2}^{3m_\Delta(M_\Delta+1)} (j-1)v^j) \tag{1}$$

STEPs.

We also have an upper bound on the outbranching of any tableau for $X\alpha = Y\beta$. This follows from the fact that there is a uniform upper bound on the total length of any subtableau root in any tableau for $X\alpha = Y\beta$. The length of any subtableau root is bounded by

$$L = \max(2\max(||\alpha||, ||\beta||), 3m_\Delta(M_\Delta + 1))$$

By repeated applications of Proposition 3.2 we see that any node in a subtableau has a length of at most $2m_\Delta(M_\Delta + 1) + L$. By Proposition 3.3 this means that there is a uniform upper bound on the number of STEP consequents at any point in any tableau for $X\alpha = Y\beta$ of

$$\max\{B_{X,Y} \mid X, Y \in Var\} \sum_{j=2}^{2m_\Delta(M_\Delta+1)+L} (j-1)v^j \tag{2}$$

This means that any $X\alpha = Y\beta$ has finitely many possible tableaux, so we get the main result

Theorem 3.4 *For any weakly normed Δ it is decidable whether or not $\alpha \approx_b \beta$ for $\alpha, \beta \in Var^*$.*

The naive decision procedure for $\approx_b$ constructs all the finitely many tableaux for $\alpha = \beta$, answering 'yes' if a successful tableau occurs and 'no' otherwise.

4 Conclusions and directions for further work

We have here shown that the branching bisimilarity of [vGW89] is decidable for the class of normed BPA processes with silent actions by giving a tableau system. This system has exponential complexity in terms of the longest possible path of a generated tableau; however, in the case of a successful tableau we get additional information in the form of a finite relation whose congruence closure w.r.t. sequential composition is a bisimulation containing the initial equation.

The results of [GH91] show that all known strong equivalences except bisimilarity are undecidable for normed BPA. This means that their weak counterparts also are undecidable, but there are still several open questions for the weak versions of bisimulation equivalence. For branching bisimulation, the restriction to processes with strictly positive norms is rather strong, as it rules out the possibility of a process terminating silently. A problem with having nullary norms in the tableau system is that we no longer are guaranteed that α and β persist throughout an eliminating subtableau for $X\alpha = Y\beta$, since a match for $X\alpha \xrightarrow{a}$ may require access to observable actions inside β. So the natural question is whether there is a way of introducing nullary norms. Moreover, we would of course also want to get rid of the restriction of normedness altogether. However, since this problem also needs to be tackled for strong bisimulation equivalence, it seems that progress must first be made here before we can give any answer for the branching bisimulation case. Last, but not least the questions for weak bisimilarity all remain open. As we saw, Lemma 2.1 does not hold for this equivalence so a different approach must be used in that case.

Finally, it would be interesting if we could give a syntax-directed version of our tableau system for branching bisimulation since this could give us an equational theory of $\approx_b$ over normed BPA^τ_{rec} along the lines of [HS91]. A naive approach would be to add the τ-laws for branching bisimulation to the equational theory for strong bisimilarity of [HS91], where a proof system is given that consists of rules that can simulate the tableau construction. However, this theory would *not* be powerful enough for this; the problem lies in simulating the STEP rule.

References

[BBK87] J.C.M. Baeten, J.A. Bergstra, and J.W. Klop. Decidability of bisimulation equivalence for processes generating context-free languages. In *LNCS 259*, pages 93–114. Springer-Verlag, 1987.

[BK88] J.A. Bergstra and J.W. Klop. Process theory based on bisimulation semantics. In J.W. de Bakker, W.P de Roever, and G. Rozenberg, editors, *LNCS 354*, pages 50–122. Springer-Verlag, 1988.

[Cau90] D. Caucal. Graphes canoniques de graphes algébriques. *Informatique théorique et Applications (RAIRO)*, 24(4):339–352, 1990.

[GH91] J.F. Groote and Hüttel. Undecidable equivalences for basic process algebra. Technical Report ECS-LFCS-91-169, Department of Computer Science, University of Edinburgh, August 1991.

[HS91] H. Hüttel and C. Stirling. Actions speak louder than words: Proving bisimilarity for context-free processes. In *Proceedings of 6th Annual Symposium on Logic in Computer Science (LICS 91)*, pages 376–386. IEEE Computer Society Press, 1991.

[HU79] J. Hopcroft and J.D. Ullman. *Introduction to Automata Theory, Languages, and Computation*. Addison-Wesley, 1979.

[KH66] A.J. Korenjak and J.E. Hopcroft. Simple deterministic languages. In *Proceedings of Seventh Annual IEEE Symposium on Switching and Automata Theory*, pages 36–46, 1966.

[Mil80] R. Milner. *A Calculus of Communicating Systems, LNCS 92*. Springer-Verlag, 1980.

[Mil89] R. Milner. *Communication and Concurrency*. Prentice-Hall International, 1989.

[vGW89] R.J. van Glabbeek and W.P. Weijland. Branching time and abstraction in bisimulation semantics (extended abstract). In G.X. Ritter, editor, *Information Processing 89*, pages 613–618. North-Holland, 1989.

Computing Distinguishing Formulas for Branching Bisimulation

Henri Korver

Department of software technology, CWI

P.O. Box 4079, 1009 AB Amsterdam, The Netherlands

e-mail: henri@cwi.nl

Abstract

Branching bisimulation is a behavioral equivalence on labeled transition systems which has been proposed by Van Glabbeek and Weijland as an alternative to Milner's observation equivalence. This paper presents an algorithm which, given two branching bisimulation inequivalent finite state processes, produces a distinguishing formula in Hennessy-Milner logic extended with an 'until' operator. The algorithm, which is a modification of an algorithm due to Cleaveland, works in conjunction with a partition-refinement algorithm for deciding branching bisimulation equivalence. Our algorithm provides a useful extension to the algorithm for deciding equivalence because it tells a user *why* certain finite state systems are inequivalent.

Note: The research of the author is supported by the European Communities under RACE project no. 1046, Specification and Programming Environment for Communication Software (SPECS). This article does not necessarily reflect the view of the SPECS project.

1 Introduction

The complexity of concurrent systems (parallel chips, computer networks) is still increasing every day. To cope with this problem a lot of research has been spent on the development of formal verification techniques that guarantee the reliability of these systems.

At the moment, the use of *behavioral equivalences* is considered as a promising approach towards system verification. In this approach, concurrent systems are modeled as transition graphs, and verification amounts to establishing that the graph representing the implementation of the system is equivalent to (*behaves the same as*) the graph representing the specification of the system. The main advantage of this approach is that behavioral equivalences can be decided fully automatically on finite transition graphs and that several equivalences can be decided efficiently.

A number of equivalences have been proposed in the literature [3], and several automated tools include facilities for computing them [8]. One particularly interesting equivalence is (strong) *bisimulation equivalence* [10], which serves as the basis for a number of other equivalences that can be described in terms of it. Bisimulation equivalence has a *logical* characterization: two systems are equivalent exactly when they satisfy the same formulas in a simple modal logic due to Hennessy and Milner [6]. This fact suggests a useful diagnostic methodology for tools that compute bisimulation equivalence: when two systems are found not to be equivalent, one may explain why by giving a (distinguishing) formula satisfied by one and not by the other.

Recently, Cleaveland developed an advanced technique to generate such distinguishing formulas automatically. His method works in conjunction with the efficient partition-refinement algorithm for computing bisimulation equivalence and is described in [1]. The formulas generated by this algorithm are often minimal in a precisely defined sense.

In this paper, we apply this technique to *branching bisimulation equivalence* [4] which is a more suitable for practical purposes than (strong) bisimulation equivalence. Branching bisimulation equivalence resembles the well-known *observation equivalence* [10] and can be decided more efficiently [5].

Branching bisimulation is characterized in terms of Hennessy-Milner Logic with an Until-operator (HMLU) [2] and we develop a technique for determining a HMLU-formula that distinguishes two branching bisimulation inequivalent finite-state systems, using the idea of the advanced method of Cleaveland. To this end, we show how to use information generated by an adapted version of the partition-refinement algorithm of Groote and Vaandrager [5] to compute such a formula efficiently. On the basis of this result, tools using branching bisimulation may be modified to give users diagnostic information in the form of a distinguishing formula when a system is found not to be equivalent to its specification.

The remainder of the paper is organized as follows. The next section defines branching bisimulation equivalence and examines the connection between it and the Hennessy-Milner Logic with Until. Section 3.1 describes the algorithm of Groote and Vaandrager to compute branching bisimulation equivalence on the states of a transition graph. Then section 3.2 describes how to generate a block tree which retains information computed by the equivalence algorithm. Finally, in section 3.3 it is shown how to compute distinguishing formulas on the basis of this block tree; a small example is also presented to illustrate the working of the new algorithm.

For proofs, the reader is referred to the full version of this paper [9].

Acknowledgements

In the first place, I would like to thank Rance Cleaveland for writing his article and for answering all my questions. Special thanks to Jan Friso Groote for reading the previous draft of this paper very carefully.

2 Transition Graphs, Branching Bisimulation and HMLU

Concurrent systems are often modeled by *transition graphs*. Vertices in these graphs correspond to the states a system may enter as it executes, with one vertex being distinguished as the start state. The edges, which are directed, are labeled with actions and represent the state transitions a system may undergo. The formal definition is the following.

Definition 2.1 *A labeled transition graph is a quadruple $<S, s, Act, \rightarrow>$, where:*

- *S is a set of states;*

- *$s \in S$ is the start state;*

- *Act is a set of actions; the silent action τ is not in Act; and*

- *$\rightarrow \subseteq S \times Act_\tau \times S$ is the transition relation where $Act_\tau = Act \cup \{\tau\}$. An element $(p, \alpha, q) \in \rightarrow$ is called a transition, and is usually written as $p \xrightarrow{\alpha} q$.*

The silent action τ is unobservable for the environment and is used to symbolize the internal behavior of the system.

When a graph does not have a start state indicated, we shall refer to the corresponding triple as a *transition system*. A state in a transition system gives rise to a transition graph in the obvious way: let the given state be the start state, with the three components of the transition graph coming from the transition system.

Transition graphs are often too concrete for representing concurrent systems. Mostly one is only interested in the observational behavior of a complicated system and one is not interested in the internal (low-level) computations. Branching bisimulation, which is an interesting alternative for the well-known observation equivalence [10], remedies this shortcoming. In [4] several definitions of branching bisimulation are given, which all lead to the same equivalence. The following definition is in our setting most suitable.

Definition 2.2 *(Branching bisimulation)*

- *Let $<S, Act, \rightarrow>$ be a transition system. A relation $R \subseteq S \times S$ is called a **branching bisimulation** if it is symmetric and satisfies the following transfer property:*

  If rRs and $r \xrightarrow{\alpha} r'$, then either $\alpha = \tau$ and $r'Rs$ or; $\exists s_0, .., s_n, s' \in S : s = s_0$, $[\forall_{0 < i \leq n} : s_{i-1} \xrightarrow{\tau} s_i]$ and $s_n \xrightarrow{\alpha} s'$ such that $\forall_{0 < i \leq n} rRs_i$ and $r'Rs'$.

- *Two states r and s are branching bisimilar, abbreviated $r \approx_B s$ or $s \approx_B r$, if there exists a branching bisimulation relating r and s.*

The arbitrary union of branching bisimulation relations is again a branching bisimulation; $\approx_B$ is the maximal branching bisimulation and is an equivalence relation.

Let $T_1 = < S_1, s_1, Act, \rightarrow_1>$ and $T_2 = < S_2, s_2, Act, \rightarrow_2>$ be two transition graphs satisfying $S_1 \cap S_2 = \emptyset$. Then T_1 and T_2 are branching bisimilar exactly when the two start states, s_1 and s_2 are branching bisimilar in the transition graph $< S_1 \cup S_2, Act, \rightarrow_1 \cup \rightarrow_2>$.

Branching bisimulation has a *logical* characterization in terms of the Hennessy-Milner Logic with Until (HMLU): two states are equivalent exactly when they satisfy the same set of HMLU-formulas (see [2]). In [2] also two other logics are given that characterize branching bisimulation. We think that HMLU is the most natural choice in this setting. HMLU is a simple modal logic; the syntax of formulas is defined by the following grammar, where $\alpha \in Act_\tau$.

$$\Phi ::= tt \mid \neg \Phi \mid \Phi \wedge \Phi \mid \Phi\langle\alpha\rangle\Phi$$

The semantics of the logic is given with respect to a transition system $T = \langle S, Act, \rightarrow\rangle$

$$[\![tt]\!]_T \;=\; S$$

$$[\![\neg\Phi]\!]_T \;=\; S - [\![\Phi]\!]_T$$

$$[\![\Phi_1 \wedge \Phi_2]\!]_T \;=\; [\![\Phi_1]\!]_T \cap [\![\Phi_2]\!]_T$$

$$[\![\Phi_1 \langle\alpha\rangle \Phi_2]\!]_T \;=\; \{s \in S|\; (\alpha = \tau \text{ and } s \in [\![\Phi_2]\!]_T) \text{ or}$$
$$(\exists s_0,\dots,s_n \in [\![\Phi_1]\!]_T, \exists s' \in [\![\Phi_2]\!]_T : s_0 = s,$$
$$[\forall_{0<i\leq n} : s_{i-1} \xrightarrow{\tau} s_i] \text{ and } s_n \xrightarrow{\alpha} s')\}$$

Figure 1: The semantics of formulas in Hennessy-Milner Logic with Until.

and appears in Figure 1. In this figure each formula is mapped to the set of states for which the formula is 'true'. We shall omit explicit reference to the transition system used to interpret formulas when it is clear from the context. Intuitively, the formula tt holds in any state, and $\neg\Phi$ holds in a state if Φ does not. The formula $\Phi_1 \wedge \Phi_2$ holds in a state if both Φ_1 and Φ_2 do. The until-proposition $\Phi_1 \langle\alpha\rangle \Phi_2$ holds in a state, if this state can reach via α, a state in which Φ_2 holds while moving through intermediate states in which Φ_1 holds.

Let $\mathcal{H}(s)$ be the set of HMLU-formulas that are valid in state s:

$$\mathcal{H}(s) = \{\Phi | s \in [\![\Phi]\!]\}.$$

The next theorem is a specialization of a theorem proved in [2].

Theorem 2.3 *Let* $< S, Act, \rightarrow >$ *be a finite-state transition system, with* $s_1, s_2 \in S$. *Then* $\mathcal{H}(s_1) = \mathcal{H}(s_2)$ *if and only if* $s_1 \approx_B s_2$.

It follows that if two states in a (finite-state) transition system are inequivalent, then there must be a HMLU-formula satisfied by one and not the other. This is the basis of our definition for distinguishing formula, although we shall in fact use the following, slightly more general formulation taken from [1].

Definition 2.4 *Let* $< S, Act, \rightarrow >$ *be a transition system, and let* $S_1 \subseteq S$ *and* $S_2 \subseteq S$. *Then HMLU-formula* Φ *distinguishes* S_1 *from* S_2 *if the following hold.*

  1. $S_1 \subseteq [\![\Phi]\!]$.

  2. $S_2 \cap [\![\Phi]\!] = \emptyset$.

So Φ distinguishes S_1 from S_2 if every state in S_1, and no state in S_2, satisfies Φ. Theorem 2.3 thus guarantees the existence of a formula that distinguishes $\{s_1\}$ from $\{s_2\}$ if $s_1 \not\approx_B s_2$.

Finally, we take the following criterion from [1] to indicate whether a distinguishing formula contains extraneous information.

Definition 2.5 *Let* Φ *be a HMLU-formula distinguishing* S_1 *from* S_2. *Then* Φ *is minimal if no* Φ' *obtained by replacing a non-trivial subformula of* Φ *with the formula* tt *distinguishes* S_1 *from* S_2.

Intuitively, Φ is a minimal formula for S_1 with respect to S_2 if each of its subformulas plays a role in distinguishing the two. This notion of minimality is rather naive, but at the moment we are not aware of a better definition.

3 Computing Distinguishing Formulas

In this section, we describe a partition refinement algorithm for computing branching bisimulation equivalence and show how to alter it to generate a block tree. Then given such a block tree, we describe how to generate distinguishing formulas. Finally, a small example is given that illustrates the use of the algorithm.

3.1 Computing Branching Bisimulation

At the moment, 'partition-refinement' is the most efficient method to compute bisimulation equivalences [7]. A partition-refinement algorithm exploits the fact that an equivalence relation on the set of states may be represented as a partition, or a set of pairwise-disjoint subsets (called blocks) of the state set whose union is the whole state set. In this representation blocks correspond to the equivalence classes, so two states are equivalent exactly when they belong to the same block. Beginning with the partition containing one block (representing the trivial equivalence relation consisting of one equivalence class), the algorithm repeatedly *refines* a partition by splitting blocks until the associated equivalence relation becomes a bisimulation.

In [5] the refinement strategy to obtain branching bisimulation is described. To refine the current partition, the algorithm of Groote and Vaandrager looks at each block in turn. If a state in block B can reach via action α, possibly after some initial stuttering, a state in block B' and another state in B does not, then the algorithm splits B into two blocks. The first block contains all the states which can reach via action α, possibly after some initial stuttering, a state in block B'. The second block contains all the other states. When no more splitting is possible, the resulting equivalence corresponds exactly to branching bisimulation on the given transition system.

Below we present the definitions and the algorithm in more formal notation; the description is a slight modification of the one in [5].

Definition 3.1

Let $\langle S, Act, \rightarrow \rangle$ be a transition system.

1) A collection $\{B_j | j \in J\}$ of nonempty subsets of S is called a partition if $\bigcup_{j \in J} B_j = S$ and for $i \neq j : B_i \cap B_j = \emptyset$. The elements of a partition are called blocks.

2) If $\mathcal{P}$ and $\mathcal{P}'$ are partitions of S then $\mathcal{P}'$ refines $\mathcal{P}$, if any block of $\mathcal{P}'$ is included in a block of $\mathcal{P}$.

3) The equivalence $\sim_{\mathcal{P}}$ on S induced by a partition $\mathcal{P}$ is defined by:
$r \sim_{\mathcal{P}} s \Leftrightarrow \exists B \in \mathcal{P} : r \in B \land s \in B$.

4) For B, B' we define the set $pos_\alpha(B, B')$ as the set of states in B from which, after some internal τ-stuttering, a state in B' can be reached:
$pos_\alpha(B, B') = \{s \in B | \exists s_0, ..., s_n \in B, \exists s' \in B' :$
$$s_0 = s, [\forall_{0 < i \leq n} : s_{i-1} \xrightarrow{\tau} s_i] \text{ and } s_n \xrightarrow{\alpha} s'\}$$
5) We say that B' is a splitter of B with respect to action α iff

$B \neq B'$ or $\alpha \neq \tau$, and $\emptyset \neq pos_\alpha(B, B') \neq B$.

6) If $\mathcal{P}$ is a partition of S and B' is a splitter of B with respect to α, then $Ref_p^\alpha(B, B')$ is the partition $\mathcal{P}$ where B is replaced by $pos_\alpha(B, B')$ and $B - pos_\alpha(B, B')$.

7) $\mathcal{P}$ is stable with respect to block B' if for no block B and for no action α, B' is a splitter of B with respect to α. $\mathcal{P}$ is stable if it is stable with respect to all its blocks.

Algorithm 3.2 *The algorithm to compute branching bisimulation maintains a partition $\mathcal{P}$ that is initially $\mathcal{P}_0 = \{S\}$. It repeats the following step, until $\mathcal{P}$ is stable:*

> *Find blocks $B, B' \in \mathcal{P}$ and a label $\alpha \in Act_\tau$ such that B' is a splitter wrt. α;*
> $\mathcal{P} := Ref_p^\alpha(B, B')$.

In [5] it is proved that the equivalence induced by the last partition computed by algorithm 3.2 corresponds exactly to branching bisimulation equivalence. Also, the complexity bounds given in [5] are presented.

Theorem 3.3 *Let $\langle S, Act, \rightarrow \rangle$ be a finite transition system. Let $\mathcal{P}_f$ be the final partition obtained by the algorithm above. Then $\sim_{\mathcal{P}_f} = \approx_B$.*

Theorem 3.4 *The time complexity of algorithm 3.2 is $O(|S| * | \rightarrow |)$. And the space complexity is $O(| \rightarrow |)$.*

3.2 Generating The Block Tree

In addition to computing the partition as described above, we now retain information about *how* and *why* the blocks are split by construction of a labeled block 'tree'. The following definitions are used to describe the generation procedure of such a block tree.

Definition 3.5 *(Parent and its children)*
$\mathcal{P}(B)$ is the parent of block B in the block tree. $\mathcal{L}(B)$ is the left child of block B. $\mathcal{R}(B)$ is the right child of block B. When B has a single child or no children at all then $\mathcal{L}(B)$ and $\mathcal{R}(B)$ are undefined.

Definition 3.6 *(Height of a block)*
The height of a block B in the block tree is defined as follows:
$h(B) := 0$ where B is the root block.
$h(B) := 1 + h(\mathcal{P}(B))$.

Definition 3.7 *(Parent Partition)*
The Parent Partition of block B in the block tree, is the partition where B is created.
$\mathcal{PP}(B) := \{C| h(C) = h(\mathcal{P}(B))\}$.

Definition 3.8 *(Blocks that can be reached from block B)*
Let B be a block in the block tree.

- $r_\alpha(B) := \{C \in \mathcal{PP}(B)| \exists s \in B, s' \in C : s \xrightarrow{\alpha} s'\}$; $r_\alpha(B)$ contains all the blocks in the parent partition of B that can be reached from a state in B via α.

- $r_\tau^p(B) := \{C \in \mathcal{PP}(B)| \exists s \in B, s' \in C : s \xrightarrow{\tau} s' \wedge C \neq \mathcal{P}(B)\}$; $r_\tau^p(B)$ contains all the blocks in the parent partition of B that can be reached from a state in B via τ. The superscript 'p' indicates that the parent of B is not included.

Algorithm 3.2 is modified as follows. Rather than discarding an old partition after it is refined, the new procedure constructs a tree of blocks as follows. The children of a block are the new blocks that result when the algorithm splits the block; accordingly, the root is labeled with the block S, and after each refinement the leaves of this tree represents the current partition.

When a block P is split due to splitter block B' and action α, we position the new block $L=pos_\alpha(P, B')$ as the left child and the new block $R=P-pos_\alpha(P, B')$ as the right child, and we label the arc connecting P to L with α and B'. We label the arc connecting P to R with $r_\tau^p(R)$ and $r_\alpha(R)$, these block-sets are given in definition 3.8. The blocks in $r_\tau^p(R)$ bear witness to the states in R that cannot evolve in internal stuttering. The blocks in $r_\alpha(R)$ bear witness to the states in R that cannot reach the splitter block by an α-step.

Recall that every state in L can reach via α, possibly after some initial stuttering, a state in B' and no state in R does. If a block is not split during a refinement, it is assigned a copy of itself as its only child Figure 3 contains an example of such a tree.

The construction of the block tree during the partition-refinement algorithm does not influence the time complexity. The space complexity has changed slightly from $O(|\rightarrow|)$ to $O(|S|^2)$ due to the following theorem (note that $|\mathcal{P}_f| \leq |S|$).

Theorem 3.9 *The space requirement of the labeled block tree is $O(|S| + |\mathcal{P}_f|^2)$.*

Proof. Strictly speaking, only the leaves in the tree need to be labeled with the corresponding sets of states.

3.3 Generating Distinguishing Formulas

Given a block tree computed by the extended partition-refinement algorithm above, and two disjoint blocks B_1 and B_2, the following postprocessing step builds a formula $\Delta(B_1, B_2)$ that distinguishes the states in B_1 from those in B_2.

First we compute the lowest common ancestor of B_1 and B_2 (and call it P). By lemma 3.11 we know that a formula distinguishing the children of P, also distinguishes B_1 from B_2.

Definition 3.10 *(Lowest Common Ancestor)*
The function $\mathcal{LCA}$ returns the Lowest Common Ancestor of two disjoint blocks B_1 and B_2 in the block tree.

Lemma 3.11
$$\left.\begin{array}{l} P = \mathcal{LCA}(B_1, B_2) \\ \Phi \text{ distinguishes } \mathcal{L}(P) \text{ and } \mathcal{R}(P) \end{array} \wedge \right\} \implies \Phi \text{ distinguishes } B_1 \text{ and } B_2.$$

Proof. B_1 and B_2 are subsets of respectively $\mathcal{L}(P)$ and $\mathcal{R}(P)$.

For easy notation, let $L = \mathcal{L}(P)$ be the left child and $R = \mathcal{R}(P)$ the right child of P. The arc connecting blocks P and L is labeled with α and B'; and the arc connecting blocks P and R is labeled with respectively the block-sets $r_\tau^p(R)$ and $r_\alpha(R)$ (call these block-sets respectively r_1 and r_2).

From the way that the block tree is generated, we know that every state in L can reach via action α, possibly after some initial stuttering, a state in B' and that no state in R

does. Accordingly, one recursively builds formulas that distinguish P and blocks in r_1, and takes their conjunction (call it Φ_1). And, if one also recursively builds formulas that distinguish B' from each block in r_2 and also takes their conjunction (call it Φ_2), then every state in L satisfies $\Phi_1\langle\alpha\rangle\Phi_2$ (call this formula Φ) and no state in R does. In case $\alpha = \tau$, one has to add the extra conjunct $\Delta(B', R)$, to ensure that Φ is a distinguishing formula; this is caused by the first disjunct at the right hand side of the last mapping in figure 1. The details are given below.

Algorithm 3.12
  When B_1 and B_2 are disjoint, $\Delta(B_1, B_2)$ can be computed recursively as follows.

  1. *Compute $P := \mathcal{LCA}(B_1, B_2)$.*

  2. *Let $L := \mathcal{L}(P);\ R := \mathcal{R}(P)$.*
     (Notice that $B_1 \subseteq L$ and $B_2 \subseteq R$, or $B_2 \subseteq L$ and $B_1 \subseteq R$.)

  3. *Let α and B' be the labels on the arc connecting P and L; and let $r_1 := r_\tau^P(R)$ and $r_2 := r_\alpha(R)$ be the labels on the arc connecting P and R;*

     - *if $r_1 = \emptyset$ then $\Phi_1 := tt$ else $\Phi_1 := \bigwedge_{C \in r_1} \Delta(P, C)$;*
     - *if $r_2 = \emptyset$ then $\Phi_2 := tt$ else $\Phi_2 := \bigwedge_{C \in r_2} \Delta(B', C)$.*

  4. *If $\alpha \neq \tau$ then $\Phi := \Phi_1\langle\alpha\rangle\Phi_2$.*
     else $\Phi_3 := \Delta(B', R)$;
     $\Phi := \Phi_1\langle\tau\rangle(\Phi_2 \wedge \Phi_3)$.

  5. *If $B_1 \subseteq L$ then return Φ else return $\neg\Phi$.*

We now have the following theorem.

Theorem 3.13 $B_1 \cap B_2 = \emptyset \implies \Delta(B_1, B_2)$ *distinguishes B_1 and B_2.*

Proof. By induction on the depth of B_1 and B_2 in the block tree.

It should be noted that exponential length formulas may be generated. However, one may present such a formula (as a set of propositional equations) in space proportional to $|\mathcal{P}_f|^2$, where $\mathcal{P}_f$ is the final partition computed by the algorithm (note that $|\mathcal{P}_f| \leq |S|$). This results from the fact that there can be at most $|\mathcal{P}_f| - 1$ recursive calls generated by the above procedure and the fact that each distinguishing formula is of the form $(\neg)\Phi_1\langle\alpha\rangle\Phi_2$, where Φ_1 and Φ_2 contain together at most $|\mathcal{P}_f| - 1$ conjuncts, each of the form $\Delta(B_i, B_j)$ for some B_i and B_j.

Theorem 3.14 *An equational representation of $\Delta(B_1, B_2)$ may be calculated in $O(|\mathcal{P}_f|^2)$ time, once the tree of blocks has been computed.*

Proof. At each recursive call, computing the lowest common ancestor requires at most $O(|\mathcal{P}_f|)$ work. $\square$

In general a formula $\Delta(s_1, s_2)$ will not be minimal in the sense of definition 2.5. In [1] the following straightforward procedure is proposed to minimize $\Delta(s_1, s_2)$ once it has been computed. Repeatedly replace subformulas in the formula by tt and see if the resulting formula still distinguishes s_1 from s_2. If so, the subformula may either be omitted (if it is one of several conjuncts in a larger conjunction) or left at tt. The result of this would be a minimal formula. The computational tractability of this procedure remains to be examined.

We close this subsection with a general remark about our method. Our method generates a formula that distinguishes blocks that may contain more than one state, but mostly one is only interested in a formula that distinguishes two particular states. In this case, algorithm 3.12 can also be used to construct a formula distinguishing two inequivalent states s_1 and s_2; first locate the disjoint blocks B_1 and B_2 such that $s_i \in B_i$ ($i = 1, 2$), then build $\Delta(B_1, B_2)$.

3.4 An Example

To illustrate our algorithm we consider two transition graphs that are not branching bisimulation equivalent. Figure 2 shows the transition system that includes the two transition graphs. It is interesting to notice that these two graphs are an instance of the second τ-law of observation equivalence (see e.g. [10]); so they are not differentiated by HML without Until-operator. State s_1 is the start state of one graph, while state s_5 is the start state of the other. Figure 3 contains a tree of blocks generated by the altered partition-refinement algorithm. Notice that $s_1 \not\approx_B s_5$, as they are in different blocks. In order to build a formula that s_1 satisfies and s_5 does not, it suffices to generate $\Delta(B_6, B_5)$, the formula that distinguishes block B_6 and B_5. To do so, the algorithm first locates the lowest common ancestor of the two blocks (B_3, in this case). The left child is B_5 and the right child is B_6. The labels on the left arc indicate that the action causing the split is a, and the splitter block is B_2. The labels on the right arc indicate that $r_\tau^p(R)=\{B_4\}$ and $r_\alpha(R)=\emptyset$. The formula that will be returned, then, will be

$$\neg(\Delta(B_3, B_4)\langle a\rangle tt);$$

this formula holds of s_1 and not of s_5. By repeating this process, it turns out that

$$\Delta(B_3, B_4) \quad = \quad tt\langle b\rangle tt$$

So the formula distinguishing s_1 from s_5 is

$$\neg((tt\langle b\rangle tt)\langle a\rangle tt).$$

This formula explains why s_1 and s_5 are inequivalent because s_5 may engage in an a-transition while in all the intermediate states (only s_5 here) a b-transition is available. This is not the case for state s_1. Note that this formula is minimal in the sense of definition 2.5.

4 Conclusions and Future Work

This paper has shown how it is possible to alter the partition-refinement of Groote and Vaandrager for computing branching bisimulation equivalence to compute a formula in the Hennessy-Milner Logic with Until that distinguishes two inequivalent states. The generation of the formula relies on a postprocessing step that is invoked on a tree-based

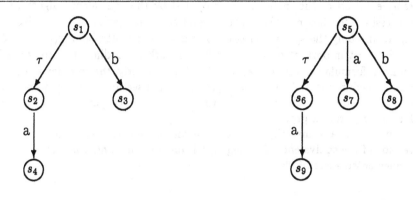

Figure 2: Two branching bisimulation inequivalent transition graphs.

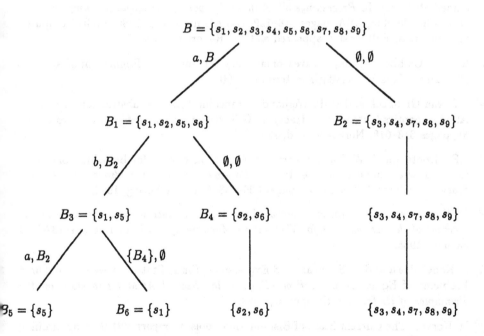

Figure 3: The generated tree of blocks.

representation of the information computed by the equivalence algorithm. The post-processing step has no effect on the worst-case complexity of the equivalence-checking algorithm, only the space complexity has changed slightly from $O(|\rightarrow|)$ to $O(|S|^2)$.

The most important direction for future work is tackling the problem of generating minimal formulas and moreover its complexity. Clearly, the complexity of the minimization procedure mentioned in passing at the end of section 3.3 needs to be analyzed fully; if this procedure is efficient enough, then it may be incorporated into the distinguishing formula generation procedure.

Another area of investigation would be an implementation of our technique, as an extension of the equivalence-checking algorithm of Groote and Vaandrager which is already implemented successfully.

References

[1] R. Cleaveland: On Automatically Distinguishing Inequivalent Processes. In *Proceedings: 1990 Workshop on Computer-Aided Verification (R. Kurshan and E.M. Clarke, editors)*, DIMACS technical report 90-31, Vol. 2, New Yersey, 1990. To appear in Lecture Notes in Computer Science.

[2] R. DeNicola and F.W. Vaandrager: Three logics for branching bisimulation (extended abstract). In *Proceedings 5th Annual Symposium on Logic in Computer Science*, Philadelphia, USA, pages 118–129, Los Alamitos, CA, 1990. IEEE Computer Society Press. Full version appeared as CWI Report CS-R9012.

[3] R.J. van Glabbeek: Comparative Concurrency Semantics and Refinement of Actions. *PhD thesis*, Free University, Amsterdam, 1990.

[4] R.J. van Glabbeek and W.P. Weijland: Branching time and abstraction in bisimulation semantics (extended abstract). In G.X. Ritter, editor, *Information Processing 89*, pages 613–618. North-Holland, 1989.

[5] J.F. Groote and F.W. Vaandrager: An efficient algorithm for branching bisimulation and stuttering equivalence. In M.S. Paterson, editor, *Proceedings 17th ICALP*, Warwick, volume 443 of *LNCS*, pages 626–638. Springer-Verlag, 1990.

[6] M. Hennessy and R. Milner: Algebraic Laws for Nondeterminism and Concurrency. *Journal of the Association for Computing Machinery*, v. 32, n. 1, pages 137-161, January 1985.

[7] P. Kanellakis and S.A. Smolka: CCS Expressions, Finite State Processes, and Three Problems of Equivalence. In *Proceedings of the Second ACM Symposium on the Principles of Distributed Computing*, 1983.

[8] H. Korver: The Current State of Bisimulation Tools. In *report P9101*, Programming Research Group, Univerisity of Amsterdam, 1991.

[9] H. Korver: Computing Distinguishing Formulas for Branching Bisimulation (Full Version). In *report CS-R9121*, CWI, Amsterdam, 1991.

[10] R. Milner: *Communication and Concurrency*. Prentice Hall, 1989.

Compositional Checking of Satisfaction*

Henrik Reif Andersen   Glynn Winskel

Department of Computer Science, Aarhus University, Denmark

Abstract: We present a compositional method for deciding whether a process satisfies an assertion. Assertions are formulae in a modal ν-calculus, and processes are drawn from a very general process algebra inspired by CCS and CSP. Well-known operators from CCS, CSP, and other process algebras appear as derived operators.

The method is *compositional in the structure of processes* and works purely on the syntax of processes. It consists of applying a sequence of *reductions*, each of which only take into account the top-level operator of the process. A reduction transforms a satisfaction problem for a composite process into equivalent satisfaction problems for the immediate subcomponents.

Using process variables, systems with undefined subcomponents can be defined, and given an overall requirement to the system, *necessary and sufficient conditions* on these subcomponents can be found. Hence the process variables make it possible to specify and reason about what are often referred to as *contexts*, *environments*, and *partial implementations*.

As reductions are algorithms that work on syntax, they can be considered as forming a bridge between traditional non-compositional model checking and compositional proof systems.

1   Introduction

In this paper we present a compositional method for deciding whether a finite state process satisfies a specification. Processes will be described in a very general and rich process algebra, which includes common operators from process algebras as CCS and CSP. This algebra contains primitive operators to reflect sequentiality (by the well-known operation of prefixing), non-deterministic choice, asynchronous and synchronous parallel composition, recursion, relabelling, and restriction. Specifications will be drawn from a modal ν-calculus with negation, in which a variety of properties can be specified. These include the usual *liveness*, *safety*, and *fairness* properties, as well as all operators from ordinary linear and branching time temporal logics (see e.g. [Sti91] and [Dam90]).

The method we advocate is *compositional in the structure of processes* and works purely on the syntactical level without any explicit references to the underlying transition system. Compositionality is important for at least the following two reasons. Firstly, it makes the verification *modular*, so that when changing a part of a system only the part of the verification concerning that particular component must be redone. Secondly, when designing a system or *synthesizing* a process the compositionality makes it possible to have undefined parts of a process and still be able to reason about it. For instance, it might be possible to reveal inconsistencies in the specification or prove that with the choices already taken in the design no component supplied for the missing parts will ever be able to make the overall system satisfy the original specification.

This approach is unlike traditional model checking where a transition system model of a process is built and the specification formula is checked by applying some algorithm to the transition system. There are several versions of this basic idea in the literature, e.g. Emerson and Lei [EL86], Clarke et al [CES86], Stirling and Walker [SW89], Larsen [Lar88], Winskel [Win89], Cleaveland [Cle90], and Arnold and Crubille [AC88]. Recently there have been attempts to extend some of these methods based on transition systems to compositional methods by Clarke,

---

*This work is supported by the ESPRIT Basic Research Actions CEDISYS and CLICS, and for the first author also by the Danish Natural Science Research Council.

Long, and McMillan [CLM89] and Larsen and Xinxin [LX90], but none of these are compositional in the structure of processes.

Our method consists of applying a sequence of *reductions* each of which removes the top-most operator of the process, i.e. a reduction transforms a satisfaction problem for a composite process to satisfaction problems for the immediate subcomponents of the process – without inspecting these. Starting with a process term one can repeatedly use the reductions until a trivial process, for which satisfaction is easily decided, or a variable remains.

2 The Languages

2.1 Syntax

Assume given a set of *state names Nam*, and a finite set of *actions Act*. Processes are denoted by syntactic terms t constructed from the following grammar:

$$t ::= nil \mid at \mid t_0 + t_1 \mid t_0 \times t_1 \mid t \upharpoonright \Lambda \mid t\{\Xi\} \mid rec \ P.t \mid P,$$

where P is an element in *Nam*, i.e. a state identifier. The usual notion of free and bound will apply to state identifiers P, so that P will be bound in *rec P.t* but free in $P + nil$.

Nil is the inactive process, and at is the usual prefix and $t_0 + t_1$ the usual sum operations known from CCS. The product term $t_0 \times t_1$ denotes a very general kind of parallel composition which allows the components t_0 and t_1 to proceed both synchronously and asynchronously. The exact semantics is defined below.

A state identifier P in the body of *rec P.t* works as a *recursion point*, and in effect will behave as the normal recursion in CCS: A term *rec P.t* has the same behaviour as the *unfolded* term $t[rec \ P.t/P]$ (the result of substituting *rec P.t* for all free occurrences of P in t). We impose the syntactic restriction on recursive terms, that no product must appear in the body, which ensures all definable processes are finite state, and for technical reasons we also require every occurrence of P in *rec P.t* to be *strongly guarded*, i.e. appear immediately under a prefix.

In the prefix at, a denotes an action in *Act*. For a given set of actions *Act* we define a set of *composite actions*. Let $*$ be a distinguished symbol not contained in *Act*. The symbol $*$ is called the *idling action* and interpreted as 'no action' or 'inaction'. Define Act_* to be the least set including $Act \cup \{*\}$ and such that $\alpha, \beta \in Act_*$ implies $\alpha \times \beta \in Act_*$ taking $* \times * = *$. Now $\Xi : Act_* \to Act_*$ is a *relabelling* which is a partial function, with finite domain, mapping non-idling actions to non-idling actions. This relabelling can be extended to a total function on Act_* by taking it to behave as the identity outside the domain. The term $t \upharpoonright \Lambda$ is a *restriction* where Λ is a finite subset of Act_*.

Properties of processes are denoted by assertions A from a modal ν-calculus:

$$A ::= \neg A \mid A_0 \vee A_1 \mid \langle \alpha \rangle A \mid X \mid \nu X.A \mid (t : A),$$

where X ranges over a set of assertion variables. In the maximal fixed-point formula $\nu X.A$ any free occurrence of X must be within an even number of negations in order to guarantee the existence of a unique maximal fixed-point. The action name α belongs to the set of composite actions Act_*. The *correctness assertion* $(t : A)$ denotes true if t satisfies A and false otherwise. An assertion is said to be *pure* if it does not contain any correctness assertions.

A lot of derived operators can easily be defined in terms of the core language and will be used throughout the paper:

$$
\begin{array}{llll}
[\alpha]A & = & \neg \langle \alpha \rangle \neg A & \qquad \mu X.A & = & \neg \nu X.\neg A[\neg X/X] \\
T & = & \nu X.X & \qquad A \to B & = & \neg A \vee B \\
F & = & \neg T & \qquad A \leftrightarrow B & = & (A \to B) \wedge (B \to A)
\end{array}
$$

Here we have used the notation $A[B/X]$ which denotes the assertion resulting from substituting B for all free occurrences of X in A. We will say that an assertion A is *closed* if it contains no free variables. Furthermore for a finite set $K \subseteq Act_*$ we define $\langle K \rangle A = \bigvee_{\kappa \in K} \langle \kappa \rangle A$ where disjunction over an empty set gives false (F).

The correctness assertions $(t : A)$ are atoms in a propositional logic which will be used to express reductions. A grammar for the logic is:

$$L ::= T \mid \neg L \mid L_0 \vee L_1 \mid (t : A)$$

In the logical language L we are able to express complex relationships between properties of different processes. For example

$$(p + q : \langle \alpha \rangle A) \leftrightarrow (p : \langle \alpha \rangle A) \vee (q : \langle \alpha \rangle A),$$

expresses a very simple example of a reduction. It states that the process $p + q$ can do an α and get into a state that satisfies A if and only if p or q can do an α and get into a state that satisfies A. It is a reduction because the formula is valid for all p's and q's, and the validity of $(p + q : \langle \alpha \rangle A)$ is reduced to validity of correctness assertions over the subterms p and q. Although this reduction is almost trivial, in general, it might be quite difficult to get reductions. Consider for example the problem of choosing a B such that

$$(rec\ P.t : \nu X.A) \leftrightarrow (t : B)$$

holds. The aim of this paper is to describe a method for supplying such a B and analogous assertions for all the other operators.

2.2 Semantics

In order to define the semantics we first recall some well-known definitions of transition systems.

Definition 1 A *transition system* T is a triple $(S, L, \rightarrow)$ where S is a set of states, L a set of labels, and $\rightarrow \subseteq S \times L \times S$ a transition relation. The *set of reachable states* R_p from a state $p \in S$ is defined as the least subset of S containing p and closed under $\xrightarrow{L}$, where $\xrightarrow{L} = \bigcup_{l \in L} \xrightarrow{l}$. A *pointed transition system* T is a quadruple $(S, L, \rightarrow, i)$ where $(S, L, \rightarrow)$ is a transition system, $i \in S$ is an initial state, and all states in S must be reachable from i, i.e. S must equal R_i.

Given a pointed transition system $T = (S, L, \rightarrow, i)$ the *rooting of* T is a pointed transition system $\underline{T} = (S \cup \{\underline{i}\}, L, \rightarrow', \underline{i})$ where $\underline{i}$ is a new state assumed not to be in S, and the transition relation $\rightarrow' \subseteq (S \cup \{\underline{i}\}) \times L \times (S \cup \{\underline{i}\})$ is defined by:

$$\rightarrow'\ =\ \rightarrow \cup\ \{(\underline{i}, \alpha, q) \mid i \xrightarrow{\alpha} q\}.$$

Pictorially the rooting of a pointed transition system is constructed by adjoining a new initial state with the same out-going transitions as the old initial state.

The rooting of a transition system T is just as good as T with respect to satisfaction in our logic. A claim made precise by the rooting lemma below.

The semantics of process terms is given by the transition system $T = (S, Act_*, \rightarrow)$, where S is the set of closed process terms, Act_* the set of composite actions, and $\rightarrow \subseteq S \times Act_* \times S$ is the transition relation given as the least relation satisfying the following rules.

$$p \xrightarrow{*} p \qquad a p \xrightarrow{a} p \qquad \frac{p \xrightarrow{\alpha} p'}{p + q \xrightarrow{\alpha} p'} \qquad \frac{q \xrightarrow{\alpha} q'}{p + q \xrightarrow{\alpha} q'}$$

$$\frac{p \xrightarrow{\alpha} p' \quad q \xrightarrow{\beta} q'}{p \times q \xrightarrow{\alpha \times \beta} p' \times q'} \qquad \frac{t[rec\ P.t/P] \xrightarrow{\alpha} t'}{rec\ P.t \xrightarrow{\alpha} t'}$$

$$\frac{p \xrightarrow{\alpha} p'}{p\{\Xi\} \xrightarrow{\beta} p'\{\Xi\}} \quad \Xi(\alpha) = \beta \qquad \frac{p \xrightarrow{\alpha} p'}{p \upharpoonright \Lambda \xrightarrow{\alpha} p' \upharpoonright \Lambda} \quad \alpha \in \Lambda$$

Note in particular the rule for product. One of the components in the product may *idle* by means of the idling action $*$ allowing the other component to proceed independently, as in the transition

$$p \xrightarrow{\alpha \times *} p'$$

where the left component of p performs an α-action and the right component idles.

For a transition system $T = (S, L, \rightarrow)$ an assertion A denotes a *property* of T which we take to be a subset of S, hence the set of all properties of T is the powerset $\mathcal{P}(S)$. As assertions may contain free variables we introduce the notion of an environment which describes the interpretation of the variables. An *environment of assertions* for T is a map

$$\phi : Var_A \rightarrow \mathcal{P}(S)$$

which assigns properties to assertion variables. The environment $\phi[U/X]$ is like ϕ except that the variable X is mapped to U.

Formally, relative to the transition system $T = (S, L, \rightarrow)$ the assertion A denotes the property $[\![A]\!]_T \phi$ defined inductively on the structure of A.

$$
\begin{aligned}
[\![\neg A]\!]_T \phi &= S \setminus [\![A]\!]_T \phi \\
[\![A_0 \vee A_1]\!]_T \phi &= [\![A_0]\!]_T \phi \cup [\![A_1]\!]_T \phi \\
[\![\langle \alpha \rangle A]\!]_T \phi &= \{s \in S \mid \exists s' \in S.\ s \xrightarrow{\alpha} s' \ \&\ s' \in [\![A]\!]_T \phi\} \\
[\![X]\!]_T \phi &= \phi(X) \\
[\![\nu X.A]\!]_T \phi &= \nu U \subseteq S.\ \psi(U) \\
&\qquad \text{where } \psi : U \mapsto [\![A]\!]_T \phi[U/X] \\
[\![(t : A)]\!]_T \phi &= \begin{cases} S & \text{if } t \in [\![A]\!]_T \phi \\ \emptyset & \text{otherwise} \end{cases}
\end{aligned}
$$

The powerset $\mathcal{P}(S)$ ordered by inclusion is a complete lattice and as we require all variables to appear under an even number of negations the map ψ will always be monotonic, so by Tarski's lemma [Tar55] ψ will have a maximum fixed-point (the *largest postfixed point*) which we denote by $\nu U \subseteq S.\ \psi(U)$.

Define $[\![A]\!]\phi = [\![A]\!]_T \phi$. This gives the standard *global interpretation* of assertions over all states S.

For a transition system $T = (S, L, \rightarrow)$, and a subset Q of S we have the induced transition system

$$T_Q = (Q, L, \rightarrow \cap (Q \times L \times Q)),$$

which is T restricted to the set of states Q. Writing $[\![A]\!]_Q \phi$ for $[\![A]\!]_{T_Q} \phi$ we get a *local interpretation* of A. For particular choices of the subset Q the local and global interpretations coincide, as is captured by the locality lemma below. Let ϕ_Q denote the environment which on the variable X gives $\phi(X) \cap Q$.

Lemma 2 *(Locality lemma.)*
Let $T = (S, L, \rightarrow)$ be a transition system. Given an assertion A, an environment ϕ, and a subset Q of S. Suppose Q satisfies the closedness criterion: Q is closed under $\xrightarrow{K}$, where K is the set of actions appearing inside diamonds in A. Then the following equality holds

$$[\![A]\!]_{T_Q} \phi_Q = [\![A]\!]_T \phi \cap Q.$$

With the transition system T one particularly interesting choice of Q is the set of reachable states R_p from a state p which by definition satisfies the closedness criterion of the locality lemma. Suppose we wanted to check whether a particular state p belongs to the set of states denoted by an assertion A, then by the locality lemma we obtain:

$$p \in [\![A]\!] \phi \quad \text{iff} \quad p \in [\![A]\!] \phi \cap R_p$$
$$\text{iff} \quad p \in [\![A]\!]_{R_p} \phi_{R_p}$$

As mentioned previously, the rooting of a transition system T is 'just as good as' T with respect to satisfaction in our logic – which is the intuitive content of the following lemma.

Lemma 3 *(Rooting lemma.)*
Given a pointed transition system, $T = (S_T, L_T, \rightarrow_T, i_T)$, with the rooting $\underline{T}$. Let $r : \mathcal{P}(S_T) \rightarrow \mathcal{P}(S_{\underline{T}})$ be the map on properties that take the initial state of T to the two copies of it in $\underline{T}$ and take all other states to their obvious counterparts. Let $\phi : Var_A \rightarrow \mathcal{P}(S)$ be an environment of assertions. Then

$$r([\![A]\!]_T \, \phi) \; = \; [\![A]\!]_{\underline{T}} (r \circ \phi).$$

The connection given by the rooting lemma between pointed transition systems T and their rootings $\underline{T}$ is very useful: The set of states satisfying an assertion will be the same in both interpretations up to application of the map r. In particular the initial state of T will satisfy A if and only if the initial state of $\underline{T}$ satisfies A; an observation central to our development of reductions in section 3.

There is another technical lemma stating a close relationship between syntactic and semantic substitution on assertions which will be used frequently in the proofs.

Lemma 4 *(Substitution lemma.)*
For B a closed assertion, X a variable, A an arbitrary, pure assertion, and ϕ an environment for T, we have
$$[\![A[B/X]]\!]_T \, \phi = [\![A]\!]_T \, \phi [[\![B]\!]_T \, \phi/X].$$

For the propositional logic we define the satisfaction predicate $\models_\phi$ relative to an environment ϕ:

$$
\begin{array}{lll}
\models_\phi T & \text{always} \\
\models_\phi \neg L & \text{iff} \quad \text{not} \models_\phi L \\
\models_\phi L_0 \vee L_1 & \text{iff} \quad \models_\phi L_0 \text{ or } \models_\phi L_1 \\
\models_\phi t : A & \text{iff} \quad t \in [\![A]\!] \phi
\end{array}
$$

Furthermore we define the derived predicate $\models$ as:

$$\models L \quad \text{iff} \quad \text{for all } \phi \models_\phi L.$$

Taking $\bullet$ to be the trivial transition system with one state (denoted $\bullet$) and no transitions, we observe that the set of assertions built from correctness assertions, negations, and conjunctions when interpreted over $\bullet$ is essentially a copy of the logic L, i.e. for such an assertion A we have $[\![A]\!]_\bullet \phi = \{\bullet\}$ if and only if $\models_\phi A$ where A is interpreted as a formula in the propositional logic.

3 Reductions

Our method for compositional checking of satisfaction is based on the notion of a *reduction*, which we explain in terms of the prefix operator.

Given a pure and closed assertion A and a prefix at we would like to find a propositional expression B over atoms $(t : B_i)$ such that the following holds:

$$\models (at : A) \leftrightarrow B$$

Having found such a B the validity of $(at : A)$ has been *reduced* to validity of a propositional expression containing only atoms on the subterm t. In order words: B is a *necessary* and *sufficient* condition on the subterm t ensuring that at satisfies A. By the word *reduction* we will henceforth understand *an algorithmic description of how to find B given A and at.*

It is not obvious that such a B exists. Although we can easily express the set of processes that will make the correctness assertion valid as

$$\{t \in S \mid \models at : A\},$$

it is not necessarily the case that this set can be expressed *within the logic* as an assertion B over atoms $(t : B_i)$ such that

$$\{t \in S \mid \models B\} = \{t \in S \mid \models at : A\}.$$

In general, the ability to do so, will depend on the expressive power of the logic, and the kind of operation for which we are trying to find a reduction. We will show that for our modal logic and all operators of our process algebra, such a B does indeed exist, and furthermore we give for each operator an algorithm that computes one particular choice of B.

In providing this B the most difficult part concerns – not surprisingly – the fixed-points. The single most important property of fixed-points around which all the reductions are centered, is expressed by the reduction lemma. Recall that a map on a complete meet semilattice is ω-anticontinuous if it preserves meets of all decreasing ω-chains.

Lemma 5 *(Reduction lemma.)*
Suppose D and E are powersets over countable sets, and $in : D \to E$ an ω-anticontinuous function with $in(\top_D) = \top_E$. Suppose $\psi : E \to E$ and $\theta : D \to D$ are both monotonic and have the property

$$\psi \circ in = in \circ \theta.$$

We can then conclude that

$$\nu\psi = in(\nu\theta).$$

To understand the role of the reduction lemma, take E to be the lattice of properties of a compound process and D to be a lattice built from properties of immediate subprocesses. The lemma allows us to express a fixed-point property of the original compound process in terms of fixed-points of functions over properties of its immediate subcomponents via the transformation *in.*

For example, the properties of a process at can be identified with certain subsets of the states S_{at} in the rooting of the transition system pointed by at, and the properties of t with subsets of the states S_t of the transition system pointed by t. Now we take the transformation to be

$$in : \mathcal{P}(S_t) \times \mathcal{P}(\{\bullet\}) \to \mathcal{P}(S_{at})$$

where $in(V_0, V_1) = V_0 \cup \{\underline{at} \mid \bullet \in V_1\}$. The role of the extra product component is to record whether or not the property holds at the initial state $\underline{at}$ of S_{at}. (The rooting is required to ensure that the initial state at is not confused with later occurrences.)[1]

---

[1] Because of the isomorphism $\mathcal{P}(A_0) \times \cdots \times \mathcal{P}(A_n) \times \cdots \cong \mathcal{P}(A_0 + \cdots + A_n + \cdots)$ we can still meet the conditions of the reduction lemma when D is a countable product of powersets of countable sets.

An assertion with a free variable occurring positively essentially denotes a monotonic function $\psi : \mathcal{P}(S_{at}) \rightarrow \mathcal{P}(S_{at})$. The definition of the reduction is given by structural induction on assertions ensuring that assertions denoting such functions ψ, and their reductions denoting monotonic functions $\theta : \mathcal{P}(S_t) \times \mathcal{P}(\{\bullet\}) \rightarrow \mathcal{P}(S_t) \times \mathcal{P}(\{\bullet\})$ are related by in in the manner demanded by the transformation lemma. The lemma then allows the reduction to proceed for fixed-points. As this case of prefixing makes clear reductions of fixed-points can be simultaneous fixed-points. However the use of Bekić's theorem ([Bek84]) replaces the simultaneous fixed-points by fixed-points in the individual components. In the case where these individual components lie in powersets of singletons they end up being replaced by boolean values for closed assertions.

In the course of this definition by structural induction we will be faced with the problem of giving a reduction for assertion variables. One solution to this problem can be found by introducing a syntactic counterpart of in called IN and define a *change of variables* σ to be a map taking all variables X to $IN(X_0, X_1)$. An application of such a substitution to an assertion A has to satisfy certain technical requirements: It should be *fresh i.e.* for an assertion A when (i) for all variables X at which σ is defined the free variables in $\sigma(X)$ are disjoint from those in A, and (ii) for distinct variables X and X', at which σ is defined, the free variables in $\sigma(X)$ and $\sigma(X')$ are disjoint. It is emphasised that while the syntactic counterparts IN of the transformations play the important part in reductions of expressing relationships between variables they do *not* appear in the reductions themselves.

Reductions for all operators can be established along the lines sketched. Each operator involves a judicious choice of in, which IN is to denote. In the following sections we present this choice and the accompanying reductions.

3.1 Prefix

The reduction for prefix is defined inductively on the structure of assertions and shown in figure 1. Note that $\text{red}^0(at : A; \sigma)$ just renames the variables of A from X to X_0. The transformation in was explained in the previous section.[2]

$$
\begin{aligned}
\text{red}^0(at : X; \sigma) \quad &= \quad X_0 \\
&\quad \text{where } \sigma(X) = IN(X_0, X_1) \\
\text{red}^0(at : \nu X.A; \sigma) \quad &= \quad \nu X_0.\text{red}^0(at : A; \sigma) \\
&\quad \text{where } \sigma(X) = IN(X_0, X_1) \\
\text{red}^0(at : (\alpha)A; \sigma) \quad &= \quad (\alpha)\text{red}^0(at : A; \sigma) \\
\text{red}^0(at : \neg A; \sigma) \quad &= \quad \neg\text{red}^0(at : A; \sigma) \\
\text{red}^0(at : A \vee B; \sigma) \quad &= \quad \text{red}^0(at : A; \sigma) \vee \text{red}^0(at : B; \sigma) \\[2mm]
\text{red}^1(at : X; \sigma) \quad &= \quad X_1 \\
&\quad \text{where } \sigma(X) = IN(X_0, X_1) \\
\text{red}^1(at : \nu X.A; \sigma) \quad &= \quad \text{red}^1(at : A; \sigma)[\text{red}^0(at : \nu X.A; \sigma)/X_0][T/X_1] \\
&\quad \text{where } \sigma(X) = IN(X_0, X_1) \\
\text{red}^1(at : (\alpha)A; \sigma) \quad &= \quad \begin{cases} t : \text{red}^0(at : A; \sigma) & \text{if } \alpha = a \\ F & \text{if } \alpha \neq a \end{cases} \\
\text{red}^1(at : \neg A; \sigma) \quad &= \quad \neg\text{red}^1(at : A; \sigma) \\
\text{red}^1(at : A \vee B; \sigma) \quad &= \quad \text{red}^1(at : A; \sigma) \vee \text{red}^1(at : B; \sigma)
\end{aligned}
$$

Figure 1: Reduction for prefix defined inductively on the structure of assertions.

---

[2] For this and the following reductions we have that $\text{red}(at : \langle * \rangle A; \sigma) = red(at : A; \sigma)$ and henceforth we will omit these trivial cases from the presentation.

The reduction is constructed in such a way that the two components are related to A through *in* by

$$[\![A[\sigma]]\!]_{\underline{at}} \phi = in([\![red^0(at : A; \sigma)]\!]_t \phi, [\![red^1(at : A; \sigma)]\!]_\bullet \phi), \tag{1}$$

where σ is a change of variables for A. From the rooting lemma we know that

$$at \in [\![A]\!]_{at} \phi \quad iff \quad \underline{at} \in [\![A]\!]_{at} \phi$$

and from the definition of *in* and (1) we get

$$at \in [\![A]\!]_{at} \phi \quad iff \quad \bullet \in [\![red^1(at : A; \sigma)]\!]_\bullet \phi.$$

As $red^1(at : A; \sigma)$ consists of correctness assertions, negations, and conjunctions only, we can consider it to be a formula in our propositional logic, yielding our reduction

$$\models (at : A) \leftrightarrow red^1(at : A; \sigma).$$

Theorem 6 *(Reduction for prefix.) Given a closed, pure assertion A, a change of variables σ which is fresh for A, and an arbitrary process term t, then $\models (at : A) \leftrightarrow red^1(at : A; \sigma)$.*

3.2 Nil

The reduction for nil is defined inductively on the structure of assertions and shown in figure 2. The definitions of $\neg$ and $\vee$ are similar to the definitions for prefix and therefore omitted. The transformation $in : \mathcal{P}(\{\bullet\}) \to \mathcal{P}(\{nil\})$ is just the direct image of the obvious isomorphism between $\{\bullet\}$ and $\{nil\}$. Note that the reduction for *nil* is quite trivial and just gives true (T) or false (F).

$$
\begin{aligned}
red(nil : X; \sigma) &= Y \text{ where } \sigma(X) = IN(Y) \\
red(nil : \nu X.A; \sigma) &= red(nil : A; \sigma)[T/Y] \text{ where } \sigma(X) = IN(Y) \\
red(nil : \langle \alpha \rangle A; \sigma) &= F
\end{aligned}
$$

Figure 2: Reduction for nil.

Theorem 7 *(Reduction for nil.) Given a closed, pure assertion A and a change of variables σ which is fresh for A, then $\models (nil : A) \leftrightarrow red(nil : A; \sigma)$.*

3.3 Sum

The reduction for sum is presented in figure 3. The definitions for $\neg$ and $\vee$ are omitted as they are similar to the definitions for prefix.

To understand the transformation first note that we have a map $j : S_{t_0} + S_{t_1} \to S_{t_0+t_1}$ taking the initial states of t_0 and t_1 to the state $t_0 + t_1$ in $S_{t_0+t_1}$ and taking all other states to their obvious counterparts. Let $f : (S_{t_0} + S_{t_1}) + \{\bullet\} \to S_{t_0+t_1}$ be the map that takes $\bullet$ to the initial state of $S_{t_0+t_1}$ and on $S_{t_0} + S_{t_1}$ behaves like j. We take the transformation to be

$$in : \mathcal{P}(S_{t_0} + S_{t_1}) \times \mathcal{P}(\{\bullet\}) \to \mathcal{P}(S_{t_0+t_1})$$

where $in(V_0, V_1) = \{j(s) \mid s \in V_0\} \cup \{t_0 + t_1 \mid \bullet \in V_1\}$.

Theorem 8 *(Reduction for sum.) Given a closed, pure assertion A, a change of variables σ which is fresh for A, and arbitrary process terms t_0 and t_1, then*

$$\models (t_0 + t_1 : A) \leftrightarrow red^1(t_0 + t_1 : A; \sigma).$$

$$\begin{aligned}
\text{red}^0(t_0 + t_1 : X; \sigma) &= X_0 \\
&\text{where } \sigma(X) = IN(X_0, X_1) \\
\text{red}^0(t_0 + t_1 : \nu X.A; \sigma) &= \nu X_0.\text{red}^0(t_0 + t_1 : A; \sigma) \\
&\text{where } \sigma(X) = IN(X_0, X_1) \\
\text{red}^0(t_0 + t_1 : \langle \alpha \rangle A; \sigma) &= \langle \alpha \rangle \text{red}^0(t_0 + t_1 : A; \sigma) \\
\\
\text{red}^1(t_0 + t_1 : X; \sigma) &= X_1 \\
&\text{where } \sigma(X) = IN(X_0, X_1) \\
\text{red}^1(t_0 + t_1 : \nu X.A; \sigma) &= \text{red}^1(t_0 + t_1 : A; \sigma)[\text{red}^0(t_0 + t_1 : \nu X.A; \sigma)/X_0][T/X_1] \\
&\text{where } \sigma(X) = IN(X_0, X_1) \\
\text{red}^1(t_0 + t_1 : \langle \alpha \rangle A; \sigma) &= (t_0 : \langle \alpha \rangle A^0) \vee (t_1 : \langle \alpha \rangle A^0) \\
&\text{where } A^0 = \text{red}^0(t_0 + t_1 : A; \sigma)
\end{aligned}$$

Figure 3: Reduction for sum.

3.4 Relabelling

For relabelling we take the transformation to be $in : \mathcal{P}(R_t) \to \mathcal{P}(R_{t\{\Xi\}})$ where $in(V) = \{p\{\Xi\} \mid p \in V\}$.

$$\begin{aligned}
\text{red}(t\{\Xi\} : X; \sigma) &= Y \text{ where } \sigma(X) = IN(Y) \\
\text{red}(t\{\Xi\} : \nu X.A; \sigma) &= \nu Y.\text{red}(t\{\Xi\} : A; \sigma) \text{ where } \sigma(X) = IN(Y) \\
\text{red}(t\{\Xi\} : \langle \alpha \rangle A; \sigma) &= \langle \Xi^{-1}(\alpha) \rangle \text{red}(t\{\Xi\} : A; \sigma)
\end{aligned}$$

Figure 4: Reduction for relabelling.

Theorem 9 *(Reduction for relabelling.) Assume A closed and pure, a change of variables σ which is fresh for A, and an arbitrary process term t, then $\models (t\{\Xi\} : A) \leftrightarrow (t : \text{red}(t\{\Xi\} : A; \sigma))$.*

3.5 Restriction

For restriction we take the transformation to be $in : \mathcal{P}(R_t) \to \mathcal{P}(R_{t\restriction\Lambda})$ where $in(V) = \{p \restriction \Lambda \mid p \in V\} \cap R_{t\restriction\Lambda}$.

$$\begin{aligned}
\text{red}(t \restriction \Lambda : X; \sigma) &= Y \text{ where } \sigma(X) = IN(Y) \\
\text{red}(t \restriction \Lambda : \nu X.A; \sigma) &= \nu Y.\text{red}(t \restriction \Lambda : A; \sigma) \text{ where } \sigma(X) = IN(Y) \\
\text{red}(t \restriction \Lambda : \langle \alpha \rangle A; \sigma) &= \begin{cases} \langle \alpha \rangle \text{red}(t \restriction \Lambda : A; \sigma) & \text{if } \alpha \in \Lambda \\ F & \text{if } \alpha \notin \Lambda \end{cases}
\end{aligned}$$

Figure 5: Reduction for restriction.

Theorem 10 *(Reduction for restriction.) Assume A closed and pure, a change of variables σ which is fresh for A, and an arbitrary process term t, then $\models (t \restriction \Lambda : A) \leftrightarrow (t : \text{red}(t \restriction \Lambda : A; \sigma))$.*

3.6 Recursion

In order to define the reduction for recursion, we will need to extend our assertion language with an assertion $\hat{P}$ to identify recursion points. The semantics of $\hat{P}$ is simply:[3]

---

[3] The general semantics should be $[\![\hat{P}]\!]_T \phi = \{P, \underline{P}\} \cap S_T$, but due to our requirement of guardedness, we will never be involved with rooting a state identifier, so the stated semantics is sufficient.

$$\llbracket \hat{P} \rrbracket_T \phi \;=\; \{P\} \cap S_T.$$

It can be verified that the locality and the rooting lemma still hold. All the reductions mentioned in the previous sections should be extended to take care of the assertions $\hat{P}$ and this is easily done – they should all give F. Furthermore, we add a reduction for P, which is like the one for *nil*, except that it gives T on $\hat{P}$.

For the first time we will need to put in extra correctness assertions in our reductions, which furthermore might contain free assertion variables. These correctness assertions can however be closed by a *closure lemma* and then 'pulled out' by a *purifying lemma* yielding an expression which belongs to the propositional language without any correctness assertions appearing inside other assertions, hence being applicable for further reductions.

Theorem 11 *(The purifying lemma.)*
Let A be an assertion with all correctness assertions closed and let t be a process term. Then there exists an expression B over unnested correctness assertions such that, $\models (t : A) \leftrightarrow B$.

Moreover, the proof of the lemma gives an algorithm for computing such a B. The closure lemma can be found in [Win90].

$$
\begin{aligned}
\mathrm{red}(rec\ P.t : X; \sigma) \quad &= \quad Y \ \ \text{where } \sigma(X) = IN(Y) \\
\mathrm{red}(rec\ P.t : \nu X.A; \sigma) \quad &= \quad \nu Y.\mathrm{red}(rec\ P.t : A; \sigma) \ \text{where } \sigma(X) = IN(Y) \\
\mathrm{red}(rec\ P.t : \langle \alpha \rangle A; \sigma) \quad &= \quad \langle \alpha \rangle A' \vee (\hat{P} \wedge (t : \langle \alpha \rangle A')) \\
&\qquad \text{where } A' = \mathrm{red}(rec\ P.t : A; \sigma)
\end{aligned}
$$

Figure 6: Reduction for recursion. The definitions for $\neg$ and $\vee$ are omitted as they again are similar to the definitions for prefix.

Take $f : S_t \to S_{rec\ P.t}$ to be the map that takes $\underline{t}$ to $rec\ P.t$ and all other states s to $s[rec\ P.t/P]$. The transformation for recursion $in : \mathcal{P}(S_{\underline{t}}) \to \mathcal{P}(S_{rec\ P.t})$ is defined to be the direct image of f.

Theorem 12 *(Reduction for recursion.) Given a closed, pure assertion A, a change of variables σ which is fresh for A, and an arbitrary process term t then*

$$\models (rec\ P.t : A) \leftrightarrow (t : \mathrm{red}(rec\ P.t : A; \sigma)).$$

3.7 Product

A reduction for a product $q \times p$ should be an assertion B over atoms $(q : B_i)$ and $(p : C_j)$ such that

$$\models q \times p : A \quad \textit{iff} \quad \models B.$$

Unfortunately, if we insist on finding such a B without inspecting either p or q, we can get a very complex expression which, in the case of fixed-points will even become infinite unless assumptions on the possible sizes of p and q are made (cf. the remarks at the end of [Win90]). In [Win90] it is shown how a very reasonable sized B can be found, when the assertion language is restricted rather severely, excluding disjunctions, negations, minimal fixed-points, and general box formulas, but still having maximal fixed-points, diamond formulas, a strong version of box formulas, and conjunctions.

Here we present another approach. We give a reduction when p is a process term without restrictions and relabellings, i.e. we find a B (depending on p) s.t.

$$\models q \times p : A \quad \textit{iff} \quad \models q : B.$$

Let $R_p = \{p_1, \ldots, p_n\}$ be the finite set of reachable states of p in some fixed enumeration. We define the map $in : \underbrace{\mathcal{P}(R_q) \times \ldots \times \mathcal{P}(R_q)}_{n} \to \mathcal{P}(R_{q \times p})$ as

$$in(U_{p_1}, \ldots, U_{p_n}) = (U_{p_1} \times p_1) \cup \ldots \cup (U_{p_n} \times p_n).$$

As usual we have a change of variables σ with $\sigma(X) = IN(X_{p_1}, \ldots, X_{p_n})$. As a notational convenience we write A/p for $red(q \times p : A; \sigma)$ omitting the σ which is always assumed to map an X into $X_{p_1}, \ldots, X_{p_n}$. The reduction is shown in figure 7.

$$
\begin{array}{lcl}
\neg A/p & = & \neg(A/p) \\
A_0 \vee A_1/p & = & (A_0/p) \vee (A_1/p) \\
X/p & = & X_p \\
\nu X.A/p & = & C_k(\nu(X_{p_1}, \ldots, X_{p_n}).(A/p_1, \ldots, A/p_n)) \\
& & \text{where } \{p_i\}_i \text{ denotes the set of reachable} \\
& & \text{states from } p \text{ with } p = p_k. \\
A/q \times r & = & (A/r)/q \\
& & \text{with the actions in the modalities of } A \text{ reassociated} \\
\langle \alpha \times \beta \rangle A/nil & = & \left\{ \begin{array}{ll} \langle \alpha \rangle(A/nil) & \text{if } \beta = * \\ F & \text{if } \beta \neq * \end{array} \right. \\
\langle \alpha \times \beta \rangle A/\gamma q & = & \left\{ \begin{array}{ll} \langle \alpha \rangle(A/\gamma q) & \text{if } \beta = * \\ \langle \alpha \rangle(A/q) & \text{if } \beta = \gamma \\ F & \text{otherwise} \end{array} \right. \\
\langle \alpha \times \beta \rangle A/q + r & = & (\langle \alpha \times \beta \rangle A/q) \vee (\langle \alpha \times \beta \rangle A/r) \\
\langle \alpha \times \beta \rangle A/rec\ P.t & = & \langle \alpha \times \beta \rangle A/t[rec\ P.t/P]
\end{array}
$$

Figure 7: Reduction for product. $C_k(\nu \underline{X}.\underline{A})$ denotes the k'th component of the n-ary fixed-point $\nu \underline{X}.\underline{A}$, closed by repeated application of Bekić's theorem[4].

Theorem 13 *(Reduction for product.)*
Assume given a pure and closed assertion A, a change of variables σ, and a term p with no restrictions and relabellings. We then have for an arbitrary term q:

$$\models (q \times p : A) \leftrightarrow (q : red(q \times p : A; \sigma)).$$

The case of the maximal fixed-point is established by repeated application of Bekić's theorem, and the resulting assertion might become rather complex, as in the worst case a fixed-point will appear for each reachable state of p, and on top of this, Bekić's theorem might increase the size of the assertion considerably. We are currently investigating methods to control the potential blow-up in general. We present in the next section an example, that indicates that in practice this need not be the case.

---

[4]Termination is ensured by the well-founded order consisting of the number of products in the process term combined lexicographically with the structure of assertions again combined lexicographically with the maximal depth to a prefix in the process term

4 Examples

It is an important property of all our reductions (except product) that they only dependent on the top-most operator of the process term, hence we can leave part of a process unspecified and still apply the reductions. Technically this can be done by adding *process variables* to our language of processes. Given an assertion and a process with variables, we can then compute a propositional expression with correctness assertions over the variables, expressing what relationship there should be between them in order to make the process satisfy the assertion. In this way the reductions compute what corresponds to weakest preconditions in Hoare logic.

As pointed out in the previous section, the reductions for product has the potential of becoming rather complex. In this section we show by a small example, that in practice, the reductions need not turn out to be too complex.

First we define a binary parallel operator $\|_{K,L}$ which allows its left and right components to independently perform the actions indicated by the sets K and L, except that they are required to synchronise on common actions of K and L. The precise definition is

$$p \|_{K,L} q \stackrel{\text{def}}{=} (p \times q) \upharpoonright \Lambda\{\Xi\}$$

where $\Lambda = \{a \times a \mid a \in K \cap L\} \cup \{a \times * \mid a \in K \setminus L\} \cup \{* \times a \mid a \in L \setminus K\}$ and

$$
\begin{aligned}
\Xi(a \times a) &= a, \quad \text{for all } a \in K \cap L \\
\Xi(a \times *) &= a, \quad \text{for all } a \in K \setminus L \\
\Xi(* \times a) &= a, \quad \text{for all } a \in L \setminus K \\
\Xi(\alpha) & \quad \text{undefined otherwise.}
\end{aligned}
$$

Now assume that we want to construct a small system consisting of a coffee vending machine and a researcher. The coffee machine should be able to accept money and then supply a cup of coffee. The researcher should be able to pay out money, drink coffee, and publish papers. Suppose we know how the researcher behaves, specified by a process term r, but would like to find out what kind of coffee machine x to put into the system, such that eventually the researcher has no other choice than to publish a paper.

In general a property of the form 'eventually only the action α can happen' can be expressed by the assertion

$$\mu X.\langle - \rangle T \wedge [-\alpha]X$$

where

$$\langle - \rangle A = \langle Act \rangle A \qquad [-K]A = [Act \setminus K]A.$$

Our problem can now be restated.

Assume the actions to be p for publish, c for taking/giving coffee, m for taking/giving money, and define $K = \{m, c\}, L = \{m, c, p\}$. Which values of x make the following correctness assertion valid

$$x \|_{K,L} r : \mu X.\langle - \rangle T \wedge [-p]X? \tag{2}$$

Suppose the researcher r behaves as *rec* $P.m.c.(m.c.P + p.P)$. Then expanding the definition of $\|_{K,L}$ and applying the reduction for restriction and relabelling, we get the equivalent correctness assertion

$$x \times r : \mu X.\langle m \times m, c \times c, * \times p \rangle T \wedge [m \times m, c \times c]X$$

and then, by applying the reduction for product, the equivalent

$$x : \mu X.\langle m \rangle T \wedge [m](\langle c \rangle T \wedge [c][m](\langle c \rangle T \wedge [c]X)). \tag{3}$$

One can now use (3) to verify different proposals for coffee machines, without redoing the first two steps. This might be done by our method, or for closed terms by other model checking algorithms.

An interesting point to note about the assertion in (3) is that, although the researcher r had *four* reachable states, and then potentially four fixed-points could appear, only *one* fixed-point appears in the resulting assertion.

Returning to the example, we can verify that a successful choice of x is $m.c.nil$, i.e. a coffee machine that accepts money and give coffee once, and then breaks down, whereas $rec\ P.m.c.P$ is an unsuccessful choice. Reading the assertion in (3) carefully, we can express the requirement to the machine as 'after having offered a finite and odd number of m's followed by c's, no m should be offered.'

Changing the behaviour of the researcher slightly and taking $r = rec\ P.m.c.P + m.c.p.P$ and performing the reductions for restriction, relabelling, and product, we arrive at the correctness assertion $x : F$, i.e. there are no coffee machines that will make the system fulfill the requirement.

References

[AC88] André Arnold and Paul Crubille. A linear algorithm to solve fixed-point equations on transitions systems. *Information Processing Letters*, 29:57–66, 1988.

[Bek84] H. Bekić. Definable operations in general algebras, and the theory of automata and flow charts. *Lecture Notes in Computer Science*, 177, 1984.

[CES86] E.M. Clarke, E.A. Emerson, and A.P. Sistla. Automatic verification of finite-state concurrent systems using temporal logic specifications. *ACM Transactions on Programming Languages and Systems*, 8(2):244–263, 1986.

[Cle90] Rance Cleaveland. Tableau-based model checking in the propositional mu-calculus. *Acta Informatica*, 27:725–747, 1990.

[CLM89] E.M. Clarke, D.E. Long, and K.L. McMillan. Compositional model checking. In *Procedings of 4th Annual Symposium on Logic in Computer Science*. IEEE, 1989.

[Dam90] Mads Dam. Translating CTL* into the modal μ-calculus. Technical Report ECS-LFCS-90-123, Laboratory for Foundations of Computer Science, Uni. of Edinburgh, November 1990.

[EL86] E. Allen Emerson and Chin-Luang Lei. Efficient model checking in fragments of the propositional mu-calculus. In *Symposium on Logic in Computer Science, Proceedings*, pages 267–278. IEEE, 1986.

[Lar88] Kim G. Larsen. Proof systems for Hennessy-Milner logic with recursion. In *Proceedings of CAAP*, 1988.

[LX90] Kim G. Larsen and Liu Xinxin. Compositionality through an operational semantics of contexts. In M.S. Paterson, editor, *Proceedings of ICALP*, volume 443 of *LNCS*, 1990.

[Sti91] Colin Stirling. Modal and Temporal Logics. In S. Abramsky, D. Gabbay, and T. Maibaum, editors, *Handbook of Logic in Computer Science*. Oxford University Press, 1991.

[SW89] Colin Stirling and David Walker. Local model checking in the modal mu-calculus. In *Proceedings of TAPSOFT*, 1989.

[Tar55] A. Tarski. A lattice-theoretical fixpoint theorem and its applications. *Pacific Journal of Mathematics*, 5, 1955.

[Win89] Glynn Winskel. A note on model checking the modal ν-calculus. In *Proceedings of ICALP*, volume 372 of *LNCS*, 1989.

[Win90] Glynn Winskel. On the compositional checking of validity. In J.C.M. Baeten and J.W. Klop, editors, *Proceedings of CONCUR '90*, volume 458 of *LNCS*, 1990.

An action based framework for verifying logical and behavioural properties of concurrent systems

R. De Nicola ✵✩, A. Fantechi ✩, S. Gnesi ✩, G. Ristori ☌

✵ Università La Sapienza Roma

✩ I.E.I. - C.N.R. Pisa

☌ C.P.R. Pisa

Abstract

A system is described which supports proofs of both behavioural and logical properties of concurrent systems; these are specified by means of a process algebra and its associated logics. The logic is an action based version of the branching time logic CTL which we call ACTL; it is interpreted over transition labelled structures while CTL is interpreted over state labelled ones. The core of the system are two existing tools, AUTO and EMC. The first builds the labelled transition system corresponding to a term of a process algebra and permits proof of equivalence and simplification of terms, while the second checks validity of CTL logical formulae. The integration is realized by means of two translation functions from the action based branching time logic ACTL to CTL and from transition-labelled to state-labelled structures. The correctness of the integration is guaranteed by the proof that the two functions when coupled preserve satisfiability of logical formulae.

1. Introduction

Process algebras [Mil89, BW90, Hoa85, Hen88] are generally recognized as a convenient tool for describing concurrent systems at different levels of abstraction. They rely on a small set of basic operators which correspond to primitive notions of concurrent systems and on one or more notions of behavioural equivalence or preorder. The operators are used to build complex systems from more elementary ones. The behavioural equivalences are used to study the relationships between different descriptions (e.g. specification and implementation) of the same system at different levels of abstractions and thus to perform part of the analysis.

In this paper we want to propose a general framework for verifying properties of any process algebra by relying on the fact that they all have a single underlying model: Labelled Transition Systems.

There are already a few verification environments in which properties of concurrent systems specified by means of process algebras can be proved [CPS90, GLZ89, dSV90, BC89, GS90]. All of them provide tools for verifying equivalences or preorders on process algebras specifications. This equivalence-based approach to system verification has a major disadvantage: specifications, even at the most abstract level, tend to be too concrete; they are, anyway, descriptions of system behaviours even when it is assumed that some of the actual actions are invisible.

Logic is a good candidate to provide more abstract specifications; it permits describing systems properties rather than systems behaviours. Indeed, different types of temporal and modal logics have been proposed for the abstract specification of concurrent systems; in particular, modal and temporal logics

Note: The research has been partially supported by the CEC under ESPRIT project 2304 LOTOSPHERE and EBRA project 3011 CEDISYS and by "Progetto Finalizzato Sistemi Informatici e Calcolo Parallelo" of CNR.

have been recognized as suitable for specifying system properties [EH86, HM85, MP89] due to their ability to deal with the notions of *necessity, possibility, eventuality,* etc.. Logics have been equipped with model checkers to prove satisfiability of formulae and thus systems properties: a system is considered as a potential model for the formula expressing the desired property. Actually, very interesting logics like CTL and CTL* which require formulating properties of systems in terms of their states, have been put forward [BCG88, EH86, ES89]; also, sophisticated and efficient model checkers have been developed for them [CES86].

Thus, the behavioural and logical approaches to system specification and verification can be seen as complementary; the first is more fruitfully used to specify abstract properties while the second permits describing more naturally behavioural and structural properties of systems. It would be of great importance to have a uniform setting for reasoning with the support of the tools made available by both methods. Unfortunately, up to now the most successful representatives of the two approaches have been based on different semantic models which take a different standpoint for looking at specifications. State changes and state properties are the base for interpreting logical specifications. Actions causing state changes are the key for interpreting systems behaviours described via process algebras. The semantic models used in the two cases are Kripke Structures and Labelled Transition Systems, respectively. In the first kind of structures, states are labelled to describe how they are modified by the transitions, while in the second, transitions are labelled to describe the actions which cause state changes. Temporal and modal logics and the associated complexity issue have been thoroughly investigated in the setting of Kripke Structures while combinators for transition systems and the issue of behavioural equivalences have received more attention in the setting of Labelled Transition Systems. Due to the success of process algebras, other logics have been proposed (see e.g. [HM85, BGS88, Lar88, Sti89]) which are interpreted over LTS's and tools have been developed to support reasoning with them. However in this case either we have logics, like Hennessy-Milner logic [HM85], that are not sufficiently expressive or logics, like the μ-calculus [Koz83], that require exponential time for model checking.

A recent result from [DV90a] has brought the world of modal logic and process algebras closer. A new logic for process algebras has been defined which is very similar to CTL* but based on actions and interpreted over Labelled Transition Systems. This new logic, ACTL*, is the natural analogue of CTL* but contains relativized modalities like $X_a\varphi$ - to be read "the next transition is labelled by action a and the remaining path satisfies φ"- as demanded by the interpretation model. Like it has been done for CTL*, a purely branching time subset of ACTL*, called ACTL, has been introduced; it is more expressive than Hennessy-Milner Logic and can describe safety and liveness properties [DV90b].

The question is now whether it is possible to have an efficient model checker for ACTL. We show how to use existing model checkers for CTL also to check validity of ACTL formulae. This is done by means of two translation functions, one from ACTL to CTL formulae, the other from Labelled Transition Systems to Kripke Structures. Both translations are linear; this, coupled with the linear algorithm used by the EMC [CES86], guarantees linear model checking.

Indeed, by relying on the translation functions, we define a verification environment that permits both to verify equivalences on systems described by means of a process algebra and properties of such systems expressed in ACTL. The environment consists of two existing tools, AUTO [dSV90] and EMC model checker [CES86], and of two modules, the *model translator* and the *logic translator*, performing the necessary translations. AUTO builds the labelled transition systems corresponding to process algebra terms and permits minimizing and checking equivalences of transition systems. The model translator transforms the transition systems built by AUTO into Kripke structures. The latter are used as models to verify, via EMC model checker, satisfiability of ACTL formulae which have been translated into CTL by the logic translator.

The rest of the paper is organized as follows. In the next section, the relevant definitions of the used logics are summarized. Section 3, the core of the paper, contains the description of our verification environment. In Section 4, a specification and verification example is presented to give a flavour of the potentiality of the verification environment.

2. ACTL: An action based version of CTL

In this section we present the logic CTL [EH86] whose interpretation domains are Kripke Structures and the logic ACTL proposed in [DV90b], based on actions rather than states, whose interpretation domains are Labelled Transition Systems.

A *Kripke Structure* (or *KS*) is a 4-tuple $\mathcal{K} = (S, AP, L, \rightarrow)$ where:
- S is a set of *states*;
- AP is a finite, nonempty set of *atomic proposition names* ranged over by p, q, ...;
- L: $S \rightarrow 2^{AP}$ is a function that labels each state with a set of atomic propositions true in that state;
- $\rightarrow \subseteq S \times S$ is the *transition relation*; an element (r, s)$\in \rightarrow$ is called a *transition* and is written as r$\rightarrow$s.

A *Labelled Transition System* (or *LTS*) is a structure $\mathcal{A} = (S, A, \rightarrow)$ where:
- S is a set of *states*;
- A is a finite, non-empty set of *actions*; the *silent action* τ is not in A;
- $\rightarrow \subseteq S \times (A \cup \{\tau\}) \times S$ is the *transition relation*; an element (r,α,s)$\in \rightarrow$ is called a *transition*, and is written as r$-\alpha\rightarrow$s.

We let $A_\tau = A \cup \{\tau\}$; $A_\varepsilon = A \cup \{\varepsilon\}$, $\varepsilon \notin A_\tau$. Moreover, we let r, s, ... range over states; a, b, ... over A; α, β, ... over A_τ and k, ... over A_ε.

Let us now introduce the notion of paths and runs over a LTS, $\mathcal{A} = (S, A, \rightarrow)$:
- A sequence (s_0,α_0,s_1) $(s_1,\alpha_1,s_2)... \in \rightarrow^\infty$ is called a *path* from s_0; a path that cannot be extended, i.e. is infinite or ends in a state without outgoing transitions, is called a *fullpath*;
- a *run* from $s \in S$ is a pair $\rho = (s,\pi)$, where π is a path from s; we write first(ρ) = s and path(ρ) = π; if π is finite then last(ρ) denotes the last state of π; a *maximal run* is a run whose second element is a fullpath;
- concatenation of runs is denoted by juxtaposition: $\eta = \rho\theta$; it is only defined if ρ is finite and last(ρ)=first(θ). When $\eta = \rho\theta$ we say that θ is a suffix of η; it is a proper suffix if $\rho \neq \varepsilon$.

We write run(s) for the set of runs from s and let π, ... range over paths and ρ, σ, η ... over runs.

The notation for runs that we have introduced for LTS's carries over to Kripke Structures $\mathcal{K} = (S, AP, L, \rightarrow)$ in the obvious way. The only difference is that transitions are no longer triples but pairs.

CTL is a language of state formulae interpreted over Kripke Structures and it is just a subset of CTL* [EH86]; CTL* combines linear and branching time operators; its syntax is given in terms of path formulae that are interpreted over full paths and state formulae that are true or false of a state. CTL is the branching time subset of CTL* in which every linear time operator is immediately preceded by a path quantifier; it is defined as the set of state formulae φ given by the following grammar, where γ ranges on path formulae and p ranges on AP:

$$\varphi \ ::= \ p \mid \neg\varphi \mid \varphi \wedge \varphi \mid \exists\gamma \mid \forall\gamma$$
$$\gamma \ ::= \ X\varphi \mid \varphi U \varphi$$

We write **true** for $\neg(p_0 \wedge \neg p_0)$ where p_0 is some arbitrarily chosen atomic proposition name.

As usual, a set of logic operators and modalities can be derived from the basic ones: **false**, $\varphi \vee \varphi'$ (*or*), $\varphi \Rightarrow \varphi'$ (*implies*), $F\varphi$ (*eventually*), $G\varphi$ (*always*) [EH86].

Let $\mathcal{K} = (S, AP, \mathcal{L}, \rightarrow)$ be a Kripke Structure. We give below a maximal interpretation of CTL formulae, that is we suppose that all maximal runs in $\mathcal{K}$ have infinite length. *Satisfaction* of a CTL formula φ (γ) by a state s (run ρ), notation $s \vDash_{\mathcal{K}} \varphi$ or just $s \vDash \varphi$ ($\rho \vDash_{\mathcal{K}} \gamma$, or $\rho \vDash \gamma$), is defined inductively by:

$s \vDash p$	iff	$p \in \mathcal{L}(s)$;
$s \vDash \neg\varphi$	iff	$s \nvDash \varphi$;
$s \vDash \varphi \wedge \varphi'$	iff	$s \vDash \varphi$ and $s \vDash \varphi'$;
$s \vDash \exists\gamma$	iff	there exists a run $\theta \in$ run(s) such that $\theta \vDash \gamma$;
$s \vDash \forall\gamma$	iff	for all runs $\theta \in$ run(s) $\theta \vDash \gamma$;
$\rho \vDash \varphi U \varphi'$	iff	there exists a suffix θ of ρ such that first(θ) $\vDash \varphi'$ and for all suffixes η of ρ, which have θ as proper suffix: first(η) $\vDash \varphi$;
$\rho \vDash X\varphi$	iff	there exist s, s', θ such that $\rho = (s, (s, s'))\theta$ and $s' \vDash \varphi$.

In order to define the logic ACTL, in [DV90b], a tiny auxiliary logic of actions is introduced.

The collection *Afor* of *action formulae* over A is defined by the following grammar where χ, χ', range over action formulae, and a$\in$ A:

$$\chi ::= \ a \mid \neg\chi \mid \chi \wedge \chi'$$

We write **true** for $\neg(a_0 \wedge \neg a_0)$, where a_0 is some arbitrarily chosen action, and **false** for $\neg$ **true**.

The *satisfaction* of an action formula χ by an action a, notation $a \vDash \chi$, is defined inductively by:

$a \vDash b$	iff	$a = b$;
$a \vDash \neg\chi$	iff	$a \nvDash \chi$;
$a \vDash \chi \wedge \chi'$	iff	$a \vDash \chi$ and $a \vDash \chi'$.

The syntax of the logic ACTL, a subset of ACTL*, is defined by the state formulae generated by the following grammar, where $\varphi, \varphi', \ldots$ range over state-formulae, γ over path formulae and χ and χ' are action formulae:

$$\varphi ::= \textbf{true} \mid \neg\varphi \mid \varphi \wedge \varphi' \mid \exists\gamma \mid \forall\gamma$$
$$\gamma ::= X_\chi\varphi \mid X_\tau\varphi \mid \varphi_\chi U_{\chi'}\varphi' \mid \varphi_\chi U\varphi'$$

We give below the satisfaction relation for ACTL formulae; as above we assume a maximal interpretation, that is, we suppose all maximal runs in the LTS are infinite in length.

Let $\mathcal{A} = (S, A, \rightarrow)$ be a LTS. *Satisfaction* of an ACTL-formula φ (γ) by a state s (run ρ), notation $s \vDash_{\mathcal{A}} \varphi$ or just $s \vDash \varphi$ ($\rho \vDash_{\mathcal{A}} \gamma$, or $\rho \vDash \gamma$), is given inductively by:

$s \models$ **true**		always;
$s \models \neg\varphi$	iff	$s \not\models \varphi$;
$s \models \varphi \wedge \varphi'$	iff	$s \models \varphi$ and $s \models \varphi'$;
$s \models \exists\gamma$	iff	there exists a run $\theta \in run(s)$ such that $\theta \models \gamma$;
$s \models \forall\gamma$	iff	for all runs $\theta \in run(s)$ $\theta \models \gamma$;
$\rho \models \varphi_{\chi}U_{\chi'}\varphi'$	iff	there exists $\theta = (s,(s,a,s'))\theta'$, suffix of ρ, s.t. $s' \models \varphi'$, $a \models \chi'$, $s \models \varphi$
		and for all $\eta = (r,(r,\beta,r'))\eta'$, suffixes of ρ, which have θ as proper
		suffix, we have $r \models \varphi$ and ($\beta \models \chi$ or $\beta = \tau$);
$\rho \models \varphi_{\chi}U\varphi'$	iff	there exists a suffix θ of ρ s. t. $first(\theta) \models \varphi'$ and for all $\eta = (r,(r,\beta,r'))\eta'$
		which have θ as proper suffix we have $r \models \varphi$ and ($\beta \models \chi$ or $\beta = \tau$);
$\rho \models X_{\chi}\varphi$	iff	$\rho = (s,(s,a,s'))\theta$ and $s' \models \varphi$ and $a \models \chi$;
$\rho \models X_{\tau}\varphi$	iff	$\rho = (s,(s,\tau,s'))\theta$ and $s' \models \varphi$.

As usual, derived modalities such as **false**, $\varphi \vee \varphi'$, $\varphi \Rightarrow \varphi'$, $F\varphi$, $G\varphi$ are introduced. Other derived modalities similar to those of Hennessy-Milner logic with until defined in [DV90a] are:

$\varphi <a> \varphi'$	for	$\exists(\varphi_{\text{ false}}U_a \varphi')$,
$\varphi <\varepsilon>\varphi'$	for	$\exists(\varphi_{\text{ false}}U \varphi')$,
$<k> \varphi$	for	**true** $<k> \varphi$,
$[k] \varphi$	for	$\neg <k>\neg\varphi$.

The indexed next modalities $X_{\chi}\varphi$, $X_{\tau}\varphi$ say that in the next state of the run, reached respectively with an action in χ or with a τ, the formula φ holds.

In [DV90b] it has been proved that every formula in ACTL can be translated in one of CTL. In order to define the mapping *lt* between them, they need to introduce a corresponding translation **mt** between their models, that is Labelled Transition Systems and Kripke Structures. In the next section the complete definition of the translation functions **mt** and *lt* is given; these are variants of the original ones *lts* and *lts'*.

3. The Verification Tool

To obtain a general verification environment which enables the user to verify both bisimulation based equivalences and ACTL properties of terms of a process algebras, we have chosen to integrate two tools: AUTO [dSV90] and EMC [CES86]. AUTO is able to generate a Labelled Transition System from a CCS [Mil89] or Meije [AB84] specification and permits verification of bisimulation based equivalences and minimization of states. EMC permits to verify the validity of a CTL formula over a Kripke Structure. Indeed, to perform the check of an ACTL formula φ on a Labelled Transition System M, the following steps are needed:

1) Input M and φ;
2) Translate M into the corresponding Kripke Structure M';
3) Translate φ into the corresponding CTL formula φ';
4) Perform the Model Checking of φ' on M'.

The architecture of our environment is summarized by the picture below:

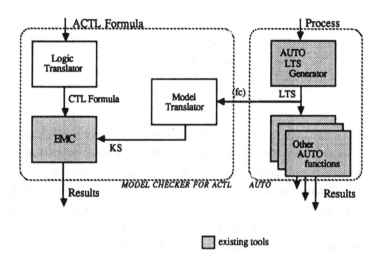

■ existing tools

3.1. Generating the Labelled Transition System

To build the Labelled Transition System corresponding to a term we use AUTO. It must be said that the actual construction phase starts only if a finiteness test is passed. Indeed, some terms might lead to generating an infinite number of states and AUTO; before starting the actual construction of the LTS, takes advantage of the sufficient conditions for finiteness given in [MV90].

The LTS provided by AUTO can be written in a number of different formats; one of these is called *format commun*; it has been proposed as standard format for representing automata.

3.2. The Model Translator

The Model Translator transforms the LTS produced by AUTO into a suitable input for the EMC, i.e. a Kripke Structure. In order to provide this functionality we have implemented the T1 algorithm given below.

Given a Labelled Transition System the corresponding Kripke Structure is obtained by splitting the transitions labelled by visible actions and creating a new state for each of them, labelled by the label of the original transition; the generated system has almost the same structure of the original one. In the picture below, the translations of an observable and of an unobservable transition are shown:

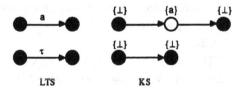

LTS   KS

T1 *(From LTS's to KS's)*
Let $\mathcal{A} = (S, A, \rightarrow)$ be a LTS, S_d the subset of states of S without successors, and $\bot$ be a fresh symbol not in A. The KS, $mt(\mathcal{A})$, is defined as $(S', AP, \mathcal{L}, \rightarrow')$ where:
• $S' = S \cup \{(r,a,s) \mid a \in A \text{ and } r -a \rightarrow s\} \cup N$,   with $N = \{s_f\}$ if $S_d \neq \{\}$ and $N = \{\}$ otherwise;

- $AP = A \cup \{\bot\}$;
- $\rightarrow' = \{(r,s) \mid r -\tau\rightarrow s\} \cup \{(r,(r,a,s)) \mid r -a\rightarrow s\} \cup \{((r,a,s),s) \mid r -a\rightarrow s\} \cup T$,
  with $T = \{(t,s_f) \mid t \in S_d\} \cup \{(s_f, s_f)\}$ if $S_d \neq \{\}$ and $T = \{\}$ otherwise;
- For $r, s \in S$ and $a \in A$: $L(s) = \{\bot\}$, $L((r,a,s)) = \{a\}$
- $L(s_f) = \{\bot\}$.

Note that the translation produces a Kripke Structure with a larger number of states; new states are labelled with the same label of the corresponding transition while old ones are labelled with a *fresh* symbol, $\bot$, which can be interpreted as: *no visible actions occurred*. To comply with maximal interpretation of ACTL formulae, we have added an additional step to the original translation in [DV90b]: if there exist finite maximal runs in the LTS then in the corresponding KS a self looping new state s_f is created, labelled by $\bot$ and finite paths are extended to relate deadlocked states with s_f.

The size of the sets of states and transitions of the Kripke Structure produced by the above algorithm is given by the following formulae, where $n = |S|$, $d = |S_d|$, $m = |\rightarrow|$, and u is the number of unobservable transitions in $\rightarrow$:

$$|S'| = \begin{cases} n + m - u & \text{if } d = 0 \\ n + m - u + 1 & \text{if } d \neq 0 \end{cases} \quad \text{and} \quad |\rightarrow'| = \begin{cases} 2m - u & \text{if } d = 0 \\ 2m - u + 1 + d & \text{if } d \neq 0 \end{cases}$$

3.3. The Logic-Translator

This module transforms an ACTL formula into a suitable input formula for the EMC, i.e. a CTL formula. This translation step has been implemented by parsing the ACTL formula before presenting it to EMC; once an ACTL formula is parsed, its translation into CTL is given according to the following $\mathfrak{lt}$ function. We have modified the original function presented in [DV90b] in order to take into account quantifications over linear time operators.

T2 (*From ACTL to CTL*)

The mapping $\mathfrak{lt}$: ACTL $\rightarrow$ CTL is inductively defined by:

- $\mathfrak{lt}(true)$ = true,
- $\mathfrak{lt}(\neg\varphi)$ = $\neg \mathfrak{lt}(\varphi)$,
- $\mathfrak{lt}(\varphi\wedge\varphi')$ = $\mathfrak{lt}(\varphi) \wedge \mathfrak{lt}(\varphi')$,
- $\mathfrak{lt}(\exists(\varphi_\chi U_{\chi'} \varphi'))$ = $\exists(((\bot \wedge \mathfrak{lt}(\varphi)) \vee (\neg\bot \wedge\chi)) U ((\neg\bot \wedge \chi') \wedge \exists X(\bot \wedge \mathfrak{lt}(\varphi'))))$,
- $\mathfrak{lt}(\exists(\varphi_\chi U \varphi'))$ = $(\bot \wedge \mathfrak{lt}(\varphi')) \vee \exists(((\bot \wedge \mathfrak{lt}(\varphi)) \vee (\neg\bot \wedge\chi)) U (\bot \wedge \mathfrak{lt}(\varphi')))$,
- $\mathfrak{lt}(\exists X_\chi\varphi)$ = $\exists X(\neg\bot \wedge \chi \wedge \exists X(\mathfrak{lt}(\varphi)))$,
- $\mathfrak{lt}(\exists X_\tau\varphi)$ = $\bot \wedge \exists X(\bot \wedge \mathfrak{lt}(\varphi))$,
- $\mathfrak{lt}(\forall(\varphi_\chi U_{\chi'} \varphi'))$ = $\forall(((\bot \wedge \mathfrak{lt}(\varphi)) \vee (\neg\bot \wedge\chi)) U ((\neg\bot \wedge \chi') \wedge \forall X(\bot \wedge \mathfrak{lt}(\varphi'))))$,
- $\mathfrak{lt}(\forall(\varphi_\chi U \varphi'))$ = $(\bot \wedge \mathfrak{lt}(\varphi')) \vee \forall(((\bot \wedge \mathfrak{lt}(\varphi)) \vee (\neg\bot \wedge\chi)) U (\bot \wedge \mathfrak{lt}(\varphi')))$,
- $\mathfrak{lt}(\forall X_\chi\varphi)$ = $\forall X(\neg\bot \wedge \chi \wedge \forall X(\mathfrak{lt}(\varphi)))$,
- $\mathfrak{lt}(\forall X_\tau\varphi)$ = $\bot \wedge \forall X(\bot \wedge \mathfrak{lt}(\varphi))$.

The key result about $\mathfrak{L}t$ is that it preserves truth, that is if $\mathcal{A}$ is a LTS and φ is an ACTL-formula then $\mathcal{A}\models\varphi$ if and only if $mt(\mathcal{A})\models\mathfrak{L}t(\varphi)$. An interesting property of the T2 algorithm is that the size of $\mathfrak{L}t(\varphi)$ is linear in the size of φ.

Proposition: Let $\mathcal{A}$ an LTS, $\mathcal{K}$ the corresponding KS obtained by means of algorithm T1, and $s\in S$; then $s\models_{\mathcal{A}}\varphi$ if and only if $s\models_{\mathcal{K}}\mathfrak{L}t(\varphi)$.

Sketch of the proof:

This proof is made by induction on the length of the ACTL formulae. We show for every formula φ that $s\not\models_{\mathcal{A}}\varphi$ implies $s\not\models_{\mathcal{K}}\mathfrak{L}t(\varphi)$ and $s\models_{\mathcal{A}}\varphi$ implies $s\models_{\mathcal{K}}\mathfrak{L}t(\varphi)$.

Note that in the construction of $mt(\mathcal{A})$ to every state in S there corresponds a state in S' with the same name; moreover, only states corresponding to existing ones are labelled with $\perp$. New states in $mt(\mathcal{A})$ are labelled with the action associated to the corresponding transition; then, if the label of the transition satisfies a given action formula χ we have that the corresponding state satisfies the CTL formula χ. We refer the interested reader to the forthcoming version of the paper.

3.4. Model Checking

The output of the Model Translation phase is given as input to EMC. The ACTL expressions to be verified can be given as input to the EMC prompt; any time an ACTL formula is given, EMC calls the Logic Translator providing the corresponding CTL formula; then EMC checks the CTL formula on the Kripke Structure, giving as result true or false.

It is not difficult to see that we can perform model checking for ACTL with time complexity $O((|S|+|\rightarrow|) \times |\varphi|)$. Indeed, if we let $\mathcal{A}$ be a finite LTS, s be a state of $\mathcal{A}$ and φ be an ACTL formula, in order to determine whether $s\models_{\mathcal{A}}\varphi$ it suffices to check whether $s\models_{\mathcal{K}}\mathfrak{L}t(\varphi)$. We can compute $mt(\mathcal{A})$ in $O(|S|+|\rightarrow|)$-time and the number of states and transitions of $mt(\mathcal{A})$ will be of order $|S|+|\rightarrow|$. The formula $\mathfrak{L}t(\varphi)$ can be computed in $O(|\varphi|)$-time and its size will be of order $|\varphi|$. Model checking of formula φ on $\mathcal{A}$ with the algorithm for CTL of [CES86] can be therefore performed in $O((|S|+|\rightarrow|) \times |\varphi|)$-time.

4. The Crossing example

We present now an example starting from the CCS specification in [BS90], in which a road crossing a railway is specified. This crossing is such that the barriers on the road are usually kept down and lifted when a car approaches and tries to cross; the traffic lights on the railway are usually red and turn green when a train approaches and tries to cross. In the CCS-Meije specification below the actions 'train' and 'car' represent respectively the action of a train and a car approaching, 'tcross' and 'ccross' the passage of a train and the passage of a car. The process Semaphore controls the barriers and the traffic lights. The notation a? represents the complementary action of a.

```
let rec {Rail = train: green: tcross: red?: Rail} in Rail;
let rec {Road = car: up: ccross: down?: Road} in Road;
let rec {Semaphore = green?: red: Semaphore + up?: down: Semaphore} in Semaphore;
let rec {Crossing = (Road // Rail // Semaphore)\green\red\up\down} in Crossing;
```

Our aim is checking wether the process Crossing satisfies the safety property (mutual exclusion):

it never happens that both a car and a train are able to cross, and the following liveness property (fairness):

whenever a train (a car) approaches, it eventually crosses.

To express mutual exclusion, we need describing by means of an ACTL formula that whenever a car can cross then trains cannot cross until the car does it and viceversa:

$$\forall G((\exists X_{ccross}\ \mathbf{true} \rightarrow \forall(\mathbf{true}\ _{\neg tcross}U_{ccross}\ \mathbf{true})) \wedge (\exists X_{tcross}\mathbf{true} \rightarrow \forall(\mathbf{true}\ _{\neg ccross}U_{tcross}\ \mathbf{true}))) \qquad (1)$$

We can express the liveness property with the following ACTL formula:

$$\forall G(([train]\ \forall(\mathbf{true}\ _{\neg train}U_{tcross}\ \mathbf{true})) \wedge ([car]\ \forall(\mathbf{true}\ _{\neg car}U_{ccross}\ \mathbf{true}))) \qquad (2)$$

Below we show the LTS produced by AUTO and the Kripke Structure resulting from the Model Translation phase.

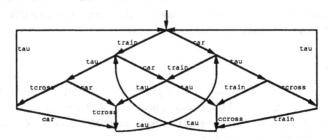

Figure 1: the LTS for Crossing

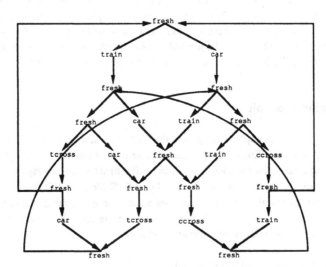

Figure 2: the Kripke Structure in the EMC format.

After the Logic Translation phase, the EMC can be used to check whether the formulae (1) and (2) hold on the Kripke Structure. The result of the model checking phase is that the level crossing does not enjoy the liveness property (2), while it does enjoy the safety property (1).

5. Conclusions

We have presented a uniform environment for the verification of logical and behavioural properties of Process Definition Languages; both classes of properties are interpreted over a single model, namely Labelled Transition Systems. The verification environment is the result of the integration of two existing tools, the EMC model checker [CES86] and AUTO [dSV90], by means of two translation functions from Labelled Transition Systems to Kripke Structures, and from the logic ACTL to the logic CTL. A work similar to ours in this respect is presented in [JKP90]. These authors use CTL as a logic for Labelled Transition Systems but substantially change the satisfaction relation; they have a relativized satisfaction relation $<a, s> \models \varphi$ instead of the relativized modality $X_a \varphi$. The expressive power of the two languages is similar, but the satisfaction relation used here is more immediate. Besides, they do not consider invisible actions and we have not yet seen a generalization of their approach to systems with silent steps in a way that would preserve some behavioural equivalence.

We see our tool as an experiment and as a means of assessing the expressivity of the action logic, if it proves fruitful then we would certainly write a direct model checker for ACTL.

In this way we could implement the useful "counterexample" facility provided by EMC: if a formula does not hold in the model, EMC looks for a path in the model which falsifies the given formula. We have considered the possibility of importing this functionality in our framework, but it is not an easy task to reinterprete all the CTL formulae provided by the EMC counterexample facility as ACTL ones. The effort needed to reverse both the logic and the transition system translators appears not smaller than that needed to build a new model checker for ACTL from the scratch.

Acknowledgements
The first author would like to thank Frits Vaandrager for joint work and discussions on the topics of the paper.

References

[AB84] D. Austry, G. Boudol: Algèbre de Processus et Synchronization. *Theoretical Computer Science*, **30**, (1) 1984, pp. 91-131

[BC89] T. Bolognesi, M. Caneve: Squiggles: a Tool for the Analysis of LOTOS Specifications, in "Formal Description Techniques" (K. Turner, ed.), North-Holland, 1989.

[BCG88] M.C. Browne, E.M. Clarke, O. Grümberg: Characterizing Finite Kripke Structures in Propositional Temporal Logic. *Theoretical Computer Science*, **59** (1,2), 1988, pp. 115-131.

[BGS88] A. Boujjani, S. Graf, J. Sifakis: A Logic for the Description of Behaviours and Properties of Concurrent Systems. In *Linear Time, Branching Time and Partial Order in Logics and Models for Concurrency*, (de Bakker, J.et al., eds.) LNCS **354**, Springer-Verlag, 1989, pp. 398-410.

[BS90] J. Bradfield, C. Stirling: Verifying Temporal Properties of Processes. in *Concur 90*(J. C. P. Baeten, J. W. Klop, eds), LNCS **458**, Springer-Verlag, 1990, pp. 115-125.

[BW90] J. C. M. Baeten, W. P. Weijland: Process Algebra. Cambridge Tracts in *Theoretical Computer Science* 18. Cambridge University Press, 1990.

[CES86] E.M. Clarke, E.A. Emerson, A.P. Sistla: Automatic Verification of Finite State Concurrent Systems using Temporal Logic Specifications. *ACM Toplas*, **8** (2), 1986, pp. 244-263.

[CPS90] R. Cleaveland, J. Parrow, B. Steffen: The Concurrency Workbench. In *Automatic Verification Methods for Finite State Systems* (J. Sifakis, ed.) LNCS **407**, Springer-Verlag, 1990, pp. 24-37.

[dSV90] R. de Simone, D. Vergamini: Aboard AUTO, I.N.R.I.A. Technical Report 111 (1990).

[DV90a] R. De Nicola, F. W. Vaandrager: Three Logics for Branching Bisimulations (Extended Abstract) in *LICS '90*, IEEE Computer Society Press, 1990, pp. 118-129.

[DV90b] R. De Nicola, F. W. Vaandrager: Action versus State based Logics for Transition Systems. In *Semantics of Systems of Concurrent Processes* (I. Guessarian,ed.), LNCS **469**, 1990, pp. 407-419.

[EH86] E. A. Emerson, J. Y. Halpern: "Sometimes" and "Not Never" Revisited: on Branching Time versus Linear Time Temporal Logic. *Journal of ACM*, **33**, 1, 1986, pp. 151-178.

[ES89] E. A. Emerson, J. Srinivasan: Branching Time Temporal Logic. In *Linear Time, Branching Time and Partial Order in Logics and Models for Concurrency*, (de Bakker et al., eds.) LNCS **354**, Springer-Verlag, 1989, pp. 123-172.

[GLZ89] J. C. Godskesen, K. G. Larsen, M. Zeeberg: TAV Users Manual, Internal Report, Aalborg University Center, Denmark, (1989).

[GS90] H. Garavel, J Sifakis: Compilation and Verification of LOTOS Specifications, in *Protocol Specification, Testing and Verification*, X, (L. Logrippo et al., eds.) North Holland , 1990.

[Hen88] M. Hennessy: *An Algebraic Theory of Processes*, MIT Press, Cambridge, 1988.

[HM85] M. Hennessy, R. Milner: Algebraic Laws for Nondeterminism and Concurrency. *Journal of ACM*, **32**, 1985, pp. 137-161.

[Hoa85] C. A. R. Hoare: *Communicating Sequential Processes*. Prentice Hall International, 1985.

[JKP90] B. Jonsson, A.H. Khan, J. Parrow: Implementing a model checking algorithm by adapting existing automated tools. In *Automatic Verification Methods for Finite State Systems* (J. Sifakis, ed.) LNCS **407**, Springer-Verlag, 1990, pp. 179-188.

[Koz83] D. Kozen: Results on the Propositional μ-calculus, *Theoretical Computer Science*, **27**, 1983.

[Lar88] K. G. Larsen: Proof Systems for Hennessy-Milner Logic with Recursion, in Proceedings *CAAP '88* (M. Dauchet & M. Nivat eds) LNCS **299**, Springer-Verlag, 1988.

[Mil89] R. Milner: *Communication and Concurrency*, Prentice Hall International,1989.

[MP89] Z. Manna, A. Pnueli: The Anchored Version of the Temporal Framework, in *Linear Time, Branching Time and Partial Order in Logics and Models for Concurrency*, (de Bakker et al., eds.) LNCS **354**, Springer-Verlag, 1989.

[MV90] E. Madeleine, D. Vergamini: AUTO: A Verification Tool for Distributed Systems Using Reduction of Finite Automata Networks, in *Formal Description Techniques II* (S.T. Vuong, ed.), North-Holland, 1990.

[Sti89] C. Stirling: Temporal Logics for CCS, in *Linear Time, Branching Time and Partial Order in Logics and Models for Concurrency*, (de Bakker et. al., eds.) LNCS **354**, Springer-Verlag, 1989, pp. 660-672.

[vGW89] R. J. van Glabbeek, W. P. Weijland: Branching Time and Abstraction in Bisimulation Semantics. In *Information Processing '89* (G.X. Ritter, ed.), North Holland, 1989, pp. 613-618.

A Linear-Time Model-Checking Algorithm for the Alternation-Free Modal Mu-Calculus

Rance Cleaveland*   Bernhard Steffen[†]

Abstract

We develop a model-checking algorithm for a logic that permits propositions to be defined with greatest and least fixed points of mutually recursive systems of equations. This logic is as expressive as the alternation-free fragment of the modal mu-calculus identified by Emerson and Lei, and it may therefore be used to encode a number of temporal logics and behavioral preorders. Our algorithm determines whether a process satisfies a formula in time proportional to the product of the sizes of the process and the formula; this improves on the best known algorithm for similar fixed-point logics.

1 Introduction

Behavioral equivalences and preorders, and temporal logics, have been used extensively in automated verification tools for finite-state processes [CES, Fe, MSGS, RRSV, RdS]. The relations are typically used to relate a high-level *specification* process to a more detailed *implementation* process, while temporal logics enable system designers to formulate collections of properties that implementations must satisfy. Decision procedures have been developed for computing different behavioral relations and for determining when processes satisfy formulas in several temporal logics, and they have been incorporated into various automated tools. Typically, these tools support only one of these verification methods. However, recent results point to advantages of using the methods together (cf. [CS1, GS]), and therefore to the need for tools, like the Concurrency Workbench [CPS1, CPS2], which support all three. Moreover, such combined tools are not necessarily more complex than single-purpose tools, as e.g. preorder checking may be efficiently reduced to model checking [CS2]; the model-checking algorithm in [CS2] leads to the most efficient algorithm known for preorder checking.

In this paper, we extend the algorithm of [CS2] to deal with a logic whose propositions are defined by least, as well as greatest, fixed points of mutually recursive systems of equations. This logic is strictly more expressive than the logic of [CS2]; it has the same power as the alternation-free fragment of the modal mu-calculus [EL], and therefore a number of different branching-time logics, including Computation Tree Logic [CES] and Propositional Dynamic Logic [FL], have uniform, linear-time encodings in it. Moreover, the time complexity of our new algorithm is proportional to the product of the sizes of the process and the formula under consideration, and therefore matches the complexity of the algorithm in [CS2].

The remainder of the paper develops along the following lines. Section 2 describes transition systems, which serve as our process model, and presents our logic. The section following then gives our model-checking algorithm, and Section 4 shows how the algorithm may be applied to model checking in other logics as well as to the calculation of behavioral preorders. The final section contains our conclusions and directions for future research.

---

*Department of Computer Science, North Carolina State University, Raleigh, NC 27695-8206, USA. Research supported by National Science Foundation/DARPA Grant CCR-9014775.

[†]Lehrstuhl für Informatik II, Rheinisch-Westfälische Technische Hochschule Aachen, D-5100 Aachen, GERMANY.

Formulas are interpreted with respect to a fixed labeled transition system $\langle S, Act, \rightarrow \rangle$, a valuation $\mathcal{V} : \mathcal{A} \rightarrow 2^S$, and an environment $e : Var \rightarrow 2^S$.

$$
\begin{aligned}
[\![A]\!]e &= \mathcal{V}(A) \\
[\![X]\!]e &= e(X) \\
[\![\Phi_1 \vee \Phi_2]\!]e &= [\![\Phi_1]\!]e \cup [\![\Phi_2]\!]e \\
[\![\Phi_1 \wedge \Phi_2]\!]e &= [\![\Phi_1]\!]e \cap [\![\Phi_2]\!]e \\
[\![\langle a \rangle \Phi]\!]e &= \{\, s \mid \exists s'.\, s \xrightarrow{a} s' \wedge s' \in [\![\Phi]\!]e \,\} \\
[\![[a]\Phi]\!]e &= \{\, s \mid \forall s'.\, s \xrightarrow{a} s' \Rightarrow s' \in [\![\Phi]\!]e \,\}
\end{aligned}
$$

Figure 1: The semantics of basic formulas.

2 Processes and the Modal Mu-Calculus

We use *labeled transition systems* to model processes. These may be formally defined as follows.

Definition 2.1 *A labeled transition system $\mathcal{T}$ is a triple $\langle S, Act, \rightarrow \rangle$, where:*

- *S is a set of states;*

- *Act is a set of actions; and*

- *$\rightarrow \subseteq S \times Act \times S$ is the transition relation.*

Intuitively, a labeled transition system encodes the operational behavior of a process. The set S represents the set of states the process may enter, and Act contains the set of actions the process may perform. The relation $\rightarrow$ describes the actions available to states and the state transitions that may result upon execution of the actions. In the remainder of the paper we use $s \xrightarrow{a} s'$ in lieu of $\langle s, a, s' \rangle \in \rightarrow$, and we write $s \xrightarrow{a}$ when there is an s' such that $s \xrightarrow{a} s'$. If $s \xrightarrow{a} s'$ then we say that s' is an *a-derivative* of s.

Given a labeled transition system $\mathcal{T} = \langle S, Act, \rightarrow \rangle$, we define processes as *rooted transition systems*, i.e. as pairs $\langle \mathcal{T}, s \rangle$, where $s \in S$ is a distinguished element, the "start state". If the transition system is obvious from the context, we omit reference to it; in this case, processes will be identified with their start states. Finally, when S and Act are finite, we say that the labeled transition system is *finite-state*.

2.1 Syntax and Semantics of Basic Formulas

The logic we consider may be viewed as a variant of the modal mu-calculus [Ko], or the Hennessy-Milner Logic with recursion [La]. Let Var be a (countable) set of variables, $\mathcal{A}$ a set of atomic propositions, and Act a set of actions. In what follows, X will range over Var, A over $\mathcal{A}$, and a over Act. Then the syntax of *basic* formulas is given by the following grammar.

$$\Phi ::= A \mid X \mid \Phi \vee \Phi \mid \Phi \wedge \Phi \mid \langle a \rangle \Phi \mid [a]\Phi$$

The formal semantics appears in Figure 1. It is given with respect to a labeled transition system $\langle S, Act, \rightarrow \rangle$, a valuation $\mathcal{V}$ mapping atomic propositions to subsets of S, and an environment e mapping variables to subsets of S. Intuitively, the semantic function maps a formula to the set of states for which the formula is "true". Accordingly, a state s satisfies $A \in \mathcal{A}$ if s is in the valuation of A, while s satisfies X if s is an element of the set bound to X in e. The propositional constructs are interpreted in the usual fashion: s satisfies $\Phi_1 \vee \Phi_2$ if it satisfies one of the Φ_i and $\Phi_1 \wedge \Phi_2$ if it satisfies both of them. The constructs $\langle a \rangle$ and $[a]$ are *modal operators*; s satisfies $\langle a \rangle \Phi$ if it has an a-derivative satisfying Φ, while s satisfies $[a]\Phi$ if each of its a-derivatives satisfies Φ.

2.2 Syntax of Equational Blocks

Formulas may also be defined using sets of *blocks* of (mutually recursive) equations. A *block* of equations has one of two forms — $min\{E\}$ or $max\{E\}$ — where E is a list of equations

$$X_1 = \Phi_1$$
$$\vdots$$
$$X_n = \Phi_n$$

in which each Φ_i is a basic formula and the X_i are all distinct. Intuitively, a block defines n mutually recursive propositions, one per variable; the precise role played by the *max* and *min* indicators will become clear in a moment. Several blocks may be used to define formulas, and the right-hand sides of an equation in one block may refer to variables appearing on the left-hand sides of equations in other blocks. In what follows we assume that all the variables that appear on the left-hand sides in a set of blocks are distinct, and we also impose an additional syntactic restriction. Define $B_i \rightarrow B_j$ if B_i and B_j are distinct and a left-hand-side variable in B_i appears in a right-hand-side expression of B_j. Then the "block graph" induced by $\rightarrow$ must be acyclic. This ensures that there are no *alternating fixed points* [EL]; we shall have more to say on this later.

2.3 Semantics of Equational Blocks

To define the semantics of a set B of blocks, we first define the semantics of an individual block. Let E be the set of equations

$$X_1 = \Phi_1$$
$$\vdots$$
$$X_n = \Phi_n.$$

Then, given a fixed environment e, we may build a function $f_E^e : (2^S)^n \rightarrow (2^S)^n$ as follows. Let $\overline{S} = \langle S_1, \ldots, S_n \rangle \in (2^S)^n$, and let $e_{\overline{S}} = e[X_1 \mapsto S_1, \ldots, X_n \mapsto S_n]$ be the environment that results from e by updating the binding of X_i to S_i. Then

$$f_E^e(\overline{S}) = \langle \llbracket \Phi_1 \rrbracket e_{\overline{S}}, \ldots, \llbracket \Phi_n \rrbracket e_{\overline{S}} \rangle.$$

$(2^S)^n$ forms a complete lattice, where the ordering, join and meet operations are the pointwise extensions of the set-theoretic inclusion $\subseteq$, union $\cup$ and intersection $\cap$, respectively. Moreover, for any equation system E and environment e, f_E^e is monotonic with respect to this lattice and therefore, according to the Tarski fixed-point theorem [Ta], has both a *greatest* fixed point, νf_E^e, and a *least* fixed point, μf_E^e. In general, these may be characterized as follows.

$$\nu f_E^e = \bigcup \{ \overline{S} \mid \overline{S} \subseteq f_E^e(\overline{S}) \}$$
$$\mu f_E^e = \bigcap \{ \overline{S} \mid f_E^e(\overline{S}) \subseteq \overline{S} \}$$

When the labeled transition system is finite-state f_E^e is continuous, and the fixed points also have an iterative characterization. Let

$$f_0 = \langle S, \ldots, S \rangle$$
$$\hat{f}_0 = \langle \emptyset, \ldots, \emptyset \rangle$$
$$f_{i+1} = f_E^e(f_i) \text{ for } i \geq 0$$
$$\hat{f}_{i+1} = f_E^e(\hat{f}_i) \text{ for } i \geq 0.$$

Then $\nu f_E^e = \bigcap_{i=0}^{\infty} f_i$, and $\mu f_E^e = \bigcup_{i=0}^{\infty} \hat{f}_i$.

Blocks $max\{E\}$ and $min\{E\}$ are now interpreted as *environments* in the following fashion.

$$[\![max\{E\}]\!]e = e_{\nu f_B^e}$$
$$[\![min\{E\}]\!]e = e_{\mu f_B^e}$$

So $max\{E\}$ represents the "greatest" fixed point of E, while $min\{E\}$ represents the least.

We now give the semantics of a (finite) set of blocks B satisfying our syntactic condition. Let $B_1, \ldots, B_m$ be a topological sorting of the blocks in B according to the relation $\rightarrow$ defined above. Notice that the syntactic restriction ensures the following: the variables that can appear on the right-hand side of an equation in B_j can only appear on the left-hand side of equations in blocks B_i with $i \leq j$, if they appear on any left-hand side at all. We now define the following sequence of environments, where e is given.

$$e_1 = [\![B_1]\!]e$$
$$\vdots$$
$$e_m = [\![B_m]\!]e_{m-1}$$

Then $[\![B]\!]e = e_m$. Note that the syntactic restriction ensures that $[\![B]\!]e_m = e_m$.

It is possible to define what it means for a state in a transition system to satisfy a formula whose variables are "bound" by a set of equations. First, we say that a basic proposition Φ is *closed* with respect to a set of blocks B if every variable in Φ appears on the left-hand side of some equation in some block in B. We also refer to a set of blocks B as closed if each right-hand side in each block in B is closed with respect to B. Then it turns out that for any e and e' and closed B, $[\![B]\!]e = [\![B]\!]e'$. This is a corollary of the following, more general result.

Proposition 2.2 *Let B be a closed set of blocks, and Φ be a proposition being closed with respect to B. Then for any environments e and e',* $[\![\Phi]\!]([\![B]\!]e) = [\![\Phi]\!]([\![B]\!]e')$

When B is closed with respect to itself we often omit reference to e and speak of $[\![B]\!]$, and we write $s \models \Phi \ where \ B$ when Φ and B are closed with respect to B and $s \in [\![\Phi]\!][\![B]\!]$.

To illustrate how properties may be formulated using sets of blocks of equations, consider the following set containing two blocks.[1]

$$B_1 \equiv min\{X_1 = P \wedge [a]X_1 \wedge \langle a \rangle tt\}$$
$$B_2 \equiv max\{X_2 = X_1 \wedge [a]X_2\}$$

Intuitively, the proposition X_2 where $\{B_1, B_2\}$ represents the CTL formula $AG\,AF\,P$ — "it is always the case that eventually, P will hold" — for labeled transition systems in which $Act = \{a\}$. Notice that $B_1 \rightarrow B_2$, since X_1 is mentioned in the right-hand side of the equation in B_2.

2.4 Blocks and Alternated Nesting

In this section we establish a correspondence between the logic introduced in Sections 2.1 and 2.2 and the alternation-free modal mu-calculus. Emerson and Lei [EL] define the notion of alternation depth of a formula in the modal mu-calculus. Intuitively, the alternation depth of a formula refers to the "level" of mutually recursive greatest and least fixed-point operators. When no such mutual recursion exists, the alternation depth is one, and the formula is said to be *alternation-free*. They refer to $L\mu_1$ as the alternation-free fragment of the full logic. We have the following.

Theorem 2.3 (Expressivity)
Let $\mathcal{T}$ be a transition system, and let e be an environment mapping formula variables to sets of states in $\mathcal{T}$. Then:

---

[1] Here tt is an atomic proposition that holds of every state in every labeled transition system.

1. *Every formula Γ in $L\mu_1$ can be translated in time proportional to the size of Γ into a block set B with $[\![\Gamma]\!]e = [\![X]\!]([\![B]\!]e)$ for some left-hand-side variable X of B.*

2. *For every block set B and variable X there is a formula Γ in $L\mu_1$ with $[\![X]\!]([\![B]\!]e) = [\![\Gamma]\!]e$.*

Thus our logic is as expressive as the alternation-free modal mu-calculus.

3   A Linear-Time Model Checker

In this section we present an algorithm for computing $[\![B]\!]$ for a closed set of blocks B with acyclic block graph, given a finite-state transition system. The algorithm, **solve**, extends the algorithm of [CS2], which only deals with maximum fixed points. The main alterations include:

- Adding the (dual) initialization and update rules for the minimum fixed points.

- Developing a method for *hierarchically* computing maximum and minimum fixed points.

The resulting algorithm still exhibits complexity that is linear in the size of the transition system and B.

Following [AC, CS2], we restrict our attention to equations whose right-hand sides are *simple*, i.e. have only variables as nontrivial subterms and do not just consist of a variable. So $X_4 \vee X_3$ is simple, while $(a)(X_4 \vee X_3)$ and X_4 are not. Any equation set E may be transformed in linear time into a simple equation set E' with at most a linear blow-up in size. Accordingly, **solve** has the same complexity for our full logic as it does for the simple sublogic.

3.1   Overview

As with the algorithms in [AC, CS2], **solve** is bit-vector-based. Each state in S has a bit vector whose i^{th} entry indicates whether or not the state belongs to the set associated with X_i in the current stage of the analysis. The algorithm then repeatedly updates the bit vectors until they correspond to $[\![B]\!]$. Given B, **solve** first initializes every component in each state's bit vector as follows.

- If the variable corresponding to the component is a left-hand side in a *max* block then the component is set to *true*, with the following exceptions.

  - The right-hand side of the corresponding equation is atomic, and the state does not satisfy the atomic proposition.

  - The right-hand side of the corresponding equation is of the form $(a)X_j$, and the state has no a-derivatives.

- *Dually*, if the variable corresponding to the component is a left-hand side in a *min* block then the component is set to *false*, with the following exceptions.

  - The right-hand side of the corresponding equation is atomic, and the state satisfies the atomic proposition.

  - The right-hand side of the corresponding equation is of the form $[a]X_j$, and the state has no a-derivatives.

The procedure then topologically sorts the blocks in B with respect to the relation $\rightarrow$, yielding $B_1, \ldots, B_m$. Subsequently, the blocks are processed one at a time in this order until consistency of the bit-vector annotation with the semantics of formulas is achieved; this is done by successively setting components to *false* (in the case of *max* blocks) or *true* (in the case of *min* blocks) that cause inconsistency. Notice that because of the order of processing, after initialization each component may change value at most once.

3.2 Data Structures

Let B be a set of m blocks, and assume that the list of equations in B is of the form $X_i = \Phi_i$, where i ranges between 1 and n. As in [AC, CS2], each state s will have the following fields associated with it.

- An array $X[1..n]$ of bits. Intuitively, $s.X[i]$ is true if s belongs to the set associated with proposition variable X_i. The array is initialized as described above.

- An array $C[1..n]$ of counters. The role played by $C[i]$ depends on the kind of block B in which X_i is a left-hand side. If B is a *max* block, then $C[i]$ contains the following.

    - If $X_i = X_j \vee X_k$ is an equation in B, then $s.C[i]$ records the number of disjuncts (0,1 or 2) of the right-hand side that are true for s. In this case, $s.C[i] = 2$ initially.
    - If $X_i = \langle a \rangle X_j$ is in B then $s.C[i]$ records the number of a-derivatives of s that are in the set associated with X_j. In this case, $s.C[i]$ is initially set to the number of a-derivatives that s has.
    - For other kinds of equations, $C[i]$ is not used.

    Dually, if B is a *min* block, then $C[i]$ contains the following.

    - If $X_i = X_j \wedge X_k$ is an equation in B, then $s.C[i]$ records the number of conjuncts (0,1 or 2) of the right-hand side that are false for s. In this case, $s.C[i] = 2$ initially.
    - If $X_i = [a]X_j$ is in B then $s.C[i]$ records the number of a-derivatives of s that are not in the set associated with X_j. In this case, $s.C[i]$ is initially set to the number of a-derivatives that s has.
    - Otherwise, $C[i]$ is not used.

- A field $s.A$ for every atomic proposition A that indicates whether s satisfies A or not. This is assumed to be given at the start of the algorithm.

In addition, the algorithm maintains two other data structures that allow one to determine efficiently which state/variable pairs must be reinvestigated as a result of changes that have been made to bit-vector components.

- An array $M[1..m]$ of *lists* of state-variable pairs; $\langle s, X_i \rangle$ is in $M[j]$ if X_i is a left-hand side in block B_j and $s.X[i]$ has just been changed.

- An edge-labeled directed graph G with n vertices, one for each left-hand-side variable in B. The edges are defined as follows.

    - $X_i \overset{\vee}{\to} X_j$ if there is an X_k such that either $X_j = X_i \vee X_k$ or $X_j = X_k \vee X_i$ is an equation in B.
    - $X_i \overset{\wedge}{\to} X_j$ if there is an X_k such that either $X_j = X_i \wedge X_k$ or $X_j = X_k \wedge X_i$ is an equation in B.
    - $X_i \overset{\langle a \rangle}{\to} X_j$ if $X_j = \langle a \rangle X_i$ is in B.
    - $X_i \overset{[a]}{\to} X_j$ if $X_j = [a]X_i$ is in B.

Intuitively, there is an edge from X_i to X_j if the set of states associated with X_i directly influences the set of states associated with X_j. This graph may be constructed in $O(|B|)$ time from B, and it contains no more than $2n$ edges, where n is the total number of equations in B, since the right-hand sides in B are simple.

3.3 The Algorithm

The procedure solve computes $[\![B]\!]$ as follows.

- Initialize the bit-vector X and counter array C for each state as described above, and the array M of lists as follows. For each *max* block B_j, add pair $\langle s, X_i \rangle$ to $M[j]$ if X_i is a left-hand side of B_j and $s.X[i]$ has been set to *false*. For each *min* block B_j, add pair $\langle s, X_i \rangle$ to $M[j]$ if X_i is a left-hand side of B_j and $s.X[i]$ has been set to *true*.

- Topologically sort B, yielding $B_1, \ldots, B_m$.

- Process each block B_i in order.

Block processing is performed by the procedures **max** and **min**, depending on the form of the block. Each of these routines "applies" the semantics of formulas to compute the meaning of the block. We describe each procedure in turn.

3.3.1 Processing Max Blocks

Given *max* block B_j as an argument, routine **max** repeatedly deletes a pair $\langle s, X_i \rangle$ from the list $M[j]$ and processes it as follows until the $M[j]$ is empty.

- For every X_k such that $X_i \overset{\vee}{\to} X_k$, if X_k a is left-hand side in a *max* block B_l then the counter $s.C[k]$ is decremented by one. If $s.C[k]$ is now 0, then none of the disjuncts on the right-hand side of X_k are satisfied by s, and s must be removed from the set associated with X_k. Accordingly, $s.X[k]$ is set to *false* and the pair $\langle s, X_k \rangle$ is added to $M[l]$.

- For every X_k such that $X_i \overset{\wedge}{\to} X_k$, if X_k is a left-hand side in a *max* block B_l and $s.X[k]$ is *true* the component $s.X[k]$ is set to *false* and the pair $\langle s, X_k \rangle$ is added to $M[l]$.

- For every X_k with $X_i \overset{\langle a \rangle}{\to} X_k$, if X_k is a left-hand side in a *max* block B_l then each counter $C[k]$ for each s' that has s as an a-derivative is decremented by one, and if it becomes 0 (meaning that s' now has no a-derivatives satisfying X_i), then $s'.X[k]$ is set to *false* and $\langle s', X_k \rangle$ is added to $M[l]$.

- For every X_k with $X_i \overset{[a]}{\to} X_k$ that is a left-hand side in a *max* block B_l, each state s' having s as an a-derivative has its $X[k]$-component examined, and if it is *true* then it is changed to *false* and $\langle s', X_k \rangle$ is added to $M[l]$.

When $M[j]$ is empty, the bit-vector entries for each state corresponding to *max* block B_j contain their final fixed-point values. They are guaranteed not to change further because of the order in which blocks are processed. Procedure **max** also updates bit-vector entries, counters and lists associated with yet-to-be processed *max* blocks. On the other hand, bit-vector entries, counters and lists corresponding to *min* blocks are not modified by the procedure above, because approximate values generated by the maximum fixed-point computations can not be safely used for *min* block variables. Accordingly, the data structures for these blocks must be updated in a separate pass; **max** does this by performing the following for each $\langle s, X_i \rangle$ pair for which X_i is a left-hand side in B_j and $s.X[i]$ is *true*.

- For every X_k such that $X_i \overset{\vee}{\to} X_k$, if X_k is a left-hand side in a *min* block B_l and $s.X[k]$ is *false* the component $s.X[k]$ is set to *true* and the pair $\langle s, X_k \rangle$ is added to $M[l]$.

- For every X_k such that $X_i \overset{\wedge}{\to} X_k$, if X_k is a left-hand side in a *min* block B_l then the counter $s.C[k]$ is decremented by one. If $s.C[k]$ is now 0, then both of the conjuncts on the right-hand side of X_k are satisfied by s, and s must be added to the set associated with X_k. Accordingly, $s.X[k]$ is set to *true* and the pair $\langle s, X_k \rangle$ is added to $M[l]$.

- For every X_k with $X_i \xrightarrow{(a)} X_k$, if X_k is a left-hand side in a *min* block B_l each state s' having s as an a-derivative has its $X[k]$-component examined, and if it is *false* then it is changed to *true* and $\langle s', X_k \rangle$ is added to $M[l]$.

- For every X_k with $X_i \xrightarrow{[a]} X_k$, if X_k is a left-hand side in a *min* block B_l then each counter $C[k]$ for each s' that has s as an a-derivative is decremented by one, and if it becomes 0 (meaning that all the a-derivatives of s' satisfy X_i), then $s'.X[k]$ is set to *true* and $\langle s', X_k \rangle$ is added to $M[l]$.

3.3.2 Processing Min Blocks

The procedure **min** works in a completely dual fashion to **max**. Again, the routine successively deletes pairs $\langle s, X_i \rangle$ from the list $M[j]$ until it is empty and processes them as follows.

- For every X_k such that $X_i \xrightarrow{\triangle} X_k$, if X_k is in a *min* block B_l then the counter $s.C[k]$ is decremented by one. If $s.C[k]$ is now 0, then all of the conjuncts on the right-hand side of X_k are satisfied by s, and s must be added to the set associated with X_k. Accordingly, $s.X[k]$ is set to *true* and the pair $\langle s, X_k \rangle$ is added to $M[l]$.

- For every X_k such that $X_i \xrightarrow{\vee} X_k$, if X_k is in a *min* block B_l and $s.X[k]$ is *false* the component $s.X[k]$ is set to *true* and the pair $\langle s, X_k \rangle$ is added to $M[l]$.

- For every X_k with $X_i \xrightarrow{[a]} X_k$, if X_k is in a *min* block B_l then each counter $C[k]$ for each s' that has s as an a-derivative is decremented by one, and if it becomes 0 (meaning that all the a-derivatives of s' now satisfy X_i), then $s'.X[k]$ is set to *true* and $\langle s', X_k \rangle$ is added to $M[l]$.

- For every X_k with $X_i \xrightarrow{(a)} X_k$ that is in a *min* block B_l, each state s' having s as an a-derivative has its $X[k]$-component examined, and if it is *false* then it is changed to *true* and $\langle s', X_k \rangle$ is added to $M[l]$.

As before, when $M[j]$ is empty the bit vectors corresponding to *min* block B_j contain their final values, and the bit vectors, counters and lists corresponding to *min* blocks have been appropriately updated. The bit vectors, counters and lists corresponding to *max* blocks must be updated subsequently in a separate pass. **min** does this by performing the following for each s/X_i pair for which X_i is a left-hand side in B_j and $s.X[i]$ is false.

- For every X_k such that $X_i \xrightarrow{\triangle} X_k$, if X_k is in a *max* block B_l and $s.X[k]$ is *true* the component $s.X[k]$ is set to *false* and the pair $\langle s, X_k \rangle$ is added to $M[l]$.

- For every X_k such that $X_i \xrightarrow{\vee} X_k$, if X_k is in a *max* block B_l then the counter $s.C[k]$ is decremented by one. If $s.C[k]$ is now 0, then both of the disjuncts on the right-hand side of X_k are not satisfied by s, and s must removed from the set associated with X_k. Accordingly, $s.X[k]$ is set to *false* and the pair $\langle s, X_k \rangle$ is added to $M[l]$.

- For every X_k with $X_i \xrightarrow{[a]} X_k$, if X_k is in a *max* block B_l each state s' having s as an a-derivative has its $X[k]$-component examined, and if it is *true* then it is changed to *false* and $\langle s', X_k \rangle$ is added to $M[l]$.

- For every X_k with $X_i \xrightarrow{(a)} X_k$, if X_k is in a *max* block B_l then each counter $C[k]$ for each s' that has s as an a-derivative is decremented by one, and if it becomes 0 (meaning that none of the a-derivatives of s' satisfy X_i), then $s'.X[k]$ is set to *false* and $\langle s', X_k \rangle$ is added to $M[l]$.

3.4 Correctness and Complexity

The algorithm solve consists of a call to an initialization procedure, a call to a topological sorting routine, and calls to max and min. It always terminates, since the number of states is finite and for any state s and any i, the component $s.X[i]$ can be changed at most once during its execution. Moreover, upon termination (i.e. when all lists in M are empty), the bit-vector annotations represent $[\![B]\!]$; this follows from the fact that max computes the appropriate νf_E^c, while min computes the appropriate μf_E^c.

Theorem 3.1 (Correctness)
Let $T = \langle S, Act, \rightarrow \rangle$ *be a labeled transition system and* B *be a closed set of blocks with acyclic block graph. Then for any left-hand-side variable* X_i *in* B, $s \in [\![X_i]\!]([\![B]\!])$ *if and only if* $s.X[i] =$ true.

Finally, we state and prove our complexity result, which is a straightforward extension of the complexity result stated in [CS2].

Theorem 3.2 (Complexity)
Let $T = \langle S, Act, \rightarrow \rangle$ *be a labeled transition system and* B *be a closed set of blocks of simple equations. Then the worst-case time complexity of* solve *is* $O(|T| * |B|)$, *where* $|T| = |S| + |\rightarrow|$ *and* $|B|$ *is the total number of equations in* B.

4 Applications

In this section we show how the model-checking algorithm presented in the previous section may be used to implement efficiently different verification methodologies on finite-state labeled transition systems. In the first subsection we illustrate how our model checker may be used to compute behavioral preorders. Subsequently, we indicate how various kinds of temporal logics may be model-checked with our algorithm using CTL as an example.

4.1 Computing Behavioral Preorders

In this section we briefly outline how one may use the model-checking algorithm of the previous section to compute the prebisimulation preorder [Wa]. In addition to being interesting in its own right, this preorder may also be used as a basis for defining other preorders, including various testing preorders [CH, CPS1, CPS2]. This account is essentially a distillation of one found in [CS2, Ste][2]. The interested reader is referred to these papers for details.

The prebisimulation preorder, $\precsim$, is defined in terms of *extended labeled transition systems*. An extended labeled transition system T has the form $\langle S, Act, \rightarrow, \{\downarrow a \mid a \in Act\} \rangle$, where $\langle S, Act, \rightarrow \rangle$ is a labeled transition system and the $\downarrow a$ are atomic formulas. Intuitively, s satisfies $\downarrow a$ if the behavior of s in response to action a is *completely defined*.

The model-checking approach to verifying whether $s_1 \precsim s_2$, where s_1 is a state in extended labeled transition system T_1 and s_2 a state in T_2, works in two steps:

- construct a *characteristic block set* B for T_1, which consists of a single *max* block containing one equation for each state in T_1, and

- check whether $s_2 \models X_1$ *where* B, where X_1 is the variable associated with s_1.

The correctness of this approach relies on the main theorem of [Ste], which may be phrased as follows.

---

[2]The logic considered in these papers differs from the one considered here in the interpretation of the $[a]$ modalities. However, it is a simple matter to "code up" these modal operators in our logic, given the $\downarrow a$ atomic propositions.

Theorem 4.1 *Let T be an extended labeled transition system and s one of its states. Also let E be the characteristic equation set of T and X_s the variable in E associated with s. Then for any state s' in any extended labeled transition system, $s \sqsubseteq s'$ if and only if $s' \models X_s$ where$\{max\{E\}\}$.*

The complexity of this preorder-checking procedure is proportional to the product of the numbers of transitions of the two transitions systems involved, which improves published complexity results about preorder checking.

4.2 Other Logics

Emerson and Lei have shown how various logics, including Propositional Dynamic Logic (PDL) and Computation Tree Logic (CTL), may be translated in linear-time into the alternation-free part of the modal mu-calculus. Our logic has the same expressive power as this fragment (Theorem 2.3), and since the same linear-time translations may be used (with slight modifications), our algorithm delivers linear-time model checkers for PDL and CTL. In the remainder of this section we illustrate this by giving the translation of CTL into our logic.

We first assume that CTL formulas are in *positive normal form*, meaning that all negations have been "pushed" inside formulas until they reach atomic formulas. To illustrate the translation of CTL formulas, then, it suffices to give accounts of the following formulas: $A(PuQ)$, $E(PuQ)$, $A(PUQ)$ and $E(PUQ)$. Here A is the universal path quantifier, and E is the existential path quantifier; u and U represent "weak" and "strong" *until* path operators, respectively. So a state satisfies $A(PuQ)$ if along every computation path beginning with s, P holds until Q does; moreover Q is not required ever to hold, in which case P will hold everywhere.

The translation is as follows.

$$
\begin{aligned}
A(PuQ) &= X \text{ where } \{max\{X = Q \vee (P \wedge [a]X)\}\} \\
E(PuQ) &= X \text{ where } \{max\{X = Q \vee (P \wedge \langle a \rangle X)\}\} \\
A(PUQ) &= X \text{ where } \{min\{X = Q \vee (P \wedge [a]X \wedge \langle a \rangle tt)\}\} \\
E(PUQ) &= X \text{ where } \{min\{X = Q \vee (P \wedge \langle a \rangle X)\}\}
\end{aligned}
$$

This translation is linear-time, and hence our model-checking algorithm yields a linear-time model-checking algorithm for CTL. This matches the complexity for existing CTL model checkers [CES].

5 Conclusions and Future Work

In this paper, we have presented a linear-time algorithm for model checking in a logic that is equivalent in expressiveness to the alternation-free modal mu-calculus. The algorithm extends one given in [CS2] for a logic that only includes greatest fixed points, and it does so while maintaining the same time complexity; it runs in time proportional to the product of the sizes of the process and the formula under consideration. The algorithm may also be used to compute behavioral preorders and to model-check other logics.

A major challenge is to extend of our algorithm to handle the full modal mu-calculus including *alternating* fixed points. We conjecture that it is possible to achieve an algorithm in this fashion whose worst case time complexity is $O((|T| * \frac{|\Phi|}{ad(\Phi)})^{ad(\Phi)})$, where $|T| = |S| + |\rightarrow|$, $|B|$ is the size of Φ, and $ad(\Phi)$ is the alternation depth of Φ. This would outperform the model-checking algorithm of Emerson and Lei [EL], which is the most efficient algorithm in the literature for the full mu-calculus. Their algorithm is $O((|T| * |\Phi|)^{ad(\Phi)+1})$. In support of this conjecture, we note that in the special case of alternation-free formulas our approach is linear, while theirs is quadratic. We also plan to implement this algorithm as an extension of the Concurrency Workbench [CPS1, CPS2].

References

[AC] Arnold, A., and P. Crubille. "A Linear Algorithm To Solve Fixed-Point Equations on Transition Systems." *Information Processing Letters* 29:57–66, 30 September 1988.

[CES] Clarke, E.M., E.A. Emerson and A.P. Sistla. "Automatic Verification of Finite State Concurrent Systems Using Temporal Logic Specifications." *ACM TOPLAS* 8(2):244–263, 1986.

[CH] Cleaveland, R. and M.C.B. Hennessy. "Testing Equivalence as a Bisimulation Equivalence." In *Proc. Workshop on Automatic Verification Methods for Finite-State Systems*. LNCS 407.

[CPS1] Cleaveland, R., J. Parrow and B. Steffen. "The Concurrency Workbench." In *Proc. Workshop on Automatic Verification Methods for Finite-State Systems*, 1989, LNCS 407. To appear in *ACM TOPLAS*.

[CPS2] Cleaveland, R., J. Parrow and B. Steffen. "A Semantics-based Verification Tool for Finite-State Systems", In *Proc. 9th Symp. on Protocol Specification, Testing, and Verification*, 1989.

[CS1] Cleaveland, R. and B. Steffen. "When is 'Partial' Complete? A Logic-Based Proof Technique using Partial Specifications." In *Proc. LICS '90*, 1990.

[CS2] Cleaveland, R. and B. Steffen. "Computing Behavioural Relations, Logically." In *Proc. ICALP '91*, 1991.

[EL] Emerson, E.A. and C.-L. Lei. "Efficient Model Checking in Fragments of the Propositional Mu-Calculus." In *Proc. LICS '86*, 1986.

[Fe] Fernandez, J.-C. *Aldébaran: Une Système de Vérification par Réduction de Processus Communicants*. Ph.D. Thesis, Université de Grenoble, 1988.

[FL] Fischer, M., and R. Ladner. "Propositional Dynamic Logic of Regular Programs." *Journal of Computer and System Sciences* 18:194–211, 1979.

[GS] Graf, S. and B. Steffen. "Using Interface Specifications for Compositional Reduction." In *Computer-Aided Verification '90*.

[Ko] Kozen, D. "Results on the Propositional μ-Calculus." *Theoretical Computer Science* 27:333–354, 1983.

[La] Larsen, K. "Proof Systems for Hennessy-Milner Logic with Recursion." In *Proc. CAAP*, 1988.

[MSGS] Malhotra, J., S.A. Smolka, A. Giacalone and R. Shapiro. "Winston: A Tool for Hierarchical Design and Simulation of Concurrent Systems." In *Proc. Workshop on Specification and Verification of Concurrent Systems*, University of Stirling, Scotland, 1988.

[RRSV] Richier, J., C. Rodriguez, J. Sifakis, J. and Voiron. "Verification in Xesar of the Sliding Window Protocol." In *Proc. 7th Symp. on Protocol Specification, Testing, and Verification*, 1987.

[RdS] Roy, V. and R. de Simone. "Auto/Autograph." In *Computer-Aided Verification '90*, 1990.

[Ste] Steffen, B.U. "Characteristic Formulae for CCS with Divergence." In *Proc. ICALP '89*, 1989. With A. Ingólfsdóttir, to appear in *Theoretical Computer Science*.

[Ta] Tarski, A. "A Lattice-Theoretical Fixpoint Theorem and its Applications." *Pacific Journal of Mathematics* 5, 1955.

[Wa] Walker, D. "Bisimulations and Divergence." In *Proc. LICS '88*, 1988.

Automatic Temporal Verification of Buffer Systems

A. Prasad Sistla

Dept of Electrical Engineering and Computer Science, University of Illinois at Chicago

e-address: sistla@uicbert.eecs.uic.edu

Lenore D. Zuck

Department of Computer Science, Yale University

e-address: zuck@cs.yale.edu

October 16, 1991

1 Introduction

Propositional Linear Time Temporal Logic (TL) was introduced in [Pnu77] as a formal system for reasoning about concurrent programs. Since then it has been widely used for specification and verification of concurrent systems.

Most formal systems that allow temporal-like reasoning use the eventuality operator as the main modal operator. In this paper we consider a temporal logic that uses $\diamondsuit$ (sometimes in the future) and $\diamondsuit$ (sometimes in the past) as the only modal operator; we term this logic RTL (Restricted Temporal Logic). At first glance RTL seems to be a very limited language. Yet, if we are concerned with properties of concurrent programs, there are convincing indications that RTL is an adequate language:

Owicki and Lamport, when giving proof rules for liveness properties, considered only formulae of the form $\square(p \rightarrow \diamondsuit q)$ ([OL82]) which are RTL formulae; Chandy and Misra conjectured that there is essentially one class of liveness properties of concurrent programs, namely, the class of *progress* properties ([CM86]); in their propositional version, progress properties are easily definable by RTL. Other specification techniques ([Lam83]) use state transition systems to specify safety properties and RTL to specify liveness properties. It is hardly surprising that most temporal properties of distributed programs discussed in the literature are given in RTL.

A natural problem associated with choosing a specification language for programs is how easy is it to verify that programs satisfy their specification. Ideally, we would like an automatic verifier that, given a program and its specification, would decide whether the program satisfies its specification. There are several *model checking* methods that are proposed in the literature for obtaining this goal which use (the full) temporal logic as the specification language (cf. [CES86, EL85, LP85]). Recently, Wolper and Vardi ([VW86]) have advocated the *automata theoretic approach* which is a variant of model checking. There, both the program and the specification are brought to the form of a finite-state graph, and model checking reduces to the emptiness problem for (ω-) finite-state automata.

All the model checking techniques that we are aware of apply only to programs which are either finite-state or those that, for verification purposes, can be considered finite-state. Many programs for distributed systems are, however, infinite-state. In particular, systems of (possibly finite-state) processes that communicate over unbounded message buffers are inherently infinite-state.

A major obstacle in verifying properties of systems that use message buffers is the complexity of the axiomatization of the behavior of the buffers used. As shown in [SCFM84], the theory of unbounded fifo buffers in the full TL is Π_1^1 complete. Hence, one cannot hope to have a model-checking procedure for verifying TL properties of systems that use unbounded fifo message buffers. However, once TL is replaced with a version of RTL that has $\diamondsuit$ as a single modal operator, the theory of unbounded message buffers is co-NP-complete ([SZ90]).

In this paper, we modify the result in [SZ90] and show that the theory of unbounded message buffers in RTL is also co-NP-complete. Based on this, we present a "simple" automatic verification method that applies to a certain class of RTL formulae and (not necessarily finite-state) programs of distributed systems whose processes communicate by means of fifo message buffers. Our method is based on the principle that can be roughly stated as follows:

Given a system of n processes, $P_1, \ldots, P_n$ that communicate over unbounded message buffers and a formula ψ in an admissible logic L, then in order to show that ψ holds over all the executions of the system, it suffices to find n formulae $\phi_1, \ldots, \phi_n$ in L such that:

1. each P_i satisfies ϕ_i, and

2. $(\bigwedge_i \phi_i \rightarrow \psi)$ is in the theory of the message buffers in the logic L.

In order for the above idea to be applicable the logic L has to be admissible. Admissible logics are defined in section 2. RTL is an admissible logic and since the theory of fifo buffers in RTL is co-NP-complete, we can use the above principle for proving RTL properties of systems that communicate through unbounded fifo buffers. Intuitively, we can think of the above method to be approximating the behavior of each process P_i by the formula ϕ_i. This gives us a sound proof method for proving RTL properties of systems that communicate through unbounded fifo buffers.

It can easily be shown that the above method is *complete* for a class of processes if the logic L is expressive for this class. By taking the logic L to be the Propositional Temporal Logic without the "nexttime" operator and by considering unbounded unordered[1], we can use the above method for proving properties of systems of processes that communicate through unbounded *unordered* buffers whose message alphabet is finite. In this case, it can easily be shown L is admissible and the theory of unbounded unordered buffers in L has been shown to be decidable in [SCFM84]. If we are only considering finite state processes then L is expressive for this class, and we get a complete and fully automatic proof method for this class of processes.

Temporal logics are usually interpreted over sequences of states, and formulae that express properties of message buffers use the *send* and *receive* actions to the buffers as atomic propositions. We therefore have to interpret the logic over both states and actions. Consequently, we consider executions sequences that explicitly have the two. A natural such model is the I/O automaton model (cf. [LT87, LT89]). This model also allows to abstract away the (application) programs run by the processes and to concentrate on the interaction between the buffers and the processes. Finally, the model has inherent compositionality properties. We therefore chose it as the model on which to demonstrate our ideas. We would like to stress that this choice is for purposes of convenience of exposition, and our results do not depend on the I/O automaton model.

2 The Formal Framework

2.1 Admissible Logics

Let Φ be a finite set of *state assertions*. We are interested in logics for specifying properties of computations which include states as well as actions. With this as our motivation, we assume that the set Φ is partitioned into two nonempty disjoint sets, denoted by Φ_s and Φ_a. Intuitively, the members of Φ_s can be true only in states that represent states of processes and those in Φ_s can be true only in states that represent actions.

We define *admissible logics*, which are logics that satisfy certain properties defined later in this section. The formulas of such logics are constructed from state assertions in Π using the boolean connectives $\neg$ and $\vee$, and some other operators (e.g., temporal ones), and are interpreted over sequences of subsets of Φ.

Let L be such a logic. For a formula φ of L (an *L-formula*), let $\text{prop}(\varphi)$ denote the set of state assertions in φ. A *model* $\mathcal{M}$ for a logic is a triple (Π, S, I) where $\Pi \subseteq \Phi$, S is a (possibly infinite) set of *states* and $I: S \rightarrow (2^\Pi - \emptyset)$ is an *evaluation* mapping each state $s \in S$ to a nonempty set $I(s)$, the set of state assertions true in s and such that either $I(s) \cap \Phi_s$ is empty or $I(s) \cap \Phi_a$ is empty. We say that a state $s \in S$ is *regular* if $I(s) \cap \Phi_s$ is nonempty; we say that a state $s \in S$ is *action* if $I(s) \cap \Phi_a$ is nonempty. It should be clear that every state in S is either regular or action. Given a model $\mathcal{M} = (\Pi, S, I)$, a *computation* σ is an infinite sequence of states, i.e.,

$$\sigma : s_0, s_1, \ldots \qquad s_i \in S.$$

We assume that a satisfiability relation $\models_L$, between a model $\mathcal{M} = (\Pi, S, I)$, a computation σ, and an L-formula φ, where $\text{prop}(\varphi) \subseteq \Pi$, is defined so that the following properties are satisfied:

- $(\mathcal{M}, \sigma) \models_L$ true and $(\mathcal{M}, \sigma) \not\models_L$ false for every $\sigma \in S^\omega$.

---

[1] In unordered buffers the messages can be delivered in any order.

- For a state assertion $Q \in \Phi$, $(\mathcal{M}, \sigma) \models_L Q$ iff $Q \in I(s_0)$.

- $(\mathcal{M}, \sigma) \models_L \neg\varphi$ iff $(\mathcal{M}, \sigma) \not\models_L \varphi$.

- $(\mathcal{M}, \sigma) \models_L \varphi_1 \vee \varphi_2$ iff $(\mathcal{M}, \sigma) \models_L \varphi_1$ or $(\mathcal{M}, \sigma) \models_L \varphi_2$.

- For every model $\mathcal{M}' = (\Pi' \supseteq \mathrm{prop}(\varphi), S', I')$ and computation $\sigma' = s'_0, \ldots, s'_i, \ldots$ over S' such that $I'(s'_i) \cap \mathrm{prop}(\varphi) = I(s_i) \cap \mathrm{prop}(\varphi)$ for every $i \geq 0$,

$$(\mathcal{M}, \sigma) \models_L \varphi \quad \text{iff} \quad (\mathcal{M}', \sigma') \models_L \varphi.$$

In other words, the satisfaction of a φ by σ only depends on the evaluation of $I(\sigma) \cap \mathrm{prop}(\varphi)$.

(Additional boolean connectives (such as $\wedge$, $\rightarrow$, $\leftrightarrow$) are defined in the usual way.)
If $(\mathcal{M}, \sigma) \models_L \varphi$, we say that σ satisfies φ in $\mathcal{M}$.
For any sequence α whose elements are from a set A, we let $\alpha|A'$ denote the *restriction of α to A'*. In other words, $\alpha|A'$ is the subsequence of α that includes all the A' elements of α.
Let $\mathcal{M} = (\Pi, S, I)$ be a model. For any $s \in S$ and $\Pi' \subseteq \Pi$, we say that s is a Π'-*state* if $I(s) \cap \Pi' \neq \emptyset$. We use $\sigma|\Pi'$ to denote σ's restriction to the Π'-states, that is,

$$\sigma|\Pi' = \sigma|\{s \in S : s \text{ is a } \Pi'\text{-state}\}.$$

We say that L has *projection property* if for every L-formula φ and every finite set Π such that $\Pi \subseteq \Phi$, there exists a formula $\varphi_{(\Pi)}$ such that for every model $\mathcal{M} = (\Pi', S, I)$ where $\Pi' \supseteq (\mathrm{prop}(\varphi) \cup \Pi)$ and every computation σ such that $\sigma|\Pi$ is infinite and the first state in σ is a Π-state,

$$(\mathcal{M}, \sigma) \models_L \varphi_{(\Pi)} \quad \text{iff} \quad (\mathcal{M}, \sigma|\Pi) \models \varphi$$

The logic L is *admissible* if it has the projection property. In the sequel we will only consider admissible logics. The projection property does not imply a unique projected formula $\varphi_{(\Pi)}$. However, we fix such a formula and let $\varphi_{(\Pi)}$ denote it. It easily follows from the definition that for every L-formula φ, $\varphi \leftrightarrow \varphi_{(\Pi)}$ holds in every model $\mathcal{M}$ whose states are all Π-states.
Let $\sigma = s_0, s_1, \ldots$ be a computation over S. If σ' is obtained from σ by possibly duplicating some of the regular states in σ, then we say that σ' is a *stuttered extension of σ*. We say that an L-formula φ is *invariant under stuttering* if for every model $\mathcal{M}$, a computation σ satisfies φ (in $\mathcal{M}$) iff every stuttered extension of σ satisfies φ (in $\mathcal{M}$).

2.2 I/O Automata

A concurrent system is often described by the specification of its possible interactions with the environment, i.e., its *observable behavior*. In the I/O automaton model, the interface between the system and its environment is described as interleaved sequences of *actions* which are called *behaviors*. When the system runs in a certain environment, certain behaviors may arise. The *specification* says which are the allowed behaviors.
Actions at the interface between the system and its environment are of two kinds. *Input* actions originate in the environment and are imposed by the environment on the system. This means that they can occur at any time and are not under the control of the system. *Output* actions are generated by the system and are imposed by it on the environment.
Formally, given two disjoint sets of actions, $inp(S)$ and $out(S)$, a specification S is a subset $beh(S)$ of the set of (finite or infinite) sequences over $acts(S) = inp(S) \cup out(S)$.
While a specification describes the interaction of a system with its environment, an *I/O automaton* is a state machine which models the system. An I/O automaton A therefore has input actions, $inp(A)$, and output actions, $out(A)$. In addition, it has *internal actions*, $int(A)$, which are not observable by the environment. Let $acts(A)$ denote the union of these three (mutually disjoint) sets of actions. The automaton also has *states*, $states(A))$, *transitions*, $trans(A) \subseteq states(A) \times acts(A) \times states(A)$, *initial states*, $i\text{-}state(A) \subseteq states(A)$, and a fairness condition, $fair(A)$, described as a partition on $out(A) \cup int(A)$. See [LT87, LT89, AAF$^+$] for an elaborate discussion.
An *execution* η of A is a (possibly infinite) sequence of the form:

$$s_0, a_1, s_1, a_2, \ldots$$

where s_0 is an initial state of A and for every $i \geq 0$, (s_i, a_{i+1}, s_{i+1}) is a transition of A. The execution η is *fair* if it is infinite, and for every set of actions $acts' \in fair(A)$, either actions from $acts'$ are taken infinitely many times in η (i.e., for infinitely many i's, $a_i \in acts'$), or actions from $acts'$ are disabled infinitely many times in η (i.e., for infinitely many i's, for all actions $a \in acts'$, there is not s' such that $(s_i, a, s') \in trans(A))$.[2]

If A and B are both I/O automata whose only mutual actions are input of one and output of the other, then the composition of A and B, $A \circ B$, is an I/O automaton such that:

1. $out(A \circ B) = out(A) \cup out(B)$, $int(A \circ B) = int(A) \cup int(B)$, and $inp(A \circ B) = inp(A) \cup inp(B) - (out(A) \cup out(B))$.

2. $states(A \circ B) = states(A) \times states(B)$, and $A \circ B$'s initial states are the cartesian product of its components' initial states.

3. $A \circ B$'s transitions are such that only the components to which the action belongs is affected, i.e., $((s_A, s_B), a, (s'_A, s'_B)) \in trans(A \circ B)$ if $(s_A, a, s'_A) \in trans(A)$ when $a \in acts(A)$ and $s_A = s'_A$ otherwise, and similarly for s'_B.

4. The fairness condition on $A \circ B$ is the union of the fairness conditions of its components.

The definition of composition of two I/O-automata is extended in the obvious way to the definition of the composition of and n I/O automata.

Let α be an execution of the composition of $A_1, \ldots, A_n$. For every $i = 1, \ldots, n$, let $\alpha[i]$ denote the execution of A_i which is defined by α. That is, $\alpha[i]$ is obtained from α by eliminating all the actions which are not in $acts(A_i)$, eliminating states which are not preceded by actions, and replacing each remaining state with its ith component.

3 Communication Systems

Consider a distributed network of n processes, $P_1, \ldots, P_n$ that communicate by means of k message buffers $B_1, \ldots, B_k$. Each process P_i is an I/O automaton and each message buffer B_j is a specification. Let $acts(B)$ denote the union $\cup_{j=1}^{k} acts(B_j)$. In the next section we define (specification of) message buffers precisely. For the purpose of this section, message buffers are specifications that share actions with the processes. The actions of the processes, however, are assumed to be mutually disjoint.

Let P denote the composition $P_1 \circ \ldots \circ P_n$. From the definition of fair executions it follows that in every fair execution of P, each process has infinitely many actions. Since the processes communicate through the message buffers, we only want to consider executions of P that obey the buffers' specification. Let $\mathcal{P}_B$ denote this set, i.e.,

$$\mathcal{P}_B = \{\eta : \eta \text{ is a fair execution of } P \text{ and } (\eta|acts(B_j)) \in beh(B_j) \text{ for every } j = 1, \ldots, k\}.$$

Fix some admissible logic L. For any model $\mathcal{M} = (\Pi, S, I)$, we say that M is *acceptable* if for every $s \in S$, if $s \in acts(B)$ then $I(s) = \{s\}$, otherwise $I(s) \cap acts(B) = \emptyset$.

We now interpret L-formulae over the executions in $\mathcal{P}_B$. With each process P_i we associate an acceptable model

$$\mathcal{M}_i = (\Pi_i \subseteq \Phi, S_i = acts(P_i) \cup states(P_i), I_i)$$

such that each for every $s \in states(P_i)$, $I_i(s) \subseteq \Phi_s$ and for every $a \in acts(P_i)$, $I_i(a) \subseteq \Phi_a$. Given an L-formula φ, we say that φ is *i-valid* if for every fair execution η of P_i, $(\mathcal{M}_i, \eta) \models_L \varphi$. We assume that the Π_is are mutually disjoint. Let $\mathcal{M} = (\Pi, S, I)$ be the model where:

1. $\Pi = \cup_{i=1}^{n} \Pi_i$,

2. $S = states(P) \cup acts(P)$,

3. for every $(s_1, \ldots, s_n) \in states(P)$, $I(s) = \cup_{i=1}^{n} I_i(s_i)$.

4. for every $a \in acts(P)$, if $a \in acts(P_i)$, then $I(a) = I_i(a)$. (Recall that each action is "owned" by a unique P_i.)

---

[2] This definition of fairness diverges from the usual one which allows for finite fair executions

Obviulsy, $\mathcal{M}$ is an acceptable model. Also, each $s \in states(P)$ is a regular state and each $a \in acts(P)$ is an action state. We say that an L-formula φ is $\mathcal{P}_B$-valid if $(\mathcal{M}, \eta) \models_L \varphi$ for every execution η of $\mathcal{P}_B$.

We next define the theory of B—the set of L-formulae that are valid over all executions of systems of processes that communicate through $B_1, \ldots, B_k$. The theory of B, denoted by $T(B)$, is the set of all formulae φ such that for all acceptable models $\mathcal{M}' = (\Pi', S', I')$, where $\Pi' \supseteq (prop(\varphi) \cup acts(B))$ and $(S' \cap acts(B)) \neq \emptyset$, and for all $\sigma \in (S')^\omega$ such that $(\sigma|acts(B_j)) \in beh(B_j)$ for $j = 1, \ldots, k$, $(\mathcal{M}', \sigma) \models_L \varphi$. Obviously, φ is $\mathcal{P}_B$-valid for every $\varphi \in T(B)$.

We now formally state and prove our main theorem. Roughly speaking, the theorem states that if every process satisfies some local L-specification, and if the formula "χ: the conjunction of the local L-specifications implies ψ" is in the theory of B, then the whole system satisfies ψ. Since we want to guarantee that the "local" specifications above are indeed local, we replace their occurrence in χ by their projected form (see Section 2).

Theorem 3.1 *Given L-formulae $\psi, \varphi^1, \ldots \varphi^n$ over $\Pi, \Pi_1, \ldots, \Pi_n$, respectively, which are invariant under stuttering, such that:*

1. *φ^i is i-valid for every $i = 1, \ldots, n$, and*

2. *the formula $(\bigwedge_{i=1}^n \varphi^i_{(\Pi_i)} \to \psi)$ is in $T(B)$.*

Then ψ is $\mathcal{P}_B$-valid.

Proof Let $\eta = \eta_0, \ldots$ be an execution in $\mathcal{P}_B$. Our goal is to show that $(\mathcal{M}, \eta) \models_L \psi$. We first show that $(\mathcal{M}, \eta) \models_L \varphi^i_{(\Pi_i)}$ for ever $i = 1, \ldots, n$, and then show how this implies that $(\mathcal{M}, \eta) \models_L \psi$.

Assume $1 \leq i \leq n$. Let $\eta' = \eta'_0, \ldots$ be the sequence obtained from η by deleting every action which is not in $acts(P_i)$, and let $\eta'' = \eta''_0, \ldots$ be the sequence obtained from η' by replacing every state by its ith component. Since φ^i is i-valid, $(\mathcal{M}_i, \eta[i]) \models_L \varphi^i$. Since φ^i is invariant under stuttering and since η'' is a stuttered extension of $\eta[i]$, we have

$$(\mathcal{M}_i, \eta'') \models_L \varphi^i.$$

¿From the definition of $\mathcal{M}_i$s and $\mathcal{M}$, it follows that $I(\eta'_j) \cap prop(\varphi^i) = I_i(\eta''_j) \cap prop(\varphi)$ for every $j \geq 0$. Hence, it now follows from the assumption on $\models_L$ that

$$(\mathcal{M}, \eta') \models_L \varphi^i.$$

The sequence η' is exactly the sequence $\eta|\Pi_i$. Since η is an execution of P, $\eta_0 \in states(P)$. From the definition of I it now follows η_0 is a Π_i state. Consequently, η'_0 is also a Π_i-state. Moreover, since η is a fair execution of P, it has infinitely many Π_i states, hence η' is infinite. It now follows from the projection property that

$$(\mathcal{M}, \eta) \models_L \varphi^i_{(\Pi_i)}.$$

The above argument shows that $(\mathcal{M}, \eta) \models_L \varphi^i_{(\Pi_i)}$ for every $i = 1, \ldots, n$. Consequently,

$$(\mathcal{M}, \eta) \models_L \bigwedge_{i=1}^n \varphi^i_{(\Pi_i)}.$$

Since $(\bigwedge_{i=1}^n \varphi^i_{(\Pi_i)} \to \psi) \in T(B)$, it follows that

$$(\mathcal{M}, \eta) \models_L (\bigwedge_{i=1}^n \varphi^i_{(\Pi_i)} \to \psi).$$

We can therefore conclude that

$$(\mathcal{M}, \eta) \models_L \psi.$$

$\blacksquare$

For each $i = 1, \ldots, n$, we say that a formula φ^i characterizes the process P_i with respect to the model $\mathcal{M}_i$ if φ^i is invariant under stuttering and for any $\sigma \in S^\omega_i$, $(\mathcal{M}_i, \sigma) \models_L \varphi^i$ iff either σ is an execution of P_i or it is a stuttered extension of such an execution. Now the following theorem states that if the logic L is expressive enough to characterize the processes $P_1, \ldots, P_n$ then any L-formula that is $\mathcal{P}_B$-valid can be proven so by using the method given in theorem 3.1.

Theorem 3.2 *If* $\psi, \varphi^1, \ldots \varphi^n$ *are L-formulae such that:*

1. $\psi, \varphi^1, \ldots \varphi^n$ *are invariant under stuttering,*

2. φ^i *characterizes* P_i *with respect to* $\mathcal{M}_i$ *for every* i, *and*

3. ψ *is* $\mathcal{P}_B$-*valid*

then $(\bigwedge_{i=1}^n \varphi^i_{(\Pi_i)} \rightarrow \psi)$ *is in* $T(B)$.

4 Temporal Logics and Message Buffers

In Section 2 we introduced *admissible logics*. In Section 3 we defined communication systems and showed how to verify some properties of admissible logics in them. In this section we show that two variants of temporal logic, termed here PTL and RTL, are admissible. PTL is the usual propositional temporal logic with past operators. RTL is PTL without the Until, Since and Nexttime operators, i.e., a temporal logic that uses only the (past and future) eventuality operators.

4.1 PTL and RTL

Propositional Temporal Logic (PTL) is one of the logics defined in Section 2. In addition to the boolean connectives, PTL-formulae can include the temporal operators U (*until*), S (*since*) and $\bigcirc$ (*nexttime*) operators.

Before defining the satisfiability relation $\models_{PTL}$ (denoted by $\models_P$), we define an auxiliary satisfiability relation, $\models'$, between a model $\mathcal{M} = (\Pi, S, I)$, a computation $\sigma = s_0, s_1, \ldots$ over S, and a PTL-formula φ. The relation $\models'$ is defined inductively as follows:

$(\mathcal{M}, \sigma, j) \models'$ true and $(\mathcal{M}, \sigma, j) \not\models'$ false for every $\sigma \in S^\omega$ and $j \geq 0$.

For a state assertion $Q \in \Pi$, $(\mathcal{M}, \sigma, j) \models' Q$ iff $Q \in I(s_j)$.

$(\mathcal{M}, \sigma, j) \models' \neg\varphi$ iff $(\mathcal{M}, \sigma, j) \not\models' \varphi$.

$(\mathcal{M}, \sigma, j) \models' \varphi_1 \vee \varphi_2$ iff $(\mathcal{M}, \sigma, j) \models' \varphi_1$ or $(\mathcal{M}, \sigma, j) \models' \varphi_2$.

$(\mathcal{M}, \sigma, j) \models' \varphi_1 U \varphi_2$ iff for some $j' \geq j$, $(\mathcal{M}, \sigma, j') \models' \varphi_2$ and for all i, $j \leq i < j'$, $(\mathcal{M}, \sigma, i) \models' \varphi_1$.

$(\mathcal{M}, \sigma, j) \models' \varphi_1 S \varphi_2$ iff for some j' such that $0 \leq j' \leq j$, $(\mathcal{M}, \sigma, j') \models' \varphi_2$ and for all i, $j' < i \leq j$, $(\mathcal{M}, \sigma, i) \models' \varphi_1$.

$(\mathcal{M}, \sigma, j) \models' \bigcirc\varphi$ iff $(\mathcal{M}, \sigma, j+1) \models' \varphi$.

Additional boolean connectives (such as $\wedge$, $\rightarrow$, $\leftrightarrow$) can be defined in the usual way. We define additional temporal operators, $\Diamond$ (*eventually in the future*), its dual $\Box$ (*always in the future*), and their past counterparts, $\Diamondblack$ (*eventually in the past*) and $\boxminus$ (*always in the past*) by:

$$\Diamond\varphi \leftrightarrow \text{true}U\varphi \qquad \Diamondblack\varphi \leftrightarrow \text{true}S\varphi$$
$$\Box\varphi \leftrightarrow \neg\Diamond\neg\varphi \qquad \boxminus\varphi \leftrightarrow \neg\Diamondblack\neg\varphi$$

The satisfiability relation $\models_P$ is defined by:

$$(\mathcal{M}, \sigma) \models_P \varphi \qquad \text{iff} \qquad (\mathcal{M}, \sigma, 0) \models' \varphi.$$

RTL (Restricted Temporal Logic) formulae are PTL formula that only do not use the U, S and $\bigcirc$ operators, that is, they only use the $\Diamond$, $\Diamondblack$, and their duals as temporal operators. We denote $\models_{RTL}$ by $\models_R$.

4.2 Admissibility of PTL and RTL

We now show that both PTL and RTL are admissible logics. We first note that both $\models_P$ and $\models_R$ trivially satisfy all the five requirements of a satisfiability relation of admissible logics listed in Section 2. We next show that both logics have the projection property.

Theorem 4.1 *PTL has the projection property.*

Proof We prove the claim by defining, for every PTL-formula φ and set $\Pi \subseteq \Phi$, a projected formula $\varphi_{(\Pi)}$ and showing that the defined $\varphi_{(\Pi)}$ satisfies the requirements of a projected formula.

For every finite set $\Pi \subseteq \Pi$, let $\overline{\Pi}$ denote the formula $\bigvee_{\pi \in \Pi} \pi$. Given a PTL-formula φ, we define $\varphi_{(\Pi)}$ by induction on the structure of φ as follows:

- If $\varphi \in \Phi$ or $\varphi \in \{\text{true}, \text{false}\}$, , then $\varphi_{(\Pi)} = \varphi$.

- If $\varphi = \neg \varphi'$, then $\varphi_{(\Pi)} = \neg \varphi'_{(\Pi)}$.

- If $\varphi = \varphi' \vee \varphi''$, then $\varphi_{(\Pi)} = \varphi'_{(\Pi)} \vee \varphi''_{(\Pi)}$.

- If $\varphi = \varphi' U \varphi''$, then $\varphi_{(\Pi)} = (\overline{\Pi} \rightarrow \varphi'_{(\Pi)}) U (\overline{\Pi} \wedge \varphi''_{(\Pi)})$.

- If $\varphi = \varphi' S \varphi''$, then $\varphi_{(\Pi)} = (\overline{\Pi} \rightarrow \varphi'_{(\Pi)}) S (\overline{\Pi} \wedge \varphi''_{(\Pi)})$.

- If $\varphi = \bigcirc \varphi'$, then $\varphi_{(\Pi)} = \bigcirc(\neg \overline{\Pi} U (\overline{\Pi} \wedge \varphi'_{(\Pi)}))$

It remains to show that for every model $\mathcal{M} = (\Pi', S, I)$ where $\Pi' \supseteq (\text{prop}(\varphi) \cup \Pi)$ and every computation $\sigma = s_0, s_1, \ldots$ such that $\sigma|\Pi$ is infinite and s_0 is a Π-state,

$$(\mathcal{M}, \sigma) \models_P \varphi_{(\Pi)} \qquad \text{iff} (\mathcal{M}, \sigma|\Pi) \models_P \varphi.$$

Let $\mathcal{M} = (\Pi', S, I)$ such a model and σ be such a computation. Let h be a mapping between indices of $\sigma|\Pi$ to indices of σ states such that $\sigma|\Pi = s_{h(0)}, s_{h(1)}, \ldots$. We claim that for every $i \geq 0$,

$$(\mathcal{M}, \sigma, h(i)) \models' \varphi_{(\Pi)} \qquad \text{iff} (\mathcal{M}, \sigma|\Pi, i) \models' \varphi.$$

The proof of the claim is by induction on the structure of φ and is left to the reader. Since s_0 is a Π-state, $h(0) = 0$, we therefore conclude that

$$(\mathcal{M}, \sigma) \models_P \varphi_{(\Pi)} \qquad \text{iff} (\mathcal{M}, \sigma|\Pi) \models_P \varphi.$$

■

Theorem 4.2 *RTL has the projection property.*

Proof The proof is similar to that of Theorem 4.1. The only difference is the definition of the projected formula: Since RTL formula do not have U and S operators, neither should projected formulae have them. We therefore add to the definitions given in the proof of Theorem 4.2 the following:

- If $\varphi = \Diamond \varphi'$ then $\varphi_{(\Pi)} = \Diamond(\overline{\Pi} \wedge \varphi'_{(\Pi)})$.

- If $\varphi = \ominus \varphi'$ then $\varphi_{(\Pi)} = \ominus(\overline{\Pi} \wedge \varphi'_{(\Pi)})$.

The proof that $\varphi_{(\Pi)}$ as defined above satisfies the requirements from a projected formula follows immediately from the proof of Theorem 4.1. ■

We can therefore conclude:

Theorem 4.3 *Both PTL and RTL are admissible logics.*

5 Message Buffers

In Section 3 we considered message buffers to be arbitrary specifications. In this section we study four examples of unbounded message buffers with finite message alphabets: first-in-first-out (fifo) buffers, fifo buffers with deletions, unordered buffers without liveness, and unordered buffers with liveness. As we show, the theory of the first two message buffers in RTL is decidable (in fact, in co-NP), and the theory of the last two message buffers in PTL is decidable. Hence, Theorem 3.1 can be used to prove properties of systems that communicate through these buffers. We should note that the theory of fifo message buffers in the full temporal logic is Π_1^1-complete and thus not axiomatizable ([SCFM84]).

5.1 Specifications of Message Buffers

A message buffer is characterized by the sequences of read/write actions it admits. These sequences depend on the properties of the buffer (e.g., fifo) and on the message alphabet. We denote a message buffer of type x with message alphabet M by $x(M)$. For every $x(M)$, we have

$$inp(x(M)) = \{\text{write}(m) : m \in M\} \quad \text{and} \quad out(x(M)) = \{\text{read}(m) : m \in M\}.$$

Since all the buffers of type x over M have the same input and output actions, we omit 'x' when discussing these actions.

Recall the system presented in Section 3. There we assume k message buffers of the same type whose actions are mutually disjoint, hence their message alphabets are mutually disjoint. Given such k disjoint message alphabets $M_1, \ldots, M_k$, we denote by $x(\hat{M})$ the joint system of the k buffers of type x that communicate over these alphabets. We also assume that:

- $inp(\hat{M}) = \bigcup_{i=1}^{k} inp(M_i))$,

- $out(\hat{M}) = \bigcup_{i=1}^{k} out(M_i)$, and

- $beh(x(\hat{M})) = \{\alpha \in (acts(x(\hat{M})))^{\infty} : \alpha|acts(x(M_i))$ is in $beh(x(M_i))$ for every $i = 1, \ldots, k\}$.

For every buffer type x, (mutually disjoint) message alphabets $M_1, \ldots, M_k$, and admissible logic L, let $T_L(x(\bar{M}))$ denote the theory of $x(\hat{M})$ in L. That is, the set of L-formulae φ such that for every acceptable model $\mathcal{M}' = (\Pi', S', I')$ ($\Pi' \supseteq (prop(\varphi) \cup acts(\bar{M}))$), for every computation σ over S' such that $(\sigma|acts(\hat{M}))$ is in $beh(x(M))$, $(\mathcal{M}', \sigma) \models_L \varphi$.

We abbreviate $T_{PTL}(x(\hat{M}))$ to $T_P(x(\hat{M}))$ and $T_{RTL}(x(\hat{M}))$ to $T_R(x(\hat{M}))$

We now describe the four buffer types and some results about their theories.

Fifo Buffers

Fifo buffers are message buffers where every read operation returns the value of the oldest unread message. Moreover, in every sequence of observable behaviors, if there are infinitely many write actions in the sequence then there are also infinitely many read actions in the sequence. Formally, for every message alphabet M, $beh(\text{fifo}(M))$ is the set of all sequences α over $acts(M)$ such that the following holds:

1. for every finite prefix α' of α, $\alpha'|out(M)$, is a prefix of $\alpha'|inp(M)$, and

2. if the $\alpha|inp(M)$ is infinite, then $\alpha|out(M)$ is infinite.

In the full version of the paper we prove the following theorem, which is an extension of a similar theorem of [SZ90].

Theorem 5.1 $T_R(\text{fifo}(\hat{M}))$ *is in co-NP, i.e., there exists a procedure in NP that decides whether a given RTL formula φ is not in $T_R(\text{fifo}(\hat{M}))$.*

Fifo Buffers with Deletions

Fifo buffers with deletions (fifod buffers) are fifo buffers that can delete messages. From such buffers we require that every message that is written infinitely many times is read infinitely many times. Formally, for every message alphabet M, $beh(\text{fifod}(M))$ is the set of all sequences α over $acts(M)$ such that the following holds:

1. for every finite prefix α' of α, $\alpha'|out(M)$, is a subsequence of $\alpha'|inp(M)$, and

2. for every $m \in M$, if the $\alpha|\text{write}(m)$ is infinite, then $\alpha|\text{read}(m)$ is infinite.

In the full version of the paper we prove the following theorem, which is an extension of a similar theorem of [SZ90].

Theorem 5.2 $T_R(\text{fifod}(\hat{M}))$ *is in co-NP, i.e., there exists a procedure in NP that decides whether a given RTL formula φ is not in $T_R(\text{fifod}(\hat{M}))$.*

Unordered Buffers

Unordered buffers (unor) are buffers that can deliver messages in any order. As before, let M denote a message alphabet. Formally, for every message alphabet M, $beh(unor(M))$ includes all the sequences α over $acts(M)$ such that there exists a one-to-one mapping, h_α, that maps each $read(m)$ event in α to a $write(m)$ event in α that precedes it.

The following theorem is proven in [SCFM84]:

Theorem 5.3 $T_P(unor(\hat{M}))$ *is elementary decidable.*

Unordered Buffers with Liveness

Unordered buffers with livenness (unorl) are unor buffers cannot read finitely many messages if infinitely many messages were written. Formally, for every message alphabet M, $beh(unorl(M))$ includes all the sequences α in $beh(unor(M))$ such that if there are infinitely many write events in α, then there are infinitely many read events in α.

The following theorem can be proved using the techniques as those given in [SCFM84].

Theorem 5.4 $T_P(unorl(\hat{M}))$ *is decidable.*

5.2 A Note about Finite Systems

Let A be an I/O automaton such both $states(A)$ adn $acts(A)$ are finite. Following the method preseted in Section 3, we can associate with A a model $\mathcal{M} = (\Pi, S, I)$ such that every $s \in states(A)$ (resp., $a \in acts(A)$) is mapped to a distinct unique state assertion in Π. It is now possible to give a PTL-formula which characterizes the A's behavior with respect to $\mathcal{M}$. Hence PTL is expressive for the process P with respect to the model $\mathcal{M}$.

Using Theorems 3.2, 5.4, and 5.3, it is easily seen that the method presented in Theorem 3.1 gives us complete and fully automatic proof methods for proving temporal properties of systems of finite state concurrent processes that communicate through unordered buffers with and without liveness properties.

6 Alternating Bit Protocol

Assume a two process system, where one process, the *sender* tries to reliably communicate a sequence of data items X over a domain D of data items, to another process, the *receiver*. The receiver has to write the data items into Y. The sender and the receiver communicate via fifod message buffers.

The Alternating Bit Protocol (ABP), introduced in [BSW69], offers a solution to the problem, namely, protocols for both sender and receiver that guarantees that at any given time, Y is a prefix of X, and that eventually $Y = X$. Presented in the terminology introduced in the previous sections, ABP uses two message buffers, one from sender to receiver with message alphabet $M_{sr} = D \times \{0, 1\}$, and the other from receiver to sender with a message alphabet $M_{rs} = \{0, 1\}$. Let A_s denote the sender's automaton, and let A_r denote the receiver's automaton. ABP proceeds as follows:

If $= x_0, \ldots$, then, for every A_s writes $(x_i, \bar{i})$ messages onto its outgoing buffer ($\bar{i}$ denotes the parity of i), until it reads a $\neg \bar{i}$ message, at which point it knows that A_r had set $y_i := x_i$ and is awaiting x_{i+1}. A_s then increments i and proceeds to the next data item. A_r is similar.

Formally, A_s's states include the input sequence $x_0, \ldots$ and an index i, initially 0, denoting the index of the data item currently transmitted. Similarly, A_r's states include the output sequence $y_0, \ldots$ and an index j, initially 0, denoting the index of the data item that A_r is waiting for.

The code for the sender and receiver appears in Figure 1.

Although we cannot express (and, consequently, prove) all the properties of the Alternating Bit protocol in RTL, we can use the fifod version of Theorem 3.1 to show some of its properties. Recall that the evlauation of any buffer action is the action itself. We use the following abbreviations for every $d \in D$:

$$
\begin{aligned}
inp_s &= \bigvee_{a \in inp(A_s)} a & inp_r &= \bigvee_{a \in inp(A_r)} a \\
out_s &= \bigvee_{a \in out(A_s)} a & out_r &= \bigvee_{a \in out(A_r)} a \\
acts_s &= inp_s \vee out_s & acts_r &= inp_r \vee out_r \\
past0_s(d) &= \boxminus(out_s \rightarrow write(d, 0)) & past0_r(d) &= \boxminus(inp_r \rightarrow read(d, 0)) \\
first_s(d) &= \diamondsuit(write(d, 0) \wedge past0_s(d)) & first_s(d) &= \diamondsuit(read(d, 0) \wedge past0_r(d))
\end{aligned}
$$

A_s	A_r

write(x, b) $((x, b) \in M_{sr})$:
    precondition:
        $x = x_i$ and $b = \bar{i}$
 	
read(b) $(b \in M_{rs})$:
    effect:
        if $b \neq \bar{i}$ then
            $i := i + 1$
	write(b) $(b \in M_{rs})$:
	    precondition:
	        $b = \bar{j}$
	
	read(y, b) $((y, b) \in M_{sr})$:
	    effect:
	        if $b = \bar{j}$ then
	            $y_j := y;\ j := j + 1$

Figure 1: The Alternating Bit Protocol

The formula

$$\psi : \text{first}_s(x) \rightarrow \text{first}_r(x)$$

therefore asserts that the first message read by the received is same as the first message written by the sender. Using Theorem 3.1, we can prove ψ by setting φ^s to:

$$\boxminus\left(\left(\text{write}(x, 0) \wedge \text{past0}_s(x)\right) \rightarrow \left(\left(\boxminus(\text{acts}_s \rightarrow \text{write}(x, 0)) \wedge \boxminus \diamondsuit \text{acts}_s\right) \vee \diamondsuit\left(\text{read}(1) \wedge \text{post0}_s(x)\right) \right) \right)$$

and φ^r to

$$\boxminus\left(\text{write}(1) \rightarrow \diamondsuit\left(\bigvee_{d \in D} \text{read}(d, 0)\right)\right)$$

If Π_s and Π_r denote all the propositions of the sender and the receiver, it can be shown that φ^s and φ^r can be replaced by $(\varphi^s_{(\Pi_s)}$ and $\varphi^r_{(\Pi_r)})$ respectively. It can also be shown that $(\varphi^s \wedge \varphi^r) \rightarrow \psi$ is in the theory of the system of two buffers with deletions connecting the sender and receiver in the two directions.

7   Conclusions

In this paper we have presented a formal model for processes that communicate through fifo message buffers and have given a sound automatic proof system for verifying RTL definable properties of such systems. The proof method is modular. Although our method is not complete, we feel, as illustrated by the example, that it can be applied to some practical examples. Theorem 3.1 holds for any fragment L of temporal logic as long as the formulae in L do not distinguish between two computations one of which is a stuttered extension of the other. In this case, we can use our approach for proving properties given by formulae in L as long as the theory of fifo buffers in the logic L is decidable.

References

[AAF+]   Y. Afek, H. Attyia, A. Fekete, M. Fischer, N. Lynch, Y. Mansour, D.-W. Wang, and L. Zuck. Reliable communication using unreliable channel. to appear in JACM.

[BSW69] K. A. Bartlett, R. A. Scantlebury, and P. T. Wilkinson. A note on reliable full-duplex transmission over half-duplex links. *Communcation of the ACM*, 12:260–261, 1969.

[CES86] E. M. Clarke, E. A. Emerson, and A. P. Sistla. Automatic verification of finite-state concurrent systems using temporal logic specifications. *Transactions on Programming Languages and Systems*, 8(2), 1986.

[CM86]   K. M. Chandy and J. Misra. *Parallel Program Design: A Fundation*. (A draft), 1986.

[EL85]   E. A. Emerson and C. L. Lei. Modalities for model checking: Branching time strikes back. In *Proc. 12th ACM Symp. on Principles of Programming Languages*, pages 84–96, 1985.

[Lam83]   L. Lamport. Specifying concurrent program modules. *ACM TOPLAS*, 5(2):190–222, 1983.

[LP85]   O. Lichtenstein and A. Pnueli. Checking that finite-state concurrent programs satisfy their linear specifications. In *Proc. 12th ACM Symp. on Principles of Programming Languages*, pages 97–107, 1985.

[LT87]   N.A. Lynch and M. R. Tuttle. Hierarchical correctness proofs for distributed algorithms. In *Proc. 6th ACM Symp. on Principles of Distributed Computing*, pages 137–151, 1987.

[LT89]   N.A. Lynch and M. R. Tuttle. An introduction to input/output automata. *CWI Quarterly*, 2(3):219–246, 1989.

[OL82]   S. Owicki and L. Lamport. Proving liveness properties of concurrent programs. *TOPLAS*, 4(3):455–495, 1982.

[Pnu77]   A. Pnueli. The Temporal Logic of programs. In *Proc. 18th IEEE Symp. on Foundation of Computer Science*, pages 46–57, 1977.

[SCFM84] A. P. Sistla, E. M. Clarke, N. Francez, and A. R. Meyer. Can message buffers be axiomatized in linear temporal logic? *Information and Control*, 63(1/2):88–112, 1984.

[SZ90]   A. P. Sistla and L. D. Zuck. Reasoning in a restricted temporal logic. submitted for publication, parts appeared in [SZ87], 1990.

[VW86]   M. Y. Vardi and P. Wolper. An automata-theoretic approach to automatic program verification (preliminary report). In *Proc. 1st IEEE Symp. on Logics in Computer Science*, 1986.

Mechanically Checked Proofs of Kernel Specifications[*][‡]

William R. Bevier[§]   Jørgen F. Søgaard-Andersen[¶]

Abstract

This paper describes an experiment in the use of the Boyer-Moore logic to specify a non-finite state operating system kernel, and in the use of the Boyer-Moore theorem prover to prove the correctness of an implementation. The kernel specification had first been given in terms of a labeled transition system. It was transcribed into the Boyer-Moore logic so that an attempt could be made to mechanically check correctness proofs.

Keywords: Kernel, mechanical proof checking, Boyer-Moore Theorem Prover, stepwise development, labeled transition systems, safety properties.

1   Introduction

An approach to specifying a multiprogramming kernel is given in [8]. It describes several levels of abstraction in the specification of a kernel implementing occam2–like [4] processes on a single machine. It also explores the question of what it means for one level to be a correct implementation of another. The underlying semantic model used in [8] is the well-known notion of labeled transition systems (see section 2 below).

This paper describes an attempt to use the Boyer-Moore logic to state the kernel specifications, and use the Boyer-Moore theorem prover to mechanically check proofs of correctness of kernel levels. The Boyer-Moore approach was chosen largely because of its use in an earlier kernel specification and implementation project described in [1].

Section 2 of this paper briefly describes the notion of labeled transition systems and what it means for one transition system to be a safe implementation of another. Section 3 describes the kernel specification given in [8]. The translation of the specification into the Boyer-Moore logic is discussed in Section 4. The correctness theorems are presented in Section 5. Section 6 contains some observations on this exercise.

---

[*]This work was supported in part at Computational Logic, Inc., by the Defense Advanced Research Projects Agency, ARPA Order 7406. The views and conclusions contained in this document are those of the authors and should not be interpreted as representing the official policies, either expressed or implied, of Computational Logic, Inc., the Defense Advanced Research Projects Agency or the U.S. Government.

[‡]This work was also supported in part at the Technical University of Denmark by the Commision of the European Communities (CEC) under the ESPRIT programme in the field of Basic Research Action proj. no. 3104: "ProCoS: Provably Correct Systems" and by The Danish Technical Research Council under the "RapID" programme.

[§]Computational Logic Inc., 1717 W. 6th St. Suite 290, Austin, Texas 78703, email: bevier@cli.com

[¶]Department of Computer Science, Building 344, Technical University of Denmark, DK-2800 Lyngby, Denmark, email: jsa@id.dth.dk

This paper contains no introduction to the Boyer-Moore logic or its theorem prover. See [3] for this information. Anyone familiar with Lisp should have little problem following the presentation. We occasionally give what we hope are helpful footnotes.

2 Labeled Transition Systems

In [8] several levels of abstraction in the specification of a multiprogramming kernel are given semantics in the style of Plotkin's Structural Operational Semantics, SOS [7].

The method uses *labeled transition systems* (LTS) as the underlying semantic model. This is a way of describing the steps of a computer program during its execution and captures the intuitive understanding of a program as transitions between states. Formally, an LTS, S^α, where α is the program, is a quadruple $(\Gamma_S^\alpha, I_S^\alpha, \Lambda_S^\alpha, \underset{S^\alpha}{\longrightarrow})$, where Γ_S^α is the set of states, I_S^α is the set of initial states, Λ_S^α is the set of labels, and $\underset{S^\alpha}{\longrightarrow}$ is the transition relation $(\underset{S^\alpha}{\longrightarrow} \subseteq \Gamma_S^\alpha \times \Lambda_S^\alpha \times \Gamma_S^\alpha)$. A transition in S^α is usually written $\alpha \vdash s \underset{S}{\overset{\lambda}{\longrightarrow}} s'$ which denotes a transition from the state s to s' in the context of the program code α. λ denotes the nature of the step. We shall return to this. Below we let α be a given program and omit it as index on LTSs and transitions.

2.1 The Correctness Notion

Since each level of abstraction in the kernel specification is described by a LTS, correctness of each step of development is expressed as a refinement relation between LTSs. In [8] this relation is divided into both a safety and a fairness part. Here we concentrate on the safety part based on simulation between LTSs[1]. We say that a step goes from an *abstract* LTS to a *concrete* LTS (which is then abstract wrt. the next development step).

Part of the safety correctness notion deals with showing correspondence between concrete and abstract transitions. Since we are only interested in investigating concrete transitions emanating from reachable states, it suffices to show the correspondence for transitions emanating from states satisfying an arbitrary concrete invariant[2]. To relate concrete and abstract states the correctness notion requires the existence of an *abstraction function*, $\mathcal{R}$, mapping states of the concrete LTS to states of the abstract LTS.

Definition 1 (SAFE implementation)

A concrete LTS C is a **safe implementation** *of an abstract LTS $\mathcal{A}$ if an abstraction function $\mathcal{R}$ and a concrete invariant $\mathcal{I}_C$ exist such that the following conditions hold:*

(i) $(\forall s \in I_C)(\mathcal{R}(s) \in I_\mathcal{A})$

(ii) $(\forall s, s' \in \Gamma_C, \lambda \in \Lambda_C)$
$(\mathcal{I}_C(s) \wedge s \underset{C}{\overset{\lambda}{\longrightarrow}} s' \implies (\lambda \in \Lambda_\mathcal{A} \wedge \mathcal{R}(s) \underset{\mathcal{A}}{\overset{\lambda}{\longrightarrow}} \mathcal{R}(s')) \vee (\lambda \notin \Lambda_\mathcal{A} \wedge \mathcal{R}(s) = \mathcal{R}(s')))$

∎

---

[1]Since the presentation in [8] includes a step of compilation, the correctness notion given there is more general than the one used here.

[2]An invariant is a predicate which is satisfied by all states reachable from an initial state.

Informally, the definition states that (i) all initial concrete states must have a corresponding initial abstract state, and (ii) each concrete transition (emanating from a state satisfying the invariant) with a label that exists at the abstract level must have an abstract counterpart, whereas new concrete transitions (indicated by new labels) must not change the abstract state.

Since Definition 1 only requires *simulation* and not *bisimulation* [6] between the LTSs, an LTS with an empty transition relation is a safe implementation of any LTS. This inconvenience can be taken care of by introducing fairness into the correctness notion, as it is done in [8].

3 A Kernel Specification

Several levels of abstraction in the specification of the kernel, implementing multiple processes on a single machine, are described in [8]. The diagram below depicts some of the levels ranging from the most abstract at the top to the most concrete at the bottom.

$$
\begin{array}{ll}
\text{Assembly Language} & \boxed{\text{AL}} \\
& \downarrow \\
\text{Global Machine} & \boxed{\text{GM}} \\
& \downarrow \\
\text{Kernel Level 1} & \boxed{\text{KL}_1} \\
& \downarrow \\
\text{Kernel Level 2} & \boxed{\text{KL}_2}
\end{array}
$$

The Assembly Language level gives the abstract semantics of an assembly language where each process is considered to be running on its own machine. The Global Machine gives the semantics of processes running on one machine but without any explicit scheduling. The two Kernel Levels introduce kernel aspects like *current process, ready queue*, etc.

This section describes parts of the GM and KL_1 levels. These are given with a high degree of detail in order to show how the subsequent translation into Boyer-Moore logic corresponds to the specification given here.

We first introduce an assembly language for a stack machine.

3.1 A Sample Assembly Language, SAL

An assembly language program is a (nonempty) list of process codes, each of which is a list of instructions. The instructions are partitioned into *kernel instructions* dealing with communication, and *private instructions* like jump etc. The instructions are inspired by the Transputer instruction set [5], i.e. we have synchronous communication on channels.

$$
\begin{array}{llr}
SAL & = Process^{+} & (1) \\
Process & = Ins^{*} & (2) \\
Ins & = KernelIns \mid PrivateIns & (3) \\
KernelIns & = \text{in}(Ch) \mid \text{out}(Ch) \mid \text{alt}(Alts) & (4) \\
PrivateIns & = \text{ldc}(Const) \mid \text{stl}(Addr) \mid \text{jump}(Label) & (5) \\
Alts & = (Ch1 \times Label)^{+} & (6) \\
Ch & = \mathbb{N}_1 & (7) \\
Ch1, Const, Addr, Label & = \mathbb{N}_0 & (8)
\end{array}
$$

We briefly describe a few of the instructions. The in instruction is used to input a value to the top position of the stack from a channel. Correspondingly, out outputs (and pops) the top value of the stack to a channel. The alt (alternation) instruction takes as parameter a list of pairs. The first component of a pair is a channel number (if this number is zero, the guard is considered to be a SKIP guard), and the second component is a label (address) where execution should continue if that alternative is chosen. ldc pushes a constant onto the stack, stl stores the top value of the stack in workspace, and jump changes the flow of control within a process. In the remainder of this paper, α is a given *SAL* program.

3.2 The Global Machine, GM

The private state of each process in GM is given by *Pstate*. It consists of a workspace, a stack, an instruction pointer, and a status.

$$Pstate \qquad = \quad Workspace \times Stack \times Ip \times Status \qquad (9)$$
$$Workspace, Stack \quad = \quad \mathrm{N_0}^* \qquad (10)$$
$$Ip \qquad = \quad \mathrm{N_0} \qquad (11)$$
$$Status \qquad = \quad \underline{ready} \mid \underline{error} \qquad (12)$$

A state in the GM LTS is simply a list[3] of private process states. The length of the list is the same as the length of the list of process codes. A process code is then connected with its state via the index into the lists. In an initial state each process has an empty stack and a <u>ready</u> status, and its instruction pointer is zero.

$$\Gamma_{GM} \quad = \quad \{<s_0, \ldots, s_n> \mid n = \underline{len}\alpha - 1 \wedge s_i \in Pstate\} \qquad (13)$$
$$I_{GM} \quad = \quad \{<s_0, \ldots, s_n> \in \Gamma_{GM} \mid \underline{s\text{-}Stack}(s_i) = <> \wedge \underline{s\text{-}Ip}(s_i) = 0 \wedge \underline{s\text{-}Status}(s_i) = \underline{ready}\} \ (14)$$
$$\Lambda_{GM} \quad = \quad \{\tau(i) \mid 0 \leq i < \underline{len}\alpha\} \cup \{ch : v(i,j) \mid ch \in Ch \wedge v \in \mathrm{N_0} \wedge 0 \leq i,j < \underline{len}\alpha\} \qquad (15)$$

The function <u>s-Stack</u> selects the stack component from a state. Similarly, <u>s-Ip</u> and <u>s-Status</u> select the instruction pointer resp. the status field. A label $\tau(i)$ denotes that the ith process is executing a private instruction, whereas $ch : v(i,j)$ denotes that process i sends the value v on channel ch to process j.

We describe some of the transition rules which define the transition relation. Here is the transition rule for the jump instruction.

$$\frac{\alpha[i][\underline{s\text{-}Ip}(s_i)] = \mathrm{jump}(lab)}{<s_0, \ldots, s_i, \ldots, s_n> \xrightarrow[GM]{\tau(i)} <s_0, \ldots, s_i', \ldots, s_n>} \qquad (16)$$

$$\mathbf{if} \ \ 0 \leq i \leq n \wedge$$
$$\quad \underline{let} \ (ws_i, st_i, ip_i, stat_i) = s_i \ \underline{in}$$
$$\quad \quad stat_i = \underline{ready} \wedge ip_i < \underline{len}\alpha[i] \wedge$$
$$\quad \quad s_i' = (ws_i, st_i, lab, stat_i)$$

---

[3]List notation: A list with elements $a_0, \ldots, a_n$ is written $<a_0, \ldots, a_n>$. $<>$ is the empty list. If l is a list, then $\underline{hd}l$, $\underline{tl}l$, and $\underline{len}l$ denote head, tail, and length of l respectively. $l[i]$ accesses the ith element of l with $l[0]$ being the head element. $l + [i \mapsto v]$ replaces the ith element of l with v. Concatenation of l_1 and l_2 is written $l_1\hat{\ }l_2$.

In order for the transition below the line to be possible, the condition above the line and the side condition (after if) must both be satisfied.

This rule states that any process whose instruction pointer points to a jump instruction and whose status is <u>ready</u> can make a step in which the instruction pointer is changed to the label in the instruction. Only the state of the chosen process is changed.

The following rule defines synchronous communication between two processes.

$$\frac{\alpha[i][\underline{s-}Ip(s_i)] = \text{in}(ch) \qquad \alpha[j][\underline{s-}Ip(s_j)] = \text{out}(ch)}{<s_0, \ldots, s_i, \ldots, s_j, \ldots, s_n> \xrightarrow[GM]{ch:v(j,i)} <s_0, \ldots, s'_i, \ldots, s'_j, \ldots, s_n>} \qquad (17)$$

$\text{if } 0 \leq i \leq n \wedge 0 \leq j \leq n \wedge$
$\quad \underline{\text{let }} (ws_i, st_i, ip_i, stat_i) = s_i, (ws_j, st_j, ip_j, stat_j) = s_j \underline{\text{ in}}$
$\qquad stat_i = \underline{\text{ready}} \wedge stat_j = \underline{\text{ready}} \wedge$
$\qquad ip_i < \underline{\text{len}}\alpha[i] \wedge ip_j < \underline{\text{len}}\alpha[j] \wedge$
$\qquad \underline{\text{len}}st_j > 0 \wedge v = \underline{\text{hd}}st_j \wedge$
$\qquad s'_i = (ws_i, <v>\hat{\ }st_i, ip_i + 1, stat_i) \wedge$
$\qquad s'_j = (ws_j, \underline{\text{tl}}st_j, ip_j + 1, stat_j)$

This rule defines transitions from states where two processes are ready to execute an in resp. an out instruction on the same channel, and the outputting process has a nonempty stack. The resulting states are obtained by incrementing the instruction pointers of the two processes and moving the value from the top of the stack of the outputting process to the top of the stack of the inputting process.

The complete definition of the transition relation at this level consists of nine rules including rules dealing with errors, like a process trying to output with an empty stack.

3.3 The Kernel Level 1, KL$_1$

At the KL$_1$ level we introduce explicit process scheduling. To do this we add a *kernel state* consisting of a *current process* identifier and a *global instruction pointer*. The private instruction pointer is then only used to store the global instruction pointer when the process is not current. We also introduce an explicit waiting status denoting that a process is waiting to communicate.

$$
\begin{array}{llll}
Kstate1 & = & Id \times Ip & (18) \\
Pstate1 & = & Workspace \times Stack \times Ip \times Status1 & (19) \\
Id & = & \mathbb{N}_0 & (20) \\
Status1 & = & Status \mid \underline{\text{waiting}} & (21)
\end{array}
$$

A state of the KL$_1$ LTS now includes a kernel state and a list of private process states.

$$
\begin{array}{lll}
\Gamma_{KL1} & = & \{(ks, psl) \mid ks \in Kstate1 \wedge psl \in Pstate1^+ \wedge \underline{\text{len}}psl = \underline{\text{len}}\alpha\} \qquad (22) \\
I_{KL1} & = & \{((id, ip), psl) \in \Gamma_{KL1} \mid id = 0 \wedge ip = 0 \wedge \qquad\qquad\qquad\qquad (23) \\
& & \quad (\forall(ws, st, pip, stat) \in psl)(st = <> \wedge pip = 0 \wedge stat = \underline{\text{ready}})\} \\
\Lambda_{KL1} & = & \{\tau(i), \kappa(i), \kappa \mid 0 \leq i < \underline{\text{len}}\alpha\} \cup \qquad\qquad\qquad\qquad\qquad\qquad (24) \\
& & \{ch : v(i, j) \mid ch \in Ch \wedge v \in \mathbb{N}_0 \wedge 0 \leq i, j < \underline{\text{len}}\alpha\} \qquad\qquad (25)
\end{array}
$$

The new label $\kappa(i)$ denotes that the kernel is performing a step in the ith process. A κ label denotes a process switch transition (see below).

In the complete definition of the KL_1 transition relation, 14 transition rules are needed. In this section we present only a few. Here is the KL_1 jump transition rule.

$$\frac{\alpha[i][ip] = \text{jump}(lab)}{((i, ip), psl) \xrightarrow[KL1]{\tau(i)} ((i, ip'), psl)} \tag{26}$$

$\text{if } \underline{\text{let}}\ (ws_i, st_i, ip_i, stat_i) = psl[i]\ \underline{\text{in}}$
$\quad stat_i = \underline{\text{ready}} \wedge ip < \underline{\text{len}}\alpha[i] \wedge$
$\quad ip' = lab$

This rule is similar to rule (16) at the GM level. Note, however, that the jump transition at this level changes the *global* instruction pointer.

At the GM level one transition rule is required to specify the synchronous communication transitions. Here, several transition rules are needed. We only show the rules where the current process wishes to execute an in instruction.

If the current process wishes to execute an in instruction and another process is already waiting to output on the same channel, the communication can be performed. Part of the state change is to give the waiting process a **ready** status.

$$\frac{\alpha[i][ip] = \text{in}(ch)}{((i, ip), psl) \xrightarrow[KL1]{ch:v(j',i)} ((i, ip'), psl')} \tag{27}$$

$\text{if } \underline{\text{let}}\ (ws_i, st_i, ip_i, stat_i) = psl[i]\ \underline{\text{in}}$
$\quad stat_i = \underline{\text{ready}} \wedge ip_i < \underline{\text{len}}\alpha[i] \wedge$
$\quad (\exists 0 \le j < \underline{\text{len}}psl)$
$\qquad (\underline{\text{let}}\ (ws_j, st_j, ip_j, stat_j) = psl[j]\ \underline{\text{in}}$
$\qquad\quad stat_j = \underline{\text{waiting}} \wedge \alpha[j][ip_j] = \text{out}(ch) \wedge$
$\qquad\quad v = \underline{\text{hd}}st_j \wedge j' = j \wedge$
$\qquad\quad ip' = ip + 1 \wedge$
$\qquad\quad psl' = psl + [i \mapsto (ws_i, <v>\hat{}st_i, ip_i, stat_i),$
$\qquad\qquad\qquad\qquad j \mapsto (ws_j, \underline{\text{tl}}st_j, ip_j + 1, \underline{\text{ready}})])$

If, on the other hand, another process is not waiting to output on the same channel, the current process is given a **waiting** status. Such transitions have no GM counterparts.

$$\frac{\alpha[i][ip] = \text{in}(ch)}{((i, ip), psl) \xrightarrow[KL1]{\kappa(i)} ((i, ip), psl')} \tag{28}$$

$\text{if } \underline{\text{let}}\ (ws_i, st_i, ip_i, stat_i) = psl[i]\ \underline{\text{in}}$
$\quad stat_i = \underline{\text{ready}} \wedge ip < \underline{\text{len}}\alpha[i] \wedge$
$\quad \neg(\exists 0 \le j < \underline{\text{len}}psl)$
$\qquad (\underline{\text{let}}\ (ws_j, st_j, ip_j, stat_j) = psl[j]\ \underline{\text{in}}$
$\qquad\quad stat_j = \underline{\text{waiting}} \wedge$
$\qquad\quad \alpha[j][ip_j] = \text{out}(ch)) \wedge$
$\quad psl' = psl + [i \mapsto (ws_i, st_i, ip_i, \underline{\text{waiting}})]$

Since we have introduced the notion of current process at the KL_1 level, we need transitions to introduce a new current process. The next transition rule defines such *process switch* transitions. The global instruction pointer is stored in the private state of the old current process and then restored from the private state of the new current process.

$$((i, ip), psl) \xrightarrow[KL_1]{\kappa} ((j, ip'), psl') \tag{29}$$

$$\textbf{if } \; 0 \leq j < \underline{\text{len}}\, psl \wedge$$
$$i \neq j \wedge$$
$$\underline{\text{s-}}Stat(psl[j]) = \underline{\text{ready}} \wedge$$
$$ip' = \underline{\text{s-}}Ip(psl[j]) \wedge$$
$$\underline{\text{let}} \; (ws_i, st_i, ip_i, stat_i) \; \underline{\text{in}}$$
$$psl' = psl + [i \mapsto (ws_i, st_i, ip, stat_i)]$$

4 Translation into the Boyer-Moore Logic

In this section we describe the translation into the Boyer-Moore logic of the specification for the GM and KL_1 levels. We follow an approach to modeling finite state machines similar to that described in [2] (even though the specifications described here are non-finite state). A state set is defined by a predicate which recognizes elements of the set. An LTS transition rule is translated into a predicate which determines if a transition defined by the rule is possible in the given state, and a function from the state to a *list* of labeled states, which represents the set of possible resulting states. It is necessary to return a list since a transition rule generally defines several transitions emanating from the same state. In all the examples shown below the lists are, however, of length one.

4.1 The Global Machine, GM

The state of a GM process is defined in the Boyer-Moore logic by two events[4]. The add-shell event pstate defines a record structure[5]. It carries the information contained in Equation (9) — that the state of a GM process contains a workspace (ws), stack (st), instruction pointer (ip), and a status field (stat). In addition, we have made the process's code (pr) a part of its state.

```
(add-shell pstate nil pstate-shell
          ((ws   (none-of) false)
           (st   (none-of) false)
           (ip   (none-of) false)
           (stat (none-of) false)
           (pr   (none-of) false)))
```

The predicate gm-pstatep imposes type restrictions on the fields of a pstate. A GM process must satisfy the requirements that the workspace and stack are lists of numbers,

---

[4]We use the term *event* to refer to function definitions, lemmas, etc. which have meaning in the Boyer-Moore logic.

[5]An add-shell introduces a new data type. The first argument gives the name of the constructor function for the type. The third argument identifies the recognizer for objects of this type. The fourth argument is a list of the fields. Each field is a triple (*fieldname recognizers defaultvalue*). The (none-of) notation used in this example indicates no type restriction.

the instruction pointer is a number, and the status is one of the literals {ready, error}. The function gm-statep captures the requirements contained in Equations (10)–(12) of Section 3.2. In addition, the program must satisfy the predicate processp. processp expresses the well-formedness of a process's code as described in Equations (2)–(8).

```
(defn gm-pstatep (x)
  (and (pstate-shell x)
       (every-numberp (ws x))
       (every-numberp (st x))
       (numberp (ip x))
       (member (stat x) '(ready error))
       (processp (pr x))))
```

The GM state space is a list of GM processes. This is recognized by the predicate gm-statep, which requires its argument to be a non-empty list of gm-pstateps. This corresponds to Equation (13).

```
(defn gm-statep (gm)
  (and (every-gm-pstatep gm)
       (listp gm)))
```

In addition to this a predicate gm-initial-statep must be defined which captures the meaning of Equation (14).

We define transition rules in the logic with two functions as explained above. One is a predicate which characterizes the enabling condition of a transition rule. The other is a function from a GM state to a list of cons pairs. The car of each pair is a label and the cdr is a GM state.

The translation of rule (17) is described as follows. The predicate gm-in-out-enabled recognizes the enabling conditions for a GM in-out transition. The arguments to this predicate are a GM state gm and process identifiers i and j. The predicate requires the ith process to be in a ready state with its instruction pointer addressing the in instruction, and the jth process to be ready to do an output with a non-empty stack. Furthermore, they must be communicating on the same channel.[6]

```
(defn gm-in-out-enabled (gm i j)
  (let ((pi (nth i gm))
        (pj (nth j gm)))
    (and (lessp i (length gm)) (lessp j (length gm))
         (equal (stat pi) 'ready) (equal (stat pj) 'ready)
         (lessp (ip pi) (length (pr pi))) (lessp (ip pj) (length (pr pj)))
         (listp (st pj))
         (let ((instri (gm-fetch pi)) (instrj (gm-fetch pj)))
           (and (equal (opr instri) 'in) (equal (opr instrj) 'out)
                (equal (arg instri) (arg instrj)))))))
```

---

[6] Here are a few of the primitive functions defined in the Boyer-Moore logic upon which this specification is based. (length l) returns the number of (top-level) elements in list l. (nth i l) fetches the ith element (zero based) from l. (put i v l) replaces the ith element of l with v.

The communication transitions are now defined by `gm-in-out-transition`. As indicated by rule (17), it returns a list containing only the pair `((tau i) . s')`, where `s'` is the state resulting from the transition. The top value is popped from j's stack and pushed onto i's. The instruction pointer of both processes is advanced by 1. Both processes remain ready.

```
(defn gm-in-out-transition (gm i j)
  (let ((pi (nth i gm)) (pj (nth j gm)))
    (let ((instri (gm-fetch pi)) (instrj (gm-fetch pj)))
      (list (cons (list 'comm j i (arg instrj) (car (st pj)))
                  (put i
                       (pstate (ws pi)
                               (cons (nth 0 (st pj)) (st pi))
                               (add1 (ip pi))
                               (stat pi)
                               (pr pi))
                  (put j
                       (pstate (ws pj)
                               (nthcdr 1 (st pj))
                               (add1 (ip pj))
                               (stat pj)
                               (pr pj))
                  gm)))))))
```

Compare these definitions with rule (17). The predicate `gm-in-out-enabled` contains the requirement which occurs above the inference line (that i's current instruction is `in`, and j's current instruction is `out`), as well as requirements described in the side condition.

The side condition in (17) is used in part to describe the details of the transitions defined. These aspects of the transition rule occur in the function `gm-in-out-transition`.

4.2   The Kernel Level 1, KL₁

The kernel level KL₁ is described in the Boyer-Moore logic in the same style as the GM level. The KL₁ state space is defined by a shell `kl`, and a predicate `kl-statep` which imposes type restrictions on the KL₁ fields. Recall that KL₁ introduces explicit process scheduling by including a current process id `kid`, and a global instruction pointer `kip` for the current process. The `psl` field is a list of KL₁ private process states. A private state at this level differs from a GM private state only in that a new process status `waiting` is introduced.

```
(add-shell kl nil kl-shellp
           ((kid (one-of numberp) zero)
            (kip (one-of numberp) zero)
            (psl (none-of) false)))

(defn kl-statep (x)
  (and (kl-shellp x)
       (kl-pstate-listp (psl x))
       (listp (psl x))))
```

Here is the translation of the KL$_1$ transition rule (27). Such a communication transition is enabled if the current process is ready to receive on a channel, and some other process is waiting to send on the same channel. In place of the existential quantifier, we write a recursive function, here called some-process-pow-channel, which recognizes when some process is in the enabling in-out relation with the current process.

```
(defn kl-in-out-enabled (s)
  (let ((p (nth (kid s) (psl s))))
    (and (equal (stat p) 'ready)
         (lessp (kip s) (length (pr p)))
         (let ((instruction (kl-fetch s)))
           (and (equal (opr instruction) 'in)
                (some-process-pow-channel (psl s) (arg instruction)))))))
```

kl-in-out-transition describes the transition on the current process and on a process j which is sending to the current process.

```
(defn kl-in-out-transition (s j)
  (let ((pi (nth (kid s) (psl s))) (instri (kl-fetch s)) (pj (nth j (psl s))))
    (let ((instrj (nth (ip pj) (pr pj))))
      (list (cons (list 'comm j (kid s) (arg instrj) (car (st pj)))
                  (kl (kid s)
                      (add1 (kip s))
                      (put (kid s)
                           (pstate (ws pi)
                                   (cons (nth 0 (st pj)) (st pi))
                                   (ip pi)
                                   (stat pi)
                                   (pr pi))
                           (put j
                                (pstate (ws pj)
                                        (nthcdr 1 (st pj))
                                        (add1 (ip pj))
                                        'ready
                                        (pr pj))
                                (psl s)))))))))
```

5 The Correctness Theorems

A correctness theorem for each KL$_1$ transition rule was derived from Definition 1 in Section 2.1. A mapping function map defines the abstraction from a KL$_1$ state to a GM state. The abstraction changes the status of every waiting process to ready. The current KL$_1$ instruction pointer is installed into the state of the current process. The KL$_1$ instruction pointer and current process identifier vanish in the mapping.

```
(defn map-pstate (p)
  (pstate (ws p) (st p) (ip p) (if (equal (stat p) 'error) 'error 'ready)
          (pr p)))
```

```
(defn map-states (1)
  (if (listp l)
      (cons (map-pstate (car l)) (map-pstates (cdr l)))
      nil))

(defn map (kl)
  (let ((p (nth (kid kl) (map-pstates (psl kl)))))
    (put (kid kl)
         (pstate (ws p) (st p) (kip kl) (stat p) (pr p))
         (map-pstates (psl kl)))))
```

Using this mapping function, we state a pair of correctness theorems for each transition rule in KL_1. The first theorem requires that a GM transition is enabled if the corresponding KL_1 transition is enabled. Here is an example of this theorem proved for the communication transition rules. This theorem says that for a valid KL_1 state s (as defined by kl-statep), a GM communication transition is enabled on the mapping of s if the KL_1 communication transition is enabled on s.

```
(prove-lemma gm-in-out-enabled-map
  (implies (and (kl-statep s)
                (inv-kl s)
                (kl-in-out-enabled s)
                (channel-wo-process (arg (kl-fetch s)) j (psl s)))
           (gm-in-out-enabled (map s) (kid s) j)))
```

A second theorem states the correctness of the transition. Let s be a valid KL_1 state on which a communication transition is enabled, and let s1 be a possible outcome of such a transition on s. (s1 is a (label . state) pair.) Then the pair (label . (map state)) is a possible outcome of the GM communication transition performed on (map s).

```
(prove-lemma kl-in-out-correctness
     (implies (and (kl-statep s)
                   (inv-kl s)
                   (kl-in-out-enabled s)
                   (member s1 (kl-in-out-transition s j))
                   (channel-wo-process (arg (kl-fetch s)) j (psl s))
                   (numberp j))
              (member (cons (car s1) (map (cdr s1)))
                      (gm-in-out-transition (map s) (kid s) j))))
```

inv-kl is the invariant on reachable KL_1 states which we use throughout the correctness proofs. It contains the fact that any process waiting to output has a non-empty stack, and that the kernel's current process identifier is "valid", i.e. identifies an existing process.

The $KL1_1$ process switch transition (29) has no corresponding transition at the GM level. We prove that this transition is invisible at the GM level. This is contained in the theorem kl-switch-correctness.

```
(prove-lemma kl-switch-correctness
  (implies (and (kl-statep s)
                (numberp z)
                (inv-kl s)
                (kl-switch-enabled s z)
                (member s1 (kl-switch-transition s z)))
           (equal (map (cdr s1))
                  (map s))))
```

The correctness theorems above are all derived from (ii) of Definition 1. The theorems are stronger than (ii) since, given a GM transition, we only search for a corresponding KL_1 transition among transitions defined by a certain rule. This is, however, also the way a hand proof would be done.

The correctness theorem for (i) of Definition 1 is simply

```
(prove-lemma initial-correctness
  (implies (kl-initial-statep s) (gm-initial-statep (map s))))
```

For each KL_1 transition which has a corresponding GM transition, we completed a proof of correspondence of the enabling condition and the transition rule. Where a KL_1 transition has no corresponding GM transition we completed a proof that the transition rule is invisible at the GM level. The simple measure of the size of our script, 162 function definitions and 287 proved lemmas, should be taken as an upper bound on the size necessary to complete the project, since we experimented with a macro language for the Boyer-Moore theorem prover.

6 Observations

The purpose of this experiment was to discover if the kernel specifications given in [8] could be translated in a satisfactory way into the Boyer-Moore logic, and to discover how difficult the correctness proofs would be.[7]

We feel that the translation was a success. There was little problem defining functions in the logic which capture the meaning of the specification given in terms of a labeled transition system. Also, the correctness theorems as expressed in the logic were clearly instances of the correctness notion developed for relating LTSs.

The correctness theorems were a good candidate for mechanical checking. Their proofs involve many cases, none of which are very difficult. Hand proofs of these theorems are mistake-prone. In fact, only a few had been attempted by hand because of the tedium involved in writing them down.

A number of similar mapping proofs have been previously checked with the theorem prover [2], all involving much more complicated mappings from concrete to abstract

---

[7]We hope that the comments about the prover in this section are intelligible. One point worth noting is that one of the central proof strategies used by the theorem prover is term rewriting. The user builds up a database of facts by stating lemmas of the form $H \rightarrow L = R$. An instance of L will be rewritten to the corresponding instance of R if condition H holds. A user can give the theorem prover hints indicating which rewrite rules to apply or which ones to ignore. Alternatively, the user can just let the theorem prover try every applicable rule in the current database.

machines. We expected the KL_1 correctness proofs to be straightforward exercises, particularly considering that one of the authors is an experienced user of the Boyer-Moore prover. This expectation was only partially realized. Some of the proofs, particularly those concerning the I/O transition rules, were far more difficult than we expected. This is disappointing, since the reasoning steps seem elementary when done by hand.

The proofs of the private transition rules were simple and followed a pattern familiar to users of the Boyer-Moore prover. The first proof took some effort, but proofs of subsequent private transition rules were structured in a way similar to the first. These proofs were easily accomplished simply by adjusting the set of supporting rewrite lemmas.

The difficult proofs involved reasoning about specifications where existential quantifiers over process identifiers occur in the LTS version. The existential quantifiers were replaced by recursive functions in the Boyer-Moore translation, thereby introducing an additional level of recursion. We made several attempts before we achieved a formulation that was clear enough to incorporate into the prover's rewrite algorithm. Our solution also involved creation of a more complete set of lemmas for the supporting theories, primarily lists, than we had before.

Is it worthwhile to expend such effort in solving problems of prover control? Our experience is that it is. The base theories which are developed and the insight gained into the problem domain pay off whenever a related problem is addressed.

Acknowledgement: We would like to thank Bill Young of Computational Logic for his contributions in formulating the Boyer-Moore version of the kernel specifications.

References

[1] William R. Bevier. Kit: A study in operating system verification. *IEEE Transactions on Software Engineering*, 15(11):1368–81, November 1989.

[2] William R. Bevier, Jr. Warren A. Hunt, J Strother Moore, and William D. Young. An approach to systems verification. *Journal of Automated Reasoning*, 5(4):411–428, December 1989.

[3] R. S. Boyer and J S. Moore. *A Computational Logic Handbook*. Academic Press, Boston, 1988.

[4] INMOS Limited. occam2 *Reference Manual*. Series in Computer Science. Prentice Hall, 1988.

[5] INMOS Limited. *Transputer Instruction Set: A compiler writer's guide*. Prentice Hall, 1988.

[6] Robin Milner. *Communication and Concurrency*. Series in Computer Science. Prentice Hall, 1989.

[7] G. D. Plotkin. An operational semantics for CSP. *Formal Description of Programming Concepts - II*, pages 199–225, 1983.

[8] Camilla Østerberg Rump and Jørgen F. Søgaard-Andersen. Specification and verification of kernels. Master's thesis, Department of Computer Science, Technical University of Denmark, August 1990.

A Top Down Approach
to the Formal Specification of
SCI Cache Coherence

Stein Gjessing, Stein Krogdahl, Ellen Munthe-Kaas
Department of Informatics, University of Oslo
P.O.Box 1080 Blindern, N–0316 Oslo 3, Norway
Phone: +47 245 3444   Fax: +47 245 3401
Internet: gjessing@ifi.uio.no

Abstract

The paper gives an introduction to an ongoing effort of formally specifying and verifying the cache coherence protocol of the new IEEE interconnect standard called the Scalable Coherent Interface. We first give the the most abstract (top level) specification of a memory system. We then introduce a private cache for each processor, and specify the notion of cache coherence. We refine the specifications of the memory operations for use with caches, and finally outline the more complex bottom layers where directory structures and concurrency are introduced.

1 Introduction

SCI – Scalable Coherent Interface – is a new standard defined by IEEE working group P1596 for the interconnect in shared memory multiprocessors [9, 10]. The interconnect is scalable, meaning that up to (a theoretical limit of) 64 000 processor-, memory- or I/O-nodes can interface to.

In order for a processor to operate at high speed, it needs a cache that contains copies of the memory entities in use at the moment. Because different processor nodes share memory, SCI defines a cache coherence protocol that ensures that all caches are coherent, i.e. at any time all processor nodes agree upon the state of the memory. In present buses coherence is achieved by eavesdropping or snooping: all processor nodes listen to the bus and invalidate or update their caches when they hear that memory is written into [6]. This snooping scheme does not work well when there are many (e.g. more than 10) processors connected to the same bus. SCI therefore defines a directory based cache coherency scheme that is intended to work for a large number of processors with shared memory.

In a directory based cache coherence protocol cache updating is based on information sent to a directory instead of observations on a bus. This directory then keeps track of which nodes cache copies of a given memory entity, and hence the directory knows which caches are affected by a modification of this entity. Directory based cache coherence protocols were suggested quite a long time ago [2, 15]. Only recently, however, is communication speed so fast and components so cheap that further development of such cache protocols is interesting. In addition to the protocol that is the topic of this paper, there are currently several directory based protocols under development [1, 10, 12, 16].

The SCI cache coherence protocol designates a directory to each line of memory (a line is 64 bytes). Each directory is implemented as a doubly linked list that starts at the memory and contains all nodes that cache that memory line. The protocol must ensure that concurrent memory operations on the same memory line keep the directory data structure for that line consistent.

The cache coherence protocol is implemented by message passing between the nodes. The interconnect does not preserve the order of messages sent between two nodes, and there are basically few assumptions about the speed of the interconnect (except some time-out parameters).

The SCI cache coherence protocol is intended for hardware implementation. To specify and verify its specification is far from a trivial task. The specification is written in the programming language C. The full code consists of approximately 5000 lines, which specify the behavior of the memory as well as the processors nodes. This program has been reviewed and tested at the University of Oslo for some time, and errors have been found and corrected. Because of the complexity of the protocol, and its asynchronous nature, a formal specification and verification effort also seems worth while. Such an effort (for a large subset of the protocol) is being undertaken by the authors of this report [4, 5]. So far, we have had few automated tools available for this formal effort, and must rely on a certain amount of proofs by hand, so errors have also made this work unreliable. We however believe that other classes of errors are found in formal verification than in simulation and debugging. We believe that the total reliability of the protocol is increased by using a versatile set of testing and verification methods. We also plan to look into computer aided verification tools, and believe that the approach presented in this paper is well suited for semi-automated verification [7, 8, 13].

Aside from the fact that our formal verification effort probably will contain faults, there are also other limitations to such an effort. Firstly the SCI cache coherence protocol is defined on top of a message passing protocol. We assume that this protocol is correct, in the sense that it among other things ensures that communication can be conducted without deadlocks due to capacity problems. Secondly we must emphasize that verifying the SCI specification is not the same as verifying the final hardware. The specification will be implemented in hardware by different computer manufacturers. A complete new set of verification tools must be deployed in order to ensure that hardware correctly implements the SCI cache coherence protocol.

In this paper we outline some of the results of the most formal part of the SCI verification effort. We emphasise the top layers of the specification, and only briefly outline the more detailed and concrete layers.

In our most abstract model, processes execute read and write operations on a shared memory without cache. We refine this model by introducing a cache in front of each processor. At first we add little structure to the set of caches. Later we refine the model by organizing the cache lines into sequences, finally to be replaced by doubly linked lists with pointers in the most concrete model. Different aspects of concurrency is introduced as the model is refined; full concurrency is specified for the bottom level.

The data structure specified at the bottom level is almost the same as the one in the C-code specification. An effort remains to show that our bottom functional specification is implemented by the C code specification of the SCI protocol.

2 An Abstract Store

Our most abstract specification of a memory system consists of several processors that execute Load and Store operations on a byte addressable store. At this most abstract level there is no cache. We divide our byte addresses into two parts. The first part addresses a block or line of memory (typically 32 or 64 bytes), while the second part gives the byte number within the memory line. We then have the following domains:

Addr : global address space
Bid : domain of byte addresses within a line
Word : domain of word values
Line = **Bid** → **Word** (e.g. 4 bytes)
Pid : the set of processors

At the most abstract level, our store S is a function that takes an address as an argument and delivers a word value as the result (tacitly assuming proper alignment):

$$T_S = \mathbf{Addr} \times \mathbf{Bid} \to \mathbf{Word}$$
$$S : T_S$$

The interface between the processors and the memory system is specified through the Load and Store operations. The signatures of these operations are:

Store : $(\mathbf{Pid} \times \mathbf{Addr} \times \mathbf{Bid} \times \mathbf{Word} \times T_S) \to T_S$
Load : $(\mathbf{Pid} \times \mathbf{Addr} \times \mathbf{Bid} \times T_S) \to \mathbf{Word}$

The effect these operations have on the store is defined by:

Store$(p, a, b, w, S) = S[(a, b) \leftarrow w]$
Load$(p, a, b, S) = S(a, b)$

where $S[(a, b) \leftarrow w]$ is the function that is identical to S, except at the point (a, b), where its value is w. Hence a Store operation redefines the store at the given address, while the Load operation returns the stored value at the given address. The p parameter identifies the processor issuing the Load or Store. It is superfluous at this levelof abstraction, but is needed when caches are introduced.

3   A Distributed Cache

In order to decrease the overall latency for Load and Store operations, we introduce a cache for each processor. Each cache line can contain a copy of one memory line. When the processor Loads a word, it first checks if a copy of the memory line containing that word, already resides in the cache. If it does, then the operation is purely local. Otherwise (called a cache-miss) the data has to be fetched from the memory or from some other cache.

Our more concrete state space then consists of a memory, M, and the caches, C. M is a function that takes a memory line address as an argument and returns the contents of that line. C is a function that takes a processor identification and a memory line address as parameters and delivers the contents of that line if it exists in the cache of that processor. We choose to make both functions total. Thus, if the memory does not contain the most recent value of an address, the function M returns the special value **gone**. In this case, some cache line must contain a valid copy of this line. If a processor does not cache that address, C returns the value **invalid**.

The types of the functions C and M are then:

$$T_C = \mathbf{Addr} \times \mathbf{Pid} \to (\mathbf{Line} \cup \{\mathbf{invalid}\})$$
$$T_M = \mathbf{Addr} \to (\mathbf{Line} \cup \{\mathbf{gone}\})$$

4 Multiprocessor cache coherence invariants

Our primary concern is that all cached copies of the same memory line have equal contents. The **cache/cache coherence invariant** states that when the same address, a, is cached by two processors, p and p', then the contents are equal:

$$\forall p, p' \in P, a \in A : \ C(a,p) \neq \text{invalid} \wedge C(a,p') \neq \text{invalid} \ \Rightarrow \ C(a,p) = C(a,p')$$

Memory may have a valid copy of its line. The **cache/memory coherence invariant** says that in this case, any cache-line with the same address must contain the same value as memory:

$$\forall a \in A, \forall p \in P : \ M(a) \neq \text{gone} \wedge C(a,p) \neq \text{invalid} \ \Rightarrow \ M(a) = C(a,p)$$

Finally there must exist an Owner for every memory line. We express this by the **data-must-exist invariant**, that says that if a memory line is invalid then there must exist a cached copy:

$$\forall a \in A : \ M(a) = \text{gone} \ \Rightarrow \ \exists p \in P : C(a,p) \neq \text{invalid}$$

We say that the memory system is **sound** whenever all three cache coherence invariants hold. In a real implementation where Load and Store operations are executed concurrently, these equations need not necessarily hold all the time. There may be intermediate cache states where the invariants are temporarily invalid. This is acceptable as long as they are reestablished as soon as the system reenters a stable state.

5 M and C implements S

We must implement the operations Load and Store (to work on M and C) such that the new system with distributed cache is an implementation of the store of section 2.

A general technique to prove that a system is an implementation (refinement) of another, is to define an **abstraction function**. This function maps the more detailed state space (in this case the memory system with caches) into the abstract state space (the memory system without caches) in a way that demonstrates the correspondence between the two models.

Preservation of the cache coherence invariants is crucial for the existence of such an abstraction function for our models. Without these restrictions on the caches and the memory, it would have been difficult to give a precise definition of a "shared memory image" [14].

Given the model of a memory with distributed cache, the abstraction function $\hat{S}$ defines our old store with no cache (S) in terms of the new memory (M) and the distributed cache (C). The signature of $\hat{S}$ is:

$$\hat{S} : T_M \times T_C \to T_S$$

In order to define $\hat{S}$, we will first define a function Image that finds the data in (M, C), regardless whether the memory-line is cached or not. This is the "shared memory image" as defined in [14]. This function has the signature:

$$\text{Image} : T_M \times T_C \to \textbf{Addr} \to \textbf{Line}$$

The semantics of Image are defined by:

Image$(M, C) =$
    $\lambda a.$ **if** $M(a) \neq$ **gone then** $M(a)$
        else some $v \in$ **Line** such that $\exists p \in$ **Pid** $: C(a, p) \neq$ invalid $\land C(a, p) = v$ **fi**

We then define the abstraction function $\hat{S}$:

$$\hat{S}(M, C) = \lambda a, b.\text{Image}(M, C, a)(b)$$

It is easy to see that **Image** and thus $\hat{S}$ is a well-defined function as long as the parameters (M, C) obey the cache coherence invariants. The interesting case is when $M(a) =$ **gone** and the **else** branch is evaluated. Then the data-must-exist invariant says that such a $p \in$ **Pid** really does exist, and the cache/cache-coherence invariant says that if more than one exists, then they all give the same value.

What remains to be proven for an actual realization of the **Load** and **Store** operations for the memory system with caches, is that they implement the corresponding operations for the more abstract model. Visualized, the **Store** operations obey the following correspondence:

$$\hat{S}(\text{Store}(p, a, b, w, M, C)) = \text{Store}(p, a, b, w, \hat{S}(M, C))$$

where the **Store** on the left hand side is the new operation.

6   A specification with write invalidate

We are going to define **Load** and **Store** operations for the refined system. A new operation, **Delete**, is added. We do not assume infinite caches, rather some kind of background (unspecified) system that calls **Delete** whenever there is a need.

To maintain cache coherence on write we decide to use the write invalidate strategy. In each operation we first test if there will be a cache hit, and if so the operation is purely local, reading a word from or writing a word into the cache line. If there is a cache miss then we execute **GetLoadable** or **GetStorable** respectively in order to fill the local cache with a copy of the memory line that the processor can use. To test for a cache hit on a **Load** or a **Store** we use the functions **HasLoadable** and **HasStorable** respectively. The signatures of these four functions are

    HasLoadable, HasStorable : **Pid** $\times$ **Addr** $\times T_M \times T_C \to$ **Bool**
    GetLoadable, GetStorable : **Pid** $\times$ **Addr** $\times T_M \times T_C \to T_M \times T_C$

The semantics of **HasLoadable** and **HasStorable** is defined by

    HasLoadable$(p, a, M, C) = C(a, p) \neq$ invalid

    HasStorable$(p, a, M, C) = M(a) =$ gone $\land C(a, p) \neq$ invalid $\land \forall p' \neq p. \, C(a, p') =$ invalid

GetLoadable and **GetStorable** are defined by

    GetLoadable$(p, a, M, C) = (M, C[(a, p) \to \text{Image}(M, C, a)])$

    GetStorable$(p, a, M, C) =$
        $(M[a \to \text{gone}],$
        $(C[a \to (\lambda p'.\text{invalid})[p \to \text{Image}(M, C, a)]]))$

Using these functions we implement Load, Store, and Delete operations on M and C:

$$\text{Load} : \textbf{Pid} \times \textbf{Addr} \times \textbf{Bid} \times T_M \times T_C \rightarrow T_M \times T_C \times \textbf{Word}$$
$$\text{Store} : \textbf{Pid} \times \textbf{Addr} \times \textbf{Bid} \times \textbf{Word} \times T_M \times T_C \rightarrow T_M \times T_C$$
$$\text{Delete} : \textbf{Pid} \times \textbf{Addr} \times T_M \times T_C \rightarrow T_M \times T_C$$

$\text{Load}(p, a, b, M, C) =$
    if $\text{HasLoadable}(p, a, M, C)$ then $(M, C, C(a, p)(b))$
    else let $(M', C') = \text{GetLoadable}(p, a, M, C) : \ (M', C', C'(a, p)(b))$ fi

$\text{Store}(p, a, b, w, M, C) =$
    if $\text{HasStorable}(p, a, M, C)$
    then $(M, C[(a, p) \rightarrow C(a, p)[b \rightarrow w]])$
    else let $(M', C') = \text{GetStorable}(p, a, M, C) :$
      $(M', C'[(a, p) \rightarrow C'(a, p)[b \rightarrow w]])$ fi

$\text{Delete}(p, a, M, C) =$
    if $\text{HasStorable}(p, a, M, C)$
    then $(M[a \rightarrow C(a, p)], C[(a, p) \rightarrow \text{invalid}])$
    else $(M, C[(a, p) \rightarrow \text{invalid}])$ fi

The above definitions of Load, Store, and Delete are not operational. A simple way to achieve this is to collect all cached lines for a given memory address in a sequence, rather than describing the set through a function. This involves redefining

$$T_C = \textbf{Addr} \rightarrow \textit{sequence of } (\textbf{Pid} \times \textbf{Line})$$

and taking advantage of the fact that for any a the sequence $C(a)$ can be traversed constructively.

7 Modeling Concurrency

In the previous sections Load, Store, and Delete for a given address are assumed to be atomic (indivisible) operations. We however want to execute memory operations issued by different processor to the same address, with a high degree of concurrency. This is achieved through two steps of refinement, briefly explained in the present and the next section. First, the operations are split into suboperations which are to be the new indivisible entities. We thereby specify concurrency in the sense that the top level operations Load, Store, and Delete to some extents may interleave. Finally, to obtain full concurrency as specified by the IEEE standard, we specify the top level memory operations based on several indivisible actions, where one action modify the state of one cache- or memory-line only.

For each address/processor pair (a, p) we introduce a **continuation**. A continuation in this case is a sequence which describes what suboperations remain to be carried out in order to complete the top level operation (Load, Store or Delete) for p at a.

A domain of continuations is added to the global state space, which now is described by

$$\textbf{T}_{\textbf{global}} = \textbf{Addr} \rightarrow T_M \times T_C \times \textbf{T}_{\textbf{Ops}}$$

where

$$T_C = \textbf{Pid} \rightarrow (\textbf{Line} \cup \{\text{invalid}\})$$
$$T_M = (\textbf{Line} \cup \{\text{gone}\}$$
$$\textbf{T}_{\textbf{Ops}} = \textbf{Pid} \rightarrow sequence\ of\ \textbf{T}_{\textbf{oper}}$$

(In essence T_M and T_C are unchanged.) *sequence of* $\textbf{T}_{\textbf{oper}}$ is the continuation sequence. At any point in time and for a given address, none, one or more processors may be ready to execute their next suboperation. At this level, at most one is actually chosen. A relation $\succ$ describes all possible global state transitions for a given address:

$$\succ: \textbf{Addr} \rightarrow (T_M \times T_C \times \textbf{T}_{\textbf{Ops}}) \times (T_M \times T_C \times \textbf{T}_{\textbf{Ops}})$$

As an example, consider the continuation $\text{Ops}(p)$ of a processor p at address a with the contents $< \text{Load}(b) >$, thus indicating that a Load operation should be initiated. The first tiny part of a Load operation consists in testing whether or not the line is cached. If so, the value is simply returned. If there is a cache miss, GetReadable is marked as the next suboperation to be executed.

> **assume** $\text{Ops}(p) =< \text{Load}(b) >$:
> **let** $(\text{ops}, w) = \text{InitLoad}(p, a, M, C)$:
> $(M, C, \text{Ops}) \succ_a (M, C, \text{Ops}[p \rightarrow \text{ops}])$

where

> $\text{InitLoad} : \textbf{Pid} \times \textbf{Addr} \times T_M \times T_C$
> $\rightarrow sequence\ of\ \textbf{T}_{\textbf{oper}} \times \textbf{Word}$

> $\text{InitLoad}(p, a, M, C) =$
>   **if** $\text{HasLoadable}(p, a, M, C)$ **then** $(<>, C(a, p)(b))$
>   **else** $(< \text{GetReadable} >, \text{nil})$ **fi**

8 Full concurrency

To obtain full concurrency, all necessary state information must be distributed to the memory- and cache-lines. At the previous level, a suboperation changed the state of more than one cache- or memory-line. Full concurrency is supported when message passing is used to invoke indivisible operation prescriptions (executed by memory or cache controllers) in different memories and caches.

In accordance with this, we introduce a message pool being the only shared part of the global state space. The message pool contains the requests and responses that have not yet been recognized by their addressees.

The global state space is changed to

$$\textbf{Addr} \rightarrow T_M \times T_C \times \textbf{T}_{\textbf{pool}}$$

Here the continuations have been included in T_C. $\textbf{T}_{\textbf{stat}}$ is the rest of the local state (caches and memories really have differenet $\textbf{T}_{\textbf{stat}}$):

$$T_M = \textbf{Line} \times \textbf{T}_{\textbf{stat}}$$
$$T_C = \textbf{Pid} \rightarrow \textbf{Line} \times \textbf{T}_{\textbf{stat}} \times sequence\ of\ \textbf{T}_{\textbf{oper}}$$
$$\textbf{T}_{\textbf{pool}} = set\ of\ \textbf{T}_{\textbf{pck}}$$

Here too we define a relation ≻ which for a given address describes all possible global state changes. The definition of ≻ is based upon a one cache- or memory-line state change description, ≻^{pr}:

$$\succ^{pr}: \mathbf{Addr} \to (\mathbf{Pid} \times \mathbf{Line} \times \mathbf{T_{stat}} \times \text{sequence of } \mathbf{T_{oper}} \times \mathbf{T_{pool}}) \times$$
$$(\mathbf{Pid} \times \mathbf{Line} \times \mathbf{T_{stat}} \times \text{sequence of } \mathbf{T_{oper}} \times \mathbf{T_{pool}})$$

For instance, p sending a request to its successor (p's local state s, defines the successor, succ(s)) in the list of cache-lines sharing the same address, a, indicating that p intends to delete its cache line at this address, will result in the pool being extended with a **Delete** message:

$$(p, v, s, < \mathsf{RequestDelete}, \mathsf{ReceiveDelete} > +\text{ops}, \text{pool}) \quad \succ^{pr}_a$$
$$(p, v, s, < \mathsf{ReceiveDelete} > +\text{ops}, \text{pool} \cup \{\mathsf{Delete}?(\text{succ}(s), p, a, v, s)\})$$

Among the other definitions that specify ≻^{pr}, there is one that defines how the addressee fetches this message from the pool, changes its own local state according to the contents of the message, and puts a response message back into the pool.

9 Discussion and Conclusion

The specification presented in this paper is currently being used in an effort to prove that the detailed cache coherence protocol of the Scalable Coherent Interface [9], is correctly specified according to an abstract view of a memory system. In order to prove that a system is correct, one needs a high level, abstract formulation of the intent of the system. The abstract memory system without a cache is used to define the intent of the SCI cache coherence protocol. It is shown that adding more details does not destroy the correctness of the system, the details are added simply to increase performance.

Among the added details are intermediate cache states and more fine-grained atomic actions. The equations that define cache coherence are refined to take care of the intermediate states as well. This could make it possible to access the data in the caches at an earlier stage, hence allowing for other types of ordering of events than the sequential one, defined by the top level specification of the present paper [11, 3]. Non-sequential event ordering models must be defined using more complex methods, for example historic sequences (traces) of events. It is important to investigate such specification methods, but this is beyond the scope of the present paper.

It might also, for fault-tolerant reasons, be useful to take special care that the so called Data-Must-Exist equation (section 4) holds when the system is in a non-stable state as well. For example in the SCI cache coherence protocol, no transient state exists, in which the only valid copy of a line is transported in the interconnect. This ensures that after a transmission failure, data can always be recovered from some cache-line (or from memory).

When making hardware (and software) systems, there are several important factors to be considered. One of these is correctness. Correctness is usually assured by informal reasoning and by simulation. The specification and verification methods presented in this paper aim at making new systems and components correct by design. Present systems are so complex and consist of components with so many combinations of states, that informal reasoning and exhaustive testing is literally impossible. This calls for new and more formal design methods. We believe that a lot is to be gained by making mathematical models of the system to be implemented, and then reasoning about the systems at different levels of abstraction, with different sets of implementation details.

References

[1] Anant Agarwal et al.: APRIL: A Processor Architecture for Multiprocessing. 17th Annual International Symposium on Computer Architecture, IEEE Computer Society Press, May, 1990.

[2] Lucien M. Censier and Paul Feautrier: A New Solution to Coherence problems in Multicache Systems. IEEE Trans. on Computers, Vol. C-27, No. 12, December 1978.

[3] Kourosh Gharachorloo et al.: Memory Consistency and Event Ordering in Scalable Shared-Memory Multiprocessors. 17th Annual International Symposium on Computer Architecture, IEEE Computer Society Press, May, 1990.

[4] Stein Gjessing, Stein Krogdahl and Ellen Munthe-Kaas: Approaching Verification of the SCI Cache Coherence Protocol Research Report in Informatics, University of Oslo, No. 145, August 1990.

[5] Stein Gjessing, Stein Krogdahl and Ellen Munthe-Kaas: A Top Down Approach to the Formal Specification of SCI Cache Coherence. Research Report in Informatics, University of Oslo, No. 146, August 1990.

[6] James R. Goodman: Using cache Memory to Reduce Processor-Memory Traffic. 10th International Symposium on Computer Architecture, 1983.

[7] M.J.C. Gordon: HOL: A Proof Generating System for Higher-Order Logic. In G. Birtwistle and P.A. Subrahmanyam (eds.): VLSI Specification, Verification and Synthesis. Kluwer Academic Publishers, Boston, 1988.

[8] John V. Guttag, James J. Horning, Andrés Modet: Report on The Larch Shared Language: Version 2.3. Digital SRC, Research Report 58, April 1990.

[9] IEEE Working Group P1596 of MSC, Scalable Coherent Interface, D1.00, January 23, 1991.

[10] David V. James, Anthony T. Laundrie, Stein Gjessing and Gurindar S. Sohi: New Directions in Scalable Shared-Memory Multiprocessor Architectures: Scalable Coherent Interface. IEEE Computer, June 1990.

[11] Leslie Lamport: How to Make a Multiprocessor Computer that Correctly Executes Multiprocess Programs. IEEE Trans. on Computers, Vol. 28, No. 9, pp 690–691, Sept. 1979.

[12] Daniel Leonski et al.: The Directory-Based Cache Coherence Protocol of the DASH Multiprocessor. Computer System Laboratory, Stanford University, Technical Report No. CSL-TR-89-404, December 1989.

[13] J Staunstrup and M.R Greenstreet: Synchronized Transitions. In IFIP WG 10.5 SUMMER SCHOOL on Formal Methods for VLSI Design. Lecture Notes.

[14] P. Sweazey and A.J. Smith: A Class of Compatible Cache Consistency Protocols and their Support by the IEEE Futurebus. 13th International Symposium on Computer Architecture, 1986.

[15] C. K. Tang: Cache system design in the tightly coupled multiprocessor system. AFIPS National Computer Conference Proceedings, Vol. 45, 1976.

[16] Manu Thapar, Bruce Delagi: Stanford Distributed Directory Protocol. IEEE Computer, June 1990.

Integer Programming in the Analysis of Concurrent Systems[1]

George S. Avrunin
University of Massachusetts
at Amherst
Amherst, MA 01003
avrunin@math.umass.edu

Ugo A. Buy
University of Illinois
at Chicago
Chicago, IL 60680
buy@figaro.eecs.uic.edu

James C. Corbett
University of Massachusetts
at Amherst
Amherst, MA 01003
corbett@cs.umass.edu

1 Introduction

Large computer systems are frequently organized as collections of cooperating asynchronous processes. Their size and the presence of nondeterminacy make it extremely difficult to understand and predict the behavior of such systems. Rigorous analysis methods with automated support will therefore be necessary for the production of reliable software. In this paper, we describe a method for generating and solving systems of inequalities that can be used effectively in the analysis of large computer systems. We also briefly discuss our experience in using this approach in the analysis of concurrent system designs written in an Ada-based design language.

Underlying our approach to analysis is a model in which each asynchronous process in such a system is represented by a finite state automaton (FSA) accepting a language over an alphabet of symbols corresponding to events occurring in executions of that process. An execution of the concurrent system involves executions of each of its component processes, subject to additional restrictions imposed by the appropriate concurrency and communication primitives. These additional restrictions are represented by a set of recursive languages over alphabets contained in the union of the alphabets of the FSAs. A string over the union of the FSA alphabets corresponds to the trace of an execution of the concurrent system if its projection on the alphabet of each FSA lies in the language accepted by that automaton, so the string represents the trace of an execution of the corresponding process, and if its projection on the alphabet of each of the additional recursive languages lies in that language, so the string satisfies the additional restrictions imposed by the concurrency and communication primitives. (For simplicity, in this paper we will regard the executions of concurrent systems as represented by traces, and so as totally ordered in time. Our model and our analysis techniques are, however, compatible with viewing the executions as corresponding only to partial orders of events.)

---

[1]The research described here was partially supported by National Science Foundation grant CCR-8806970 and Office of Naval Research grant N00014-89-J-1064.

An example of this type of model is the constrained expression formalism [8, 14, 15], which has been used to represent concurrent systems given by Petri nets and by programs in a variety of programming and design languages, involving both synchronous and asynchronous communication [3, 6, 9].

Our approach to analysis is based on the following paradigm. First, we generate a set of linear equations for each FSA. Second, additional linear inequalities are generated that reflect the additional restrictions on the behavior of the model imposed by the recursive languages. Third, inequalities representing the analyst's assumptions or queries are added to the system. Finally, we apply integer programming (IP) techniques to solve the resulting system of equalities and inequalities. If no integer solutions to the linear system exist, we conclude that our conditions are inconsistent and that no trace satisfies the restrictions imposed by the analyst's assumptions. If an integer solution is found, it may or may not correspond to the trace of an actual execution. In this case, however, the solution can be used to guide a highly constrained reachability-based analysis of the concurrent system under consideration.

This approach to analysis has several advantages. It can be applied to the analysis of system descriptions written in a variety of specification and implementation languages. By contrast with reachability-based approaches, this approach does not require the enumeration of the complete state space for the system being analyzed. Finally, the approach has been implemented in the *constrained expression toolset*, a set of prototypes that carry out the analysis of concurrent system designs written in an Ada-based design language. Performance results have been very encouraging and compare favorably with other approaches to analysis [3].

This paper is organized as follows. The model underlying our approach is described in section 2. The analysis method we use is discussed in section 3. The toolset implementing constrained expression analysis of designs is described in section 4 along with some performance results. The last section discusses some related techniques as well as ongoing and planned extensions of our method.

2 The Model

We require the following definitions. For any sets of symbols Σ and S with $S \subseteq \Sigma$, let $\rho_A : \Sigma^* \to S^*$ be the homomorphism, called *projection on S*, defined by extending the map $\Sigma \to S$ given by:

$$\rho_S(\alpha) = \begin{cases} \alpha & \text{if } \alpha \in S \\ \lambda & \text{otherwise} \end{cases}$$

Let $L(M)$ be the language recognized by machine M. The *shuffle* of the languages L_1 and L_2, written $L_1 \otimes L_2$, is the language consisting of the strings $x_1 y_1 x_2 y_2 \ldots x_n y_n$ formed by concatenating substrings such that $x_1 x_2 \ldots x_n \in L_1$ and $y_1 y_2 \ldots y_n \in L_2$ for some n (the substrings x_1 and y_n may be empty). Finally, let *dagger* (†) be the closure of the shuffle operation: $L^\dagger = \{w | \text{for some } n: w = w_1 \otimes w_2 \otimes \ldots \otimes w_n, w_i \in L \text{ for all } i\}$.

We model a concurrent system as a collection of coupled finite state automata (FSAs) with additional restrictions expressed as a set of recursive languages on the alphabets of the FSAs. The acceptance of a symbol by an automaton represents the occurrence of an event in the concurrent system. An event may represent a normal action of a component, such as initiating a communication with another component, or an error, such as waiting forever for a communication that never takes place. An execution of the concurrent program is thus modeled by a string of event symbols.

Formally, a concurrent system is a triple (M, R, T) where M is a set of FSAs $M_1, \ldots, M_n$ with alphabets $\Sigma_1, \ldots, \Sigma_n$, R is a set of recursive *restriction* languages $R_1, \ldots, R_m$ with alphabets $A_1, \ldots, A_m$, where $A_i \subseteq \Sigma$ for all i, and $T \subseteq \Sigma = \bigcup_i \Sigma_i$ is a terminal alphabet. A string $t \in T^*$ represents a legal behavior or trace of the concurrent system if there exists a string $s \in \Sigma^*$ with $\rho_T(s) = t$ where $\rho_{\Sigma_i}(s) \in L(M_i)$ for all i and $\rho_{A_j}(s) \in R_j$ for all j. An example of the use of this model to describe a system of two processes communicating by asynchronous message passing is given in the next section.

This formulation is a somewhat more general version of the formal definition of *constrained expressions* given in [3]. That formulation allows as restriction languages only those generated by the standard regular operators (concatenation, union, and Kleene star) plus shuffle and dagger. It follows from [1] that all recursively enumerable languages are given by constrained expressions. Allowing arbitrary recursive languages as restrictions, as in our model, thus represents no increase in power, although it may make application of the model somewhat simpler and more convenient.

3 The Method

Given a concurrent program represented in the above model, we generate a system of linear inequalities reflecting much, but not all, of the semantics of the representation to determine if any executions of the concurrent program exist that satisfy certain properties. Essentially, the method finds a possible execution of the concurrent program by finding traces of each process and then enforcing a weaker consistency criterion between these traces than is specified in the restriction languages.

When generating equations for the FSAs $M_1, \ldots, M_n$, it is useful to picture each FSA as a directed graph in the standard way. An execution of the concurrent program will correspond to a path through each FSA from the start state to a final state. We assign a *transition variable* x_a to each transition arc a in the FSAs of the concurrent program. The variable associated with an arc will represent the number of times that arc is crossed in the paths. We also assign an *accept variable* f_i to each final state i of the FSAs that will be one if and only if the path through that FSA ends at this final state and will be zero otherwise. We then generate a *flow equation* for each state i in an FSA stating that the flow into the state (i.e., the total number of times paths enter the state) must equal the flow out of the state (i.e., the total number of times paths leave the state). The start state of each FSA has an implicit flow in of one, and each final state has an extra flow out represented by its accept variable. The flow equations imply that, in any nonnegative integer solution, exactly one accept variable in each FSA will have the value one.

Suppose that a symbol α belongs to two alphabets Σ_i and Σ_j. Then an occurrence of α in a string corresponding to an execution represents the occurrence of an event in the processes corresponding to M_i and M_j. In such a case, we must add an equation stating that the numbers of occurrences of α in the traces of those processes is the same. In other words, we must equate the sum of the transition variables for arcs of M_i labeled by α with the corresponding sum for M_j.

In addition to the equations generated in this fashion from the FSAs $M_1, \ldots, M_n$, we generate equations and inequalities reflecting the restrictions imposed by the R_j. If a restriction language R_j is regular, we can generate equations from an FSA accepting it, exactly as described above. (Indeed, even expressions involving the shuffle and dagger operators can be handled this way: by ignoring order, shuffle can be treated as concatenation and dagger can be treated as Kleene star). Then, for each symbol $\alpha \in A_j$ and each i such that $\alpha \in \Sigma_i$, we add an equation stating that the sum of the variables for arcs labeled by α is the same in the FSA accepting R_j and in M_i, just as for symbols belonging to two FSA alphabets. In practice, we have made use of restriction languages that are simple enough that the additional inequalities can be expressed directly in terms of the variables from the M_i, avoiding the creation of many new variables and equations and reducing the size of the IP problems that must be solved. (An example of this is given below.) We have not attempted to formalize a procedure for efficiently generating inequalities from arbitrary recursive languages.

Figure 1 shows the equations for a simple concurrent program with two processes that use channels with infinite message buffers to communicate. Here, $+a$ represents the sending of a message to channel a and $-a$ represents the reception of a message from channel a. Consistent communication over a channel a is enforced by the restriction $(+a - a)^\dagger \otimes (+a)^*$ (this expression generates strings having the property that, in any prefix, the number of $-a$'s never exceeds the number of $+a$'s). From this we extract the relation that the number of $+a$ event symbols must be greater than or equal to the number of $-a$ event symbols in any string representing an execution. (This is exactly the relation that would be generated by treating the dagger as a Kleene star, but we express it in terms of the transition variables already associated with the $+a$ and $-a$ symbols.)

Every execution trace will have a corresponding solution to the inequality system we generate. However, not all solutions to the inequality system correspond to actual traces. The conditions represented by the inequality system are thus necessary, but not sufficient. There are two reasons for this. First, we ignore information about the order of event symbols given by the restriction languages. In the example of Figure 1, there is no execution in which process 1 executes $-a, +b$ and process 2 executes $-b, +a$ since any interleaving of these two strings violates the restriction for channel a or b, but since the number of events is consistent with relations derived from the restrictions, this would correspond to a solution to the inequality system. The second reason that the conditions are not sufficient is that the flow equations do not completely capture the semantics of the FSAs. The events in which a process engages in a legal execution must lie along a single path, however, the presence of cycles in the FSA graph can allow extra circular flows. An example of this is the solution to the inequalities of Figure 1 in which $x_1 = x_4 = x_6 = x_7 = f_2 = f_5 = 1$ and all other variables are zero.

The analyst usually searches for traces with certain properties by adding additional inequalities to the system. For example, an analyst might ask whether there is an execution in which more messages are sent to channel b than are received from that channel by adding the inequality $x_2 + x_3 - x_5 > 0$. Similarly, if we added transitions labeled with symbols representing permanent blocking of the process to the example, the analyst would seek executions in which a process waits forever to receive a message by adding an inequality stating that the sum of the variables corresponding to the particular symbol is greater than or equal to one.

The flow equations can also be generated directly from regular expressions. For this algorithm, picture the regular expression parsed into a tree where leaf nodes are labeled

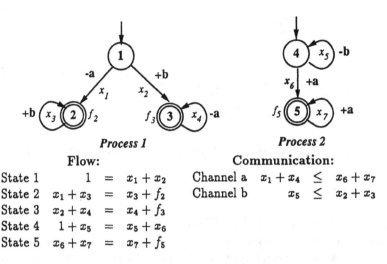

Figure 1: Example of Inequality System

with event symbols and other nodes are labeled with one of the regular operators (SE-QUENCE, OR, or Kleene STAR) whose operands are its child nodes. Figure 2 shows the regular expression $(ab)^*(a \vee cb)$ so parsed. We create *environment variables* for the nodes representing the number of times the node "occurs" in the derivation of the trace (e.g., the lower left sequence node in Figure 2 occurs twice in the derivation of the string *ababcb*). Each variable has an associated *scope* consisting of a set of nodes that must occur the same number of times (e.g., a sequence node and its operands). To accomplish this, we assign an environment variable to the root node and the children of OR and STAR nodes. Then we let the scope of each environment variable be the node to which it belongs and all descendants of that node down to but not including the next node with its own environment variable. In Figure 2, the nodes with assigned variables are labeled with the variable and the nodes in the scope of a particular variable are labeled with that variable in parentheses.

We write the following equations in these variables. First, we set the variable of the root node to one, indicating that exactly one string is to be generated for this process. Second, for each OR node, we generate an equation stating that the number of times that the OR node occurs equals the sum of the numbers of times that its operand nodes occur. At STAR nodes, the appropriate inequality expressing the fact that an operand of the STAR does not occur unless the STAR node does is of the form $x_s x_o - x_o \geq 0$, where x_s is the variable associated with the STAR node and x_o is the variable associated with the operand. (Since our variables are constrained to be nonnegative, this says that x_o must be zero if x_s is.) Since solving systems of nonlinear inequalities is very much more difficult than solving linear systems, in our application of this method we have simply ignored these quadratic inequalities. (We have defined, but not used, a technique for approximating this quadratic inequality with a linear one.) Just as with cycles in the generation of equations from FSAs, this can produce solutions that will not correspond to any legitimate execution of the process. Figure 2 shows the equations generated from the given regular expression. Additional inequalities would be generated from the restriction

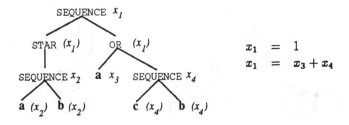

Figure 2: Example of Inequality System From Regular Expression

languages as before.

4 Implementation and Application

This method for generating inequalities reflecting necessary conditions that must be satisfied by system traces has been implemented as part of the *constrained expression toolset* [3] and applied to a variety of concurrent systems. Our experiments with the toolset clearly show that these necessary conditions are strong enough to settle many of the questions arising in analysis of concurrent systems. Furthermore, the results also show that the method can be used effectively with concurrent systems that are far too large for most other existing analysis methods to be practically applied. Here, we briefly describe the toolset, focusing on the components that generate and solve inequalities, and give some of the experimental results. More detailed descriptions of the tools and discussion of additional experiments are given in [3].

The constrained expression toolset is intended for use in analyzing concurrent system designs written in an Ada-like design notation called CEDL, and has five major components. In normal use, an analyst would first use the *deriver* to produce a constrained expression from a CEDL design. The restriction languages (called *constraints*) needed for the constrained expression representation of CEDL systems are all regular; the output of the deriver thus consists of a set of regular expressions. This constrained expression would then be supplied as input to the *constraint eliminator*, which uses regular language intersection techniques to produce an equivalent constrained expression that can be analyzed more effectively. For reasons of efficiency, the constrained expression produced by the eliminator consists of regular languages represented as regular expressions, FSAs, or in a hybrid form we call *regular expression deterministic finite automata* (REDFAs) [3, 7] that yields particularly compact systems of inequalities. The *inequality generator* then produces systems of inequalities from this constrained expression using the methods just described, augmented by inequalities representing the analyst's queries about the behavior of the concurrent system. An *integer programming package* determines whether the system of inequalities has any integer solutions and, if it does, produces one with appropriate properties (typically, in our applications, one that minimizes some measure of size). Finally, if a solution is found, a *behavior generator* performs a highly constrained reachability analysis to determine whether the solution corresponds to a trace of the concurrent system being analyzed, and to produce such a trace if one exists.

Input to the inequality generator is a constrained expression produced by the deriver from a CEDL design and possibly modified by the constraint eliminator. Each task (asynchronous process) in the design is represented by a regular expression, an FSA, or an REDFA. The inequality generator produces a system of equations for each task, as described above. It then generates additional inequalities reflecting the constraints arising in the constrained expressions derived from CEDL designs. (For reasons of efficiency, we have chosen to sacrifice some of the language independence and build some knowledge of the CEDL constraints into the inequality generator.) The inequality generator provides a menu-driven interface that allows the analyst to formulate queries and to specify one of several objective functions for integer linear programming, and facilities that assist the analyst in interpreting the solutions found by the integer programming tool. The inequality generator is written in Common LISP. A complete description of this tool can be found in [2].

The integer programming component of the toolset is a branch-and-bound integer programming system that uses the MINOS optimization package [12] to solve the LP-relaxations of the integer programming problems. We refer to the tool that incorporates our branch-and-bound code and MINOS as IMINOS (Integer MINOS). The IMINOS tool takes an inequality system and associated objective function in the standard MPS file format as input. The input file is produced by the inequality generator. At each branch-and-bound iteration, IMINOS uses depth-first search to determine which active tree node to examine. We have experimented with three relatively naive strategies for selecting branching variables. Although we have obtained fairly good results with one of these strategies, we have begun to implement a strategy based on special ordered sets that makes use of semantic information from the constrained expression to choose branching variables [4].

We chose to base the integer programming component of the toolset on MINOS for several reasons, including the availability and robustness of MINOS and the relative ease of adding the branch-and-bound mechanism to it, despite some drawbacks. While the performance of IMINOS has been very satisfactory for demonstrating the feasibility of the general approach, further development of the toolset will require improved integer programming methods. We are therefore also investigating special-purpose algorithms for the solution of the network flow problems with side constraints that are generated by our method.

As mentioned above, the constrained expression toolset has been applied to analyze a variety of concurrent system designs, including designs for some standard problems like the dining philosophers and readers-and-writers, a protocol for distributed mutual exclusion, and an automated self-service gas station. Many of these experiments are described in [3]; here we briefly describe some of the results of experiments with several sizes and versions of the dining philosophers problem.

In the basic CEDL system, each fork and each philosopher is represented by a separate task, and a philosopher picking up or putting down a fork is modeled by a rendezvous at the up or down entry, respectively, of the fork task. Thus, in the system with n philosophers, there are $2n$ tasks. This system can deadlock when each philosopher picks up one fork. One of the standard ways to prevent this deadlock is to introduce a "host" or "butler" who ensures that all the philosophers do not attempt to eat at the same time. We have modeled this by introducing an additional host task and modifying the philosopher tasks so that a philosopher calls the enter entry of the host before attempting to pick up the first fork and calls the leave entry of the host after putting down the second fork.

	phils	tasks	size	IG time	IMINOS time	total time
basic	60	120	1141 × 960	158	74	629
	80	160	1521 × 1280	248	75	883
	100	200	1901 × 1600	399	120	1249
host	20	41	603 × 1261	157	65	467
	30	61	903 × 2491	538	58	1223
	40	81	1203 × 4121	1516	81	2941
incorrect	20	41	607 × 1305	222	54	716
host	30	61	905 × 2523	537	119	1540
	40	81	1205 × 4163	1603	865	4070

Figure 3: Performance on Dining Philosophers Problems

The host accepts calls at enter as long as no more than $n - 2$ philosophers are currently attempting to eat, and accepts calls at leave at any time.

The first 3 lines of the table in Figure 3 give some information about the performance of the toolset on versions of the basic system having 60, 80, and 100 philosophers when analyzed to determine whether a philosopher can be permanently blocked after picking up a fork. The columns of the table give the number of philosophers, the number of tasks, the size of the system of inequalities produced by the inequality generator (inequalities × variables), the time used by the inequality generator, the time used by IMINOS, and the total time used by the constrained expression toolset. (All times are given in CPU seconds on a DECstation 3100, and include both system and user time.) In each case, the toolset produces a system trace displaying a deadlock in which each philosopher has picked up one fork.

The next three lines of Figure 3 give the same information for 20- 30- and 40- philosopher versions of the system with host, also analyzed to determine whether a philosopher can be permanently blocked after picking up a fork. In each case, the toolset correctly reports that such blocking is impossible. In these cases, the constraint elimi- nator is used to modify the constrained expressions produced by the deriver in order to allow the inequality system to better reflect the dependence of control flow in the host task on the value of the variable counting the number of philosophers attempting to eat. This process, together with the additional entry calls in the philosopher tasks, results in a significantly larger system of inequalities for the dining philosophers with host than for the system without host having the same number of philosophers. For comparison, the last three lines of the figure give the results of the same analysis on systems in which the host task was modified to erroneously allow all the philosophers to attempt to eat at the same time (the condition guarding the enter entry was changed). In the cases with the incorrect host, the toolset produces a trace displaying deadlock.

5 Discussion

The approach to analysis of concurrent systems we have described is based on a formal model in which the possible traces of the executions of a concurrent system are repre- sented by a language over an alphabet of event symbols. The model is powerful enough to represent all recursively enumerable sets, and has been used with a variety of design and programming languages and notations, including languages with asynchronous and synchronous communication primitives and Petri nets. The approach involves the generation and solution of systems of inequalities that must be satisfied by all execution traces of the particular system being analyzed; the inequalities thus represent necessary, but, in general, not sufficient, conditions for a string to correspond to an execution.

The approach has been implemented as part of the constrained expression toolset, a collection of prototype tools for automated analysis of concurrent system designs written in an Ada-based design language. Experiments with this toolset, some of which are described above, have demonstrated that the necessary conditions represented by our inequalities are strong enough to answer many of the questions of interest in the analysis of concurrent systems. For example, our method of generating inequalities can be used to answer such questions as whether a component process can become permanently blocked or whether a resource will always be used in the intended mutually exclusive fashion [3]. The experiments have also shown that the method is practical for use with systems that approach, or even exceed, realistic sizes for concurrent system designs, in marked contrast with the results reported for most other analysis methods that have been implemented.

Because the inequalities represent only necessary, but not sufficient, conditions, solutions to the system of inequalities may not correspond to execution traces of the system being analyzed. Thus, when the system of inequalities is inconsistent, our method rigorously establishes that no execution of the system has the particular property of interest to the analyst. When a solution to the system of inequalities is found, however, we do not know that an execution with the desired property exists. (The behavior generator in the constrained expression toolset uses heuristic search to settle this question in many cases, as illustrated by the dining philosophers experiments reported above.) Our method is thus less accurate than methods based on construction of the full state space of the concurrent system. In general, however, the number of states that such methods must examine is exponential in the number of processes in the system. Because our method avoids constructing the full state space, it can be practically applied to much larger systems than such reachability-based methods. For example, Karam and Buhr [10] indicate that their approach "is effective for designs with a complexity in the order of 10-20 tasks" and suggest the use of a knowledge-based system for designs with 50 to 100 tasks. Similarly, Young et al. [16] suggest that a reasonable granularity for analysis of designs is "in the neighborhood of 8 processes." As indicated in the previous section, our method has been successfully used with systems having 200 or more processes.

Various methods have been proposed to reduce the complexity of determining the full state space. Among the most promising of such methods is the "stubborn sets" approach of Valmari [13]. By systematically reducing the number of states that need to be examined in order to establish a particular property of the system, this method can, for example, detect deadlock in the basic dining philosophers system in time that is linear in the number of philosophers. The range of useful application of this method is not completely clear at the present time — for the dining philosophers with host, for example, deadlock detection remains exponential in the number of philosophers.

Other methods for analyzing concurrent systems include those based on proving theorems in some logical structure associated with the system, those approaches that examine executions of a completed system or some simulation of it, and the T-invariant method proposed by Murata, Shenker, and Shatz [11]. In general, the theorem-proving methods are hard to automate, and it is difficult to assess their complexity and generality. Although testing and simulation methods are relatively straightforward to implement, they are limited in the extent to which they can explore the space of potential executions of a system. This limitation, problematic even for sequential software systems, is more severe in concurrent or distributed systems, since the nondeterministic interleaving of concurrent activities in such systems dramatically increases the number of possible executions.

The method of Murata, Shenker, and Shatz [11] is very close in spirit to ours. In their approach, certain Petri nets are derived from Ada tasking programs, and the *T-invariants* of these nets are determined. These *T*-invariants are integer solutions to homogeneous systems of linear equations that represent necessary conditions for deadlock-free execution of the original programs, and are first used to detect and remove certain "inconsistency" deadlocks and then to guide the construction of a reachability graph to determine whether "circular" deadlocks are possible. At present, this approach has not been fully automated.

Our approach has also been extended to analyze timing properties of concurrent systems [5]. Ongoing and planned research includes the extension of our method to infinite executions, so that it can be used to answer questions about fairness and starvation, improvements in the way our method handles questions involving the order of occurrences of events, and the development of special techniques for analyzing concurrent systems containing arbitrary numbers of copies of some processes.

The approach to analysis of concurrent systems described in this paper thus has a number of advantages in comparison to other proposed approaches. It can be used with a variety of programming and design notations, and does not involve the enumeration of the full state space of the concurrent system being analyzed. Experiments with an implementation have shown that the approach can be effectively applied to systems that approach or exceed realistic sizes for concurrent system designs and that it can be used to answer a variety of interesting questions about those systems. Furthermore, by converting questions about the behavior of concurrent systems into ones of linear algebra and integer programming, our method brings a large and well-developed body of mathematical methods to bear on the concurrent system analysis problem.

Acknowledgment The work described here was conducted as part of a larger project on constrained expression analysis. We are grateful to Susan Avery, Laura Dillon, Michael Greenberg, RenHung Hwang, G. Allyn Polk, George Walden, and Jack Wileden for their contributions.

References

[1] T. Araki and N. Tokura. Flow languages equal recursively enumerable languages. *Acta Inf.*, 15:209–217, 1981.

[2] G. S. Avrunin, U. Buy, and J. Corbett. Automatic generation of inequality systems for constrained expression analysis. Technical Report 90-32, Department of Computer and Information Science, University of Massachusetts, Amherst, 1990.

[3] G. S. Avrunin, U. A. Buy, J. C. Corbett, L. K. Dillon, and J. C. Wileden. Automated analysis of concurrent systems with the constrained expression toolset. *IEEE Trans. Softw. Eng.*, November 1991, to appear.

[4] G. S. Avrunin, U. A. Buy, J. C. Corbett, L. K. Dillon, and J. C. Wileden. Experiments with an improved constrained expression toolset. In *Proceedings of the Symposium on Testing, Analysis, and Verification*, Oct. 1991, to appear.

[5] G. S. Avrunin, J. C. Corbett, L. K. Dillon, and J. C. Wileden. Automated constrained expression analysis of real-time software. Submitted for publication. Available as Technical Report 90-117, Department of Computer and Information Science, University of Massachusetts, Dec. 1990.

[6] G. S. Avrunin, L. K. Dillon, J. C. Wileden, and W. E. Riddle. Constrained expressions: Adding analysis capabilities to design methods for concurrent software systems. *IEEE Trans. Softw. Eng.*, 12(2):278–292, 1986.

[7] J. C. Corbett. On selecting a form for inequality generation in the constrained expression toolset. Constrained Expression Memorandum 90-1, Department of Computer and Information Science, University of Massachusetts, Amherst, 1990.

[8] L. K. Dillon. *Analysis of Distributed Systems Using Constrained Expressions*. PhD thesis, University of Massachusetts, Amherst, 1984.

[9] L. K. Dillon, G. S. Avrunin, and J. C. Wileden. Constrained expressions: Toward broad applicability of analysis methods for distributed software systems. *ACM Trans. Prog. Lang. Syst.*, 10(3):374–402, July 1988.

[10] G. M. Karam and R. J. Buhr. Starvation and critical race analyzers for Ada. *IEEE Trans. Softw. Eng.*, 16(8):829–843, 1990.

[11] T. Murata, B. Shenker, and S. M. Shatz. Detection of Ada static deadlocks using Petri net invariants. *IEEE Trans. Softw. Eng.*, 15(3):314–326, 1989.

[12] M. A. Saunders. MINOS system manual. Technical Report SOL 77-31, Stanford University, Department of Operations Research, 1977.

[13] A. Valmari. A stubborn attack on state explosion. In E. M. Clarke and R. P. Kurshan, editors, *Computer-Aided Verification '90*, number 3 in DIMACS Series in Discrete Mathematics and Theoretical Computer Science, pages 25–41, Providence, RI, 1991. American Mathematical Society.

[14] J. C. Wileden. *Modelling Parallel Systems with Dynamic Structure*. PhD thesis, University of Michigan, 1978.

[15] J. C. Wileden. Constrained expressions and the analysis of designs for dynamically-structured distributed systems. In *Proceedings of the International Conference on Parallel Processing*, pages 340–344, August 1982.

[16] M. Young, R. N. Taylor, K. Forester, and D. Brodbeck. Integrated concurrency analysis in a software development environment. In R. A. Kemmerer, editor, *Proceedings of the ACM SIGSOFT '89 Third Symposium on Software Testing, Analysis and Verification*, pages 200–209, 1989. Appeared as *Software Engineering Notes*, 14(8).

THE LOTOS MODEL OF A FAULT PROTECTED SYSTEM AND ITS VERIFICATION USING A PETRI NET BASED APPROACH

Michel Barbeau

Département de mathématiques et d'informatique

Université de Sherbrooke, Sherbrooke, Canada J1K 2R1

and

Gregor v. Bochmann

Département d'IRO, Université de Montréal

C.P. 128, Succ. "A", Montréal, Canada H3C 3J7

Abstract

Having introduced a novel Petri net based method for the verification of Lotos specifications [Barb 90a], this paper demonstrates its practical interest. Contrary to other similar Petri net based techniques, our approach avoids to build the whole Petri net from the Lotos specification before verification. In contrast to finite automata based methods, our method can analyse Lotos systems with unbounded state spaces. Our method is founded on a Place/Transition-net Lotos semantics. The method is applied to the verification of the Lotos model of fault protected system.

1. Introduction

Lotos [ISO 88] is a specification language for protocols and distributed applications. In this paper, we consider a Lotos specification which models the fault protection aspect of a small system. This system consists of two unreliable pieces of equipment and a standby equipment. Initially, the system is working and protected. When a failure occurs, the standby is substituted for the failed piece of equipment and the whole system moves to the "working-unprotected" state. If a second equipment failure occurs, the whole system moves to the "failed" state. To describe this model, only a subset of Lotos called *Basic Lotos* is required. Basic Lotos is introduced in § 2 whereas the Lotos model of the fault protected system is presented in § 3.

The dynamic semantics of Lotos is defined formally. This means that formal verification is possible. Our verification method is based on Petri net theory. Petri net verification techniques are transferred to Lotos. So far, two transfer approaches have been proposed. A first approach consists of translating Lotos specifications into Petri nets and evaluating the properties on the equivalent Petri net models [Gara 90, and Marc 89].

We proposed a second approach which involves no translation from one formalism to another [Barb 90a]. We adapted to Lotos the well known Place/Transition-net (P/T-net) reachability analysis technique, namely, the Karp and Miller procedure [Karp 69]. In § 4 of this paper, we apply this technique for the verification of the Lotos specification of a fault protected system.

2. Basic Lotos

Lotos consists of two sub-languages. First, there is a sub-language, based on Act One [Ehri 85], dealing with the description of data structures. Second, there is a sub-language, based on CCS [Miln 89], concerned with the description of dynamic discrete event processes. Basic Lotos is a core subset of the second sub-language. A Basic Lotos behavior expression is formed out of the following terms:

Inaction	**stop**
Action prefix	$a; B$
Choice	$B_1[]B_2$
Process instantiation	$p[g_1, ..., g_n]$
Pure interleaving	$B_1|||B_2$
General parallel composition	$B_1|[g_1, ..., g_n]|B_2$
Successful termination	**exit**
Sequential composition	$B_1 >> B_2$
Disabling	$B_1[> B_2$
Hiding	**hide** $g_1, ..., g_n$ **in** B_1

where B, $B1$ and $B2$ are behavior expressions. The formal semantics of Lotos is given in [ISO 88].

3. The Lotos Specification

To present the specification of the fault protected system, we adapted to Lotos Knuth's literate programming style [Knut 84].

1. The purpose of this Lotos specification is to define the model of a system which is composed of two pieces of equipment that can fail. The system is protected by one piece of standby equipment that can fail as well. When either two pieces of equipment or one piece of equipment and the standby are failed, the whole system is failed. The Lotos specification describes the failure as well as the repair of pieces of equipment.

2. For readability, we define the following lists of gates:

$L_0 \equiv fl1, fl2, rp1, rp2, sfl, srp1, srp2, swsucc, swfl$

$L_1 \equiv res, fl1, fl2, rp1, rp2, sfl, srp1, srp2, swsucc, swfl$

$L_2 \equiv fl1, rp1, sfl, srp1, srp2, swsucc, swfl$

$L_3 \equiv fl1, fl2, rp1, rp2, swsucc, swfl$

Lotos gates are synchronization points where atomic events occur. We interpret the above gates as follows:

res (restart): The system had a breakdown and is restarted in the protected state.

fl1 (failure1): A piece of equipment fails while the standby is available.

fl2 (failure2): A piece of equipment fails while the standby is not available.

rp1 (repair1): A piece of equipment is repaired while the system is working but unprotected.

rp2 (repair2): A piece of equipment is repaired while the system is failed.

sfl (standby failure): The standby fails, the system moves to the failed state.

srp1 (standby repair): The standby is repaired while the system is unprotected.

srp2 (standby repair): The standby is repaired while the system is failed.

swsucc (switch successful): This event models the successful substitution of the standby for a failed piece of equipment.

swfl (switch failure): This event models the unsuccessful substitution of the standby for a failed piece of equipment.

3. Here is an outline of the Lotos specification:

specification ProtectedSystem [res]:**noexit**
behavior
< Initial system behavior 4 >
where
< Definition of the system component 5 >
< Definition of the piece of standby 6 >
< Definition of a piece of equipment 7 >
endspe

In accordance with the classification of Vissers et al. [Viss 87], the style of this Lotos specification is *resource-state* oriented. In the resource oriented style, the behavior of the system is defined as the composition of interacting components. Actually, we define the components "system", "piece of standby" and "piece of equipment". The components are specified using a state oriented approach. Every entity internal state is modelled as one Lotos process.

4. The fault protected system initial behavior is defined as the parallel composition of four process instances. The instances correspond to the initial states of one system component, one piece of standby component and two pieces equipment components. Internal interactions are hidden.

< Initial system behavior 4> ≡
hide L_0 **in** ((protected [L_1]
      |[L_2]|
      available [L_2])
      |[L_3]|
      (equip_work [L_3] ||| equip_work [L_3]))

5. The initial state of the system component is protected and may change to switching (i.e., sys_switch) if a piece of equipment detects a failure. The standby is switched for the failed piece of equipment. The standby then does the work of the original piece of equipment. Next, there are two alternatives. If the standby does not detect a problem, the original piece of equipment is declared as failed and the switching phase is complete. However, if the standby also detects a failure, the conclusion is that the malfunction origin is not the piece of equipment. And, the system moves to the breakdown state. In the latter situation, the system requires service and may then be restarted in the protected state.

The system status may change from unprotected to failed (sys_failed) if either another piece of equipment fails or the standby fails. Two other alternatives are repair of a piece of equipment or repair of the standby. The system remains in the failed state until either a piece of equipment or the standby is repaired. Five processes are defined to model the five internal states of a "system" entity.

$<$ Definition of the system component 5 $> \equiv$
process protected $[\ L_1\ ]$:**noexit**:=
fl1;sys_switch $[\ L_1\ ]$
where

        process breakdown $[\ L_1\ ]$:**noexit**:=
        res;protected $[\ L_1\ ]$
        endproc
        process sys_switch $[\ L_1\ ]$:**noexit**:=
        swsucc;unprotected $[\ L_1\ ]$ $[]$ swfl;breakdown $[\ L_1\ ]$
        endproc
        process unprotected $[\ L_1\ ]$:**noexit**:=
        fl2;sys_failed $[\ L_1\ ]$ $[]$ sfl;sys_failed $[\ L_1\ ]$ $[]$ rp1;protected $[\ L_1\ ]$ $[]$ srp1;protected $[\ L_1\ ]$
        endproc
        process sys_failed $[\ L_1\ ]$:**noexit**:=
        rp2;unprotected $[\ L_1\ ]$ $[]$ srp2;unprotected $[\ L_1\ ]$
        endproc
endproc

6. The standby entity is initially inactive and available. When a piece of equipment failure occurs, it becomes active. If the switching phase succeeds, it behaves as a piece of equipment. Four processes are defined to model the four internal states of the standby.

$<$ Definition of the piece of standby 6 $> \equiv$
process available $[\ L_2\ ]$:**noexit**:=
fl1;stan_switch $[\ L_2\ ]$
where

        process stan_switch $[\ L_2\ ]$:**noexit**:=
        swsucc;stan_work $[\ L_2\ ]$ $[]$ swfl;available$[\ L_2\ ]$
        endproc
        process stan_work $[\ L_2\ ]$:**noexit**:=
        sfl;stan_failed $[\ L_2\ ]$ $[]$ rp1;available $[\ L_2\ ]$
        endproc
        process stan_failed $[\ L_2\ ]$:**noexit**:=

srp1;available [L_2] [] srp2;stan_work [L_2]

endproc

endproc

7. A piece of equipment is initially working and has four internal states modelled by four Lotos processes.

< Definition of a piece of equipment 7 > ≡
process equip_work [L_3]:**noexit**:=
fl1;equip_switch [L_3] [] fl2;equip_failed [L_3]
where

        process equip_switch [L_3]:**noexit**:=
        swsucc;equip_failed [L_3] [] swfl;equip_work [L_3]
        endproc
        process equip_failed [L_3]:**noexit**:=
        rp1;equip_work [L_3] [] rp2;equip_work [L_3]
        endproc

endproc

8. The goal of this model is to mimic the behavior of a real fault protected system. We expect some properties from this model which are listed below:

P1: If the system is in the protected state then the standby is available and two pieces of equipment are working.

P2: If the system is in the unprotected state then either: (1) the standby and one piece of equipment are working, or (2) two pieces of equipment are working.

P3: If the system is in the failed state then either: (1) two pieces of equipment are failed, or (2) the standby and one piece of equipment are failed.

P4: If the system is in the breakdown state then the standby is available and two pieces of equipment are working.

Correctness of the specification means that the aforementioned properties are satisfied. The assessment of correctness is the topic of next section.

4. Verification Based on a P/T-net Semantics

Our approach is based on a P/T-net semantics for Lotos. That is, the execution of Lotos specifications is modelled by P/T-nets. We first outline in § 4.1 the P/T-net semantics for Lotos. The verification method itself is discussed in § 4.2 and § 4.3.

4.1. Overview of the P/T-net Semantics

We slightly deviate from the usual notation for P/T-nets [Pete 81]. We represent a P/T-net as a tuple (P, T, Act, M_0) where:

- P is a set of places $\{p_1, ..., p_n\}$,

- $T \subseteq \mathcal{N}^P \times Act \times \mathcal{N}^P$, is a transition relation,

- Act is a set of transition labels, and

- $M_0 \in \mathcal{N}^P$, is the initial marking.

A P/T-net has a **finite structure** if the sets P, T and Act are finite.

$\mathcal{N}$ is the set of non-negative integers. $\mathcal{N}^P$ denotes the set of multi-sets over the set P. A multi-set is a set that can contain multiple instances of the same element. An element $t = (X, a, Y) \in T$ is also denoted as $X - a \rightarrow Y$. Its **preset** is X, its **postset** is Y and **action** is a. The operators $\leq$, $+$ and $-$ denote respectively multi-set inclusion, summation and difference. A Petri net marking is also a multi-set. We denote by $M(p_i)$ $(X(p_i)/Y(p_i))$ the number of instances of the element p_i in the multi-set M (preset/ postset). Instances of the element p_i are also called tokens inside place p_i.

Full Basic Lotos cannot be modelled by finite structure P/T-nets [Barb 90b]. There is a theoretical limitation. Basic Lotos has the computational power of Turing machines, this is not the case of P/T-nets. Furthermore, data structures and their operations are difficult to model concisely into P/T-nets. We identified a subset of Basic Lotos, called PLotos, that can be modelled by P/T-nets, with bisimulation equivalence [Miln 83]. It consists of Basic Lotos plus easy to verify syntactical constraints.

Definition of PLotos

Let p_1 be a process and B_{p_1} the body of the definition of p_1. We say that p_1 **calls** p_2 if instantiation of p_2 is a subterm of B_{p_1}. This relation is denoted as:

$$C = \{(p_1, p_2) : p_1 \text{ calls } p_2\}$$

Let C^+ be the transitive closure of C. We define in terms of C^+ the **mutual recursion** relation as follows:

$$M = \{(p_1, p_2) : (p_1, p_2) \in C^+ \wedge (p_2, p_1) \in C^+\}$$

The **functionality** of a behavior B is equal to *exit iff* every alternative in B terminates with the successful termination action δ, otherwise it is equal to *noexit*. The **execution paths** of behavior expressions are defined, as usual, by selective statements, namely, choice terms for Basic-Lotos.

PLotos is defined as the subset of Basic Lotos that satisfies the following syntactical constraints:

1. *Guarded recursive processes:* A process instantiation term is guarded if it is in the scope of a prefixing operator "$;$", or a sub-term of B_2 of a sequential composition $B_1 >> B_2$ or of a disabling $B_1 [> B_2$.

2. *Noexit functionality in independent parallelism:* Operands B_1 and B_2 in a parallel composition $B_1 ||| B_2$ must have the *noexit* functionality.

3. For every pair $(p_1, p_2) \in M$ we must have:

    3.1. The general parallel operator $||[g_1, ..., g_n]||$ does not occur on the execution path of B_{p_1} which leads to instantiation of p_2.

    3.2. If $B_1 >> B_2$ (or $B_1[> B_2$) is a sub-term of B_{p_1} then instantiation of p_2 is not a sub-term of B_1, also B_1 must have the *exit* functionality.

Stronger constraints, than constraints 2 and 3.1, are stated in [Gara 90] which disallow mutual recursion in sub-terms of the form "$B_1|||B_2$" and "$B_1|[g_1, ..., g_n]|B_2$". They are such that the control can be modelled by a finite state automaton. In our case the operator "$|[g_1, ..., g_n]|$" is disallowed on recursive paths, but mutual recursion is possible in sub-terms of the form "$B_1|||B_2$", with functionality *noexit* operands, the control is not finite state but can still be represented by a finite structure P/T-net.

It is possible to simulate an arbitrarily large stack if the constraint 3.2 is not satisfied. Arbitrarily large stacks cannot be simulated by finite structure P/T-nets.

The Lotos to P/T-nets mapping is based on the work of Olderog [Olde 87] and has two aspects i) a decomposition function, and ii) a set of inference rules.

A Lotos behavior expression B generally represents the composition of several concurrent components. B is decomposed into a multi-set of behavior expressions which, when B is activated, may be interpreted as P/T-net tokens. P/T-net tokens are unstructured elements. The place in which a token is contained is named after the concurrent component that it denotes. For instance, let $B = u; v; stop|[u]|v; stop$, then:

$$dec(B) = \{u; v; stop|[u]|, |[u]|v; stop\}$$

This means that instantiation of B is modelled as tokens deposited into places labelled $u; v; stop|[u]|$ and $|[u]|v; stop$.

Inference rules are used to infer, from subsets of concurrent components, executable transitions. For instance, by application of appropriate inference rules we can infer that the following transition is executable from $dec(B)$:

$$\{u; v; stop|[u]|, |[u]|u; stop\} - u \rightarrow \{u; stop|[u]|\}$$

Moreover, from the component set $\{u; stop|[u]|\}$ the following transition is executable:

$$\{u; stop|[u]|\} - u \rightarrow \{\}$$

The head of each rule is a term of the form:

$$\{p_1, ..., p_m\} - a \rightarrow \{q_1, ..., q_n\}$$

Each rule can be used to infer, as a function of component structures, a transition with preset $\{p_1, ..., p_m\}$, action a and postset $\{q_1, ..., q_n\}$. For instance the rule:

if $M_1 - a \rightarrow M_1'$ and $a \notin \{S, \delta\}$

then $M_1.|[S]|_k - a \rightarrow M_1'.|[S]|_k$

has been used to infer the second above transition: We substituted $\{u; stop\}$, u and v to respectively M_1, S and a. M_1' is empty because the decomposition of "stop" is defined as the empty set. The decomposition function and the inference rules are defined in [Barb 90a, Barb 90b].

Finally, note that we have also shown that conversely P/T-nets can be simulated in our Lotos subset, with language equality equivalence [Barb 90b]. This means that our Lotos subset and P/T-nets have the same computational power. Proofs of correctness can also be found in [Barb 90b].

4.2. Karp and Miller Graphs for Lotos

Given a Lotos specification, it is possible to construct an equivalent P/T-net model by successive applications of the inference rules discussed above. This P/T-net then becomes the input of the reachability analysis algorithm to evaluate the properties. In our approach, we skip the intermediate Lotos to P/T-nets translation step. We derive the reachability graph directly from the Lotos specification, then properties are evaluated. The syntax of the reachability graph slightly deviates from the usual syntax for Karp and Miller graphs. We first discuss the derivation of Karp and Miller graphs for Lotos.

P/T-nets as well as PLotos are not finite state systems. This means that classical finite state/transition system reachability analysis [Boch 78] does not work for P/T-nets. Karp and Miller graphs are finite representations of in general infinite reachability graphs. As other reachability graphs, vertices are labelled with states and edges with transitions. However, a single state in the coverability graph may represent an unbounded number of "equivalent" reachable states.

In our case, states are multi-sets of Lotos behavior expression components. We label the root of the graph with the decomposition of the Lotos expression that represents the initial system behavior. For example, the initial behavior B_0 of the protected system is[1]:

$$(protected[L_1]\|[L_2]\|available[L_2])\|[L_3]\|(equip\_work[L_3]\|\|\|equip\_work[L_3]))$$

The decomposition of B_0, $dec(B_0)$, yields the state represented as the following box:

$$
\begin{array}{|l|}
\hline
1/protected[L_1]\|[L_2]\|\|[L_3]\| \\
1/\|[L_2]\|available[L_2]\|[L_3]\| \\
2/\|[L_3]\|equip\_work[L_3] \\
\hline
\end{array}
$$

Every line in the box defines the number of instances of one process type in the current state. In case there is an unbounded number of occurrences, the process is paired with the ω symbol.

We go from one state to another by application of the inference rules. An inference rule is applicable from one state if a finite subset of the expression component multi-set matches the preset of the transition in the head of the rule. The successor state is obtained by removing this preset from the current state and adding the postset defined by the transition (reformulation of the usual P/T-net transition firing rule). Every edge is labelled with the number of the inference rule, which has been applied to derive the transition, and the action name of the transition. A Karp and Miller graph is also called a coverability graph because for every reachable state s of the

---

[1]We choose the unhidden version of the behavior in order to obtain meaningful transition labels in the graph.

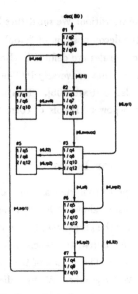

Figure 1: Fault protected system coverability graph

model, there exists a state s' in the Karp and Miller graph such that $s \leq s'$ (the operator $\leq$ denotes multi-set inclusion). The Karp and Miller procedure adapted to Lotos is precisely defined in [Barb 90a].

The coverability graph of the fault protected system is shown if Fig 1. For conciseness, Lotos expression components are shown as $q_1, ..., q_{12}$ which are equivalent to:

$q_1 \equiv breakdown[L_1]||[L_2]|||[L_3]||$, system in the breakdown state.

$q_2 \equiv protected[L_1]||[L_2]|||[L_3]||$, system in the protected state.

$q_3 \equiv sys\_switch[L_1]||[L_2]|||[L_3]||$, system in the switching phase.

$q_4 \equiv unprotected[L_1]||[L_2]|||[L_3]||$, system in the unprotected state.

$q_5 \equiv sys\_failed[L_1]||[L_2]|||[L_3]||$, system in the failed state.

$q_6 \equiv ||[L_2]|available[L_2]||[L_3]||$, standby is available.

$q_7 \equiv ||[L_2]|stan\_switch[L_2]||[L_3]||$, standby in the switching phase.

$q_8 \equiv ||[L_2]|stan\_work[L_2]||[L_3]||$, standby in the working state.

$q_9 \equiv ||[L_2]|stan\_failed[L_2]||[L_3]||$, standby in the failed state.

$q_{10} \equiv ||[L_3]|equip\_working[L_3]$, a working piece of equipment.

$q_{11} \equiv ||[L_3]|equip\_switch[L_3]$, a piece of equipment in the switching phase.

$q_{12} \equiv ||[L_3]|equip\_failed[L_3]$, a failed piece of equipment.

4.3. Verification of Properties

Verification consists of determining if the model is "correct" and satisfies certain properties. The properties can be classified into two groups: (1) general properties, and (2) specific properties. General properties are independent of the goal of the modelled system whereas specific properties are strongly related to the system function. In the field of communication protocols, deadlock freeness and conformity with the service are examples of, respectively, general and specific properties.

By examination of Fig. 1, we can identify the following general properties: (1) The fault protected system is *finite state* because there is no marking that contains a component paired with the ω symbol, (2) for the same reason the *bounded process instantiation* property is satisfied, and (3) every state has successors, consequently the model contains *no deadlock*.

The goal of our model is to mimic the behavior of a real system, with respect to the fault protection aspect. The real system properties are listed under item 8 in § 3, they are evaluated with the help of the coverability graph. First, these specific properties have to be expressed formally. We use logical formulae, i.e. assertions, to formalize the properties. The expression "$s(q_x)$" denotes the number of occurrences of the Lotos expression component q_x in state s. The expression "$s(q_x) = n$" is true if state s contains n occurrences of q_x, otherwise the expression evaluates to false. We sometimes consider $s(q_x)$ as a predicate which is true if "$s(q_x) > 0$" and false if "$s(q_x) = 0$". We denote as RS the set of reachable states. The above four properties are formally stated as follows:

P1: $\forall s \in RS.s(q_2) \Rightarrow s(q_6) \wedge s(q_{10}) = 2$

P2: $\forall s \in RS.s(q_4) \Rightarrow [(s(q_8) \wedge s(q_{10})) \vee s(q_{10}) = 2]$

P3: $\forall s \in RS.s(q_5) \Rightarrow [s(q_{12}) = 2 \vee (s(q_9) \wedge s(q_{12}))]$

P4: $\forall s \in RS.s(q_1) \Rightarrow s(q_6) \wedge s(q_{10}) = 2$

To verify the properties, we must check that every reachable state satisfies the assertions. A quick visual inspection of the coverability graph of Fig. 1 reveals that the above assertions are satisfied by the model.

5. Conclusion

We introduced a novel verification method for Basic Lotos specifications based on Petri net theory. The method can handle non-finite state systems although the example presented in this paper has the finiteness property.

The verification method consists of building a coverability graph. We use a notation slightly different from the usual syntax for Karp and Miller graphs. Properties are stated by logical formulae and evaluated by visual inspection of the coverability graph associated with the Lotos specification. In contrast to other similar approaches, no intermediate Petri net coding is required. That means: (1) a verification procedure of lower complexity, and (2) reachability graphs that are easier to interpret since states contain Lotos expressions nearly in their original form.

Acknowledgements. This work was performed within a research project on object-oriented specifications funded by Bell Northern Research and the Computer Research Institute of Montréal. The authors thank the members of this project for many fruitful discussions.

References

[Barb 90a] M. Barbeau, G. v. Bochmann, *Extension of the Karp and Miller Procedure to Lotos Specifications*, Computer Aided Verification'90, ACM/AMS DIMACS Series in Discrete Mathematics and Theoretical Computer Science, Vol. 3, 1991, pp. 103-119.

[Barb 90b] M. Barbeau, G. v. Bochmann, *Verification of Lotos Specifications: A Petri Net Based Approach*, Proc. of Canadian Conference on Electrical and Computer Engineering, Ottawa, September 1990 (Full paper: *Deriving Analysable Petri Nets from Lotos Specifications*, Research Report No. 707, Dept. d'IRO, Université de Montréal, 1990).

[Boch 78] G. v. Bochmann, *Finite State Description of Communication Protocols*, Computer Networks, Vol. 2, October 1978, pp. 361-372.

[Ehri 85] H. Ehrig, B. Mahr, *Fundamentals of Algebraic Specifications 1*, Springer-Verlag, Berlin, 1985.

[Gara 90] H. Garavel, J. Sifakis, *Compilation and Verification of Lotos Specifications*, PSTV X, Ottawa, 1990.

[ISO 88] ISO, *Lotos - A Formal Description Technique Based on the Temporal Ordering of Observational Behavior*, IS 8807, E. Brinksma (Ed.), 1988.

[Karp 69] R. M. Karp, R. E. Miller, *Parallel Program Schemata*, J. Computer and System Sciences, Vol. 3, 1969, pp. 147-195.

[Knut 84] D. Knuth, *Literate Programming*, Computer Journal, Vol. 27, No. 2, May 1984, pp. 97-111.

[Marc 89] S. Marchena, G. Leon, *Transformation from Lotos Specs to Galileo Nets*, in: K. J. Turner (Ed.), Formal Description Techniques, North-Holland, 1989.

[Miln 83] R. Milner, *Calculi for Synchrony and Asynchrony*, TCS 25, 1983, pp. 267-310.

[Miln 89] R. Milner, *Calculus for Communication and Concurrency*, Prentice-Hall, 1989.

[Olde 87] E.-R. Olderog, *Operational Petri Net Semantics for CCSP*, LNCS 266, Springer-Verlag, 1987.

[Viss 87] C. A. Vissers, G. Scollo, M. van Sinderen, *Architecture and Specification Style in Formal Description of Distributed Systems*, Proc. of PSTV VIII, Atlantic City, 1987.

Error diagnosis in finite communicating systems

Anne RASSE[*]

Abstract

We present an error diagnosis method for parallel communicating systems with branching temporal specifications. Verification is done by model checking on the finite graph of the executions. We consider errors whose diagnostics are sequences of the graph. We define a minimality criterium for the diagnostics such that a finite number of minimal diagnostics give all the reasons of the error. Diagnostics are produced in a simplified form according to a given abstraction. We define an equivalence on models which preserves the simplified diagnostics.

Introduction

The complexity and the growing importance of parallel and reactive systems [Pnu86] requires the development of validation tools. Validation consists successively in detecting the errors, localizing, then correcting them. Error detection is done by comparing the executions of the program against a reference obtained from the service specifications. It can be performed either by verification, simulation or test. When an error is detected, it is necessary to find out the reasons for the error in order to correct it. We present a diagnosis method for verification by model checking, a method used by systems like MEC [Arn89], EMC [CES83], XESAR [RRSV87] : a state graph of the behaviour of the program is compared to specifications given by formulas of temporal logic. Our diagnostics explain the non-validity of the specifications in terms of sequences of the model. It has been shown that every specification of a system can be expressed in terms of safety and liveness properties [AL88]. Intuitively, a safety property expresses that something bad can never happen, and a liveness property expresses that something good eventually happens. They concern all executions of the program : if they are not satisfied, there exists an execution where something bad happens or something good does not happen. Such an execution is called an explicative sequence.

The diagnosis method presented here has been implemented in the framework of XESAR, a verification tool for communication protocols. The model for the executions of the program is a finite state graph. Specifications are expressed in the branching temporal logic CTL [CES83]. The semantics of CTL is defined by a satisfaction relation $\models$ between states of the graph and the formulas. The verification examines if all the states satisfy f. If it is not the case, an error diagnostics is generated, which is an *explanation* of an *assertion* $s \models \neg f$: it expresses properties of the graph proving $s \models \neg f$, such as explicative sequences.

---

[*]LGI IMAG Campus BP53X 38041 Grenoble cedex France; e-mail: {rasse}@imag.imag.fr

This paper is organized as follows. In section 1, we give the model of the program, and the language of formulas. Section 2 is devoted to the generation of explanations. An assertion has generally an infinite number of explanations, but we show that every assertion has a finite number of minimal one giving all the reasons explaining it. In section 3, we are interested in simplification of explanations according to a set of visible actions. We define an equivalence relation between models of a formula f, the *explanational equivalence*, which preserves the simplified explanations of f. In section 4, we present computation of explanations by the diagnostics tool of XESAR, called CLÉO, which implements our diagnosis method.

1   Model of programs - Language of specifications

• **Model of programs.** Let S be a finite set of states, s_0 the initial state, Act a set of identifiers associated by the user to actions of the program, $\rightarrow \subset S \times Act \times S$ a transition relation labelled with elements of Act, $\mathcal{P}$ a set of propositional variables, and a total labelling function $\Pi : S \rightarrow 2^{\mathcal{P}}$. $\mathcal{P}$ contains a variable $sink$ which labels the states whithout successors. The model of the program is the execution structure $M = (S, \rightarrow, s_0, Act, \mathcal{P}, \Pi)$. We write :
$s_1 \xrightarrow{\alpha} s_2$ iff $(s_1, \alpha, s_2) \in \rightarrow$ and $s_1 \xrightarrow{\sigma} s_n$ with $\sigma = \alpha_1 \ldots \alpha_{n-1}$ iff $\exists s_2, \ldots s_{n-1} \mid \forall i \leq n-1. s_i \xrightarrow{\alpha_i} s_{i+1}$. If $w \in S^*$, $w(i)$ is the i-th element of w. An execution sequence is a non empty sequence w of states s. t. $\forall i. w(i+1) \rightarrow w(i)$. If w is finite, $last(w)$ is its last element. w is maximal if w is infinite or $last(w)$ is a sink state. $Ex(s)$ is the set of execution sequences of state s and $Mx(s)$ the set of maximal ones. S^c s the set of the infinite cyclic sequences : $S^c = \{w_1(w_2)^\omega \mid w_1, w_2 \in S^*\}$.

• **Specification language** : CTL without next time operator [EC82].

- **Syntax.** The formulas of CTL are defined by the abstract grammar :
$$f ::= T \mid p \in \mathcal{P} \mid \neg f \mid f \vee f \mid E(f\mathcal{U}f) \mid A(f\mathcal{U}f)$$

- **Semantics.** The semantics is defined by a satisfaction relation between states and formulas. We write $M, s \models f$, or $s \models f$ when M is clear from the context, if the state s satisfies f. The relation $\models$ is defined inductively over the structure of the formulas as follows :

$$\forall s \in S, s \models T$$
$$s \models p \quad \Leftrightarrow \quad p \in \Pi(s)$$
$$s \models \neg f \quad \Leftrightarrow \quad s \not\models f$$
$$s \models f_1 \vee f_2 \quad \Leftrightarrow \quad (s \models f_1 \text{ or } s \models f_2)$$
$$s \models E(f_1\mathcal{U}f_2) \quad \Leftrightarrow \quad (\exists w \in Mx(s), \exists k \geq 1 \mid (\forall i < k. w(i) \models f_1) \text{ and } w(k) \models f_2)$$
$$s \models A(f_1\mathcal{U}f_2) \quad \Leftrightarrow \quad (\forall w \in Mx(s), \exists k \geq 1 \mid (\forall i < k. w(i) \models f_1) \text{ and } w(k) \models f_2)$$

For convenience, in the following, we use the abbreviations :
$$f_1 \wedge f_2 = \neg(\neg f_1 \vee \neg f_2) \quad f_1 \Rightarrow f_2 = \neg f_1 \vee f_2 \quad pot[f_1]f_2 = E(f_1\mathcal{U}f_2)$$
$$inev[f_1]f_2 = A(f_1\mathcal{U}f_2) \quad al[f_1]f_2 = \neg pot[f_1]\neg f_2 \quad some[f_1]f_2 = \neg inev[f_1]\neg f_2$$

and we write $op\, f$ instead of $op[T]f$ for $op = pot, some, al$ or $inev$.

The program satisfies the formula f iff $\forall s \in S, s \models f$. Thus, the specifications are not valid if there exists a state s and a formula f in the specifications such that $s \models \neg f$. The aim of our method is to explain why an assertion $s \models \neg f$ is true.

2 The method for generation of explanations

2.1 Principle

We produce explanations for the formulas whose satisfaction can be shown by giving a single execution sequence. This allows to explain the non satisfaction of formulas constructed from the propositional variables, their negations, operators $\land$, $\lor$, al and $inev$. Most of the usefull specifications can be expressed by such formulas. In fact, a safety property meaning that something bad can never happen, is generally expressed by a formula like $al\neg$ "bad". A liveness property meaning that someting good does eventually happen is generally expressed by formulas like $inev$ "good" or $al\ inev$ "good". The negation of these formulas contains only the modalities pot and $some$ in the explication of which we are especially interested.

The method is extended to the other formulas of CTL. A propositional variable p or its negation does not require any explanation : the assertions $s \models p$ (or $s \models \neg p$) are their own explanation. Formulas like $al[f_1]f_2$ or $inev[f_1]f_2$ cannot be explained in terms of execution sequences, because they express properties of all executions sequences : to explain $s \models al[f_1]f_2$ or $s \models inev[f_1]f_2$, we have to give all execution sequences from s, which would be an information too large to be useful. So, $s \models al[f_1]f_2$ and $s \models inev[f_1]f_2$ are their own explanation. We call *basic formulas* the formulas which we do not explain : the propositional variables, their negations, and the formulas equivalent to a formula $al[f_1]f_2$ or $inev[f_1]f_2$.

The first step of the generation of an explanation of $s \models f$ is to write f in a canonical form $\bigvee_i \bigwedge_j (f_{i,j})$, where all $f_{i,j}$ are basic formulas, or of the form $op[g_1]g_2$ ($op = pot$ or $some$), g_1 and g_2 being in canonical form. Then, the generation of explanations is based on a stepwise explanation of the sub-formulas : s satisfies f because some sub-formulas of f are satisfied in some states reachable from f. Explanations are terms built from assertions of the form $s_i \models f_i$. An explanation of $s \models f$ is obtained by using a rewrite system : a rule rewrites $s \models f$ into a term whose the assertions concern sub-formulas of f, which have to be explained at their turn. The generation of an explanation terminates when the formulas appearing in the assertions are basic formulas. Consider for example the assertion $s \models pot[f_1]f_2$:

$s \models pot[f_1]f_2$ because   *there exists* an execution sequence w from s in which a

state satisfies f_2 and each previous state on w satisfies f_1.

The explanation of this assertion (and also of $s \models some[f_1]f_2$) requires to exhibit a particular sequence *explaining* this assertion. We study these *explicative sequences* (es) in the next section.

2.2 Explicative sequences

If $f = pot[f_1]f_2$ or $f = some[f_1]f_2$, we denote by $W(s \models f)$ the set of es of $s \models f$. We show that there exists a partial order over $W(s \models f)$, compatible with the natural order induced by the notion of sub-sequences, such that there is a finite number of minimal elements, and that every es has a lower bound which is a minimal element. Consequently, if the sequence w explains $s \models f$, there exists a minimal es comparable with w which explains also $s \models f$.

2.2.1 Explicative sequences of $s \models pot[f_1]f_2$

• **Definition.** $s \models pot[f_1]f_2$ is the case iff $\exists s_1 \ldots s_i \ldots \in Mx(s)$ and $\exists k > 0$ s.t. $s_1 = s$ and $(\forall i < k.\ s_i \models f_1)$ and $s_k \models f_2$. Let a be the assertion $s \models pot[f_1]f_2$, then

$$W(a) = \{s_1 \ldots s_k \in Ex(s) \mid (\forall i < k.\ s_i \models f_1) \text{ and } s_k \models f_2\}$$

• **Properties.** If $w = s_1 \ldots s_k \in W(a)$, some shorter es of a may be extracted from w :
- by prefix : if $\exists i < k \mid s_i \models f_2$, then $s_1 \ldots s_i$ is also an es of a.
- by pruning away a cycle : if $\exists i < j \mid s_i = s_j$, then $s_1 \ldots s_i s_{j+1} \ldots s_k$ is also an es of a.

This leads us to define an order relation $\leq_{fi}$ on finite sequences : $\leq_{fi}$ is the transitive closure of $\leq_{fi}^0$, s.t. $w_1 \leq_{fi}^0 w_2$ iff w_1 is a prefix of w_2, or w_1 is obtained from w_2 by pruning a cycle away. Let $W^0(a)$ be the subset of $W(a)$ whose elements have no cycle, and such that none of their strict prefixes belongs to $W(a)$. The following properties are straighforward :

Proposition 1 *If $a = s \models pot[f_1]f_2$: $W^0(a)$ is the finite set of elements of $W(a)$ minimal for $\leq_{fi}$. Every element of $W(a)$ has a minimal lower bound in $W^0(a)$.*

2.2.2 Explicative sequences of $s \models some[f_1]f_2$

• **Definition.** If $s \models some[f_1]f_2$, i.e. $s \not\models inev[f_1]\neg f_2$, there exists an execution sequence from s which cannot reach $\neg f_2$ through states always satisfying f_1. In other words there exists, either : an execution sequence having an occurence of a state satisfying $\neg f_1$ before reaching a state satisfying $\neg f_2$, or an execution sequence ending without having an occurence of a state satisfying $\neg f_2$, or an infinite execution sequence without an occurence of a state satisfying $\neg f_2$. The graph of the program being finite, the existence of an infinite sequence is related to the existence of a cycle in this graph. Let a be the assertion $s \models some[f_1]f_2$. $W(a)$ is the union of a set of finite sequences : $W_{fi}(a) = \{s_1 \ldots s_k \in Ex(s) \mid (\forall i < k.\ s_i \models \neg f_1 \wedge f_2)$ and $(s_k \models \neg f_1 \wedge f_2$ or $s_k \models f_1 \wedge f_2 \wedge sink)\}$ and a set of cyclic sequences : $W_{in}(a) = \{s_1 \ldots s_k (s_{k+1} \ldots s_n)^\omega \in Ex(s) \mid s_k = s_n$ and $(\forall i.\ s_i \models f_1 \wedge f_2)\}$

• **Properties of $W_{fi}(s \models some[f_1]f_2)$.** In the same way as for $pot[f_1]f_2$, every es obtained from a finite explicative sequence of a by pruning away a cycle is an es of a (notice that it is never the case for their strict prefixes) Let $W_{fi}^0(a)$ contain the elements of $W_{fi}(a)$ without cycles. This set has similar properties as $W^0(s \models pot[f_1]f_2)$:

Proposition 2 *If $a = s \models some[f_1]f_2$: $W_{fi}^0(a)$ is the finite set of elements of $W_{fi}(a)$ minimal for $\leq_{fi}$. Every element of $W_{fi}(a)$ has a minimal lower bound in $W_{fi}^0(a)$.*

• **Properties of $W_{in}(s \models some[f_1]f_2)$.** We define an order relation on cyclic sequences such that the set of minimal elements of $W_{in}(a)$ has similar properties as the minimal finites es of $s \models pot[f_1]f_2$ or $s \models some[f_1]f_2$. The minimal cyclic es of a must explain this assertion with a minimal information : it should prove the existence of an infinite execution of the program whith only one elementary cycle of the graph. Then, the order on cyclic sequences to be considered should take into account the number of elementary cycles covered by the sequences. To compare cyclic sequences, we define a canonical form for them :

Definition 1 $\forall w \in S^c$, there exists a unique pair of finite sequences (w_1, w_2) s. t. w_2 is the first shortest period of w satisfying : $w = w_1(w_2)^\omega$ and $last(w_1) = last(w_2)$. $w_1(w_2)^\omega$ is the canonical form of w.

From now on, we suppose always a cyclic sequence to be given in canonical form. Let $nc(w_1(w_2)^\omega)$ be the number of elementary cycles covered by the finite sequence $w_1 w_2$:

$$nc(w_1(w_2)^\omega) = Card(\{(i,j) \mid 1 \leq i < j \leq n \text{ and } w_3(i) = w_3(j)\}), \text{ where } w_3 = w_1 w_2$$

We want to introduce an order relation $\leq_{in}$ on cyclic sequences such that : $w \leq_{in} w' \Rightarrow nc(w) \leq nc(w')$. There is a simple way to define such an order, in terms of the relation $\leq_{fi}$:

$$\forall w_1(w_2)^\omega, w_1'(w_2')^\omega \in S^c, w_1'(w_2')^\omega \leq_{in} w_1(w_2)^\omega \Leftrightarrow w_1' w_2' \leq_{fi} w_1 w_2$$

Indeed, if $W_{in}^0(a) = \{w \in W_{in}(a) \mid nc(w) = 1\}$, we have the following properties :

Proposition 3 If $a = s \models some[f_1]f_2$: $W_{in}^0(a)$ is the finite set of elements of $W_{in}(a)$ minimal for $\leq_{in}$. Every element of $W_{in}(a)$ has a minimal lower bound in $W_{in}^0(a)$.

2.3 Building the explanations

The set of explanations is the least set defined by the set of rules described by the following table. The rule corresponding to a row must be understood as "if *condition* is true then *explanation* is an explanation of the assertion *assertion* ".

condition	explanation	assertion	name
$s \models f$	$s \models f$	$s \models f$	(I)
$s \models f_i$	$s \models f_i$	$s \models f_1 \vee \ldots \vee f_n$	(D)
$s \models f_1 \wedge \ldots \wedge f_n$	$(s \models f_1 \& \ldots \& s \models f_n)$	$s \models f_1 \wedge \ldots \wedge f_n$	(C)
$w \in W(s \models pot[f_1]f_2)$	$pot[f_1]f_2 : e(w, pot[f_1]f_2)$	$s \models pot[f_1]f_2$	(P)
$w \in W(s \models some[f_1]f_2)$	$some[f_1]f_2 : e(w, some[f_1]f_2)$	$s \models some[f_1]f_2$	(S)
x is an expl. of $s \models f$ x contains $s' \models f'$ x' is an expl. of $s' \models f'$	$x[x'/s' \models f']$	$s \models f$	(X)

where $e(w, f)$ is defined by :

$$e(s_1 \ldots s_n, pot[f_1]f_2) = s_1 \models f_1 \rightarrow \ldots s_{n-1} \models f_1 \rightarrow s_n \models f_2$$

$$e(s_1 \ldots s_n, some[f_1]f_2) = \begin{cases} s_1 \models f_1 \wedge f_2 \ldots s_{n-1} \models f_1 \wedge f_2 \rightarrow s_n \models \neg f_1 \wedge f_2 & \text{if } s_n \not\models f_1 \\ s_1 \models f_1 \wedge f_2 \rightarrow \ldots s_{n-1} \models f_1 \wedge f_2 \rightarrow s_n \models f_1 \wedge f_2 \wedge sink & \\ & \text{if } s_n \models f_1 \end{cases}$$

$$e(s_1 \ldots s_k (s_{k+1} \ldots s_n)^\omega, some[f_1]f_2) = s_1 \models f_1 \wedge f_2 \rightarrow \ldots s_k \models f_1 \wedge f_2 (\rightarrow \\ \models f_1 \wedge f_2 \rightarrow \ldots \rightarrow s_n \models f_1 \wedge f_2)^\omega$$

Complete explanations contain only assertions $s \models f$ where f is a basic formula. $X(s \models f)$ denotes the set of explanations of $s \models f$.

Remark : propositional variables in XESAR. When using CTL to express properties of programs, the propositional variables are interpreted as basic predicates which express properties of the states. In the following, we consider the generation of explanations in the case of XESAR. The set $\mathcal{P}$ includes predicates of the form $enable(\alpha)$ and $after(\alpha)$, where $\alpha \in Act$. For these predicates, the function Π is such that : $(enable(\alpha) \in \Pi(s)$ iff $\exists s' \mid s \xrightarrow{\alpha} s')$ and $(after(\alpha) \in \Pi(s)$ iff $\exists s' \mid s' \xrightarrow{\alpha} s$ and $\forall s'. \; s' \to s \Rightarrow s' \xrightarrow{\alpha} s)$.

Example. Consider the specification for the program on figure 1 : "every transmission(tm) is inevitably followed by a reception(rc)", expressed by the formula $f = al(after(tm) \Rightarrow inev\ after(rc)))$. We build an explanation of $s_0 \models \neg f = pot(after(tm) \wedge some\neg after(rc))$:

figure 1.

$$s_0 \models \neg f \overset{(P)}{\longmapsto} \neg f : (s_0 \models T \to s_1 \models after(em) \wedge some\neg after(rc))$$

$$s_1 \models after(em) \wedge some\neg after(rc) \overset{(C)}{\longmapsto} (s_1 \models after(em) \& s_1 \models some\neg after(rc))$$

$$s_1 \models some\neg after(rc) \overset{(S)}{\longmapsto} some\neg after(rc) : (s_1 \models \neg after(rc) \to s_2 \models \neg after(rc) \wedge sink)$$

$$s_2 \models \neg after(rc) \wedge sink \overset{(C)}{\longmapsto} (s_2 \models \neg after(rc) \& s_2 \models sink)$$

For convinience, we represent in the sequel the assertions like $s \models T$ appearing in the explanations only by s (in the same way as we forget these assertions appearing in terms like $s \models T\&x$). More, it is often desirable that action names also appear in explanations so as to establish a more direct correspondence with the program, as action names appear in the program, but not the states. Using these conventions, the explanation obtained in the preceding example is the following (rule (X)):

$$pot(after(tm) \wedge some\neg after(rc)) : (s_0 \overset{em}{\to} (s_1 \models after(em) \& some\neg after(rc) :$$
$$(s_1 \models \neg after(rc) \overset{lost}{\to} (s_2 \models \neg after(rc) \& s_2 \models sink))))$$

• **Properties of the system of rules.**

- Termination : any complete explanation of an assertion $s \models f$ is finite.

- Completeness : if $s \models f$ then $X(s \models f) \neq \emptyset$

- Soundness : if $s \not\models f$ then $X(s \models f) = \emptyset$

• **Minimal explanations**

Consider the following restrictions of the rules (P) and (S), where the explanations of $pot[f_1]f_2$ and $some[f_1]f_2$ are built with minimal es :

$w \in W^0(s \models pot[f_1]f_2)$	$pot[f_1]f_2 : e(w, pot[f_1]f_2)$	$s \models pot[f_1]f_2$	(P^0)
$w \in W^0(s \models some[f_1]f_2)$	$some[f_1]f_2 : e(w, some[f_1]f_2)$	$s \models some[f_1]f_2$	(S^0)

The explanations obtained by applying only the rules (I), (D), (C), (P^0), (S^0) and (X) are called minimal. Because of the properties of minimal explicative sequences, only a finite number of rules (P^0) (resp. (S^0)) can be applied to an assertion $s \models pot[f_1]f_2$ (resp. $s \models some[f_1]f_2$). This system of rules has the same properties as the general one, in particular, it is complete : every assertion has a minimal explanation.

3 Simplification of the explanations

As the programs into considerations and therefore the explanations may be large, it is important to be able to compress the explanations. We provide the user with the possibility to define an observation criterion by defining a sub-set V of visible actions of Act, which are the only to appear in the explanations, and we associate the label λ with the transitions without visible action. In the es of $s \models f$, there can be states s_1, s_2, which cannot be distinguished with respect to f and V in the following sense : they satisfy the same sub-formulas of f, and s_2 is reached from s_1 by a λ-path. A transition between two such states is a silent transition. In simplified execution sequences every maximal sequence of states related by silent transitions is replaced by exactly one of these states. The simplified es do not contain silent transitions. There are two possible methods to obtain simplified explanations. The first method is the one described above consisting of computing first an explanation and then simplifying it. A second method consists of first simplifying the model, and then computing the explanations in this simplified model. This is possible if we find a reduction method allowing to find the same simplified explanations than by using the first method. In this section, we define an observation criterion for a model, the simplified explanations, and then an *explanational equivalence* on models which preserves the simplified explanations.

3.1 Observation criterion

$\phi(f)$ is the set of formulas which can appear in an explanation of f, defined by :

$$\text{if } f \text{ is a basic formula, } \phi(f) = \{f\}, \quad \phi(pot[f_1]f_2) = \{pot[f_1]f_2\} \cup \phi(f_1) \cup \phi(f_2)$$
$$\phi(some[f_1]f_2) = \{some[f_1]f_2\} \cup \phi(f_1) \cup \phi(f_2) \cup \phi(\neg f_1) \cup \{sink\}$$
$$\phi(f_1 \wedge \ldots \wedge f_n) = \phi(f_1) \cup \ldots \cup \phi(f_n), \quad \phi(f_1 \vee \ldots \vee f_n) = \phi(f_1) \cup \ldots \cup \phi(f_n)$$

An *observation criterion* is a pair $C = (V, f)$ where V is a sub-set of Act, and f a formula. C specifies which informations the user is interested in, by defining :

- A labelling of the transitions restricted to the visible actions. Let $V_\lambda = V \cup \{\lambda\}$ and $\leadsto \subseteq S \times (V_\lambda \cup \{\tau\}) \times S$ be the transition relation such that :

$$s_1 \overset{\beta}{\leadsto} s_2 \Leftrightarrow s_1 \overset{\alpha}{\to} s_2 \text{ and } \begin{cases} \text{if } \alpha \notin V \text{ and } \phi(s_1) = \phi(s_2) & \text{then } \beta = \tau \\ \text{if } \alpha \notin V \text{ and } \phi(s_1) \neq \phi(s_2) & \text{then } \beta = \lambda \\ \text{if } \alpha \in V & \text{then } \beta = \alpha \end{cases}$$

τ-transitions are the above defined silent transitions.

- A labelling of the states, restricted to the elements of $\mathcal{P}_f = \mathcal{P} \cap \phi(f)$.

By labelling the transitions and the states of M according to C, we define a new model $M_C = (S, \leadsto, s_0, V_\lambda \cup \{\tau\}, \mathcal{P}_f, \Pi)$. In this model, the satisfaction relation for the sub-formulas of f is the same : $\forall g \in \phi(f)$. $M, s \models g$ iff $M_C, s \models g$. Thus, the explanations of $s \models f$ in the model M and in the model M_C are the same, up to the labelling of the transitions.

3.2 Simplification of the explanations

Simplifying an explanation means generating a more compact form of it without losing any useful information. We define more formally the notion of simplified explanations defined above. The transformations concern the sequences of explanations, sub-terms of the explanation to simplify, where the corresponding es contains a τ-path. There are three transformations depending on the form of the sequences :

Initial sequence of explanations	Simplified sequence
(1) $\ldots x_1 \overset{\tau}{\leadsto} \ldots \overset{\tau}{\leadsto} x_{n-1} \overset{\alpha}{\leadsto} x_n$ where $\forall i < n.\ x_i \in X(s_i \models g)$	$\ldots x_1 \overset{\alpha}{\leadsto} x_n$
(2) $\ldots x_1 \overset{\tau}{\leadsto} \ldots x_k (\overset{\tau}{\leadsto} \ldots \overset{\tau}{\leadsto} x_n)^{\omega}$ where $\forall i.\ x_i \in X(s_i \models g)$	$\ldots (x_1 \& \Delta(s_1))$
(3) $\ldots x_1 \overset{\tau}{\leadsto} \ldots \overset{\tau}{\leadsto} x_{n-1} \overset{\tau}{\leadsto} x_n$ where $x_i \in X(s_i \models g_1)_{i<n}$ and $x_n \in X(s_n \models g_2)$	$\ldots x_1'$ where $x_1' \in X(s_1 \models g_2)$

(1) It is not necessary to explain the satisfaction of g for each of the s_i on a τ-path. The sequence $x_1 \ldots x_{n-1}$ will be reduced to only one of these explanations, say the first one.

(2) We say that a state s_1 *diverges*, denoted by $\Delta(s_1)$, if it is possible to reach from s_1 a cycle of silent transitions, without executing any visible transition. On the τ-path $s_1 \ldots s_k (\ldots s_n)^{\omega}$, the s_i are not distinguished, but we do not want to lose the information of the existence of an infinite sequence. The sequence of explanations is reduced to x_1, supplied with the fact that s_1 diverges, denoted by $(x_1 \& \Delta(s_1))$.

(3) This case happens for explanations of an assertion $s \models pot[g_1]g_2$; the transitions (s_i, s_{i+1}) are silent, thus, if $s_n \models g_2$, $\forall i.\ s_i \models g_2$ (the corresponding es is not minimal). Then, there exists $x_1' \in w(s_1 \models g_2)$ with which the sequence $x_1 \ldots x_n$ can be identified (see [Ras90]).

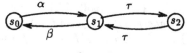

figure 3.

Example (figure 2). Let $f = pot\ some\neg after(\beta)$, the explanation of $s_0 \models f$:

$f : (s_0 \overset{\alpha}{\leadsto} s_1 \overset{\tau}{\leadsto} some\neg after(\beta) : (s_2 \models \neg after(\beta) \overset{\tau}{\leadsto} s_1 \models \neg after(\beta)$
$\qquad\qquad (\overset{\tau}{\leadsto} s_2 \models \neg after(\beta) \overset{\tau}{\leadsto} s_1 \models \neg after(\beta))^{\omega}))$

can be simplified to : $f : (s_0 \overset{\alpha}{\leadsto} some\neg after(\beta) : (s_1 \models \neg after(\beta) \& \Delta(s_1)))$

3.3 Explanational equivalence

We define an equivalence between models which satisfies the following conditions :

1) it preserves the useful properties for the simplified explanations of f : the satisfaction of the formulas appearing in an explanation of f, the sequences of visible actions on the es,

and the properties of divergence.

2) it is done as weak as possible in order to allow efficient simplifications.

Definition 2 *The explanational equivalence for f, $\approx_f$, is the weakest binary relation on S such that :*

$$s \approx_f s' \Leftrightarrow \phi(s) = \phi(s')$$
$$\Delta(s) \Leftrightarrow \Delta(s')$$
$$\forall \alpha \in V_\lambda : [\forall s_1 : (s \overset{\tau * \alpha}{\leadsto} s_1) \Rightarrow (\exists s_1' \mid s' \overset{\tau * \alpha}{\leadsto} s'1 \text{ and } s_1 \approx_f s_1')]$$
$$and \quad [\forall s_1' : (s' \overset{\tau * \alpha}{\leadsto} s_1') \Rightarrow (\exists s_1 : s \overset{\tau * \alpha}{\leadsto} s_1 \text{ and } s_1 \approx_f s_1')]$$

Let $\leftrightarrow$ be the weakest congruence between explanations satisfying the rules :

$$\forall s_1, s_2 : s_1 \models f \leftrightarrow s_2 \models f, \quad \Delta(s_1) \leftrightarrow \Delta(s_2)$$
$$\text{if } x_1 \leftrightarrow x \text{ and } x_2 \leftrightarrow x, \text{ then } x_1 \& x_2 \leftrightarrow x, \quad \text{if } x_1 x_2 \leftrightarrow x, \text{ then } (x_1 x_2)^\omega \leftrightarrow (x)^\omega$$

The following property of the explanational equivalence has been proven in [Ras90] :

Proposition 4 *If $s \approx_f s'$, then for every simplified explanation x of $s \models f$, there exists a simplified explanation x' of $s' \models f$ such that $x \leftrightarrow x'$*

Consequently, simplified explanations can be computed in any model of an equivalence class. The transition relation of the normal form of the model (the smallest equivalent model) is the τ-closure of the transition relation, a silent loop beeing added for each diverging state. In computing such a model, the first step is $O(n_\tau^3)$, where n_τ is the number of silent transitions, the second one is of order of the size of the reduced model.

4 Automatic generation of explanation

We present hereafter an example of an explanation generation by CLÉO, which implements the method described in section 2. This tool is integrated in a verification tool in order to help the user in case of non validity of the specifications. An explanation of an assertion is built step by step, each step being the application of a rewrite rule (§2.3). After one step, the user selects an assertion in the partial explanation obtained, and get an explanation of this assertion. We consider in this example a program describing a token ring protocol.

• **Short description of the Chang-Roberts algorithm [CR79].**

The goal of this protocol is to realize a resource sharing with mutual exclusion between a set of stations $S_{i(i=1...n)}$ connected trough a virtual ring. A token moves along the ring. If S_i wants to have acces to the resource, it waits for the token and transmits it to the next station after it has released the resource, The transmission lines are not reliable, thus the token may be lost. In this case, the stations elect one of the station who produces a new token. The only visible action at the higher level are the acces ($open_i$) and the release ($close_i$) of the resource from the station S_i. The mutual exclusion property is expressed by the formulas :

$$after(open_i) \Rightarrow \neg pot[\neg after((close_i)]after(open_j), \text{ for every pair } (S_i, S_j) \text{ of stations.}$$

• **Verification and diagnostics**

This protocol has been described in LOTOS. It is known that the Chang-Roberts algorithm is correct, but our description in LOTOS was not. By using the CÆSAR system [GS90], it was possible to generate a graph for a fixed number of stations. For a ring of two stations, the formula : $after(open_1) \Rightarrow \neg pot[\neg after((close_1)]after(open_2)$ was not valid for our program. The verification tool gives us the list of the states (coded as integers) which do not satisfy it, i.e. who satisfy its negation $f = after(open_1) \wedge pot[\neg after(close_1)]after(open_2)$. Among this list, the user chooses a state s, for example $s = 369$, in order to obtain an explanation of $s \models f$. First, CLÉO computes a sequence from the initial state ($s_0=1$) to the chosen state, and applies of one rewrite rule to the assertion $s \models f$:

```
ACCES SEQUENCE : 1-3-6-13-25-40-61-84-110-136-172-219-283-(open1)->369

              369   |==    (after(open1) and pot[not after(close1)]after(open2))
BECAUSE :     369   |==    after(open1)
              &
              369   |==    pot[not after(close1)]after(open2)
```

After that, the user selects an assertion in this partial explanation, and CLÉO computes the corresponding rewrite rule :

```
              369   |==    pot[not after(close1)]after(open2)
BECAUSE :     369   |==    not after(close1)
               :    |==    not after(close1)
              824   |==    after(open2)      VIA :369-487-643-(open2)->824
```

This explanation is build with the es 369.487.643.842 of $369 \models pot[\neg after(close_1)]after(open_2)$. The acces sequence followed by the es forms an execution sequence where one can observe the sequence of actions : $open_1$ $open_2$ whithout seeing the action $close_1$. Then, the mutual exclusion is not satisfied. CÆSAR allows to get the meaning of the silent transitions (the internal actions of the network) in terms of the source program. With the help of the explanation and of these actions, we could understand the cause of the error in the election process : it was possible to generate two tokens in the ring, and correct it.

Conclusion

We propose an error diagnosis method for specifications expressed in a branching time logic. The results are given for a particular logic, but our approach can be generalized to other specification formalisms.

In the set of the explanations, we have pointed out a finite subset of minimal explanations, sufficient to show all the reasons of non-satisfaction of f. The cost of computing an explanation of $s \models f$ is the cost of a derivation of this assertion in the rewrite system. The generation of a minimal explicative sequence is the search of a shortest path in the graph of the program, and possibly for strongly connected components.

The explanations can be given in a simplified form depending on of visible actions defined by the user. For this aim, we have defined the explanational equivalence, such that the set of the simplified explanations of f is the same in equivalent models. This equivalence relation depends on the formula, in order to be enough weak to allow efficient reductions.

An interesting application of our diagnosis method could be the generation of test sequences directed by the properties. In fact, the two problems are very close. Testing an implantation amounts to verifying that it has the same properties as its abstract model. By extracting from the model a finite set of sequences such that the property to verify is true because of them, one defines a set of test sequences for the property.

References

[AL88]   M. Abadi and L. Lamport. *The existence of refinement mappings*. SRC 29, Digital Equipment Corporation, August 1988.

[Arn89]   A. Arnold. MEC : a System for Constructing and Analysing Transition Systems. In *Proceedings Workshop on Automatic Verification Methods for Finite State Systems, Grenoble, France*, 1989.

[CES83]   E. Clarke, E. A. Emerson, and A. P. Sistla. Automatic Verification of Finite State Concurrent Systems using Temporal Logic. In *10th Annual Symposium on Principles of Programming Languages*, ACM, 1983.

[CR79]   Ernest Chang and Rosemary Roberts. An Improved Algorithm for Decentralized Extrema-Finding in Circular Configurations of Processes. *Communications of the ACM*, 22(5):281–283, may 1979.

[EC82]   E.A. Emerson and E.M. Clarke. *Using branching time logic to synthtize synchronization skeletons*. In *Sci. Comput. Programming*. Volume 2, 1982.

[GS90]   Hubert Garavel and Joseph Sifakis. Compilation and Verification of LOTOS Specifications. In L. Logrippo, R. L. Probert, and H. Ural, editors, *Proceedings of the 10th International Symposium on Protocol Specification, Testing and Verification (Ottawa, Canada)*, IFIP, North-Holland, Amsterdam, June 1990.

[Pnu86]   A. Pnueli. Specification and Development in Reactive Systems. In *Conf IFIP 86*, North-Holland, 1986.

[Ras90]   Anne Rasse. *CLEO : diagnostic des erreurs en XESAR*. Thèse de Doctorat, Institut National Polytechnique de Grenoble, June 1990.

[RRSV87] Jean-Luc Richier, Carlos Rodríguez, Joseph Sifakis, and Jacques Voiron. Verification in XESAR of the Sliding Window Protocol. In Harry Rudin and Colin H. West, editors, *Proceedings of the 7th International Symposium on Protocol Specification, Testing and Verification (Zurich)*, IFIP, North-Holland, May 1987.

Temporal Precondition Verification of Design Transformations

Ranga Vemuri and **Anuradha Sridhar**

Laboratory for Digital Design Environments
Department of Electrical and Computer Engineering
University of Cincinnati, ML 30
Cincinnati, Ohio 45221-0030, USA

Abstract: Design transformations are ubiquitous in design derivation systems. Many such transformations have elaborate conditions of applicability known as *preconditions*. Usually, preconditions have both spatial and temporal components. The temporal (components of the) preconditions are usually specified by associating a dynamic interpretation with the design description at hand. Such dynamic interpretations have a semantic content which is based on interpreting the design description over the domain of natural numbers. Thus the problem of precondition verification is just as difficult as the problem of design verification itself.

This paper is an informal exposition to the techniques we have used in verifying preconditions of the design transformations in a transformational exploration system for register-level hardware designs. These techniques are based on a purely syntactic interpretation of the design description and avoid the difficulties associated with the theorem proving techniques one could employ when a semantic interpretation is associated. While not as powerful as theorem proving methods, we found these techniques to be adequate for most cases of precondition verification of useful design transformations, at least within the design domain, namely register-level hardware, considered.

1   Introduction

Transformational design methods have been proposed for both program derivation (eg. [4]) and hardware design derivation (eg. [3, 5, 9]). In such systems, a design transformation can be applied to the current design to derive a functionally equivalent design. Many design transformations have elaborate preconditions which must be satisfied by the design before the transformation can be applied. For example, two values can be assigned to the same memory location, only if the *life-spans* of the values do not overlap; two ALU's can be folded into one only if they are never used at the same time and if the wires to connect the sources and destinations to the ALU's already exist. Clearly, preconditions of transformations have a *spatial* component and a *temporal* component. The spatial preconditions are predicated upon the static composition and connectivity among the various modules in the design description and are relatively easy to verify. The temporal preconditions are predicated upon a dynamic interpretation of the design representation. Such dynamic interpretation is usually based on the input data typically encoded as (streams of) natural numbers (or an equivalent domain of values) and on interpreting the design entities (such as the functional units) as functions over the domain of interpretation. Then, in general, automated verification of the temporal preconditions is as difficult as verifying design (against its functional specifications) itself.

While building a register-level design-space exploration system [7], we have developed several techniques for precondition verification of design transformations. These techniques do not use conventional theorem proving techniques directly and are not based on any semantic interpretation of the design representation. Rather, they exploit any information available about the set of possible *traces* (execution paths) to effectively verify the preconditions. *Partial evaluation* is the main technique we used for this purpose. When combined with two other methods, namely using *symbolic equivalence* rules and *comparison rules*, we found that partial evaluation is a very effective technique for precondition verification. The preconditions themselves are specified in terms of what we call *t-expressions*. A *t-expression* essentially encapsulates all the time-steps at which the various *control points* in the design can be executed given different traces. Verification of temporal preconditions then amounts to determining the truth value of various predicates on one or more t-expressions. Specification of preconditions using t-expressions was the subject of an earlier work [7, 8]. In this paper, after providing an introduction to t-expressions, we concentrate on the evaluation of t-expressions while partial or no trace information is available.

In this paper, we use *flow chart programs* as the designs being manipulated in the design derivation system. Flow chart programs prescribe a sequencing of assignment statements and no-ops. An assignment statement can be executed in one time-step; like-wise a no-op can be executed in one time-step. The sequencing operators themselves do not consume any time-steps. [1] We do not explicitly deal with the internals of the assignment statement in the flow chart. It is enough to say that during an assignment statement several resources (such as ALU's, memory locations, wires etc.) are used. Some of these resources (such as ALU's) are occupied or live only during execution of the assignment statement. Other resources (such as memory locations) are occupied over many time steps (as long as the values stored in them are live). Assignment statements abstract register transfers in hardware design and program statements in software design. Similarly, no-ops represent control delays. (Manipulating the occurrences of no-ops is the primary way to schedule the design operations over the resources available.)

In Section 2 we introduce the flow charts. We introduce t-expressions which describe the time-step assignment to the control points in the flow charts. We describe a notation for describing execution traces. In Section 3 we describe the evaluation process of a t-expression at a given execution trace. In Section 4 we briefly discuss the symbolic equivalence of t-expressions. In Section 5, we introduce partial evaluation of t-expressions as a mechanism to verify the preconditions by utilizing any partial trace information that might be available to the designer. Often, in temporal preconditions we are only interested in relative scheduling of the resources rather than the absolute time-steps at which they are used. Verification of such preconditions involves comparing two t-expressions. We introduce several *comparison rules* to compare t-expressions through relation operators without evaluating the expressions. Section 7 contains a very brief sketch of our precondition verification system and two small examples to explain how these techniques fit together. The verification system itself is discussed in [6]; in this paper we concentrate on the underlying techniques.

2 Flow Charts, T-Expressions and Traces

Our *flow chart programs* (or, simply, flow charts) contain the following types of statements: *assignment*, *noop*, *parallel*, *case*, and *while*. A flow chart has exactly one *enter* node and one *exit* node. We use the icons shown in Figure 1 to write flow chart programs. Figure 1 also defines the syntax rules for the flow chart programs. Figure 2 shows an example flow chart program. Informally, an *assignment* statement is used to assign to one or more *variables* values computed using certain resources and the values currently stored in the variables. For the purposes of this paper, we are not concerned with the semantics or the internals of the assignment statement any further.

---

[1] It is straight forward to extend our techniques to incorporate the case where sequencing operators as well as assignments take multiple time-steps.

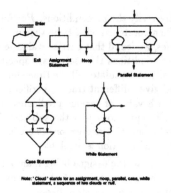

Figure 1: **Statements in Flow Chart Programs**

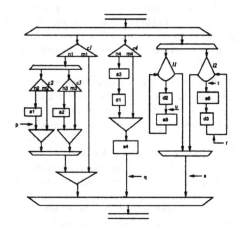

Figure 2: **An Example Flow Chart Program**

A *control point* is an edge in a flow chart. A *t-expression* is associated with each control point, as per the derivation rules shown in Figure 3. For the purposes of the t-expressions, we associate a unique symbol, called the *c-variable*, with each *case* statement and a unique symbol, called the *l-variable* with each *while* statement in the flow chart. (C-variables and l-variables are used to bind the trace information to the preconditions without making references to the execution paths themselves explicitly.) We also label each branch of each *case* statement with a unique symbol called the *branch id*. Using the derivation rules, the following t-expressions can be derived at the control points p, q, r and s of the flow chart shown in Figure 2:

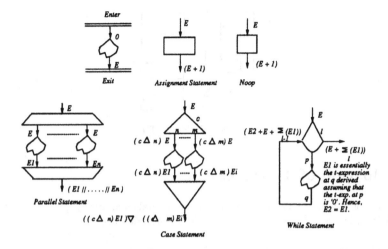

Figure 3: **T-Expression Derivation Rules**

$$E_p = (c2\Delta n2)((c1\Delta n1)0 + 1) \tag{1}$$

$$E_q = (((c4\Delta n4)(0 + 1 + 1))\nabla((c4\Delta m4)0)) + 1 \tag{2}$$

$$E_r = 0 + 1 + 1 + \sum_{l2-1}(0 + 1 + 1) \tag{3}$$

$$E_s = ((0 + \sum_{l1}(0 + 1 + 1)))\|((0 + \sum_{l2}(0 + 1 + 1))) \tag{4}$$

Informally, a *trace* of a flow chart is an execution path through the flow chart beginning at the *enter* node and ending at the *exit* node. [2] For example,
{a1,a4,d2,a6},{a5,d3},{d2,a6},{a5,d3},{a6},{d3} is a trace of the flow chart shown in Figure 2. In this trace, *a1, a4, d2,* and *a6* are executed in the first step, *a5* and *d3* are executed in the second step and so on. We use a visual notation, called *trace diagrams*, to denote traces. Intuitively, the trace diagrams denote an assignment of integer values to l-variables and branch ids to c-variables. [3] For example, Figure 4 is the trace diagram corresponding to the above trace. The trace diagram indicates that the c-variable *c1* diverged on the branch id *n1* and in that *context* the c-variables *c2* and *c3* diverged on *n2* and *m3* respectively. It also shows that the l-variables *l1* and *l2* took the values 2 and 3 respectively indicating the number of iterations of the corresponding *while* statements.

---

[2]Note that a trace cannot be defined as a *path* in the graph theoretic sense because of the parallel statements whose branches are executed simultaneously.

[3]Only well-formed trace diagrams denote valid traces. To be well-formed, a trace diagram must assign an integer value to each l-variable for each context of invocation of the corresponding *while* statement and a *branch id* to each c-variable for each context of invocation of the corresponding *case* statement. In this paper we consider only well-formed trace diagrams. When in doubt, the reader should try to 'walk through' the trace denoted by the trace diagram.

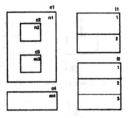

Figure 4: **Example Trace Diagram**

3 Evaluation of T-Expressions

A t-expression of a control point in a flow chart can be evaluated at any given trace of the flow chart to yield an integer. We use the following rules when evaluating the t-expressions:

1. '+' and '-' denote integer addition and subtraction respectively.

2. $\|$ denotes integer *'maximum-of'* operation.

3. $\sum$ denotes multiple instantiations.

4. Δ denotes selective instantiation:
   $(x\Delta y) = x\ if\ x = y;\ undefined\ otherwise.$

5. ∇ denotes mutual exclusion. For any given trace, all but one of the operands of the ∇ operator evaluate to 'undefined'. The value of the ∇ then is same as the value of that one operand.

For example, given the trace shown in Figure 4, the t-expressions (Eqs. 1-4) can be evaluated to, $E_p = 1$, $E_q = 1$, $E_r = 6$, $E_s = 6$. The evaluation can be better understood by viewing the snapshots of the decorated parse-trees of the t-expression E_q and E_s shown in Figure 5. The evaluation process involves iteratively substituting, at the leaves of the parse tree, the values of l-variables and c-variables and propagating these values up the tree using the evaluation rules given above until the root of the tree is assigned with an integer (or the special 'undefined' value). Note that new leaves are created during the reduction process due to the multiple instantiations resulting from evaluating the $\sum$ operator. These new leaves get appropriate values from the trace diagram. For any valid trace of the flow chart, any t-expression in the flow chart can be so evaluated [7, 8].

Informally, the integer to which a t-expression is reduced indicates the time-step (relative to the *enter* node) at which the corresponding control point is reached by a controller executing the flow chart. There is one complication however. The control points inside *while* statements may be traversed several times during the execution of the flow chart. This leads to the notion of *series evaluation* of the t-expressions for control points inside *while* statements.

A *series evaluation* of a t-expression of a control point inside a *while* statement yields a series of integers. If the *while* statement is not nested within any other *while* statement then the series evaluation procedure involves repeating, with $l = 0, 1, 2, \cdots lval$ where *lval* is the value assigned to the l-variable l by the given trace, the procedure illustrated in Figure 5. If the *while* statement is

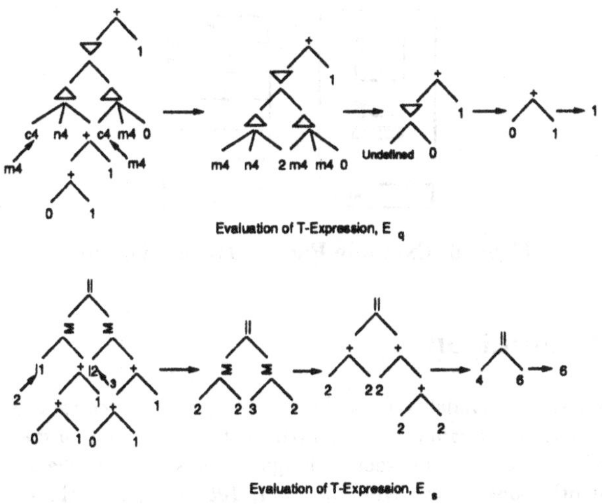

Evaluation of T-Expression, E_q

Evaluation of T-Expression, E_s

Figure 5: **Evaluation of T-Expressions**

nested within another *while* then this procedure is recursively applied. Each such evaluation of the t-expression yields an integer (or 'undefined' value) in the series. For example, given the trace in Figure 4, the t-expression E_r shown in the previous section evaluates to the series [2,4,6].

Hence forth, when we say 'evaluation' of t-expressions we mean series evaluation for expressions of control points within a *while* statement the usual integer evaluation for other expressions.

4   Symbolic Equivalence

In general, evaluation of a t-expression requires a complete trace. However, during the process of design derivation no information about trace (or the set of possible traces) is available. Even so, it is sometimes possible to reduce the t-expressions using certain equivalence rules. Two t-expressions (or subexpressions) are equivalent if and only if, for any t-trace, both expressions evaluate to the same value. Following are some of the equivalence rules often used in our system: [4]

1. $(E\|E) = E$

2. $((c\Delta n)E\nabla(c\Delta m)E) = E$

3. $(((c\Delta n)i_1\nabla(c\Delta m)i_2))\|i_3 = i_3$, where i_1, i_2, and i_3 are integers and if $max(i_1,i_2) \leq i_3$

At any time during the evaluation process, an equivalence rule can be applied to reduce a subexpression of a t-expression into a simpler form. Examples illustrating the use of these rules appear in Section 7.

[4]Actually, these rules are used in some what more general forms where associativity and commutativity of some of the t-expression operators is implicitly taken into account.

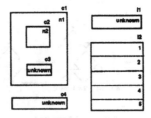

Figure 6: **Example Partial Trace Diagram**

5 Partial Evaluation

If partial trace information is available, it can be effectively used to reduce t-expressions through a technique known as *partial evaluation* [1]. Such partial trace information may be available in the design description or, more often in interactive design systems, through the designer. For example, for fixed iteration-depth loops (of the type *for i = 1, 100 do ()*) the values of the corresponding l-variables are known. In a flow chart with two successive *case* statements with m and n branches respectively, of the $m * n$ possible traces, the designer, knowing the values the variables on which the *case* statements are predicated assume, may be able exclude several. In general, partial evaluation of a t-expression yields a *residual* t-expression. The residual expression is subject to symbolic reduction as well as the other techniques discussed in this paper.

A partial trace is specified by a trace diagram in which a special *unknown* symbol is used to specify one's ignorance about the assignments of values to specific instances of the l-variables and c-variables. For example, Figure 6 shows a partial trace of the flow chart given in Figure 2.

The procedure for partial evaluation is similar to the total evaluation procedure discussed in Section 3 except that, in general, by the end of the evaluation process the root may not receive any value. The available l-values and c-values are substituted at the leaves and propagated through the internal nodes by applying as many t-expression evaluation rules as possible. At the end of this process, a part of the parse tree remains intact where as the other part is decorated and reduced. For example, the t-expressions 1-4 can be partially evaluated at the partial trace shown in Figure 6 to yield the following residual t-expressions:

$$
\begin{aligned}
E_p &= 1 \\
E_q &= (((c4 \triangle n4)2) \nabla ((c4 \triangle m4)0)) + 1 \\
E_r &= 10 \\
E_s &= \sum_{l1} (2) \| (10)
\end{aligned}
$$

6 Comparison of T-Expressions

Most of the time, in verifying the preconditions, evaluation of one t-expression in itself is of little use. More important is to evaluate two t-expressions and compare the results. For example, to substitute a resource r_1 used in an assignment statement s by another resource r_2 it is necessary to verify, for each execution of s, whether r_2 is being used elsewhere. This can be done by comparing the t-expression E associated with s and the t-expressions E_i associated with the assignment statements in which r_2 is used; the objective is to verify whether E and any E_i evaluate to the same value at some trace of the flow chart. Resource folding, where a resource can be a memory location, an ALU, a wire, a register etc., is the most important class of optimizing transformations found in design derivation systems.

In our precondition verification framework, the following operators are provided to compare t-expressions: $E_1 \ op \ E_2 \ iff \ eval(E_1) \ op \ eval(E_2)$ for all the c-traces (of interest) of the flow chart, where $eval$ stands for the result of evaluating the expression and op is any of the following relational operators: $<, >, =, \leq, \geq, and \neq$.

For example, consider the t-expressions at the control points t and r in the flow chart shown in Figure 2:

$$E_t = \sum_{l2-1}(0+1+1)+0$$

$$E_r = \sum_{l2-1}(0+1+1)+0+1+1$$

For any trace where E_t and E_r are defined it can be shown that $E_t < E_r$. Similarly, for control points t and u it can be shown that $E_t \neq E_u$ for any trace where both expressions are defined. Hence, for example, certain types of resource folding transformations can be applied to assignment statements $a5$ and $a6$ (say, using the same ALU for the computations in the assignment statements).

In addition to the techniques discussed in the previous sections, we use several rules, called *comparison rules* to compare t-expressions when the entire trace information is unavailable. Some of the comparison rules often used in our system are given below:

1. $E < k + E$ where k is a positive integer and E is a t-expression.

2. $\sum_{l1} i \neq \sum_{l2}(i+j)$ where i, j are positive integers and $l1$ and $l2$ are l-variables.

3. $(c\Delta m)i_1 \nabla(c\Delta n)i_2) \neq i_3$, where i_1, i_2 and i_3 are integers and $i_3 \neq i_1$ and $i_3 \neq i_2$

The next section has an example to show the application of these rules.

7 Examples and Implementation

This section has two more examples to illustrate the applications of the techniques discussed in the previous sections. Figure 7 shows a flow chart in which we are interested in finding the time step at which control point x is reached. The t-expression at x is,

$E_x = \sum_l((((c2\Delta2)((c1\Delta1)1\nabla(c1\Delta2)1) + 1)\nabla(c2\Delta3)((c1\Delta1)1\nabla(c2\Delta2)1))\|(((c1\Delta1)1\nabla(c2\Delta2)1) + 1 + 1))$

Using the second symbolic equivalence rule given in Section 4 this expression can be reduced to,
$E_x = \sum_l((((c2\Delta2)(1) + 1)\nabla(c2\Delta3)(1))\|((1) + 1 + 1))$

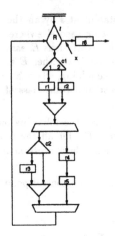

Figure 7: **An Example Flow Chart Program**

By partial evaluation, this is evaluated to,

$E_x = \sum_l ((((c2\Delta2)(2)\nabla(c2\Delta3)(1))\|(3))$

Using the third symbolic equivalence rule given in Section 4 this can be reduced to,

$E_x = \sum_l (3)$

This cannot be reduced any further without some information on the trace. Specifically, a partial trace which assigns a value to the l-variable, l, is sufficient to evaluate this expression.

As another example, consider the flow chart shown in Figure 8. Suppose we are interested in resource folding involving assignment statements $r11$ and $r12$, such as using the same ALU in both statements. The t-expressions at control points y and z are given below:

$E_y = (c3\Delta2)(((c1\Delta1)1\nabla(c1\Delta2)2) + 1)\nabla(c3\Delta3)(((c1\Delta1)1\nabla(c1\Delta2)2) + 1 + 1 + 1)$

$E_z = (c2\Delta1)3\nabla(c2\Delta2)1$

In the absence of any knowledge of the set of possible traces, resource folding is not possible, because we cannot verify that $E_y \neq E_z$ for all possible traces. (In fact, $E_y = E_z$ at the trace where $c1$ diverges on 2, $c3$ on 2 and $c2$ diverges on 1). Suppose that the designer can assert that (say, for example, because the same register is tested to take the branching decision involving both $c1$ and $c2$ *case* statements) whenever $c1$ diverges on 1, $c2$ also diverges on 1 and whenever $c1$ diverges on 2, $c2$ also diverges on 2. However, no information is available about $c3$. Even with partial information, the above expressions can be reduced using partial evaluation to (when $c1$ diverges on 1),

$E_y = (c3\Delta2)(2)\nabla(c3\Delta3)(4)$

$E_z = 3$

Using the third comparison rule given in Section 6 one can assert that $E_y \neq E_z$ at this partial trace. Similarly the two expressions can be reduced to, (when $c1$ diverges on 2),

$E_y = (c3\Delta2)(3)\nabla(c3\Delta3)(5)$

$E_z = 1$

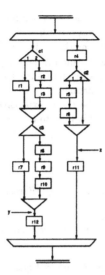

Figure 8: **An Example Flow Chart Program**

Again, using the third comparison rule we can assert that $E_y \neq E_z$ at this partial trace. Therefore, without any further knowledge of the trace information, we can positively verify the resource folding precondition.

We have implemented all the techniques discussed in this paper in a precondition verification system, called PV. PV is implemented in Prolog on a Unix workstation and is part of a transformational design system for register-level hardware designs. PV is described in [6].

8 Discussion

We have successfully used the techniques presented here in a precondition verification system which can verify the preconditions of a set of 18 design transformations used in a register-level design system. In our experience, designers (or programmers) can in most occasions supply partial information about the possible traces. By using the partial evaluation technique in conjunction with symbolic equivalence and comparison rules we could successfully exploit that information leading to better optimization of the design.

Various extensions to the t-expressions are possible: assignments taking multiple time steps, control operators taking one or more time-steps etc. can be easily incorporated.

Temporal logic can also be used to specify temporal preconditions. However, verification of temporal logic expressions is more time consuming. We have abstracted away, by using c- and l-variables, references to the data values which decide the trace of execution. Use of temporal logic would perhaps force one to make references to the data values; we believe that the mechanism based on c- and l-variables and trace diagrams is cleaner and the associated verification techniques are faster as opposed to those using temporal logic based theorem provers.

Finally, having argued the case against the use of general purpose theorem proving for precondition verification, we *are* currently exploring ways of using, in a limited way, such theorem proving techniques, to enhance the power of the methods discussed in this paper. It seems that after applying several rounds of partial evaluation and symbolic equivalence, even if certain precondition could not be verified, it can almost certainly be reduced to a form where theorem proving can be applied in a computationally efficient manner; On the other hand, theorem proving, specifically those based on temporal logic, would have been very expensive (and, preconditions are to be verified on the fly during design transformation) if it were to be used on the unreduced preconditions.

References

[1] D. Bjorner, A. P. Ershov, and N. D. Jones (eds.), "Partial Evaluation and Mixed Computation", North-Holland, 1988.

[2] R. S. Boyer and J. S. Moore, "The Correctness Problem in Computer Science", Academic Press, 1981.

[3] Steven Johnson, "Digital Design from Recursion Equations" MIT Press, 1982.

[4] L. Meertens (ed.), "Program Specification and Transformations, North-Holland, 1987.

[5] W. Rosentiel, "Optimizations in High-level Synthesis", Microprocessing and Microprogramming, pp. 347-352, 1986.

[6] A. Sridhar and R. Vemuri, "Automatic Precondition Verification for High-Level Design Transformations", Proc. International Symposium on Circuits and Systems, 1990.

[7] R. R. Vemuri, "A Transformational Approach to Register Transfer Level Design-Space Exploration", Ph.D. Thesis, Case Western Reserve University, January 1989.

[8] R. Vemuri and C.A. Papachristou, "On the Control-Step Assignment in A Transformational Synthesis System" in G. Saucier and P. McLellan (ed.), Logic and Architecture Synthesis for Silicon Compilers, Elsevier, 1988.

[9] R. A. Walker and D. E. Thomas, "Design Transformation for Algorithmic Level IC Design", IEEE Trans. on Computer-Aided Design, pp. 1115-1128, October 1989.

PAM: A Process Algebra Manipulator

Huimin Lin
Computer Science
School of Cognitive and Computing Sciences
University of Sussex

Abstract

PAM is a general proof tool for process algebras. It allows users to define their own calculi and then perform algebraic style proofs in these calculi by directly manipulating process terms. The logic that PAM implements is equational logic plus recursion, with some features tailored to the particular requirements of process algebras. Equational reasoning is implemented by rewriting, while recursion is dealt with by induction. Proofs are constructed interactively, giving users the freedom to control the proof processes.

1 Introduction

It has been gradually recognized that computer assistance is essential for the analysis of concurrent systems. There are already a number of proof tools, among them are the Concurrency Workbench [CPS 89], TAV [GLZ 89], and Auto [BRSV 89]. Most of these tools are behaviourally based and perform proofs automatically. They interpret processes as labelled transition systems and proofs are established by automatically searching the resulting spaces.

More recently, efforts have been devoted to implementing algebraic proof systems for process calculi. One such system is being developed in Pisa for CCS [NIN 89], and another one is in Amsterdam for ACP [MV 91]. But building a proof system takes considerable efforts as one has to implement the parser, user interface, proof strategy, proof environment management, and so on. Since there are quite a few process calculi around and each is evolving (new operators are emerging, with new axioms characterizing them), it is desirable to have a general system which allows users to define their own calculi, so that much of the implementation efforts can be expended once and for all.

A well-developed technique for general theorem proving in equational logic is term-rewriting [DJ 89]. But there are some difficulties involved in applying existing term rewriting systems to process algebras:

- With pure equational logic one can only reason about finite processes. Infinite processes are defined recursively, and there is no way to handle recursion by rewriting.

- Some "equations" in process algebras, such as the *expansion laws*[Mil 89], are not simple equations but rather *equation schemes*, i.e. they are common patterns of infinitely many equations. This is beyond the power of existing rewriting systems which can only handle finite set of equations.

- Some calculi have "indexed operators", such as the parallel operators indexed by a set of actions in LOTOS and CSP. They represent classes of infinitely many operators and as such cann't be handled by existing rewriting systems which only allow finite signatures.

PAM (Process Algebra Manipulator) is a general proof tool for process algebras using rewriting techniques. The logic it implements is essentially equational logic plus recursion, with some features tailored to the particular requirements of process algebras. At the core of PAM is a rewrite machine which is capable of handling associative and commutative operators. A pattern is provided for defining interleaving (or expansion) laws in various calculi, and applications of these laws are treated as special forms of rewriting. Infinite processes can be defined by mutual recursion, and some forms of induction, such as Scott Induction and Unique Fixpoint Induction, have been built into the system to cope with such recursively defined processes. The syntax for signature definitions is powerful enough to allow "indexed operators".

It is possible in PAM to designate as theorems proved conjectures and then use them in subsequent proofs. This allows users to decompose a big problem into subproblems, prove these separately, and then combine all the small proofs together to establish a proof of the original problem. This is an important feature for any proof tool to be practically useful.

One disadvantage of interactive theorem proving is that proofs can get quite tedious, and it is desirable to interface PAM with other automatic proof tools for process algebras so that some parts of proofs can be "submitted" to such tools for automatic verification. An experimental interface from PAM to the Concurrency Workbench has been implemented which allows calls to the Workbench from within PAM for checking various congruence/equivalence relations between CCS agents.

The process algebras which have been successfully defined in PAM include *CCS* [Mil 89], *CSP* [Hoa 85], *ACP* [BK 89] and *EPL* [Hen 88]. We have been experimenting with some small examples such as the Scheduling problem [Mil 89] and Alternating Bit Protocol [BK 89] in different calculi.

The rest of the paper is organized as follows: Section 2 shows how to use the system by giving examples; The meta language for calculus definition is explained in Section 3; Section 4 presents the implementation of unique fixpoint induction. Section 5 describes the problem definition format and proof commands available at the present; Finally, future work is outlined in Section 6.

2   How to Use The System: An Example

PAM accepts a process calculus definition file, yielding a proof manipulator for the calculus. The meta-language for defining calculi is explained in Section 3 . Here we only take *CCS* as an example to show how to use the system.

2.1   Defining A Calculus

A calculus definition consists of two sections: *signature* and *axiom*. The signature section starts with type declarations:

```
signature
type     Label Action  Process
with     Label < Action
```

Here three types `Label`, `Action` and `Process` are introduced, with `Label` declared as a subtype of `Action`.

After type declarations come operator descriptions:

```
operator
  _ + _ :: Process Process -> Process 120 AC LEFT    -- choice
  _ . _ :: Action Process -> Process 200 RIGHT       -- prefixing
  NIL :: -> Process
  _ \ _ :: Process Action set -> Process   300       -- restriction
  ~ _ :: Label -> Label                              -- inverse
  tau :: -> Action
  _ | _ :: Process Process -> Process 150 AC LEFT    -- parallel
  _ [ _ / _ ] :: Process Label Label -> Process 300 -- renaming
```

Here we have 8 operators defined. As an example, the choice operator + is infix, has priority 120, is associative and commutative (AC), and associates to the left. Note that _ is used as *place holder* to indicate where the actual arguments should go, and set is a built-in postfixing type constructor. Anything after -- in a line is a comment.

In the axiom section we first list basic axioms of the calculus:

```
axiom
A1   x + x = x
A2   x + NIL = x
PN   x | NIL = x
R0   (x + y)\A = x\A + y\A
R1   (a.x)\A = a.(x\A)          if not(a in A or ~a in A)
R2   (a.x)\A = NIL              if a in A or ~a in A
R3   NIL\A = NIL
R4   (x|y)\A = (x\A)|y     if Sort(y) inter (A union (map ~ A)) eq {}
N1   (x + y)[a/b] = x[a/b] + y[a/b]
N2   (c.x)[a/b] = c.(x[a/b])        if not(c eq b) and not(c eq ~b)
```

```
N3    (c.x)[a/b] = a.(x[a/b])         if c eq b
N4    (c.x)[a/b] = ~a.(x[a/b])        if c eq ~b
N5    NIL[a/b] = NIL
T1    a.tau.x = a.x
T2    x + tau.x = tau.x
T3    a.(x + tau.y) + a.y = a.(x + tau.y)
```

Each axiom consists of a name, an equation, and possibly a side condition.

A subset of axioms can be designated as an *action algebra* which defines the structural behaviour of actions:

```
action algebra
        ~(~a) = a
```

The expansion law is separated from the ordinary axioms and is written in a particular format since they are treated differently from normal equations:

```
expansion law
let x = a1.x1 + ... + an.xn        y = b1.y1 + ... + bm.ym
then
    (x|y)\A = NIL   if sync_move(x,y) eq nil and async_move(x,y) eq nil
    (x|y)\A = Sum(+,async_move(x,y))      if sync_move(x,y) eq nil
    (x|y)\A = Sum(+,sync_move(x,y))       if async_move(x,y) eq nil
    (x|y)\A = Sum(+,async_move(x,y)) + Sum(+,sync_move(x,y))
                                          otherwise
with communication function
            sync(a, b) = tau        if a eq (~b) or b eq (~a)
            async(a) = true         if not(a in A or ~a in A)
```

where sync, async, sync_move, async_move and Sum are built-in primitives and are explained in Section 3.4.

The rules for computing *syntactic sort*[Mil 89] can be placed after the keywords **sort computation**:

```
sort computation

        Sort(NIL) = {}
        Sort(tau.P) = Sort(P)
        Sort(a.P) = {a} union Sort(P)
        Sort(P + Q) = Sort(P) union Sort(Q)
        Sort(P | Q) = Sort(P) union Sort(Q)
        Sort(P \ A) = Sort(P) diff (A union (map ~ A))
```

2.2   Proving A Conjecture

Having defined a calculus, one can prove theorems in it. The problems one wants to prove are given in problem definition files. The following is a definition file of the two bit buffer problem in *CCS*:

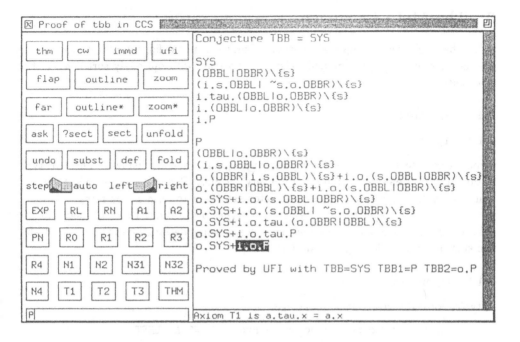

Figure 1: A Proof Window

```
conjecture
        TBB = SYS
where
        TBB = i.TBB1
        TBB1 = i.TBB2 + o.TBB
        TBB2 = o.TBB1

        SYS = (OBBL|OBBR)\{s}
        OBBL = i.s.OBBL
        OBBR = ~s.o.OBBR
end
```

The system reads in the above problem definition file (assuming the calculus *CCS* has already been compiled), creating a proof window for it. Proofs are constructed by clicking suitable command buttons which correspond to *proof steps*. The available proof steps are explained in Section 5. Figure 1 shows a proof window with a complete proof for the two bit buffer problem.

3   The Meta Language

As can be seen in the example of the last section, a calculus definition in this proof system basically consists of *signature* and *axiom* descriptions, with optionaly sort computation rule specification.

3.1   Signature

3.1.1   Types

Type names are listed after the keyword type, separated by blanks. The two types Action and Process must be present in every calculus. There is a pre-defined type Bool and a pre-defined postfixing type constructor set (used to form action sets).

It is possible to specify some types as subtypes of others. "T1 < T2" says T1 is a subtype of T2. A blank-separated list of such subtyping declarations can be placed after the keyword with following type declaration.

3.1.2   Operators

A typical operator declaration looks like

    _ + _ :: Process Process -> Process 120 AC LEFT

The symbol _ is used as a *place-holder* to indicate where the actual arguments should go. So + is a binary infix operator, left-associative and commutative, with priority 120.

It is possible to declare *operator schemes*, or *indexed operators*. At the present only associative and commutative operator schemes are allowed, i.e., all parameterized operators must be of attribute AC, and arguments other than the first and the last ones are regarded as indexes. For example, the family of parallel operators indexed by sets of actions may be declared as follows:

    _ |[_]| _ :: Process Action set Process -> Process
                   100 AC LEFT

Here a scheme for a family of infix, left-associative and commutative operators is specified. For instance, |[{a,b}]| and |[{c}]| are two such operators. Each operator in this family will take two processes as arguments and return another process as result.

3.2   Axioms

An axiom is a named equation, or inequation, possibly with a side-condition.

The language for side-conditions is simple, involving equality test eq between two actions or two action sets, boolean operations true, false, not, and and or, and (finite) set operations in (membership), union, diff (difference) and inter (intersection). When the rules for sort computation are presented, the operator Sort can also be used in side-conditions to compute the syntactic sorts of processes.

A side condition is a boolean expression built up from action names and/or sets of action names using the above operators. It follows the keyword if after an equation.

3.3 Action Algebra

A subset of axioms on terms of type Action may be grouped under the keywords action
algebra. These are the laws governing the structural behaviour of actions.

The equations in the action algebra of a calculus, when it is present, are automatically
applied as left-right oriented rewrite rules to evaluate the action expressions in the side-
condition every time a conditional equation is used as a rewrite rule. Hence it is crucial
to ensure that the action algebra, when left-right oriented, constitutes a confluent and
terminating rewrite system (modulo associativity and commutativity).

3.4 Expansion Law

The definition of an expansion law in this meta language consists of three clauses: the
let clause, then clause, and with clause, as shown in the example of Section 2.

In the let clause the form of the components of the parallel composition is specified.
It must be the sum of a list of processes prefixed by actions. Ellipsis... is used to make
it more comfortable to read. The summation (or *choice*) operator must be associative
and commutative.

The with clause defines the synchronization mechanism. In this meta language such
a mechanism is determined by three parameters: two functions (sync and async) and
one communication style (handshake or broadcast).

- async maps actions to the boolean constant true, and may have a side condition
  attached. The actions satisfying the side condition can occur asynchronously, while
  the others can not.

- sync is the synchronization function. It takes two actions as arguments and, if
  they satisfy the side condition, gives the action resulting from the communication
  between them.

- *communication style* decides how the components of a parallel composition par-
  ticipate in communication. There are two communication styles: handshake and
  broadcast. The default is handshake.

The then clause consists of a list of (conditional) equations with identical left handsides which are parallel compositions, or restricted parallel compositions, of the process
terms specified in the let clause. The right handsides are the terms into which the left
handsides will be expanded. The system provides three primitives that can be used in
the right handside terms.

- sync_move takes two processes as specified in the let clause, and returns a (possibly
  empty) list of processes resulting from all possible communications between them.
  The result of sync_move depends on sync and the communication style.

- async_move takes two processes as specified in the let clause, and returns a (possibly empty) list of processes resulting from all possible asynchronous movement of
  these two processes. The result of async_move depends on async.

- Sum is a term constructor. It takes a summation operator (which must be associative and commutative) and a non-empty list of processes, and returns the sum of these processes.

For some technical reasons, the cases that sync_move and/or async_move are empty must be specified separately. A constant nil is provided to test whether they are empty in side conditions.

Usually there would be one expansion law for each parallel operator.

3.5 Sort Computation

The *sort* or *alphabet* information is useful in proofs involving infinite processes [BK 89, Mil 89]. Although the sort of an arbitrary process is uncomputable in general, it is not difficult to calculate the *syntactic sorts* of processes. In PAM the rules for compute syntactic sorts can be listed after the keywords sort computation. The top level symbol of the left handside of each rule must be the built-in operator Sort which has type Process -> Action set. When sort computation is enabled (see Section 5.1), an algorithm is invoked to calculate the least sorts determined by these rules.

4 Unique Fixpoint Induction

Unique fixpoint induction allows one to assert that two process terms are equal if they satisfy the same set of equations. Its practical application usually involves a pair of process terms, one of which is the specification defined by recursive equations, and the other one is the implementation which has been shown to satisfy a set of equations that are structurally the same as (or similar to) the definitional equations of the specification. Applying unique fixpoint induction to prove the equality of two such processes amounts to match two sets of equations. The algorithm for unique fixpoint induction is outlined in Figure 2 using pseudo-ml code.

With unique fixpoint induction one can prove problems involving infinite state processes. Here is the *counter* problem (in *CCS*) which can be proved in PAM with only a few steps:

conjecture

        C = P
where
        C = up.(down.NIL | C)
        P = up.(~s.P | B) \ {s}
        B = s.down.NIL

need sort computation
end

```
fun ufi(spec,impl,spec_defs,impl_eqs) =
let fun matching(matched,to_match) =
    let val to_do = diff(to_match,matched)
        fun match_one(sp,im) =
        let val sd = lookup(spec_defs,sp) handle Lookup => sp
            val id = lookup(impl_eqs,im) handle Lookup => im
        in  match_term(id,sd)
        end
    in  if to_do = nil then (matched,[])
        else let val m = map match_one to_do
                 val new_to_match = fold union m []
                 val new_matched = union(matched,to_do)
             in matching(new_matched, new_to_match)
             end  handle Match_term => (matched,to_match)
    end
in  matching([],[(spec,impl)])
end
```

Figure 2: The pseudo-ml code for unique fixpoint induction

As is well-known unique fixpoint induction is unsound. However it is applicable when some condition, called guardedness, is satisfied [Hoa 85, Hen 88, Mil 89, BK 89]. At the present we leave to the users the responsibility of checking these conditions.

5 Proofs

5.1 Problem Definition

To start a proof, one must present the conjecture to the system in a problem definition file. We have already seen an example in Section 2.

The formula (equation or inequation) to prove follows the keyword **conjecture**. The recursive definitions of the process constants, if any, are listed after the keyword **where**. Macros may be defined after the keyword **macro**. They are used to shorten inputs/outputs and have no computational effect.

Sort computation can be enabled by the keywords **need sort computation**. It is disabled otherwise.

5.2 Proof Sections

The proof system relies heavily on term rewriting techniques. A proof usually consists of several sections, each starts with a process term followed by some terms transformed from it by applying equational reasoning rules or folding/unfolding recursive definitions.

Such transformations are invoked by performing the corresponding *proof steps* explained in the following subsection.

5.3 Proof Steps

A proof proceeds when one performs proof steps. The proof steps already implemented so far can be classified into three groups:

transformation steps The basic transformation steps are rewriting, applying expansion law, and folding/unfolding recursive definition.

assertion steps Here we have proof commands such as unique fixpoint induction, proving by transitivity, and proving by the concurrency workbench. The last one is only meaningful for *CCS*. These commands are needed to confirm that a conjecture has been proved so that it can be admitted as theorem by the proof system.

auxiliary steps These include the commands for making auxiliary definitions, commands for opening new sections, and commands for making proved conjectures as theorems so that they can be used in subsequent proofs.

Proof steps are invoked by clicking command buttons in the window interface. The behaviour of rewriting commands are controlled by two switches: The left-right switch determines in which direction an axiom is used as a rewrite rule, while the step-auto switch decides if rewriting should be performed for just one-step, or go as far as possible.

6 Conclusions and Future Work

We have described a general process algebra manipulation system which is based on equational axiomatization. It allows the users to define their own process algebras and carry out proofs for problems in the defined calculi. During the proofs terms can be simplified automatically by rewriting, and assertions about recursively defined processes can be verified by induction.

Only the kernel part of PAM has been implemented. Much more efforts at both design level and implementation level are still needed to make it a practically useful system.

Attempts have been made to integrate PAM with the Concurrency Workbench. At the moment we have only one direction of such linkage, i.e. to call the Workbench from within PAM, and the experiments gained are encouraging. More efforts are needed to investigate how to cooperate between these two kinds of proof tools so that each of them can take the advantages of the other: the indentities proved by algebraic manipulations can be exploited to reduce the state space of behavioural proof systems, while some parts of algebraic proofs can be checked automatically by behavioural tools to reduce the amount of tedious manipulations in algebraic proofs.

Acknowledgements

Many thanks to Matthew Hennessy for initiating and overseeing this project and detailed comments on an early draft of this paper, to Luca Aceto for help in process algebra and particularly in formulating the expansion law, to Robin Milner for remarks on fair abstraction rule and on the integration with the Concurrency Workbench, to Faron Moller for detailed comments on the paper, to Simon Bainbridge for discussions on the proof system, to Astrid Kiehn and Anna Ingólfsdóttir for their helps during the implementation of PAM.

This project has been carried out with the financial support from the Science and Engineering Research Council of UK, and the ESPRIT II BRA project CONCUR.

References

[BK 89]   Bergstra, J.A., Klop, J.W., "Process Theory Based on Bisimulation Semantics", in *Linear Time, Branching Time and Partial Order in Logics and Models for Concurrency*, LNCS 354, 1989.

[BRSV 89]   Boudol, G., Roy, V., de Simone, R., Vergamini, D., *Process Calculi, From Theory to Practice: Verification Tools*, INRIA Report No 1098, 1989.

[CPS 89]   Cleaveland, R., Parrow, J. and Steffen, B., "The Concurrency Workbench", *Proc. of the Workshop on Automated Verification Methods for Finite State Systems*, LNCS 407, 1989.

[DJ 89]   Dershowitz, N., Jouannaud, J.-P., "Rewrite Systems", in *Handbook of Theoretical Computer Science* North-Holland, 1989.

[GLZ 89]   Godskesen, J.C., Larsen, K.G., Zeeberg, M., *TAV Users Manual*, Internal Report, Aalborg University Centre, Denmark, 1989.

[Hen 88]   Hennessy, M., *Algebraic Theory of Processes*, MIT Press, 1988.

[MV 91]   Mauw, S., Veltink, G.J., *A proof Asisteant for PSF*. Programming Research Group, University of Amsterdam, 1991. In this Volume.

[Hoa 85]   Hoare, C.A.R., *Communicating Sequential Processes*, Prentice-Hall, 1985.

[Mil 89]   Milner, R., *Concurrency and Communication*, Prentice-Hall, 1989.

[NIN 89]   De Nicola, R., Inverardi, P., Nesi, M., "Using the Axiomatic Presentation of Behavioural Equivalences for Manipulating CCS Specifications", *Proc. Workshop on Automatic Verification Methods for finite State Systems*, LNCS 407, 1989.

The Concurrency Workbench with Priorities

Claus Torp Jensen *ctjmrr@daimi.dk*
Computer Science Department
Aarhus University
DK 8000 Aarhus C.

Abstract

This paper presents an extension of Milner's CCS with a priority choice operator accompanied by a suitable notion of bisimulation and a characterizing modal logic. It is implemented in an extension of the analysis tool the Edinburgh-Sussex Concurrency Workbench.

1 Background

Many everyday systems include alternative activities with different priorities. Consider a nuclear reactor - if something goes wrong, the shutdown of the reactor should have the highest priority of all. Some recent programming languages (like OCCAM) include the possibility of giving some actions priority over others, but when modelling in CCS there is no way in which one could force an agent to choose a particular one of the two subagents in a sum, so what is actually needed in CCS, is a new constructor.

A priority choice constructor $>$ named PRISUM (it has some resemblance to the construction PRI ALT in OCCAM - see OCC[84]) is chosen, which gives the left agent preference to the right, and otherwise behaves like a sum. So $A > B$ means: "Perform as A if you can - if no transitions for A are possible, then perform as B"

This construct is extendable to multiple levels of priorities where the PRISUM construct chooses a transition for the leftmost agent possible. The control system for the nuclear reactor could now be modelled by $shutdown.nil > GO$.

The theoretical part of this paper is based on Milner's CCS and on work done by Juanito Camilleri (Camilleri[90]). Camilleri's work on priorities is reformulated and simplified, so that it now constitutes a practical basis for an implementation of a state space analysis tool. A key improvement of the present formulation is that the number of possible transitions is dramatically decreased without losing information. The forthcoming paper Camilleri/Winskel[91] is closely related, and presents a complete equational proof system for the equivalence used here, although based on a different operational semantics. The actual implementation is done by modifying the existing analysis tool the Edinburgh-Sussex Concurrency Workbench (called CW - see CW[1-3] for details). The changes are conservative, so that without priorities the system behaves exactly as it did before.

All proofs are left out because of lack of space, but will appear in a forthcoming report.

2 Construction of transition-system for CCS with priorities

In the rest of the paper, let *Act* be the set of actions (including τ), *A* the set of input actions (not necessarily *physical* input actions), *Agt* the set of $CCS^>$ agents, and for a set *S* let S^n be the set of vectors of length n over *S* and $P(S)$ the powerset of *S*.

2.1 The extended language

If $X \in VS$, where VS is a set of variables (restriction to just one variable would prohibit nesting of fixpoints), $CCS^>$ expressions have the following regular syntax:

$$G ::= X \mid nil \mid a.E \mid \tau.E \mid G \setminus L \mid G[f] \mid G + G \mid G > G \mid (G|G) \mid fix(X = G)$$
$$E ::= X \mid nil \mid \alpha.E \mid E \setminus L \mid E[f] \mid E + E \mid G > G \mid (E|E) \mid fix(X = E)$$

where the symbols from CCS have their usual meaning, $a \in A$, $L \in P(A)$ and $\alpha \in Act$. f is an injective relabeling function. Only *guarded* recursions are allowed.

The syntax restricts guards (the agents in priority constructs) so that they do not contain output actions on the top level (this is consistent with OCCAM). The reason is, that looking at an agent like $A \mid B \equiv (\alpha.nil > \overline{\beta}.nil) \mid (\beta.nil > \overline{\alpha}.nil)$ it is not clear what its transitions should be. *A* can do an α transition in a handshake with *B*, but this can only be the case if *B* cannot do a β transition, which can only be the case if a possible α transition for *A* prevents the $\overline{\beta}$ transition. Similarly *B* can do a β transition if *A* cannot do an α transition, which can only be the case if a possible β transition for *B* prevents the $\overline{\alpha}$ transition. What choice should one make then?

Because all recursions are guarded, one single set of recursion variables is sufficient. In a guard, any recursion variable must be guarded by an *input* action. Accordingly it is *never* possible to introduce an output action on the top level by substitution for variables (output actions in guards are allowed if they are guarded by an input action).

2.2 The environment's influence on behaviour

What kind of information about the environment is actually relevant, when it comes to deciding the possible transitions for an agent? The answer is information about what the environment cannot do, and this is captured in the notion of *refusal sets*. A refusal set is defined to be a set of input actions, for which it is known that the environment can't perform any of the matching output actions.

Since all actions in CCS are basically performed in handshakes, one expects for $A, B \in Agt$ and $\alpha \in Act$: "If *A*'s environment refuses to perform an $\overline{\alpha}$ transtion, then *A* can't perform an α-transition". Accumulating over the possible actions for *A*, one expects: "If the environment of $A > B$ refuses to match any of *A*'s transitions, then *B* can be allowed to perform its transitions".

2.3 Goals for the transition system

When automated analysis is the goal, the transition system for $CCS^>$ should be computationally tractable, and preferably intuitively understandable.

Given the informal definition of refusal sets above, it is immediately observable that a given transition would be possible under a very large (actually infinite) number of different refusal sets. This would prevent any analysis using all possible transitions for finite state agents (which is commonly used), so some kind of simplification is needed. The solution is to use transitions of the form $\vdash_R A \xrightarrow{\alpha} A'$ understood as meaning *"In an environment which refuses at least R (and possibly more actions), and is prepared to match α, the agent A can perform α to become A'"*.

Thus, the subscripted refusal set should be the *weakest condition* for a given derivation. It is *not* my intention to allow a transition to occur under all imaginable refusal sets - in order to get an efficient implementation, I just want the smallest ones.

In view of the above description, one would expect of a suitable transition system that $\vdash_R A \xrightarrow{\alpha} A' \Rightarrow \alpha \notin R$.

2.4   Transition rules

2.4.1   Preliminaries

In order to define the transition system, two functions on agents are needed (note that these functions only work properly on *guarded* recursions).

First of all, it is necessary to determine the possible actions of a guard (always input actions or taus), in order to express what the environment cannot be allowed to do, if the righthand agent in a PRISUM construct is to perform any actions.

Definition 1 *Define inActs on guards by the following structural induction:*

$$inActs(nil) = \emptyset \tag{1}$$
$$inActs(a.A) = \{a\} \tag{2}$$
$$inActs(\tau.A) = \{\tau\} \tag{3}$$
$$inActs(A_1 + A_2) = inActs(A_1) \cup inActs(A_2) \tag{4}$$
$$inActs(A \setminus L) = inActs(A) \setminus L \tag{5}$$
$$inActs(A[f]) = (inActs(A))[f] \tag{6}$$
$$inActs(G_1 > G_2) = inActs(G_1) \cup inActs(G_2) \tag{7}$$
$$inActs(A_1|A_2) = inActs(A_1) \cup inActs(A_2) \tag{8}$$
$$inActs(fix(X = A)) = inActs(A) \tag{9}$$

where $X \in VS$. Observe that τ can never be in any refusal set, since refusal sets consist of the *input* actions which the environment cannot match (and there is no such thing as an $\overline{\tau}$ action) - this expresses the fact that the *internal* τ action is *always* possible (and therefore always prevents low priority actions), and is similar to the SKIP option in the PRI ALT construction in OCCAM.

(9) is so simple because all recursions are guarded. Since only the top level actions are interesting, it is not necessary to unfold.

It might be interesting to notice, that the definition of *inActs* is independent of the environment. This is due to the fact that in $A > B$ although the environment does influence the possible transitions for A, it has to refuse *all* the handshakes, if B is to be allowed to perform any actions.

One also needs the possible output actions for an agent (note that these are always independent of the environment, since output actions are not allowed in guards), because in a parallel composition $A|B$ the environment for A is the external environment *together with B*.

Definition 2 *Define outActs on agents by the following structural induction:*

$$outActs(nil) = \emptyset \tag{10}$$
$$outActs(a.A) = \emptyset \tag{11}$$
$$outActs(\bar{a}.A) = \{a\} \tag{12}$$
$$outActs(\tau.A) = \emptyset \tag{13}$$
$$outActs(A_1 + A_2) = outActs(A_1) \cup outActs(A_2) \tag{14}$$
$$outActs(A \setminus L) = outActs(A) \setminus L \tag{15}$$
$$outActs(A[f]) = (outActs(A))[f] \tag{16}$$
$$outActs(G_1 > G_2) = \emptyset \tag{17}$$
$$outActs(A_1|A_2) = outActs(A_1) \cup outActs(A_2) \tag{18}$$
$$outActs(fix(X = A)) = outActs(A) \tag{19}$$

Note regarding (17), that output-actions are not allowed in guards.

2.4.2 The rules

The transition rules are now defined as follows:

$$\vdash_{\emptyset} \alpha.A \xrightarrow{\alpha} A \tag{20}$$

$$\frac{\vdash_R A \xrightarrow{\alpha} A'}{\vdash_R A + B \xrightarrow{\alpha} A'} \tag{21}$$

$$\frac{\vdash_R B \xrightarrow{\alpha} B'}{\vdash_R A + B \xrightarrow{\alpha} B'} \tag{22}$$

$$\frac{\vdash_R A \xrightarrow{\alpha} A' \; (\alpha \notin L \cup \bar{L})}{\vdash_{R \setminus L} A \setminus L \xrightarrow{\alpha} A' \setminus L} \tag{23}$$

$$\frac{\vdash_R A \xrightarrow{\alpha} A'}{\vdash_{R[f]} A[f] \xrightarrow{f(\alpha)} A'[f]} \tag{24}$$

$$\frac{\vdash_R G_1 \xrightarrow{\alpha} G_1'}{\vdash_R G_1 > G_2 \xrightarrow{\alpha} G_1'} \tag{25}$$

$$\frac{\vdash_R G_2 \xrightarrow{\alpha} G_2', \; \tau \notin inActs(G_1), \; \alpha \notin inActs(G_1)}{\vdash_{R \cup inActs(G_1)} G_1 > G_2 \xrightarrow{\alpha} G_2'} \tag{26}$$

$$\frac{\vdash_R A_0 \xrightarrow{\alpha} A_0', \; R \cap outActs(A_1) = \emptyset}{\vdash_R A_0|A_1 \xrightarrow{\alpha} A_0'|A_1} \tag{27}$$

$$\frac{\vdash_R A_1 \xrightarrow{\alpha} A_1', \; R \cap outActs(A_0) = \emptyset}{\vdash_R A_0|A_1 \xrightarrow{\alpha} A_0|A_1'} \tag{28}$$

$$\frac{\vdash_{R_0} A_0 \xrightarrow{\alpha} A_0', \; \vdash_{R_1} A_1 \xrightarrow{\overline{\alpha}} A_1', \; R_1 \cap outActs(A_0) = \emptyset, \; R_0 \cap outActs(A_1) = \emptyset}{\vdash_{R_0 \cup R_1} A_0|A_1 \xrightarrow{\tau} A_0'|A_1'} \quad (29)$$

$$\frac{\vdash_R A\{fix(X = A)/X\} \xrightarrow{\alpha} A'}{\vdash_R fix(X = A) \xrightarrow{\alpha} A'} \quad (30)$$

where $[A/Y]$ means syntactical substitution by A of *free* occurrences of the variable Y. An intuitive explanation of the transition-rules:

- (20) There is no requirement on the refusal set of the environment in order for the first action of a prefix to occur.

- (21) + (22) Correspond to the rules for CCS.

- (23) The refusal set has to be changed, because actions in $L \cup \overline{L}$ are not observable, so *no* environment is able to do a handshake over one of them.

- (24) To the outside world the original refusal set will look like the relabeled one (this works, because f injective implies f *bijective*).

- (25) The highest prioritized agent may always perform its transitions.

- (26) Since *inActs* gives *every* possible action for a guard, the refusal set for G_2 transitions should exactly be extended with $inActs(G_1)$. Since τ is not allowed in refusal sets, $\tau \notin inActs(G_1)$ is a necessary condition.
  Furthermore it must be the case that the G_2 action is not itself in the new refusal set - it does not make sense to have an agent perform an action that is *never* observable, because the corresponding output action is forbidden by the transition's refusal set. This is consistent with the intuitive description of $\vdash_R A \xrightarrow{\alpha} A'$ - an environment cannot both refuse α and be prepared to match it.

- (27) + (28) *outActs* gives exactly *every* possible output action for an agent, and one of the agents in a parallel composition cannot do a transition if the other one violates the refusal set condition (since the two subagents are part of each other's environments).

- (29) The refusal set for the handshake is the union of the individual refusal sets - otherwise one of the handshake transitions would be impossible.

2.5 Results for the transition system

Not surprisingly (since an environment cannot both refuse an action and match it) we do indeed have:

Theorem 1 Let R be a refusal set, $\alpha \in Act$ and $A, A' \in Agt$: If $\vdash_R A \xrightarrow{\alpha} A'$ then $\alpha \notin R$

The following result is significant because it allows refusal sets to be represented as finite lists:

Theorem 2 If the agent A respects the given syntax, then any A-transition has a finite refusal set.

Furthermore $CCS^>$ extends CCS (since CCS is a syntactic subclass of $CCS^>$):

Theorem 3 Let A be a CCS agent (without any PRISUM that is): $\vdash_\emptyset A \overset{\alpha}{\to} A'$ iff $A \overset{\alpha}{\to} A'$

The relation to Camilleri[90] and Camilleri/Winskel[91] is established by:

Theorem 4 Let R, R' be refusal sets, $A, A' \in Agt^{JC}$, $\alpha \in Act$ and $\alpha \notin R'$:

$$\vdash_{R'}^{JC} A \overset{\alpha}{\to} A' \quad iff \quad \exists R \subseteq R'. \ \vdash_R A \overset{\alpha}{\to} A'$$

where $\vdash^{JC}$ represents the transition system used in Camilleri[90], and Agt^{JC} is the class of agents considered in Camilleri[90] (where the syntax is a bit more restrictive than mine).

3   A new definition of bisimulation and equivalence

The definition of strong observational equivalence is not quite so obvious as in Milner[89]. Consider the two agents P and Q defined as $P = \alpha.A + (\beta.B > \alpha.A)$ and $Q = \alpha.A + \beta.B$. Now we would of course expect P and Q to be equivalent, but for P we get the transition $\vdash_{\{\beta\}} P \overset{\alpha}{\to} A$ which *cannot* be matched directly by Q, since the only α-transition for Q is $\vdash_\emptyset Q \overset{\alpha}{\to} A$ The problem is that several subagents are syntactically equal, and therefore one gets several different refusal sets for the same action and derived agent.

Instead we would expect P and Q to be equivalent, if a transition for one of the agents under refusal set R, could be matched by the other agent under refusal set $R' \subseteq R$ (remember that refusal sets are considered to be *conditions* on transitions), since in the above example we do in fact also have $\vdash_\emptyset P \overset{\alpha}{\to} A$

Note that if every transition can be matched by a smaller or equal refusal set, then regardless of the environment the two agents do in fact have the same behaviour under the intuitive interpretation of $\to$. For closed agents (no free variables) we are lead to:

Definition 3 The symmetric relation $S \subseteq Agt \times Agt$ is a bisimulation with respect to $\to$, if $(P, Q) \in S$ implies for all $\alpha \in Act$, for all refusal sets R,
(1) Whenever $\vdash_R P \overset{\alpha}{\to} P'$ then for some Q', $\exists R'. \ R' \subseteq R \wedge \vdash_{R'} Q \overset{\alpha}{\to} Q' \wedge (P', Q') \in S$
(2) Whenever $\vdash_R Q \overset{\alpha}{\to} Q'$ then for some P', $\exists R'. \ R' \subseteq R \wedge \vdash_{R'} P \overset{\alpha}{\to} P' \wedge (P', Q') \in S$

Definition 4 Define strong observational equivalence by $\sim = \cup \{S | S \text{ is a bisimulation}\}$

Theorem 5 The relation $\sim$ is the largest bisimulation, and $\sim$ is an equivalence relation on closed agents satisfying $P \sim Q$ iff, for all $\alpha \in Act$, for all refusal sets R,
(1) Whenever $\vdash_R P \overset{\alpha}{\to} P'$ then for some Q', $\exists R'. \ R' \subseteq R \wedge \vdash_{R'} Q \overset{\alpha}{\to} Q' \wedge P' \sim Q'$
(2) Whenever $\vdash_R Q \overset{\alpha}{\to} Q'$ then for some P', $\exists R'. \ R' \subseteq R \wedge \vdash_{R'} P \overset{\alpha}{\to} P' \wedge P' \sim Q'$

We use the same approach as in Milner[89] to define strong observational equivalence for agents with free variables:

Definition 5 *Let A and B contain at most variables $\tilde{X} \subseteq VS^n$. Then*

$$A \sim B \quad iff \quad \forall \tilde{P} \subseteq Agt^n. \, A\{\tilde{P}/\tilde{X}\} \sim B\{\tilde{P}/\tilde{X}\}$$

Note that we could use Definition 5 as the general definition of equivalence, since syntactic substitution for a variable has no effect on closed terms.

We proceed to investigate the properties of $\sim$:

Theorem 6 $\sim$ *is a congruence (equivalence is preserved in all algebraic contexts).*

For the proof of Theorem 6 the following definitions and theorems are needed (partly analogously with Milner[89]):

Definition 6 *The symmetric relation $S \subseteq Agt \times Agt$ is a bisimulation up to $\sim$ with respect to $\rightarrow$, if $(P,Q) \in S$ implies for all $\alpha \in Act$, for all refusal sets R,*
(1) Whenever $\vdash_R P \xrightarrow{\alpha} P'$ then for some Q', $\exists R'. \, R' \subseteq R \land \vdash_{R'} Q \xrightarrow{\alpha} Q' \land P' \sim S \sim Q'$
(2) Whenever $\vdash_R Q \xrightarrow{\alpha} Q'$ then for some P', $\exists R'. \, R' \subseteq R \land \vdash_{R'} P \xrightarrow{\alpha} P' \land P' \sim S \sim Q'$

Theorem 7 *If S is a bisimulation up to $\sim$ then $\sim S \sim$ is a bisimulation.*

Theorem 8 *If S is a bisimulation up to $\sim$ then $S \subseteq \sim$.*

Theorem 9 *If $A \sim B$, then $inActs(A) = inActs(B) \land outActs(A) = outActs(B)$.*

As a last result (not related to Theorem 6), one might notice

Theorem 10 *On Agt^{JC} the equivalence from Camilleri[90] and Camilleri/Winskel[91] coincide with $\sim$*

4 A modal logic for priorities

I proceed to define a modal logic for analysing $CCS^>$ agents. As the labelling of transitions is changed from actions to actions combined with refusal sets, the same is done with the labelling of modalities. The logic then has the following syntax (largely taken from CW):

$$P \;::=\; X \mid T \mid F \mid \sim P \mid PorP \mid PandP \mid <\alpha,R>P \mid <.,R>P \mid [\alpha,R]P \mid [.,R]P$$
$$\mid min(X = P) \mid max(X = P)$$

where T and F mean true and false, $\alpha \in Act$, '.' means *any* action, R is a refusal set, $X \in PV$ is a propositional variable, every recursion *must* be guarded, negative occurrences of recursion variables are forbidden, $<\alpha, R>$ and $[\alpha, R]$ denote possibility and necessity respectively, and 'min' and 'max' denote minimal and maximal fixpoint.

What should the semantic meaning of modal formulae be? Most of the usual semantics can be used, but what about refusal sets? The semantics of refusal sets should have some resemblance to their meaning in the definition of bisimilarity (because intuitively the same formulae should be valid for two equivalent agents), so the following definition seems natural:

$$A \models < \alpha, R > P \quad iff \quad (\alpha \notin R) \wedge (\exists A', R' \subseteq R. \vdash_{R'} A \xrightarrow{\alpha} A' \wedge A' \models P)$$

$$A \models < ., R > P \quad iff \quad \exists \alpha \in Act. A \models < \alpha, R > P$$

This agrees with the intuitive idea, that if $A \models < \alpha, R > P \wedge R \subseteq R'$, then $A \models < \alpha, R' > P$ (if a formula is valid under a condition R, then it is also valid under a *stronger* condition R'). The reason for $\alpha \notin R$ is the implicit relation between α and R, that α cannot occur if the environment refuses α (represented by Theorem 1).

Furthermore the reductions $[\alpha, R]P \rightarrow \sim < \alpha, R > \sim P$ and $[., R]P \rightarrow \sim < ., R > \sim P$ are needed. The semantics of the rest of the syntax is not changed.

The following characterization theorem then holds:

Theorem 11 *The modal logic presented above is characteristic for $CCS^>$. That is, for all $P, Q \in Agt$: $P \sim Q$ iff $\forall$logic formulae $F. (P \models F \Leftrightarrow Q \models F)$*

5 Implementation of priorities in The Concurrency Workbench

5.1 Why the Concurrency Workbench?

CW is a tool for analysing CCS agents that provides a large number of different analysis methods. It is built in a modular way that better enables changing only the relevant parts of the code, and is state-based so the implemented transition system is relatively easy to find and change.

5.2 Objectives

First of all, a necessary objective for such an implementation is that it is conservative - if you do not consider priorities then the new CW should act exactly like the old one. This is achieved by definition and by Theorem 3: If all refusal sets are empty (no priorities are used), then the operational semantics and the logic for CCS and $CCS^>$ are the same.

Secondly, which parts of CW should in fact be changed? I have chosen for the time being to restrict my attention to the transition system, strong equivalence, logic formulae and model checking.

5.3 Changes

The main changes in basic routines and definitions are:

- Module 'BasicAgent': A definition of refusal sets has been added. The PRISUM operator has been added to the datatype representing agents. The function 'transitions', which gives the possible transitions of an agent, has been changed according to the transition system presented above.

- Module 'AgentIO': The PRISUM operator has been added to the IO-syntax of agents (including the restriction on guards).

- Module 'PolyGraph': It was mainly the function 'mkgraph' (generates stategraphs from agents), that needed change. The list of possible successors to a state under a given action has been changed from a list of states to a list of (refusal set,state). The refusal set from each possible transition is attached to the successor state (*not* to the action) in order to follow the original structure of CW as closely as possible (thereby minimizing changes and easing the conservativity).

- Module 'PolyGraphOp': The generic equivalence check between agents is done by block partioning (see CW[1] for brief description of algorithm and further references) comparing so-called capabilities (a capability is a list of actions together with a list of blocks reachable through each action). If two states in a block have different capabilities, the block is split in two - two agents are equivalent if they end up in the same block. This function has been changed according to the changes in module 'PolyGraph', and the change in definition of bisimulation presented above. The definition of capabilities has to take refusal sets into account. A list of refusal sets, through which the block is reachable, is attached to each blocknumber (only the smallest possible refusal sets are recorded - two refusal sets belonging to the same block might be included in one another, because a block may contain more than one state).

- Module 'Logics': The definition of the logic for model checking has been changed to suit the modal logic presented above.

- Module 'HMLIO': IO of the modal logic is changed according to the changes in module 'Logics'. The changes are conservative, so that it is possible to use the old logic, and forget all about refusal sets.

- Module 'HMLChecker': The function 'check', that performs the validity check of modal formulae, has been changed according to the semantics for the modal logic presented above, reinterpreting the meaning of the modalities possibility and necessity.

5.4 Examples of sessions in the new Concurrency Workbench

The example below shows that PRISUM doesn't distribute over sum. It also illustrates the use of the new modal logic:

```
Command: strong equivalence
Agent: (a.nil > b.nil) + (c.nil > b.nil)
Agent: (a.nil + c.nil) > b.nil
false

Command: check strong proposition
Agent: (a.nil > b.nil) + (c.nil > b.nil)
```

Proposition: <b,{a} >T

true

Command: check strong proposition

Agent: (a.nil + c.nil) > b.nil

Proposition: <b,{a} >T

false

Note, that the proposition <b,{a,c} >T holds for *both* the above agents, so larger refusal sets *do* in fact make a difference in the logic.

This example shows how to implement a fair (cyclic) critical region (or a scheduler "on need"). Notice, that if only one of the processes wants the critical region, it gets it regardless of whose turn it is.

Command: bind identifier

Identifier: S1

Agent: a.S2 > b.S1

Command: bind identifier

Identifier: S2

Agent: b.S1 > a.S2

Command: check strong proposition

Agent: S1

Proposition: max(X.<a,{} >X)

false

Command: check strong proposition

Agent: S1

Proposition: max(X.<a,{b} >T & [a,{b}]X)

true

6 Conclusion

A new CCS-constructor > to treat priorities has been proposed (similar to Camilleri[90]). An implementable and hopefully intuitive transition system for the extended $CCS^>$ has been presented. The definitions of strong bisimilarity and strong equivalence have been changed accordingly. An extended modal logic has been presented. These features have been implemented in an existing analysis tool, in a way that allows the user to work freely with both CCS and $CCS^>$. To my knowledge, this is the only existing automated tool for investigating processes with priority.

In the future, I shall investigate weak bisimulations in connection with priorities, and possibly other equivalence criteria as well.

I plan to extend the work to a generalised analogue of the PRI PAR construct in OCCAM (PRI PAR is fairly restrictive), where it becomes sensible to allow output actions in guards.

7 Acknowledgements

Part of this note can be viewed as an extension of the PhD work done by Juanito Albert Camilleri on the notion of priority in CCS. My debt to the work underlying the Concurrency Workbench is clear. I wish to thank Juanito Camilleri and Glynn Winskel for discussions.

8 Reference list

Milner[89]: Milner, Robin, Communication and Concurrency, C.A.R. Hoare, Series editor, Prentice Hall, 1989

Winskel[89]: Winskel, Glynn, An Note on Model Checking the Modal ν -calculus, DAIMI PB - 279, Computer Science Department, Aarhus University, 1989

Camilleri[90]: Camilleri, Juanito A., Priority in Process Calculi, Ph.D. Thesis, Computer Laboratory, University of Cambridge, 1991

CW[1]: Cleaveland, R., Parrow, J. and Steffen, B., The Concurrency Workbench: A Semantics Based Tool for the Verification of Concurrent Systems, LFCS Report Series, ECS-LFCS-89-83, Department of Computer Science, University of Edinburgh, 1989

CW[2]: Cleaveland, R., Parrow, J. and Steffen, B., The Concurrency Workbench: Operating Instructions, LFCS-TN-10, 1988

CW[3]: Morley, Matthew J., Tactics for State Space Reduction on the Concurrency Workbench, LFCS Report Series, ECS-LFCS-90-109, Department of Computer Science, University of Edinburgh, 1990

OCC[84]: inmos. OCCAM Programming Manual, International Series in Computer Science, Prentice Hall, 1984

Camilleri/Winskel[91]: Camilleri, Juanito A., Winskel, Glynn, CCS with priority choice, to appear in proceedings of LICS 91

A Proof Assistant for PSF

S. Mauw & G.J. Veltink

Programming Research Group
University of Amsterdam
Kruislaan 403
1098 SJ Amsterdam
The Netherlands

Abstract
A description of a tool to support computer-aided construction of proofs for parallel systems is given. In contrast to the conventional approach based on state space exploration, we use an axiomatic approach. The axioms we use for the construction of proofs, are based on ACP. Besides these standard axioms we also consider tactics for shortening proofs. We use PSF (Process Specification Formalism), an extension of ACP with abstract data types, to describe the processes subject to the verification.

1. INTRODUCTION

One of the advantages of the use of formal techniques for the specification of parallel systems is that it enables formal verification of the correctness of such a specification. There are several approaches towards verification. One can verify certain properties of a specification, such as deadlock-freedom, fairness or starvation-freedom. A more general approach is to verify the truth of logic propositions about the execution traces of a specified system, see for example [HM85,TT91]. We will focus on a third approach, namely verifications of equality of two specifications, as developed in [Bae90]. Equality in this context can be interpreted in many ways, depending on the desired semantics.

A common way of proving that two processes are equal is by interpreting (or defining) the processes in some model, typically a graph model, followed by testing whether the interpretations are equal with respect to some congruence relation, such as observational equivalence or weak bisimulation. For finite process graphs several more or less efficient algorithms have been developed for determining these congruences [Fer91,GV90]. All of these algorithms suffer from the so-called state explosion problem. This problem comes from the fact that the number of states in a complex system is proportional to the product of the number of states of its parallel components.

An alternative is the algebraic or axiomatic approach, where a process expression is manipulated and proven equal to another process expression at a syntactic level, using an effectively given set of axioms. The advantage of this method over exploring the state space is that one can reason about the components or subsystems at a higher level of abstraction. Subsystems can be replaced by simpler ones and this way of pruning in the state graph results in simpler proofs. Another advantage is that an algebraic approach gives more insight into the reasons why a proof works or fails. This might give clues as to how faulty specifications can be repaired, and how correct specifications can be optimized. The axiomatic approach is also used in the PAM project [Lin91].

The restriction to finite state machines, or the class of regular processes, that is implied by the state exploration methods does not apply to the axiomatic approach. This way more complex processes, such as an unbounded queue, can be considered. The main

Note: This work was partially supported by ESPRIT Project no. 3006, CONCUR.

drawback of an axiomatic approach is that an equality guaranteed by some state space exploration algorithm need not be effectively constructable in the axiomatic system.

Computer tools supporting the axiomatic approach can be divided into two classes: theorem provers and proof assistants. The distinction is based on the level of mechanization of the process of proving. A simple proof assistant will have the form of an "electronic notebook" with accompanying software, which helps in rewriting the formulas that constitute the proof and will depend heavily on the interaction between people and machines. A more sophisticated theorem prover would make use of a number of heuristics to decide automatically what axioms to apply in what order.

ACP (Algebra of Communicating Processes) [BW90] is a process theory, which has been developed from an axiomatic viewpoint. Verifications of systems specified in ACP can be found in [Bae90] for example. The process specification language PSF [MV90] is an extension of ACP with abstract data types. It has a computer readable format and several computer tools have been developed to support specification in PSF, such as a syntax checker and a simulator.

In this paper we will describe how a proof assistant for PSF can be designed and the status of current preliminary investigation. This tool will be an aid in editing process expressions, selecting axioms that are applicable and applying these axioms. Preferably, sequences of applications of axioms which are commonly used in proofs must be offered using some shorthand. We will call these sequences: *tactics*.

This article is organised in the following way. We start off with a description of the toolkit for PSF which is under development followed with a short introduction to ACP. After that we will explain what we consider a proof within the proof assistant, give the axioms that are used to construct proofs and discuss the tactics that have been implemented. We conclude with a description of the implementation and an example to demonstrate the current status of the proof assistant.

2. THE PSF PROJECT

The PAT (Process Algebra Tools) project aims at constructing an environment of computer tools for studying concurrent systems, especially in the setting of the formal concurrency theory ACP (Algebra of Communicating Processes) [BW90]. Several tools had been written before the PAT project started, but because of the lack of a unified guiding framework there were many inconsistencies between the tools. The first step towards the construction of an integrated system in PAT has been the development of a language for specifying ACP-like processes in general. The resulting language PSF (Process Specification Language) is a formal specification language suitable for specifying concurrent systems. An introduction to the subject including examples is [MV89a], and the formal definition of PSF is given in [MV90].

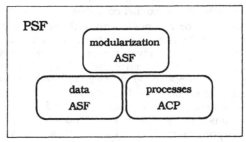

Figure 1.

PSF has been designed as the high-level specification language in the PAT project. It combines ACP with abstract data types. On the one hand PSF is based on ACP, that is for the part that is used to describe processes. The syntax of this part is kept as close as possible to the more informal syntax of ACP. On the other hand PSF is based on ASF

(Algebraic Specification Formalism) [BHK89]. This formalism is used to describe the data types with which processes can be parameterized. PSF also inherits its modularization concepts and its support of generics from ASF. Figure 1 gives a graphical representation of the constituting parts of PSF.

In contrast to PSF, a low-level language called TIL (Tool Interface Language) [MV89b] has been designed. TIL serves as a common kernel language for all the tools to be supported by the environment, including: a simulator; a proof assistant; a term rewriter and a bisimulation verifier. Although TIL was primarily intended as a dedicated interface language for the tools in the PAT project, it was designed so that it could be used on its own. From a semantical point of view TIL has the same expressive power as the combination of ACP and ASF. The main advantage of using TIL is that many parts of the toolkit can be reused. Because TIL is used mainly by tools, its readability for humans is of secondary importance.

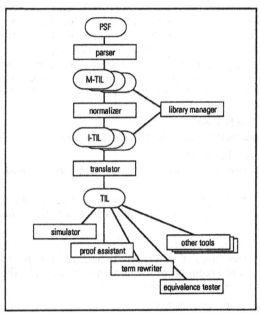

Figure 2.

At the centre of the toolkit, see figure 2, is the Tool Interface Language (TIL) through which all tools can communicate. From the picture we see that the PSF specification at the top is translated into TIL using two intermediate languages called M-TIL and I-TIL. In the course of this translation the library manager is used which supports and controls separate compilation of PSF modules.

Each PSF module is translated into exactly one M-TIL module. M-TIL is similar to TIL, but it still contains information about the modular structure of the specification. Because TIL supports no modular structure at all, a PSF specification has to flattened. This is done in the normalization phase in which the I-TIL language is used. The complete description of the translation from PSF to TIL can be found in [Vel90].

At the bottom of the picture we see the several tools. At the moment a simulator, a term rewriter and a proof assistant have been implemented. We are currently working on interfacing the toolkit with an existing tool for equivalence testing. Future plans for other tools include, for example, a compiler that compiles a PSF specification into a traditional programming language.

This approach of implementing an environment by using clearly defined intermediate languages, serves several purposes. The main reason is that it results in a layered design, in which humans can inspect specifications on a high level through PSF and in which the tools have access to the specifications through a low level representation tailored to their needs. This means in particular that the process of parsing and type checking of PSF is of no concern to the tools which will use a very simple parser to read the intermediate language. The second reason for using TIL and its derivatives is that having a definition of an intermediate language, construction of software can be started in parallel and so for example the construction of the simulator had not to wait for the parser and normalizer to be completed. The final reason for using TIL is that for new versions of PSF, or formalisms with comparable functionality, the toolkit can be easily adapted. Writing a new front-end for the specific language will be sufficient. In this way reusability of large parts of software, present in the tools, is guaranteed.

3. ACP

In this section we will give a brief introduction to ACP. This introduction is by no means intended to be complete. For more specific information on ACP we refer to [BW90]. The notation used here will differ slightly from the one used in the aforementioned book, because we have to deal with a computer readable syntax.

ACP starts from a set of objects, called atomic actions, atoms or steps. Atomic actions are the basic and indivisible elements of ACP. The (finite) set of constants is called A. On this set A there is defined a fixed partial function $\gamma : A \times A \to A$. Moreover we have two special constants:

- delta or deadlock. (delta $\notin A$)
  deadlock is the acknowledgement that there is no possibility to proceed.

- skip or silent action. (skip $\notin A$)
  skip represents the process terminating after some time, without performing any observable action.

Processes are constructed by combining constants and processes by operators. In the following introduction of the operators, a,b,c will stand for constants and x,y,z for processes.

- +, alternative composition or sum.
  $x + y$ is the process that first makes a choice between its summands x and y, and then proceeds with the execution of the chosen command. In the presence of an alternative, deadlock is never chosen.

- ·, sequential composition or product.
  $x \cdot y$ is the process that executes x first and continues with y after termination of x.

- ‖, parallel composition or merge.
  $x \parallel y$ is the process that represents the simultaneous execution of x and y.

- ⫞, left merge.
  $x \lfloor\!\lfloor y$ is the process that represents the simultaneous execution of x and y in which the first action to be performed must come from x.

- |, communication merge.
  $x \mid y$ is the process that represents the simultaneous execution of x and y in which the first action to be performed must be a communication between an action from x and an action from y.

- encaps(H,x), encapsulation.
  encaps(H,x) is the process x without the possibility of performing from the set of actions H ($H \subseteq A$).

- hide(I,x), abstraction.
  hide(I,x) is the process x without the possibility of observing actions from the set of atomic actions I ($I \subseteq A$). This is achieved by renaming all atoms from I in x into *skip*.

4. PROOFS

In this section we will shortly discuss what we consider a proof in the setting of the proof assistant. A verification of a process expression consists of a stepwise transformation of this process expression into another one. This transformation can be seen as a proof that both expressions are equal in a certain process semantics. The semantics depends on the axioms used within the proof assistant. In the current implementation we use the weak bisimulation semantics [BW90].

In the next section we will give the axioms used by the proof assistant. If every step in a proof can be motivated by one of the given axioms, it can be considered correct. Using this technique, correctness of, say, a communication protocol is demonstrated by constructing a proof that the protocol specification and the service specification denote the same process. Computer support in construction of proofs can be applied in the editing of an expression, the selection of suitable axioms, the application of trivial transformation sequences, the report generation of the proof and to check manually constructed proofs.

5. AXIOMS

The axioms for ACP, describing the operators presented in section 3, can be transformed into a complete term rewriting system modulo commutativity and associativity [AB90]. The axioms given here should also be read as a TRS in which the expressions on the lefthand-side are rewritten into the expressions on the righthand-side. Some rules are added that are not present in the standard axiomatization, but they serve to optimize the rewriting within the proof assistant. See LMRG_SEQMRG for an example of an equality that, although it can be derived from the basic axioms, is a useful property to shorten proofs.

$x + y = y + x$	ALT_COMM
$x + (y + z) = (x + y) + z$	ALT_ASOC
$x + x = x$	ALT_IDENT
$x + delta = x$	DLK_ALT

In the axioms we choose the left-associative form of an expression. See for example axiom ALT_ASOC. An exception to the this rule is SEQ_ASOC where the right-associative form is chosen because one is mostly interested in the first atom (head) of the sequential composition.

$(x + y) \cdot z = x \cdot z + y \cdot z$		SEQ_ALT
$(x \cdot y) \cdot z = x \cdot (y \cdot z)$		SEQ_ASOC
$delta \cdot x = delta$		DLK_SEQ
$x \parallel y = y \parallel x$		MRG_COMM
$x \parallel (y \parallel z) = (x \parallel y) \parallel z$		MRG_ASOC
$x \parallel y = (x \mathbb{L} y + y \mathbb{L} x) + x \mid y$		MRG_LMRG
$a \mathbb{L} x = a \cdot x$		LMRG_SEQ
$a \cdot x \mathbb{L} y = a \cdot (x \parallel y)$		LMRG_SEQMRG
$(x + y) \mathbb{L} z = x \mathbb{L} z + y \mathbb{L} z$		LMRG_ALT
$x \mathbb{L} delta = x \cdot delta$		LMRG_DLKSEQ
$delta \mathbb{L} x = delta$		DLK_LMRG
$a \mid b = \gamma(a,b)$	if γ is defined	CMM_DEF
$a \mid b = delta$	if γ is undefined	CMM_UNDEF
$x \mid delta = delta$		DLK_CMM
$x \mid y = y \mid x$		CMM_COMM
$(a \cdot x) \mid b = (a \mid b) \cdot x$		CMM_SEQ

$(a \cdot x) \mid (b \cdot y) = (a \mid b) \cdot (x \parallel y)$		CMM_SEQMRG
$(x + y) \mid z = x \mid z + y \mid z$		CMM_ALT
$encaps(H, a) = a$	if $a \notin H$	ENC_ATM
$encaps(H, a) = delta$	if $a \in H$	ENC_DLKATM
$encaps(H, skip) = skip$		ENC_SKP
$encaps(H, x + y) = encaps(H, x) + encaps(H, y)$		ENC_ALT
$encaps(H, x \cdot y) = encaps(H, x) \cdot encaps(H, y)$		ENC_SEQ
$hide(I, a) = a$	if $a \notin I$	HID_ATM
$hide(I, a) = skip$	if $a \in I$	HID_DLKATM
$hide(I, skip) = skip$		HID_SKP
$hide(I, x + y) = hide(I, x) + hide(I, y)$		HID_ALT
$hide(I, x \cdot y) = hide(I, x) \cdot hide(I, y)$		HID_SEQ
$x \cdot skip = x$		SKPACP_T1
$skip \cdot x + x = skip \cdot x$		SKPACP_T2
$a \cdot (skip \cdot x + y) = a \cdot (skip \cdot x + y) + a \cdot x$		SKPACP_T3
$x \cdot (skip \cdot y) = x \cdot y$		SKPACP_T1B

At the end of the table we have added some laws for *skip* which are known as Milner's τ-laws. Technically speaking the last axiom is not necessary, because it is a consequence of the first axiom. We have added it however because of the right-associative form used for the sequential composition.

6. TACTICS

Trying to prove facts by using only the axioms provided can be a tiresome job and therefore error-prone. As a typical example we found in one of our first experiments with the initial implementation of the proof assistant, that a simple proof that takes seven steps when done with pencil and paper takes more than sixty steps when applying only one axiom at a time. It goes without saying that a successful proof assistant should provide means to shorten such proofs. We have tried to cope with this problem by trying to mimic the reasoning used by human provers. In doing this, however, we remain exact all the time, that is we do not want to rely on *heuristics* of any kind. In this section we will discuss some of the tactics that we have found and that are implemented in the proof assistant. These tactics were developed by analyzing a number of manual ACP verifications from [Bae90].

In order to keep up with the state explosion problem it is crucial to be able to prune the state space as soon as possible. One of the strategies to follow is to try to produce and remove deadlocks as early as possible. By applying the axiom $delta \cdot x = delta$, we can prevent unnecessary rewriting within x. Deadlocks are created within encapsulation expressions when atomic actions are prohibited to occur because they are blocked. An atomic action that is blocked could escape the blocking because it can engage in a communication and get renamed. However, atomic actions that are blocked by an encapsulation operator and are not able to communicate can be renamed into deadlocks safely. We can get rid of the processes following a delta by applying the axiom: $delta \cdot x = delta$. This strategy is called *find deadlocks* in the proof assistant. A related strategy is *remove deadlocks*. This strategy removes, possibly multiple, deadlocks in one step by creating as much deadlocks as possible followed by applying: $delta + x = x$.

The next strategy is what we think one of the main strategies humans apply in constructing proofs in an ACP setting. In this strategy we try to separate a term X into a *head*, the first atom that is possible to occur, and the rest of the term, its *tail*. In analogy this strategy is called *head-tail*. In general the resulting term is not simply a head followed by a tail but it is of the form: $h_1 \cdot t_1 + h_2 \cdot t_2 + \ldots + h_n \cdot t_n$. In trying to create the head-tail expression each process variable that is encountered, is expanded. This means that the lefthand-side of a process definition is replaced by the appropriate righthand-side.

In fact this head-tail strategy is a combination of a number of axioms which relate closely to the expansion theorem from [BW90]. For brevity we state this axiom in the case we have a merge with two components X and Y, defined by

$X = a_1 \cdot X_1 + ... + a_n \cdot X_n$

$Y = b_1 \cdot Y_1 + ... + b_n \cdot Y_m$, then

$X \parallel Y = a_1 \cdot (X_1 \parallel Y) + ... + a_n \cdot (X_n \parallel Y) +$
$\qquad b_1 \cdot (X \parallel Y_1) + ... + b_m \cdot (X \parallel Y_m) +$
$\qquad (a_1 | b_1) \cdot (X_1 \parallel Y_1) + (a_1 | b_2) \cdot (X_1 \parallel Y_2) + ... + (a_n | b_m) \cdot (X_n \parallel Y_m)$

In case the merge is surrounded by an encapsulation operator, we have the following:

$$\text{encaps}(H, X \parallel Y) = \sum_{\{i | a_i \notin H\}} a_i \cdot (X_i \parallel Y) + \sum_{\{j | b_j \notin H\}} b_j \cdot (X \parallel Y_j) + \sum_{\{i,j | a_i | b_j \notin H\}} (a_i | b_j) \cdot (X_i \parallel Y_j)$$

Also other combinations of operators are supported.

As a corollary we have the *recursive head-tail* strategy. Here we have to be careful not just to try to apply head-tail on all sub-expressions otherwise we would be able to wind up in an endless recursion when we consider the following process e.g.: $X = a \cdot X$. Without explicitly stating these, a number of rules are built in that determine when to stop recursion.

Finally there are three strategies implemented that relate to the so-called conditional axioms [BBK87]. These axioms are very useful in breaking a complex specification down into subsystems. They support a modular approach towards verification.

Before giving the axioms we first have to introduce the notion of the alphabet $\alpha(x)$ of a process x. This is the collection of all atomic actions that process x can perform (see [BBK87] for a definition).

Since this notion is not decidable (see [BBK87]), the alphabet of process x will be approximated by the collection of all actions used in the specification of x or one of its sub-processes. This inexactness does not influence the validity of the axioms.

Another notation which will be used is the communication set $S \mid T$ of two sets of atoms, S and T. This is defined by

$\qquad S \mid T = \{ a | b \mid a \in S, b \in T \}$.

The first conditional axiom deals with pushing encapsulations through a merge.

$\qquad \text{encaps}(H, X \parallel Y) = \text{encaps}(H, X \parallel \text{encaps}(H', Y)),$

$\qquad\qquad$ where $H' = H - \{ a \in \alpha(Y) \mid ((\{a\} | \alpha(X)) \cap H^C) \neq \varnothing \} - \{ a \mid a \notin \alpha(Y) \}$.

The set H' is derived from H by first deleting all elements which can take part in a communication of which the resulting action is not encapsulated. Secondly we delete the actions from H that are superfluous because they do not occur in Y.

The second conditional axiom deals with pushing hiding through a merge.

$\qquad \text{hide}(I, X \parallel Y) = \text{hide}(I, X \parallel \text{hide}(I', Y)),$

$\qquad\qquad$ where $I' = I - \{ a \in \alpha(Y) \mid (\{a\} | \alpha(X)) \neq \varnothing \} - \{ a \mid a \notin \alpha(Y) \}$.

The third axiom is a combination of the first two.

$\qquad \text{hide}(I, \text{encaps}(H, X \parallel Y)) = \text{hide}(I, \text{encaps}(H, X \parallel \text{hide}(I', Y))),$

$\qquad\qquad$ where $I' = I - H - \{ a \in \alpha(Y) \mid (\{a\} | \alpha(X)) \neq \varnothing \} - \{ a \mid a \notin \alpha(Y) \}$.

These three axioms are easily proved correct for closed process expressions, using the conditional axioms from [BBK87].

The following example will clarify the use of these axioms. We consider an array of n components, serially connected to each other. Without giving a description of the behaviour of the components, we assume that each component has k states. Thus the parallel composition (before encapsulation and abstraction) has k^n states. Now assume that after encapsulation and abstraction of the complete parallel composition a fairly simple process with, say $n \cdot k$ states results, then we would have needed to visit these $n \cdot k$ states in order to reduce the system to the smaller size.

Now by applying the conditional axioms described above, we can focus on the subsystem consisting of the first two components, which has k^2 states, and reduce it to a system with $2 \cdot k$ states. The following step would be to focus on the subsystem obtained by combining this newly derived component and the third component, and so on. The result of this operation is that by restricting oneself to only sub-systems, the number of states visited decreases significantly. In this example the order of states visited would be $n^2 \cdot k^2$ instead of k^n.

7. THE IMPLEMENTATION OF THE PROOF ASSISTANT

As mentioned earlier the proof assistant is part of the PAT project. It has been developed on SUN workstations and is written in the programming language C [KR78] using the X-Windows system. The proof assistant is an interactive tool and currently we restrict ourselves to PSF specifications in which atomic actions can be parameterized with elements from finite data sets only.

The proof assistant uses TIL as input language so one has to translate a PSF specification into TIL using the PSF-compiler. After reading the TIL specification, the proof assistant interacts with the user through five windows which are described below.

PSF Window. This window displays a PSF version of the specification which is constructed by translating the input TIL back into PSF. The text can be scrolled using the mouse. *Verify Window.* This window shows all the steps of the proof constructed so far. In this window the user selects the subterms that are to be manipulated. *Operation Window.* This window contains several buttons among which the buttons to activate the tactics. The buttons are only active when there is a term selected in the Verify Window. *Rewrite Window.* Whenever a subterm is selected in the Verify Window, this window pops up and shows the rewrite actions possible according to the axioms. The desired action can be selected using the mouse. *Special Window.* This window contains some buttons for actions to: undo the last step, reset the complete verification, choose another term from the specification to rewrite, generate troff output of the proof from the Verify Window, quit the proof assistant.

8. VERIFICATION OF TWO ONE-BIT BUFFERS, AN EXAMPLE

Although an explanation of an interactive tool by means of a written text is less adequate than active hands-on experience, we will try to demonstrate the working of the proof assistant with an example. We will use the tools to construct a proof that a system of two one-bit buffers shows the same behaviour as one two-bit buffer. Facilities for handling data will not be used, since the current status of the tools will not allow this.

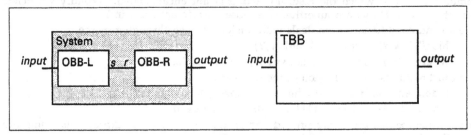

Figure 3.

THE SPECIFICATION

The system that we will consider consists of a parallel composition of two one-bit buffers, which are connected via an internal port. The left buffer (*OBB-L*) gets data from the environment via an *input*-port and sends it to the internal channel, while the right buffer reads data from this internal channel and hands it over to the environment via the *output*-port. The situation is as depicted in figure 3.

The shaded area is to indicate that we want to abstract from all actions at the internal port. In PSF the specification of this system looks as follows. First we define the behaviour of the two-bit buffer, which will be our target specification. The atomic actions *input* and *output* are defined, the process *TBB* which represents the two-bit buffer, and two auxiliary processes *TBB'* and *TBB''*.

The behaviour of the buffer is straightforward. It starts with an input action and comes in the state *TBB'* which indicates that there is one item in the buffer. *TBB'* can either do another input action and continue in state *TBB''* with two buffered items, or it can do an output action and restart with an empty buffer. Process *TBB''* can only do an output action and continue with *TBB'*.

For the system of two one-bit buffers, we define the processes *OBB-L* and *OBB-R*. Communication via the internal channel takes place by means of the r and s action. If both an r and an s action occur, this will result in a c action, which indicates successful communication.

The behaviour of the two one-bit buffers is defined straightforward. Now the System is defined as the parallel composition of these two buffers, while encapsulating unsuccessful communications (from the set H) and abstracting from communications via the internal channel (see the set I).

```
process module TBB
begin

   exports
     begin
       atoms
          input, output
       processes
          TBB, TBB', TBB''
     end

   definitions

     TBB   = input . TBB'
     TBB'  = input . TBB'' + output . TBB
     TBB'' = output . TBB'

end TBB
```

```
process module Buffers
begin

   imports
     TBB

   atoms
     s, r, c

   processes
     System, OBB-L, OBB-R

   sets of atoms
     H = { r, s }
     I = { c }

   communications
     s | r = c

   definitions

     OBB-L = input . s . OBB-L
     OBB-R = r . output . OBB-R
     System = hide(I,
              encaps(H, OBB-L || OBB-R ))

end Buffers
```

VERIFICATION

The aim is to verify that the processes *TBB* and *System* define the same process, by which one may conclude for example that a composition of two one-bit buffers can be used as an implementation for a two-bit buffer. Figure 4 contains the output of the tool.

After starting the tool one can select the process to be manipulated. This will be the System process, for which the definition is displayed. After clicking on the *hide* operator to select the entire expression, applying the head-tail operation yields expression A1. The *skip* action comes out when doing this again (A2). After selecting the first dot, an axiom can be chosen which removes internal *skip* actions in this context (A3). The last step is to attach a new name, *S'* for example, to the expression after the input action (A4).

Next we focus on the newly defined process *S'*. After three steps we have been able to prove it equal to an expression which contains a new process name *S''* and the already defined process *System*. Note that the order of the left and the right buffer in the definition of System is opposite to the order in B2. However these two subexpressions are recognized by the proof assistant as being equal.

The third step is to repeat the process for the new process name *S''*. This yields an expression in which the definition for *S'* is recognized automatically (C3).

```
System = hide(I, encaps(H, OBB-L || OBB-R ) )
( A1 )        = input . hide(I, encaps(H, s . OBB-L || OBB-R ) )
( A2 )        = input . skip . hide(I, encaps(H, OBB-L || output . OBB-R ) )
( A3 )        = input . hide(I, encaps(H, OBB-L || output . OBB-R ) )
( A4 )        = input . S'

S' = hide(I, encaps(H, OBB-L || output . OBB-R ) )
( B1 )        = input . hide(I, encaps(H, s . OBB-L || output . OBB-R ) ) +
                output . hide(I, encaps(H, OBB-L || OBB-L ) )
( B2 )        = input . S'' + output . hide(I, encaps(H, OBB-R || OBB-L ) )
( B3 )        = input . S'' + output . System

S'' = hide(I, encaps(H, s . OBB-L || output . OBB-R ) )
( C1 )        = output . hide(I, encaps(H, OBB-R || s . OBB-L ) )
( C2 )        = output . skip . hide(I, encaps(H, output . OBB-R || OBB-L ) )
( C3 )        = output . hide(I, encaps(H, output . OBB-R || OBB-L ) )
( C4 )        = output . S'
```

Figure 4.

The result of this manipulation is that we have given a derivation that the process *System* is the solution of the following set of equations.

```
System        = input . S'
S'            = input . S'' + output . System
S''           = output . S'
```

Figure 5.

Now using the Recursive Specification Principle (see [BW90]) we can conclude that *System* and *TBB* in fact define the same process. This last step of reasoning has not yet been implemented in the proof assistant.

9. CONCLUSIONS

In this article we have given the description of a system that can be used to assist in the process of proving properties of process specifications. We think of the proof assistant as it is now, more as a somewhat smart electronic notebook than a full-fledged proof constructing system. It never has been our aim to be able to generate proofs automatically.

Even so we think there are still a large number of subjects on which the proof assistant can be improved. In the current version the axioms are 'hard-wired' into the code. The system would be more flexible if the user is allowed to enter a set of axioms of his own. In this way the user would also be able to select a different process semantics than the weak bisimulation that we have implemented. To be able to achieve this, a language for representing axioms has to be developed. Moreover one can think of an extension of the PSF language that allows to express proofs, which can be checked automatically afterwards.

We think that the conventional method of state space exploration and axiomatic approach should go hand in hand. In this way the axiomatic approach can be used to cut down the state space into several components which can then be checked by state space exploration. Although the implementation of the proof assistant has not been finished yet, we are encouraged by the fact that the tool is already used by people that are not involved in the PAT project. Experiences show that even for the relatively small examples, which it has been applied to, the tool is an important aid in constructing and analyzing specifications. Several suggestions for other tactics for special classes of specification domains are under consideration.

The authors would like to thank Bob Diertens for his practical work on the proof assistant and Ben Thompson for proofreading this paper and suggesting several improvements.

10. REFERENCES

[AB90]   G.J. Akkerman & J.C.M. Baeten, Term rewriting analysis in process algebra, Report P9006, Programming Research Group, University of Amsterdam, 1990.

[Bae90]   J.C.M. Baeten (ed.), Applications of Process Algebra, Cambridge Tracts in Theoretical Computer Science 17, Cambridge University Press, 1990.

[BBK87]   J.C.M. Baeten, J.A. Bergstra & J.W. Klop, Conditional axioms and a/b-calculus in process algebra, in: Proceedings IFIP Conference on Formal Description of Programming Concepts III, Ebberup, (M. Wirsing, ed.) pp. 77-103, North-Holland, 1987.

[BHK89]   J.A. Bergstra, J. Heering & P. Klint, The algebraic specification formalism ASF, in: Algebraic specification, J.A. Bergstra, J. Heering & P. Klint (eds.), pp. 1-66, ACM Press Frontier Series, Addison-Wesley 1989.

[BW90]   J.C.M. Baeten & W.P. Weijland, Process Algebra, Cambridge Tracts in Theoretical Computer Science 18, Cambridge University Press, 1990.

[Fer91]   J.C. Fernandez, Aldébaran, A tool set for deciding bisimulation equivalences, in: Proceedings CONCUR '91, Amsterdam, (J.C.M. Beaten & J.A. Bergstra, eds.), 1991. (to appear in LNCS series).

[GV90]   J.F. Groote & F.W. Vaandrager, An efficient algorithm for branching bisimulation and stuttering equivalence, in: Proceedings 17th ICALP, Warwick, (M.S. Paterson, ed.) LNCS 443, pp. 626-638, Springer Verlag, 1990.

[HM85]   M. Hennessy & R. Milner, Algebraic Laws for Nondeterminism and Concurrency, Journal of the Association for Computing Machinery, vol. 32, nr. 1, pp. 137-161, 1985.

[KR78]   B.W. Kernighan & D.M. Ritchie, The C programming language, Prentice-Hall, 1978.

[Lin91]   H. Lin, PAM: A Process Algebra Manipulator, this volume.

[MV89a]   S. Mauw & G.J. Veltink, An introduction to PSF_d, in: Proc. International Joint Conference on Theory and Practice of Software Development, TAPSOFT '89, (J. Díaz, F. Orejas, eds.) LNCS 352, pp. 272-285, Springer Verlag, 1989.

[MV89b]   S. Mauw & G.J. Veltink, A Tool Interface Language for PSF, Report P8912, Programming Research Group, University of Amsterdam, 1989.

[MV90]   S. Mauw & G.J. Veltink, A process specification formalism, Fundamenta Informaticae XIII (1990), pp. 85-139, IOS Press, 1990.

[TT91]   B.C. Thompson & J.V. Tucker, Equational specification of Synchronous Concurrent Algorithms & Architectures, University College of Swansea, Technical Report, 1991. (in preparation)

[Vel90]   G.J. Veltink, From PSF to TIL, Report P9009, Programming Research Group, University of Amsterdam, 1990.

Avoiding state explosion by composition of minimal covering graphs[1]

Alain FINKEL
LIFAC
Ecole Normale Supérieure de Cachan
61 Avenue du Président Wilson
F-94235 CACHAN cedex

Laure PETRUCCI
CEDRIC-IIE
18 allée Jean Rostand, BP 77
F-91002 EVRY cedex

Abstract

In this paper, we study composition and decomposition of Petri nets via a common set of places or transitions. We are interested in automatic verification of Petri nets properties from the point of view of reusability of partial results already obtained. We give two algorithms which allow to compute the minimal covering graph of a Petri net by composing the minimal covering graphs of each of its modules.

1 Introduction

Composition/Decomposition of Petri nets is a key problem, as well as concerns specification as verification of properties. This problem was already tackled in [Bou90], [Hac76], [Sou90], ..., but generally sub-classes of Petri nets were studied (state machine decomposable nets, bounded nets). When a system is specified with general Petri nets, one does not know, a priori, whether the net is bounded or not. Moreover, imposing to the places to be bounded may introduce unwanted deadlocks and change the demanded service.

We studied in [FP91] the properties preserved by composition/decomposition mechanisms. The techniques considered consist in composing two nets by fusion of common transitions or fusion of common places. They are applied to Petri nets in general, i.e. without any restricition. However some properties are not shared by a net and its subnets : two subnets can have the same property P, and their composed net can eventually not satisfy P. The main analysis methods for Petri nets are the calculus of invariants or of the covering graph. The first method does not allow to automatically deduce properties of the Petri net. But we know that the covering graph of a net allows to verify most properties. However, in some cases, the computation of the covering graph is too long. Our approach

---

[1] Work supported by the Esprit Project DEMON (BRA 3148) and C[3].

consists in using the minimal covering graph (which is the smallest covering graph) and to compute it not with the usual global and centralised method, but with a local and distributed method using a given decomposition of the Petri net.

So, in this paper, we study composition of minimal covering graphs of Petri nets composed via a common set of places or a common set of transitions. More precisely, we are interested in the construction of the minimal covering graph of a net using the minimal covering graphs of its subnets. Let us notice that a first study from Bourguet ([Bou90]) dealt with composition of reachability graphs for bounded Petri nets. In the case of unbounded Petri nets, covering graphs are needed. As the minimal covering graph of a net is both unique and as small as possible, composition of minimal covering graphs can easily be performed.

Basic notions about Petri nets can be found in [Rei85]. We first recall some notions about the minimal covering graph of a net. Then, we give two new algorithms which compute the minimal covering graph of a net from those of its subnets. The efficiency of these algorithms, as concerns time, can be increased by parallelising the calculus of the minimal covering graphs of each of the subnets.

2 The minimal covering graph of a Petri net

The classical Karp-Miller covering graph ([KM69]) is sometimes too large to be computed. The minimal covering graph ([Fin90]) is the smallest covering graph which allows to verify the same properties as the usual covering graph.

Definition 2.1([Fin90])
A *coverability set* CS(PN) of a Petri net PN = $<P,T,V,M_0>$ is a subset of $(N \cup \{\omega\})^P$ such that the two following conditions hold :
(i)   for every reachable marking $m \in RS(PN)$, there is a marking $m' \in CS(PN)$ such that $m \leq m'$,
(ii)   for every marking $m' \in CS(PN)-RS(PN)$, there is an infinite strictly increasing sequence of reachable markings $\{m_n\}$ converging to m'.
A coverability set CS(PN) is *minimal* iff no proper subset of CS(PN) is a coverability set of PN.

Lemma 2.2([Fin90])
The minimal coverability set is finite and unique.

Definition 2.3([Fin90])
A *coverability graph* of a Petri net PN = $<P,T,V,M_0>$ is a labelled directed graph $<N,L,A>$ where the set of nodes N is a coverability set of PN, L=T and there is an arc $(m,t,m') \in A$ iff $m(t>m'$. The *minimal coverability graph* of a Petri net PN is the coverability graph such that its set of nodes is the minimal coverability set.

The algorithm to construct the minimal covering graph of a net can be found in [Fin90]. However, the algorithms we will present in the next sections are very similar, as they are derived versions.

Theorem 2.4 ([Fin90])
Let PN be a Petri net and MCG(PN) its minimal covering graph.
(i)   The reachability tree RT(PN) is infinite iff there is at least one circuit in MCG(PN).
(ii)   The reachability set RS(PN) is infinite iff there is at least one symbol ω in MCG(PN).
(iii) A place p is not bounded iff there is at least one marking $m \in$ MCG(PN) such that $m(p)=\omega$.
(iv)   A transition t is quasi-live iff there is at least one marking $m \in$ MCG(PN) such that for every place p, $m(p) \geq Pre(p,t)$.

Proposition 2.5 ([Fin90])
The minimal covering graph is computable, finite and unique.

We are interested in composing nets either by fusion of common transitions or by fusion of common places. The definitions and properties of these compositions were introduced in [FP91].
We first recall the composition by fusion of transitions.
We consider two nets with distinct places and two kinds of transitions : proper ones, and transitions common to both nets. So, we study two nets N_1 and N_2 such that :

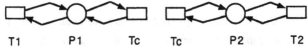

$$T_1 \qquad P_1 \qquad T_c \qquad T_c \qquad P_2 \qquad T_2$$

where T_1 (T_2) is the set of transitions proper to N_1 (N_2), T_c is the set of transitions common to both nets, and P_1 (P_2) is the set of places of N_1 (N_2).
We obtain, by fusion of transitions common to N_1 and N_2, the following net N_0 :

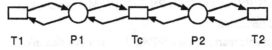

$$T_1 \qquad P_1 \qquad T_c \qquad P_2 \qquad T_2$$

Composition by fusion of places is defined in a similar way. We consider two nets with distinct transitions and two kinds of places : proper ones, and places common to both nets. So, we study two nets N_1 and N_2 such that :

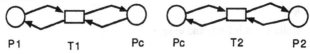

$$P_1 \qquad T_1 \qquad P_c \qquad P_c \qquad T_2 \qquad P_2$$

where P_1 (P_2) is the set of places proper to N_1 (N_2), P_c is the set of places common to both nets, and P_1 (P_2) is the set of transitions of N_1 (N_2).

We obtain, by fusion of places common to N_1 and N_2, the following net N_0 :

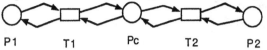

P1   T1   Pc   T2   P2

<u>Notation</u> : every marking M of N_0 can be decomposed into $M=(M_1,M_c,M_2)$ where M_1 is the marking of places of P_1, M_2 is the marking of places of P_2 and M_c is the marking of places of P_c.

3 Fusion of transitions

We now build the minimal covering graph of a net N_0 obtained by composing two subnets N_1 and N_2 by fusion of common transitions. A marking M of net N_0 can be divided into two parts : a marking M_1 corresponding to places of P_1 and a marking M_2 corresponding to places of P_2.

The construction of MCG0, minimal covering graph of net N_0, from MCG1 and MCG2, minimal covering graphs of nets N_1 and N_2, is done using the following algorithm :

```
MCG1 := minimal covering tree of N1;
MCG2 := minimal covering tree of N2;
/* construction of MCG0 := minimal covering graph of N0 */
unprocessed_nodes := {create_node(r,M0)};        /* M0=(M1,M2) is the marking of root r */
processed_nodes := Ø;
while unprocessed_nodes ≠ Ø;
    select some node n ∈ unprocessed_nodes;
    unprocessed_nodes := unprocessed_nodes - {n}; /*m is the marking of n and m' the one of n' */
    case n : [1..4] of
        1: there exists a node n' ∈ processed_nodes such that m = m' :
           processed_nodes := processed_nodes + {n};
           exit;
        2: there exists a node n' ∈ processed_nodes such that m < m' :
           remove_node(n; MCT);
           exit;
        3: there exists a node n'∈ processed_nodes such that m > m' :
           m2 := m;
           ancestor := false;
           for all ancestors n1 of n such that m1<m do
               for all places p such that m1(p)<m(p) do
                   m2(p) := ω;
               endfor
           endfor
           if there exists an ancestor n1 of n such that m1<m2
               then ancestor := true;
                    n1 := first processed node, on the path from the root to n such that m1<m2;
                    m1 := m2;
                    remove_tree(n1; MCT);
                    remove from (processednodes + unprocessednodes) all nodes of tree(n1; MCT);
                    unprocessednodes := unprocessednodes + {n1};
           endif
           for every n1∈ processednodes such that m1<m2 do
```

```
                 | remove from (processednodes + unprocessednodes) all nodes of tree(n₁; MCT);
                 | remove_tree(n₁; MCT);
                 | remove_node(n₁; MCT);
              endfor
              if ancestor = false
              |  then   unprocessednodes := unprocessednodes + {n};
              endif
              exit;
       4: otherwise :                           /* compute sons of node n with marking m=(m₁,m₂) */
              nc₁ := the node of MCG1 with marking mc₁, comparable with m₁;
              nc₂ := the node of MCG2 with marking mc₂, comparable with m₂;
              for all transitions t ∈ T₁ s.t.there exists an arc mc₁ [t> mc₁' in MCG1 and m₁ [t> m₁' do
              |  create_node+arc((n',t,(m₁',m₂)); MCT);
              |  unprocessed_nodes := unprocessed_nodes + {n'};
              |  processed_nodes := processed_nodes + {n};
              endfor
              for all transitions t ∈ T₂ s.t. there exists an arc mc₂ [t> mc₂' in MCG2 and m₂ [t> m₂' do
              |  create_node+arc((n',t,(m₁,m₂')); MCT);
              |  unprocessed_nodes := unprocessed_nodes + {n'};
              |  processed_nodes := processed_nodes + {n};
              endfor
              for all transitions t ∈ T_c s.t. there exists an arc mc₁ [t> mc₁' in MCG1
              |  and an arc mc₂ [t> mc₂' in MCG2 and m₁ [t> m₁' and m₂ [t> m₂' do
              |  create_node+arc((n',t,(m'₁,m₂')); MCT);
              |  unprocessed_nodes := unprocessed_nodes + {n'};
              |  processed_nodes := processed_nodes + {n};
              endfor
              exit;
       endcase
   endwhile
unprocessednodes := maximal(unprocessednodes);
MCS := {label(n) ; n∈ processednodes };
identify_nodes_having_same_label(MCT; MCG);
for every arc (m,t,m') of MCG do
|  if not ( m[t>m' )
|  |  then   remove_arc((m,t,m'); MCG);
|  endif
endfor
```

Informal explanation :

We start with the initial marking $M_0=(M_{0_1},M_{0_2})$ of N_0. There exists one and only one marking M_1 comparable with M_{0_1} (related by the < relation) in MCG1 (property of the minimal covering graph). Likewise, there exists a unique marking M_2 comparable with M_{0_2} in MCG2. If there exists an arc $M_1[t>\dots$ in MCG1, with $t∈T_1$, then t may be firable in N_0 and, if it is the case, a similar arc is constructed in MCG0. If there exists an arc $M_2[t>\dots$ in MCG2, with $t∈T_2$, then t may be firable in N_0 and, if it is the case, a similar arc is constructed in MCG0. If there exists an arc $M_1[t>\dots$ in MCG1 and an arc $M_2[t>\dots$ in MCG2, with $t∈T_c$, then t may be firable in N_0, and if it is the case, the arc is constructed.

This is not only valid for the initial marking, but also for any reachable marking of N_0. To build MCG0, we already know which transitions are firable, and also part of the marking - the one corresponding tothe set of places not concerned by the firing of the transition, i.e. places of P_2 for a transition of T_1 and places of P_1 for a transition of T_2.

Proposition 3.1
The algorithm terminates.

5 Fusion of places

As for composition by fusion of transitions, we are going to study composition of minimal covering graphs when using composition of nets by fusion of common places.

A marking M of N_0 can be decomposed into three parts : a marking M_1 corresponding to places of P_1, a marking M_c corresponding to places of P_c and a marking M_2 corresponding to places of P_2.

We propose the following algorithm to compute the minimal covering graph of the entire net from those of the subnets :

```
finished := false;
∀i, kcᵢ := M0(pcᵢ);                    /* initial number of tokens in common place pcᵢ */
while not finished do
    MCG1 = minimal covering tree of N₁, with M₀₁(pcᵢ)=kcᵢ;
    MCG2 = minimal covering tree of N₂, with M₀₂(pcᵢ)=kcᵢ;

    ∀i, kcᵢ₁ := maxMCG1M(pcᵢ);          /* the higher number of tokens in pci in MCG1 */

    ∀i, kcᵢ₂ := maxMCG2M(pcᵢ);          /* the higher number of tokens in pci in MCG2 */

    if ∀i, kcᵢ₁ = kcᵢ₂
        then finished := true;          /* the bounds of places pcᵢ are the same in both nets */
    endif
    ∀i, kcᵢ := max(kcᵢ₁,kcᵢ₂);
    if there exists a sequence s and i,j, i≠j, s.t.:
        M[s>M' M(pcᵢ)>M'(pcᵢ) and M(pcⱼ)<M'(pcⱼ) in MCG1 or MCG2
        then finished := true;          /* if Pc is a singleton, this is not applied */
    endif
endwhile
/* construction of MCG0 := minimal covering graph of N₀ */
unprocessed_nodes := {create_node(r,M0)};    /* M0=(M₁,M₂) is the marking of root r */
processed_nodes := Ø;
while unprocessed_nodes ≠ Ø;

    select some node n ∈ unprocessed_nodes;
    unprocessed_nodes := unprocessed_nodes - {n}; /* m is the marking of n and m' the one of n' */
    case n : [1..4] of
        1: there exists a node n' ∈ processed_nodes such that m = m' :
            processed_nodes := processed_nodes + {n};
            exit;
        2: there exists a node n' ∈ processed_nodes such that m < m' :
            remove_node(n; MCT);
            exit;
```

3: there exists a node n'∈ processed_nodes such that m > m' :
   m_2 := m;
   ancestor := false;
   <u>for</u> all ancestors n_1 of n such that m_1<m <u>do</u>
      | <u>for</u> all places p such that $m_1(p)$<m(p) <u>do</u>
      | | $m_2(p)$:= ω;
      | <u>endfor</u>
   <u>endfor</u>
   <u>if</u> there exists an ancestor n_1 of n such that m_1<m_2
      | <u>then</u> ancestor := true;
      | n_1 := first processed node, on the path from the root to n such that m_1<m_2;
      | m_1 := m_2;
      | remove_tree(n_1; MCT);
      | remove from (processednodes + unprocessednodes) all nodes of tree(n_1; MCT);
      | unprocessednodes := unprocessednodes + {n_1};
   <u>endif</u>

   <u>for</u> every n_1∈ processednodes such that m_1<m_2 <u>do</u>
      | remove from (processednodes + unprocessednodes) all nodes of tree(n_1; MCT);
      | remove_tree(n_1; MCT);
      | remove_node(n_1; MCT);
   <u>endfor</u>
   <u>if</u> ancestor = false
      | <u>then</u> unprocessednodes := unprocessednodes + {n};
   <u>endif</u>
   <u>exit</u>;
4: otherwise :   /* compute sons of node n with marking m=(m_1,m_c,m_2) */
   nc_1 := node in one of the MCG1 computed, of marking comparable with (m_1,m_c);
   nc_2 := node in one of the MCG2 computed, of marking comparable with (m_2,m_c);
              /* in both cases, value 0 is returned if the node could not be found */
   <u>if</u> nc_1 = 0
      | <u>then</u> <u>for</u> all t ∈ T_1 such that (m_1,m_c) [t▷ (m_1',m_c') <u>do</u>
      | create_node+arc((n',t,(m_1',m_c',m_2)); MCT);
      | unprocessed_nodes := unprocessed_nodes + {n'};
      | processed_nodes := processed_nodes + {n};
      | <u>endfor</u>
      | <u>else</u> <u>for</u> all t ∈ T_1 s.t. there exists an arc (mc_1,mc_c)[t▷(mc_1',mc_c')
      | in one of the MCG1 computed and (m_1,m_c) [t▷ (m_1',m_c') <u>do</u>
      | create_node+arc((n',t,(m_1',m_c',m_2)); MCT);
      | unprocessed_nodes := unprocessed_nodes + {n'};
      | processed_nodes := processed_nodes + {n};
      | <u>endfor</u>
   <u>endif</u>
   <u>if</u> nc_2 = 0   /* both "if" are similar, but they are duplicated for easier reading */
      | <u>then</u> <u>for</u> all t ∈ T_2 such that (m_2,m_c) [t▷ (m_2',m_c') <u>do</u>
      | create_node+arc((n',t,(m_1,m_c',m_2')); MCT);
      | unprocessed_nodes := unprocessed_nodes + {n'};
      | processed_nodes := processed_nodes + {n};
      | <u>endfor</u>
      | <u>else</u> <u>for</u> all t ∈ T_2 such that there exists an arc (mc_2,mc_c)[t▷(mc_2',mc_c')
      | in one of the MCG2 computed and (m_2,m_c) [t▷ (m_2',m_c') <u>do</u>
      | create_node+arc((n',t,(m_1,m_c',m_2')); MCT);
      | unprocessed_nodes := unprocessed_nodes + {n'};
      | processed_nodes := processed_nodes + {n};
      | <u>endfor</u>
   <u>endif</u>
   <u>exit</u>;

```
  | endcase
endwhile
unprocessednodes := maximal(unprocessednodes);

MCS := {label(n) ; n∈ processednodes };
identify_nodes_having_same_label(MCT; MCG);
for every arc (m,t,m') of MCG do
  | if not ( m[t>m' )
  |   | then  remove_arc((m,t,m'); MCG);
  | endif
endfor
```

Informal explanation :

In the first loop, we compute the minimal covering graphs of each module. One of the subnets can add tokens to a common place. In this case the number of tokens in this place will be greater then the initial marking. So, these tokens can be used by the other subnet. Thus, we have to take this information into account.

The union of minimal covering graphs is defined as follows. We start with the initial state M_0 of net N_0. It can be decomposed into three parts : $M_0=(M_1,M_c,M_2)$, where M_1 (resp. M_2) is the marking of places of P_1 (resp. P_2) and M_c is the marking of places of P_c, common to both nets. Let us suppose that in one of the MCG1 (resp. MCG2) computed, there exists a marking (M_1',M_c') (resp. (M_2',M_c')) comparable with (M_1,M_c) (resp. with (M_2,M_c)). Let t be a transition of T_1 such that $(M_1',M_c')[t>$ in MCG1 (for MCG2, the operation is similar). If t is firable in the global net, then, we will obtain in MCG0 an arc $(M_1,M_c,M_2)[t>(M_1'',M_c'',M_2)$. We apply the same operation for the markings obtained.

When processing a marking M, if a marking M' comparable with marking M, was found in one of the MCG1 computed, then only transitions of T_1 firable from M are transitions firable from M'. It is the same for transitions of MCG2.

Proposition 5.1
The algorithm terminates.

Proof
The problem of the algorithm termination is not as simple as for the algorithm concerning composition by fusion of transitions. So we are going to detail the proof. For that purpose, proving that the first loop of the algorithm terminates is enough.

Let s be a generic term used to denote a firing sequence such that M[s>M'. Two cases may be encountered :

• $(\forall s \in T_i^*) ((\forall p \in P_c \ M'(p) \leq M(p))$ or $(\forall p \in P_c \ M(p) \geq M(p)))$.

Let us consider the first subcase : $\forall p \in P_c \ M'(p) \leq M(p)$. The bound of places is preserved. So, the algorithm terminates.

Let us now consider the second subcase : $\forall p \in P_c \ M'(p) \geq M(p)$. The nodes are uncomparable, by definition of the minimal covering graph. So, there exists a place p', not in P_c, such that $M(p')>M'(p')$, i.e. the marking of p' decreases when firing s. So, the algorithm stops.

• $\exists s \in T_i^*$ tq $((\exists p \in P_c \text{ tq } M'(p) > M(p))$ and $(\exists p' \in P_c \text{ tq } M'(p') < M(p')))$: in this case, we force the algorithm termination by setting variable finished to true. ◆

6 Example

Let us consider a railway with a two-way section. Trains circulate from East to West and from West to East. The driving rules on the two-way part of the railway are the following :
• there cannot be two trains going in opposite ways (otherwise, there would be collisions);
• there can be one or several trains going in the same direction;
• there are at most two trains on the section (for security reasons).
We model this problem with the following Petri net.

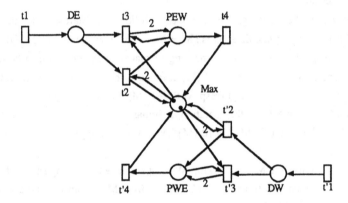

Trains going from East to West (from West to East) are generated by transition t1 (t'1) and are then in their departure place, DE (DW). The first train to go on the critical section fires transition t2 (t'2), while the following one would fire transition t3 (t'3). Place PEW (PWE) contains the trains going from East to West (from West to East) on the two-way part of the railway. Place Max contains the maximal number of trains which can still be allowed on this part. When a train wants to exit this system, it fires transition t4 (t'4).

We are going to calculate the minimal covering graph of this net. We use, in order to compare the different methods, two time criteria : the tests of transitions (is a transition firable?) and the calculus of the marking of a place (what is the new marking of a place p?).

First, we do the direct construction of the graph. The cost of this operation is 56 tt (tests of transitions) and 76 pm (calculus of places markings).

Secondly, we decompose the net into two nets communicating via place Max : the first net NP1 is composed of places DE, PEW, Max and transitions t1, t2, t3, t4; the second net NP2 is composed of places DW, PWE, Max and transitions t'1, t'2, t'3, t'4. The cost of the whole operation is 38 tt and 37 mp, when the covering graphs of the components are computed sequentially. When computed in parallel, the cost becomes 22 tt and 20 mp.

Thirdly, we decompose the net into three nets communicating via transitions : the first net NT1 is composed of place DE and transitions t1, t2, t3; the second net NT2 is composed of places PEW, PWE, Max and transitions t2, t3, t'2, t'3; the third net NT3 is composed of place DW and transitions t'1, t'2, t'3. The cost of the whole operation is 50 tt and 33 mp, when the covering graphs of the components are computed sequentially. When computed in parallel, the cost is 38 tt and 31 mp.

7 Conclusion

In this paper, we studied the composition of Petri nets by fusion of a set of common transitions or a set of common places. The goal of this work was to make verification of properties easier by reusing already computed results.

We presented two new algorithms to compute the minimal covering graph of a Petri net, knowing the minimal covering graphs of its modules.

The complexity (in terms of tests of firability for transitions) mainly depends on the chosen decomposition. If the decomposition of the net is badly chosen, the calculus by composition can be worse than a direct computation. The problem is thus to find out an optimal decomposition for a more efficient covering graph computation. In general, it would certainly be possible to obtain a decomposition such that the parallel computation of the n modules covering graphs would have almost the complexity of the direct computation divided by n. This problem was examplified in the previous section.

From a practical point of view, these algorithms will be implemented within the Petri nets environment PAPETRI ([BJP90]).

8 Bibliography

[BJP90] G. Berthelot, C. Johnen, L. Petrucci : *PAPETRI : Environment for the Analysis of PETRI nets*. Proceedings of the 2nd Computer-Aided Verification Workshop, New-Brunswick, USA, 18-21 June 1990.

[Bou90] A. Bourguet : *Etude de la concordance de comportement de deux réseaux de Petri. Application à la validation des protocoles : détection automatique des erreurs de conception*. Thesis of University Pierre et Marie Curie (Paris 6), September 1990.

[Bra83] G.W. Brams : *Réseaux de Petri : théorie et pratique*. Masson Ed, 1983.

[Fin90] A. Finkel : *The minimal coverability graph for Petri nets*. Proceedings of the 11th International Conference on Application and Theory of Petri nets, Paris, June 1990.

[FP91] A. Finkel, L. Petrucci : *Verification of net properties by composition/decomposition*. Research report CEDRIC, January 1991.

[Hac76] M. Hack : *Decidability questions for Petri nets*. PhD Thesis, Technical Report 161, MIT, Laboratory for Computer Science, Juin 1976.

[KM69] R.M. Karp, R.E. Miller : *Parallel program schemata*. JTSS 4, 1969, pp 147-195.

[Rei85] W. Reisig : *Petri nets*. Springer-Verlag, 1985.

[Sou90] Y. Souissi : *Une étude de la préservation de propriétés par composition de réseaux de Petri. Quelques extensions aux réseaux à files. Application à la validation de protocoles de communication*. Thesis of University Pierre et Marie Curie (Paris 6), February 1990.

Minimal covering graph of net N:

(DE, PEW, Max, DW, PWE)

(0,0,2,0,0)

t_1 t'_1

(1,0,2,0,0)   (0,0,2,1,0)

$\Rightarrow$

t_1 ↺ (ω,0,2,0,0)

t'_1 t_2

(ω,0,1,1,0)   (ω,1,1,0,0)

$\Rightarrow$

t_1, t'_1 ↺ (ω, 0, 2, ω, 0)

t_2 t'_2

t_1, t'_1 ↺ (ω,1,1,ω,0)   (ω,0,1,ω,1) ↻ t_1, t'_1

t_4 ⇅ t_3 t'_4 ⇅ t'_3

t_1, t'_1 ↺ (ω,2,0,ω,0)   (ω,0,0,ω,2) ↻ t_1, t'_1

cost:

transitions: 56

places: 76

Minimal covering graph of net NP1:   (NP2 with t' instead of t and markings (DW,PWE,Max))

(DE, PEW, Max)

(0,0,2)

t_1 ↓

(1,0,2)

$\Rightarrow$

(ω,0,2) ↻ t_1

t_2 ⇅ t_4

(ω,1,1) ↻ t_1

t_3 ⇅ t_4

(ω,2,0) ↻ t_1

cost:

transitions: 16

places: 17

Composition of minimal covering graphs of NP1 and NP2:

(DE, PEW, Max, DW, PWE)

(0,0,2,0,0)

t_1 t'_1

(1,0,2,0,0)   (0,0,2,1,0)

$\Rightarrow$

t_1 ↺ (ω,0,2,0,0)

t'_1 t_2

(ω,0,2,1,0)   (ω,1,1,0,0)

$\Rightarrow$

t_1, t'_1 ↺ (ω, 0, 2, ω, 0)

t_2 t'_2

t_1, t'_1 ↺ (ω,1,1,ω,0)   (ω,0,1,ω,1) ↻ t_1, t'_1

t_4 ⇅ t_3 t'_4 ⇅ t'_3

t_1, t'_1 ↺ (ω,2,0,ω,0)   (ω,0,0,ω,2) ↻ t_1, t'_1

cost:

transitions: 6

places: 3

Minimal covering graph of net NT1:   (NT3 with t' instead of t and markings (DW))

(DE)
(0)
t1 ↓
(1)

⇒   t1,t2,t3
      ↻ (ω)

cost:
transitions: 6
places: 1

Minimal covering graph of net NT2:

(PEW, Max, PWE)
(0,2,0)
t2 ↗ ↖ t'2
   t4 t'4
(1,1,0)   (0,1,1)
t3 ↕ t4   t'3 ↕ t'4
(2,0,0)   (0,0,2)

cost:
transitions: 30
places: 24

Composition of minimal covering graphs of NT1 and NT2:

(DE, PEW, Max, PWE)
(0,0,2,0)
t1 ↗   ↖ t'2
(1,0,2,0)   (0,0,1,1)

⇒

t1 ↻ (ω,0,2,0)
t2 ↗   ↖ t'2
   t4 t'4
t1 ↻ (ω,1,1,0)   (ω,0,1,1) ↺ t1
t3 ↕ t4   t'3 ↕ t'4
t1 ↻ (ω,2,0,0)   (ω,0,0,2) ↺ t1

cost:
transitions: 2
places: 1

Composition with the minimal covering graph of NT3:

(DE, PEW, Max, DW, PWE)
(0,0,2,0,0)
t1 ↗   ↖ t'1
(1,0,2,0,0) (0,0,2,1,0)

⇒

t1 ↻ (ω,0,2,0,0)
t'1 ↗   ↖ t2
(ω,0,2,1,0)   (ω,1,1,0,0)

t1,t'1 ↻ (ω,0,2,ω,0)
t2 ↗   ↖ t'2
   t4 t'4
t1,t'1 ↻ (ω,1,1,ω,0) (ω,0,1,ω,1) ↺ t1,t'1
t3 ↕ t4   t'3 ↕ t'4
t1,t'1 ↻ (ω,2,0,ω,0) (ω,0,0,ω,2) ↺ t1,t'1

cost:
transitions: 6
places: 6

"On the Fly" Verification of Behavioural Equivalences and Preorders

Jean-Claude Fernandez   Laurent Mounier
IMAG–LGI BP53X 38041 GRENOBLE Cedex

Abstract

This paper describes decision procedures for bisimulation and simulation relations between two transition systems. The algorithms proposed here do not need to previously construct them: the verification can be performed during their generation. In addition, a diagnosis is computed when the two transitions systems are not equivalent.

1 Introduction

One of the successful approaches used for the verification of systems of communicating processes is provided by behavioral equivalence and preorder relations, which allow to compare different descriptions of a given system. More precisely, if we note S (Specification) the most abstract description of the system and I (Implementation) the most detailed one, it is possible to check whether I is in fact an implementation of S in the following manner: from S and I, generate two Labeled Transition Systems (LTS for short) S_1 and S_2. Let R be an appropriate equivalence relation or preorder relation on LTS. Then, I implements S if and only if S_1RS_2.

Among the different equivalence relations which have been proposed, *bisimulations* appear to be the most attractive ones: these equivalences have a suitable semantics, are well defined, and for each of them a normal form exists which is minimal in number of states and transitions. An efficient algorithm [PT87] allows to compute the normal form of a LTS S for the strong bisimulation relation. This algorithm consists in refining a partition of its states until it becomes "compatible" with its transition relation. If n is the number of states of S, and m is the cardinality of its transition relation, then the time requirement for this algorithm is $O(m \log(n))$. Thus, an efficient decision procedure for the equivalence of two transition systems consists in computing the normal form of the union of the LTS.

Other equivalence relations are based on simulation preorders like *safety equivalence*, which characterizes exactly safety properties [BFG*91]. In this case, I implements S if and only if S_1RS_2 and S_2RS_1. A decision procedure for safety equivalence is based on the Paige & Tarjan algorithm [Fer89].

However, the main drawback of these methods is that the whole LTS have to be stored (i.e, the sets of states and transitions). Consequently, the size of the graphs which can be compared is limited, and this limit is easily reached when verifying real examples.

In this paper we extend the decision procedure for bisimulation equivalence relation, presented in [FM90], to simulation based equivalence or preorder. In fact, we show that it is sufficient to define a particular synchronous product between two LTS parametrized by a simulation or a bisimulation. Thus, the verification can be done during the process of the two transition systems ("on the fly" verification). In addition, in the case where two LTS are not comparable under the relation R, we produce as a *diagnosis* an execution sequence which leads in a *failure state*. This approach is similar to the one proposed in [JJ89], [BFH90] and [CVWY90], which deals with "on the fly" verification of linear temporal logic properties.

A version of our algorithm for a weaker bisimulation, for safety equivalence and for simulation preorder have been implemented in the tool ALDÉBARAN which allows to compare and reduce LTS with respect to several equivalence relations (strong bisimulation, observational equivalence [Mil80], acceptance model equivalence [GS86] and safety equivalence).

The paper is organized as follows: in section 2 we give the definitions used in the following pages, in section 3 the verification method for simulations and bisimulations is described, in section 4 we give the algorithm, and in section 5 we show how it can be adapted to provide a diagnostic. The results obtained when applying the usual algorithm and our improved one are also compared in this section.

2 Definitions

2.1 Labeled Transition Systems

Let *States* be a set of states, A a set of names (of actions), and τ a particular name of A, which represents an internal or hidden action. For a set X, X^* will represent the set of finite sequences on X.

A LTS is a tuple $S = (Q, A, T, q_0)$ where: Q is the subset of *States* reachable from q_0 with respect to T, A is a set of actions (or labels), $T \subseteq Q \times A \times Q$ is a labeled transition relation, and q_0 is the initial state.

For $a \in A$ and each state q, we consider the image set: $T^a[q] = \{q' \in Q \mid (q, a, q') \in T\}$.
We also use the notation $p \xrightarrow{a}_T q$ for $(p, a, q) \in T$. We consider the set of the actions which can be performed in a state q: $\mathcal{A}ct(q) = \{a \in A \mid \exists q' \in Q . q \xrightarrow{a} q'\}$.

Definition 2.1 *Let $S = (Q, A, T, q_0)$ be a LTS and q a state of Q.*
The set of the finite execution sequences from q (noted $Ex(q)$) is defined as follows:

$$Ex(q) = \{\sigma \in Q^* . \sigma(0) = q \ \wedge \ \forall i . 0 \le i < |\sigma| - 1, \exists a_i \in A . \sigma(i) \xrightarrow{a_i}_T \sigma(i+1)\}.$$

In the following, for a LTS S, the term *execution sequences* of S represents the set $Ex(q_0)$ (where q_0 is the initial state of S). Furthermore, an execution sequence is *elementary* if and only if all its states are distinct. The subset of $Ex(q)$ containing the elementary execution sequences of a state q will be noted $Ex_e(q)$.

2.2 Equivalences and Preorders

We recall the definition of the simulation and the bisimulation relations.

Notation 1 *Let $\lambda \subseteq A^*$, and let $p, q \in Q$. We write $p \xrightarrow{\lambda}_T q$ if and only if:*
$\exists u_1 \cdots u_n \in \lambda \ \wedge \ \exists q_1, \cdots, q_{n-1} \in Q \ \wedge \ p \xrightarrow{u_1}_T q_1 \xrightarrow{u_2}_T q_2 \cdots q_i \xrightarrow{u_{i+1}}_T q_{i+1} \cdots q_{n-1} \xrightarrow{u_n}_T q$.
$T^\lambda[q] = \{q' \in Q \mid q \xrightarrow{\lambda}_T q'\}$. *Let Π be a family of disjoint languages on A.*
$\mathcal{A}ct_\Pi(q) = \{\lambda \in \Pi \mid \exists q' . q \xrightarrow{\lambda} q'\}$.

Definition 2.2 *(simulation) Let Π be a family of disjoint languages on A. We define inductively a family of simulations R_k^Π by:*

$$R_0^\Pi = Q \times Q$$
$$R_{k+1}^\Pi = \{(p_1, p_2) \mid \forall \lambda \in \Pi . \forall q_1 . (p_1 \xrightarrow{\lambda}_T q_1 \Rightarrow \exists q_2 . (p_2 \xrightarrow{\lambda}_T q_2 \ \wedge \ (q_1, q_2) \in R_k^\Pi))\}$$

The simulation preorder is $\sqsubseteq^\Pi = \bigcap\limits_{k=0}^{\infty} R_k^\Pi$, *the simulation equivalence is* $\approx^\Pi = \sqsubseteq^\Pi \cap \sqsubseteq^{\Pi^{-1}}$.

Definition 2.3 *(bisimulation) Let Π be a family of disjoint languages on A. We define inductively a family of bisimulations R_k^Π by:*

$$
\begin{aligned}
R_0^\Pi \ &= \ Q \times Q \\
R_{k+1}^\Pi \ &= \ \{(p_1, p_2) \mid \forall \lambda \in \Pi . \ \forall q_1 . \ (p_1 \xrightarrow{\lambda}_T q_1 \ \Rightarrow \ \exists q_2 . \ (p_2 \xrightarrow{\lambda}_T q_2 \ \wedge \ (q_1, q_2) \in R_k^\Pi)) \\
& \qquad\qquad\qquad \forall q_2 . \ (p_2 \xrightarrow{\lambda}_T q_2 \ \Rightarrow \ \exists q_1 . \ (p_1 \xrightarrow{\lambda}_T q_1 \ \wedge \ (q_1, q_2) \in R_k^\Pi))\}
\end{aligned}
$$

The bisimulation equivalence for Π is $\sim^\Pi = \bigcap\limits_{k=0}^{\infty} R_k^\Pi$.

Remark 1 From these general definitions, several simulation and bisimulation relations can be defined. The choice of a class Π corresponds to the choice of an *abstraction criterion* on the actions. The *strong simulation* and the *strong bisimulation* are defined by $\Pi = \{\{a\} \mid a \in A\}$, the *w-bisimulation* is the bisimulation equivalence defined by $\Pi = \{\tau^* a \mid a \in A \ \wedge \ a \neq \tau\}$, the *safety preorder* is the simulation preorder defined by $\Pi = \{\tau^* a \mid a \in A \ \wedge \ a \neq \tau\}$ and the *safety equivalence* is the simulation equivalence where $\Pi = \{\tau^* a \mid a \in A \ \wedge \ a \neq \tau\}$.

Each equivalence relation R^Π defined on states can be extended to an equivalence relation comparing LTS in the following manner: let $S_i = (Q_i, A_\tau, T_i, q_i)$, for $i = 1, 2$ be two LTS such that $Q_1 \cap Q_2 = \emptyset$ (if it is not the case, this condition can be easily obtained by renaming). Then we define $S_1 \ R^\Pi \ S_2$ if and only if $(q_1, q_2) \in R^\Pi$ and $S_1 \ \not R^\Pi \ S_2$ if and only if $(q_1, q_2) \notin R^\Pi$.

3 Verification of Simulations and Bisimulations "On the Fly"

In this section, we describe the principle of a decision procedure which allows to check if two LTS S_1 and S_2 are similar or bisimilar without explicitly constructing the two graphs. We define the product $S_1 \times_{R^\Pi} S_2$ between two LTS S_1 and S_2, and then we show how the existence of R^Π between these two LTS can be expressed as a simple criterion which must hold on the execution sequences of this product. In the rest of the section, we consider two LTS $S_i = (Q_i, A_i, T_i, q_{0i})$, for $i = 1, 2$. We use p_i, q_i, p_i', q_i' to range over Q_i. We use R^Π and R_k^Π to denote either simulations or bisimulations $(R^\Pi = \bigcap\limits_{k=0}^{\infty} R_k^\Pi)$.

The LTS $S_1 \times_{R^\Pi} S_2$ is defined as a synchronous product of S_1 and S_2: a state (q_1, q_2) of $S_1 \times_{R^\Pi} S_2$ can perform a transition labeled by an action a if and only if the state q_1 (belonging to S_1) and the state q_2 (belonging to S_2) can perform a transition labeled by a. Otherwise,

- in the case of a simulation, if **only** the state q_1 can perform a transition labeled by a, then the product has a transition from (q_1, q_2) to the sink state noted *fail*.

- in the case of a bisimulation, if **only one** of the two states (q_1 or q_2) can perform a transition labeled by a, then the product has a transition from (q_1, q_2) to the sink state *fail*.

Definition 3.1 *We define the LTS $S = S_1 \times_{R^\Pi} S_2$ by:*
$S = (Q, A, T, (q_{01}, q_{02}))$, *with* $Q \subseteq (Q_1 \times Q_2) \cup \{fail\}$, $A = (A_1 \cap A_2) \cup \{\phi\}$, *and* $T \subseteq Q \times A \times Q$, *where* $\phi \notin (A_1 \cup A_2)$ *and fail* $\notin (Q_1 \cup Q_2)$.
T and Q are defined as the smallest sets obtained by the applications of the following rules: R0, R1 and R2 in the case of a simulation, R0, R1, R2 and R3 in the case of a bisimulation.

$$(q_{01}, q_{02}) \in Q \qquad\qquad [R0]$$

$$\frac{(q_1, q_2) \in Q,\ Act_\Pi(q_1) = Act_\Pi(q_2),\ q_1 \xrightarrow{\lambda}_{T_1} q_1',\ q_2 \xrightarrow{\lambda}_{T_2} q_2'}{\{(q_1', q_2')\} \in Q, \{(q_1, q_2) \xrightarrow{\lambda}_T (q_1', q_2')\} \in T} \qquad [R1]$$

$$\frac{(q_1, q_2) \in Q,\ q_1 \xrightarrow{\lambda}_{T_1} q_1',\ T_\lambda^2[q] = \emptyset}{\{fail\} \in Q, \{(q_1, q_2) \xrightarrow{\phi}_T fail\} \in T} \qquad [R2]$$

$$\frac{(q_1, q_2) \in Q,\ q_2 \xrightarrow{\lambda}_{T_2} q_2',\ T_\lambda^1[q] = \emptyset}{\{fail\} \in Q, \{(q_1, q_2) \xrightarrow{\phi}_T fail\} \in T} \qquad [R3\ bisimulation]$$

Let's notice that $(p_1, p_2) \xrightarrow{\phi}_T fail$ if and only if $(p_1, p_2) \notin R_1^\Pi$.

The following proposition allows to express that S_1 and S_2 are not comparable against R^Π in terms of the execution sequences of $S_1 \times_{R^\Pi} S_2$.

Proposition 3.1 *Let $S = (Q, A, T, q_0)$ be the product $S_1 \times_{R^\Pi} S_2$. Then, $(q_{01}, q_{02}) \notin R^\Pi$ if and only if it exists an elementary execution sequence σ of S ($\sigma \in Ex_e(q_{01}, q_{02})$) such that:*

- $\sigma = \{(q_{01}, q_{02}) = (p_0, q_0), (p_1, q_1), \dots (p_k, q_k), fail\}$.
- $\forall i.\ 0 \le i \le k,\ (p_i, q_i) \notin R_{k-i+1}^\Pi$ and $(p_i, q_i) \in R_{k-i}^\Pi$.

If one of the two LTS is deterministic, proposition 3.1 can be improved.

Proposition 3.2 *Let $S = (Q, A, T, q_0)$ be the product $S_1 \times_{R^\Pi} S_2$ and let us suppose that S_2 is deterministic (or S_1 if the $(R_k^\Pi)_{k \ge 0}$ are bisimulations). Then:*
$S_1 \not\!\!R^\Pi S_2 \Leftrightarrow \exists \sigma \in Ex(q_{01}, q_{02}) . \exists k > 0 . \sigma(k) = fail$.

According to this proposition, if at least one of the two LTS S_1 or S_2 (resp. S_2) is deterministic then S_1 and S_2 are not bisimilar (resp. similar) if and only if it exists an execution sequence of $S_1 \times_{R^\Pi} S_2$ containing the state *fail*.

4 Algorithms

In the previous section, we have expressed the bisimulation and the simulation between two LTS S_1 and S_2 in terms of the existence of a particular execution sequence of their product $S_1 \times_{R^\Pi} S_2$. Now we show that this verification can be realized by performing depth-first searches (DFS for short) on the LTS $S_1 \times_{R^\Pi} S_2$. Consequently, the algorithm does not require to construct the two LTSpreviously : the states of $S_1 \times_{R^\Pi} S_2$ are generated during the DFS ("on the fly" verification), but not necessarily all stored. And the most important is that transitions do not have to be stored.

We note n_1 (resp. n_2) the number of states of S_1 (resp. S_2), and n the number of states of $S_1 \times_{R^\Pi} S_2$ ($n \le n_1 \times n_2$). We describe the algorithm considering the two following cases:

Deterministic case: if R^Π represents a simulation (resp. a bisimulation) and if S_2 (resp. either S_1 or S_2) is deterministic, then, according to proposition 3.2, it is sufficient to check whether or not the state *fail* belongs to $S_1 \times_{R^\Pi} S_2$, which can be easily done by performing a usual DFS of $S_1 \times_{R^\Pi} S_2$. The verification is then reduced to a simple reachability problem in this graph. Consequently, if we store all the visited states during the DFS, the time and memory complexities of this decision procedure are $O(n)$. Several memory efficient solutions exist to manage such a DFS ([Hol89]).

General case: in the general case, according to the proposition 3.1, we have to check the existence of an execution sequence σ of $S_1 \times_{R^\Pi} S_2$ which contains the state *fail* and which is such that for all states (q_1, q_2) of σ, $(q_1, q_2) \notin R_k^\Pi$ for a certain k. According to the definition of R_k^Π, this verification can be done during a DFS as well if:

- the relation R_1^Π can be checked.
- for each visited state (q_1, q_2), the result $(q_1, q_2) \in R_k^\Pi$ is synthesized for its predecessors in the current sequence (the states are then analyzed during the back tracking phase).

More precisely, the principle of the general case algorithm is the following: if R^Π is a simulation (resp. a bisimulation) we associate with each state (q_1, q_2) a bit_array M of size $|T_1[q_1]|$ (resp. $|T_1[q_1]| + |T_2[q_2]|$). During the analysis of each successor (q_1', q_2') of (q_1, q_2), whenever it happens that $(q_1', q_2') \in R^\Pi$ then $M[q_1']$ (resp. $M[q_1']$ and $M[q_2']$) is set to 1. Thus, when all the successors of (q_1, q_2) have been analyzed, $(q_1, q_2) \in R^\Pi$ if and only if all the elements of M have been set to 1.

As in the deterministic case algorithm, to reduce the exponential time complexity of the DFS the usual method would consist in storing all the visited states (including those which do not belong to the current sequence) together with the result of their analysis (i.e, if they belong or not to R^Π). Unfortunately, this solution cannot be straightly applied:

During the DFS, the states are analyzed in a postfixed order. Consequently, it is possible to reach a state which has already been visited, but not yet analyzed (since the visits are performed in a prefixed order). Therefore, the result of the analysis of such a state is unknown (it is not available yet). We propose the following solution for this problem:

Notation 2 We call the *status* of a state the result of the analysis of this state by the algorithm. The status of (q_1, q_2) is "$\sim$" if $(q_1, q_2) \in R^\Pi$, and is "$\not\sim$" otherwise.

Whenever a state already visited but not yet analyzed (i.e, which belongs to the stack) is reached, then we assume its status to be "$\sim$". If, when the analysis of this state completes (i.e, when it is popped), the obtained status is "$\not\sim$", then a TRUE answer from the algorithm is not reliable (a wrong assumption was used), and another DFS has to be performed. On the other hand, a FALSE answer is always reliable.

Consequently, the following data structures are required:

- A stack St_1, to store the states already visited of the current execution sequence. Each element of St_1 is a couple $((p, q), l)$, where (p, q) is a state and l the list of its direct successors which remains to explore.

- A stack St_2, to store the bit_arrays associated to each state of the current execution sequence. We assume that whenever a new array is pushed into St_2, then it is initialized with the value 0.

- a set V, to mark all the visited states.

- a set R, to store all the states of the current sequence visited more than once.

- a set W, to store all the states for which the obtained status is "$\not\sim$".

The list of all direct successors of a state (p, q) is obtained by the function *succ*:
$$succ(p, q) = \{(a, (p', q')) \cdot p \xrightarrow{a}_{T_1} p' \wedge q \xrightarrow{a}_{T_2} q'\}.$$
$succ(p, q)$ can be incrementally computed in the following manner:

- calculate the direct successors of p and q applying the transition rules of the description language of S_1 and S_2.

- calculate the direct successors of (p, q), applying the rules given in definition 3.1.

We also consider the function $partial\_DFS$, which performs a DFS storing all the visited states and analyzing only the states which do not belong to $V \cup W$. The result returned by this function may be TRUE, FALSE or UNRELIABLE. The algorithm then consists in a sequence of calls of $partial\_DFS$ (each call increasing the set W), until the result belongs to $\{TRUE, FALSE\}$.

The algorithm dealing with the bisimulation relation is the following:

Algorithm
```
    W := ∅
    repeat
        result := partial_DFS  { perform a DFS }
    until result ∈ {TRUE, FALSE}
    return result
end.
```

function partial_DFS
```
    V := ∅ ; R := ∅ ; stable := false
    St₁ := {((q₀₁, q₀₂), succ(q₀₁, q₀₂))}
    St₂ := ∅
    push into St₂ a bit_array of size 2  { in order to deal with (q₀₁, q₀₂) }
    push into St₂ a bit_array of size (|T₁[q₀₁]| + |T₂[q₀₂]|) (1)
    while St₁ ≠ ∅
        stable := true
        ((q₁, q₂), l) := top(St₁)
        M := top(St₂)
        if l ≠ ∅
            choose and remove (q'₁, q'₂) in l
            if (q'₁, q'₂) ∉ V ∪ W
                if (q'₁, q'₂) ∉ St₁  { it's a new state }
                    if ¬ ((q'₁, q'₂) ──ᵩ→_T fail)
                        push {(q'₁, q'₂), succ(q'₁, q'₂)} in St₁
                        push into St₂ a bit_array of size (|T₁[q'₁]| + |T₂[q'₂]|) (1)
                    endif
                else  { (q'₁, q'₂ ∈ St₁) }
                    insert (q'₁, q'₂) in R  { this state has been visited more that once }
                    M[q'₁] := 1 ; M[q'₂] := 1 (2)
                endif
            else  { (q'₁, q'₂) ∈ V ∪ W (i.e, visited in a previous DFS) }
                if (q'₁, q'₂) ∉ W
                    M[q'₁] := 1 ; M[q'₂] := 1 (2)  { q'₁ ∼ q'₂ }
                endif
            endif
        else  { l ≠ ∅ }
            pop(St₁) ; pop(St₂)
            insert (q₁, q₂) in V  { a new state has been analyzed }
            M' := top(St₂)
            if M[q'] = 1 for all q' in (T₁[q₁] ∪ T₂[q₂]) (3)
                M'[q₁] := 1 ; M'[q₂] := 1 {q₁ ∼ q₂ } (2)
            else
                insert (q₁, q₂) in W  { q₁ ≁ q₂ }
                if (q₁, q₂) ∈ R
                    stable := false  { we assumed a wrong status }
```

```
                endif
            endif
        endif
    endwhile
    M := top(St₂)
    if M[q₀₁] ≠ 1 and M[q₀₂] ≠ 1 (4)
        return FALSE  { q₀₁ ≁ q₀₂ }
    else
        if stable
            return TRUE  { q₀₁ ∼ q₀₂ }
        else
            return UNRELIABLE  { another DFS has to be performed }
        endif
    endif
end.
```

The algorithm dealing with the simulation is straightly obtained by replacing:

(1) by push into St_2 a bit_array of size $(|T_1[q_{01}]|)$

(2) by $M[q_1'] := 1$

(3) by if $M[q'] = 1$ for all q' in $T_1[q_1]$

(4) by if $M[q_{01}] = 1$

Proposition 4.1 *Algorithm terminates, and it returns TRUE if and only if the two LTS are bisimilars.*

Proof We use the following notations: let DFS_i representing the ith execution of the function *partial_DFS*, and let R_i (resp. W_i) representing the set R (resp. W) at the end of DFS_i. When DFS_i terminates, the following property holds:

  $stable = False \Leftrightarrow R_k \cap W_k \neq \emptyset$ (1)

Algorithm terminates: From (1), $\forall i . DFS_i$ returns UNRELIABLE $\Leftrightarrow$

  $\exists (q_1, q_2) \in Q . ((q_1, q_2) \in W_i \cap R_i)$.

Moreover, as during DFS_i the states of W_{i-1} aren't pushed, we also have:

  $\forall i . \forall (q_1, q_2) \in Q . ((q_1, q_2) \in R_i \Rightarrow (q_1, q_2) \notin W_{i-1})$.

From these two assertions, we can deduce :

$\forall i . DFS_i$ returns UNRELIABLE $\Rightarrow$

  $\exists (q_1, q_2) \in Q . ((q_1, q_2) \in W_i \land (q_1, q_2) \notin W_{i-1})$.

Consequently, the set W increases strictly $(\forall i . W_i \subset W_{i+1})$ and, as Q is finite, it exists a k such that DFS_k doesn't return UNRELIABLE, which ensures the termination of Algorithm. Moreover, the number of calls to the function *partial_DFS* is less or equal to n.

It remains to prove the correctness. Let DFS_k be the last DFS performed. From (1), $R_k \cap W_k = \emptyset \lor DFS_k$ returns FALSE. But,

- if $R_k \cap W_k = \emptyset$, then all the assumptions made during DFS_k are correct. Consequently, the obtained result is correct too.

- Whenever the status of a state is unknown, it's assumed to be $\sim$. Thus, the relation computed by the algorithm contains the relation $\sim$ (it's a weaker relation). It follows that if the algorithm returns FALSE then the LTS aren't bisimilar.

□.

The time requirement for the function *partial_DFS* is $O(n)$. In the worst case, as pointed out in the proof of proposition 4.1 the number of calls of this function may be n. Consequently, the theoretical time requirement for this algorithm is $O(n^2)$. In practice, it turns out that only 1 or 2 DFS are required to obtain a reliable result. Moreover, whenever the LTS are not bisimilar, the time requirement is always $O(n)$.

In both cases, the memory requirement for the algorithm is $O(n)$. However, the data structures required can be divided into *sequentially accessed* memory (St_1 and St_2) and *randomly accessed* memory (R, V and W). Furthermore, as it is not critical to store all the already visited states, memory efficient implementations can be found for the set V, like hash-based caches.

5   Applications and Results

From this general algorithm several decision procedures for bisimulation and simulation based relations have been implemented in the tool ALDÉBARAN, like strong and w-bisimulation, strong simulation, safety preorder and safety equivalence. However, as it is the case for the Paige & Tarjan algorithm, such decision procedures are really useful in a verification tool – from a user's point of view – only if they allow to build a *diagnosis* whenever the two LTS are not related. We show how the previous algorithm has been modified in order to allow this computation. Then, we give some results obtained when applying it to the verification of LOTOS specifications.

Remark 2 In this draft implementation, the verification is not performed "on the fly" straightly from the LOTOS specifications: the LTS are previously generated and the verification phase consists in simultaneously building the LTS product and deciding whether or not they are related, as described in the algorithm. Thus, the obtained results can be compared with the classical verification procedure (based on the Paige & Tarjan algorithm) already implemented in ALDÉBARAN.

5.1   Diagnosis

Several formalisms have been proposed in order to express the "non bisimulation" of two LTS (for example Hennessy-Milner Logic in [Cle90]). We present here a more intuitive solution, suitable either for bisimulation or simulation relations (both denoted by R^{Π}): whenever the two LTS S_1 and S_2 are not related, we build an *explanation sequence* consisting of an execution sequence σ of $S_1 \times_{R^{\Pi}} S_2$ terminated by a failure state (p_k, q_k) which is not in R_1^{Π} (i.e, from which it clearly appears that S_1 and S_2 are not related) and such that for each (p_i, q_i) of σ, $(p_i, q_i) \notin R^{\Pi}$.

Definition 5.1 *Let S_1 and S_2 be two LTS. An explanation sequence of $S_1 \not{R}^{\Pi} S_2$ is an execution sequence σ of $S_1 \times_{R^{\Pi}} S_2$ such that:*

- $\sigma = \{(q_{01}, q_{02}) = (p_1, q_1), (p_2, q_2), ..., (p_k, q_k)\}$
- $\forall i . 0 \leq i \leq k, (p_i, q_i) \notin R_{k-i+1}^{\Pi}.$
- $(p_k, q_k) \notin R_1^{\Pi}$

In fact, the explanation sequences are exactly the execution sequences which are looked for during the verification phase, see proposition 3.1.

We show how such a sequence can be obtained (and therefore printed) without modifying the time and memory complexities of the previous algorithm:

deterministic case: Obviously, when a state *fail* is reached during the DFS of $S_1 \times_{R^\Pi} S_2$ the stack St_1 contains an *explanation sequence* (proposition 3.2).

general case: In this case, the sequence has to be explicitly built during the verification phase. In the previous algorithm, all the visited states (p, q) of $S_1 \times_{R^\Pi} S_2$ which do not belong to R^Π are inserted in the set W. To obtain an *explanation sequence*, it is then sufficient to modify the algorithm in the following manner: whenever a new state is inserted in W, it is linked with one of its successor already in W (which always exists). Thus, if the initial state of the product belongs to W (i.e, the two LTS are not related), an *explanation sequence* is straightly available from its associated linked list.

5.2 Results

Two examples are studied here: the first one is an alternating bit protocol called Datalink protocol [QPF88], and the second one is a more realistic example, the rel/REL_{fifo} protocol [SE90]. For each example, the verification was performed as follows:

- generating the LTS S_1 (*Implementation*) from the LOTOS description, using the LOTOS compiler CÆSAR [GS90].

- building the LTS S_2 (*Specification*), representing the expected behavior of the system.

- comparing S_1 and S_2 with respect to w-bisimulation or safety equivalence, using both the usual decision procedure of ALDÉBARAN and the improved one described in this paper.

5.2.1 Datalink protocol

The Datalink protocol is an example of an alternating bit protocol. The LOTOS specification provided to CÆSAR is described in [QPF88]. By varying the number of the different messages (noted N), LTS of different sizes can be obtained. These LTS have been compared, with respect to w-bisimulation, with the LTS describing the expected behavior of the protocol. However, for $N > 40$, the memory required by the classical decision procedure of ALDÉBARAN becomes too large, and consequently the verification can no longer be performed with this procedure.

The following notations are used:

- n_i and m_i denote the number of states and transitions of the two LTS ($i = 1, 2$).

- n denotes the number of states of the product which have been effectively analyzed.

- $t1$ is the time needed by the usual decision procedure of ALDÉBARAN.

- $t2$ is the time needed by the decision procedure described in this paper.

The times given here are elapsed times, obtained on a SUN 3-80 Workstation.

N	n1	m1	n2	m2	n	t1	t2
20	7241	10560	41	440	1661	0:24	0:19
30	15661	23040	60	930	3691	0:57	0:55
40	27281	40320	80	1640	6521	2:07	1:45
50	42101	62400	101	2600	10151	—	2:27
60	60121	89280	121	3720	14581	—	3:42
70	81341	120960	140	4970	19811	—	6:42
80	105761	157440	161	6560	25841	—	9:23

5.2.2 rel/REL_{fifo} protocol

This algorithm has also been used for the verification of a "real" protocol, rel/REL_{fifo} ([SE90]), carried out in Hewlett-Packard Laboratories [MB90]. This *reliable multicast protocol* provides the following service:

Atomicity: If a multicast from a transmitter is received by a functioning receiver, then all the other functioning receivers will also receive it, even if the transmitter crashes during the multicast.

Fifo: All the multicasts from the same transmitter are received by the functioning receivers in the order of the multicasts were made.

This protocol has been modeled in LOTOS, and a LTS of 680 000 states and 1 900 000 transitions has been generated by CÆSAR. The **Fifo** requirement has been verified by comparing (with respect to safety equivalence) this LTS in which only the actions performed by one receiver were visible, with the expected behavior of a single receiver. Although the size of the graphs prevented a verification by using the Paige & Tarjan algorithm, this comparison was carried out by using the algorithm described in this paper in less than 3 hours on a HP-9000 Workstation.

6 Conclusion

Several applications can be obtained from the algorithm described in this paper.

First, it can be viewed as a new decision procedure (in the usual sense) for bisimulation equivalence, simulation equivalence and simulation preoders between LTS.

The results obtained, from a draft implementation in ALDÉBARAN, show that this algorithm can be more efficient than the usual one. As this algorithm requires less memory, verifications of larger LTS become possible.

Moreover, the diagnosis capability of this decision procedure is very useful from the user's point of view for the specification of communicating processes (as a debugging tool for a sequential language).

But one of the major improvement provided by this algorithm is that "on the fly" verification of bisimulation and simulation relations are allowed. In this framework, our project is to modify the LOTOS compiler CÆSAR to compare LOTOS specifications (with respect to these relations) without explicitly storing the whole LTS of the LOTOS specifications. Consequently, checking of real size examples could be carried out.

References

[BFG*91] A. Bouajjani, J.C. Fernandez, S. Graf, C. Rodriguez, and J. Sifakis. Safety for Branching Time Semantics. In *18th ICALP*, july 1991.

[BFH90] A. Bouajjani, J. C. Fernandez, and N. Halbwachs. *On the verification of safety properties*. Tech. report, Spectre L 12, IMAG, Grenoble, march 1990.

[Cle90] R. Cleaveland. On Automatically Distinguishing Inequivalent Processes. In *Workshop on Computer-Aided Verification*, june 1990.

[CVWY90] C. Courcoubetis, M. Vardi, P. Wolper, and M. Yannakakis. Memory Efficient Algorithms for the Verification of Temporal Properties. In *Workshop on Computer-Aided Verification*, june 1990.

[Fer89]   J. C. Fernandez. *Aldébaran: A tool for verification of communicating processes.*
           Tech. report Spectre C14, LGI-IMAG Grenoble, 1989.

[FM90]   J. C. Fernandez and L. Mounier. Verifying Bisimulations on the Fly. In *Proceedings
           of the Third International Conference on Formal Description Techniques FORTE'90
           (Madrid, Spain)*, pages 91–105, North-Holland, November 1990.

[GS86]   S. Graf and J. Sifakis. *Readiness Semantics for Regular Processes with Silent Action.*
           Technical Report Projet Cesar RT-3, LGI-IMAG Grenoble, 1986.

[GS90]   Hubert Garavel and Joseph Sifakis. Compilation and Verification of LOTOS Spec-
           ifications. In L. Logrippo, R. L. Probert, and H. Ural, editors, *Proceedings of the
           10th International Symposium on Protocol Specification, Testing and Verification
           (Ottawa)*, IFIP, North-Holland, Amsterdam, June 1990.

[Hol89]   Gerard J. Holzmann. Algorithms for Automated Protocol Validation. In *Proceed-
           ings of the 1st International Workshop on Automatic Verification Methods for Finite
           State Systems (Grenoble, France)*, Springer Verlag, jun 1989.

[JJ89]   Claude Jard and Thierry Jeron. On-Line Model-Checking for Finite Linear Tem-
           poral Logic Specifications. In *International Workshop on Automatic Verification
           Methods for Finite State Systems, LNCS 407*, Springer Verlag, 1989.

[MB90]   Laurent Mounier and Simon Bainbridge. *Specification and Verification of a Reliable
           Multicast Protocol.* Technical Report (In preparation), Hewlett-Packard Laborato-
           ries, Bristol, U.K, 1990.

[Mil80]   R. Milner. A Calculus of Communication Systems. In *LNCS 92*, Springer Verlag,
           1980.

[PT87]   R. Paige and R. Tarjan. Three Partition Refinement Algorithms. *SIAM J. Comput.,
           No. 6*, 16, 1987.

[QPF88]   Juan Quemada, Santiago Pavón, and Angel Fernández. Transforming LOTOS Spec-
           ifications with LOLA: The Parametrized Expansion. In Kenneth J. Turner, editor,
           *Proceedings of the 1st International Conference on Formal Description Techniques
           FORTE'88 (Stirling, Scotland)*, pages 45–54, North-Holland, Amsterdam, Septem-
           ber 1988.

[SE90]   Santosh K. Shrivastava and Paul. D. Ezhilchelvan. *rel/REL: A Family of Reliable
           Multicast Protocol for High-Speed Networks.* Technical Report (In preparation),
           University of Newcastle, Dept. of Computer Science, U.K, 1990.

Bounded-memory Algorithms for Verification On-the-fly *

Claude JARD and Thierry JÉRON
IRISA, Campus de Beaulieu, F-35042 Rennes, France.
jard@irisa.fr

1 Introduction

1.1 Motivation

Program verification is a branch of computer science whose business is "to prove programs correctness". It has been studied in theoretical computer science departments for a long time but it is rarely and laboriously applied to real world problems. As a matter of fact, we must pay much more attention to practical problems like the amount of space and time needed to perform verification. Let us recall that proofs of correctness are proofs of the relative consistency between two formal specifications: those of the program, and of the properties that the program is supposed to satisfy. Such a formal proof tries to increase the confidence that a computer system will make it right when executing the program under consideration.

A considerable need for such methods appeared these last ten years in different domains, such as design of asynchronous circuits, communication protocols and distributed software in general. A lot of us accepted the challenge to design automated verification tools, and many different theories have been suggested for the automated analysis of distributed systems. There now exist elaborate methods that can verify quite subtle behaviors.

A simple method for performing automated verification is symbolic execution which is the core of most existing and planned verification systems. The practical limits of this method are the size of the state space and the time it may take to inspect all reachable states in this state space. Those quantities can dramatically rise with the problem size.

1.2 Current state-of-art

Reachability analysis is basically an exhaustive search yielding a rooted graph of global states. This technique is often called *perturbation* [22]. Starting from some specified initial state, successor states are generated and stored in the computer. The process stops when no new state (i.e. one not previously stored) can be generated. Termination is guaranteed if all the program variables (including communication channels) are bounded.

---

*This work was partly funded by the french national project C^3 on parallelism.

The state graph is usually very large and for example, any protocol of practical relevance will have a state space in the order of one million states. There are two major problems when handling systems of this size: state matching (to avoid double work and to ensure termination), and state storing.

We will suppose that the memory is arranged as a balanced tree, that reachable states are numbered from 1 to R, and that states are of constant size S. The memory size M needed is then at least $R.S$. Let $C(S)$ be the time needed for the comparison of two states. The first time a state i is generated, the memory contains $i - 1$ states, thus its insertion in the tree is carried out in time at worst $C(S).\log(i)$. If d is the average degree of nodes, each node is re-generated $d - 1$ times and searched in a memory which contains at least i states. The time needed for those searches can be approximated by $(d - 1).C(S).\log(i)$. Coarsely approximating $\log(R!)$ by $R.\log(R)$, we say that the time complexity of the perturbation technique is

$$T \simeq d.C(S).\Sigma_{i=1}^{R} \log(i) \simeq d.C(S).\log(R!) \simeq d.C(S).R.\log(R)$$

If $M = 10^7$ bytes and $S = 10^2$ bytes, the size of the graphs that can actually be analysed is less than $R = 10^5$ states. If $d = 2$, $C(S) = 10^{-4}$ seconds, and trees are binary trees, the time needed is $T \simeq 6$ minutes.

In order to master the "state explosion", different works have been conducted to reduce the size of the graph [3, 21, 2, 8, 7]. Obviously, reduction must be performed during the graph generation. The other constraint is that the validity of properties to be verified must not be changed. For that reason, we do not consider simulation methods which provide only partial verification [14, 9, 23, 19, 13, 10].

1.3 Verification on-the-fly

The key idea is that, for a large class of properties, storing all the reachability graph is not mandatory. It is enough to visit all the states and/or all the transitions. A depth-first traversal of the reachability graph performs such an exhaustive search. Only the current path has to be stored but the time needed to perform a verification can be catastrophic, due to the re-generation of forgotten states.

We propose an intermediate method which offers a good compromise between time and space requirements. It is based on a depth-first traversal but uses all the available space in order to store not only the current path, but also the greatest possible number of already visited states. We will prove that bounding memory to a smaller size than the state space may not significantly increase the time complexity. Such algorithms allow us to build efficient verifiers, able to handle large graphs. This approach is often called "verification on-the-fly".

It was first proposed in terms of "on-line model-checking" by the authors in [15]. Since then, similar ideas have been advocated in [4] and [5]. [4] presents efficient algorithms to compare Büchi automata and thus proposes a new solution to the verification of temporal properties on infinite behaviors of finite state programs. [5] extends the technique to verify on-the-fly bisimulation equivalences on transitions graphs. The core of the method is to traverse (during its generation) a kind of product of finite transitions systems. Unifying these different views would be an interesting prospect.

The remainder of the paper is organized as follows. We present in detail a class of bounded-memory algorithms that traverse exhaustively the state space of the program to be verified. Upper bounds for space and time complexities are computed and different experiments show the average behavior of our algorithms. Another part of the paper discusses applications, namely verification of safety properties and testing unboundedness of Fifo channels. We conclude with some prospects.

2 Depth-first traversal with replacement

We saw above that the main drawback of a perturbation technique is the memory size needed to perform the graph generation of real size systems. Now, there are some verifications for which a traversal of all states and transitions is enough. It is then unnecessary to store the whole graph. An algorithm performing this exhaustive traversal is a depth-first traversal in which we theoretically only need to detect cycles, provided that the memory is large enough to store the longest acyclic sequence. Unfortunately, visited states which no longer behave to the current sequence are forgotten and can be visited again in many other sequences. In the best case the number R_{gen} of generated states is R. But in the worst case R_{gen} can reach $R!.e$ for a complete graph with R states (e is the basis of natural logarithms). If the number of states in the memory is bounded by the length of the longest acyclic sequence D_{max}, the time needed to complete the traversal is in the scale

$$C(S).R.\log(D_{max}) \leq T \leq C(S).R!.e.\log(D_{max})$$

However, a depth–first traversal can significantly be improved if the whole memory amount is used [16]. Actually, since $D_{max}.S < M$, one can use the remainder of the memory to store already visited states, and then avoiding re-traversing some states. We present this technique and show with examples that it can be efficiently used to analyse real size graphs which are too large to fit in memory.

2.1 The algorithm

An algorithm performing a depth–first traversal with replacement is described above. It is very similar to a classical depth–first traversal except for the set $Visited$ of already visited states and the execution phase when the memory is full.

The traversal with replacement algorithm can be used on every graph such that $D_{max}.S \leq M$. But, contrarily to the simple traversal, it is not a necessary condition for the termination because states of the longest acyclic sequences can be reached by shortest sequences. A necessary condition is $G_{max}.S \leq M$ where G_{max} is the maximal length of a geodesic with initial state S_0 (a geodesic from S to S' is an acyclic sequence from u

to v with minimum length). We have $G_{max} \le D_{max}$ but if $G_{max}.S \le M \le D_{max}.S$ the algorithm may or may not terminate, depending on the order of transitions evaluations.

```
St_Stack:=nil; (* -- states of the current sequence -- *)
Tr_Stack:=nil; (* -- stack of sets of pending transitions -- *)
Visited:=∅; (* -- already visited states -- *)
push (S₀, St_Stack); push(fireable(S₀), Tr_Stack);
while St_Stack ≠ ∅ do begin
    S:=top(St_Stack); (* -- current state -- *)
    if top(Tr_Stack) ≠ ∅ then begin
        t:=extract_one_elt_of(top(Tr_Stack)); (* -- choose and remove -- *)
        S':=succ(S,t);
        if S' ∉ St_Stack ∪ Visited then begin
            if memory_full then begin (* -- replacement -- *)
                S_del:=one_state_from(Visited);
                Visited:=Visited - {S_del};
                end;
            push(S',St_Stack);
            push(fireable(S'), Tr_Stack);
            end;
        end
    else begin (* -- top(Tr_Stack) = ∅ -- *)
        pop(St_Stack);
        pop(Tr_Stack);
        Visited:=Visited ∪{S};
        end;
    end;
```

2.2 Time complexity

Let us remark that we always have $(|St\_Stack| + |Visited|).S \le M$ and the boolean variable $Memory\_full$ is equal to $(|St\_Stack|+|Visited|).S = M$ and is a stable property. Let R_{ins} be the number of insertions of states in the memory i.e. $St\_Stack \cup Visited$. The behavior of the algorithm in the case $R.S \le M$ is almost the same as a perturbation, except for the generation order. Each state is inserted once, so $R_{ins} = R$. The time complexity is then approximately the same.

Now if $R.S > M$, R_{ins} exceeds R because an already visited state may have been forgotten. Due to the stability of the property $memory\_full$, we can separate the algorithm into two phases:

- in the first phase, when $\neg memory\_full$, all visited states are in $St\_Stack \cup Visited$ and the algorithm behaves like a perturbation,

- in the second phase, when $memory\_full$, each time a state S' is generated and not found in $St\_Stack \cup Visited$, we must remove one state S_{del}

from $Visited$ before pushing S' in St_Stack. The way this replacement is performed influences the total number of generated states R_{gen}.

We also suppose that the whole memory $St\_Stack \cup Visited$ is arranged as a balanced tree, which supports access, insertion and deletion operations in logarithmic worst case. The number of states in that memory is always less than M/S. Each generated state must be searched in that memory. Thus, the total time of the traversal is approximately

$$T \simeq C(S).R_{gen}.\log(\frac{M}{S})$$

Recall that for the perturbation technique, time complexity is $C(S).d.R.\log(R)$. If $M \leq R.S$, we have $R_{gen} \simeq d.R$, thus complexities are identical. If $M > R.S$, a perturbation technique is no longer possible. We have $\log(M/S) < \log(R)$ thus, if R_{gen} is in the same order of magnitude that $d.R$, time complexity of the depth–first traversal is close to the complexity that a perturbation would have with a memory of size $R.S$.

The relation between R_{gen} and R_{ins} is almost the same that the one between $d.R$ and R. So, we expect that R_{ins} will stay close to R.

The choice of a replacement strategy is then essential in such an algorithm. Several strategies have been looked at. As noticed in [11], the best one seems to be random replacement. It is easily performed and has no performance drop for particular graphs.

2.3 Experiments

The depth–first traversal with replacement has been used with different kinds of graphs. Some of them are accessibility graphs of communication protocols modelled by communicating finite state machines, and others are random graphs. The parameters of these random graphs are R_{max} a bound on the number of states and d_{max} the maximum degree of a node. They are generated in a breadth–first way. The degree of each node is chosen uniformly between 0 and d_{max}. If g is the number of already generated states, each successor of the current state has probability $1 - g/min(2.g, R_{max})$ to be a new state. Among those random graphs, we only considered those with R close to R_{max}.

The two curves of figure 1 represent the behavior of the algorithm on a random graph when decreasing the memory size. Starting from $M_{max} = R.S$, the memory size is decreased down to the minimal possible value M_{min} for which the algorithm terminates. The two bounds M_{max}/S and M_{min}/S are figured by the two dashed vertical lines.

The two first curves represent the evolution of the number of insertions R_{ins} of states in $St\_Stack \cup Visited$ and the execution time. If $M = M_{max} = R.S$ then $R_{ins} = R$. When M decreases, R_{ins} increases. But it increases very slowly until M comes very near from M_{min}. The number R_{ins} is then less than twice R. Finally R_{ins} explodes but the memory has been significantly reduced before explosion. The execution time T has then a similar form. For that example, with a memory size of 40% of $R.S$ we have only 70% more insertion of states, which give only 50% time increase.

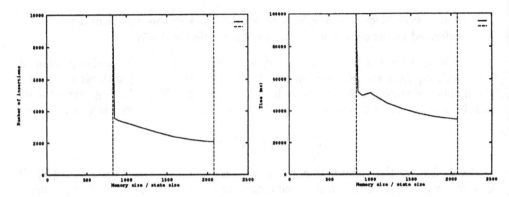

Figure 1: Number of generated states and execution time

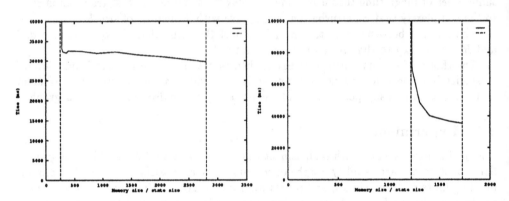

Figure 2: Execution time in extremal cases

Many examples have been tested with this traversal. They almost gave the same type of curves. But we can only decrease the memory size downto a value between $D_{max}.S$ and $G_{max}.S$. Thus when D_{max} is small with respect to R, one can reduce M very significantly, and the increase of R_{ins} and T are very slow. In the left example of figure 2, $M_{min} = M_{max}/10$, and we have an increase of only 1% of R_{ins} and 11% of T (see the left hand curve of figure 2). However, for graphs in which D_{max} is close to R as in the right hand curve of figure 2, that is when graphs are very connected (a complete graph is the worst case) results are not so good. The domain in which M/S can vary is very tight and R_{ins} and T increase very quickly.

3 Application to on–line model–checking

The first application of the depth–first traversal with replacement was introduced in [15]. The purpose was to verify that a protocol specification satisfied a property f. Properties were expressed in event based linear temporal logic (LTL) [20] and translated into finite states automata. But the idea can be generalized to other formalisms such as Büchi automata.

Let $S_1 =< Q_1, A, T_1, q_{01} >$ be the labelled transition system associated to the specification $Spec$ where Q_1 is a finite set of states, A a finite set of actions, $T \subseteq Q_1 \times A \times Q_2$ the transition relation, and q_{01} the initial state.

Suppose that a property $\mathcal{P}$ can be expressed by a deterministic Büchi automaton $\mathcal{B} =< Q_2, A, T_2, q_{02}, F_2 >$ where Q_2 is its finite set of states, A its set of actions, $T_2 \subseteq Q_2 \times A \times Q_2$ its transition relation, q_{02} the initial state and F_2 a set of designated states. An infinite word $a_1 \ldots a_n \ldots \in A^\omega$ is recognized by $\mathcal{B}$ if and only if there exists an infinite run of $\mathcal{B}$: $q_{02} \xrightarrow{a_1} q_1 \ldots q_{n-1} \xrightarrow{a_n} q_n \ldots$ such that $q_i \in F_2$ for infinitely many i's.

We say that $Spec$ satisfies $\mathcal{P}$ written $Spec \models \mathcal{P}$ if and only if every infinite word labelling an infinite transition sequence of S_1 is recognized by $\mathcal{B}$.

When the Büchi automaton is not necessarily deterministic, the usual way to verify that $Spec \models \mathcal{P}$ is to consider S_1 as a Büchi automaton (its set of designated states is Q_1), make the product of S_1 with the complement automaton $\overline{\mathcal{B}}$ of $\mathcal{B}$ and check if $S_1 \times \overline{\mathcal{B}}$ is empty (accepts no word). This can be done by computing the strongly connected components.

In the case of a deterministic Büchi automaton, we will show that there is a very simple algorithm which performs this verification without complementation and without computation of strongly connected components [16].

We consider S_1 as a Büchi automaton with Q_1 as its set of designated states. We suppose that $\mathcal{B}$ is complete. This can always be done by adding a new state.

The synchronous product of S_1 and $\mathcal{B}$ is $S =< Q, A, T, q_0, F >$ with:

- $Q = Q_1 \times Q_2$,
- $q_0 = (q_{01}, q_{02})$,
- $F = Q_1 \times F_2$,
- $T \subseteq Q \times A \times Q$ is defined by

$$((q_1, q_2), a, (q_1', q_2')) \in T \text{ if and only if } (q_1, a, q_1') \in T_1 \text{ and } (q_2, a, q_2') \in T_2$$

Since $\mathcal{B}$ is complete, the infinite sequences of executable actions of S_1 are exactly the words labelling the infinite runs of S. And according to the definition of S, $Spec \models \mathcal{P}$ if and only if every infinite run of S contains infinitely many states of F. Considering S as a directed graph, it is equivalent to say that every cycle of the graph contains a vertice in F. But this is equivalent to say that the sub-graph S' obtained from S by removing all vertices of F (and the correponding edges) is acyclic. And S' is acyclic if and only if a depth-first traversal of S' doesn't detect any cycle.

But we don't want to first build S and then remove vertices of F. We would like to check whether that S' is acyclic during a traversal of S. This can be done by a traversal of S which is composed of depth-first traversals of sub-graphs of S in the following way. We need a set W initialized with $\{q_0\}$ which contains the roots of the depth-first traversals not yet performed. These roots are q_0 and all states of F. For each traversal initiated in a state $q_{init} \in W$, remove q_{init} from W and add the following to the traversal with replacement: if a new state $q \in F$ is reached, it is added to W and successors of q are not explored now (they will be in the traversal initiated in q) and if a cycle is detected in $q \notin F$ this simply signifies that a cycle of S' is detected.

The algorithm stops when W is empty and $Spec \models \mathcal{P}$ if and only if no cycle of S' is detected. This algorithm is described below:

```
Visited:=∅;
W:={S₀};
while W ≠ ∅ do begin
    St_Stack:=nil;
    Tr_Stack:=nil;
    qinit:=extract_one_elt_of(W);
    push(qinit, St_Stack);
    push(fireable(qinit), Tr_Stack);
    while St_Stack ≠ ∅ do begin
        q:=top(St_Stack);
        if top(Tr_Stack) ≠ ∅ then begin
            t:=extract_one_elt_of(top(Tr_Stack));
            q':=succ(q,t);
            if q' ∈ St_Stack then
                if q' ∉ F then ERROR
            else if q' ∉ Visited then
                if q' ∈ F then W:=W ∪{q'}
                else begin
                    if memory_full then begin
                        qdel:=one_state_from(Visited);
                        Visited:=Visited - {qdel};
                        end;
                    push(q',St_Stack);
                    push(fireable(q'), Tr_Stack);
                    end;
            end;
        else begin (* -- top(Tr_Stack) = ∅ -- *)
            pop(St_Stack);
            pop(Tr_Stack);
            Visited:=Visited ∪{q};
            end;
        end;
    end;
```

The depth–first traversal with replacement is very efficient for the on–line model-checking of deterministic finite states and Büchi automata. It avoids constructing the complete reachability graph. Moreover, you can choose to stop as soon as an error is detected.

It appears in the litterature that different kinds of verification can be performed on–the–fly, since then they are based on a depth-first traversal. We found the [5] paper, which presents a new technique to verify strong bisimulation equivalence. In the paper [4] also, the authors define a method for the verification of a temporal logic property f on a finite state program P which combines a depth–first traversal with a partial search with hashing [10]. Finally, in [17] our traversal with replacement has also been proposed for the test of unboundedness of fifo channels in some specification models such as communicating finite state machines [1], fifo–nets [18, 6] and even Estelle programs [12].

4 Conclusion and prospects

Dealing with the state space explosion problem, we have presented an alternative to the exhaustive construction of state graphs. The depth–first traversal insures an exhaustive traversal of all states and/or transitions of a reachability graph. It requires less memory since it theoretically only needs a memory large enough to store the longest acyclic sequence. In order to improve this technique, it is necessary to store some visited states. When the memory is full, visited states are randomly replaced by new states of the current sequence. We have shown that this method can significantly increase the size of the state graphs that can actually be analysed without excessively increasing the computation time.

As we saw, this method can be used for different kinds of verification. A few application examples have pointed out that it can certainly improve the verification tools in various domains such as bisimulation, Büchi acceptance, on–the–fly verification of temporal properties and test for unboundedness.

However, this technique does not solve all the problems. We still don't know the whole applicability domain of that method. For example, is it possible to verify branching time temporal logic properties with a depth–first traversal with replacement, and, if the answer is positive, is it efficient? We also know that this algorithm is not quite suited for all kinds of graphs. Perhaps an interesting problem would be to carefully study the structure of graphs for which it is well suited. We could then infer on the convenience of the method on some classes of transitions systems. Within a tool, the choose of the depth–first traversal in a particular verification could then be guided by the expected structure of graphs.

References

[1] G.V. Bochmann. Finite state description of communication protocols. *Computer Networks*, 2, October 1978.

[2] A. Bouajjani, J.-C. Fernandez, and N. Halbwachs. Minimal model generation. In *Workshop on Computer Aided Verification DIMACS 90*, June 1990.

[3] E.M. Clarke and O. Grumberg. Avoiding the state explosion problem in temporal logic model checking algorithms. *6th ACM SIGACT-SIGOPS Symposium on Principles of Distributed Computing, Vancouver, Canada*, August 1987.

[4] C. Courcoubetis, M. Vardi, P. Wolper, and M. Yannakakis. Memory efficient algorithms for the verification of temporal properties. In *Workshop on Computer Aided Verification, DIMACS 90*, June 1990.

[5] J.-C. Fernandez and L. Mounier. Verifying bisimulation on the fly. In *Third International Conference on Formal Description Techniques, FORTE'90*, Madrid, November 1990.

[6] A. Finkel and G. Memmi. An introduction to fifo nets – monogeneous nets: a subclass of fifo nets. *Theoretical Computer Science*, 35:191–214, 1985.

[7] P. Godefroid and P. Wolper. A partial approach to model checking. In *6th IEEE Symposium on Logic in Computer Science, Amsterdam*, July 1991.

[8] S. Graf and B. Steffen. Compositional minimization of finite state processes. In *Workshop on Computer Aided Verification DIMACS 90*, June 1990.

[9] G. Holzmann. Tracing protocols. *ATT Technical Journal*, 64(10):2413–2434, 1985.

[10] G.J. Holzmann. Algorithms for automated protocol validation. In *Proceedings of the International Workshop on Automatic Verification Methods for Finite State Systems*, Grenoble, France, June 1989.

[11] G.J. Holzmann. Automated protocol validation in ARGOS, assertion proving and scatter searching. *IEEE trans. on Software Engineering, Vol 13, No 6*, June 1987.

[12] ISO 9074. *Estelle: a Formal Description Technique based on an Extented State Transition Model*. ISO TC97/SC21/WG6.1, 1986.

[13] C. Jard, R. Groz, and J.F. Monin. Development of VEDA: a prototyping tool for distributed algorithms. In *IEEE Trans. on Software Engin.*, March 1988.

[14] C. Jard, R. Groz, and J-F. Monin. Véda : a software simulator for the validation of protocol specifications. In *COMNET'85, Hungary*, October 1985.

[15] C. Jard and T. Jéron. On-line model-checking for finite linear temporal logic specifications. In *Proceedings of the International Workshop on Automatic Verification Methods for Finite State Systems*, Grenoble, France, June 1989. Springer–Verlag, LNCS #407, pages 275–285.

[16] T. Jéron. Contribution à la validation des protocoles : test d'infinitude et vérification à la volée. Ph.D Thesis, University of Rennes I, May 1991.

[17] T. Jéron. Testing for unboundedness of fifo channels. In *STACS 91 : Symposium on Theoretical Aspects of Computer Science, Hamburg, Germany*, February 1991. Springer–Verlag, LNCS #480, pages 322–333.

[18] R. Martin and G. Memmi. *Spécification et validation de systèmes temps réel à l'aide de réseaux de Petri à files*. Technical Report 3, Revue Tech. Thomson–CSF, Sept. 1981.

[19] J.-M. Pageot and C. Jard. Experience in guiding simulation. *Protocol Specification, Testing and Verification, VIII, IFIP*, 207–218, June 1988.

[20] A. Pnueli. Applications of temporal logic to the specification and verification of reactive systems: a survey of current trends. *LNCS #224, Current Trends in Concurrency*, 510–584, 1986.

[21] A. Valmari. A stubborn attack on state explosion. In *Workshop on Computer Aided Verification DIMACS 90*, June 1990.

[22] C.H. West. General techniques for communication protocols. *IBM J. Res. Develop.*, 22, july 1978.

[23] C.H. West. Protocol validation by random state exploration. In 6th *IFIP International Workshop on Protocol Specification, Testing and Verification, Montréal, Gray rock*, North Holland, June 1986.

Extended Abstract

Generating BDDs for Symbolic Model Checking in CCS

Reinhard Enders, Thomas Filkorn, Dirk Taubner

Siemens AG, Corporate Research and Development (ZFE IS INF2)
Otto-Hahn-Ring 6, W-8000 München 83, F.R. Germany
email: { reinhard, thomas%apollo21, taubner } @ztivax.uucp

Abstract Finite transition systems can easily be represented by binary decision diagrams (BDDs) through the characteristic function of the transition relation. Burch et al. have shown how model checking of a powerful version of the μ-calculus can be performed on such BDDs.

In this paper we show how a BDD can be generated from elementary finite transition systems given as BDDs by applying the CCS operations of parallel composition, restriction, and relabelling. The resulting BDDs only grow linearly in the number of parallel components. This way bisimilarity checking can be performed for processes out of the reach of conventional process algebra tools.

1 Introduction

A binary decision diagram as described by Bryant [1] is a normal form representation of boolean functions $f : \mathbb{B}^n \to \mathbb{B}$, where $\mathbb{B} = \{0, 1\}$. It is often much smaller than other normal form representations. Moreover boolean operations can be applied efficiently.

Transition systems have states and transitions leading from one state via some action to another state. They underly many semantics for concurrent systems, e.g. bisimulation equivalence for CCS [10]. They also underly semantics of modal logics, which allow to reason about concurrent systems.

Burch, Clarke, McMillan, Dill, and Hwang [2] have shown how model checking of a powerful version of the μ-calculus including existential quantification and λ-abstraction can be performed for a boolean domain using BDDs for internal representation. They call the approach *symbolic model checking*. They also indicate how other finite domains can be treated through binary encoding.

In particular for a finite transition system the set of states S and the set Act of actions can be encoded as subsets of $\mathbb{B}^{\lceil \log_2 |S| \rceil}$ and $\mathbb{B}^{\lceil \log_2 |Act| \rceil}$ respectively. The transition relation $D \subseteq S \times Act \times S$ can be encoded as a function $\chi : \mathbb{B}^{2 \cdot \lceil \log_2 |S| \rceil + \lceil \log_2 |Act| \rceil} \to \mathbb{B}$ which in turn can be represented as a BDD. Burch et al. show how weak and strong bisimilarity can be expressed as formulas in their μ-calculus and hence can be checked for transition systems given as BDDs.

However they do not indicate how the BDDs are generated. If they were generated from the list of state-action-state triples of the transition relation (which is straightforward) the approach would immediately suffer the well-known explosion problem, namely that a system of N parallel components, with n states each, may have n^N transitions.

The question arises whether the BDD which represents the transition system of the compound system could be generated more efficiently directly from the N components given as BDDs without enumerating all resulting transitions. This question is the topic of this paper. It is answered in the following way: We give a certain encoding of transition systems as BDDs. We show how the CCS [10] operators of parallel composition, restriction, and relabelling can be applied to BDDs. We prove that for a fixed set of actions the BDD for representing N parallel communicating processes grows only linearly in N. Worst case boundaries for the size of BDDs are rare in literature, hence this bound is interesting. However it has to be pointed out that it concerns only the resulting BDD which represents the system of N parallel component processes. It does not concern intermediate BDDs which are used during the generation or during the model checking. Nevertheless a benchmark example shows that bisimilarity checking can be performed for systems out of the reach of conventional tools such as [3, 4, 7, 9, 6].

Note that the μ-calculus of [2] is more powerful than that of e.g. [5, 11]. Hence all formulas checked with the latter approaches can be checked in the framework of this paper. We expect to be able to handle larger transition systems.

On the other hand it should be noted that BDDs are efficient only in a heuristic sense, the worst case may still be catastrophic. For circuit verification experience has shown that indeed BDDs can serve as an efficient representation in many practical cases. This paper gives evidence that this is also the case for verification of parallel processes. Possible applications are communication protocols, operating system tasks, and distributed control systems.

Before we start with the technical part of this paper let us explain with an example the basic idea, i.e. how to represent relations by BDDs and why this is promising for the parallel composition of transition systems. Consider the relation D of Fig. 1 where $D \subseteq S \times S$ for $S = \{0, 1, 2, 3\}$. We omit the actions for the moment. An obvious boolean encoding of S is $0 \mapsto 00, 1 \mapsto 01, 2 \mapsto 10, 3 \mapsto 11$. The relation D may then be represented by a function $\chi : \mathbb{B}^4 \to \mathbb{B}$, such that $\chi(r_1, r_2, s_1, s_2) = 1$ if and only if the state encoded by $r_1 r_2$ has an edge to the state encoded by $s_1 s_2$. This boolean function χ can in turn be represented as a BDD.

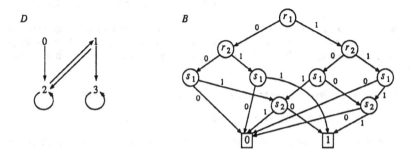

Figure 1: A relation (left) and its BDD representation (right)

For a given set of boolean variables which are totally ordered by $\prec$ a BDD is a rooted directed acyclic graph, each node is either terminal, then it is labelled by a truthvalue and has no successor, or it is nonterminal, then it is labelled by some variable and has two successors which are terminal or labelled by a larger ($\prec$) boolean variable. One successor corresponds to 0, the other to 1.

Taking the ordering $r_1 \prec r_2 \prec s_1 \prec s_2$ the function χ is represented by the BDD B given in Fig. 1.

Now assume we want to represent the relation[1]

$$\{ \langle (r, r'), (s, s') \rangle \in S \times S \mid (r, s) \in D \land (r', s') \in D \}$$

as a BDD C. We can take a copy B' of B with fresh variables r_1', r_2', s_1', s_2' and calculate C as $B \land B'$ where the conjunction of BDDs is as described in [1].

However the size of C depends on the chosen variable ordering. If $r_1 \prec r_2 \prec s_1 \prec s_2 \prec r_1' \prec r_2' \prec s_1' \prec s_2'$ is chosen it has 20 nodes, approximately $2 \cdot |B|$, where $|B|$ denotes the number of nodes in B. It is formed simply by attaching B' to the 1-exit of B. If, on the other hand, $r_1 \prec r_2 \prec r_1' \prec r_2' \prec s_1 \prec s_2 \prec s_1' \prec s_2'$ is chosen it has 47 nodes (approximately $|B|^2/2$).

This ends our introductory example. We wanted to indicate that if the ordering of variables is chosen carefully the BDD only grows additively while the number of elements in the represented relation grows multiplicatively. However be aware that the encoding as presented in Section 4 uses a different ordering in order to also serve the asynchronous case well.

---

[1] This relation resembles the synchronization part of parallel composition, cf. the next section. In general, of course, one wants to combine two relations and not twice the same.

2 Operators on transition systems

Our language for composing parallel processes is taken from the process algebra CCS [10]. Let *Act* be the finite set of actions which contains the invisible action τ and all other actions in two copies, a and $\overline{a}$, which are complementary, i.e. $\overline{\overline{a}} = a$. A transition system $T = \langle S, D, z \rangle$ has states S, initial state $z \in S$, and transitions $D \subseteq S \times Act \times S$ leading from one state with some action to another state. Throughout we assume S to be finite.

Next we give operators on transition systems which correspond to CCS parallel composition, restriction, and relabelling. In [12] it is shown that they are correct (consistent) in the following sense. Given two closed CCS terms P_1 and P_2 and let T_1, T_2 be their respective transition systems according to the transitional semantics [10], then $T_1 \mid T_2$ as defined below is strongly bisimilar to the transition system of $P_1 \mid P_2$ according to the transitional semantics. Similar results hold for restriction and relabelling.

The *CCS parallel composition* for given $T_1 = \langle S_1, D_1, z_1 \rangle$ and $T_2 = \langle S_2, D_2, z_2 \rangle$ is defined as $T_1 \mid T_2 = \langle S_1 \times S_2, D, \langle z_1, z_2 \rangle \rangle$ where

$$D = \Big\{ \langle \langle r_1, r_2 \rangle, \alpha, \langle s_1, s_2 \rangle \rangle \mid \quad \langle r_1, \alpha, s_1 \rangle \in D_1 \wedge r_2 = s_2 \ \vee \ \langle r_2, \alpha, s_2 \rangle \in D_2 \wedge r_1 = s_1$$
$$\vee \ \alpha = \tau \wedge \exists a \neq \tau : \langle r_1, a, s_1 \rangle \in D_1 \wedge \langle r_2, \overline{a}, s_2 \rangle \in D_2 \Big\}.$$

The condition $\langle r_1, \alpha, s_1 \rangle \in D_1 \wedge r_2 = s_2$ and its symmetric version represent an *asynchronous* move, only one component proceeds. On the other hand the condition $\langle r_1, a, s_1 \rangle \in D_1 \wedge \langle r_2, \overline{a}, s_2 \rangle \in D_2$ represents a *synchronous* move. The latter in a simplified version has already been discussed in the introduction.

Let $T = \langle S, D, z \rangle$ be given. *Restriction* of a subset $A \subseteq Act - \{\tau\}$ is defined as

$$T \backslash A = \langle S, \quad \{\langle r, \alpha, s \rangle \in D \mid \alpha \notin A \wedge \overline{\alpha} \notin A\}, \quad z \rangle.$$

Relabelling of a visible action a ($a \neq \tau$) into the action b is defined as $T[b/a] = \langle S, D', z \rangle$ where

$$D' = \{\langle r, \beta, s \rangle \mid \exists \alpha : \langle r, \alpha, s \rangle \in D \wedge (\beta = \alpha \notin \{a, \overline{a}\} \vee \beta = b \wedge \alpha = a \vee \beta = \overline{b} \wedge \alpha = \overline{a})\}.$$

3 Symbolic model checking using BDDs

Burch, Clarke, McMillan, Dill, and Hwang [2] show how model checking can be performed using BDDs. They call their approach 'symbolic' as it proceeds without supplying an interpretation for the individual variables. The result of model checking a formula is a BDD which represents the result of the formula for all interpretations. Given a particular interpretation taking choices according to the values of the variables under this interpretation leads from the root of the BDD to a truthvalue. This is the truthvalue of the formula under the particular individual variable interpretation. Additionally in [2] BDDs are used to represent relations internally with the intention that this is more efficient than the corresponding lists of tupels.

The version of the μ-calculus used in [2] includes individual variables, n-ary relational variables ($n > 0$), existential quantification, abstraction (λ-binding) of individual variables, and fixpoint binding of relational variables. The reader is referred to [2] for the details of syntax and semantics.

In general, given a structure of a domain and interpretations I_P and I_D of relational and individual variables, model checking performs the task of checking, whether a formula F is true in this structure (i.e. $\mathcal{D}(F)(I_P)(I_D) = 1$), in other words, whether the structure is a model for F.

From a different point of view the model checker of Burch et al. may be seen as a certain approach to work with relations which are represented as BDDs. The actual model checking of a formula F proceeds by first calculating as a BDD the relation which contains a tuple $\langle d_1, \ldots, d_n \rangle$ iff F is true for the individual variable interpretation which maps the first variable to $d_1 \ldots$ and the last variable to d_n. The model checking is finished (and yields a truthvalue) by instantiating this BDD to a particular individual variable interpretation.

However the interpretation of the relational variables have to be supplied before the symbolic model checker can start. They have to be supplied as BDDs. In particular for model checking CCS-terms

[2, Sect. 8] the transition relations of the transition systems to be checked have to be supplied by the relational variable interpretation, i.e. as BDDs. Burch et al. leave open where the BDDs for the transition relations come from. The following two sections propose an approach for generating these BDDs.

4 Encoding of transition systems as BDDs

In principle given a certain enumeration $e_0, e_1, \ldots, e_{|S|-1}$ of a finite set S the boolean encoding is obvious, one needs $\#S := \lceil \log_2 |S| \rceil$ boolean variables and lets $s_1, \ldots, s_{\#S}$ denote e_i where i is the number one gets when interpreting $s_1 \ldots s_{\#S}$ as a binary digit.

We will use this encoding for the state sets of elementary[2] transition systems and for the set of actions. For the latter we additionally assume that Act is enumerated $\tau, a, b, \ldots, \bar{a}, \bar{b}, \ldots$, i.e. that τ is encoded as all zeros and any visible action a as $0x_2 \ldots x_{\#A}$ and its complement $\bar{a}$ as $1y_2 \ldots y_{\#A}$ such that for all $i \in \{2, \ldots, \#A\}$ we have $x_i = y_i$. Here $\#A := \lceil \log_2 |Act| \rceil$.

In order to work with BDDs one has to fix a global ordering on the boolean variables used to encode the information. This ordering has great influence on the size of the BDDs. If nothing is known on the structure of a relation to be represented as a BDD not much can be done. However in our case we can use knowledge about the transition relation and in particular about the operations performed on them, most importantly the parallel composition.

For explanation let us consider a binary relation $D \subseteq S \times S$ as in the introduction. If we need $\#S$ bits to encode S we need $2 \cdot \#S$ bits to encode D, say $r_1, \ldots, r_{\#S}$ to encode the first element of a pair in D and $s_1, \ldots, s_{\#S}$ for the second. In the introduction we demonstrated for the synchronization case of parallel composition of two such relations that we get small BDDs if all variables of one relation are ordered before those of the other.

However in the asynchronous case where only one component proceeds while the other (say the first) stays in its state we have to check for $\langle \langle r, r' \rangle, \langle s, s' \rangle \rangle$ whether $r = s \wedge \langle r', s' \rangle \in D$, i.e. we have to check whether $r_1 = s_1 \wedge r_2 = s_2 \wedge \ldots \wedge r_{\#S} = s_{\#S}$. But with the variable ordering $r_1 \prec r_2 \prec \ldots r_{\#S} \prec s_1 \prec \ldots \prec s_{\#S}$ for the bits of a relation the BDD for this check explodes.

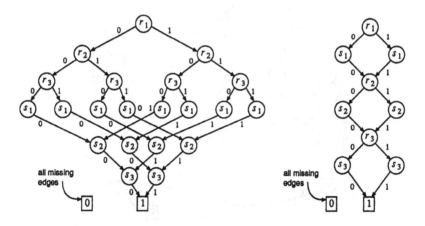

Figure 2: BDD for $(r_1 = s_1) \wedge (r_2 = s_2) \wedge (r_3 = s_3)$ with poor (left) and good (right) variable ordering

Figure 2 gives an example for $\#S = 3$. In general it has $\Omega(2^{\#S})$ nodes. Therefore we choose a different ordering, namely

$$r_1 \prec s_1 \prec r_2 \prec s_2 \prec \ldots \prec r_{\#S} \prec s_{\#S}.$$

---

[2] We call a transition system elementary if it is not formed by parallel composition, restriction, or relabelling but is given as a list of transitions.

With this improved ordering the BDD for the above example is as given on the right of Figure 2, i.e. it grows only linearly.

We are now ready to present our encoding for a transition relation $D \subseteq S \times Act \times S$. We choose the variable ordering

$$a_1 \prec a_2 \prec \ldots a_{\#A} \prec r_1 \prec s_1 \prec r_2 \prec s_2 \prec \ldots \prec r_{\#S} \prec s_{\#S}$$

where $a_1 \ldots a_{\#A}$ encodes the action of the transition, $r_1 \ldots r_{\#S}$ encodes the source state of the transition, and $s_1 \ldots s_{\#S}$ encodes the target state. We always understand that $00 \ldots 0$ is the initial state. Fig. 3 gives an example transition system and Fig. 4 shows the representation of its transition relation as a BDD.

States				Actions		
0	$\mapsto$	000		τ	$\mapsto$	000
1	$\mapsto$	001		a_0	$\mapsto$	001
2	$\mapsto$	010		$\overline{a}_0$	$\mapsto$	101
3	$\mapsto$	011		c_0	$\mapsto$	010
4	$\mapsto$	100		$\overline{c}_0$	$\mapsto$	110
				c_1	$\mapsto$	011
				$\overline{c}_1$	$\mapsto$	111

Figure 3: A transition system and the encoding of its states and actions

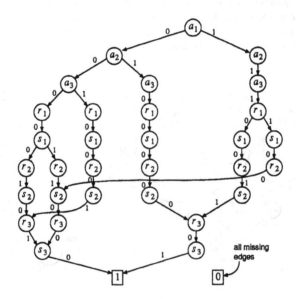

Figure 4: BDD encoding of the transition relation of the system of Fig. 3

The reason to put the bits for the actions above those for the states is that in the worst case this leads to only $|Act|$ r_1-labelled nodes in the BDD, each corresponding to one action. If the bits were below those of the states the worst case of a_1-labelled nodes would be $2^{|Act|}$, each corresponding to a subset of Act. However this is an intuitive reason only. As it stands it does not imply that the resulting BDD is smaller.

5 Operators on BDDs

In this section we describe the operators of CCS parallel composition, restriction, and relabelling on BDDs. Note that this comprises the practically most important case of a parallel composition of N processes

$$(P_1 \mid P_2 \mid \ldots \mid P_N)\backslash A$$

where the restriction imposes the wanted synchronization.

We assume that the elementary processes (transition systems) are given as BDDs. The BDD for an elementary transition system may easily be formed from the list of triples in the transition relation as follows. Each transition $\langle r, a, s \rangle$ which has encodings $br_1, \ldots, br_{\#S}$, $ba_1, \ldots, ba_{\#A}$, and $bs_1, \ldots, bs_{\#S}$, is considered as one BDD with only the path $a_1 \overset{ba_1}{\to} a_2 \overset{ba_2}{\to} \ldots a_{\#A} \overset{ba_{\#A}}{\to} r_1 \overset{br_1}{\to} s_1 \overset{bs_1}{\to} \ldots r_{\#S} \overset{br_{\#S}}{\to} s_{\#S} \overset{bs_{\#S}}{\to} 1$ leading to 1. All other branches directly lead to 0. The BDD for the transition relation is calculated by performing the disjunction (cf. [1]) of all these BDDs. In the worst case this yields a BDD with approximately $2^{2 \cdot \#S + \#A}$ nodes.

CCS parallel composition

Let B_1 and B_2 be two BDDs representing transition relations D_1 and D_2 over the same set of actions but over disjoint sets of states encoded as described in the previous section. The BDD $B_1|B_2$ representing the transition relation of the parallel composition is calculated as follows.

Let $a_1, \ldots, a_{\#A}$ be the boolean variables for the actions in both, B_1 and B_2. Let r_i, s_i ($i \in \{1, \ldots, \#S_1\}$) and r'_j, s'_j ($j \in \{1, \ldots, \#S_2\}$) be the boolean variables for the source and target states of D_1 and D_2 respectively. According to the previous section we have the following ordering dependencies

$$a_1 \prec \ldots \prec a_{\#A} \prec r_1 \prec s_1 \prec \ldots \prec r_{\#S_1} \prec s_{\#S_1}$$

and

$$a_1 \prec \ldots \prec a_{\#A} \prec r'_1 \prec s'_1 \prec \ldots \prec r'_{\#S_2} \prec s'_{\#S_2}.$$

We additionally impose that

$$s_{\#S_1} \prec r'_1$$

this leaves the previous orderings and hence B_1, B_2 unchanged.

Note that this choice of combined ordering ensures that the BDD for $B_1 \mid B_2$ again fulfills our encoding convention for transition systems, i.e. we use the first $\#A$ variables for the actions and than alternatingly one bit for the source and one for the target state of the transition.

We now may calculate $B_1 \mid B_2$ as

$$B_1 \wedge Stab_2 \quad \vee \quad B_2 \wedge Stab_1 \quad \vee \quad C$$

where the missing components are explained below. The $\wedge$ and $\vee$ are operations on BDDs as described in [1]. $Stab_1$ is the BDD for $r_1 = s_1 \wedge \ldots \wedge r_{\#S_1} = s_{\#S_1}$ (cf. Fig. 2). It corresponds to the condition that the first component stays in its state ($Stab_2$ is analogous). Let E be the BDD calculated as

$$B_1|_{a_1=0} \wedge B_2|_{a_1=1} \quad \vee \quad B_1|_{a_1=1} \wedge B_2|_{a_1=0}.$$

$B_1|_{a_1=0}$ denotes the subgraph of B_1 one gets when restricting the variable a_1 to 0 (see [1] for details) again $\wedge$ and $\vee$ are operations on BDDs. The BDD E expresses the condition that complementary actions match. The last component C of the parallel composition above is calculated as

$$(a_1 = 0) \wedge \ldots \wedge (a_{\#A} = 0) \wedge (\exists a_3 \exists a_3 \ldots \exists a_{\#A} E).$$

Here $\exists a_i G$ for some BDD G is short for $G|_{a_i=0} \vee G|_{a_i=1}$, i.e. it represents an existential quantification of the boolean variable a_i. The existential quantification of $a_2, \ldots, a_{\#A}$ can be implemented directly as a BDD operator. Applied to E it yields a BDD without nodes labelled by variables $a_1, \ldots, a_{\#A}$. The first part of C puts this BDD below the encoding of τ.

Restriction

Given a BDD B representing the transition relation of T and a BDD C for the set of actions A (it may be generated straightforward from the list of actions in A) the BDD for the transition relation of $T\backslash A$ is simply $B \wedge \neg(C|_{a_1=0} \vee C|_{a_1=1})$, where $\wedge, \vee, \neg$, and $|_{a_1=b}$ on BDDs are as described in [1].

Relabelling

For B as above let the binary encoding of actions a and b be $ba_1, \ldots, ba_{\#A}$ and $bb_1, \ldots, bb_{\#A}$ respectively. The BDD for the transition relation of $T[b/a]$ is

$$B \ \wedge \ \neg(a_2 = ba_2 \wedge \ldots \wedge a_{\#A} = ba_{\#A})$$
$$\vee \ (a_2 = bb_2 \wedge \ldots \wedge a_{\#A} = bb_{\#A}) \ \wedge \ B|_{a_2=ba_2}|_{a_3=ba_3}|\cdots|_{a_{\#A}=ba_{\#A}}.$$

6 Complexity of resulting BDDs

We have the following results on the size of the generated BDDs.

Theorem 6.1 Let $T_i = \langle S_i, D_i, z_i \rangle$ for $i \in \{1, \ldots, N\}$ be transition systems where the transition relation is represented as BDD B_i according to Section 4.
The number of nodes of the BDD $B := B_1 \mid B_2 \mid \ldots \mid B_N$ is

$$O(2^{|Act|} \cdot \sum_{i=1}^{N} |S_i|^2).$$

Proof   We will use $\vec{a}, \vec{r}_i, \vec{s}_i$ as abbreviations such that $\vec{a} = \langle a_1, \ldots, a_{\#A} \rangle$ is the variable vector encoding the actions of Act and such that $\vec{r}_i = \langle r_{i,1}, \ldots, r_{i,\#S_i} \rangle$ and $\vec{s}_i = \langle s_{i,1}, \ldots, s_{i,\#S_i} \rangle$ are the variable vectors encoding source and target state of the transition relation D_i. The BDD B_i ranges over the variables $\vec{a}, \vec{r}_i, \vec{s}_i$ and the BDD B over the variables $\vec{a}, \vec{r}_1, \vec{s}_1, \ldots, \vec{r}_N, \vec{s}_N$. The variable ordering is $\vec{a} \prec \vec{r}_1, \vec{s}_1 \prec \ldots \prec \vec{r}_N, \vec{s}_N$ where the ordering within $\vec{r}_i, \vec{s}_i$ is as described in Section 4.

For the proof we have a layered view of B. Let us say that all variables for states of transition system T_l belong to level l.

For instances $\vec{ba} \in \mathbb{B}^{\#A}$ and $\vec{br}_i, \vec{bs}_i \in \mathbb{B}^{\#S_i}$ let σ_l denote the instantiation $\langle \vec{ba}, \vec{br}_1, \vec{bs}_1, \ldots, \vec{br}_{l-1}, \vec{bs}_{l-1} \rangle$. Let $\sigma_l(B)$ denote the BDD one gets by instantiating B to σ_l, i.e.

$$\sigma_l(B) := B|_{\vec{a}=\vec{ba}, \vec{r}_1=\vec{br}_1, \vec{s}_1=\vec{bs}_1, \ldots, \vec{r}_{l-1}=\vec{br}_{l-1}, \vec{s}_{l-1}=\vec{bs}_{l-1}}.$$

This BDD $\sigma_l(B)$ denotes a boolean function of arity $2 \cdot \sum_{i=l}^{N} \#S_i$.

To count the nodes of B on level l we determine the number of different such functions one gets by varying σ_l over all instances. This number is called $width(l)$. Since BDDs are a normal form for boolean functions and they are reduced (i.e. have no two isomorphic subgraphs) [1] this number immediately gives an upper bound for the number of nodes in B which are labeled with variables of level l. For $j \in \{1, \ldots, \#S_l\}$ this bound is $width(l) \cdot 2^{2 \cdot (j-1)}$ for the label $r_{l,j}$ and $width(l) \cdot 2^{2 \cdot (j-1)+1}$ for the label $s_{l,j}$. Note that we do not make any assumptions about the part of B within level l hence we have to allow the exponential growth in this part. Knowing an upper bound W for $\max_l width(l)$ we get an upper bound for $|B|$, the number of nodes in B.

$$
\begin{aligned}
|B| &\leq 2^{\#A} + \sum_{l=1}^{N} \sum_{j=1}^{\#S_l} width(l) \cdot (2^{2 \cdot (j-1)} + 2^{2 \cdot (j-1)+1}) \\
&\leq 2^{\#A} + \sum_{l=1}^{N} width(l) \cdot 2^{2 \cdot \#S_l} \\
&\leq 2^{\#A} + W \cdot \sum_{l=1}^{N} 2^{2 \cdot \#S_l} \\
&\leq 2 \cdot |Act| + W \cdot \sum_{l=1}^{N} 4 \cdot |S_l|^2 \\
&= O(|Act| + W \cdot \sum_{l=1}^{N} |S_l|^2)
\end{aligned}
$$

The rest of the proof is given in the appendix. It calculates W to be $4 \cdot 2^{|Act|}$ which in turn proves the stated bound. □

For a fixed set of actions and $n := \max_i |S_i|$ this bound is simply $O(N \cdot n^2)$ which compares favourably to the straightforward worst case bound $O(n^{N+2} \cdot N^2)$ for the number of transitions in $T_1 \mid \ldots \mid T_N$.

If we know more on the structure of the transition systems we are able to give the following tighter bound. See the appendix for details.

Corollary 6.2 For T_i and B as above let c be the number of sets of visible actions which occur in transitions between any two states of any component, i.e.

$$c := \left| \left\{ A \subseteq Act \mid \exists j \in \{1, \ldots, N\} : \exists r, s \in S_j : A = \{\alpha | \alpha \neq \tau \wedge \langle r, \alpha, s \rangle \in D_j\} \right\} \right|.$$

If no component contains a visible self-loop, i.e. if for all $j \in \{1, \ldots, N\}$ there exists no $s \in S_j$, $\alpha \in Act - \{\tau\}$ such that $\langle s, \alpha, s \rangle \in D_j$, then

$$|B| = O\left((c + |Act|) \cdot \sum_{i=1}^{N} |S_i|^2\right). \qquad \Box$$

We expect c to be close to $|Act|$ in typical cases.

Let us remark that the same bounds are true for any relabelling of the B_i's and for arbitrary restrictions (as for example in $((B_1 \mid B_2) \backslash A_1 \mid (B_3 \mid B_4) \backslash A_2) \backslash A_3$). In particular this comprises the most important practical case given at the beginning of the previous section.

7 Implementation

We have implemented the described generation of BDDs for elementary transition systems and the operators of CCS parallel composition, restriction, and relabelling. Furthermore we implemented the symbolic model checker of Burch et al. [2]. The implementations are based on a Prolog system extended by unification in finite algebras [8].

Our implementation captures the powerful version of the μ-calculus as used in [2]. In particular the μ-calculus formulas for strong and weak bisimilarity can be checked. Note that special care is needed for the ordering of the boolean variables encoding the variables in these μ-calculus formulas in order to avoid exponential explosion of the involved BDDs.

8 Example

Milner's example of a simple distributed scheduler has become a benchmark for process algebra tools [7, 9]. The scheduler consists of one starter process and N processes which are scheduled. The communication is organized in a ring. Expressed in CCS [10] the processes are as follows.

$$
\begin{aligned}
Starter &\stackrel{\text{def}}{=} \overline{c_0}.0 \\
C_0 &\stackrel{\text{def}}{=} c_0.a_0.(\tau.\overline{c_1}.C_0 + \overline{c_1}.\tau.C_0) \\
C_1 &\stackrel{\text{def}}{=} c_1.a_1.(\tau.\overline{c_2}.C_1 + \overline{c_2}.\tau.C_1) \\
&\vdots \\
C_{N-1} &\stackrel{\text{def}}{=} c_{N-1}.a_{N-1}.(\tau.\overline{c_0}.C_{N-1} + \overline{c_0}.\tau.C_{N-1})
\end{aligned}
$$

Each cycler process C_i awaits the permit c_i to start, performs action a_i, and passes the permit to the next cycler either before or after some internal computation. The transition system for C_0 is given in Fig. 3. The compound process for N cyclers is

$$SCHED_N \stackrel{\text{def}}{=} (Starter \mid C_0 \mid C_1 \mid \ldots \mid C_{N-1}) \backslash \{c_0, \ldots, c_{N-1}\}$$

it is weakly bisimilar to $SPEC_N \stackrel{\text{def}}{=} a_0.a_1. \ldots a_{N-1}.SPEC_N$.

Table 1 shows the size of the BDD for $SCHED_N$ and the times needed to check the weak bisimilarity between $SCHED_N$ and $SPEC_N$ compared to conventional tools. The number of states and transitions for $N > 12$ as well as the times for the conventional tools for $N = 20$ are extrapolated estimates. The times for AUTO and BB are taken from [9], those for Aldébaran from [7]. Times for our system were obtained on an Apollo with 16MBs memory. It is approximately as fast as a SUN 3/60.

To be better comparable one would have to add the times needed for computing the transition relation of $SCHED_N$ to the columns for AUTO, Aldébaran, and BB. Additionally the time needed to compute the transitive closure with respect to τ-transitions has to be added for AUTO and Aldébaran, it is not needed for branching bisimulation. Only the column for this paper includes all these times.

Applying Corollary 6.2 to $SCHED_N$ yields $c = O(|Act|)$ and hence the size of the BDD representing the transition system of $SCHED_N$ is $O(N \cdot \sum_{i=0}^{N-1} |S_i|^2) = O(N^2)$.

N	states	transitions	nodes in BDD	AUTO [4]	Aldébaran [7]	BB [9]	BDD
6	577	2017	424	3.3s	1.9s	0.2s	177s
8	3073	13825	654	57s	24s	1.2s	345s
10	15361	84481	908	-	-	7.4s	665s
12	73729	479233	1213	-	-	53s	1147s
14	300000	2000000	1549	-	-	-	1928s
16	1200000	8000000	1960	-	-	-	2972s
18	4800000	32000000	2337	-	-	-	3259s<1h
20	18000000	128000000	2810	$(10^9 s)$	$(7 \cdot 10^7 s)$	(50000s)	4927s<1.5h

Table 1: Benchmarks for the scheduler

9 Conclusion

We have presented the missing link, namely the generation of transition relations as BDDs, for exploiting symbolic model checking as a tool for process algebras. The example shows that processes out of the reach of conventional tools can be checked for bisimilarity this way.

We have shown that the BDD for N parallel transition systems grows only linearly in N. Such a worst case bound for BDDs is rare in the literature. On the other hand it is not clear how the BDDs grow during the symbolic model checking.

Another open problem is the question whether other process algebra operators, in particular recursion can be performed on BDDs similarly efficiently.

Acknowledgement We thank Peter Warkentin, his fast implementation of operations on BDDs is used for the larger experiments reported in Table 1.

Appendix

This appendix shows how to calculate the bound W needed for the proof of Theorem 6.1. For the BDD B recall that $\sigma_l(B) = B|_{\vec{a}=\vec{ba}, \vec{r}_1=\vec{br}_1, \vec{s}_1=\vec{bs}_1, \ldots, \vec{r}_{l-1}=\vec{br}_{l-1}, \vec{s}_{l-1}=\vec{bs}_{l-1}}$. For arbitrary l we want W to be an upper bound for the number of different relations (i.e. characteristic functions) $\sigma_l(B)$ for any instantiation $\sigma_l = \langle \vec{ba}, \vec{br}_1, \vec{bs}_1, \ldots, \vec{br}_{l-1}, \vec{bs}_{l-1} \rangle$.

In the following the relations $\sigma_l(B)$ will be stated in terms of the relations $stab_l$, $move_l(A)$ and $SyncAsync_l$. The relation $stab_l$ expresses that all components T_i on level l or lower are stable, i.e. perform no change of state.

$$stab_l \stackrel{\text{def}}{=} \{ \langle \vec{br}_l, \vec{bs}_l, \ldots, \vec{br}_N, \vec{bs}_N \rangle \mid \forall i, l \leq i \leq N : \vec{br}_i = \vec{bs}_i \}$$

For a set A of actions $move_l(A)$ expresses that one component T_j on level l or lower performs a transition with an action of A while all other processes are stable.

$$move_l(A) \stackrel{\text{def}}{=} \{ \langle \vec{br}_l, \vec{bs}_l, \ldots, \vec{br}_N, \vec{bs}_N \rangle \mid \exists \alpha \in A, j, l \leq j \leq N : \langle \vec{br}_j, \alpha, \vec{bs}_j \rangle \in D_j \\ \wedge \forall i, i \neq j, l \leq i \leq N : \vec{br}_i = \vec{bs}_i \}$$

The relation $SyncAsync_l$ states that some process T_j on level l or lower performs an asynchronous τ-transition or that two processes T_j, T_k perform synchronizing transitions. In both cases all other processes are stable.

$$SyncAsync_l \stackrel{\text{def}}{=} move_l(\{\tau\}) \cup \{ \langle \vec{br}_l, \vec{bs}_l, \ldots, \vec{br}_N, \vec{bs}_N \rangle \mid \exists \alpha \in Act, j, k, j \neq k, l \leq j, k \leq N : \\ \langle \vec{br}_j, \alpha, \vec{bs}_j \rangle \in D_j \wedge \langle \vec{br}_k, \overline{\alpha}, \vec{bs}_k \rangle \in D_k \wedge \\ \forall i, k \neq i \neq j, l \leq i \leq N : \vec{br}_i = \vec{bs}_i \}$$

Instantiations σ_l can be divided into non-τ- and τ-transitions (cases **a** and **b** below). The former are always asynchronous. Depending on the number of unstable components in σ_l (a component k of σ_l is unstable if $\vec{br}_k \neq \vec{bs}_k$) we distinguish the cases **a0** (no unstable components), **a1** (one unstable component), and **a2** (two or more unstable components).

Case a $\vec{ba} \neq \tau$

Case a0 $\vec{br}_i = \vec{bs}_i$ for all $i \in \{1,\ldots,l-1\}$

$$\sigma_l(B) = \begin{cases} move_l(\{\vec{ba}\}) \cup stab_l & \text{if } \exists j, 1 \leq j < l : \langle \vec{br}_j, \vec{ba}, \vec{br}_j \rangle \in D_j \\ move_l(\{\vec{ba}\}) & \text{otherwise} \end{cases}$$

Case a1 $\exists j : \vec{br}_j \neq \vec{bs}_j$ and $\forall i, i \neq j : \vec{br}_i = \vec{bs}_i$ where $1 \leq i, j < l$

$$\sigma_l(B) = \begin{cases} stab_l & \text{if } \langle \vec{br}_j, \vec{ba}, \vec{bs}_j \rangle \in D_j \\ \emptyset & \text{otherwise} \end{cases}$$

Case a2 $\exists j, k, j \neq k : \vec{br}_j \neq \vec{bs}_j \land \vec{br}_k \neq \vec{bs}_k$ where $1 \leq j, k < l$

$$\sigma_l(B) = \emptyset$$

The τ-transitions are more complicated because we have to consider transitions resulting from two synchronizing processes as well as asynchronous τ-transitions of a single process. Depending on the number of unstable components in σ_l we distinguish cases **b0**, **b1**, **b2** and **b3**. The case **b3** covers those σ_l which contain three or more unstable components.

The cases **b0**, **b1** and **b2** have to check whether for σ_l a process can proceed asynchronously and whether two processes can synchronize. For this purpose we define the predicates Async-τ and Sync-τ.

$$\text{Async-}\tau(j) \stackrel{\text{def}}{\Longleftrightarrow} \langle \vec{br}_j, \tau, \vec{bs}_j \rangle \in D_j$$
$$\text{Sync-}\tau(j,k) \stackrel{\text{def}}{\Longleftrightarrow} \exists \alpha \in Act : \langle \vec{br}_j, \alpha, \vec{bs}_j \rangle \in D_j \land \langle \vec{br}_k, \overline{\alpha}, \vec{bs}_k \rangle \in D_k$$

Case b $\vec{ba} = \tau$

Case b3 $\exists M \subseteq \{1,\ldots,l-1\}, |M| > 2 : \forall i \in M : \vec{br}_i \neq \vec{bs}_i$

This means that three or more processes perform a transition in B, which is impossible from the definition of the parallel composition operator.

$$\sigma_l(B) = \emptyset$$

Case b2 $\exists j, k, j \neq k : \vec{br}_j \neq \vec{bs}_j, \vec{br}_k \neq \vec{bs}_k, \forall i, k \neq i \neq j : \vec{br}_i = \vec{bs}_i$ where $1 \leq i, j, k < l$

If two processes are making a transition they are synchronizing, i.e. the remaining components must be stable.

$$\sigma_l(B) = \begin{cases} stab_l & \text{if } \text{Sync-}\tau(j,k) \\ \emptyset & \text{otherwise} \end{cases}$$

Case b1 $\exists j : \vec{br}_j \neq \vec{bs}_j \ \forall i, i \neq j : \vec{br}_i = \vec{bs}_i$ where $1 \leq i, j < l$

If process T_j can perform an asynchronous τ-transition or synchronize with a process $T_i, i < l$ the relation $stab_l$ is contained in $\sigma_l(B)$. The other part of $\sigma_l(B)$ stems from synchronisations of T_j with a process $T_i, i \geq l$.

For the latter case we define the set $A_1 := \{\overline{\alpha} \mid \langle \vec{br}_j, \alpha, \vec{bs}_j \rangle \in D_j \land \alpha \neq \tau\}$.

$$\sigma_l(B) = \begin{cases} move_l(A_1) \cup stab_l & \text{if Async-}\tau(j) \text{ or } \exists k, j \neq k < l : \text{Sync-}\tau(j,k) \\ move_l(A_1) & \text{otherwise} \end{cases}$$

Case b0 $\vec{br}_i = \vec{bs}_i$ for all $i \in \{1,\ldots,l-1\}$

Again we have the same possibilities as in case **b1**, but the value of j is not fixed, it may be in the range of 1 to $l-1$. As components 1 to $l-1$ are stable we also have the possibility that processes $T_l,\ldots,T_N$ perform an asynchronous transition or a pair of synchronizing transitions.

Let $A_0 := \{\overline{\alpha} \mid \exists j, 1 \leq j < l : \langle \vec{br}_j, \alpha, \vec{br}_j \rangle \in D_j \land \alpha \neq \tau\}$.

$$\sigma_l(B) = \begin{cases} move_l(A_0) \cup SyncAsync_l & \text{if } \exists j, 1 \leq j < l : \text{Async-}\tau(j) \text{ or} \\ \quad \cup stab_l & \quad \exists j, k, j \neq k, 1 \leq j, k < l : \text{Sync-}\tau(j,k) \\ move_l(A_0) \cup SyncAsync_l & \text{otherwise} \end{cases}$$

By counting all possibilities for $\sigma_l(B)$ in cases **a0** to **a2** and **b0** to **b3** and allowing any subset of Act for A_0 and A_1 we get the upper bound $W = 4 \cdot 2^{|Act|}$.

Critical cases for a better approximation are **b0** and **b1** from which we can get a smaller upper bound W. If no process contains a visible self-loop the set A_0 in case **b0** is empty. We then get $W = 2 \cdot |Act| + 4 + 2 \cdot c$ with c as stated in Corollary 6.2.

References

[1] R. E. Bryant. Graph-based algorithms for boolean function manipulation. *IEEE Transactions on Computers*, C-35(8):677–691, 1986.

[2] J. R. Burch, E. M. Clarke, K. L. McMillan, D. L. Dill, and L. J. Hwang. Symbolic model checking: 10^{20} states and beyond. In *Proceedings of the 5th IEEE Symposium on Logic in Computer Science, Philadelphia*, pages 428–439, 1990.

[3] R. Cleaveland, J. Parrow, and B. Steffen. The concurrency workbench. In J. Sifakis, editor, *Automatic Verification Methods for Finite State Systems. Proceedings, Grenoble, 1989*, volume 407 of *Lecture Notes in Computer Science*, pages 24–37, Berlin et al., 1990. Springer.

[4] R. de Simone and D. Vergamini. Abord auto. Rapports Techniques 111, INRIA, Sophia Antipolis, 1989.

[5] E. A. Emerson and C.-L. Lei. Efficient model checking in fragments of the propositional mu-calculus. In *Proc. of the First Annual Symp. on Logic in Computer Science*, pages 267–278. Computer Society Press, 1986.

[6] K. Estenfeld, H.-A. Schneider, D. Taubner, and E. Tidén. Computer aided verification of parallel processes. In A. Pfitzmann and E. Raubold, editors, *VIS '91 Verläßliche Informationssysteme. Proceedings, Darmstadt 1991*, volume 271 of *Informatik Fachberichte*, pages 208–226, Berlin, 1991. Springer.

[7] J.-C. Fernandez. An implementation of an efficient algorithm for bisimulation equivalence. *Science of Computer Programming*, 13:219–236, 1989/90.

[8] T. Filkorn. Unifikation in endlichen Algebren und ihre Integration in Prolog, Master's Thesis, Techn. Universität München, 1988.

[9] J. F. Groote and F. Vaandrager. An efficient algorithm for branching bisimulation and stuttering equivalence. In *ICALP '90*, Lecture Notes in Computer Science, Berlin, 1990. Springer.

[10] R. Milner. *Communication and Concurrency*. Prentice Hall, New York, 1989.

[11] C. Stirling and D. Walker. Local model checking in the modal mu-calculus. In J. Díaz and F. Orejas, editors, *TAPSOFT '89. Volume 1., Proceedings, Barcelona 1989*, volume 351 of *Lecture Notes in Computer Science*, pages 369–383, Berlin, 1989. Springer.

[12] D. Taubner. *Finite Representations of CCS and TCSP Programs by Automata and Petri Nets*, volume 369 of *Lecture Notes in Computer Science*. Springer, Berlin, 1989.

Vectorized Symbolic Model Checking of Computation Tree Logic for Sequential Machine Verification

Hiromi Hiraishi[†], Kiyoharu Hamaguchi[‡]
Hiroyuki Ochi[‡] and Shuzo Yajima[‡]
† Department of Information and Communication Sciences
Kyoto Sangyo University
Kita-ku, Kyoto 603, JAPAN
‡ Department of Information Science, Kyoto University
Sakyo-ku, Kyoto 606, JAPAN

Abstract

The major goal of this paper is to clarify how large and practical sequential machines can be verified with the current most powerful supercomputers. The basic algorithm used is an implicit symbolic model checking algorithm, which is shown to be 100 times and 40 times more efficient in time and space than the conventional symbolic model checking algorithms. Based on the algorithm, a vectorized symbolic model checking algorithm, which is suitable for execution on vector processors, is also proposed. Some benchmark results show that it achieves about $6 \sim 20$ acceleration ratio and it can verify a 16 bit pipelined ALU with 4 word register file, which supports 16 arithmetic/logical operations, in around 12 minutes on a vector processor HITAC S-820/80.

1 Introduction

Various kinds of formal methods for automatic verification have been widely studied. Among them, the symbolic model checking approaches based on a branching time temporal logic called CTL (Computation Tree Logic) are one of the most efficient approaches [5, 6, 7]. It uses a Boolean characteristic function, which is efficiently represented and manipulated by using *Shared Binary Decision Diagrams (SBDD)*[1, 3], to express the state transition relation of a state machine explicitly.

The size of the SBDD representation of the characteristic function, however, is apt to become very large even if the size of the SBDD representation of the state transition functions of a sequential machine is small. In order to avoid this problem, new improved algorithms (we call them as implicit symbolic model checking) are proposed [4, 10, 15]. They do not use the Boolean characteristic function to represent the state transition relation explicitly. Instead, they use the state transition functions of a sequential machine directly without generating the characteristic function representing the state transition relation of a sequential machine explicitly.

Our major goal is to clarify how large and practical sequential machines can be verified based on the symbolic model checking algorithm of CTL by using one of the most advanced current supercomputers. Aiming at verification of sequential machines, we adopted a kind of implicit symbolic model checking algorithm of CTL. It is efficiently executed not only on supercomputers but also on the current conventional workstations.

First, we implemented both algorithms, i.e. explicit and implicit ones, on SPARC Station 1+ to see the effect of the implicit symbolic model checking algorithm. Experimental results show that the implicit version achieves up to 100 times and 40 times improvements in time and space respectively compared with the explicit version.

Next, we vectorized the implicit symbolic model checking algorithm so that it can be executed efficiently on a vector processor. Since the most time consuming parts of the symbolic model checking algorithm are manipulations of SBDD, we concentrated on vectorizing manipulations of SBDD [14]. Although many SBDD manipulators have been developed up to now, most of them are implemented on workstations [2, 13]. In order to handle much larger SBDD in a reasonable time, the use of parallel machines or connection machines is studied [12]. Their algorithms are based on depth first search recursive algorithms and it is difficult to vectorize such recursive algorithms for efficient execution on vector processors. Our vectorized algorithm is based on breadth first search algorithm, instead, to enjoy the power of vector processors.

We also implemented and evaluated our vectorized symbolic model checking algorithm of CTL on a vector processor HITAC S-820/80 at the University of Tokyo. It achieves 6 to 20 acceleration ratio and it takes about 12 minutes to verify a 16 bit pipelined ALU with 4 word register file which supports 16 arithmetic/logical operations.

This paper is organized as follows: Section 2 summarizes CTL, notations of sequential machines, and SBDD. Section 3 describes our symbolic model checking algorithm of CTL for sequential machine verification. Vectorization of our algorithm is discussed in section 4. In section 5 we explain the implementation of our algorithm and show some benchmark results. Section 6 concludes this paper.

2 Preliminaries

2.1 Computation Tree Logic

Computation Tree Logic (CTL)[8] is a branching time temporal logic. Let AP be a set of atomic propositions. Let p be an atomic proposition and η, ξ be CTL formulas. Then, $p, \neg\eta, \eta \vee \xi, EX\eta, EG\eta$ and $E[\eta \mathcal{U} \xi]$ are also CTL formulas.

The semantics of CTL is defined over a Kripke structure $K = (S, R, I)$, where S is a non-empty finite set of states; $R \subseteq S \times S$ is a total binary relation on S; $I : S \rightarrow 2^{AP}$ is an interpretation function which labels each state with a set of atomic propositions true at that state.

An infinite sequence of states $\pi = s_0 s_1 s_2 \ldots$ is called a *path* from s_0 if $(s_i, s_{i+1}) \in R$ for $\forall i \geq 0$. $\pi(i)$ denotes the i-th state of the sequence π (i.e. $\pi(i) = s_i$).

The truth-value of a CTL formula is defined at a state of a Kripke structure and $K, s \models \eta$ denotes that a CTL formula η hold at a state s of a Kripke structure K. If there is no ambiguity, we will omit K and just write as $s \models \eta$. The relation $\models$ is recursively defined as follows: $s \models p \ (\in AP)$ iff $p \in I(s)$; $s \models \neg\eta$ iff $s \not\models \eta$; $s \models \eta \vee \xi$ iff $s \models \eta$ or $s \models \xi$; $s \models EX\eta$ iff there exists some next state s' of s (i.e. $(s, s') \in R$) such that $s' \models \eta$; $s \models EG\eta$ iff there exists some path π on K starting from the state s such that $\pi(i) \models \eta$ for $\forall i \geq 0$; $s \models E[\eta \mathcal{U} \xi]$ iff there exists some path π on K starting from the state s such that $\exists i \geq 0$, $\pi(i) \models \xi$ and $\pi(j) \models \eta$ for $0 \leq \forall j < i$.

2.2 Sequential Machines

Let $x_i (1 \leq i \leq l)$, $y_j (1 \leq j \leq m)$ be input variables and state variables over $B = \{1, 0\}$ respectively. x and y are vectors $< x_1, x_2, \cdots x_l >$ over B^l and $< y_1, y_2, \cdots y_m >$ over B^m respectively. A sequential machine with l binary input signals, m binary state variables and n binary output signals is defined by the set of Boolean functions as follows:

- State transition functions: $f_j \in [B^l \times B^m \to B]\ (1 \leq j \leq m)$

  $f(x, y) = < f_1(x_1, x_2, \cdots x_l, y_1, y_2, \cdots y_m), \cdots, f_m(x_1, x_2, \cdots x_l, y_1, y_2, \cdots y_m) >$ gives the next state y' of a current state y for an input x.

- Output functions:

  - $z_k \in [B^m \to B]\ (1 \leq k \leq n)$ for a Moore-type machine;
    $z(y) = < z_1(y_1, y_2, \cdots y_m), \cdots, z_n(y_1, y_2, \cdots y_m) >$ gives the current output at a state y.
  - $z_k \in [B^l \times B^m \to B]\ (1 \leq k \leq n)$ for a Mealy-type machine;
    $z(x, y) = < z_1(x_1, x_2, \cdots x_l, y_1, y_2, \cdots y_m), \cdots, z_n(x_1, x_2, \cdots x_l, y_1, y_2, \cdots y_m) >$ gives the current output at a state y for an input x.

In order to associate binary input signals, binary state variables, and binary output signals of sequential machines with atomic propositions, $p_{x_i}\ (1 \leq i \leq l)$, $p_{y_j}\ (1 \leq j \leq m)$, and $p_{z_k}\ (1 \leq k \leq n)$ are used as atomic propositions corresponding to x_i, y_j and z_k respectively. $x_i = 1$ means p_{x_i} is true and so on.

2.3 Shared Binary Decision Diagram

Boolean functions are efficiently represented by using a *Shared Binary Decision Diagram* (SBDD)[1, 3]. SBDD is a kind of labeled acyclic directed graph representing Shannon's expansion theorem according to a given fixed variable ordering, in which all isomorphic subgraphs are shared and nodes corresponding to redundant variables are removed. Each node is labeled by its corresponding variable name and has two outgoing edges called *'0' edge* and *'1' edge* respectively. It represents a Boolean function $f = x f_1 + \overline{x} f_0$, where x is its label; f_1 and f_0 are Boolean functions pointed to by its '1' edge and '0' edge respectively.

SBDD has various useful properties. If the ordering of the variables is fixed for the whole graph, the graph is canonical, i.e. there are no two different nodes representing a same Boolean function [1, 3]. In addition, the size of the graph is feasible for many practical Boolean functions [11]. The manipulations for various operations on Boolean functions represented by SBDD can be performed in time proportional to the size of the SBDD [3].

In order to guarantee the uniqueness of SBDD representation, we need to manage SBDD nodes so that no two different nodes represent a same function. This is usually done by using a hash table called *node table* [13]. In addition, in order to perform various operations on Boolean functions in time proportional to the size of their corresponding SBDD, same operations on same Boolean functions should be prevented. This is usually done by using another hash table called *operation result table*[13].

3 Symbolic Model Checking for Sequential Machines

For a Boolean function $f \in [B^n \to B]$ and a vector of variables $\mathbf{x} =< x_1, x_2, \cdots x_n >$ over B^n, we use the following notations:

$$\exists x_i . f(\mathbf{x}) \stackrel{\text{def}}{=} f(x_1, x_2, \cdots x_{i-1}, 0, x_{i+1}, \cdots, x_n) \vee f(x_1, x_2, \cdots x_{i-1}, 1, x_{i+1}, \cdots, x_n)$$

$$\exists \mathbf{x} . f(\mathbf{x}) \stackrel{\text{def}}{=} \exists x_1 \exists x_2 \cdots \exists x_n . f(\mathbf{x})$$

A subset S of B^n is represented by a Boolean characteristic function $F_S \in [B^n \to B]$ such that $F_S(\mathbf{s}) = 1$ if and only if $\mathbf{s} \in S$.

3.1 Basic Algorithm

The algorithm shown in this sub-section is based on the symbolic model checking algorithm proposed in [5, 6, 7].

Since the semantics of CTL is defined over Kripke structure, a given sequential machine has to be transformed to the corresponding Kripke structure for model checking.

Let $\mathbf{x}$ and $\mathbf{y}$ be a input vector and a state vector of a sequential machine respectively. Let $\mathbf{s}$ be a state vector of the corresponding Kripke structure. Since a state transition of a sequential machine corresponds to a state of the corresponding Kripke structure, $\mathbf{s}$ can be expressed as $\mathbf{x} \# \mathbf{y}$, where $\mathbf{x} \# \mathbf{y}$ represents a concatenation of two vectors $\mathbf{x}$ and $\mathbf{y}$ (i.e. $\mathbf{x} \# \mathbf{y} \stackrel{\text{def}}{=} < x_1, x_2, \cdots x_l, y_1, y_2, \cdots y_m >$). The set of states of the Kripke structure is $B^l \times B^m$.

By introducing new vectors of Boolean variables $\mathbf{x}' =< x'_1, x'_2, \cdots x'_l >$ and $\mathbf{y}' =< y'_1, y'_2, \cdots y'_m >$ corresponding to $\mathbf{x}$ and $\mathbf{y}$, $\mathbf{s}'$ is defined to be $\mathbf{x}' \# \mathbf{y}'$. We use $\mathbf{x}'$, $\mathbf{y}'$, and $\mathbf{s}'$ to represent the input vector and the state vector of the sequential machine and the state vector of the Kripke structure at the next time.

Let f_j be a state transition function corresponding to a state variable y_j. The Boolean function representing the Kripke structure K, denoted by F_K, is constructed as follows:

$$F_K(\mathbf{s}', \mathbf{s}) = \prod_{0 \leq j \leq m} (y'_j \equiv f_j(\mathbf{x}, \mathbf{y}))$$

This function means that $F_K(\mathbf{s}', \mathbf{s}) = 1$ if and only if $(\mathbf{s}', \mathbf{s})$ is an edge of the corresponding Kripke structure. It is easy to see that $F_K(\mathbf{s}', \mathbf{s})$ does not depend on $\mathbf{x}'$ and we can also regard it as a Boolean characteristic function which represents state transition relation of the sequential machine.

Let $F_\eta(\mathbf{s})$ be a characteristic function of a CTL formula η. It represents a set of states where η holds. We can get $F_\eta(\mathbf{s})$ in a bottom up manner as follows:

- For atomic propositions, $F_{p_{x_i}}(\mathbf{s}) \stackrel{\text{def}}{=} x_i$, $F_{p_{y_j}}(\mathbf{s}) \stackrel{\text{def}}{=} y_j$ and $F_{p_{z_k}}(\mathbf{s}) \stackrel{\text{def}}{=} z_k$.

- $F_{\eta \cdot \xi}(\mathbf{s}) \stackrel{\text{def}}{=} F_\eta(\mathbf{s}) \cdot F_\xi(\mathbf{s})$, where '$\cdot$' is any Boolean operator.

- $F_{EX\eta}(\mathbf{s}) \overset{\text{def}}{=} \exists \mathbf{s}'.(F_\eta(\mathbf{s}') \wedge F_K(\mathbf{s}', \mathbf{s}))$.

- $F_{EG\eta}(\mathbf{s})$ is obtained by the following fixed point calculations.

$$A_0(\mathbf{s}) \overset{\text{def}}{=} F_\eta(\mathbf{s}), \quad A_{i+1}(\mathbf{s}) \overset{\text{def}}{=} A_i(\mathbf{s}) \wedge \exists \mathbf{s}'.(A_i(\mathbf{s}') \wedge F_K(\mathbf{s}', \mathbf{s}))$$

- $F_{E[\eta \mathcal{U} \xi]}(\mathbf{s})$ is obtained by the following fixed point calculations.

$$A_0(\mathbf{s}) \overset{\text{def}}{=} F_\xi(\mathbf{s}), \quad A_{i+1}(\mathbf{s}) \overset{\text{def}}{=} A_i(\mathbf{s}) \vee \exists \mathbf{s}'.(A_i(\mathbf{s}') \wedge F_\eta(\mathbf{s}) \wedge F_K(\mathbf{s}', \mathbf{s}))$$

3.2 Implicit Manipulation of Transition Relation

The size of an SBDD representing the characteristic function $F_K(\mathbf{s}', \mathbf{s})$ for the transition relation can be very large, even if the total size for f_j is small. In order to improve the efficiency of the above algorithm, it is desired to prevent the calculation of $F_K(\mathbf{s}', \mathbf{s})$.

Note that $F_K(\mathbf{s}', \mathbf{s})$ is used only in the form of $\exists \mathbf{s}'.(C(\mathbf{s}') \wedge F_K(\mathbf{s}', \mathbf{s}))$. This function is equivalent to

$$\exists \mathbf{y}'.((\exists \mathbf{x}'.C(\mathbf{s}')) \wedge \prod_{1 \le j \le m} (y_j' \equiv f_j(x, y)))$$

Therefore, we can get this function without constructing $F_K(\mathbf{s}', \mathbf{s})$ explicitly as follows:
[Implicit Calculation of $\exists \mathbf{s}'.(C(\mathbf{s}') \wedge F_K(\mathbf{s}', \mathbf{s}))$]

Obtain the following $m+1$ functions D_i from D_0 to D_m sequentially. D_m is the result.

$$D_0(\mathbf{y}', \mathbf{s}) \overset{\text{def}}{=} \exists \mathbf{x}'.C(\mathbf{s}')$$

$$D_{i+1}(y_{i+2}, y_{i+3}, \cdots, y_m, \mathbf{s}) \overset{\text{def}}{=} (D_i(1, y_{i+2}, y_{i+3}, \cdots, y_m, \mathbf{s}) \wedge f_{i+1}(\mathbf{s})) \vee$$
$$(D_i(0, y_{i+2}, y_{i+3}, \cdots, y_m, \mathbf{s}) \wedge \neg f_{i+1}(\mathbf{s})), \quad 0 \le i \le m-2$$

$$D_m(\mathbf{s}) \overset{\text{def}}{=} (D_{m-1}(1, \mathbf{s}) \wedge f_m(\mathbf{s})) \vee$$
$$(D_{m-1}(0, \mathbf{s}) \wedge \neg f_m(\mathbf{s}))$$

4 Vectorization of SBDD Manipulation

Because most time consuming part of the symbolic model checking algorithm is the manipulation of Boolean functions represented by SBDD, we concentrate on vectorization of SBDD manipulation.

Vector processors achieve more than several GFLOPS by vector instructions which execute uniform operations on array-structured data using pipelined functional units, and they usually have large main memory of several hundred mega bytes. In conjunction with floating-point operations, they also support integer and bit-wise logical operations. Since the performance of programs on vector processors are strongly affected by *vectorization ratio* and *vector length*, we usually need to devise new algorithms suitable for vector execution to enjoy power of vector processors.

4.1 Vectorized Algorithm for SBDD Manipulation

The conventional algorithm for manipulating SBDD's is based on a recursive procedure (or depth-first operation), which is not suitable for vector processing. In this subsection, we propose a breadth-first algorithm for manipulating SBDD's [14].

The proposed algorithm consists of two parts; an *expansion phase* and a *reduction phase*. In the expansion phase, new nodes sufficient to represent the resultant function are generated in a breadth-first manner from the root node toward leaf nodes. In the reduction phase, the nodes generated in the expansion phase are checked and the redundant nodes and the equivalent nodes are removed in a breadth-first manner from nodes nearby leaf nodes toward the root node. The nodes generated in the expansion phase are called *temporary nodes*, while the nodes which already exist are called *permanent nodes*.

4.1.1 Expansion Phase

The input for the expansion phase is a triple (op, f, g), where op is a Boolean operator to be executed, and f and g are the root edges for operand Boolean functions. We refer to this triple as a *requirement*. The requirement (op, f, g) requires to compute the root edge for the resultant function of $op(f, g)$. During processing a requirement, new requirements will be generated for computing the operations between subfunctions or subsubfunctions $\cdots$ of the operand functions. Actually a requirement corresponds to a procedure call in the depth-first algorithm. We introduce a queue called a *requirement queue* to manage these requirements, which makes our procedure breadth-first. (The procedure would be depth-first if we use a stack instead of the queue.)

For a given requirement (op, f, g), a new root node is not always generated. We should not generate a new node if a node representing the result of $op(f, g)$ already exists. For example, if the result of $op(f, g)$ is found trivially, or found by looking up the operation result table, we do not generate a new node. These judgment can be done immediately from f and g. However, we can not tell, in general, the existence of the node of the same function as $op(f, g)$ until we construct the whole graph for the subfunctions of $op(f, g)$. In our breadth-first algorithm, we once generate a temporary node in such cases. Whether the temporary node is actually essential or not is examined in the reduction phase.

[Algorithm of the Expansion Phase]

Put the given requirement (op, f, g) to the requirement queue and repeat the following operations for every requirement in the queue until the queue becomes empty.

(1) If the root node representing the result of $op(f, g)$ is found trivially, return the edge pointing to the node.

(2) If the root node representing the result of $op(f, g)$ is found in the operation result table, return the edge found in the table.

(3) Otherwise, generate a new temporary node and return the edge pointing to the temporary node. At the same time, register the edge pointing to the temporary node to the operation result table as the result of $op(f, g)$ and put the new requirements (op, f_0, g_0) and (op, f_1, g_1) to the requirement queue, whose result will be '0' edge and '1' edge of this temporary node respectively.

Since the total number of requirements processed in the above procedure is exactly the same as the number of procedure calls in the conventional depth-first algorithm, there is no serious increase on the computation cost. The only drawback of our algorithm is the increase of the storage required for temporary nodes.

This procedure is suitable for vector processing because it is a simple reptition of processing all requirements in the queue simultaneously and all the repeated operations are vectorized.

4.1.2 Reduction Phase

After the expansion phase is finished, there may be the following type of temporary nodes:
- *Redundant node*: A temporary node whose '0' and '1' edges point to the same node.

- *Equivalent node*: A temporary node whose label, '0' and '1' edges are the same as one of the permanent nodes.

The main tasks of the reduction phase are to find redundant or equivalent nodes and to remove them. They are performed in a breadth-first manner from the nodes nearby the leaf nodes toward the root node. In addition, temporary nodes which are neither redundant nor equivalent are registered to the node table. In practice, the removal of the redundant nodes and the equivalent nodes should be done at the end of the reduction phase because these nodes could be pointed to by some edges. Therefore, the redundant nodes and the equivalent nodes are marked with *slave nodes*. Every slave node has a pointer to its *master node* which takes the place of the slave node. When a slave node is pointed to by '0' or '1' edges of other nodes, these edges are modified to point to the master node.

[Algorithm of the Reduction Phase]
Repeat the following operations while there are temporary nodes. For every temporary node whose '0' and '1' edges are not temporary nodes (i.e. permanent nodes or leaf nodes), execute the followings:

(1) If its '0' and '1' edges are the same, mark the node as a slave node whose master node is the node pointed to by its '0' edge.

(2) If there is an equivalent node registered in the node table, mark the temporary node as a slave node whose master node is the node registered in the node table.

(3) Otherwise, register the node to the node table, and change its attribute to permanent from temporary.

This procedure is also suitable for vector processing because all temporary nodes whose '0' and '1' edges are not temporary nodes can be processed at a time, and almost all operations are vectorizable.

5 Experimental Results

5.1 Pipelined ALU

The sequential machine we used as an example is an n bit pipelined ALU with a register file. Its structures is similar to the sequential circuit used by Burch et al[5, 6]. Fig. 1 shows its block diagram. The solid lines represent data paths and the dotted lines represent control signals. The register file consists of 4 registers of n bits. PRA, PRB and PRC are n bit pipeline registers. This pipelined ALU performs one of 16 arithmetic/logical operations on the register file according to the given input signals. There are 11 bit input signals; 1 bit *Enable* signal, 4 bit *Op_Code* signal, three 2 bit signals specifying source register A (*Src_Reg_A*), source register B (*Src_Reg_B*), and destination register (*Dest_Reg*) respectively. When *Enable* signal is asserted, this pipelined ALU performs its specified operation in 3 stage pipeline. In the first stage, the operands are read from the register file to PRA and/or PRB. Simple modification on the operand data may be performed during this stage if necessary. In the second stage, the specified operation is performed and its

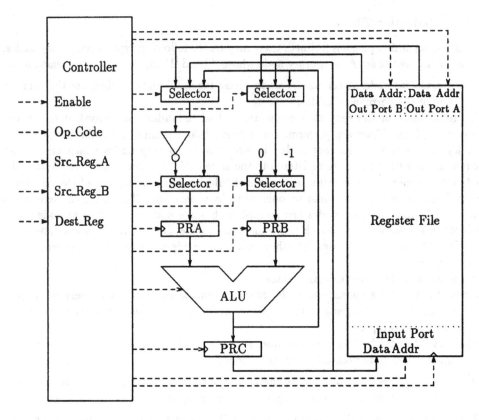

Figure 1: Block Diagram of a Pipelined ALU

result is stored in PRC. In addition, this result can be used immediately as operands of an instruction on the next clock cycle. In the third stage, the content of PRC is written into the register file, as well as it can be used as operands of an instruction on this clock cycle.

The specification of the ALU can be written as CTL formula in the similar manner stated in [5, 6]. Considering that the latency of this pipelined ALU is three, what we should verify are:

- If *Enable* is asserted, the content of the destination register at three clock later will be the result of the specified operation on the source registers at two clock later.

- For any register in the register file, if *Enable* is not asserted or it is not specified as a destination register, its content at three clock later will be the same as its content at two clock later.

We used the n bit pipelined ALU explained above as benchmark tests for our model checking algorithms. It is referred to CALUn hereafter. CALUn contains $7n + 11$ bit memory elements in total (the 4 word register file, 3 pipeline registers, a C-flag, and 10 flipflops in the controller). In addition, PADDn, which is obtained from CALUn by fixing the Op_Code input signals to *ADD* instruction and removing the C-flag. PADDn contains $7n + 6$ bit memory element in total.

Table 1: Size of SBDD representing Sequential Machines and Kripke Structures

Name	Sequential Machine (nodes)	Kripke Structure (nodes)	ratio K.S./S.M.
PADD2	132	7,514	56.9
PADD8	540	54,734	101.4
PADD16	1,084	117,694	108.6
CALU2	541	183,065	338.4
CALU8	2,194	> 1,000,000	——
CALU16	4,566	> 1,000,000	——

Table 2: Verification time and space of the implicit and explicit versions

Name	Implicit version		Explicit version		Ratio	
	time (sec)	size (nodes)	time (sec)	size (nodes)	time	size
PADD2	5.37	3,718	75.60	34,539	14.08	9.29
PADD8	90.67	8,320	6,025.88	279,746	66.46	33.62
PADD16	608.78	14,864	59,851.55	607,354	98.31	40.86
CALU2	24.35	34,527	——†	> 1,000,000	——	——
CALU8	1,879.72	252,997	——†	> 1,000,000	——	——
CALU16	16,648.28	754,465	——†	> 1,000,000	——	——

† Cannot be obtained because more than 1 million nodes are required.

5.2 Effects of the Implicit Manipulation of Transition Relation

In order to evaluate the effects of the implicit manipulation of transition relation stated in Section 3.2, we have implemented two symbolic model checker for sequential machine verification on a SPARC Station 1+: one is based on the algorithm explained in Section 3.1 (*Explicit* version); the other is based on the algorithm stated in Section 3.2 (*Implicit* version). These two model checker can use up to 1 million SBDD nodes by using about 23 M byte user area. We used SBDD package developed by Minato [13] for Boolean manipulations in the model checkers.

Table 1 shows the number of SBDD nodes used to represent a sequential machine (i.e. its state transition functions and output functions) and the size of SBDD representing a

Table 3: Benchmark results of the vectorized symbolic model checking

Name	Scalar (sec)	Vector (sec)	S/V
PADD2	4.251	0.659	6.45
PADD8	56.132	6.718	8.36
PADD16	387.178	38.730	10.00
CALU2	18.686	1.874	9.97
CALU8	833.253	40.991	20.33
CALU16	——†	741.420	——

† Not experimented because it may exceed CPU time limit.

characteristic function for transition relations of their corresponding Kripke structures. Kripke structures require much more space than sequential machines.

Table 2 shows the comparison of the experiments of the two implementations. It shows the required time and the required number of SBDD nodes for verification. We can see from this table that the *Implicit* version is dramatically efficient compared with the *Explicit* version. It achieves up to 100 times and 40 times improvements in time and space respectively. The amount of improvements seems to become much larger if a sequential machine under verification becomes more complex.

5.3 Effects of the Vectorization

Considering the experimental results stated in the previous subsection, we adopt the *Implicit* mode checking algorithm to implement the vectorized symbolic model checker for sequential machines on a vector processor HITAC S-820/80. We call this implementation as *Vector* version. The *Vector* version uses the vectorized manipulation algorithms for SBDD proposed in Section 4.1. It can use 5 million SBDD nodes with 256 M byte user area.

Table 3 shows the scalar execution and the vector execution of the *Vector* version on HITAC S-820/80. It achieves about 6 to 20 vector acceleration ration. It verified CALU16 in about 12 minutes.

6 Concluding Remarks

In this paper, we first compared the implicit and the explicit symbolic model checking algorithms of CTL for sequential machine verifications. It is shown that the implicit one is dramatically efficient and achieved $14 \sim 98$ times and $9 \sim 38$ improvement in time and space. The more complex sequential machines become, the more improvement factor it achieves.

Next we proposed the vectorized symbolic model checking algorithm based on the new algorithm. It achieved $6 \sim 20$ acceleration ratio and succeeded to verify a 16 bit pipelined ALU of 16 arithmetic/logical operations on 4 word register file in only 12 minutes.

Our current implementations do not support *frontier set simplification* [5, 6, 9] which is effective in fixed point calculations. We think it is not difficult to realize it in our model checkers. We would also like to support *fairness constraint* [5, 6] in the near future.

Acknowledgments The authors would like to express their appreciations to Prof. E. M. Clarke of CMU, Dr. N. Takagi of Kyoto Univ., Dr. N. Ishiura of Osaka Univ., and Dr. S. Kimura of Kobe Univ. for their valuable discussions. This research is supported partially by Japan-U.S.A. cooperative research of JSPS and NSF. It is also supported partially by a grant-in-aid for scientific research of the Ministry of Education of Japan.

References

[1] S. B. Akers. Binary decision diagrams. *IEEE Transactions on Computers*, C-27(6):509–516, June 1978.

[2] K. S. Brace, R. L. Rudell, and R. E. Bryant. Efficient implementation of a BDD package. In *Proc. 27th Design Automation Conference*, pages 40–45, June 1990.

[3] R. E. Bryant. Graph-based algorithms for boolean function manipulation. *IEEE Transactions on Computers*, C-35(8):677–691, August 1986.

[4] J. R. Burch, E. M. Clarke, and D. E. Long. Representing circuits more efficiently in symbolic model checking. In *Proc. 28th Design Automation Conference*, June 1991.

[5] J. R. Burch, E. M. Clarke, K. L. McMillan, and D. L. Dill. Sequential circuit verification using symbolic model checking. Technical report, Carnegie Mellon University, November 1989.

[6] J. R. Burch, E. M. Clarke, K. L. McMillan, and D. L. Dill. Sequential circuit verification using symbolic model checking. In *Proc. 27th Design Automation Conference*, pages 46–51, June 1990.

[7] J. R. Burch, E. M. Clarke, K. L. McMillan, D. L. Dill, and J. Hwang. Symbolic model checking: 10^{20} states and beyond. In *Proc. Logic in Computer Science*, June 1990.

[8] E. M. Clarke and E. A. Emerson. Synthesis of synchronization skeletons for branching time temporal logic. In *Proc. Workshop on Logic of Programs*, pages 52–71. Springer-Verlag, 1981.

[9] O. Coudert, C. Berthet, and J. C. Madre. Verification of sequential machines using functional vectors. In *Proc. IMEC-IFIP Intrn. Workshop on Applied Formal Methods for Correct VLSI Design*, pages 111–128, November 1989.

[10] O. Coudert, J. C. Madre, and C. Berthet. Verifying temporal properties of sequential machines without building their state diagrams. In *Proc. Workshop on Computer-Aided Verification*, June 1990.

[11] N. Ishiura and S. Yajima. A class of logic functions expressible by polynomial-size binary decision diagrams. In *Proc. the Synthesis and Simulation Meeting and International Interchange*, pages 48–54, October 1990.

[12] S. Kimura and E. M. Clarke. A parallel algorithm for constructing binary decision diagrams. In *Proc. IEEE ICCD'90*, September 1990.

[13] S. Minato, N. Ishiura, and S. Yajima. Shared binary decision diagram with attributed edges for efficient boolean function manipulation. In *Proc. 27th Design Automation Conference*, pages 52–57, June 1990.

[14] H. Ochi, N. Ishiura, and S. Yajima. Breadth-first manipulation of SBDD of boolean functions for vector processing. In *Proc. 28th Design Automation Conference*, June 1991.

[15] H. J. Touati, H. Savoj, B. Lin, R. K. Brayton, and A. Sangiovanni-Vincentelli. Implicit state enumeration of finite state machines using BDD's. In *Proc. ICCAD*, 1990.

Functional Extension of Symbolic Model Checking

Thomas Filkorn

Siemens AG, Corporate Laboratories for Information Technology, ZFE IS INF 2
Otto-Hahn-Ring 6, D-8000 Munich 83, F.R.G.

Abstract

Burch, Clarke, McMillan, Dill and Hwang describe in [4] a symbolic model checking procedure for μ-calculus formulas. The algorithm is based on the representation of relations by binary decision diagrams (BDDs) [1]. In the area of synchronous digital circuits a functional instead of a relational representation results in more compact BDDs. This is the reason for extending the μ-calculus and the symbolic model checking procedure with functions.

1 Introduction

Errors in the design phase of systems, like communication protocols or digital circuits, are a major reason for unexpected delays, costs and lack of reliability. Verification is today performed by techniques based on simulation and testing. However these are far away from being exhaustive and hence correctness can not be guaranteed. This has stimulated interest in formal verification techniques which can guarantee correctness with respect to the verified properties.

The behaviour of many systems can be modeled adequately as finite-state systems and verification of them can often be performed automatically by examining their state-graphs. Based on this a number of methods, e.g., testing for various equivalences or model checking on finite-state systems, have been proposed and are further researched. Since all of the methods rely on an explicit representation of the state-graph in a table or something similar they are limited to systems with at most approximately 10^6 states. A principal problem in the application to larger realistic examples is the so called *state explosion problem*, that is the number of states grows exponentially with the number of components in the system. One approach to avoid the state explosion problem is to represent the state space symbolically.

One kind of symbolic representation are binary decision diagrams (BDDs) [1]. BDDs are a canonical representation of boolean formulas by directed acyclic graphs and Bryant described in [1] efficient algorithms for manipulating them. Based on BDDs Burch, Clarke et al. described in [3] a model checking algorithm for a branching time temporal logic, CTL, and generalized the idea in [4] to a powerful version of the μ-calculus. Their model checking algorithm is restricted to relations. From a theoretical point of view this is not really a restriction, since every function $f : A \to B$ can be seen as a relation $r_f \subseteq A \times B$. But, for a compact representation, BDDs exploit regularities in the structure of a function and often these regularities can not be exploited by BDDs in the corresponding relation. From our experiences in the area of digital circuits the BDD representations for the functions of circuits are in general more compact than the representation of the corresponding relations.

This is the reason why I extended the μ-calculus presented by Burch, Clarke et al. in [4] with functions. Section 2 describes the extended μ-calculus and in Section 3 the BDD based symbolic evaluation algorithm is presented. Section 4 will give results about the practical examples, including the simple pipeline design from [3], where the functional BDD representation is more efficient than the BDD representation of the model by relations.

2 The Extended μ-Calculus

The semantic model of the extended μ-calculus formulas will be vectors and functions over vectors. Since functions are normally defined only for vectors of a certain length, we have to introduce simple typing in the calculus in order to interpret the formulas in the semantic model. The set of basic types is Γ. Let X be a set of variable symbols, where each $x \in X$ has a basic type $\tau \in \Gamma$. F is a set of function symbols and every $f \in F$ has a type $\tau_1 \times ... \times \tau_n \rightarrow \tau_{n+1}$ with basic types $\tau_i \in \Gamma$. There are two syntactical categories, individual terms and functional terms, both typed and inductively defined as follows.

individual terms

x where $x \in X$. The type of this individual term is the type of the variable symbol x.

$g(t_1, ..., t_n)$ where t_i are individual terms with types τ_i and g must be a functional term with type $\tau_1 \times ... \times \tau_n \rightarrow \tau$. The type of this individual term is τ.

$\forall x\, t$ where t is an individual term with type τ and $x \in X$. The resulting type is τ.

functional terms

f where $f \in F$. The type of this functional term is the type of the functional symbol f.

$\lambda x_1, ..., x_n\, t$ where t is an individual term and $x_1, ..., x_n \in X$. The type of this functional term is $\tau_1 \times ... \times \tau_n \rightarrow \tau$, when τ_i is the type of x_i and τ the type of t.

$\mathrm{rec} f.g$ where g is a functional term and $f \in F$, both with type $\tau_1 \times ... \times \tau_n \rightarrow \tau$, which is also the resulting type.

The individual and functional terms are interpreted with respect to a semantic structure $\mathcal{M} = (D, I_\Gamma, I_X, I_F)$. The *domain* D is a finite, non-empty, totally ordered set. I_Γ gives an interpretation of the basic types $\tau \in \Gamma$ as sets of vectors over D, $I_\Gamma(\tau) = D^{n_\tau}$. Individual variables $x \in X$ with basic type τ are mapped by the variable interpretation I_X to vectors over D, $I_X(x) \in I_\Gamma(\tau) = D^{n_\tau}$. In the same way function symbols $f \in F$ are interpreted by the functional variable interpretation I_F as functions over D-vectors. Let $\tau_1 \times ... \times \tau_n \rightarrow \tau$ be the type of f, then $I_F(f) \in (I_\Gamma(\tau_1) \times ... \times I_\Gamma(\tau_n) \rightarrow I_\Gamma(\tau))$.

The semantic interpretation $I_{(I_X, I_F)}$ for a semantic structure (D, I_Γ, I_X, I_F) maps individual terms t to vectors over D, $I_{(I_X, I_F)}(t) \in D^{n_t}$, and functional terms g to functions over D-vectors, $I_{(I_X, I_F)}(g) \in (D^{n_1} \times ... \times D^{n_k} \rightarrow D^{n_{k+1}})$. $I_{(I_X, I_F)}$ is inductively defined on the syntactic structure of individual and functional terms. In the following x is a variable, f a functional symbol, g a functional term, and $t_1, ..., t_n, t$ are individual terms. $\tau(x_i)$ is the type of a variable symbol x_i. The definition of $I_{(I_X, I_F)}$ on individual terms is given by the following equations:

$$
\begin{aligned}
I_{(I_X, I_F)}(x) &= I_X(x) \\
I_{(I_X, I_F)}(g(t_1, ..., t_n)) &= I_{(I_X, I_F)}(g)(I_{(I_X, I_F)}(t_1), ..., I_{(I_X, I_F)}(t_n)) \\
I_{(I_X, I_F)}(\forall x\, t) &= min(\{I_{(I_X \langle x \leftarrow e \rangle, I_F)}(t) \mid e \in I_\Gamma(x)\})
\end{aligned}
$$

min for a set of vectors over D is defined as a vector, in which each component is the minimal value of all the values occuring in the corresponding component of all vectors in the set. The minimal value is determined with respect to the total ordering on D. The interpretation of functional terms is also defined equationally:

$$I_{(I_X,I_F)}(f) \quad = \quad I_F(f)$$
$$I_{(I_X,I_F)}(\lambda x_1,...,x_n\ t) \quad = \quad h : I_\Gamma(\tau(x_1)) \times ... \times I_\Gamma(\tau(x_n)) \to I_\Gamma(\tau(t))$$
$$h(e_1,...,e_n) \stackrel{\mathrm{def}}{=} I_{(I_{X(x_1 \leftarrow e_1,...,x_n \leftarrow e_n)},I_F)}(t)$$
$$e_i \in I_\Gamma(\tau(x_i))$$
$$I_{(I_X,I_F)}(\mathrm{rec}f.g) \quad = \quad \mathrm{lfp}\ h \in I'_F(f)\ .\ I_{(I_X,I_{F(f \leftarrow h)})}(g)$$

$I'_F(f)$ stands as an abbreviaton for $I_\Gamma(\tau_1) \times ... \times I_\Gamma(\tau_n) \to I_\Gamma(\tau)$ when f has the type $\tau_1 \times ... \times \tau_n \to \tau$. This are all possible functions to which the function symbol f can be mapped by a semantic interpretation. lfp $h.g$ denotes the least fixpoint of the functional g with respect to the partial ordering $\sqsubseteq$ on functions, defined in the following. On the domain D a partial order $\sqsubseteq$ is defined by: $a \sqsubseteq b$ iff $a = b$ or $a = \perp$. $\perp$ denotes the minimal value of D with respect to the total ordering on D. This extends to vectors of D by: $\langle a_1,...,a_n \rangle \sqsubseteq \langle b_1,...,b_n \rangle$ iff $\forall i : a_i \sqsubseteq b_i$. The partial order $\sqsubseteq$ can further be extended to functions $f_1, f_2 \in (D^n \to D^m)$ in the usual way: $f_1 \sqsubseteq f_2$ iff $\forall x \in D^n : f_1(x) \sqsubseteq f_2(x)$. A functional g is monotone, iff $f_1 \sqsubseteq f_2$ implies $g(f_1) \sqsubseteq g(f_2)$. A least fixpoint need not exist for every functional, but for monotone functionals over a finite domain it exists and is uniquely defined. So $I_{(I_X,I_F)}$ is only well defined for functional terms rec$f.g$ where g is a monotone functional.

In this paragraph I want to outline briefly how the μ-calculus used by Burch, Clarke et al. in [4] is contained in the extended calculus. For this I assume the boolean domain, $D = \{0,1\}$, with the ordering $0 < 1$, thus 0 serving as the bottom element $\perp$. Any relation $r \subseteq D^n$ can be represented by its characteristic function $f_r : D^n \to D$ with $f(x) = 1 \Leftrightarrow x \in r$. For characteristic functions f_r the ordering $\sqsubseteq$ is exactly the set inclusion ordering on the corresponding relations r and so the rec operator is identical to the μ operator. From the previous it is clear that the relational terms defined in Section 3 of [4] are a subset of the functional terms used in the calculus here. Also the formulas of [4] are special cases of the individual terms described here, if the boolean operators $\lor, \neg, =$ are available with their usual interpretation in I_F.

By using a finite domain D and the ordering $\sqsubseteq$ we have a general calculus in which also e.g., 3-valued logic or recursively defined functions can be expressed directly. However the examples of Section 4 will only use the boolean domain $D = \{0,1\}$.

3 Symbolic Evaluation

Evaluation of a term t means computing the semantic interpretation $I_{(I_X,I_F)}(t)$ with respect to a semantic structure (D, I_Γ, I_X, I_F). An explicit representation of functions $g : D^{n_1+...+n_k} \to D^m$ by tables, would implicate the state explosion problem, as mentioned in the introduction. To avoid this problem BDDs are used here as a symbolical representation of functions.

In [1] Bryant described binary decision diagrams (BDDs) as a normal form representation for boolean functions and efficient algorithms for manipulating them. BDDs are directed acyclic graphs with internal nodes labeled by variables $x_1,...,x_n$ and encode the truth table of a boolean function by exploiting some regularities in the function. For a given variable ordering a boolean function has a unique BDD. In most cases the ordering of the variables is very critical for the size of the BDD. For certain boolean functions (e.g., integer multiplication [1]) the size of a BDD grows exponentially in the number of variables for every variable ordering, which is not surprising since the NP-complete satisfiability problem can be solved with BDDs. However from our experience the sizes of the BDDs representing boolean functions realized by digital circuits are small in most cases. The extension of BDDs to functions $f : D^n \to D^m$, where D is a finite set is straigthforward.

The symbolic evaluation algorithm described in the next part is based on a few operations on BDDs. *BDD_var* maps variable symbols $x \in X$ to vectors of BDD variables. Since BDDs are normal forms for functions the equivalecnce check *BDD_equal* is a trivial operation. *BDD_forall* gets two arguments, a set of BDD variables and a BDD-vector, and evaluates a BDD-vector according to the semantic given in Section 2. The basic operation during the evaluation process is *BDD_compose*. Given the BDD-vectors for $g(x_1, ..., x_n), f_1, ..., f_n$ it computes the BDD-vector of the composite function $g|_{(x_1=f_1,...,x_n=f_n)}$. The apply operation, as described in [1], can be seen as a special case of function composition.

Based on BDDs, symbolic evaluation of individual terms and functional terms is performed by the routines *eval_it* and *eval_ft* as defined in the Figure below. The definitions of the semantic interpretation $I_{(I_X,I_F)}$ from Section 2 are directly computed, but for all possible variable interpretations instead of only a specific one.

Hence, the result of the routine *eval_it* for an individual term t is not a value from D^n, but a BDD-vector t_{BDD} with variables from X. For a specific variable interpretation I_X the interpretation $I_{(I_X,I_F)}(t)$ can be obtained from the BDD-vector t_{BDD} by substituting all the BDD variables in t_{BDD} with their values according to I_X, resulting in a vector over D. $I_{(I_X,I_F)}(t) = t_{BDD}|_{x_i=I_X(x_i)}$. In the first case of *eval_it* a variable is just mapped to its corresponding vector of BDD variables. In the two other cases the parts of the individual term are evaluated first and afterwards the BDD operation, realizing the semantic (see Section 2), is applied.

$$
\begin{aligned}
\text{eval\_it}(x, I_F) &= \text{BDD\_var}(x) \\
\text{eval\_it}(f(t_1, ..., t_n), I_F) &= \text{BDD\_compose}(\text{eval\_ft}(f, I_F), \\
&\qquad \text{eval\_it}(t_1, I_F), ..., \text{eval\_it}(t_n, I_F)) \\
\text{eval\_it}(\forall x\, t, I_F) &= \text{BDD\_forall}(\text{BDD\_var}(x), \text{eval\_it}(t, I_F))
\end{aligned}
$$

The result of the routine *eval_ft* for a functional term g is a BDD-vector g_{BDD} and a vector of variables, indicating that these variables are serving as placeholders for the functions arguments. Again the interpretation $I_{(I_X,I_F)}(g)$ for a variable interpretation I_X is obtained from g_{BDD} by substituting all variables not marked as placeholders by their values, according to I_X. The resulting BDD-vector, containinig only placeholder variables, is a representation for the function $I_{(I_X,I_F)}(g)$. When g is a function symbol its BDD representation is obtained by a simple table lookup in I_F. In the second case the individual term t is evaluated first, resulting in a BDD t_{BDD} with variables of X. For the lambda abstraction it is sufficient to mark the variables $x_1, ..., x_n$ as placeholders without affecting the BDD-vector t_{BDD}. The least fixpoint $\text{rec} f.g$ of a monotone functional g is calculated by the standard fixpoint iteration, starting with the bottom element $\vec{\perp}$. $\vec{\perp}$ is a vector of $\perp$'s, when $\perp$ is the minimal element of the domain D, with respect to the total ordering on D. The next function h_{i+1} of the iteration is calculated from h_i and g by evaluating the functional term g with the interpretation of the function symbol f set to h_i. Monotonicity of g and finiteness of D guarantees termination of the iteration with the least fixpoint lfp $f.g = h_{f_p+1} = h_{f_p}$.

$$
\begin{aligned}
\text{eval\_ft}(f, I_F) &= I_F(f) \\
\text{eval\_ft}(\lambda x_1, ..., x_n\, t, I_F) &= \langle \text{eval\_it}(t, I_F), \langle \text{BDD\_var}(x_1), ..., \text{BDD\_var}(x_n) \rangle \rangle \\
\text{eval\_ft}(\text{rec} f.g, I_F) &= h := \vec{\perp};
\end{aligned}
$$

```
          do
                h_old := h;
                h := eval_ft(g, I_F⟨f ← h_old⟩);
          until BDD_equal(h, h_old);
          return h
```

4 Empirical Results

Using BDDs is only efficient in a heuristic sense, and so it is difficult to give estimates for the sizes of the BDDs. Therefore empirical results from practical circuits are needed in order to evaluate the method and to compare it with other approaches. For this reason two examples of synchronous digital circuits, reported previously in the literature, were considered: The MinMax circuit [8], which is a small signal processor proposed by IMEC as a benchmark for formal system design methods, and the simple pipeline used by Burch, Clarke et al. in [3].

4.1 MinMax Circuit

This Section shows how equivalence of functionally represented automata can be expressed as a term in the extended μ-calculus. So a symbolic comparison of the automata can be performed by evaluating that term with the symbolic evaluation algorithm of Section 3. Specification and implementation of synchronous digital circuits like the MinMax example can be modeled by finite-state systems, more precisely Mealy automata. A Mealy automaton is a tuple $(S, \Sigma, \Delta, \delta, \lambda, r)$, where S is the set of states, Σ the input alphabet, Δ the output alphabet and $r \in S$ the initial state. The behaviour of a Mealy automaton is defined by the transition function $\delta : S \times \Sigma \rightarrow S$ and the output function $\lambda : S \times \Sigma \rightarrow \Delta$. In the case of digital circuits the domain of the states, inputs, and outputs are bitvectors.

Behavioural equivalence of two Mealy automata $\mathcal{M}_{spec}$ and $\mathcal{M}_{impl}$ can be defined with respect to their initial states: $r_{spec} \approx r_{impl}$. Two states are behavioural equivalent iff for every input sequence the generated output sequences are equal. The relation $\approx \subseteq S_{spec} \times S_{impl}$ of behavioural equivalent states is defined inductively as the largest relation with the following property:

$$s_1 \approx s_2 \text{ iff } \forall \sigma \in \Sigma : (\lambda_{spec}(s_1, \sigma) = \lambda_{impl}(s_2, \sigma) \text{ and } \delta_{spec}(s_1, \sigma) \approx \delta_{impl}(s_2, \sigma)).$$

The largest fixpoint $\nu f.g(f)$ of an recursive definition, as above, can also be expressed by a least fixpoint: $\neg \mu f.\neg g(\neg f)$. With this simple syntactic transformation the above equivalence definition for Mealy automata can be expressed directly in our calculus by the individual term $\neg \not\approx (r_{spec}, r_{impl})$, where $\not\approx$ stands as an abreviation for the following functional term:

$$rec \not\approx . \lambda x_1, x_2 \neg \forall \sigma (\lambda_{spec}(s_1, \sigma) = \lambda_{impl}(s_2, \sigma) \wedge \neg \not\approx (\delta_{spec}(s_1, \sigma), \delta_{impl}(s_2, \sigma)))$$

This formula was evaluated for different bitsizes of the MinMax circuit and the results are listed in Table 1. The first five columns give some characteristics about the circuit. *width* is the width of the data path, *states* is an approximation for the number of possible states, these are those reachable from initial states. The execution times, measured in minutes, of column *time* have been obtained on a Sun 3/60 workstation with the described method, implemented in a Prolog extended by unification in finite algebras [6]. As a comparison, the times in column *time*[7] are the ones Berthet, Coudert and Madre obtained with their approach for BDD-based automata equivalence checking [5] on a DPX5000 mini computer (about twice as fast as a VAX/780).

width	states	time	time [7]
8	$2.8 * 10^6$	3	1.5
9	$2.5 * 10^7$	4	5
10	$1.8 * 10^8$	6	23
16	$4.4 * 10^{13}$	20	
32	$9.3 * 10^{27}$	109	

Table 1: MinMax Empirical Results

The time for evaluating the above term, expressing automata equivalence, grows polynomially with the bitsize N, about $N^{2.5}$, whereas execution times in [7] seem to grow exponentially, about 4^N.

4.2   Synchronous Pipeline

This section gives an example for the verification of a simple pipeline design. The circuit was first described in [3] and also verified with the symbolic model checker of [3]. However Burch, Clarke et al. used relations for representing the circuit. In contrast to them in the following approach functions are used for the same task.

The pipeline performs simple arithmetic and logical operations on a register file, according to an instruction register. The instruction register contains the source register addresses, the destination register address, the operation code, and a special stall bit. The operations are performed in three stages. In the first step the operands are read from the register file. In the next step an ALU operation is performed and in the third step the result is written back to the register file. Since the result of an operation can be used immediately in the next step as an operand there are register bypass paths. If the stall bit in the instruction register is set a "no-operation" is propagated through the pipe. A simple block diagram of the pipeline is shown below.

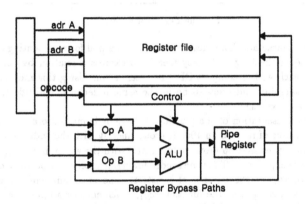

Register Bypass Paths

The pipeline can be modeled as a finite-state system. The state is composed of the register file state, the pipe registers and the state of the control part. A transition function δ gives for each state and input, the state in the next step. From Table 2 the great difference in the representation by a transition relation, as done in [3], and the functional representation is evident.

A specification of the pipeline can be obtained by taking into account the latency of the pipe which is three clock cycles. The result of an operation will not affect the register file until three cycles in the future, and the inputs of the operation should correspond to the state of the register file two cycles in the future. reg is a simple projection, giving the register file part of a pipeline state. The function $select$, selects the i-th part of an array of values. $reg_2(i)$, $reg_3(i)$ are used as abbreviations for the value of the i-th register two, three steps in the future.

$$reg_2(i) \ = \ select(reg(\delta(\delta(s,\sigma_1),\sigma_2),i))$$
$$reg_3(i) \ = \ select(reg(\delta(\delta(\delta(s,\sigma_1),\sigma_2),\sigma_3),i))$$

The function $aluop(op,x,y)$ gives the result of the operation op applied on the arguments x and y. With this abreviations the whole specification can be expressed by the following term in our calculus.

$$\forall s,\sigma_1,\sigma_2,\sigma_3,x \quad \neg stall \quad \Rightarrow \ reg_3(c) = aluop(op,reg_2(a),reg_2(b))$$
$$\wedge$$
$$stall \vee x \neq c \ \Rightarrow \ reg_3(x) = reg_2(x)$$

The above formula was evaluated for different versions of the pipeline. The pipeline performed addition and exor operations and was used with various register widths and numbers of registers. The first column *width* gives the width of the registers in bits. In the following columns the results for register files with 4, 8, and 16 registers are listed. *BDD* gives the number of nodes in the BDD-vector for representing the transition function δ. The execution times, measured in seconds, of column *time* have been obtained on a Sun 3/60 workstation with the described method, implemented in a Prolog extended by unification in finite algebras [6]. As a comparison, the columns *BDD*[3] and *time*[3] are the results Burch, Clarke et al. obtained with their approach for the same task also on a Sun 3.

width	4 registers				8 registers		16 registers	
	BDD	*BDD* [3]	*time*	*time* [3]	*BDD*	*time*	*BDD*	*time*
2	161	18429	21	188	355	141	757	1178
4	329	53924	66	1706	715	433	1517	
8	665		308		1435	1683	3037	
16	1337		1905		2875		6077	
32	2681				5755		12157.0	

Table 2: Pipeline Empirical Results

In a new paper Burch, Clarke and Long described in [2] a method for representing circuits more efficiently in symbolic model checking. The key idea is to express a relation by conjunctions or disjunctions of relations, each with a compact BDD representation. Using this method the results have been improved considerably and seem to be in the same order of magnitude then the ones achieved with the functional extension.

The functional BDD representation of the pipelines behaviour is much more compact than the pure relational one, by a factor of more than 100. It grows linearly with the width and the number of registers. The relational representation grows only linearly with the width, but cubically with the number of registers from our experience. The time needed for verification grows between quadratically and cubically with the width and the number of registers. The most time consuming operation during verification consists in computing the function reg_3, which encodes all possible operand, i.e., register, combinations. Because in the BDD for reg_3 nearly no sharing is possible between two different combinations, the BDD grows at least quadratically with the number of registers.

References

[1] R. E. Bryant. Graph-based algorithms for boolean function manipulation. *IEEE Transactions Computer*, C-35(12):1035–1044, 1986.

[2] J.R. Burch, E.M. Clarke, and D.E. Long. Representing circuits more efficiently in symbolic model checking. In *ACM/IEEE Design Automation Conference*, 1991.

[3] J.R. Burch, E.M. Clarke, K.L. McMillan, and David L. Dill. Sequential circuit verification using symbolic model checking. In *ACM/IEEE Design Automation Conference*, 1990.

[4] J.R. Burch, E.M. Clarke, K.L. McMillan, David L. Dill, and L.J. Hwang. Symbolic model checking: 10^{20} states and beyond. In *LICS*, 1990.

[5] Olivier Coudert, Christian Berthet, and Jean-Christophe Madre. Verification of sequential machines using boolean functional vectors. In *IMEC-IFIP International Workshop on Applied Formal Methods For Correct VLSI Design*, 1989.

[6] Thomas Filkorn. Unifikation in endlichen Algebren und ihre Integration in Prolog. Master's thesis, Technical University Munich, 1988.

[7] Jean-Christophe Madre, Olivier Coudert, Michel Currat, Alain Debreil, and Christian Berthet. The formal verification chain at BULL. In *EURO ASIC 90*, 1990.

[8] Diederik Verkest, Luc Claesen, and Hugo De Man. Special benchmark session on formal system design. In *IMEC-IFIP International Workshop on Applied Formal Methods For Correct VLSI Design*, 1989.

An Automated Proof Technique for Finite-State Machine Equivalence *

Wenbo Mao [†]   George J Milne

HardLab, Department of Computer Science, University of Strathclyde
26 Richmond Street, Glasgow G1 1XH, Scotland U.K.

Abstract

This paper presents a mechanical technique which allows behavioural equivalence proof between (nondeterministic) finite-state machines (FSMs). Given a pair of FSMs which are recursively described in the syntax of a process algebra, a third FSM which represents the concurrent behaviour of the two original FSMs is constructed. An algorithm is engineered for comparing the two FSMs against this third concurrent FSM. A self-evident proof of the equivalence between the FSMs will be produced; if the two FSMs are not equivalent, a sequnce of events will be returned which distinguishes between them.

1 Introduction

Finite-State Machines (FSMs) are common components of hardware designs. Proof of FSM correctness is a frequently occurring task in hardware design verification. By using process algebras such as CCS [19], CSP [11], and ACP [3] the task of proving FSM correctness may be helped in two ways. Firstly, from a descriptive point of view an FSM may be described by two processes at two different abstraction levels, high and low. The high level (usually referred to as the *specification*) stipulates the abstract behaviour of the FSM, while the low level (usually referred to as the *implementation*) may provide detailed hardware design information. Proof of FSM correctness can then be addressed as the proof of behavioural equivalence between two processes which respectively represent the specification and an implementation of an FSM. Secondly, the process algebra approach helps to develop new computational methods. Using process algebras, powerful algebraic techniques based either on the processes *semantic transitions* or based on their *syntactic transformations* may be applied to provide a proof.

Nice features of the proof method based on semantic reasoning include low computational complexity and fully decidable proof. *State Space Partitioning* [13], [5] is one of the well-known techniques for finding bisimulations between two processes. However, there is a commonly known drawback with the partitioning technique. Namely, a proof delivered by the state partitioning technique is merely a "yes/no" answer which is not accompanied

---

*Supported in part by the EEC under contract ESPRIT BRA 3216 "CHARME"
[†]Supported by a University of Strathclyde Postgraduate Studentship

by any easily-understandable explanation. Such an explanation is important especially when a "no" results since this can be used as the diagnostic information for identifying the design error.

Recent research developments in proof technique based on syntactic manipulation include the term rewriting strategy seen in [12]. This strategy is based on the principle of transforming the syntax (i.e., CCS expressions) into a *canonical* syntactic structure or *normal form*. A canonical system basically demands that objects under transformation have the terminating property. In real applications, such as digital hardware, most FSMs do not necessarily terminate and are expressed by recursive process descriptions. For these recursive processes a canonical rewriting procedure will not halt. Therefore a rewriting system for finite-state processes only works in an interactive way. In [7], a term rewriting system is given which allows the user to *interactively* build his/her own (recursive rewriting) strategy. The consequence of this is that a term rewriting system cannot provide automatic proof of behavioural equivalence/inequivalence between finite-state processes; especially when inequivalence is the case.

TAV (Tools for Automatic Verification) [14], [10] is a distinct verification tool which can provide a self-evident explanation when two processes are not equivalent. An inequivalence is explained by TAV as a Hennessy-Milner Logic formula [9]. In order to compute such a formula, Hillerstöm [10] applied a backtracking algorithm (see e.g., [1]) when implementing TAV. Since backtracking techniques work on the principle of finding a solution by exhaustively searching data structures, it is commonly regarded as computationally inefficient.

In this paper we present a new approach to constructing an equivalence proof between a pair of processes; in fact processes belonging to the Circal process algebra [18]. The Circal concurrent composition operator "*" plays an important role in this approach. Given two nondeterministic, finite-state processes, we use this operator to compose them into a third process. Due to a property that two equivalent processes may synchronise and run concurrently to yield a concurrent process with equivalent behaviour, this concurrent process is used as a standard by which to compare the two original processes. In case two processes are not equivalent, a sequence of events will be automatically generated from the concurrent composition, which can distinguish between the different behaviour of the two processes.

This paper is organised as follows. In Section 2, we introduce the Circal process algebra and go through necessary theoretic preliminaries. In Section 3, the concurrent composition method is presented. In Section 4, we discuss how to extend the work to nondeterministic processes. Finally, Section 5 gives our conclusions.

2 Preliminaries

Circal is a process algebra and a formal language. One of its operators, concurrent composition, makes Circal suitable for describing the concurrent communicating behaviour of interacting FSMs. This operator is also essential to the technique presented in this paper. We therefore wish to use Circal as the language with which to describe the operation of FSMs. For details about Circal and recent research on its semantics and proof techniques see [16], [17], [18], [20] and [2]. Related process algebras include the work of [8], [19], [11] and [3].

A sublanguage of Circal which we choose for presenting our investigation in this paper has the following syntax:

$$P \quad ::= \quad \Delta \mid x \mid aP \mid P+P \mid P \oplus P \mid P * P \mid \mu x.P(x)$$

We denote this sublanguage by $\mathcal{P}$. The *terminal* operator Δ accepts no events; each *prefix* operator a represents an arbitrary event from an alphabet Σ, the *prefix* term aP accepts the event a; the *external choice* term $P+Q$ acts either like P or like Q; the *internal choice* term $P \oplus Q$ behaves similarly as $P + Q$, except the behaviour is not determined by the external event stimulus; the *concurrent* term $P * Q$ synchronise events in the alphabet of P and in that of Q simultaneously; finally x is a variable from a set of variables (denoted by X) and the *recursive* term $\mu x.P(x)$ repeats the behaviour stipulated by P.

We use a *labelled transition system* for providing this sublanguage with a formal semantics. Transition $P \xrightarrow{a} P'$ means that P accepts the event a and is thereby transformed into P'. We often write $P \xrightarrow{a}$ to mean that there exists some P' with $P \xrightarrow{a} P'$ and write $P \not\xrightarrow{a}$ if no such P' exists. As we will deal separately with deterministic and nondeterministic systems, we first define the *structured operational semantic (SOS)* rules [22] for the transition relation $\longrightarrow$ on deterministic processes.

$$\frac{}{aP \xrightarrow{a} P} \qquad \frac{P \xrightarrow{a} P'}{P+Q \xrightarrow{a} P'} \qquad \frac{P \xrightarrow{a} P'}{P+Q \xrightarrow{a} Q'} \qquad \frac{P([\mu x.P(x)/x]) \xrightarrow{a} P'}{\mu x.P(x) \xrightarrow{a} P'}$$

$$\frac{P \xrightarrow{a} P' \wedge Q \xrightarrow{a} Q'}{P*Q \xrightarrow{a} P'*Q'} \quad \frac{P \xrightarrow{a} P' \wedge a \notin \Sigma(Q)}{P*Q \xrightarrow{a} P'*Q} \quad \frac{Q \xrightarrow{a} Q' \wedge a \notin \Sigma(P)}{P*Q \xrightarrow{a} P*Q'}$$

These transition rules have a straightforward meaning along the lines of those given by various authors on the semantics of process algebras (for example in [8] and [20]). In the rules concerning the concurrent operator "$*$", the notation $\Sigma(P)$ means the alphabet of the term P. In the rule concerning recursion, $E[F/x]$ denotes the expression which results from substituting every free occurrence of x in E, with F. We often use an abbreviated notation to denote a recursive term. We write $x \Leftarrow E(x)$ as an abbreviation for $\mu x.E(x)$, e.g., $\mu x.(ax + b\Delta)$ will be displayed as $x \Leftarrow ax + b\Delta$. We call the $E(x)$ the *definition body* of the process $x \Leftarrow E(x)$.

We apply *strong bisimulation* equivalence [21], [19] to determine the behavioural equivalence between processes.

Definition 2.1 Strong Bisimulation:

A binary relation $\sim \subseteq \mathcal{P} \times \mathcal{P}$ is a strong bisimulation, if $\forall P, Q \in \mathcal{P}, \forall a \in \Sigma$:

$$\text{if } P \xrightarrow{a} P' \text{ then } (\exists Q' : Q \xrightarrow{a} Q' \text{ and } P' \sim Q')$$

$$\text{if } Q \xrightarrow{a} Q'' \text{ then } (\exists P'' : P \xrightarrow{a} P'' \text{ and } P'' \sim Q'')$$

P and Q are said to be strong bisimilar, if $P \sim Q$.

From this equivalence, axioms which equate deterministic processes of $\mathcal{P}$ are derived as follows:

$(+_0) \ x + \Delta = x \quad (+_1) \ x + x = x \quad (+_2) \ x + y = y + x \quad (+_3) \ x + (y + z) = (x + y) + z$
$(+_a) \ ax + ay = a(x + y) \qquad\qquad (rec) \ x = y \text{ if } x \Leftarrow f(g(x)), \ y \Leftarrow f(z) \wedge z \Leftarrow g(y)$

Using axiom (rec), for a deterministic recursive process $P \Leftarrow E(P)$, we may *normalise* it into a set of mutually defined recursive definitions $P_i \Leftarrow E_i$ (for $i \in I$), where each definition body E_i is a summation of form $\sum_{j=1}^{J_i} a_j^i P_j^i \equiv a_1^i P_1^i + a_2^i P_2^i + \cdots + a_{J_i}^i P_{J_i}^i$, and each $P_k^i \in \{P_i | i \in I\}$ is defined by another summation. Owing to axiom $(+_a)$, we may transform a summation $\cdots + aP' + \cdots aP'' + \cdots$ into $\cdots + a(P' + P'') + \cdots$. So we may stipulate that there exists no two identical guarding actions in each summation. For example, a recursive term $P \Leftarrow abP + \Delta + acP + abP$ can be normalised into $P \Leftarrow aP_1$; $P_1 \Leftarrow bP + cP$. We call elements appearing in the left-hand sides of symbols $\Leftarrow$ *states*. A *start state* is associated with a *process name* in the form of *process-name* $\overset{def}{=}$ *start-state*. In the rest of this paper, when there is no specific indication, a deterministic process is viewed as such a normalised process. Here is an example of a deterministic normal process (together with a directed graph representation):

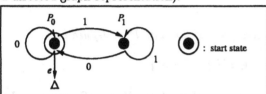

$$Div_2 \overset{def}{=} P_0$$
$$P_0 \Leftarrow 0P_0 + 1P_1 + e\Delta$$
$$P_1 \Leftarrow 0P_0 + 1P_1$$

where Div_2 is the name of the process and P_0, P_1 are states, P_0 is the start state. The process Div_2 represents the behaviour of an FSM; it accepts strings of binary digits which are ended by symbol e; the digital part of an accepted string forms an even binary number (or divisible by 2). For example, Div_2 accepts strings $\{0,1\}^*0e$ but not $\{0,1\}^*1e$, where symbol S^* denotes the transitive and reflexive closure of the set S.

The concurrent composition operator "$*$" has the following axiomatisation [17], [18], [20]: for $P \overset{def}{=} \sum_{i \in I} a_i P_i$, $Q \overset{def}{=} \sum_{j \in J} b_j Q_j$,

$$(con) \qquad P * Q \overset{def}{=} \sum_{i \in I, \, a_i \notin \Sigma(Q)} a_i (P_i * Q) + \sum_{j \in J, \, b_j \notin \Sigma(P)} b_j (P * Q_j) + \sum_{i \in I, \, j \in J, \, a_i = b_j} a_i (P_i * Q_j)$$

This axiomatisation provides us with a algorithmic way to generate a concurrent composition out of two given processes.

Definition 2.2 Trace Transition :
For $s = a_1 a_2 \cdots a_n$, *transition relation* $\overset{s}{\longrightarrow}$ *is defined by* $\overset{a_1}{\longrightarrow} \overset{a_2}{\longrightarrow} \cdots \overset{a_n}{\longrightarrow}$

Lemma 2.1 *Let P and Q be deterministic processes. If $\Sigma(P) = \Sigma(Q)$ then for any s : $P_0 * Q_0 \overset{s}{\longrightarrow} P' * Q'$ iff $P_0 \overset{s}{\longrightarrow} P'$ and $Q_0 \overset{s}{\longrightarrow} Q'$ where P_0, Q_0 are start states of P, Q respectively.*

Proof: When $\Sigma(P) = \Sigma(Q)$, the axiom (con) can only be applied under the condition that $a_i = b_j$ where a_i and b_j are guarding actions of P_0 and Q_0 respectively. Let $P_0 \overset{a_i}{\longrightarrow} P_1$ and $Q_0 \overset{a_i}{\longrightarrow} Q_1$ respectively. From (con) we see that this is equivalent to say $P_0 * Q_0 \overset{a_i}{\longrightarrow} P_1 * Q_1$. Since $\Sigma(P_1) = \Sigma(Q_1)$, step by step, we can extend the above result into that $\forall s : P_0 * Q_0 \overset{s}{\longrightarrow} P' * Q'$ iff $P_0 \overset{s}{\longrightarrow} P'$ and $Q_0 \overset{s}{\longrightarrow} Q'$. $\qquad \square$

Theorem 2.1 *Let P, Q be deterministic processes. If $P \sim Q$ then for each $P' * Q'$ being a state in $P * Q$, we have $P' \sim Q'$.*

Proof: $P' * Q'$ as a state of $P * Q$ implies that there exists a string s such that $P_0 * Q_0 \xrightarrow{s} P' * Q'$. By $P \sim Q$, we can derive $\Sigma(P) = \Sigma(Q)$. So by lemma 2.1, $P_0 * Q_0 \xrightarrow{s} P' * Q'$ iff $P_0 \xrightarrow{s} P'$ and $Q_0 \xrightarrow{s} Q'$. Note that P, Q are deterministic processes, so transitions $P_0 \xrightarrow{s} P'$ and $Q_0 \xrightarrow{s} Q'$ are unique. Hence $P' \sim Q'$ due to $P_0 \sim Q_0$. $\square$

3 The Concurrent Composition Method

Theorem 2.1 leads to our new approach for checking the equivalence/inequivalence between two deterministic processes.

Definition 3.1 Successor Set:
Let P' be a state of a process P. The successor set of the state P' is defined by

$$S(P') = \{ a \mid \forall a \in \Sigma(P) : P' \xrightarrow{a} \}$$

Let P and Q be two deterministic processes with start states P_0 and Q_0 respectively. We compose P and Q using the Circal concurrent composition operator. The following algorithm proves equivalence/inequivalence for finite-state deterministic processes by matching the successor sets of any pair of states which appear in the concurrent composition. In case of inequivalence, the algorithm returns a distinguishing trace as the obvious explanation for the inequivalence.

Algorithm — Concurrent Composition Method (CCM) :

1. if $\Sigma(P) \neq \Sigma(Q)$ then print "$P \neq Q$"; halt; otherwise compute their concurrent composition $P * Q$;

2. traverse $P * Q$; for each state $P' * Q'$, if $S(P') \neq S(Q')$ then go to 3; otherwise, when $P * Q$ has been completely traversed, print "$P = Q$"; halt;

3. search for path s from $P_0 * Q_0$ to $P' * Q'$ such that $P_0 * Q_0 \xrightarrow{s} P' * Q'$; if $S(P') \backslash S(Q') \neq \emptyset$ then choose $\forall a \in S(P') \backslash S(Q')$; print "$P \neq Q$ because $P_0 \xrightarrow{sa}$ and $Q_0 \xrightarrow{sa}\!\!\!\!/\,$"; otherwise choose $\forall a \in S(Q') \backslash S(P')$; print "$P \neq Q$ because $Q_0 \xrightarrow{sa}$ and $P_0 \xrightarrow{sa}\!\!\!\!/\,$"; halt;

Now we argue that the CCM algorithm works properly.

Theorem 3.1 *The CCM algorithm proves strong bisimulation/non-bisimilarity between finite state deterministic processes correctly and completely.*

Proof:
(Correctness) Firstly we assume that in the composition $P * Q$, we find a state $P' * Q'$ satisfying that $S(P') \neq S(Q')$. In such a case P and Q cannot be equivalent. Otherwise, by Theorem 2.1, we get $P' = Q'$ which is impossible due to $S(P') \neq S(Q')$. Moreover, using a path searching technique (such as the depth-first searching algorithm [1]), we can

find a path s from the start state $P_0 * Q_0$ to the state $P' * Q'$. Then $\forall a \in S(P')\backslash S(Q')$ (or $\forall a \in S(Q')\backslash S(P')$), we have $P_0 \xrightarrow{sa}$ and $Q_0 \xrightarrow{sa}\!\!\!\!\!/\,$ (or $Q_0 \xrightarrow{sa}$ and $P_0 \xrightarrow{sa}\!\!\!\!\!/\,$). Thus this sa forms an evident explanation as to why $P \neq Q$. We call a string with such a property a *distinguishing trace*.

Then, conversely, we assume that for every state $P' * Q'$ in $P * Q$, we always meet $S(P') = S(Q')$. Then from $S(P_0) = S(Q_0)$ (P_0, Q_0: start states), we derive that $\forall a$: $P_0 \xrightarrow{a} P_1$ iff $Q_0 \xrightarrow{a} Q_1$ (two deterministic transitions). Let $\approx$ denote a binary relation satisfying that $U \approx V$ if $S(U) = S(V)$ and $\forall a : U \xrightarrow{a} U'$ iff $V \xrightarrow{a} V'$. We have $P_0 \approx Q_0$. Now by the transition rule for concurrency, we have $P_0 * Q_0 \xrightarrow{a} P_1 * Q_1$, and by our assumption, we have $S(P_1) = S(Q_1)$. The latter implies that $\forall a : P_1 \xrightarrow{a} P_2$ iff $Q_1 \xrightarrow{a} Q_2$ for some P_2, Q_2, i.e., $P_1 \approx Q_1$. Comparing the relation $\approx$ with the strong bisimulation we see that $\approx$ is exactly the strong bisimulation relation $\sim$. Therefore $P_0 \sim Q_0$.

(Completeness) We note that when P, Q are finite state processes, so is $P * Q$. Therefore the traversal in step 2 will terminate in finite steps. □

Examples: We give two examples to illustrate this technique.

1. Proof of Inequivalence: For $P \stackrel{def}{=} P_0$, $P_0 \Leftarrow aP_0 + b\Delta$ and $Q \stackrel{def}{=} Q_0$, $Q_0 \Leftarrow aQ_1 + b\Delta$, $Q_1 \Leftarrow aQ_0$. Prove that $P \not\sim Q$.

Composing P and Q we get $P * Q \stackrel{def}{=} P_0 * Q_0$, $P_0 * Q_0 \Leftarrow a(P_0 * Q_1) + b\Delta$, $P_0 * Q_1 \Leftarrow a(P_0 * Q_0)$. For $P_0 * Q_1$ as a state in the composition, we see $S(P_0) = \{a, b\} \neq \{a\} = S(Q_1)$. Hence $P \neq Q$, with an evident explanation : $P_0 \xrightarrow{ab}$ but $Q_0 \xrightarrow{ab}\!\!\!\!\!/\,$.

2. Proof of Equivalence: Using a method provided in [15], for an arbitrary number n, we may design a machine Div_n to accept binary numbers which are divisible by n. Similar to the process Div_2 given in Section 2, we give Div_3 and Div_6 as follows.

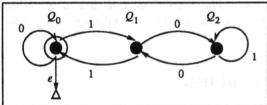

$$Div_3 \stackrel{def}{=} Q_0$$
$$Q_0 \Leftarrow 0Q_0 + 1Q_1 + e\Delta$$
$$Q_1 \Leftarrow 1Q_0 + 0Q_2$$
$$Q_2 \Leftarrow 0Q_1 + 1Q_2$$

It is easy to check that Div_3 accepts strings $0e$, $11e$, $110e$, $\cdots$. Then Div_6 is designed by:

$Div_6 \stackrel{def}{=} S_0$

$S_0 \Leftarrow 0S_1 + 1S_2 + e\Delta$		$S_4 \Leftarrow 0S_1 + 1S_2$		$S_8 \Leftarrow 1S_4 + 0S_5$	
$S_1 \Leftarrow 1S_3 + 0S_0 + e\Delta$		$S_5 \Leftarrow 0S_8 + 1S_9$		$S_9 \Leftarrow 1S_{10} + 0S_{11}$	
$S_2 \Leftarrow 1S_4 + 0S_5$		$S_6 \Leftarrow 1S_{10} + 0S_{11}$		$S_{10} \Leftarrow 0S_8 + 1S_9$	
$S_3 \Leftarrow 0S_6 + 1S_7$		$S_7 \Leftarrow 1S_3 + 0S_0$		$S_{11} \Leftarrow 0S_6 + 1S_7$	

Indeed, Div_6 accepts strings of binary digits ended by the symbol e. The digital part forms a number divisible by 6; for instance, for $(6)_2 = 110$, we have $S_0 \xrightarrow{1} S_2 \xrightarrow{1} S_4 \xrightarrow{0} S_1 \xrightarrow{e} \Delta$; for $(12)_2 = 1100$, we have $S_0 \xrightarrow{110} S_1 \xrightarrow{0} S_0 \xrightarrow{e} \Delta$ and for $(42)_2 = 101010$, we have $S_0 \xrightarrow{1} S_2 \xrightarrow{0} S_5 \xrightarrow{1} S_9 \xrightarrow{0} S_{11} \xrightarrow{1} S_7 \xrightarrow{0} S_0 \xrightarrow{e} \Delta$.

Note that for any number n which is divisible by 6 *if and only if* it is divisible by both 2 and 3. Also note that the Circal operator $*$ builds a composition from its two operands; the composition behaves like the two operands interacting concurrently. Owing to these two facts, we expect to avoid using Div_6 by using the simpler machine $Div_2 * Div_3$. We therefore wish to prove

$$Div_2 * Div_3 \sim Div_6$$

Firstly, it is easy to obtain $Div_2 * Div_3$ using the (mechanisation of the) composition operator:

$Div_2 * Div_3$	$\overset{def}{=}$	R_0					
R_0	$\Leftarrow$	$0R_0 + 1R_1 + e\Delta$	R_2	$\Leftarrow$	$0R_0 + 1R_1$	R_4	$\Leftarrow$	$1R_2 + 0R_3$
R_1	$\Leftarrow$	$1R_2 + 0R_3$	R_3	$\Leftarrow$	$0R_4 + 1R_5$	R_5	$\Leftarrow$	$0R_4 + 1R_5$

Then composing $Div_2 * Div_3$ with Div_6, the following composition can be obtained mechanically:

$(Div_2 * Div_3)$	$*$	$Div_6 \overset{def}{=} R_0 * S_0$			
$R_0 * S_0$	$\Leftarrow$	$0R_0 * S_1 + 1R_1 * S_2 + e\Delta$	$R_3 * S_6$	$\Leftarrow$	$0R_4 * S_{11} + 1R_5 * S_{10}$
$R_0 * S_1$	$\Leftarrow$	$0R_0 * S_0 + 1R_1 * S_3 + e\Delta$	$R_2 * S_7$	$\Leftarrow$	$0R_0 * S_0 + 1R_1 * S_3$
$R_1 * S_2$	$\Leftarrow$	$0R_3 * S_5 + 1R_2 * S_4$	$R_4 * S_8$	$\Leftarrow$	$0R_3 * S_5 + 1R_2 * S_4$
$R_1 * S_3$	$\Leftarrow$	$0R_3 * S_6 + 1R_2 * S_7$	$R_5 * S_9$	$\Leftarrow$	$0R_4 * S_{11} + 1R_5 * S_{10}$
$R_3 * S_5$	$\Leftarrow$	$0R_4 * S_8 + 1R_5 * S_9$	$R_4 * S_{11}$	$\Leftarrow$	$0R_3 * S_6 + 1R_2 * S_7$
$R_2 * S_4$	$\Leftarrow$	$0R_0 * S_1 + 1R_1 * S_2$	$R_5 * S_{10}$	$\Leftarrow$	$0R_4 * S_8 + 1R_5 * S_9$

Now it is easy to check that for any state $R_i * S_j$ in the composition $(Div_2 * Div_3) * Div_6$, $S(R_i) = S(S_j)$ (we have $S(R_0) = S(S_0) = S(S_1) = \{0, 1, e\}$ and R_0 is only composed with S_0, S_1 and conversely S_0, S_1 are only composed with R_0; also for $1 \leq i \leq 5$ and for $2 \leq j \leq 11$, we have $S(R_i) = S(S_j) = \{0, 1\}$). Therefore indeed $Div_2 * Div_3 \sim Div_6$.

In this example, two properties of the Circal composition operator are utilised. The first one is its modelling property which we use to build the simpler machine $Div_2 * Div_3$. The second is its proof property which we use to generate the composition as required by the CCM algorithm.

4 Dealing with Nondeterminism

In order to deal with nondeterminism, we apply the equivalence notion of *testing* suggested by De Nicola and Hennessy [6], [8]. The SOS transition rules for nondeterministic processes are as follows:

$$\frac{}{P \oplus Q \longrightarrow P} \qquad \frac{}{P \oplus Q \longrightarrow Q} \qquad \frac{P \longrightarrow P'}{P + Q \longrightarrow P' + Q} \qquad \frac{Q \longrightarrow Q'}{P + Q \longrightarrow Q' + P}$$

where transition $P \longrightarrow Q$ means that P takes a non-observable transition and evolves to Q; the action for such a transition is not visible. A list of the axioms abstracted from the testing semantics is sufficient to understand this treatment of nondeterminism and the testing equivalence relation.

$(\oplus_1)$ $x \oplus x = x$ $(\oplus_2)$ $y \oplus x = x \oplus y$

$(\oplus_3)$ $x \oplus (y \oplus z) = (x \oplus y) \oplus z$ $(+\oplus)$ $x + (y \oplus z) = (x + y) \oplus (x + z)$

$(\oplus+)$ $(x \oplus y) + (x \oplus z) = x \oplus (y + z)$ $(+\oplus_\alpha)$ $(ax + u) \oplus (ay + v) =$
$$= (a(x \oplus y) + u) \oplus (a(x \oplus y) + v)$$

Applying this set of axioms together with those for deterministic processes (excluding $(+_\alpha)$), it is straightforward that we may transform the syntactic structure of a process into so-called *disjunctive form* of [16]. A disjunctive form satisfies the following: (i) operator $\oplus$'s is distributed over operator $+$'s (by $(+\oplus)$ and $(\oplus+)$); (ii) subterms guarded under the same actions are unified (by $(+\oplus_\alpha)$). For example, let

$$P \stackrel{def}{=} P_0 \qquad P_0 \Leftarrow aP_0 + (aP_1 \oplus bP_2) \qquad P_1 \Leftarrow aP_0 \qquad P_2 \Leftarrow bP_2$$

Applying the testing axioms, this process can be transformed into the following disjunctive form:

$$Q \stackrel{def}{=} Q_0 \qquad Q_0 \Leftarrow aQ_1 \oplus (aQ_1 + bQ_2) \qquad Q_1 \Leftarrow aQ_1 \oplus (aQ_1 + bQ_2) \qquad Q_2 \Leftarrow bQ_2$$

Now we look at how to generate a *deterministic* labelled transition system out of a *non-deterministic* one. In order to achieve this, we introduce the following notions.

Definition 4.1 Transition $\longmapsto$:
A transition relation $\longmapsto \subseteq \mathcal{P} \times Act \times \mathcal{P}$ is defined as follows :

$$P \stackrel{a}{\longmapsto} Q \quad \text{iff} \quad \exists P' : \ P \longrightarrow^* P' \stackrel{a}{\longrightarrow} Q$$

The definition of $\longmapsto$ stipulates that transition $P \stackrel{a}{\longmapsto} Q$ consists of a series of transition steps with the last step being restricted to be a labelled, observable one. Note that in a disjunctive form, the same actions guards the same subterms, therefore:

Lemma 4.1 *If P is in disjunctive form and a is a guarding action of P, then transition $P \stackrel{a}{\longmapsto} P'$ exist and P' is unique.* $\qquad\qquad\square$

Taking the disjunctive form Q given in the above as an example, we have $Q_0 \stackrel{a}{\longmapsto} Q_1, Q_0 \stackrel{b}{\longmapsto} Q_2$.

Definition 4.2 Acceptance Set, Saturation : [8]
An acceptance set of a process P, $\mathcal{A}(P)$ is defined by :

$$\mathcal{A}(P) = \{\ S(P') \mid P \longrightarrow^* P' \wedge \forall P'' : P' \longrightarrow P'' \ \text{implies} \ P'' \equiv P'\ \}$$

$\mathcal{A}$ is union closed, if for every pair of sets $S_1, S_2 \in \mathcal{A}$, $S_1 \cup S_2 \in \mathcal{A}$;
$\mathcal{A}$ is convex closed, if for every pair $S_1, S_2 \in \mathcal{A}$, whenever $S_1 \subseteq S \subseteq S_2$ then $S \in \mathcal{A}$;
$\mathcal{A}$ is saturated, if it is both union closed and convex closed.

The definition of saturation actually provides us with a method to saturate an acceptance set $\mathcal{A}$. We denote the procedure of saturation by $Sat(\mathcal{A})$. For example $Sat(\{\{a\}, \{b\}\}) = \{\{a\}, \{b\}, \{a, b\}\}$ is a saturated acceptance set. The notion of saturation reflects the following two equations which are derivable from the testing axioms:

$(uc) \quad x \oplus y = x \oplus y(x + y) \qquad\quad (cc) \quad x \oplus (x + y + z) = x \oplus (x + y) \oplus (x + z) \oplus (x + y + z)$

Therefore to saturate the acceptance set of a process can be thought of as transforming the process using these two equations; the testing semantics of the process will not be changed. In the Concurrency Workbench [5], [4] a type of deterministic transition system called T-graph forms the basis for computing testing equivalence as bisimulation equivalence. The following graph is similar to the T-graph.

Definition 4.3 Acceptance Graph :
Let P be in disjunctive form. An acceptance graph of P (denoted by $G(P)$) is a collection of nodes and edges, which are constructed as follows:

1. *construct a starting node to be* $Sat(\mathcal{A}(P_0))$

2. *for* $i \geq 0$, *if* $P_i \overset{a}{\longmapsto} P_j$ *then construct only one edge labelled by a going out from the node* $Sat(\mathcal{A}(P_i))$

3. *construct a node* $Sat(\mathcal{A}(P_j))$, *and let it be pointed by the edge labelled by a, go to step 2*

Lemma 4.2 *For a disjunctive form P, G(P) gives a deterministic transition system.* □

Since an acceptance graph is still a labelled transition system, we may view it as a process and simply use P to denote it. The relationship between a graph and its nodes is thought of as similar to that between a process and its states; thus we may say that P' is a node of graph P. Also when we write $P' \overset{a}{\longmapsto} P''$ we mean that the transition takes place from node P' to another node P''; finally for a node P', we use $P'.acc$ to denote the *saturated* acceptance set of the node P'.

Definition 4.4 Bisimulation between Acceptance Graphs:
Let P', Q' *be two nodes of one/two acceptance graphs. They are said to be bisimilar, which we denote by* $P' \sim_{\mathcal{A}} Q'$, *if:*

1. $P'.acc = Q'.acc$
2. $\forall a \in \Sigma :$ *if* $P' \overset{a}{\longmapsto} P_1$ *then* $(\exists Q_1 : Q' \overset{a}{\longmapsto} Q_1$ *and* $P_1 \sim_{\mathcal{A}} Q_1)$
                                  if $Q' \overset{a}{\longmapsto} Q_2$ *then* $(\exists P_2 : P' \overset{a}{\longmapsto} P_2$ *and* $P_2 \sim_{\mathcal{A}} Q_2)$

Two acceptance graphs P, Q are said to be bisimilar, which we denote by $P \sim_{\mathcal{A}} Q$, *if* $P_0 \sim_{\mathcal{A}} Q_0$ *where* P_0, Q_0 *are two start nodes of the graphs P, Q respectively.*

Theorem 4.1 *When P and Q are disjunctive forms, then P is testing equivalent to Q if and only if* $G(P) \sim_{\mathcal{A}} G(Q)$. □

Due to that the testing equivalence relation has not been defined in this paper, we omit the proof of this theorem. Nevertheless, we refer the reader to [4], where the testing equivalence relation between two processes is computed by a bisimulation between two T-graphs; the bisimulation there is similar to the bisimulation $\sim_{\mathcal{A}}$ in this paper. Now since acceptance graphs are deterministic transition systems, we can compose them using the Circal concurrent composition operator in the same way as we compose two deterministic processes. Theorem 2.1 can then be re-stated as follows:

Theorem 4.2 *Let P, Q be acceptance graphs. If* $P \sim_{\mathcal{A}} Q$ *then for each* $P' * Q'$ *as a state in* $P * Q$, *we have* $P' \sim_{\mathcal{A}} Q'$. □

The CCM algorithm now can be applied to decide the equivalence/inequivalence in terms of bisimulation $\sim_{\mathcal{A}}$ between two acceptance graphs. Step 2 in the original algorithm needs to be slightly modified to include checking for equality of acceptance sets.

2. traverse $P * Q$; for each state $P' * Q'$, if $S(P') \neq S(Q')$ then go to 3; if $P'.acc \neq Q'.acc$ then

search for path s from $P_0 * Q_0$ to $P' * Q'$ such that $P_0 * Q_0 \xrightarrow{s} P' * Q'$; print "$P \neq Q$ because after transitions $P_0 \xrightarrow{s} P'$ and $Q_0 \xrightarrow{s} Q'$, we find different internal choices"; print $P'.acc$; print $Q'.acc$; halt;

otherwise, when $P * Q$ has been completely traversed, print "$P = Q$"; halt;

Using the same reasoning as we did for proving Theorem 3.1, we have the following theorem:

Theorem 4.3 *The CCM algorithm proves the equivalence relation $\sim_\lambda$ between acceptance graphs correctly and completely.* □

For two finite state, nondeterministic processes, to transform them into disjunctive forms and then into acceptance graphs, the testing semantics is preserved. We therefore have the following theorem:

Theorem 4.4 *The CCM algorithm is sound and complete for proving testing equivalence relation between finite state, nondeterministic processes.* □

Example : For $\mu x.a(ax + bx)$ and $\mu y.a(ay \oplus by)$, their two acceptance graphs are :
$P \stackrel{def}{=} P_0$, $P_0 \Leftarrow aP_1$, $P_1 \Leftarrow aP_0 + bP_0$ and $Q \stackrel{def}{=} Q_0$, $Q_0 \Leftarrow aQ_1$, $Q_1 \Leftarrow aQ_0 + bQ_0$.
The concurrent composition of the two systems is: $P * Q \stackrel{def}{=} P_0 * Q_0$, $P_0 * Q_0 \Leftarrow aP_1 * Q_1$, $P_1 * Q_1 \Leftarrow a(P_0 * Q_0) + b(P_0 * Q_0)$. Since $P_1 * Q_1$ is a state in $P * Q$ and $P_1.acc = \{\{a, b\}\} \neq \{\{a\}, \{b\}, \{a, b\}\} = Q_1.acc$, therefore the algorithm returns $P \neq Q$ due to the difference between internal action choices after the two systems executing a.

5 Conclusions

We have taken a new approach to proving the equivalence or in-equivalence between finite-state, deterministic *and* nondeterministic processes. The Circal concurrent composition operator plays a central role in engineering this technique. It composes states in pairs, two states which are composed together must execute the *same observable/non-observable* actions and thus provides us with a concise algorithm to check the bisimilarity/non-bisimilarity between two finite-state processes. The merit of the approach is that the behavioural inequivalence between two processes can be demonstrated by an evident, diagnostic explanation, which helps the user to locate errors in the systems and aids redesign.

Acknowledgement : We should like to thank Andrew Bailey, Paul Cockshott, Jim MacIntosh, George McCaskill and Faron Moller for their comments and help with this paper.

References

[1] A.V. Aho, J. E. Hopcroft, and J.D. Ullman. *Data Structures and Algorithms.* Series in Computer Science and Information Processing. Addison-Wesley, Reading, MA, 1983.

[2] A. Bailey, G.A. McCaskill, J. McIntosh, and G.J. Milne. The description and automatic verification of digital circuits in CIRCAL. In *Advanced Research Workshop on Correct Hardware Design Methodologies*, pages 265–280, Turin, Italy, June 1991.

From data structure to process structure[*]

Ed Brinksma

Tele-Informatics Group

Dept. of Computer Science, University of Twente

PO Box 217, 7500 AE Enschede, The Netherlands

brinksma@cs.utwente.nl

Abstract

This paper deals with transformations in a process algebraic formalism that has been extended with an abstract data type language. We show how for a well-known class of processes (bags, queues, stacks, etc.) descriptions in terms of simple process definitions and complex state parameters can be transformed in a stepwise fashion into equivalent systems of interacting processes with state parameters of reduced complexity. The key to the solution are so-called *context equations*.

0   Introduction

Interchanging the complexity of the control structure and the parameter structure of a program is a well-known program transformation principle. In this paper we investigate this principle in the particular setting of a process algebraic formalism that has been complemented with an abstract data type (ADT) language for the definition of data structures. The formalism resembles the ISO specification language LOTOS [BoBr87,ISO89], which contains a dialect of the ADT language ACT ONE [EhMa85]. It abstracts from the concrete syntactic structure of LOTOS, which has been optimized for the structured representation of the functionality of large distributed systems. Our results, however, can be directly translated back to any process algebraic formalism that has a sufficiently related abstract syntactic and semantic definition.

Transformations that exchange the complexity of the state parameters for complexity of the control structure of processes or vice versa are widely studied as methods to improve their structure and/or efficiency. In the design of concurrent systems it is of interest to find transformations that can be used to decompose specifications of processes that are described in terms of an explicit global state into a number of concurrently interacting processes with less complicated local states. In fact, the various formal definitions can be differentiated in terms of their *specification styles* which relate the use of different operator signatures to the (informal) purpose of a specification, e.g. specification-oriented or implementation-oriented, see [VSSB90].

---

[*]This work has been partly supported by the CEC as part of the ESPRIT/LOTOSPHERE project (ESPRIT project 2304)

[3] J.A. Bergstra and J.W. Klop. Process algebra for synchronous communication. *Information and Computation*, 60(1/3), 1984.

[4] R. Cleaveland and M.C.B. Hennessy. Testing equivalence as a bisimulation equivalence. In J. Sifakis, editor, *Lecture Notes in Computer Science 407*, pages 11–23. Springer-Verlag, 1989.

[5] R. Cleaveland, J. Parrow, and B. Steffen. The concurrency workbench. In J. Sifakis, editor, *Lecture Notes in Computer Science 407*, pages 24–37. Springer-Verlag, 1989.

[6] R. de Nicola and M.C.B. Hennessy. Testing equivalence for processes. *Theoretical Computer Science*, 34(1 and 2), 1984.

[7] R. de Nicola, P. Inverardi, and M. Nesi. Using the axiomatic presentation of behavioural equivalences for manipulating ccs specifications. In J. Sifakis, editor, *Lecture Notes in Computer Science 407*, pages 54–67. Springer-Verlag, 1989.

[8] M.C.B. Hennessy. *Algebraic Theory of Processes*. The MIT Press, 1988.

[9] M.C.B. Hennessy and R. Milner. Algebraic laws for nondeterminism and concurrency. *Jounal of the Association of Computing Machinery*, 32(1):137–161, 1985.

[10] M. Hillerstöm. *Verification of CCS-Processes*. PhD thesis, Aalborg University Centre, Denmark, 1987. R 87-27.

[11] C.A.R. Hoare. *Communicating Sequential Processes*. Series in Computer Science. Prentice Hall International, 1985.

[12] P. Inverardi and M. Nesi. A rewriting strategy to verify observational congruence. *Information Processing Letters*, 35:191–199, 1990.

[13] P. C. Kanellakis and S. A. Smolka. CCS expressions, finite state processes, and three problems of equivalence. *Information and Computation*, 86(1):43–68, May 1990.

[14] K.G. Larsen. Proof systems for hennessy-milner logic with recursion. *Jounal of Theoretical Computer Science*, 72:265–288, 1990.

[15] L.S. Levy. *Fundamental Concepts of Computer Science, Methematical Foundations of Programming*. Dorset House Publishing, 1988.

[16] G.J. Milne. The representation of communication and concurrency. Technical Report 4088, Caltech, 1980.

[17] G.J. Milne. Circal: A calculus for circuit description. *Integration, the VLSI Journal*, 1(2,3):121–160, 1983.

[18] G.J. Milne. Circal and the representation of communication, concurrency and time. *ACM Transactions on Programming Languages and Systems*, 7(2), 1985.

[19] R. Milner. *Communication and Concurrency*. Series in Computer Science. Prentice Hall International, 1989.

[20] F.G. Moller. The semantics of Circal. Technical Report HDV-3-89, University of Strathclyde, Department of Computer Science, Glasgow, Scotland, 1989.

[21] D. Park. Concurrency and automata in infinite strings. In *Lecture Notes in Computer Science 104*, pages 167–183. Springer-Verlag, 1981.

[22] G.D. Plotkin. A structural approach to operational semantics. Technical Report DAIMI-FN-19, Computer Science Dept, Aarhus Univ, Denmark, 1981.

So far, the main contributions of the process algebraic approach to distributed systems has been in providing useful semantic frameworks for proving the *correctness* of such transformations, see e.g. the implementation of a queue in [Mil80] and the correctness of the AB-protocol in [LaMi87]. It is, however, of great methodological interest to have methods to obtain such transformations. It is to this area that we claim to contribute. We show how for a well-known class of processes (bags, queues, stacks, etc.) descriptions in terms of simple process definitions and complex state parameters can be replaced by a systems of interacting processes whose parameters do not exceed the complexity of a single data element. This is done by deriving *context equations* (from the complex-state descriptions) as in [Lar90], but with the important difference that in our set-up the context is the unknown entity. By solving the equations we obtain the building bricks for the desired transformations.

1   A process algebraic calculus

We use a process algebraic language that is an abstract version of ISO specification language LOTOS [ISO89]. It is also strongly related to other process algebraic calculi, most notably to TCSP [Hoa85], CIRCAL [Mil85] and CCS [Mil80,Mil89]. Parts of our results will therefore be, *mutatis mutandis*, transferable to other calculi. A more detailed account of the language than is given here can be found in the full paper [BrKa91] and [EhMa85,Bri88,ISO89].

The basic calculus is built around a set *Act* providing the alphabet of *actions*, and a set *PId* of process identifiers. The set *BExpr* of behaviour expressions is defined by the following BNF-schema:

$$B ::= \textbf{stop} \mid a; B \mid \tau; B \mid \sum\{B_i \mid i \in I\} \mid B_1 \parallel_A B_2 \mid B//A \mid B[S] \mid p$$

where $a \in Act$, $\tau \notin Act$, $\{B_i \mid i \in I\}$ an indexed set of behaviour expressions, $A \subseteq Act$, $S : Act \to Act$, and $p \in PId$. For this language we define attributes such as the label sort $L(B)$ etc. in the usual way. S is extended to $Act \cup \{\tau\}$ by defining $S(\tau) = \tau$. The meaning of the process identifiers p is given by an environment of *process definitions* $PE = \{p_j := B_j \mid j \in J\}$. The SOS-rules defining the operational semantics of the language are contained in table 1.

The main differences with respect to CCS are:

- synchronization is on the basis of *identical* labels, not complementary ones;
- synchronization does not result in the silent action τ, but the action on which was synchronized; this enables synchronization between more than two processes;
- restriction is 'built in' the (indexed) parallel combinator;
- as hiding of actions cannot be achieved via synchronization, this requires an extra combinator; the treatment of parallelism, hiding and restriction is thus closer to that in TCSP [Hoa85];
- the relabelling function S can be non-injective.

Some derived operators of this calculus are:

- $B_1 \; [] \; B_2 =_{df} \sum\{B_1, B_2\}$

B	rules	condition
stop	no rules	
$\mu; B$	$\vdash \mu; B -\mu\rightarrow B$	$\mu \in Act \cup \{\tau\}$
$\sum\{B_i \mid i \in I\}$	$B_i -\mu\rightarrow B_i' \vdash \sum\{B_i \mid i \in I\} -\mu\rightarrow B_i'$	$i \in I$
$B_1 \parallel_A B_2$	$B_1 -\mu\rightarrow B_1' \vdash B_1 \parallel_A B_2 -\mu\rightarrow B_1' \parallel_A B_2$	$\mu \notin A$
	$B_2 -\mu\rightarrow B_2' \vdash B_1 \parallel_A B_2 -\mu\rightarrow B_1 \parallel_A B_2'$	$\mu \notin A$
	$B_1 -\mu\rightarrow B_1', B_2 -\mu\rightarrow B_2' \vdash B_1 \parallel_A B_2 -\mu\rightarrow B_1' \parallel_A B_2'$	$\mu \in A$
$B//A$	$B -\mu\rightarrow B' \vdash B//A -\mu\rightarrow B'//A$	$\mu \notin A$
	$B -\mu\rightarrow B' \vdash B//A -\tau\rightarrow B'//A$	$\mu \in A$
$B[S]$	$B -\mu\rightarrow B' \vdash B[S] -S(\mu)\rightarrow B'[S]$	
p	$B -\mu\rightarrow B' \vdash p -\mu\rightarrow B'$	$p := B \in PE$

Table 1: SOS rules for the basic calculus

- $B_1 \parallel B_2 =_{df} B_1 \parallel_{Act} B_2$

- $B_1 \parallel\parallel B_2 =_{df} B_1 \parallel_\emptyset B_2$

- **exit** $=_{df} \delta$; **stop** for a reserved action name $\delta \in Act$ marking *successful termination*;

- $B_1 \gg B_2 =_{df} (B_1[ok/\delta] \parallel_{\{ok\}} ok; B_2)//\{ok\}$, where $ok \notin L(B_1) \cup L(B_2)$.

To extend this basic calculus with value-passing and parameterization constructs it is combined with an abstract data type formalism. This formalism is used to define a Σ-algebra A for a signature of sorts and operations Σ, providing a *data-type environment* for the specification of process behaviour. The signature is used to generate terms with which data-values can be represented. The sort *bool* of Boolean values with constants *true* and *false* is assumed to be predefined. For every sort s, an operation if_then_else_ : $bool, s, s \rightarrow s$ is implicitly defined.

In this setting we can endow the elements of Act and PId with some substructure, viz.

- $Act =_{df} \{a_v \mid a \in L, v \in D\}$, where L is a set of *port/gate/label-names* and D is the domain of the defined Σ-algebra A;

- $PId =_{df} \{p_v \mid p \in P, v \in D^*\}$, where P is a set of *process names*.

In the extended language the attribute $L(B)$, and indexed combinators like $\parallel_A$ and $//A$ refer to subsets of L, but should, as usual, be interpreted as their obvious extensions to Act.

The language of behaviour expressions is then extended with a number of new constructs:

- $a?x : s; B(x) =_{df} \sum\{a_v; B(t_v) \mid v \in D_s\}$, where $D_s \subseteq D$ is the subdomain of sort s in A, and t_v is a term with value v; we write $a(-); B$ if the name of the variable is immaterial (e.g. when the subsequent behaviour B does not depend on it);

- $a!t; B =_{df} a_v; B$, where v is the value of term t;

- $[t] \rightarrow B =_{df}$ if $A \models t = true$ then B else **stop**, for Boolean terms t.

Process definitions are generalized to the format

$$p(x_1:s_1,\ldots,x_n:s_n) := B(x_1:s_1,\ldots,x_n:s_n)$$

which are interpreted as sets of elementary process definitions, viz.

$$\{p_v := B(t_1,\ldots,t_n) \mid v = \langle val(t_1),\ldots,val(t_n)\rangle \in D_{s_1} \times \ldots \times D_{s_n}\}.$$

In the context of this paper we will need the equations over the behaviour expressions induced by the *strong bisimulation equivalence* $\sim$ and the *observation congruence* $\approx^c$ (see e.g. [Mil89]). The resulting laws are the expected analogies of the laws as they are known for related calculi. The full paper [BrKa90] contains a list of those that are needed for the proofs of our results. The reader may also consult [Bri88,ISO89] on this matter.

2 Context equations

In this paper an important role is played by the concept of a *context*. It can be most easily imagined as a behaviour expression with a number of *holes* in it. It is convenient to introduce a set *Var* of process variables, whose elements we will denote with $X, Y, \ldots$. A context $C[X_1,\ldots,X_n]$ then is a behaviour expression in which the variables $X_1,\ldots,X_n$ may occur as sub-behaviour expressions. To deal successfully with issues of infinity due to infinite value domains, we allow contexts C that are parameterized with possibly infinite (indexed) sets of process variables, which we denote by $C[X_i|i\in I]$. A context $C[X_i|i\in I]$ is *(weakly) guarded* if every occurrence of an X_i $(i\in I)$ in C is contained in a subexpression $\mu; B$ with $\mu \in Act \cup \{\tau\}$. $C[X_i|i \in I]$ is *observably guarded* if every occurrence of an X_i $(i\in I)$ in C is contained in a subexpression $a; B$ with $a\in Act$. A system of *context equations* is a set of the form $\{X_i = C_i[X_i|i\in I] \mid i\in I\}$ where $=$ denotes an appropriate instance of equivalence, in our case $\sim$ or $\approx^c$. The proof of the following theorem is a simple variation of analogous ones existing in the literature, e.g. the one in [Mil88].

Theorem 1
Let $\{X_i \sim C_i[X_i|i\in I] \mid i\in I\}$ be a system of weakly guarded context equations then there exists a unique set of solutions (modulo $\sim$) $\{B_i \mid i\in I\}$ such that $B_i \sim C_i[B_i|i\in I]$ for all $i\in I$, viz. $B_i = p_i$ defined by the process environment $\{p_i := C_i[p_i|i\in I] \mid i\in I\}$. □

The generalization of this theorem to the $\approx^c$ is more specific to the combinator signature of our calculus and results from the application of theorem 4.8.5 in [Bri88].

Theorem 2
Let $\{X_i \approx^c C_i[X_i|i \in I] \mid i \in I\}$ be a system of observably guarded context equations *not containing applications of the hiding operator* $//A$, then there exists a unique set of solutions (modulo $\approx^c$) $\{B_i \mid i \in I\}$ such that $B_i \approx^c C_i[B_i|i\in I]$ for all $i \in I$, viz. $B_i = p_i$ defined by the process environment $\{p_i := C_i[p_i|i\in I] \mid i\in I\}$. □

The transformations between data-oriented specifications and process-oriented specifications as studied in this paper build on solving context equations *with unknown contexts*, i.e. to determine $C[X]$ such that $C[B_1] = B_2$ for known B_1, B_2. It will be sufficient in this case to work with contexts C that contain one occurrence of a process variable. Just as behaviours can be specified by listing the involved transitions $B -a\rightarrow B'$, such contexts

$$
\begin{aligned}
Multiset(Nat) = \quad & Nat\ + \\
\textbf{sorts}: \quad & mult \\
\textbf{opns}: \quad & \emptyset :\to mult \\
& add, rem : nat, mult \to mult \\
& \_\in\_ : nat, mult \to bool \\
\textbf{eqns}: \quad & x, y : nat;\ m, n : mult \\
& add(x, add(y, m)) = add(y, add(x, m)) \\
& rem(x, \emptyset) = \emptyset \\
& rem(x, add(y, m)) = \text{if } eq(x, y) \text{ then } m \text{ else } add(y, rem(x, m)) \\
& x \in \emptyset = false \\
& x \in add(y, m) = \text{if } eq(x, y) \text{ then } true \text{ else } x \in m
\end{aligned}
$$

Table 2: *Multiset(Nat)*

may be characterized by *transductions*, see e.g. [Lar90]. Let *Con* be a set of *context variables* whose elements we denote by $C, D, E, \dots$, then we write such transductions as $C -[a/b] \to C'$, meaning that context C can change into context C' by consuming action b (from a process that is substituted for X in $C[X]$) and producing an action a. It corresponds to an SOS-inference rule of the form $X -b\to X' \vdash C[X] -a\to C'[X']$. If a context moves independently of the process in it, this is denoted by $C -[a/0] \to C'$, which corresponds to the SOS-rule $\vdash C[X] -a\to C'[X]$. The following theorem is at the heart of our transformational methods.

Theorem 3

Let *Trans* be a set of transductions over *Con* of the form $C -[a/0]\to C'$ or $C -[a/a]\to C'$. Let $M \subseteq L$, $M' =_{df} \{a' \mid a \in M\}$, where $': M \to L$ is an injection such that $M \cap M' = \emptyset$, and let $S_M : L \to L$ with $S_M(a) = a\ (a \notin M')$ and $S_M(a') = a\ (a' \in M')$, and $\{p_C\}_{C \in Con}$ a family of process identifiers defined by

$$
\begin{aligned}
p_C := \quad & \Sigma\{a'; p_{C'} \mid C -[a/0]\to C' \in Trans\}\ [] \\
& \Sigma\{a; p_{C'} \mid C -[a/a]\to C' \in Trans\}
\end{aligned}
$$

then for all $C \in Con$, and for all $X \in BExpr$ such that $L(X) \subseteq M$

$$
C[X] \sim (p_C \parallel_M X)[S_M] \tag{1}
$$

3 The bag

We will start with what is arguably the simplest of the *reactive data structures* that we will study: the *bag*. The definition of the corresponding data type, the multiset of natural numbers can be found in table 2.

The specification of the bag that we wish to transform is:

$$
\begin{aligned}
Bag \quad\quad &:= MSet(\emptyset) \tag{2} \\
MSet(v : mult) &:= in?x : nat;\ MSet(add(x, v)) \\
&\quad\ []\ \Sigma\{out!w;\ MSet(rem(w, v)) \mid w \in v\}
\end{aligned}
$$

To transform this specification we will try to find a parameterized context $C_x[X]$ with $x : nat$ and

$$
C_x[MSet(v)] \sim MSet(add(x, v)) \tag{3}
$$

The intuitive idea behind (3) is that we simulate the effect of the *add* operation on multisets by the context $C_x[X]$. By studying the transitions of $MSet(add(x, v))$ we find that it is sufficient if $C_x[X]$ satisfies the following transductions:

$$C_x -[out_x/0] \rightarrow I$$
$$C_x -[a_w/a_w] \rightarrow C_x \qquad a \in \{in, out\}, w \in D_{nat} \tag{4}$$

where I denotes the *identity context* that is completely defined by $I -[a/a] \rightarrow I$ for all $a \in Act \cup \{\tau\}$.

Applying theorem 3 we find the following solution for $C_x[X]$ under the assumption that $L(X) \subseteq \{in, out\}$:

$$C_x[X] := (p_C(x) \parallel_{\{in,out\}} X)[out/out'] \tag{5}$$
$$\text{with } p_C(x) := out'!x; p_I \; [] \; in(-); p_C(x) \; [] \; out(-); p_C(x)$$
$$p_I \qquad := in(-); p_I \; [] \; out(-); p_I$$

We can now immediately derive a solution to our transformation problem. Define

$$NewBag := in?x:nat; C_x[NewBag] \tag{6}$$

then we have the following theorem, which is obtained by applying theorem 1.

Theorem 4 $\qquad Bag \sim NewBag$

When we expand (6) in its full form we get the following definition for *NewBag*

$$NewBag := in?x:nat; (p_C(x) \parallel_{\{in,out\}} NewBag)[out/out'] \tag{7}$$
$$\text{with } p_C(x) \quad := out'!x; p_I \; [] \; in(-); p_C(x) \; [] \; out(-); p_C(x)$$
$$p_I \qquad := in(-); p_I \; [] \; out(-); p_I$$

Analysing the structure of $p_C(x)$ a bit we can prove the following lemma by application of standard laws for $\sim$ and theorem 1.

Lemma 5 $\qquad p_C(x) \sim out'!x; \textbf{stop} \parallel\mid p_I \tag{8}$

With this result we can get (7) in a much more agreeable form by using that p_I imitates the identity context I.

Theorem 6 $\qquad NewBag \sim in?x:nat; (out!x; \textbf{stop} \parallel\mid NewBag) \tag{9}$

Corollary 7 $\qquad Bag \sim NewBag \sim BestBag$
$$\text{where } BestBag := in?x:nat; (out!x; \textbf{stop} \parallel\mid BestBag)$$

This solution is of course well-known in the process-algebraic literature, and therefore we proceed with less transparent cases to show the usefulness of our method.

4 The queue

The data-oriented specification of an ordinary (FIFO) queue is parameterized by values of the main sort of the data type *String* defined in table 3.

The corresponding process definition is

$$Queue \qquad := FIFO(empty) \tag{10}$$
$$FIFO(s:string) := in?x:nat; FIFO(add(x, s))$$
$$[] \; [\neg Empty(s)] \rightarrow out!first(s); FIFO(rest(s))$$

$$
\begin{aligned}
String(Nat) = \quad & Nat\ + \\
\textbf{sorts}:\quad & string \\
\textbf{opns}:\quad & empty :\rightarrow string \\
& add : nat, string \rightarrow string \\
& rest : string \rightarrow string \\
& first : string \rightarrow nat \\
& Empty : string \rightarrow bool \\
\textbf{eqns}:\quad & x : nat;\ s, t : string \\
& Empty(empty) = true \\
& Empty(add(x, s)) = false \\
& first(empty) = 0 \\
& first(add(x, s)) = \text{if } Empty(s) \text{ then } x \text{ else } first(s) \\
& rest(empty) = empty \\
& rest(add(x, s)) = \text{if } Empty(s) \text{ then } empty \text{ else } add(x, rest(s))
\end{aligned}
$$

Table 3: $String(Nat)$

We could try to follow the same approach as with the *Bag*, i.e. to find a context $D_x[X]$ simulating the effect of the *add* operation, such that $D_x[FIFO(s)] \sim FIFO(add(x, s))$. If we try this we find that the transductions $D_x -[in_w/0]\rightarrow D_w \circ D_x$ are necessary because $add(w, add(x, s)) \neq add(x, add(w, s))$, unlike the addition of elements to a *Bag*. Instead of trying to construct contexts that satisfy such transductions we decompose the queue in a different way. We search for contexts $D_x[X]$ such that for $s \neq empty$

$$D_{first(s)}[FIFO(rest(s))] \sim FIFO(s) \tag{11}$$

The idea here is to decompose the queue into the next element that can be taken from the queue and the rest, instead of the element last put into the queue and the rest. Analysing the behaviour of $FIFO(s)$ we find that the following transductions define a context satisfying (11).

$$
\begin{aligned}
D_x &-[out_x/0]\rightarrow I \\
D_x &-[in_w/in_w]\rightarrow D_x \qquad w \in D_{nat}
\end{aligned}
\tag{12}
$$

i.e. the output is performed by the context, which then disappears, whereas the inputs are delegated to the process in the context (i.e. the rest of the queue). Again, we have transductions that satisfy the general format for which we have a standard solution under the assumption that $L(X) \subseteq \{in, out\}$, viz.:

$$D_x[X] := (p_D(x) \,\|_{\{in, out\}} X)[out/out'] \tag{13}$$
$$\text{with } p_D(x) := out'!x; p_I \;[]\; in(-); p_D(x)$$
$$\qquad p_I \quad := in(-); p_I \;[]\; out(-); p_I$$

As before, we can now derive a first solution quite simply by:

$$NewQueue := in?x{:}nat;\ D_x[NewQueue] \tag{14}$$

Theorem 8 $Queue \sim NewQueue$

As before we will try to simplify this solution by transforming it.

Lemma 9 $p_D(x) \sim (out'!x; (out(-))^\omega) \,\|\|\,(in(-))^\omega$
       where $a(-)^\omega := a(-); a(-)^\omega$

We thus obtain our simplification.

Theorem 10 $NewQueue \sim in?x\!:\!nat; (out'!x; (out(-))^{\omega} \parallel_{\{out\}} NewQueue)[out/out']$ (15)

In the case of the *Bag* we were done with our transformations after having proved simplification (9). The resulting specification *BestBag* could be regarded as a resource-oriented specification in which after each receipt of a new data element a new memory cell is allocated to store it and offer it to the environment independently (interpretation of $\parallel\parallel$) of the subsequent behaviour. The equivalence (15), however, is still constraint-oriented [VSSB90,Bri89] in style, where after the storage of a new element the subsequent behaviour is constrained via $\parallel_{\{out\}}$ by the memory cell. It is interesting as an example of how one can specify infinite FIFO-queues without using heavy parameterized process definitions and without introducing internal moves τ into the specification.

To obtain a resource-oriented variant of this specification that corresponds more closely to an implementation in terms of elementary, communicating memory cells, we want to replace the constraints in the form of continuous synchronization by a number of more sparsely exchanged signals. The basic idea is to replace the constraining behaviour $out'!x; (out(-))^{\omega}$ by $out'!x; ok;$ **stop**, where ok signals the end of constraints on the occurrence of out-actions. The synchronizing occurrence of ok is placed immediately before all out-actions that currently have to synchronize with the first out-action of $(out(-))^{\omega}$, and $\parallel_{\{out\}}$ is replaced by $\parallel_{\{ok\}}$. The new ok-action is hidden to make it invisible for the environment.

In the full paper [BrKa91] we carry out the proposed transformation in detail, where the main ingredient is the application of theorem 2, besides some more specialized operations on contexts. The resulting theorem is as follows.

Theorem 11 $NewQueue \approx^c AuxQueue/\!/\{ok\}$
    with $AuxQueue := F[AuxQueue]$
    where $F[X] =_{df} in?x\!:\!nat; ((ok'; out!x; ok; \textbf{stop} \parallel_{\{ok\}} X)/\!/\{ok\})[ok/ok']$

Corollary 12 $Queue \sim NewQueue \approx^c BestQueue$
    with $BestQueue := AuxQueue/\!/\{ok\}$
    $AuxQueue := F[AuxQueue]$

5   The stack

The monolithic specification of a stack (or LIFO queue) has the same structure as that of the ordinary (FIFO) queue. The only difference is in the definition of the operations of the corresponding data type, which is specified in table 4. For reasons of clarity we have chosen identifiers for the specification of the stack that are in most cases different from those used for the queue. We leave it to the reader to convince himself of the structural similarity between the two specifications.

$$
\begin{aligned}
Stack &:= LIFO(empty) \qquad\qquad (16)\\
LIFO(s\!:\!stack(nat)) &:= in?x\!:\!nat; LIFO(add(x,s))\\
&\quad [\![\, [\neg Empty(s)] \rightarrow out!top(s); LIFO(rest(s))
\end{aligned}
$$

The decomposition principles that were chosen for the *Bag*, building a context that depends on the last value accepted, and for the *Queue*, a context depending on the next

$$
\begin{aligned}
Stack(Nat) = \quad & Nat\ + \\
\textbf{sorts}: \quad & stack \\
\textbf{opns}: \quad & empty :\to stack \\
& add : nat, stack \to stack \\
& rest : stack \to stack \\
& top : stack \to nat \\
& Empty : stack \to bool \\
\textbf{eqns}: \quad & x : nat;\ s : stack \\
& Empty(empty) = true \\
& Empty(add(x, s)) = false \\
& top(empty) = 0 \\
& top(add(x, s)) = x \\
& rest(empty) = empty \\
& rest(add(x, s)) = s
\end{aligned}
$$

Table 4: $Stack(Nat)$

value to be output, coincide in the case of the *Stack* because of the LIFO discipline. As there is no obvious alternative, we derive the implied context transductions based on the decomposition given by

$$
G_x[LIFO(s)] \sim LIFO(add(x, s)) \tag{17}
$$

yielding

$$
\begin{aligned}
& G_x -[out_x/0]\to I \\
& G_x -[in_w/0]\to G_w \circ G_x \qquad\qquad w \in D_{nat}
\end{aligned} \tag{18}
$$

These transductions do satisfy the requirements for a general solution as defined by theorem 3. This solution is not adequate, however, for our purposes, as the second transduction generates combined contexts $G_{w_1} \circ G_{w_2} \circ \ldots \circ G_{w_n}$ of arbitrary length. This implies that the corresponding processes $p_{G \circ G \circ \ldots \circ G}$ are parameterized by an ever increasing number of parameters $w_1, \ldots, w_n$, i.e. the complexity of the process states is not a priori bounded.

To find again a solution in which the data complexity of each of the concurrent processes is at most that of one data element, we prove another type of solution for context transductions that are like the ones in (18). Their main characteristic is that all contexts that are unequal to the identity context I have only actions that are independent of the initial actions of an argument process, i.e. their transductions are of the form $C -[a/0]\to C'$.

Theorem 13

Let *Trans* be a set of transductions over *Con* of the form $C -[a/0]\to C'$ or $I -[a/a]\to I$. Let $\{p_C\}_{C \in Con}$ be a family of process definitions given by

$$
\begin{aligned}
p_C &:= \sum\{a; p_{C'} \mid C -[a/0]\to C' \in Trans\} \qquad \text{if } C \neq I \\
p_I &:= ok; \textbf{stop}
\end{aligned}
$$

then for all $C \in Con \setminus \{I\}$, $X \in BExpr$ with $ok \notin L(X)$

$$
C[X] \approx^c (p_C \parallel_{\{ok\}} ok; X)//\{ok\} \tag{19}
$$

$\square$

Taking advantage of the fact that $(p_C \parallel_{\{ok\}} ok; X)//\{ok\}$ in facts implements the LOTOS sequential composition $\gg$, redefining $p_I := \textbf{exit}$, (19) may be reformulated to

$$C[X] \approx^c p_C \gg X \qquad (20)$$

If we now turn back to solving (18) we find that there is a solution of the form

$$G_x[X] := (out!x; \textbf{exit} \; [] \; in?y; q(x,y)) \gg X \qquad (21)$$

where $q(x, y)$ corresponds to $p_{C'}$ for $C' = G_y \circ G_x$. To meet our objective of having only processes with at most parameter complexity of a single data element, we must decompose $q(x, y)$ into simpler processes. From (18) and (21) we find that for $w \in D_{nat}$

$$G_x[X] -in_w \rightarrow q(x, w) \gg X$$
$$G_x[X] -in_w \rightarrow G_w \circ G_x[X]$$

Rewriting $G_w \circ G_x[X]$, using (21), and applying the associativity of $\gg$, it follows that

$$q(x, w) \gg X \approx ((out!w; \textbf{exit} \; [] \; in?y; q(w, y)) \gg (out!x; \textbf{exit} \; [] \; in?y; q(x, y))) \gg X$$

Because X can be an arbitrary process we can conclude

$$q(x, w) \approx (out!w; \textbf{exit} \; [] \; in?y; q(w, y)) \gg (out!x; \textbf{exit} \; [] \; in?y; q(x, y))$$

whence

$$in?w; q(x, w) \approx^c in?w; (out!w; \textbf{exit} \; [] \; in?y; q(w, y)) \gg (out!x; \textbf{exit} \; [] \; in?y; q(x, y))$$

i.e., $in?w; q(x, w)$ is a solution of

$$X(x) \approx^c in?w; (out!w; \textbf{exit} \; [] \; X(w)) \gg (out!x; \textbf{exit} \; [] \; X(x))$$

whose unique solution (modulo $\approx^c$) by theorem 2 is

$$Cell(x) := in?w; (out!w; \textbf{exit} \; [] \; Cell(w)) \gg (out!x; \textbf{exit} \; [] \; Cell(x))$$

It follows that $G_x[X] \approx^c (out!x; \textbf{exit} \; [] \; Cell(x)) \gg X$. Using standard techniques we obtain our final result.

Theorem 14 $Stack \approx^c NewStack$
              where $NewStack := in?x; Top(x) \gg NewStack$
$$Top(x) \quad := (out!x; \textbf{exit} \; [] \; Cell(x))$$
$$Cell(x) \quad := in?w; Top(w) \gg Top(x)$$

Remark

We could have tried to decompose the process $q(x, y)$ corresponding to $p_{C'}$ for $C' = G_y \circ G_x$ in the context of the solution for (18) generated by theorem 3 instead of that of theorem 13, as we have done now. The reader is encouraged to check that this cannot succeed: the renaming strategy in (1) does not have the associativity properties of $\gg$.

6 Conclusion

We have developed a technique to solve certain classes of context equations with unknown contexts in a fairly general process algebraic formalism. Using this technique we have shown how we may obtain specifications with an implementation-oriented substructure by distributing the global state of a high-level monolithic specification based on a single process definition and a complicated parameter structure in a controlled step-by-step fashion. In the full paper [BrKa91] we will report on our experience in applying this technique to more involved examples, and indicate ways to extend our results.

Acknowledgements

The author gratefully acknowledges the help of SICS, Kim Larsen, Rom Langerak and Pim Kars, who all contributed to the realization of this paper.

References

[BoBr87]   Bolognesi, T., Brinksma, E.: Introduction to the ISO Specification Language LOTOS. *Computer Networks and ISDN Systems* 14, 22–59 (1987).

[Bri88]   Brinksma, E.: *On the design of Extended LOTOS*. Doctoral Dissertation, University of Twente, The Netherlands, 1988.

[Bri89]   Brinksma, E.: Constraint-Oriented Specification in a Constructive Formal Description Technique, in: LNCS 430, pp. 130–152, Springer, 1989.

[BrKa91]   Brinksma, E., Kars, W.: From data structure to process structure. Memorandum INF-91-38/TIOS-91-11, University of Twente, The Netherlands, 1991.

[EhMa85]   Ehrig, H., Mahr, B.: *Fundamentals of Algebraic Specification 1*. Springer, 1985.

[Hoa85]   Hoare, C.A.R.: *Communicating Sequential Processes*. Prentice-Hall, 1985.

[ISO89]   ISO: *LOTOS, A formal description technique based on the temporal ordering of observational behaviour*. International Standard ISO 8807, 1989.

[Lar90]   Larsen, K.G.: Ideal Specification Formalism = Expressivity + Compositionality + Decidability + Testability + ... , in: Baeten, J.C.M., Klop, J.W. (eds.): *CONCUR'90*, LNCS 458, Springer, pp. 33–56 (1990).

[LaMi87]   Larsen, K., Milner, R.: Verifying a protocol using relativized bisimulation, in: *Proc. ICALP'87*, LNCS 267, Springer, 1987.

[Mil80]   Milner, R.: *A Calculus of Communicating Systems*. LNCS 92, Springer, 1980.

[Mil85]   Milne, G.: CIRCAL and the Representation of Communication, Concurrency and Time. *ACM Trans. on Progr. Languages and Systems* 7, 270–298 (1985).

[Mil89]   Milner, R.: *Communication and Concurrency*. Prentice-Hall, 1989.

[VSSB91]   Vissers, C.A., Scollo, G., Van Sinderen, M., Brinksma, E.: Specification Styles in Distributed Systems Design and Verification, to appear in: Special Issue TCS Tapsoft'89.

Checking for Language Inclusion Using Simulation Preorders

David L. Dill, Alan J. Hu, and Howard Wong-Toi*
Department of Computer Science
Stanford University

1 Introduction

Systems involving interaction among state machines, such as protocols, concurrent algorithms, and certain kinds of hardware, often contain subtle design errors that defy detection by conventional means, such as inspection, simulation, and testing a prototype. As a result, formal verification methods for such systems are of increasing interest.

We are interested in automatic verification using finite-state models of systems, with the underlying assumption that system behavior can be represented as a set of sequences representing all the possible histories (or traces) of the system (we assume *linear-time*). In this model, verification consists of testing for *language inclusion*: the implementation describes a set of actual traces and the specification gives the set of allowed traces; the implementation meets the specification if every actual trace is allowed.

In this paper, we consider only the case where both the implementation and the specification are represented by finite-state automata. The automata used here can describe both safety properties (which intuitively say that nothing bad happens), and liveness properties (which intuitively assert that something good eventually happens). More specifically, we deal with safety automata and Büchi automata.

As specifications become more complicated, it becomes less natural to express them with deterministic automata. This occurs because a complicated specification is more likely to have invisible internal state that is not a function of the externally visible state. Although such specifications can be expressed using deterministic automata, this places an unnecessary burden on the user. Determinization algorithms may cause exponential blowups and are also difficult to program.

Deciding language inclusion for non-deterministic automata is PSPACE-complete. Therefore it is highly unlikely that a polynomial technique can be used to decide language inclusion. However, deciding language inclusion for deterministic automata is known to be polynomial. Our main goal is to provide polynomial methods that work not only for deterministic automata, but also work for non-deterministic automata in cases of practical interest.

The *simulation preorder* is one of many preorders and equivalences considered by people studying branching-time models of concurrency. Simulation preorder is decidable in polynomial time (proportional to the product of the sizes of the two automata) even when the specification automaton is nondeterministic. However, the *simulation preorder* is a stronger relation between automata than language inclusion. So from our perspective (linear time), the simulation preorder should be regarded as an approximation (sufficient condition) for language inclusion that is much easier to check.

*This work was supported by the NSF under grant MIP-8858807. The second author is also supported by an ONR Graduate Fellowship.

One automaton precedes another in the simulation preorder if there exists a certain kind of correspondence, called a simulation relation, between states of the two automata (the correspondence is defined precisely below). Hence, deciding simulation preorder involves finding a simulation relation or proving that none exists. We consider below some variants on the simulation preorder that are expensive to check directly. In such cases, it may still be useful to do "semi-automatic verification": a human defines a candidate relation, and uses a computer to check automatically whether the candidate is a simulation relation. Hence, the computational complexity of checking a given simulation is also of interest.

The verification methods presented here are all incomplete, in that they can be used to prove language inclusion (whenever a simulation relation exists), but cannot decide language inclusion (that is, an automaton may accept a subset of the language of another without any simulation relation between them). This deficiency is a necessary sacrifice in return for efficiency. Nevertheless, we provide evidence that the technique is useful in practice through some examples.

1.1 Background

State relations in one form or another have been studied for a long time, including the *weak homomorphisms* and *coverings* of Ginzburg [Gin68] and the *simulations* of Milner [Mil71]. Many verification methods consider (possibly) infinite state automata, and therefore develop proof methodologies where the human verifier supplies a relation together with a mathematical proof that it is a simulation relation (for example, Milner's simulations, Lam and Shankar's protocol *projections* [LS84], the *possibilities mappings* of Lynch and Tuttle [LT87], Klarlund and Schneider's *invariants* [KS89] and the *progress measures* of Klarlund [Kla90]).

The Concurrency Workbench [CPS89] is one of several programs that test for simulation preorder between automata. However, none of these can handle large state spaces or liveness properties.

For liveness and fairness properties, we are interested in defining simulation relations on Büchi automata (finite automata that accept infinite strings). Park proposed using simulation relations on Muller automata, which are somewhat similar to Büchi automata. Checking Park's relations can be done in polynomial time, but automatically finding the relation is NP-complete, which limits their usefulness in practice (his simulations are similar to the relation called BSR-dlc below).

Lynch and Tuttle give a manual verification technique similar in spirit to our BSR-aa's on their IO-automata, which can also express fairness properties. Since they do not consider finite-state automata, neither testing a given relation nor finding one is decidable.

1.2 Notation

Let Σ be a set. Then Σ^* is the set of all finite sequences over Σ, and Σ^ω is the set of all infinite sequences over Σ. We will use Σ^∞ for $\Sigma^* \cup \Sigma^\omega$. If σ is in Σ^∞, its i-th element, if it exists, will be denoted σ_{i-1}, and σ may be identified with the corresponding string with the same elements. We let $len(\sigma)$ be the length of any σ in Σ^∞.

Let σ be in Σ^ω. The set of prefixes of σ, $pr(\sigma)$ is defined as $\{\sigma' \in \Sigma^* \mid \text{for all } i < len(\sigma'), \sigma'_i = \sigma_i\}$. Given a set $A \subseteq \Sigma^*$, its closure $cl(A)$ is the set of strings in Σ^ω such that every prefix is in A, i.e. $cl(A) = \{\sigma \mid pr(\sigma) \subseteq A\}$. The set $B \subseteq \Sigma^\omega$ is *closed* iff $B = cl(pr(B))$.

2 Safety Automata

Intuitively, states of an automaton represent states of the system or process being modeled. A state is made up of an external visible component, and an internal invisible component. A trace of an automaton is an infinite sequence of external states, and models what an external agent could observe of the process. All automata used here are finite-state and define languages of infinite traces.

A *safety automaton* A is a tuple $\langle S, E, P, N \rangle$. S is a finite set of *internal state components* and E is a finite set of *external state components*. The set of *states* of the automaton is $S \times E$. $P \subseteq S \times E$ is a set of *initial states*, and $N \subseteq (S \times E) \times (S \times E)$ is the *next state relation*. A *run* of A on the infinite sequence $e = e_0, e_1, \ldots \in E^\omega$ is an infinite sequence of states $\langle s_0, e_0 \rangle, \langle s_1, e_1 \rangle \ldots$ such that $\langle s_0, e_0 \rangle \in P$, and for all $i \geq 0$, $(\langle s_i, e_i \rangle, \langle s_{i+1}, e_{i+1} \rangle)$ is in N. The infinite sequence e is *accepted* by A if there is a run of A on e. The language $L(A)$ is the set of all *infinite* sequences for which there are accepting runs.

A is said to be *deterministic* if P is a singleton set and if for every state $\langle s, e \rangle \in S$ and every external component $e' \in E$ there is at most one state $\langle s', e' \rangle \in S \times E$ such that $((\langle s, e \rangle, \langle s', e' \rangle)) \in N$.

2.1 Simulation Relations for Safety Automata

We consider first simulation relations between safety automata, $A_1 = \langle S_1, E, I_1, N_1 \rangle$ and $A_2 = \langle S_2, E, I_2, N_2 \rangle$. Intuitively every state in the implementation must be related to a state in the specification with the same external component. It must be possible for every transition in the implementation to be simulated by a transition in the specification. The simulation relations relate each implementation state to several specification states, like those of Park, Lynch and Tuttle, and Loewenstein and Dill [Par81, LT87, LD90].

Definition 1 (SSR) A *safety simulation relation* between safety automata A_1 and A_2 is any relation $R \subseteq S_1 \times E \times S_2$ that satisfies the following properties:

(SR1) (simulation) $\forall s_1 \in S_1, e \in E, s_2 \in S_2, s_1' \in S_1, e' \in E$,

$[\, R(s_1, e, s_2) \wedge N_1((\langle s_1, e \rangle, \langle s_1', e' \rangle)) \,] \Rightarrow \exists s_2' \in S_2 \,[\, R(s_1', e', s_2') \wedge N_2((\langle s_2, e \rangle, \langle s_2', e' \rangle)) \,].$

(SR2) (initiality) $\forall s_1 \in S_1, e \in E$,

$\langle s_1, e \rangle \in P_1 \Rightarrow \exists s_2 \in S_2 \,[\, \langle s_2, e \rangle \in P_2 \wedge R(s_1, e, s_2) \,].$

Theorem 1 (SSR soundness) *If there is an SSR between A_1 and A_2, then $L(A_1) \subseteq L(A_2)$.*

As mentioned in the introduction, one way of verifying language inclusion is to check that a user-supplied relation is actually a simulation relation.

Algorithm 1 (Checking safety simulation relations) It is straightforward to verify that a relation satisfies SR1 and SR2 independently. For example, SR1 may be verified by a simple check that outgoing transitions from implementation states are mimicked in their simulating specification states. This simple procedure is polynomial in the number of states and edges of the two automata.

2.2 Finding Simulation Relations

Because simulation relations over safety automata are closed under union, there is a largest simulation relation that contains all others. The algorithm to find simulation relations finds the largest candidate relation and then verifies it is indeed a simulation relation. This candidate relation R is the largest relation satisfying the simulation property, SR1. Since SR2 (initiality) is a monotone property (that is, if it is true in a relation R', it is true in any larger relation), there is a simulation relation over $S_1 \times E \times S_2$ iff R satisfies SR2. Computing R from the maximum relation $S_1 \times E \times S_2$ involves repeatedly deleting triples which do not locally satisfy SR1. It is then straightforward to check whether SR2 holds. The algorithm is polynomial in the size of the automata.

While safety simulation relations are in general incomplete, there are special cases where language inclusion does imply the existence of a simulation relation. A safety automaton A is *non-deadlocking* whenever every finite string σ' having a run on A is a prefix of some infinite string in $L(A)$.

Theorem 2 *If $L(A_1) \subseteq L(A_2)$, A_2 is deterministic and A_1 is non-deadlocking, then there is an SSR between A_1 and A_2.*

2.3 Symbolic Implementation

One way to contain the state explosion problem is to represent automata and relations "symbolically," using some data structure that does not expand as quickly as an explicit list of states. One such data structure is the *binary decision diagram* (BDD), which gives a compact representation for a Boolean function [Bry86]. These data structures have proven especially efficient in many cases. Using the paradigm of symbolic model checking, [BCMDH90, BCMD90] we can efficiently perform the computations specified below.

An expression for the maximum relation satisfying the simulation condition (SR1 in Definition 1) on a safety simulation relation is:

$$\nu Z.\lambda s_1, e, s_2 \left[Z(s_1, e, s_2) \wedge \forall s_1', e' \left[N_1(\langle s_1, e \rangle, \langle s_1', e' \rangle) \Rightarrow \exists s_2' \left[Z(s_1', e', s_2') \wedge N_2(\langle s_2, e \rangle, \langle s_2', e' \rangle) \right] \right] \right]$$

where $\nu Z.F[Z]$ denotes the greatest fixed point of the predicate transformer F. Let $Q(s_1, e, s_2)$ be this fixed point.

Theorem 3 *A safety simulation relation exists iff Q satisfies the initiality condition (SR2 in Definition 1).*

3 Simulation relations for liveness properties

While safety automata can express many useful properties, they cannot express simple liveness properties, such as "process A will eventually read the variable x". To handle general liveness properties, we need automata that can handle general ω-regular languages. Many such automata have been proposed: Büchi automata, Muller automata, Rabin automata, Streett automata, $\forall$-automata, and L-automata. For simplicity, we choose to work with the conceptually simplest of these, Büchi automata. The ideas expressed here can be extended to the other types of automata, as well. •

A *Büchi automaton* $A = \langle S, E, P, N, F \rangle$ is a safety automaton with an additional fifth component $F \subseteq S \times E$, a set of *accepting states*. An infinite run r over the safety automaton $A_S = \langle S, E, P, N \rangle$ is called a run of the Büchi automaton A. The run r is an *accepting run* iff an accepting state occurs infinitely often in r. The *language* accepted by A is the set of all infinite strings with an accepting run. In the following, it is assumed every state in a Büchi automaton is reachable. A safety automaton can be considered to be a Büchi automaton in which $F = S \times E$.

Our definition of Büchi automata is non-standard: while our automata have external visible state components, the usual Büchi automata have visible labeled transitions between internal states. This change makes it easy for us to model our examples. However, there is a simple correspondence between the two definitions, and the simulations we propose can easily be applied to the more conventional definition of Büchi automata, also.

We define various simulation relations between Büchi automata, as extensions of simulation relations between safety automata. A Büchi automaton accepts an infinite string iff it has a run r for that string, and r is an *accepting* run, i.e. it includes infinitely many accepting states. Thus Büchi simulation relations must guarantee the existence not only of simulating runs but of simulating accepting runs.

Throughout the following we assume $A_1 = \langle S_1, E, P_1, N_1, F_1 \rangle$ and $A_2 = \langle S_2, E, P_2, N_2, F_2 \rangle$ are non-deadlocking Büchi automata.

3.1 Accepting-accepting Büchi simulation relations

Here, safety simulation relations are augmented with a simple condition that guarantees that whenever the newly entered state of the implementation is accepting, then so must be its simulating A_2 state.

Definition 2 (BSR-aa) An *accepting-accepting Büchi simulation relation (BSR-aa)*, is any relation $R \subseteq S_1 \times E \times S_2$ that satisfies SR1 (simulation), SR2 (initiality) and the additional property:

(SR-aa) $\forall s_1 \in S_1, e \in E, s_2 \in S_2,$

$$R(s_1, e, s_2) \Rightarrow [F_1(\langle s_1, e \rangle) \Rightarrow F_2(\langle s_2, e \rangle)].$$

Theorem 4 (BSR-aa soundness) *If there is BSR-aa between A_1 and A_2, then $L(A_1) \subseteq L(A_2)$.*

Example 1

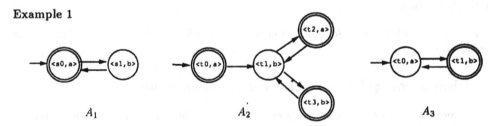

A_1 $\qquad\qquad\qquad\qquad A_2 \qquad\qquad\qquad\qquad\qquad A_3$

The relation $R = \{(s_0, a, t_0), (s_0, a, t_2), (s_1, b, t_1)\}$ is a BSR-aa between A_1 and A_2. However, there is no BSR-aa between A_1 and A_3, since the accepting states of one automaton are not "synchronized" with those of the other, even though clearly $L(A_1) \subseteq L(A_3)$.

3.2 Algorithms

As for safety simulation relations, we demonstrate algorithms for checking and finding each Büchi simulation relation. Büchi simulation relations are defined as safety simulation relations with an additional fairness property. When this additional property is of a certain form, the algorithms are trivial extensions of those for the safety case.

Suppose the fairness property determines *a priori* which pairings of automaton states are permitted in a simulation relation, independent of what other pairings appear in the simulation relation. Then a relation is a simulation relation whenever all pairings of states are permitted, or "good". Checking whether a relation is a Büchi simulation relation is then just checking it is a safety simulation relation and that all state pairings are good. Finding Büchi simulation relations is simply finding safety simulation relations among the good pairs.

Definition 3 A property P of relations in $S_1 \times E \times S_2$ is *locally-determined* if $P = 2^W$ for some $W \subseteq S_1 \times E \times S_2$.

Intuitively P is locally-determined iff R satisfies P whenever all triples in R are in some maximum relation W. We may interpret the triples in W as the good triples in $S_1 \times E \times S_2$.

Definition 4 Let BSR-P define the class of simulation relations that satisfy the properties SR1, SR2 and $SR - P$.

Lemma 1 *If $SR - P = 2^W$ is locally-determined, then a relation R is a BSR-P iff it is a safety simulation relation and contained in W.*

Theorem 5 *If $SR - P = 2^W$ is locally-determined and W is polynomially decidable, then checking whether a relation is a BSR-P is polynomial.*

Lemma 2 *If $SR - P$ is locally-determined, then BSR-P's are closed under union.*

Theorem 6 *If $SR - P = 2^W$ is locally-determined, and W is polynomially decidable, then deciding whether there is a BSR-P between two automata is polynomial.*

The property SR-aa is locally-determined, with SR-aa $= 2^W$, where $W = \{(s_1, e, s_2) \mid F_1((s_1, e)) \Rightarrow F_2((s_2, e))\}$. Determining SR-aa is linear in the sizes of S_1 and S_2, so by the above results there are polynomial algorithms for checking and finding BSR-aa's.

3.3 Live-cycles Büchi simulation relations

We may relax the condition of having to simulate every F_1 state with an F_2 state. It is sufficient to simulate F_1 states by some state in S_2 from which it is guaranteed every A_2-run will later pass through an accepting state. Equivalently, it must be impossible to continue simulation of A_1 in a cycle from $(s_1, e) \in F_1$ with a cycle of A_2 from (s_2, e) to (s_2, e) which does not pass through any states in F_2. In fact the converse is true, and this condition is also sufficient for language inclusion. Furthermore, it is locally-determined and polynomially decidable.

We first define the pseudo-product machine $A_{12} = \langle S_{12}, P_{12}, N_{12} \rangle$, where $S_{12} = S_1 \times E \times S_2$, $P_{12} = \{(s_1, e, s_2) \mid P_1((s_1, e)) \text{ and } P_2((s_2, e))\}$, and the next-state relation $N_{12} \subseteq S_{12} \times S_{12}$ is defined by $N_{12}((s_1, e, s_2), (s_1', e, s_2'))$ iff $N_1((s_1, e), (s_1', e'))$ and $N_2((s_2, e), (s_2', e'))$. A product-state (s_1, e, s_2) is an F_1 state iff $(s_1, e) \in F_1$, and likewise an F_2 state iff $(s_2, e) \in F_2$.

Definition 5 (BSR-lc) A *live-cycles Büchi simulation relation (BSR-lc)*, between A_1 and A_2 is any relation $R \subseteq S_1 \times E \times S_2$ that satisfies SR1 (simulation), SR2 (initiality) and the additional property:

(SR-lc) $\forall s_1 \in S_1, e \in E, s_2 \in S_2,$

$$R(s_1, e, s_2) \Rightarrow [F_1((s_1, e)) \Rightarrow LC((s_1, e, s_2))].$$

where $LC(\langle s_1, e, s_2\rangle)$ holds if every cycle through $\langle s_1, e, s_2\rangle$ in the pseudo-product machine A_{12} passes through an F_2 state (the cycle is "live").

Theorem 7 (BSR-lc soundness) *If there is a BSR-lc between A_1 and A_2, then $L(A_1) \subseteq L(A_2)$.*

Example 2 Here $R = \{(s_0, a, t_0), (s_1, b, t_1)\}$ is a BSR-lc, because the pseudo-product machine has the same structure as A_1. However, A_1 and A_2 have no BSR-ma.

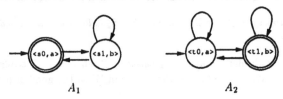

$$A_1 \qquad\qquad\qquad A_2$$

Theorem 8 (BSR-lc completeness for deterministic specifications) *If $L(A_1) \subseteq L(A_2)$ and A_2 is deterministic, then there is a BSR-lc between A_1 and A_2.*

3.4 Dynamic-live-cycles Büchi simulation relations

The fairness properties of all the Büchi simulation relations defined so far have been locally-determined, and static in the sense that they are given as predetermined safety conditions over the state-pairings allowable. They do not take into consideration exactly which state pairings appear in the relation. However, in order to guarantee simulating runs are accepting, we need only consider runs permitted by R. Consider the pseudo-machine $A'_{12} = \langle S'_{12}, P'_{12}, N'_{12}\rangle$, with state set $S'_{12} = (S_1 \times E \times S_2) \cap R$, initial states $P'_{12} = P_{12} \cap R$, and the next-state relation given by $N'_{12}(\langle s_1, e, s_2\rangle, \langle s'_1, e', s'_2\rangle)$ iff $N_1(\langle s_1, e\rangle, \langle s'_1, e'\rangle)$, $N_2(\langle s_2, e\rangle, \langle s'_2, e'\rangle)$, and $\langle s_1, e, s_2\rangle, \langle s'_1, e, s'_2\rangle \in R$. The machine A'_{12} is simply A_{12} restricted to R, so there will be fewer non-live cycles and thus more simulation relations between the automata. The SR-dlc condition is merely SR-lc with cycles taken with respect to A'_{12} instead of A_{12}.

Definition 6 (BSR-dlc) A *dynamic-live-cycles Büchi simulation relation (BSR-dlc)*, is any relation $R \subseteq S_1 \times E \times S_2$ that satisfies SR1 (simulation), SR2 (initiality) and the additional property:

(SR-dlc) $\forall s_1 \in S_1, e \in E, s_2 \in S_2,$
$$R(s_1, e, s_2) \Rightarrow [F_1(\langle s_1, e\rangle) \Rightarrow LC'(\langle s_1, e, s_2\rangle)].$$

where $LC'(\langle s_1, e, s_2\rangle)$ iff every cycle through $\langle s_1, e, s_2\rangle$ in the pseudo-product machine A'_{12} is live, i.e. it passes through an F_2 state.

Theorem 9 (BSR-dlc soundness) *If there is a BSR-dlc between A_1 and A_2, then $L(A_1) \subseteq L(A_2)$.*

Theorem 10 (BSR-dlc deterministic completeness) *If A_2 is deterministic and $L(A_1) \subseteq L(A_2)$, then there is a BSR-dlc between A_1 and A_2.*

While SR-dlc is still polynomially decidable, it is not locally-determined. Thus checking BSR-dlc's is polynomial, and in fact finding BSR-dlc's is NP-complete.

	Deterministic completeness	Checking	Finding
BSR-aa	no	poly	poly
BSR-lc	yes	poly	poly
BSR-dlc	yes	poly	exponential

Figure 1: Completeness and Complexity of Büchi simulation relations.

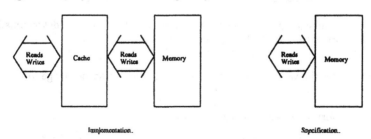

Figure 2: In the first verification example, a cached memory (nondeterministic) implements a memory (deterministic).

3.5 Summary/Comparative Expressiveness

Figure 1 summarizes the results above. Of the alternatives for Büchi simulations here, BSR-lc is the only one whose preorder is complete for deterministic specifications and decidable in polynomial time. Hence, we believe it is the one most likely to be of practical use in verification.

4 Verification Examples

The first example is adapted from an earlier paper using simulation relations [LD90]. We have a very general model of a cache (that allows prefetch, concurrent operations, etc.) and would like to show that a cached memory implements a memory. The cache model is nondeterministic and the memory model is deterministic. (See Figure 2.) Running on a DecStation 3100, finding a safety simulation relation took less than 5 seconds.

As CPU speeds have increased, the cache-memory port has become a bottleneck. Many architectures now incorporate a write buffer between the cache and the memory to reduce this problem. The second example considers a weaker memory model that allows the memory to buffer writes (delayed arbitrarily, but preserving the order of the writes) while allowing reads to bypass the buffer and read directly from memory. While this is not entirely realistic (real machines do not do it, at least intentionally), but it is similar to some consistency models used in *multi-processor* caching. We assume a finite-length write buffer.

We would like to show that the same cache from the first example can be attached to a write-buffered memory, with the result implementing a write-buffered memory. (See Figure 3.) Note that both the implementation and the specification are nondeterministic, demonstrating this important feature of simulation relations.

In under a minute, the verifier reported that no simulation relation exists. Additional queries to the system suggested the following scenario that demonstrates that in this case, the implementation is not correct with respect to the specification:

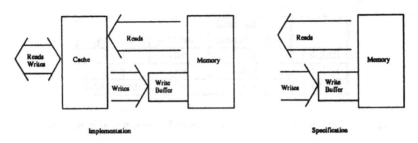

Figure 3: In the second example, a cached memory with write buffer (nondeterministic) fails to implement a memory with write buffer (nondeterministic).

1. Processor writes the value A to location X and receives an acknowledge from the memory system.

2. Processor performs operations not related to location X.

3. Processor writes a sequence of B's to location X (and receives acknowledgements for each). The number of B's written must be greater than the length of the write buffer.

4. Processor performs operations not related to location X.

5. Processor reads location X.

For the specification (a write-buffered memory), step 3 must result in a B being stored at location X because the write buffer must write B's to location X in order to keep from overflowing. Therefore, at step 5, the read must return the value B. For the cached implementation, however, consider the following possible scenario:

1. During step 1, the cache has a dirty copy of location X equal to the value A.

2. During step 2, the cache writes back its dirty copy. At some point, the write makes its way through the write buffer, so location X now equals A.

3. During step 3, the cache misses, reads a clean copy of $X = A$, and modifies its copy to a dirty copy $X = B$. Memory location X still holds value A.

4. During step 4, the cache writes back its dirty copy of $X = B$. This write gets buffered.

5. During step 5, the processor attempts to read location X. The cache misses and gets a clean copy of $X = A$ from the memory. The cache returns $X = A$.

This trace is possible in the implementation, but not in the specification.

To correct that bug, the third example again verifies that a cached, write-buffered memory implements a write-buffered memory, but the write buffer is modeled differently. We add an interlock to the memory to block a read to any location that has a write pending in the write buffer. (See Figure 4.) With this modification, the cached memory operates correctly. The verifier found a simulation relation in just over 20 seconds.

The following table summarizes the results. All runs used a DecStation 3100 with 16MB of memory. The implementation uses Brace, Rudell, and Bryant's package for boolean decision diagram manipulation. [BRB90]

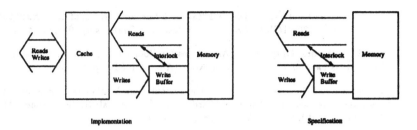

Figure 4: In the third example, a modified write buffer now blocks reads to locations that have a write pending in the buffer. Both the specification and the implementation are still nondeterministic.

Memory	Implementation (w/cache)		Specification		Simulation	Time
Model	Det	States	Det	States	Relation	(in sec)
Plain	No	64K	Yes	64	Yes	5
w/write buf	No	500K	No	500	No	41
w/interlock	No	500K	No	500	Yes	22

5 Conclusion

We have implemented an efficient verifier for language inclusion, using simulation relations as a heuristic. The examples above demonstrate the promise of this approach. Since the method is incomplete, more examples need to be verified to determine its practical usefulness. Future work along these lines includes development of improved diagnostics during verification, especially to suggest counterexamples when no simulation relation exists.

We plan to extend the implementation to find Büchi simulation relations. We are also investigating simulation relations defined over other forms of ω-automata.

Our framework deals only with the logical sequencing of events in trace traces. We are currently working on including timing properties in our specifications (cf. [LA89, Bes90]).

6 Acknowledgements

We would like to thank Andreas Drexler for his help in implementing the verifier.

References

[BCMD90] J.R. Burch, E.M. Clark, K.L. McMillan, and David L. Dill, "Sequential Circuit Verification Using Symbolic Model Checking," *27th ACM/IEEE Design Automation Conference*, 1990, pp. 46-51.

[BCMDH90] J.R. Burch, E.M. Clark, K.L. McMillan, D.L. Dill, and L.J. Hwang, "Symbolic Model Checking: 10^{20} States and Beyond," *Proceedings of the Conference on Logic in Computer Science*, 1990, pp. 428–439.

[Bes90] A.A. Bestavros, "The input-output timed automaton: a model for real-time parallel computation", Presentation at Workshop on Timing Issues in the Specification and Synthesis of Digital Systems, 1990.

[BRB90]   Karl S. Brace, Richard L. Rudell, and Randal E. Bryant, "Efficient Implementation of a BDD Package," *27th ACM/IEEE Design Automation Conference*, 1990, pp. 40-45.

[Bry86]   Randal E. Bryant, "Graph-Based Algorithms for Boolean Function Manipulation," *IEEE Transactions on Computers*, Vol. C-35, No. 8 (August 1986), pp. 677-691.

[CPS89]   R. Cleaveland, J. Parrow, B. Steffen, "The Concurrency Workbench", Proceedings of the International Workshop on Automatic Verification of Finite State Systems, June 1989, LNCS 407, J. Sifakis (ed.), Springer-Verlag 1989, pp. 24-37.

[Gin68]   A. Ginzburg, "Algebraic Theory of Automata", ACM Monograph Series, Academic Press, 1968.

[Kla90]   N. Klarlund, "Progress Measures and Finite Arguments for Infinite Computations", Ph.D Thesis, Cornell University, TR 90-1153, September 1990.

[KS89]   N. Klarlund and F.B. Schneider, "Verifying safety properties using infinite-state automata", Technical report TR-1036, Cornell University, 1989.

[Kur90]   R. Kurshan, "Analysis of discrete event coordination", in *Stepwise Refinement of Distributed Systems: Models, Formalisms, Correctness*, LNCS 430, J.W. deBakker, W.-P. de Roever, G. Rozenberg (eds.), Springer-Verlag 1990, pp. 414–453.

[LA89]   N.A. Lynch, II. Attiya, "Using mappings to prove timing properties", MIT-LCS-TM-412.b, 1989.

[LD90]   Paul Loewenstein and David Dill, "Formal Verification of Cache Systems using Refinement Relations," *IEEE International Conference on Computer Design*, 1990, pp. 228-233.

[LS84]   S.S. Lam, A.U. Shankar, "Protocol verification via projections", *IEEE Transactions on Software Engineering*, SE-10(4):325–342, July 1984

[LT87]   N.A. Lynch, M.R. Tuttle, "Hierarchical correctness proofs for distributed algorithms", in *Proceedings of the 6th Annual ACM Symposium on Principles of Distributed Computing*, 1987, pp. 137–151.

[Mil71]   R. Milner, "An algebraic definition of simulation between programs", *Proceedings of the 2nd International Joint Conference on Artificial Intelligence*, British Computer Society, 1971, pp. 481–489.

[Par81]   D.M.R. Park, "Concurrency and automata on infinite sequences", in *Proc. 5th GI conference (P. Deussen. ed.)*, LNCS 104, 1981, pp. 167–183.

A Semantic Driven Method to Check the Fineteness of CCS Processes

N. De Francesco[*] & P. Inverardi[♥]

[*] Dipartimento di Ingegneria dell'Informazione, Università di Pisa
[♥] IEI-CNR, Pisa

Abstract

In this paper we present a method to check the finiteness of CCS expressions. The method is interpretative, i.e. it is based on an extended operational semantics of CCS. According to this new operational semantics it is always possible to build a finite state transition system which, if some condition holds, is a finite representation of a process. It works on terms of the CCS signature and is able to decide the finiteness of a CCS expression in a large number of cases which are not captured by the known syntactic criteria.

1. INTRODUCTION

The problem of determining if a given CCS term is representable by a finite state automata is particularly interesting when dealing with verification environments. Most of the existing verification environments for CCS-like languages, [BC89, CPS88, DSV89, Fer88] are, in fact, based on an internal finite state representation of the process which allows for the application of efficient algorithms to decide if two processes are bisimilar [BS87, GV90, KS90].

In this paper we describe a method to check finiteness of CCS expressions. It is well known that it is undecidable if a CCS expression represents a finite state automata unless it is expressed in suitable subsets of the language [Tau89]. Therefore, either syntactic conditions are proposed which guarantee the finiteness of a CCS expression, e.g. not allowing the presence of the parallel operator and of the relabelling operator inside the body of a recursive expression [MV90], or, given a term P, a syntax-driven construction of an *equivalent* finite transition system for P is defined [Tau89]. Even if the latter is more general, i.e. it deals with a larger class of terms, than the former, it still suffers from being syntax-driven.

The method we present is, instead, *interpretative*. It is based on an extended operational semantics of CCS by means of which we actually build a finite state transition system which, if some condition holds, is a finite representation of a process. It works on terms of the CCS signature and it is able to decide the finiteness of a CCS expression in a number of cases which are not captured by the known syntactic criteria. This *non-standard* semantics defines an aproximation of the standard one, in the sense that the synchronization tree that can be built by means of it in correspondence of a given term, can be properly related with the standard one. In this respect, our approach fits in the more general framework of *non-standard interpretations* for CCS-like languages [DI91], that we will not explicitly address in this paper. The paper is structured as follows. In section 2 a general overview of the language and of the known results about the fineteness of CCS expressions are briefly surveied. Section 3, presents the method, that

Work partially supported by Progetto Finalizzato Sistemi Informatici e Calcolo Parallelo of CNR.

is the general idea of the approach and two non-standard semantics are given, together with a comparison among them. Section 4 discusses future developments and concludes.

2 SETTING THE FRAMEWORK

2.1 The language: syntax and operational semantics
We consider the following syntax for process terms (or simply processes):

$$P::= \mu.P \mid nil \mid P+P \mid P|P \mid P\backslash A \mid x$$

As usual, there is a set of actions Act=$\{a,\bar{a},b,\bar{b},...\}$ over which α ranges, while μ ranges over

Act $\cup$ $\{\tau\}$, being τ the so-called *internal action*. Moreover x ranges over a set $\{x, y, ..\}$ of *constants*. Every constant is a process defined by an equation (*constant definition*): x=P.

Constant definitions may be (mutually) recursive and this is the only way to define processes with infinite behaviour. We assume that all recursive definition are *guarded*. An *occurrence* of x in P is *guarded* if it occurs within some subexpression $\mu.F$ ($\mu \neq \tau$) of P. A recursive definition x=P is *guarded* if every occurrence of x in P is guarded.

Note that, for the sake of simplicity, we have not introduced in the language the relabelling operator, we discuss how to cope with it in section 3.4.

The operational semantics of the language, from now on referred to as SOS, is the usual one given in [Mil89]. We indicate by $\bar{\mu}$ the *action complement*: if α=a, then $\bar{\alpha} = \bar{a}$, while if $\alpha=\bar{a}$, then $\bar{\alpha}$ = a. Given two processes P_1 and P_2 such that $P_1-\mu\rightarrow P_2$ by the inference rules, P_2 is said to be an μ-*immediate derivative* of P_1. In order to represent the possible computations of a process, we use *derivation trees* [Mil80]. The derivation tree is an unorderd, possibly infinite, tree having processes as nodes and such that there is an arc labelled by μ from a node P_1 to a node P_2 if P_2 is a μ-*immediate derivative* of P_1. The tree may be infinite. In the following, we call standard semantics the SOS one to distinguish it from the *non-standard semantics* we are going to define in order to check the finiteness conditions.

2.2 Finiteness conditions
In this section we recall some of the definitions and of the results already present in the literature. For more details we refer to [Tau89].

Given a process term P and an operational semantics S, we call $DT_S(P)$ the derivation tree obtained using the rules in S. We call $TS_S(P)$ the labelled transition system obtained in a similar way than $DT_S(P)$, except that folding takes place. A new node is created in $TS_S(P)$ only when an expression is derived from P which is not the label of an already existing node of $TS_S(P)$; otherwise a transition back to such a node is added. It can easily be proved that, for each P, $TS_S(P)$ and $DT_S(P)$ are strongly equivalent.

For example, let us consider the process $P1 = x$ where x= $(a.c.nil \mid b.\bar{c}.x) \backslash \{c\}$

Its (infinite) transition system $TS_{SOS}(P1)$, built by using the standard operational semantics, is:

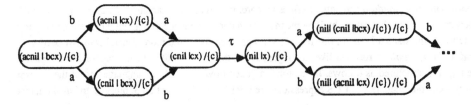

Figure 1

We say that a CCS process P is *finite state* if it exists a finite state transition system strongly bisimilar to $TS_{SOS}(P)$. For example, it is easy to see that it exists a finite state transition system strongly bisimilar to the infinite transition system shown in Figure 1. In general, it is not decidable if an arbitrary process P is finite state. Sufficient syntactic conditions exist which characterize classes of processes for which it is possible to build an equivalent finite transition system. In the following, we present only the conditions which are of interest in our framework, while we refer to [BS87, Tau89, MV90] for more details.

With our syntax, we can say, for example, that a process is finite state if no parallel operators is present inside a constant definition. Thus   x|y   where x=rec.x.ax and y=rec.y.by+cx

is finite state. It is, of course, possible to refine the syntactic conditions in order to take into account more cases. For example, we can accept recursive definitions including the parallel operators, as long as the constant name does not occur in the operands. By this new rule

x=rec.x. (a.nil I b.nil + cx) is well formed.

However, any syntactic approach, even if more and more refined, is intrinsically limited and leaves room for different methods. Our approach is *interpretative*, and the bulk of the method we are going to describe in the following section consists in constructing a finite transition system of a CCS term by means of a new operational semantics.

3 THE METHOD

The basic idea relies on the fact that if a process is finite state, while building its derivation tree it must happen that either it has finite branches or its infinite branches are *regular*, that is along an infinite path there are infinitely many repetition of the *same* node. This means that, in building the transition system, each time we reach a node *equal* to one already present in the derivation, we can stop the development of that node.

Let us for the moment be quite vague about the semantics of what a *same* or *equal* node is and let us show some examples. Consider the process P1 of the previous section which does not respect the stated syntactic conditions and whose infinite transition system has been shown in Figure 1. It is easy to see that by using the standard operational semantics the two states

(c.nil I b.$\bar{c}$.x) \ {c} and (nil I (c.nil I b.$\bar{c}$.x) \ {c}) \ {c} are different while they become equal as soon as an absorption of the nil process and of the restriction {c} is performed on the second process term. This suggests to build in the operational semantics some of the information that is usually introduced by means of axioms, with the specific purpose of directly obtaining from the resultant derivation tree a finite state transition system.

3.1 1st Non-Standard Semantics

In this section we present our first non-standard operational semantics. The attempt is to perform directly within the operational semantics some term simplifications which turn out to be useful for our purposes. To this extent we introduce a predicate *term* with the following meaning

$$\text{term(P)} = \begin{cases} true & \text{if P has no derivatives according to SOS} \\ false & \text{otherwise} \end{cases}$$

Our 1st operational semantics, shown in Figure 2, takes care of:
- the termination of a process, by deleting the terminated process when it is an operand of the parallel composition operator (rules Com_2 and Com_4). For example, a.nil I P $-a\rightarrow$ P;
- the growing of the restriction operator (rule Res_2).

```
┌─────────────────────────────────────────────────────────────────┐
│ 1st Non-Standard Semantics                                        │
│                                                                   │
│ Act                    ─────────                                  │
│                        μ.P −μ→ P                                  │
│                                                                   │
│                                                                   │
│                        P −μ→ P'                                  │
│ Con                    ─────────      x=P                         │
│                        x −μ→ P'                                  │
│                                                                   │
│                                                                   │
│                        P−μ→ P'                                   │
│ Sum                    ───────────────────────                    │
│                        P + Q −μ→ P'  and Q+ P −μ→ P'            │
│                                                                   │
│                        P −μ→ P' , term(P) =false                │
│ Com₁                   ─────────────────────────────              │
│                        P│Q −μ→ P'│Q   and   Q│P−μ→ Q│P'       │
│                                                                   │
│                        P −μ→ P' , term(P') =true               │
│ Com₂                   ─────────────────────                      │
│                        P│Q−μ→ Q  and  Q│P−μ→ Q                 │
│                                                                   │
│                        P − α→ P' , Q − ᾱ→ Q' , term(P')=term(Q')=false │
│ Com₃                   ───────────────────────────────────────    │
│                        P│Q−τ→ P'│Q'                             │
│                                                                   │
│                        P − α→ P' , Q − ᾱ→ Q' , term(P') =true  │
│ Com₄                   ─────────────────────────────────          │
│                        P│Q−τ→ Q'  and   Q│P−τ→ Q'             │
│                                                                   │
│                        P −μ→ P' , P'≠P'' \ B ,  term(P') =false │
│ Res₁                   ─────────────────────────────────  μ,μ̄ ∉ A │
│                        P\A −μ→ P'\A                             │
│                                                                   │
│                        P −μ→ P' \B , term(P') =false            │
│ Res₂                   ─────────────────────────────   μ,μ̄ ∉ A  │
│                        P\A −μ→ P'\(A∪B)                         │
│                                                                   │
│                        P −μ→ P' , term(P') =true               │
│ Res₃                   ─────────────────────────   μ,μ̄ ∉ A      │
│                        P\A −μ→ nil                              │
│                                                                   │
└─────────────────────────────────────────────────────────────────┘
```

Figure 2. 1st non-standard semantics

If we now reconsider the process P1 whose infinite transition system is shown in Figure 1, by using our new operational semantics we have that $TS_{1S}(P1)$ is finite:

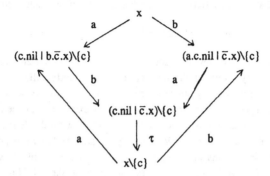

Note that we used rule **Com₄** in the derivation $(c.nil||\bar{c}.x)\backslash\{c\} \xrightarrow{\tau} x\backslash\{c\}$ and **Res₂** in $x\backslash\{c\}\xrightarrow{\tau} (c.nil \mid b.\bar{c}.x)\backslash\{c\}$. Note also that $TS_{1S}(P1)$ is not the minimal transition system, but this is not relevant to our purposes. However, it is possible to modify the rules in such a way to recognize an already reached state as soon as possible. In order to rely on our new operational semantics we must prove the following:

Theorem 1. $TS_{1S}(P)$ is strongly equivalent to $TS_{SOS}(P)$ for each P.
Sketch of the proof. It is straightforward since we have basically introduced in 1S, rules that are the operational counterpart of the axioms nil||P=P, P||nil=P, nil \ A = nil and $P\backslash A\backslash B = P\backslash(A\cup B)$.

The non-standard semantics we have given allows the construction of a finite transition system in cases in which the transition system corresponding to the standard one is infinite. However, it does not fulfill all our requirements since it still allows the construction of infinite transition systems. Consider, for example, the process P2=x, where x=a.x|b.nil, which is not representable by a finite state automaton. $TS_{1S}(P2)$ is infinite:

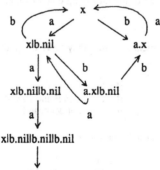

Instead, we want to have a decision procedure which, even if not complete, is always able to give an answer. In fact, the difference between the syntactic and the interpretative methods are similar to the difference between compile time and run time checking: compile time checking may give a negative response even if the program is correct because some branches of the program are never actually executed. On the other hand, the difficulty of the interpretative methods is to decide when they have to stop. In our case, this means that we have to establish a criterion which blocks potential non-regular infinite derivations.

3.2 2nd Non-Standard Semantics

Before presenting the 2nd non-standard semantics, let us introduce the intuition underlying it by using, as example, the process P2 above. In $TS_{1S}(P2)$, we see that the only infinite path starting from x is

$$x{-}a\rightarrow x|b.nil\ {-}a\rightarrow x|b.nil|b.nil\ {-}a\rightarrow\ ..\ x|b.nil|b.nil...|b.nil$$

In all the other paths the term labelling the states decreases in length. Our 2nd non-standard semantics prevents such situations by stopping the derivation of potentially infinite growing terms. As a consequence, given a term P, we may obtain a transition system which is not bisimilar to $TS_{SOS}(P)$, while, as we shall see later on, a precise approximation relation exists between the two ones. Considering our syntax, the operators that, in presence of recursion, would allow for the derivation of growing terms are the parallel composition and the restriction ones. As regards the latter it is possible, in a language with finite action set, to prevent this situation, by using an inference rule like **Res₂** in 1S. On the other hand, when dealing with the parallel operator our solution prevents the unfolding of x if it occurs as an operand in a non-empty parallel composition. Thus, we define a new semantics, 2S, shown in Figure 2, which blocks the derivation of the term x|P if it occurs inside the expansion of x.

To achieve this goal, it is necessary to manage a term like x|b.nil in a different way depending whether the parallel operator is inside or outside the recursive unfolding of x. While in the first case, we must stop the derivation, in the second one we can unfold x safely. The new semantics keeps distinct the two terms by maintaining the recursive expansion prefixed by rec.x.: parentheses are used as usual to make terms non-ambiguous, i.e. rec.x.(x|b.nil) and rec.x.x|b.nil are different processes. We use a function F that deletes from a term all the rec.x prefixes, thus obtaining a term to which it is possible to apply the predicate *term* defined at the beginning of section 3.1. For example, F(rec.x.a.nil)=a.nil.

The new semantics includes all the rules of the first non-standard semantics, except that **Con** is modified and a new set of rules is added, dealing with terms prefixed by rec.x. for some x. **Con** and the new rules are shown in Figure 3. These new rules maintain the information that a recursive term is being derived by keeping the prefix rec.x. until the rest of the unfolding contains x and we have not reached x itself, in which case rec.x. is deleted.

The square and the { } brackets are meta-notation: they serve the purpose of avoiding replication of the same rule. More precisely, if $P{\neq}P'\setminus A$,

$$[P]\quad=\quad\begin{cases}x & \text{if } P{=}x\\ rec.x.P & \text{if x occurs in P and } P{\neq}x\\ P & \text{if x does not occur in P}\end{cases}$$

Moreover, [and] push the restriction out of the prefixed expression:

$$[P\setminus A]\quad=\quad\begin{cases}x\setminus A & \text{if } P{=}x\\ (rec.x.P)\setminus A & \text{if x occurs in P and } p{\neq}x\\ P\setminus A & \text{if x does not occur in P}\end{cases}$$

This allows to omit a rule **P-Res₂**, while only **P-Res₁** is needed. For example, [a.nil]=a.nil, [a.x|b.nil]=rec.x.(a.x|b.nil) and [a.x\A]= (rec.x.a.x)\A.

For the other meta-notation, we have:

$$\{P\}\quad=\quad\begin{cases}P' & \text{if } P{=}rec.x.P'\\ P & \text{if } P{\neq}rec.x.P'\end{cases}$$

This is again a shorthand in order to avoid extra rules: the prefix of P', if present, has to be omitted because it is mantained in the conclusion of the rule; this is necessary in order to avoid the increasing of prefixes.

2nd Non-Standard Semantics

Con
$$\frac{[P]-\mu\to P'}{x-\mu\to P'} \qquad x=P$$

P-Act
$$\frac{}{rec.x.\mu P -\mu\to [P]}$$

P-Sum
$$\frac{rec.x.\,P-\mu\to P'}{rec.x.(P+Q)-\mu\to P' \quad \text{and} \quad rec.x.(Q+P)-\mu\to P'}$$

P-Com$_1$
$$\frac{rec.x.P -\mu\to P', \ Q\neq x, \ term(F(P'))=false}{rec.x.(P\,|\,Q)-\mu\to [\{P'\}|\,Q] \quad \text{and} \quad rec.x.(Q\,|\,P)-\mu\to [Q|\,\{P'\}]}$$

P-Com$_2$
$$\frac{rec.x.P -\mu\to P', \ Q\neq x, \ term(F(P'))=true}{rec.x.(P\,|\,Q)-\mu\to [Q] \quad \text{and} \quad rec.x.(Q\,|\,P)-\mu\to [Q]}$$

P-Com$_3$
$$\frac{rec.x.P - \alpha\to P', \ rec.x.Q - \bar{\alpha}\to Q', \ term(F(P'))=term(F(Q'))=false}{rec.x.(P\,|\,Q)-\tau\to [\{P'\}\,|\,\{Q'\}]}$$

P-Com$_4$
$$\frac{rec.x.P - \alpha\to P', \ rec.x.Q - \bar{\alpha}\to Q', \ term(F(P'))=true}{rec.x.(P\,|\,Q)-\tau\to Q' \quad \text{and} \quad rec.x.(Q\,|\,P)-\tau\to Q'}$$

P-Res$_1$
$$\frac{rec.x.P -\mu\to P', \ P'\neq P''\backslash B, \ term(F(P'))=false}{rec.x.(P\setminus A)-\mu\to [\{P'\}\setminus A]} \qquad \mu,\bar{\mu}\notin A$$

P-Res$_3$
$$\frac{rec.x.P -\mu\to P', \ P'\neq P''\setminus B, \ term(F(P'))=true}{rec.x.(P\setminus A)-\mu\to nil} \qquad \mu,\bar{\mu}\notin A$$

Figure 3. 2nd Non-Standard semantics

The stopping of the derivation of terms x|P inside the x unfolding is assured by rules **P-Com₁** and **P-Com₂**: when x is an operand of a parallel operator prefixed by rec.x. the whole process cannot do any move. All the other rules are similar to the corresponding ones for non-prefixed terms, except that they maintain the prefixes: thus a prefixed process rec.x.P, unless P= x|Q, can do every move P can do by using 1S (the prefix can be ignored).

Let us now show some examples.

Example 1

$TS_{2S}(P1)$ is the following:

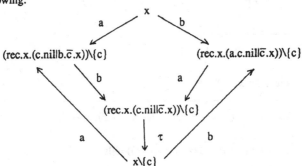

Note that it is equal to $TS_{1S}(P1)$, even if the labels of the states are not equal: for each state P in $TS_{2S}(P1)$ there is a state in $TS_{1S}(P1)$ labelled by F(P).

Example 2

Let us now consider $TS_{2S}(P2)$:

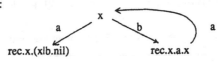

In this case we get an approximation of $TS_{1S}(P2)$ which is finite state.

Example 3

Let us consider the constant definition x=a.x|b.x. If we consider the term x, it is not finite state, while x\{a} is finite state, because it is strongly equivalent to the following transition system, obtained by 2S:

Now, if we use syntactic constructions like in [Tau89] which builds a finite state transition systems for a term by composing the transition systems corresponding to its subterms, it is very difficult to manage general terms of this kind whatever the syntactic criteria are. In this case, the fact that the parallel operator is not distributive with respect to the restriction one forbids the formulation of general syntactic criteria, being the only possible safe criterion an operational one.

3.3 Relationships between the non-standard semantics

The following theorem assures that the transition system built by means of the second non-standard semantics is always finite.

Theorem 2. $TS_{2S}(P)$ is finite for each P.

Sketch of the proof. We prove that the terms derivable from P in $DT_{2S}(P)$ are of bounded length. This is done by showing that the restriction and the parallel operators are not allowed to infinitely increase the length of the recursive terms generated by unfoldings. For what concerns \, this is proved by using the inference rule **Res₂** and the fact that the action set is finite. For the | operator, we block every potential dangerous derivation by rule **P-Com₁** and **P-Com₂**. An important point is that, the extra notation rec.x. we use to control the unfolding process does not itself contribute to the growing of a term. In fact, when we start the derivation of rec.x.P,

a) we take retrictions out of the prefixed processes; and

b) we maintain the prefix rec.x during the derivation until we reach x and at this point rec.x. is no more present and we can, if needed, use rule **Res₂**.

Now we can express the finiteness condition. We say that a state of the transition system is *terminal* if it does not have outgoing transitions. Let us consider the labels of the terminal states, if any, of the transition system obtained from a process Q by 2S: two cases may occur for the label P of a terminal state:

i.) P is a "truly" terminal situation, i.e. F(P) is not derivable also with the standard semantics: it is nil or deadlocked, where F is the function introduced in the previous section;

ii.) the derivation of P has been stopped in 2S because it is a potential source of infinite path, i.e. x|P occurs in the unfolding of x inside P.

Our algorithm gives a positive response to the finiteness of a process if all the terminal states, if any, are of the first kind. In the following, we briefly sketch the correctness proof of our method.

Well-formedness. $TS_{2S}(P)$ is *well-formed* if for the label Q of each terminal state, term(F(Q)) holds.

The following theorem states the correctness of 2S.

Theorem 3. If $TS_{2S}(P)$ is well-formed, it is strongly equivalent to $TS_{1S}(P)$.

Sketch of the proof. The only difference between 1S and 2S is that 2S does not derive terms like x|P if they are present in the expansion of x. In fact, if a rule R applies on a term P, the rule P-R applies on the term rec.x.P, allowing the same moves. The only difference regards the rules **P-Com₁** and **P-Com₂** which behave as **Com₁** and **Com₂** except in the case when an operand of the parallel composition is x. Note that, even if $TS_{2S}(P)$ is not well-formed, a relation exists between it and $TS_{1S}(P)$: $TS_{2S}(P)$ has only a subset of the states of $TS_{1S}(P)$, but these states have the same behaviour as in $TS_{1S}(P)$. This relation is described by the following definition:

Definition (*Approximation*) A transition system T is an approximation of another transition system T' if, for each state s in T there is a state s' in T' with the same incoming transitions and such that if s is not terminal, s' has the same outgoing transitions.

Theorem 4. $TS_{2S}(P)$ is an approximation of $TS_{1S}(P)$.

Proof Straightforward from the construction of $TS_{2S}(P)$.

The following result gives the correctness of the method :

Corollary. If $TS_{2S}(P)$ is well-formed, P is finite state.

Proof $TS_{2S}(P)$ is strongly equivalent to $TS_{SOS}(P)$ by theorems 1and 3.

3.4 Adding relabelling

Let us now discuss the introduction of the relabelling operator in our syntax. First of all we have, as in [Tau89], to restrict to finite relabelling, that is to relabelling functions with finite codomain. Then, once the usual operational semantics rule for relabelling is introduced in 1S and hence in 2S, we have to address the problem of avoiding the production of growing terms like for the restriction operator. This can be done similarly to what done for the restriction by including in the semantics an absorption rule for relabelling, by means of functional composition. This is not yet enough because now restriction and relabelling can occur intertwined, thus preventing the application of the absorption rules. To this extent it is necessary to add extra rules allowing for exchanging the order of consecutive restriction and relabelling operators. Note that this basically corresponds to build in the operational semantics two (correct) axioms like $P[f1][f2]=P[f1 \cdot f2]$ and $P \setminus C[f] = P[f] \setminus C$ provided that $labels(C) \neq labels(f)$.

4 CONCLUSIONS

In this paper we have presented an interpretative method for checking the finiteness of CCS expressions. We have defined a new operational semantics which allows for the construction of finite approximation of the transition system of a process P. In this way it is possible in a large number of cases to capture the finiteness nature of a process term even if it does not exhibit a particular syntactic structure. Note that due to the indecidability of the problem, it is not possible, in general, to provide a statement which assesses that our method is more powerful than whatsoever syntactic criteria. Anyhow it is possible to show that for the most widely used syntactic criteria, like those mentioned in the paper, this correspondence holds. In any case we think that our method has not to be seen as a substitutive one but mainly as an auxiliary tool which has to be used when the syntactic criteria do not apply.

The interesting point of our method is that, in order to define our finite approximations of the transition system, we have enriched the standard CCS operational semantics with a certain amount of "behavioural" information. Of course, our extent is not to use as much behavioural semantics as possible, but only to introduce as less equivalences as possible in order to make our interpretative method decidable. This is an important point of our interpretative approach. Depending on the verification problem it is going to be addressed, one can define the most appropriate extended operational semantics to solve it by using only that part of the "behavioural" semantics which is related to the solution of the problem. For example, in our case, we were interested in detecting nodes which differ only for the presence of nil operands in a parallel composition while in other cases this information may be completely irrelevant.

REFERENCES

[BC89] Bolognesi, T., Caneve, M. - A Tool for the Analysis of Lotos Specifications, in Formal Description Techniques (K. Turner, ed.), North-Holland, (1989), 201-216.

[BS87] Bolognesi, T., Smolka, S. Fundamental results for the Verification of Observational Equivalence: A Survey, in Proc. IFIP WG 6.1 7th Conference on Protocol Specification, Testing and Verification, North-Holland, (1987)

[CPS88] Cleaveland, R., Parrow, J., Steffen, B. The Concurrency Workbench: Operating Instructions, Tech. Note of Sussex University, (1988).

[DSV89] De Simone R., Vergamini D. Aboard AUTO, INRIA Technical Report 111, 1989.

[DI91] De Francesco, N., Inverardi, P. Non-standard Semantics in Process Algebras, forthcoming.

[Fer88] Fernandez J., C. Aldebaran, Un system de verification par reduction de processus communicantes, Ph.D. Thesis, Universite de Grenoble, 1988.

[GLZ89] Godskesen, J.C., Larsen, K.G., Zeeberg, M. TAV Users Manual, Internal Report, Aalborg University Center, Denmark, (1989).

[GV90] Groote, J. F., Vaandrager, F. W. An efficient algorithm for branching bisimulation and stuttering equivalence. Proc. 17th ICALP, LNCS 443, Springer-Verlag, 1990.

[KS90] Kanellakis, P.C., Smolka, S.A. CCS Expressions, Finite State Processes and Three Problems of Equivalence, Information and Computation, Vol. 86, Num. 1, May 1990.

[MV90] Madelaine, E., Vergamini, D. (1990), Finiteness Conditions and Structural Construction of Automata for All Process Algebras, in "Proceedings, Workshop on Computer-Aided Verification, DIMACS Center, Technical Report 90-31, Rutgers University.

[Mil80] Milner, R. (1980), A Calculus of Communicating Systems, Lecture Notes in Computer Science, Vol. 92, Springer-Verlag, New York/Berlin.

[Mil89] Milner, R. (1989), Communication and Concurrency, Prentice-Hall Int., 1989.

[Plo81] Plotkin, G. D. A Structural Approach to Operational Semantics, DAIMI FN-19, Computer Science Department, Aarhus University, Denmark, (September 1981).

[Tau89] Taubner, D. (1989), Finite Representations of CCS and TCSP Programs by Automata and Petri Nets, Lecture Notes in Computer Science, Vol. 369, Springer-Verlag, New York/Berlin.

Using the HOL Prove Assistant
for proving the Correctness of Term Rewriting Rules
reducing Terms of Sequential Behavior

Matthias Mutz

Universität Passau, Fakultät für Mathematik und Informatik,
Lehrstuhl für Rechnerstrukturen, Innstraße 33, D-8390 Passau, Germany

Abstract

There are several approaches of using automated theorem provers and assistants in hardware verification. It has been shown, that hardware behavior can be modelled and verified using theorem proving tools. But the task of generating a proof remains difficult and often needs a big amount of interaction. Therefore, the methods of our hardware verification system VERENA are based on term rewriting. It is shown how we use the expressive power of type theory to model circuit behavior. The crucial point in implementing a term rewriting system is to guarantee that the term rewriting rules used have specific properties like correctness, confluence, completeness, etc. It is demonstrated how we use the HOL prove assistant to prove the correctness of term rewriting rules.

1. Introduction

There are several approaches of using computer assisted theorem proving in hardware verification. For example, the Boyer-Moore prover [BoMo 79] establishes a partially automated theorem proving system. VERITAS [HaDa 85] provides a specification languange and a computational implementation for theorem proving. The HOL prove assistant [HOL 88] supports theorem proving with user-defined prove strategies.

Hardware verification by using theorem provers has been demonstrated successfully. For example, in [Pie 89, BrCa 89] the Boyer-Moore prover is used to verify the Min-Max sequential benchmark circuit and a pipeline, respectively. HOL is used in [RaC 89] to verify cascading properties of a parallel sorting circuit. But fully automated theorem proving is very difficult to achieve. To automate the verification of hardware as much as possible, algebraic simplification methods like rewriting techniques have been suggested, e.g. [Lar 88].

We developed some proof strategies for hardware verification and implemented them in our verification system VERENA [Gra 88]. We decided to use term rewriting methods to transform behavior descriptions and implementation descriptions into canonical representations, which can easily be checked for equivalence. The approach becomes practicable since the verification goals are partitioned into manageable parts. The close relationship between term representations and specifications based on type theory let us decide to use the HOL prove assistant to prove the correctness of the term rewriting rules. By this means we have a strict seperation of two tasks: a manager of VERENA establishes term rewriting rules verified by assistance of HOL while a user of VERENA is only concerned with defining algebraic specifications based on the introduced functions.

Our tools for the verification of descriptions concerning sequential designs have to deal with specific representations of temporal relationships. In similar approaches based on Temporal Logic, e.g. [BrCDM 85, FuKTM 86], also in approaches aiming at the verification of synchronous hardware, e.g. [Pai 87], the advantages by abstracting from time are shown. These approaches use modal operators for hiding the time parameter. In these approaches the user of the verification system is much concerned with theoretical aspects of specification and verification. Tools with close relationships to mathematics may be hard to handle by designers. We think, the VERENA user interface is much more oriented in hardware design.

In Paragraph 2, we motivate the use of term rewriting rules for the verification of sequential behavior descriptions. Paragraph 3 shows how we model circuit behavior expressing time relations explicitly and how we use HOL specifications to define the semantics of temporal expressions. We introduce time dependant operators and give some examples for operators used. In Paragraph 4, we introduce operators used in our hardware description language (VIOLA) based on HOL definitions hiding the time parameter. We show how to prove the correctness of term rewriting rules given in terms of VIOLA using the HOL prove assistant. As an example, a term rewriting rule is applied to a latch specification. Finally, we give some results and conclusions.

2. Hardware verification with VERENA using term rewriting techniques

The structure of a logical system is given as a hierarchical netlist: a structural refinement of a logical system has structural components (each defined as a logical system) with input, output, and bidirectional terminals and nets connecting the terminals of the components and the terminals of the refined logical system. The behavioral description of the logical system is derived from the composition of the behavioral descriptions of the components.

The verification task is to show, that an implemented behavior satisfies the restrictions established by the specification of the expected behavior. The implementation terms are derived from the implementation description defined by a netlist using our hardware description language VIOLA. The expected sequential behavior is given in terms of an *interval dependency graph* (IDG). The term representations derived from the implementation description are valid for all time instants. The IDG defines time intervals, in which input functions and expected output functions are valid in the specific interval. By this way, the verification task is partitioned into several verification goals, where for each verification goal two term representations are to be compared. A detailed description of the derivation of subgoals is behind the scope of the paper and it will be given elsewhere [Mut 91].

To make the strategy more clear we consider two extreme IDGs. An IDG consisting of two nodes t_1 and t_2 has assigned the complete behavior of the considered system. Additional assertions may define relations between the set of input and output signals of the implemented and specified behavior. Another extreme IDG has time intervals corresponding to clock cycles and establishes different behavior and relations for each clock cycle. The first approach establishes difficult specification and verification tasks while the second approach needs to much details about the implementation for specifying the behavior. Our approach intends that the user selects a description between the two extremes.

As a subgoal, we have to prove that two terms, one derived from the implemented behavior description and one derived from the specified behavior description, are equivalent. Fig. 2.1 a) shows the transformation steps used in hardware verification with VERENA.

The crucial point in implementing a term rewriting system is the guarantee that the term rewriting rules used have specific properties like correctness, confluence, completeness. Fig. 2.1 b) shows how we prove the *correctness* of term rewriting rules using the HOL prove assistant. At first, the left side of an equation defining the rewriting rule and the right side are transformed into two HOL terms depending on the interpretation given for the used operators. Then time is introduced to build a HOL theorem. If we can show that the theorem holds we have proved, that the term rewriting rule is correct with respect to the HOL-interpretation.

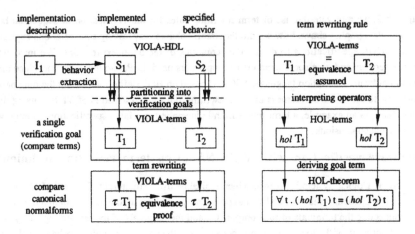

a) verification of hardware descriptions   Fig 2.1   b) verification of term rewriting rules

3. Formal behavior description: explicit time

For the definition of sequential behavior, one has to use formalisms in which to represent temporal precedence and other temporal relationships. The ad hoc way is to use an explicit time parameter t denoting an instant of time taken from a set that is isomorphic to the reals, the integers, or the natural numbers depending on the systems to be described and the manipulations of descriptions required. In our approach time is isomorphic to the integers.

In the next section we introduce operators that model sequential behavior with explicit time. All axioms, definitions, theorems, and proofs are specified or generated using the HOL prove assistant. Together they form a new theory. The reader should be familiar with standard type theory and predicate calculus notation. We will use formalisms according to [Gor 85].

3.1 Time base

The discrete time base is represented by the type *time*. The set of instants of type *time* is isomorphic to the integers. We employ the properties of integers according to [Zei 76]. The constant "-∞:time" denotes the fictitious lower bound. The operators "π:time→time" and "σ:time→time" are introduced to denote the instant (π t) directly preceeding t and the instant (σ t) directly following t. The constant -∞ and the two operators are set into relation by the following axioms:

$$\Vdash \forall t\, t'.\ (t' = \pi\, t) = (\sigma\, t' = t)\ [1] \qquad\qquad [\pi\sigma\_ax1]$$
$$\Vdash \pi\, \text{-}\infty = \text{-}\infty \qquad\qquad\qquad\qquad\quad [\pi\_\text{-}\infty]$$

---

[1] We use $\Vdash$ to denote an axiom or a definition. $\vdash$ is used to denote a theorem, derived from axioms, definitions, and previously derived theorems.

The *time functions* "tpred:num→time→time" and "tsucc:num→time→time" determining the order of instants are given as definitions satisfying the Primitive Recursion theorem [Gor 85]:

$\Vdash$ ($\forall$t. **tpred** 0 t = t) $\wedge$ ($\forall$n t. **tpred** (**suc** n) t = π (**tpred** n t)) [2]   [tpred_def]

$\Vdash$ ($\forall$t. **tsucc** 0 t = t) $\wedge$ ($\forall$n t. **tsucc** (**suc** n) t = σ (**tsucc** n t))   [tsucc_def]

For example, the following theorems are derived:

$\vdash$ ($\forall$n. **tsucc** -∞ = -∞)   [tsucc_-∞]

$\vdash$ ($\forall$n t. **tsucc** n (**tpred** n t) = t) $\wedge$ ($\forall$n t. **tpred** n (**tsucc** n t) = t)   [tsucc_tpred]

Due to the discrete time-base, the **tpred** operator may be compared with the **P** operator in [BoPP 88] describing a past occurence of a synchronizing event. We do not use the **tpred** operator to distinguish between two synchronization points. Instead, we interpret the "distance" between two instants as the smallest time between two distinguishable instants. We use explicit event functions to figure out synchronization points. Therefore, the **P** operator is better compared with the **llast** operator introduced later.

3.2 Signals and event functions

Signals are modelled by functions of type *signal* = time→num list. A signal therefore represents a time-dependant logical *vector* function.

Functions assigning each instant a boolean value are called *event functions*. Event functions are used to determine the instants of synchronizing events. The type of event functions is abbreviated as *event* = time→bool. An event function *e* defines the occurrences of an event *E*: an event *E* occurs at instant *t*, iff *e*(t)=T holds.

3.3 Sequential behavior

Besides **tpred** and **tsucc**, the basic operators for describing sequential behavior are **llast**, **llastn**, and **stable**:

llast	:	event → time → time
llastn	:	num → event → time → time
stable	:	num → signal → time → bool

The introduction of the **llast** operator is inspired by [AmCH 86] where a time base isomorphic to the reals is used. It is also closely related to the use of the **delta** function introduced by [Eve 86] where a time base isomorphic to the natural numbers is used.

The **llast** operator is defined as [llast_def]:

$\Vdash$ **llast** e t = ($\neg\exists$n. e (**tpred** n t)) $\Rightarrow$ -∞ | **tpred** (ϵn.e (**tpred** n t) $\wedge$ $\forall$m. m<n $\supset$ $\neg$(e (**tpred** m t))) t [3] [4]

---

[2] suc is the successor function defined for natural numbers (suc n = n+1)

[3] ϵ denotes the choice operator. ϵx.P(x) denotes some value of type σ, *a* say, such that P(a) is true. If there is no *a* of type σ such that P(a) is true, ϵx.P(x) denotes a fixed but unspecified value of type σ [Gor 85]. It holds ($\exists$x.P(x)) $\equiv$ P(ϵx.P(x)).

If e is the event function of an event E, e.g. a synchronization event like the edge of a trigger signal, the term "llast e t" associates with each instant t the instant of the last occurence of E loosely preceeding t. If no such event exists, we define the term to represent the fictitious lower bound of *time*. Fig 3.1 gives typical examples for the use of the **llast** function in the description of memory elements. The logical values are denoted by H (high), L (low) and Z (tristate). The range of the signals is {L,H} except *out* which has range {L,H,Z}.

$$q(t) = d(\textbf{llast}\ up(ck)\ t)$$
$$\overline{q}(t) = not(q(t))$$

$$out(t) = (en(t)=L) \Rightarrow Z \mid in(\textbf{llast}\ and(en,ck)\ t)$$

$$up(ck,t) = (ck(t)=H) \wedge (ck(\textbf{tpred}\ 1\ t)=L)$$

a) positive edge triggered D-flipflop   Fig 3.1   b) latch with enable

While **llast** determines the last occurence of an event E, we may be interested in the instant of the last occurrence strictly before "llast e t" or the nth occurence of E before t. For this sake, we introduce the **llastn** operator. The **llastn** operator is defined by Primitive Recursion :

$$\vdash (\forall e\ t.\textbf{llastn}\ 0\ e\ t = \textbf{llast}\ e\ t) \wedge (\forall n\ e\ t.\textbf{llastn}\ (n+1)\ e\ t = \textbf{llastn}\ n\ e\ (\textbf{tpred}\ 1\ (\textbf{llast}\ e\ t))) \quad \text{[llastn\_def]}$$

The boolean term "**stable** n s t" is true at an instant t, iff the value of the signal s at t is equal to the value of s at t-1, t-2, ..., t-n. The definition of the **stable** operator is:

$$\vdash (\forall s\ t.\textbf{stable}\ 0\ s\ t = T) \wedge \quad\quad\quad\quad\quad\quad \text{[stable\_def]}$$
$$(\forall n\ s\ t.\textbf{stable}\ (\text{suc}\ n)\ s\ t = (s\ t = s\ (\textbf{tpred}\ 1\ t)) \wedge (\textbf{stable}\ n\ s\ (\textbf{tpred}\ 1\ t)))$$

The stable operator is used in combinations defining event functions.

4. Hardware description language: abstracting from time

We aim at behavioral descriptions abstracting from time, i.e. there is no explicit use of the time parameter t. Time-dependency is introduced by the usage of *modal* operators, i.e. operators with implicit consideration of the time parameter. The time parameter t is explicitly used in the definitions of modal operators.

In our approach of hardware verification, we have to reduce terms only containing signal variables, combinational or modal operators. For the reduction process, we use sets of term rewriting rules depending on the nature of the verification goal. The correctness of these rules is imperative for the correctness of the verification results.

We introduce a HOL definition for each operator defined in VIOLA. It is not the actual syntax of VIOLA terms, but it is the corresponding HOL term notation.

---

[4]   The conditional operator $\Rightarrow$ is defined by $(b \Rightarrow t_1 \mid t_2) = \varepsilon t.((b=T) \supset (t=t_1)) \wedge ((b=F) \supset (t=t_2))$.

4.1 Operators

We introduce operators combining natural numbers and signals to obtain new signals:

TPRED	:	num $\rightarrow$ signal $\rightarrow$ signal
TSUCC	:	num $\rightarrow$ signal $\rightarrow$ signal
LLASTN	:	num $\rightarrow$ signal $\rightarrow$ signal $\rightarrow$ signal
STABLE	:	num $\rightarrow$ signal $\rightarrow$ signal

The HOL-definitions are given as λ-terms:

(TPRED n s)	=	λt. s (**tpred** n t)	[TPRED_def]
(TSUCC n s)	=	λt. s (**tsucc** n t)	[TSUCC_def]
(LLASTN n es s)	=	λt. s (**llastn** n (λt'. es t' = [H]) t)	[LLASTN_def]
(STABLE n s)	=	λt. (**stable** n s t) $\Rightarrow$ [H]	[L]	[STABLE_def]

[H] denotes a single digit logical vector. Single digit signals may represent event functions. We use H=2 (high) to represent T (true) and L=1 (low) to represent F (false).

4.2 Verification by theorem proving

The HOL interpretation of a term rewriting rule $T_1 = T_2$ is obtained by transforming the rule according to the given λ-term definitions of the used operators:

$$T_1 = T_2 \, [v_1, v_2, ...] \xrightarrow{\text{HOL}} \forall \, v_1 \, v_2 \, ... \, t. \, (\, T_1 \,) \, t = (\, T_2 \,) \, t$$

$[v_1, v_2, ...]$ denotes the set of free variables occuring in T_1 and T_2.

We say, that the rewriting rule is *correct with respect to the HOL-interpretation* (or simply *correct*), iff the HOL-term obtained is a theorem of our theory that is based on the predefined theories (like theories on natural numbers, lists, booleans). To prove the correctness of a term rewriting rule, we enter the HOL representation of the rule containing the combinational and modal operators as a goal for theorem proving. Then we use the definitions of the modal operators to get an equation with an explicit time parameter t.

Unlike other theorem provers like Boyer-Moore, there are no automated proof generation strategies in the HOL system. To generate the theorems that follow the user has to tell the system how to do the proofs. There is much support to do this job. The next examples illustrate some tools typically used in the verification of our term rewriting rules supporting the construction of a proof.

4.3 Verification examples

One way to prove a term to be a theorem of a given theory is to derive T (true) using the inference rules, definition, axioms, and pre-proved theorems given by the HOL proof assistant. This kind of theorem proving is called *goal directed*. In our examples, we illustrate the use of some *tactics* defining how to use previously derived theorems and inference rules.

As an example, we give the first steps of a goal-oriented proof of the following HOL-representation of a term rewriting rule. The goal is defined by g " ∀n m s t. (TPRED n (STABLE m s)) t = (STABLE m (TPRED n s)) t "

The first step in verifying a rule is to get the term representation containing time functions. The actual command in HOL-88 is:

e (REWRITE_TAC[TPRED_def;STABLE_def] THEN BETA_TAC)

The new goal term is obtained by rewriting the goal term using the equations given as definitions of TPRED and STABLE as left to right rewriting rules and by β-conversion:

➭ ∀n m s t. (**stable** m s (**tpred** n t)) ⟹ [H] | [L] = (**stable** m (λt'. s (**tpred** n t')) t) ⟹ [H] | [L]

The proofs of theorems containing operators defined by Primitive Recursion are mostly done by induction over natural numbers. The HOL-88 command

expand (INDUCT_TAC)

splits the goal into two subgoals

➭ ∀m s t.(**stable** m s (**tpred** 0 t)) ⟹ [H] | [L] = (**stable** m (λt'.s (**tpred** 0 t')) t) ⟹ [H] | [L]

and

➭ ∀m s t.(**stable** m s (**tpred** (suc n) t)) ⟹ [H] | [L] = (**stable** m (λt'.s (**tpred** (suc n) t')) t) ⟹ [H] | [L]

with the assumption

∀m s t. (**stable** m s (**tpred** n t)) ⟹ [H] | [L] = (**stable** m (λt'. s (**tpred** n t')) t) ⟹ [H] | [L]

The first goal is solved by rewriting with the **tpred** definition and by η-conversion. The second goal is solved by induction over *m*: for P(0) we rewrite with the **stable** definition. The proof for P(m)⊃P(**suc** m) is a little bit more complicated to notate (but not very complicated to prove) and therefore behind the scope of this paper.

As a second example we give a sketch of the proof for the following rule:

g " ∀n m es s t. (TSUCC m (LLASTN n (TPRED m es) s)) t =
              (LLASTN n es (TSUCC m s)) t "

The derived goal is obtained by the basic rewritings:

e (REWRITE_TAC[TPRED_def;TSUCC_def;LLASTN_def] THEN BETA_TAC)

that results in

➭ ∀n m es s t. s (**llastn** n (λt'. es (**tpred** m t') = [H]) (**tsucc** m t))
              = s (**tsucc** m (**llastn** n (λt'. es t' = [H]) t))

We want to prove the following lemma:

$$\forall n \text{ k e t. llastn n } (\lambda t'.e(\textbf{tpred } k \text{ t'})) (\textbf{tsucc } k \text{ t}) = \textbf{tsucc } k (\textbf{llastn } n \text{ e t})$$

The lemma is formulated as a subgoal, and the subgoal term is used as a rewriting rule applied to the term of the original goal. We first have to solve the subgoal to continue with the proof of the transformed original goal:

> e (SUBGOAL_THEN
>   "∀n k e t.llastn n (λt'.e(**tpred** k t')) (**tsucc** k t) = **tsucc** k (**llastn** n e t)"
>   (λth. REWRITE_TAC[th]))

The goal derived from the original goal with the assumption of the subgoal term is

➡ ∀n m es s t. s (**tsucc** m (**llastn** n (es t = [H])) = s (**tsucc** m (**llastn** n (λt'. es t' = [H]) t))

We start with induction over *m*. For P(0) we rewrite with the definitions of **llastn** and **llast** to obtain

➡ **tsucc** k (¬∃n. e(**tpred** n t)) ⇒ -∞ | **tpred** (εn. e(**tpred** n t) ∧ ∀m. m<n ⊃ ¬e(**tpred** m t)) t)
     = (¬∃n. e(**tpred** n)) ⇒ -∞ | **tpred** (εn. e(**tpred** n t) ∧ ∀m. m<n ⊃ ¬e(**tpred** m t)) (**tsucc** k t)

This goal is solved by a boolean case decision

> e (ASM_CASES_TAC "∃n. e(**tpred** n t)")

obtaining the two subgoals

➡ **tsucc** k (**tpred** (εn. e(**tpred** n t) ∧ ∀m. m<n ⊃ ¬e(**tpred** m t)) t)
     = **tpred** (εn. e(**tpred** n t) ∧ ∀m. m<n ⊃ ¬e(**tpred** m t)) (**tsucc** k t)

and

➡ **tsucc** k -∞ = -∞

The two goals are easily proved using rewriting tactics.

4.4 Application example

To show the use of term rewriting rules, we give the term representing the function of a latch (memory element) with inputs *in* and *ck* and output *out* regarding setup, hold, and delay times:

> out   = (TPRED Δd (LLASTN 1 (OR ck↓ ck) (IF error X (LLASTN 1 ck in))))
> error = (AND (ck↓ (NOT (TSUCC Δh (STABLE (Δs+Δh) in))))
> ck↓   = (AND (NOT ck) (TPRED 1 ck))

We first consider the times of possible changes of the output *out*. If *ck* is L (low) no change can occur. If *ck* is H (high) the value of input *in* is observed at *out* delayed by Δd time units. At the falling edge (*ck* changes from H to L) the setup and hold condition must be considered: the output becomes X (undefined) if the input is not stable since Δs time units or if it is not stable for the next Δh time units. Because the input value must not change at the falling edge, we formulate the error condition as follows: the input value was not stable since $\Delta s+\Delta h$ time units Δh time units after the falling edge of *ck*.

To illustrate the effect of term rewriting we give a structural representation of terms. Each subterm with an operator *op* is represented by an one-output / multi-input component marked with *op*. Fig 4.1 is the structural representation of the latch term.

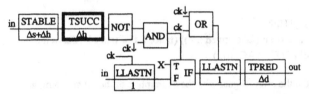

Fig. 4.1: structural representation of the latch term regarding setup, hold, and delay times

We use a confluent and noetherian set of term rewriting rules to "move" TSUCC occurences from the inputs to the outputs of components. We use this set to remove the TSUCC component.

We have proved, that an occurence of a [TSUCC n] component at any input of a *combinational component* can be moved to the output if we insert a [TPRED n] component at the other inputs. This property is used to obtain the structure of Fig 4.2.

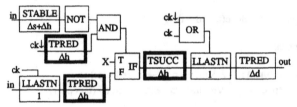

Fig. 4.2: structure obtained by moving the TSUCC component toward the outputs

The rule given as our second example in section 4.2 is applied to obtain the structure given in Fig. 4.3.

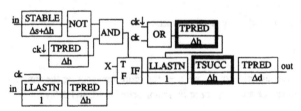

Fig. 4.3: structure after applying example term rewriting rule

In a final step we use the following rule (assuming $\Delta d \leq \Delta h$) to remove the TSUCC component:

$$n \leq m \Rightarrow (\text{TPRED } m \, (\text{TSUCC } n \, *)) = (\text{TPRED } (m-n) \, *) .$$

5. Results and conclusions

We developed and implemented (and are currently developing) tools for hardware verification based on term rewriting techniques. Most of the methods concerning the verification of complex combinational circuits are implemented in the VERENA system. Descriptions of synchronous sequential circuits with corresponding state variables can be verified automatically too. We are currently implementing the procedure to obtain verfication goals that can be handled by the term comparison methods already implemented.

To prove the correctness of term rewriting rules we had to choose a formalism both covering the low level description of hardware behavior based on time functions and the descriptions based on VIOLA providing the term rewriting rules.

The HOL proof assistant was used to specify hardware behavior based on type theory. Term rewriting rules are transformed into HOL-terms that are proved to be theorems of the theory defining the framework for specifications of hardware behavior. The use of the HOL prove assistant was very helpful in the detection of inaccuracies in hand-made proofs and it much fastens the development of new term rewriting rules concerning sequential behavior.

Currently, we are thinking about additional applications of the HOL88 system related to the development of our verification tools. For example, we want to use HOL to prove that the verification of the subgoals obtained from a sequential description is sufficient to solve the whole verification goal. The proofs are up to now done by hand.

Acknowledgements

I would like to thank Phil Windley and Sara Kalvala who sent me addresses of FTP sites to get a version of the HOL88 proof assistant for Sun 3.

References

[AmCH 86]   P.Amblard, P.Caspi, N.Halbwachs: "Use of time functions to describe and explain circuit behavior," *IEE Proceedings*, Vol.133, Pt.E, No.5, 1986, pp. 271-275

[BoMo 79]   R.Boyer, J.Moore: "A Computational Logic," Academic Press, New York, 1979

[BoPP 88]   D.Borrione, J.-L.Paillet, L.Pierre: "Formal Verification of CASCADE descriptions," *The Fusion of Hardware Design and Verification*, G.J.Milne (ed.), Elsevier Science Publishers B.V. (North-Holland), 1988, pp. 185-210

[BrCa 89]   A.Bronstein, C.L.Talcott: "Formal Verification of Pipelines based on String-Functional Semantics," *Proc. of the IMEC-IFIP International Workshop on Applied Formal Methods for Correct VLSI Design*, L.J.M.Claesen (ed.), Houlthalen Belgium, Nov., 1989, pp. 347-364

[BrCDM 85] M.Browne, E.Clarke, D.Dill, B.Mishra: "Automatic Verification of Sequential Circuits using Temporal Logic," *CHDLs and their Applications*, C.J.Koomen and T.Moto-oka (eds.), North-Holland, 1985, S.98-113

[Eve 86]   A.Eveking: "Formal Verification of Synchronous Systems," *Formal Aspects of VLSI Design*, G.J.Milne and P.A.Subrahmanyam (eds.), Elsevier Science Publishers B.V. (North-Holland), 1986, pp. 137-151

[FuKTM 86] M.Fujita, S.Kono, H.Tanaka, T.Moto-oka: "Aid to hierarchical and structural logic design using temporal logic and Prolog," *IEE PROCEEDINGS*, Vol.133, Pt.E, No.5, Sept. 1986, S283-294

[Gor 85]   M.Gordon: "HOL - A Machine Oriented Formulation of Higher Order Logic," University of Cambridge, Computer Laboratory, Technical Report no. 68, 1985

[Gra 88]   W.Grass: "VERENA - A CAD tool for designing guaranteed correct logic circuits," *Proceedings of the 2nd ABAKUS workshop*, Innsbruck-Igls, Austria, Sept.1988, pp. 41-56

[HaDa 85] F.K.Hanna, N.Daeche: "Specification and Verification using Higher-Order Logic," *Proc. CHDL*, Kommen and Moto-oka (eds.), North Holland, 1985

[HOL 88]   M.Gordon: "The HOL Reference Manual," "The HOL Description," and "The HOL Tutorial," *Documentation of the HOL88 System*, Cambridge, 1988

[Lar 88]   T.Larsson: "Hardware Verification based on Algebraic Manipulation and Partial Evolution," *The Fusion of Hardware Design and Verification*, G.J.Milne (ed.), Elsevier Science Publishers B.V. (North-Holland), 1988, pp. 231-252

[Mut 91]   M.Mutz: "Formal verification of sequential circuits with VERENA: a case study," *Proc. of the Advanced Research Workshop on Correct Hardware Design Methodologies*, Turin, Italy, June 1991, P.Prinetto and P.Camurati (eds.), Elsevier Science Publishers B.V. (North-Holland)

[Pai 87]   J.-L.Paillet: "Descriptions and Specifications of Digital Devices," *From HDL to Guaranteed Correct Designs*, IFIP, pp. 21-42,

[Pie 89]   L.Pierre: "The Formal Proof of the Min-Max sequential benchmark described in CASCADE using the Boyer-Moore Theorem Prover," *Proc. of the IMEC-IFIP International Workshop on Applied Formal Methods for Correct VLSI Design*, L.J.M.Claesen (ed.), Houlthalen Belgium, Nov., 1989, pp. 129-148

[RaC 89]   S.R.Ramirez Chavez: "Formal proof of the cascading properties of a parallel sorting circuit," *Proc. of the IMEC-IFIP International Workshop on Applied Formal Methods for Correct VLSI Design*, L.J.M.Claesen (ed.), Houlthalen Belgium, Nov, 1989, 338-346

[Zei 76]   B.Zeigler: "Theory of Modelling and Simulation", John Wiley & Sons, New York, Chichester, Brisbane, Toronto, 1976

Mechanizing a Proof by Induction of Process Algebra Specifications in Higher Order Logic *

Monica Nesi

Istituto di Elaborazione dell' Informazione, C.N.R.
via Santa Maria 46, I-56126 Pisa, Italy

&

University of Cambridge, Computer Laboratory
New Museums Site, Pembroke Street, Cambridge CB2 3QG, U. K.

Abstract

When dealing with *inductively defined systems*, correctness proofs of different specifications of the same system cannot be accomodated in a framework based on finite state automata. Instead, these systems can be naturally analysed and verified by manipulating the process algebra specifications by means of equational reasoning. In this paper, we describe an attempt to mechanize a proof by mathematical induction of the correctness of a simple buffer. To achieve this goal, we use the interactive theorem prover HOL to support the theory of observational congruence for CCS, and provide a set of axiomatic proof tools which can be used interactively.

1 Introduction

In the past few years, several verification tools based on process algebras have been proposed for proving properties of concurrent systems [15]. Most of them resort to a finite state automata representation of specifications, which is used to verify equivalences of specifications and to show that a specification satisfies a logical (modal) property by means of some reasonably efficient automatic algorithms. This completely automatic approach has, however, a few problems (e.g. state explosion) and some limitations (e.g. it can deal with only finite state specifications). In such a framework, there is no easy way to accommodate the verification of processes with infinite states or, more generally, to perform incremental or interactive proofs, even though the theory behind the process algebras supports such reasoning. Moreover, even when dealing with (finite state) parameterized systems, the specifications cannot be verified by using finite state machines.

---

*Research supported by Progetto Finalizzato Informatica, I.E.I.-C.N.R., Pisa, Italy.

In [3, 6] a verification environment which relies on the algebraic nature of the concurrent specification language CCS [13], is described and fully motivated. Such an environment provides the user with facilities to control the analysis and verification phases and to perform proofs automatically. It also allows interactive control when automation is not desirable and permits the user to define sound verification strategies, thus allowing for a better understanding of both the specifications and the correctness criteria one is attempting to verify. This verification environment for CCS is based on the interactive theorem prover HOL [7]. The formal theory for a specific semantics of CCS, namely *observational congruence*, is represented in the logic, and the resulting representation is the basis for higher level verification strategies by mechanized formal proof.

In this paper, we address a particular kind of reasoning, namely *proofs by induction*. We consider concurrent systems with inductive structure and show how a proof of correctness by mathematical induction can be mechanized in HOL. The mechanization exploits the rich set of proof tactics available in the HOL system and the facility for defining new tactics from the built-in ones. It also takes advantage of the subgoal package for backward proofs, thus resulting in quite natural and simple proofs.

In what follows, we first give a brief description of the HOL system. We then introduce the subset of CCS under consideration and show how the syntactic definitions and the axioms for the observational semantics can be formalized in HOL. Next, we illustrate how reasoning by induction can be done in the resulting framework, by proving the correctness of an implementation of a simple buffer. Finally, we discuss related work and possible extensions to the described approach.

2   The HOL System

Higher order logic is a good formalism for mechanizing other mathematical languages because it is both powerful and general enough to allow sound and practical formulations. It has been used to mechanize several logics [8] and process algebras, e.g. CSP [1, 2] and CCS [3]. The theorem prover used in these mechanizations is the HOL system [7], developed by Gordon, which is based directly on the LCF theorem prover [14].

The HOL logic is a variety of higher order logic based on Church's formulation of type theory [7]. In the HOL logic, the standard predicate calculus is extended by allowing variables to range over functions, the arguments of functions can themselves be functions, functions can be written as λ-abstractions and terms can be polymorphic.

The HOL logic is mechanized using the programming language ML [5], which is used to manipulate HOL logic terms and, in particular, to prove that certain terms are theorems. Theorems proved in the system are distinguished from ordinary terms by being assigned a built-in ML type thm. To introduce values of type thm, they must either be postulated as axioms or deduced from existing theorems by ML programs called *inference rules*.

Certain kinds of axioms are classed as *definitions*. These are axioms of the form $\vdash c = t$ where c is a constant not previously defined and t is a term containing no free variables. Definitions form a conservative extension to the logic, i.e. a sound extension.

A collection of logical types, type operators, constants, definitions, axioms and theorems is called a *theory*. To make a definition, prove a theorem, or declare a new HOL type, one must first enter a theory and, if facts from other theories are to be used, the relevant existing theories must be declared as *parents*. Theories, therefore, enable a hierarchical organization of facts. A library of theories is available in the HOL system to enable the reuse of established and commonly used theorems. The availability of such a library greatly aids the task of mechanization and reasoning.

To prove a theorem in a theory, one must apply a sequence of steps to either axioms or previously proved theorems by using inference rules (forward proof). The core of the HOL system is made up of a small set of *primitive inference rules* and a small number of definitions and axioms from which all the standard rules of logic are derived.

The HOL system supports another way of carrying out a proof called goal directed proof or backward proof. The idea is to start from the desired result (*goal*) and manipulate it until it is reduced to a subgoal which is obviously true. ML functions that reduce goals to subgoals are called *tactics* and were developed by Milner [14].

As regards goal directed proofs, the HOL system provides a *subgoal package* due to Paulson [14], which implements a simple framework for interactive proofs. A goal can be set by invoking the function g, which initializes the subgoal package with a new goal. The current goal can be expanded using the function e which applies a tactic to the top goal on the stack and pushes the resulting subgoals onto the goal stack. When a tactic solves a subgoal (i.e. returns an empty subgoal list), the package computes a part of the proof and presents the user with the next subgoal. When a theorem is proved, it can be stored in the current theory using several functions. Among the others, TAC_PROOF takes a goal and a tactic, and applies the tactic to the goal in an attempt to prove it.

The HOL system also provides functions called *conversions* [14] that map terms t to theorems expressing the equality of that term with some other term, $\vdash t = u$. Various built-in conversions and operators for constructing conversions from smaller ones, and several tactics and operators for constructing tactics from smaller ones and from conversions, played a fundamental role in our mechanization of proof strategies for CCS. Examples of the use of some of these conversions and tactics are given in later sections.

3 CCS in HOL

In this section, familiarity with some of the concepts behind CCS is assumed, so only essential information is presented. We consider *pure* CCS, a subset of the language which does not involve value passing and consists of the inactive process nil, and the following operations on processes: *prefix* (.), *summation* (+), *parallel composition* (|), *restriction* (\), *relabelling* ([ ]) and *recursion* (rec). The syntax of pure CCS is given below:

$$E ::= \mathsf{nil} \mid u.E \mid E + E \mid E|E \mid E \setminus l \mid E[f] \mid X \mid \mathsf{rec}\,X.\,E$$

where X ranges over process variables, l ranges over visible actions, called *labels*, u ranges over actions which are either labels or the invisible action τ, and f ranges over relabelling functions on labels. Labels consist of *names* and *co-names* where, for any name a, the corresponding co-name is written $\overline{a}$. The *complement* operation has the property that $\overline{\overline{l}} = l$, and relabelling co-names has the property that $f(\overline{l}) = \overline{f(l)}$.

The formal interpretation of the above operators is given via an operational semantics [13]. In addition, in the literature several behavioural semantics have been defined, and then characterized in terms of axiomatizations which have been proved sound and complete for subsets of CCS. The axioms concerning the internal action τ, referred to as τ-*laws*, distinguish the various equivalences. In this paper, we address the theory of *observational congruence* and refer to [13] for the axioms concerning this theory.

Finally, we recall a result which will be used in the correctness proof (Section 4.1). Let $E\{F/X\}$ denote the substitution of F for all free occurrences of X in E. When dealing with recursive equations, two processes P and Q which are observational congruent to the expressions $E\{P/X\}$ and $E\{Q/X\}$ respectively, denote the (unique) solution of the recursive equation $X = E$, if X is sequential and guarded in the expression E [13].

3.1 Mechanization of CCS

In this section, we recall briefly some aspects about the formalization of pure CCS in HOL; the reader should refer to [3] for more details about the mechanization of the axioms.

The CCS syntax presented earlier can be mechanized by defining in HOL a concrete data type CCS in terms of all its possible constructors. This is done by using a built-in facility for automatically defining concrete recursive data types from a specification of their syntax [11]. The type definition for CCS can be done as follows:

$$
\begin{aligned}
CCS = \ &\text{nil} \mid \\
&\text{var } string \mid \\
&\text{prefix } action\ CCS \mid \\
&\text{sum } CCS\ CCS \mid \\
&\text{restr } CCS\ label \mid \\
&\text{relab } CCS\ relabelling \mid \\
&\text{par } CCS\ CCS \mid \\
&\text{rec } string\ CCS
\end{aligned}
$$

where nil, var, prefix, sum, restr, relab, par and rec are distinct constructors, *label* and *action* are syntactic types defined as follows:

$$label = \text{const } string \mid \text{compl } label \qquad\qquad action = \text{tau} \mid \text{label } label$$

and *relabelling* is an abbreviation for the function type *label→label*.

To avoid using a verbose prefix notation, the parsing and pretty-printing facilities in HOL are extended to accept input, and print output, almost identical to that usually associated with CCS.[1] Since the above prefix constructors are therefore only used internally by the system, we re-adopt the standard CCS syntax for the rest of the paper.

The next steps in the formalization should be to mechanize the operational semantics of the CCS operators, define the notion of observational congruence, and derive its axiomatization. As stated in [3], some work has already shown that it is feasible to mechanize process algebra semantics in HOL and to mechanically prove their axiomatization [1, 2, 12]. In the present work, we are interested in practical reasoning tools at the axiomatic level. Thus, we directly assert the axioms for observational congruence in the HOL logic. We intend to mechanize the operational semantics and to derive the axioms later on, to remove the inconsistency of asserting axioms on a free type such as CCS and to ensure that our mechanization of the CCS theory is sound.

---

[1]Modulo ascii syntax, e.g. $\bar{a}$ is written $-a$, and τ is written tau.

Having defined the appropriate types and syntactic constructors in the HOL logic, it is straightforward to assert most of the axioms. Due to lack of space, we present only some of them below, namely associativity for summation, distributivity of relabelling with respect to summation and the law for the restriction of a prefix process [13, 3]:

$\vdash \forall P\, Q\, R : CCS.\ P + (Q + R) = (P + Q) + R$

$\vdash \forall (P\, Q : CCS)\,(f : relabelling).\ (P + Q)[f] = P[f] + Q[f]$

$\vdash \forall (P : CCS)\,(l : label).$
$\quad (\tau.P) \setminus l = \tau.(P \setminus l) \wedge$
$\quad \forall l_1 : label.\ (l_1.P) \setminus l = ((l_1 = l) \vee (l_1 = \bar{l})) \Rightarrow \mathsf{nil} \mid l_1.(P \setminus l)$

The above formalization demonstrates the suitability of HOL for supporting embedded notations, the axioms being very similar to their conventional presentation. On the other hand, more work than is originally expected can be involved when mechanizing some definitions or axioms, e.g. the expansion law for parallel composition and the unfolding law for recursive expressions [3], because axioms written by hand are often packed with notation which itself needs to be formalized.

4   Verification of a Simple Buffer by Induction

Below we illustrate how the formalization of CCS described in the preceding section is used to reason about CCS specifications by presenting transcripts of a HOL session. In particular, we consider inductive reasoning and apply mathematical induction to prove the correctness of an implementation of a simple buffer [13].

The behaviour $Buffer_n$ of a buffer of capacity n can be simply specified as follows:

$$Buffer_n(0) \equiv in\,.\,Buffer_n(1)$$
$$Buffer_n(k) \equiv in\,.\,Buffer_n(k+1) + \overline{out}\,.\,Buffer_n(k-1) \qquad (0 < k < n)$$
$$Buffer_n(n) \equiv \overline{out}\,.\,Buffer_n(n-1)$$

Such a specification is parameterized on the capacity n of the buffer and the number k of the values presently stored in the buffer. An implementation of the buffer can be built by composing in parallel n copies of a buffer cell

$$C \equiv \mathsf{rec}\,X.\,in\,.\,\overline{out}\,.\,X$$

and hiding the internally synchronizing actions in and out by using a new action mid, thus obtaining the chain $Impl(n)$ given by:

$$Impl(1) \equiv C$$
$$Impl(n+1) \equiv C^\frown Impl(n)$$

where, given two arbitrary processes P and Q, $\frown$ is a linking operator defined as follows:

$$P^\frown Q \equiv (P\,[mid/out] \mid Q\,[mid/in]) \setminus mid$$

To show that $Impl(n)$ is a correct implementation of the buffer $Buffer_n$, we shall prove that for all $n \geq 1$

$$Impl(n) = Buffer_n(0)$$

where $=$ stands for the observational congruence. The proof is by induction on n, and in the proof of the inductive step, a lemma is needed which is itself proved by induction.

4.1 Mechanizing the proof in HOL

One interacts with the HOL system via ML. The ML prompt is #, so lines beginning with #
show the user's input (always terminated by two successive semi-colons), and other lines
show the system's response. Terms in the HOL logic are distinguished from ML expressions
by enclosing them in double quotes. To help readability, the HOL transcripts are edited
to show proper logical symbols instead of their ascii representations.

After having entered a theory in which we reason about the buffer, and declared the
mechanized theory for CCS described earlier as a parent of this theory, we define the
behaviour of a buffer cell and the linking operator. Throughout the proof, a buffer cell
will be considered in its two possible states: as an empty cell C and as a full cell C'.

```
#new_definition ('C', "C = rec X. 'in'.-'out'.X");;
⊢ C = rec X. 'in'.-'out'.X

#new_definition ('C'', "C' = rec X. -'out'.'in'.X");;
⊢ C' = rec X. -'out'.'in'.X

#new_infix_definition
  ('Link', "∀ P Q:CCS. P Link Q = (P['mid'/'out'] | Q['mid'/'in'])\'mid'");;
⊢ ∀P Q.
  P Link Q = (P['mid'/'out'] | Q['mid'/'in'])\'mid'
```

The specification of the buffer is not primitive recursive, but it can be defined by
invoking the ML function new_constant to introduce a function BUFF_SPEC and then by
using the ML function new_axiom to assert the properties of such a BUFF_SPEC.

```
#new_constant ('BUFF_SPEC', ":num → num → CCS");;
() : void

#new_axiom ('BUFF_SPEC',
            "((0 < n) ⇒
              (BUFF_SPEC n 0 = 'in'.(BUFF_SPEC n 1)) ∧
              ((0 < k) ∧ (k < n) ⇒
              (BUFF_SPEC n k =
              'in'.(BUFF_SPEC n (SUC k)) + -'out'.(BUFF_SPEC n (PRE k)))) ∧
              (BUFF_SPEC n n = -'out'.(BUFF_SPEC n (PRE n))))");;
⊢ ∀n k.
    0 < n ⇒
    (BUFF_SPEC n 0 = 'in'.(BUFF_SPEC n 1)) ∧
    (0 < k ∧ k < n ⇒
     (BUFF_SPEC n k =
      'in'.(BUFF_SPEC n(SUC k)) + -'out'.(BUFF_SPEC n(PRE k)))) ∧
    (BUFF_SPEC n n = -'out'.(BUFF_SPEC n(PRE n)))
```

The implementation of the buffer is a primitive recursive definition starting from 1,
thus we want to apply induction starting with 1. Since recursion and induction are defined
on natural numbers in HOL, we must derive a recursive definition starting with 1 from that
starting with 0. We first prove the existence of a recursive implementation IMPL0 starting
with 0, and then prove that there exists a function fn satisfying the recursive definition

starting with 1. Finally, we give a name to fn by invoking the function **new_specification** which allows the new constant BUFF_IMPL to be introduced in a consistent way.

```
#new_prim_rec_definition
    ('IMPLO', "(IMPLO 0 = C) ∧ (IMPLO (SUC n) = (C Link (IMPLO n)))");;
⊢ (IMPLO 0 = C) ∧ (∀n. IMPLO(SUC n) = C Link (IMPLO n))

#let IMPL1 = TAC_PROOF
                ((□, "∃fn :num → CCS.
                    (fn 1 = C) ∧
                    (∀n. fn (SUC(SUC n)) = C Link (fn (SUC n)))"),
            STRIP_ASSUME_TAC IMPLO THEN
            EXISTS_TAC "λn. IMPLO (PRE n):CCS" THEN
            CONV_TAC (ONCE_DEPTH_CONV BETA_CONV) THEN
            ASM_REWRITE_TAC [PRE]);;
IMPL1 =
⊢ ∃fn. (fn 1 = C) ∧ (∀n. fn(SUC(SUC n)) = C Link (fn(SUC n)))

#new_specification 'BUFF_IMPL' [('constant','BUFF_IMPL')] IMPL1;;
⊢ (BUFF_IMPL 1 = C) ∧
  (∀n. BUFF_IMPL(SUC(SUC n)) = C Link (BUFF_IMPL(SUC n)))
```

To prove that the implementation meets the specification, we apply several tactics. Some of them are built-in and some have been implemented in the system specially for manipulating CCS specifications. The built-in tactic INDUCT_TAC applies induction on natural numbers and the induction assumption is indicated with set brackets.

```
#g "∀n. BUFF_IMPL(SUC n) = BUFF_SPEC(SUC n)0";;
"∀n. BUFF_IMPL(SUC n) = BUFF_SPEC(SUC n)0"

() : void

#e (INDUCT_TAC);;
OK..
2 subgoals
"BUFF_IMPL(SUC(SUC n)) = BUFF_SPEC(SUC(SUC n))0"
    [ "BUFF_IMPL(SUC n) = BUFF_SPEC(SUC n)0" ]

"BUFF_IMPL 1 = BUFF_SPEC 1 0"

() : void
```

To prove the basis subgoal, we expand with the definition of BUFF_IMPL and of C. Next, the resulting recursive expression is unfolded once, by means of the tactic REC_EXP_TAC derived from the unfolding law for recursion, and then the current goal is folded back by using the definition of C and the first clause of the definition of BUFF_IMPL.

```
#e (ONCE_REWRITE_TAC [BUFF_IMPL] THEN ONCE_REWRITE_TAC [C] THEN REC_EXP_TAC
        THEN ONCE_REWRITE_TAC [SYM C] THEN SUBST1_TAC (SYM IMPL_CLAUSE1));;
OK..
"'in'.-'out'.(BUFF_IMPL 1) = BUFF_SPEC 1 0"

() : void
```

Now we manipulate the specification of the buffer by expanding twice with the definition of BUFF_SPEC, each time selecting the right definition clause based on the value of k.

```
#e (ONCE_REWRITE_TAC [CONJUNCT1 SPEC_SUCO_SUCO] THEN
    ONCE_REWRITE_TAC [CONJUNCT2 SPEC_SUCO_SUCO]);;
OK..
"'in'.-'out'.(BUFF_IMPL 1) = 'in'.-'out'.(BUFF_SPEC 1 0)"

() : void
```

The next step is to check if BUFF_IMPL 1 and BUFF_SPEC 1 0 denote the (unique) solution of the same recursive equation. This can be achieved by applying the tactic UNIQUE_SOL_TAC that mechanizes the proof rule for the unique solution of recursive equations (Section 3).

```
#e (UNIQUE_SOL_TAC "BUFF_IMPL 1 :CCS" "'in'.-'out'.(BUFF_IMPL 1)"
                   "BUFF_SPEC 1 0 :CCS" "'in'.-'out'.(BUFF_SPEC 1 0)");;
OK..
goal proved
⊢ 'in'.-'out'.(BUFF_IMPL 1) = 'in'.-'out'.(BUFF_SPEC 1 0)
⊢ 'in'.-'out'.(BUFF_IMPL 1) = BUFF_SPEC 1 0
⊢ BUFF_IMPL 1 = BUFF_SPEC 1 0

Previous subproof:
"BUFF_IMPL(SUC(SUC n)) = BUFF_SPEC(SUC(SUC n))0"
    [ "BUFF_IMPL(SUC n) = BUFF_SPEC(SUC n)0" ]

() : void
```

Once the basis subgoal has been proved, the HOL system presents us with the induction step subgoal. Note that, since we started the proof by induction from 1, the inductive hypothesis holds for $n + 1$ and we prove the induction step for $n + 2$. We expand with the definition of BUFF_IMPL and of the linking operator, and we then apply the inductive hypothesis by rewriting with the equation in the assumption list of the goal.

```
#e (ONCE_REWRITE_TAC [BUFF_IMPL] THEN ONCE_REWRITE_TAC [Link] THEN
    ONCE_ASM_REWRITE_TAC []);;
OK..
"((C['mid'/'out']) | ((BUFF_SPEC(SUC n)0)['mid'/'in']))\'mid' =
 BUFF_SPEC(SUC(SUC n))0"
    [ "BUFF_IMPL(SUC n) = BUFF_SPEC(SUC n)0" ]

() : void
```

At this point, the goal will be proved if we show that the two sides of the above equivalence denote the (unique) solution of the same recursive expression. This means that we have to prove that the defining equations of $Buffer_{n+2}$ are satisfied when replacing

$$
\begin{array}{llll}
Buffer_{n+2}(k) & \text{by} & C^\frown Buffer_{n+1}(k) & (0 \le k \le n+1) \\
Buffer_{n+2}(n+2) & \text{by} & C'^\frown Buffer_{n+1}(n+1) & (k = n+2)
\end{array}
$$

By case analysis on k, this requires one to prove the following observational congruences:

$$
\begin{array}{lll}
C^\frown Buffer_{n+1}(0) & = & in\,.(C^\frown Buffer_{n+1}(1)) \\
C^\frown Buffer_{n+1}(k) & = & in\,.(C^\frown Buffer_{n+1}(k+1)) \qquad\qquad (0 < k < n+1) \\
& & +\ \overline{out}\,.(C^\frown Buffer_{n+1}(k-1)) \\
C^\frown Buffer_{n+1}(n+1) & = & in\,.(C'^\frown Buffer_{n+1}(n+1)) \qquad\qquad (k = n+1) \\
& & +\ \overline{out}\,.(C^\frown Buffer_{n+1}(n)) \\
C'^\frown Buffer_{n+1}(n+1) & = & \overline{out}\,.(C^\frown Buffer_{n+1}(n+1))
\end{array}
$$

These congruences can be proved by rewriting each left-hand side with the definitions of the processes occurring in it and applying the axioms for relabelling, restriction and parallel composition operators, until a suitable form is reached and the key lemma of the whole proof can be applied. This lemma is the following:

$$
C'^\frown Buffer_n(k) \;=\; \tau\,.(C^\frown Buffer_n(k+1)) \qquad (0 \le k < n)
$$

The specification $Buffer_n(k)$ can be expressed as the linking of k full buffer cells C' and $(n - k)$ empty cells C. When an empty cell inputs a value and becomes a full cell, then its value can percolate to the right by a sequence of internal actions, thus obtaining $Buffer_n(k + 1)$.

The above lemma is proved by induction on k, by applying the usual rewriting strategy. Below, we present the mechanization of this proof. To help readability, the ML code for the tactic that proves the lemma has been replaced by an informal English description.

```
#let LEMMA =
  TAC_PROOF
    ((□, "∀k n :num.
            ((0 < n) ∧ (k < n)) ⇒
              (C' Link (BUFF_SPEC n k) = tau.(C Link (BUFF_SPEC n (SUC k)))))"),
      Rewrite using the definition of the linking operator
      THEN Apply mathematical induction on the variable k
      THENL [Strip off the universally quantified variable n and
              move the antecedent of implication to assumption list
              THEN Use the theorem FULL_TO_EMPTY_CELL
              THEN Rewrite using the definition of BUFF_SPEC
              THEN Apply axioms for relabelling, parallel and restriction;
              Strip off the universally quantified variable n and move
              conjuncts of antecedent of implication to assumption list
              THEN Use the theorem FULL_TO_EMPTY_CELL
              THEN Rewrite using the definition of BUFF_SPEC
              THEN Apply axioms for relabelling, parallel and restriction
              THEN Use the theorem TRANSF_FULL_CELL
              THEN Apply the inductive hypothesis
              THEN Apply the τ-law μ.τ.E = μ.E
              THEN Use the theorem EXP_ABS_THM
              THEN Apply TAU_STRAT]);;
LEMMA =
⊢ ∀k n.
    0 < n ∧ k < n ⇒
    (C' Link (BUFF_SPEC n k) = tau.(C Link (BUFF_SPEC n(SUC k))))
```

In this proof, various tactics and theorems, e.g. FULL_TO_EMPTY_CELL, TRANSF_FULL_CELL and EXP_ABS_THM, are used which we have previously defined and proved in HOL, to manipulate subexpressions of the goal and make the application of some axioms concerning the action τ possible. Moreover, we use the rewriting strategy TAU_STRAT which implements a term rewriting system equivalent to the axiomatization of observational congruence for finite CCS, [9], and which has been mechanized in HOL, [3]. In the proof of the lemma, this strategy applies the derived τ-law, $E + \tau \cdot (F + E) = \tau \cdot (F + E)$.

The above congruences can now be proved, but we do not present the proofs here. Actually, only the second congruence needs the application of the lemma; the remaining ones may also be proved by the usual rewriting strategy.

5 Conclusion

We have presented an attempt to use a verification environment based on the HOL theorem prover for reasoning about CCS specifications. In particular, we have considered inductively defined systems, and we have described how a higher level verification proof, such as a proof by induction, can be mechanized in such an environment.

We believe that this attempt demonstrates evidence that mathematical proof techniques - based on the axiomatic representation of process algebras - provide a promising approach to the mechanical verification of concurrent systems. Works on a similar approach include an investigation into mechanizing CCS using NUPRL [4], a formalization of CSP failure-divergence semantics in HOL [2], an ongoing mechanization of Milner's π-calculus in HOL [12], and the development of a process algebra manipulator [10]. With respect to these works, we are more interested in the formalization of higher level verification strategies in a theorem proving framework, where mathematical proof techniques are naturally available and the facility for defining user's verification strategies is provided.

In this paper, we have focussed attention on a subset of CCS, on the theory of observational congruence, and on the facility that HOL provides for performing proofs by induction, thus making it possible to reason about parameterized or indexed specifications. It is also possible, due to the facilities for modularity in HOL, to mechanize different process algebras, various behavioural semantics for the same process algebra, and to derive axiomatizations and proof tools for them.

Current work concerns the mechanization of the operational semantics of CCS, the definition of observational congruence, and the mechanical derivation of its axiomatization. Future work will mainly be devoted to extend the functionality of the HOL-CCS environment, e.g. enriching the language under consideration by incorporating data with processes (*value passing*).

Acknowledgements

I should like to thank several members of the Cambridge hardware verification group for many useful discussions. I am especially grateful to Mike Gordon, Tom Melham, Sara Kalvala, Brian Graham, John Van Tassel, John Harrison and Richard Boulton for their advice on mechanization in HOL. Thanks are also due to Paola Inverardi (I.E.I., Pisa) and Albert Camilleri (Hewlett-Packard Labs, Bristol) for their continued support.

References

[1] Camilleri A. J., 'Mechanizing CSP Trace Theory in Higher Order Logic', *IEEE Transactions on Software Engineering*, Special Issue on Formal Methods, N. G. Leveson (ed.), September 1990, Vol. 16, No. 9, pp. 993-1004.

[2] Camilleri A. J., 'A Higher Order Logic Mechanization of the CSP Failure-Divergence Semantics', Proc. of the *4th Banff Higher Order Workshop*, G. Birtwistle (ed.), Springer-Verlag, London, 1991, (to appear).

[3] Camilleri A. J., Inverardi P., Nesi M., 'Combining Interaction and Automation in Process Algebra Verification', Proc. of TAPSOFT '91, Lecture Notes in Computer Science, Springer-Verlag, 1991, Vol. 494, pp. 283-296.

[4] Cleaveland R., Panangaden P., 'Type Theory and Concurrency', *International Journal of Parallel Programming*, November 1988, Vol. 12, No. 2, pp. 153-206.

[5] Cousineau G., Huet G., Paulson L., 'The ML Handbook', INRIA, 1986.

[6] De Nicola R., Inverardi P., Nesi M., 'Using the Axiomatic Presentation of Behavioural Equivalences for Manipulating CCS Specifications', Proc. of the Workshop on *Automatic Verification Methods for Finite State Systems*, Lecture Notes in Computer Science, Springer-Verlag, 1990, Vol. 407, pp. 54-67.

[7] Gordon M. J. C., 'HOL—A Proof Generating System for Higher-Order Logic', *VLSI Specification, Verification and Synthesis*, G. Birtwistle and P. Subrahmanyam (eds.), Kluwer Academic Publishers, Boston, 1988, pp. 73-128.

[8] Gordon M. J. C., 'Mechanizing Programming Logics in Higher Order Logic', *Current Trends in Hardware Verification and Automated Theorem Proving*, G. Birtwistle and P. Subrahmanyam (eds.), Springer-Verlag, 1989, pp. 387-439.

[9] Inverardi P., Nesi M., 'A Rewriting Strategy to Verify Observational Congruence', *Information Processing Letters*, 1990, Vol. 35, pp. 191-199.

[10] Lin H., 'PAM: A Process Algebra Manipulator', this volume.

[11] Melham T. F., 'Automating Recursive Type Definitions in Higher Order Logic', *Current Trends in Hardware Verification and Automated Theorem Proving*, G. Birtwistle and P. Subrahmanyam (eds.), Springer-Verlag, 1989, pp. 341-386.

[12] Melham T. F., 'A Mechanized Theory of the π-calculus in HOL', Proc. of the *2nd Annual Esprit BRA Workshop on Logical Frameworks*, Univ. of Edinburgh, 1991.

[13] Milner R., *Communication and Concurrency*, Prentice Hall, 1989.

[14] Paulson L. C., *Logic and Computation—Interactive Proof with Cambridge LCF*, Cambridge Tracts in Theoretical Computer Science (2), Cambridge Univ. Press, 1987.

[15] Proc. of the Workshop on *Automatic Verification Methods for Finite State Systems*, Lecture Notes in Computer Science, Springer-Verlag, 1990, Vol. 407.

A Two-Level Formal Verification Methodology using HOL and COSMOS *

Carl-Johan H. Seger and Jeffrey J. Joyce
Department of Computer Science
University of British Columbia
Vancouver, B.C. V6T 1Z2 Canada

Abstract

Theorem-proving and symbolic simulation are both described as methods for the *formal verification of hardware*. They are both used to achieve a common goal—correctly designed hardware. However, they have different strengths and weaknesses. The main significance of this paper—and its most original contribution—is the suggestion that symbolic simulation and theorem-proving can be combined in a complementary manner. We also illustrate this combined approach on an example that neither tool can handle well.

1 Introduction

Designing complex digital system in VLSI technology usually involves working at several levels of abstraction, ranging from very high level behavioral specifications down to physical layout at the lowest. One of the main difficulties in this process is to verify the consistency of the different levels of abstraction. Simulation is often used as the main tool for "checking" the consistency. Despite major simulation efforts, serious design errors often remain undetected. Consequently, there has been a growing interest in using formal methods to verify the correctness of designs. There are three general approaches to formal hardware verification: theorem-proving, state machine analysis, and symbolic simulation. These methods all have their strengths and weaknesses. In this paper we will illustrate how theorem-proving can be used in conjunction with symbolic simulation to gain a verification methodology that draws on the strengths of each approach.

Most research on formal verification has relied on the use of computer-assisted theorem provers [3, 8, 9, 12, 16] to establish equivalence between different circuit representations. One of the main strengths of the theorem-proving approach is its ability to describe and relate circuit behaviors at many different levels of abstraction. By being able to reason about the circuit at increasingly higher levels

---

*This research was supported by operating grants from the Natural Sciences and Engineering Research Council of Canada.

of abstraction, we can eventually minimize the semantic gap between the formal high-level specification and the informal, intuitive, specification of the circuit that resides in the mind of the designer.

Unfortunately, theorem-proving based verification requires a large amount of effort on the part of the user in developing specifications of each component and in guiding the theorem prover through all of the lemmas. Also, in order to make the proofs tractable, most attempts at this style of verification have been forced to use highly simplified circuit models.

A verifier based on symbolic simulation applies logic simulation to compute the circuit's response to a series of stimuli chosen to detect all possible design errors. When a circuit has been "verified" by simulation, this means that any further simulation would not uncover any errors. Since a symbolic simulator is based on a traditional logic simulator, it is can use the same, quite accurate, electrical and timing models to compute the circuit behavior. Also—and of great significance— the switch-level circuit used in the simulator can be extracted automatically from the physical layout of the circuit. Hence, the correctness results will link the physical layout with some higher level of specification.

Recently, Bryant and Seger [6] developed a new type of symbolic simulators. Here the simulator establishes the validity of formulas expressed in a very limited, but precisely defined, temporal logic. By limiting the complexity of the logic, great efficiency is obtained. Furthermore, the verification process is highly automated. Unfortunately, the automation obtained by the symbolic simulator comes with a price. First of all, for some behaviors, the computational requirements for carrying out a correctness proof can make the approach infeasible for larger circuits. Secondly, the semantic gap between the intuitive, informal, specification the designer has in mind and the specification used in the symbolic simulator is often quite large.

When tabulating the strengths and weaknesses of theorem-proving and symbolic simulation used for formal hardware verification, it is striking to see how well the two approaches complement each other. Thus, it is very appealing to attempt to integrate them into a two-level combined approach to formal hardware verification. However, in order to achieve this integration, two problems need to be resolved: 1) a mathematically precise interface must be developed so that the rigor of the formal proof is not jeopardized, and 2) a practical interface between the two processes must to be developed. In this paper we focus on the first issue and only briefly mention ongoing work towards solving the second problem.

2 A Two-Level Approach

Symbolic simulation, as achieved by the COSMOS simulator, can be viewed as a highly specialized form of theorem-proving. COSMOS checks the validity of assertions in a specification language (which we call *CL*) with respect to a model structure Ψ. This model structure is a set of infinite state sequences determined by an extracted circuit netlist C and a built-in switch-level and delay model of circuit behavior. When viewed as a theorem-proving system, the COSMOS system can be used to prove theorems of the form, $\Psi \models f$, where f is a formula in *CL*.

A rigorous link with general-purpose theorem-proving, in particular, the Cambridge HOL system, is achieved by semantically embedding the specification language *CL* in higher-order logic. The semantic embedding of *CL* in higher-order logic allows *CL* specifications to be expanded into a term of higher-order logic and used to derive higher-level correctness results. That is, the HOL system can be used to prove theorems of the form, $\vdash f \implies t$, where f is a formula in *CL* (embedded in higher-order logic) and t is a term in higher-order logic.

Thus, the two proof results, $\Psi \models f$ and $\vdash f \implies t$ constitute a statement of correctness in our combined approach. They are obtained by symbolic simulation and general-purpose theorem-proving respectively.

3 Symbolic Simulation Viewed as Theorem-Proving

The main thesis of this section is that the verification system described in [6], based on the COSMOS symbolic simulator, can be viewed as a proof system. We use the

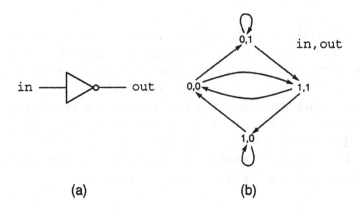

(a)   (b)

Figure 1: Inverter and corresponding state machine.

simple example of an inverter, shown in Fig. 1(a), to provide the reader with an informal account of our approach. If we assume a binary circuit model and a unit delay simulator, the inverter circuit is accurately described by the state machine shown in Fig. 1(b). The states of the machine are labelled with the current values of the two nodes in the circuit, and a transition in the state machine corresponds to a basic unit of time.

The state machine in Fig. 1(b) implies certain properties. For example, it is easy to see that we can conclude from the state machine that the value on the output is always the complement of the value that was present on the input one time unit ago. Informally, this could be written as:

$$\text{for every state sequence} \quad [(\text{in} = a) \implies X(\text{out} = \bar{a})]$$

where the X is a "next time" operator and $\bar{a}$ denotes the Boolean complement of a. The main result of [6] is that the COSMOS symbolic simulator can be used to prove this kind of statement. In other words, the COSMOS system can be used to prove that the behaviors derived from an extracted netlist, using a sophisticated switch-level and timing model, implies certain formulas described in a logic with precisely defined semantics.

3.1 Circuit State Machine and Trajectories

The circuit model used in [6] is a ternary model, i.e., nodes in the circuit can take on the values 0, 1, and X. The *circuit state machine* corresponding to some circuit C is a non-deterministic finite state machine $\mathcal{M} = (S, \Delta, \Theta)$, where S is a finite set of states, Δ, the *transition relation*, is a relation on S, and Θ is a function $\Theta: S \rightarrow \{0, 1, X\}^n$ relating every state in S to an assignment of 0s, 1s, and Xs to the nodes of the circuit. Intuitively, if the circuit currently is in the state s^i and $(s^i, s^{i+1}) \in \Delta$, then the circuit can be in the state s^{i+1} one basic time unit later. The circuit state machine is determined by three factors: 1) the extracted netlist, 2) the switch-level model, and 3) the delay model.

Given a circuit state machine, a *state trajectory*, χ, is an infinite sequence of states $s^1, s^2, \ldots$, such that $s^i \in S$ and $(s^i, s^{i+1}) \in \Delta$ for $i \geq 1$. The *circuit trajectory*, $\psi(\chi)$, corresponding to a state trajectory χ is an infinite sequence of ternary state vectors $a^1, a^2, \ldots$, such that $a^i \in \{0, 1, X\}^n$ and $a^i = \Theta(s^i)$ for $i \geq 1$. Informally, a circuit trajectory can be viewed as an infinite sequence of "snap-shots" of the operating circuit taken every unit of time. Finally, let Ψ denote the set of all possible circuit trajectories for a given circuit. Intuitively, Ψ can be viewed as the set of all possible circuit behaviors according to the switch-level and delay model used.

3.2 Logic CL

The logic CL is defined in terms of another logic called CL'. We begin by describing CL' and then consider CL.

The logic CL' is defined over a set of nodes, $\mathcal{N} = \{n_1, \ldots, n_n\}$, and over a set of symbolic Boolean variables, $\mathcal{V}$. The formulas consists of constants (UNCONST), atomic propositions ($n_i = 1$ and $n_i = 0$), conjunction ($f_1 \wedge f_2$), case restriction ($e \rightarrow f$), and next time operations (Xf). In case restriction, ($e \rightarrow f$), e is a Boolean expression over $\mathcal{V}$ and f is a CL' formula. The basic idea is to use a Boolean function to limit the cases for which the CL' formula f is of interest.

Let $\mathcal{V}$ be a set of symbolic Boolean variables. An *interpretation*, ϕ, is a function $\phi : \mathcal{V} \rightarrow \mathcal{B}$ assigning a binary value to each symbolic Boolean variable. Let Φ be the set of all possible interpretations, i.e., $\Phi = \{\phi : \mathcal{V} \rightarrow \mathcal{B}\}$.

The truth semantics of a CL' formula f is defined relative to an interpretation $\phi \in \Phi$ and a circuit trajectory $\psi = a^1, a^2, a^3, \ldots \in \Psi$. For a precise definition of the truth semantics, see [6]. Informally, the CL' formula UNCONST holds for every ϕ and ψ. The formula $n_i = 0$ ($n_i = 1$) holds if and only if $a_i^1 = 0$ ($a_i^1 = 1$). The conjunction of two CL' formulas holds if and only if both formulas hold. The CL' formula $e \rightarrow f$ holds if either the Boolean formula denoted by the Boolean expression e evaluates to 0 for interpretation ϕ, or if the CL' formula f holds. Finally, Xf holds for ϕ and circuit trajectory $a^1, a^2, a^3 \ldots \in \Psi$ if and only if f holds for ϕ and circuit trajectory $a^2, a^3 \ldots$.

The verification methodology used by the COSMOS system entails proving *assertions* about the model structure. These assertions, written in the *core logic CL*, are of the form $A \implies C$, where the *antecedent* A and the *consequent* C are CL' formulas over $\mathcal{N}$ and $\mathcal{V}$. This assertion is true, written $\Psi \models (A \implies C)$, if and only if for every interpretation, i.e., every assignment of 0s and 1s to the symbolic Boolean variables, and for every possible circuit trajectory, the CL' formula C holds or the CL' formula A does not hold.

3.3 A Decision Algorithm

A decision algorithm based on ternary symbolic simulation was given in [6] for determining the validity of formulae in CL. That is, the algorithm determines whether or not for every interpretation every circuit trajectory satisfying the antecedent A must also satisfy the consequent C. It does this by generating a symbolic simulation sequence corresponding to the antecedent, and testing whether the resulting symbolic state sequence satisfies the consequent. For details, see [6].

4 Semantically Embedding *CL* in Higher-Order Logic

As argued in [14], a major advantage of higher-order logic as a formalism for verifying hardware is the ability to semantically embed more specialized formalisms into this logic. This often results in more concise specifications and easier proofs. Furthermore, as this paper demonstrates, the ability to semantically embed another formalism in higher-order logic, in particular *CL*, provides a means of establishing a rigorous link between general-purpose theorem-provers, such as HOL, and other verification tools, such as COSMOS.

Although full details, including machine-readable syntax, are beyond the scope of this paper, a sketch of how *CL* can be embedded in higher-order logic is given below. As explained earlier, the truth semantics of a *CL'* formulae is relative to an interpretation ϕ and a circuit trajectory ψ. Thus, operators of *CL'* are defined as functions of ϕ and ψ. An interpretation ϕ is represented as a function that maps Boolean expressions to Boolean values. Circuit trajectories are also represented by functions—in this case, functions that map position in a sequence to state vectors.

$\vdash_{def}$ UNCONST $= \lambda \phi \psi.$ true

$\vdash_{def} n\_i = 0 = \lambda \phi \psi.$ (head ψ)$[i] = 0$

$\vdash_{def} n\_i = 1 = \lambda \phi \psi.$ (head ψ)$[i] = 1$

$\vdash_{def}$ f1 $\wedge$ f2 $= \lambda \phi \psi.$ (f1 $\phi \psi$) $\wedge$ (f2 $\phi \psi$)

$\vdash_{def}$ e $\rightarrow$ f $= \lambda \phi \psi.$ (ϕ(e)) $\Longrightarrow$ (f $\phi \psi$)

$\vdash_{def}$ Xf $= \lambda \phi \psi.$ f ϕ (tail(ψ))

$\vdash_{def} \Psi \models (A \Longrightarrow B) = \forall \phi \in \Phi, \forall \psi \in \Psi. (A \phi \psi) \Longrightarrow (C \phi \psi)$

To avoid a proliferation of symbols in this informal account, we have used the same symbol for conjunction and implication in both *CL'* and higher-order logic, namely, $\wedge$ and $\Longrightarrow$ respectively.

5 An Example

To illustrate our two-level approach to formal hardware verification, consider the circuit shown in Fig. 2. This is a 16-bit instance of a (pseudo) domino-logic design for a circuit that tests whether: 1) input A is greater than input B and, 2) input

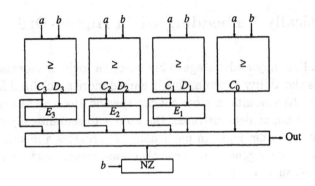

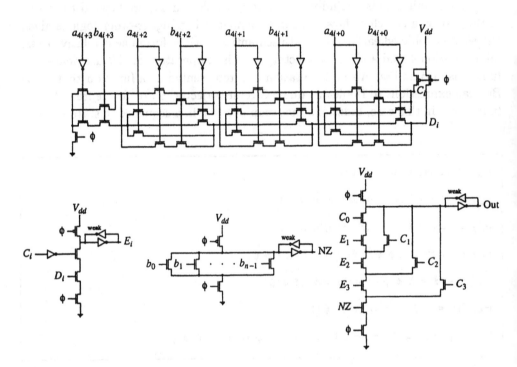

Figure 2: 16-bit circuit for computing $A > B > 0$.

B is greater than zero, when these inputs are interpreted as the unsigned binary representation of two numbers. The goal of formal verification is to relate a top-level specification of this circuit's intended function to a bottom-level specification of its implementation (based on an underlying model of hardware). The top-level specification should be sufficiently abstract to minimize the semantic gap between it and the informal, intuitive, specification of the circuit that resides in the mind of the designer. On the other hand, the bottom-level specification should be an accurate model of the circuit. This includes not only an accurate electrical model but also temporal properties of the circuit.

In the mind of the human specifier, the intended function of the circuit shown in Fig. 2 is intuitively understood in terms of an arithmetic relation, i.e., "the output should be 1 when A is greater than B and B is greater than 0". To minimize the semantic gap, the top-level formal specification should also be stated in terms of an arithmetic relation. At the bottom-level of specification, the actual operation of the circuit shown in Fig. 2 cannot be accurately described by a simple model of circuit behavior. A number of detailed features such as clocking, charge storage, charge sharing, and sized transistors, need to be included in an accurate model of this circuit. Hence, the verification problem, in this particular case, is to relate a top-level specification expressed in terms of an arithmetic relation to a bottom-level specification based on a detailed model of switch level circuit behavior.

Neither symbolic simulation or theorem-proving on their own is able to satisfactorily deal with this verification problem. Symbolic simulation would clearly be unable to support a top-level specification stated in terms of arithmetic relations. Theorem-proving is generally inappropriate for reasoning about detailed circuit behavior. Below, we will outline how this proof could be carried out using our combined verification approach. However, due to space considerations, we will not include the actual code representing the specification to the COSMOS system nor the actual HOL statements.

At the COSMOS level, we first define a function *CmpBitLevel* that takes a size parameter n and two vectors of Boolean variables A and B and returns the Boolean expression representing the bit level "compare and greater than zero operation". We then define a function *timing* that takes a Boolean expression res as argument and that essentially describes the timing conditions under which we wish to verify the circuit in Fig. 2. To paraphrase this definition: on the assumption that, 1) the clock signal phi is low for 100 time units and then is high for another 100 time units, and 2) the vectors of circuit nodes a and b are assigned the vectors of symbolic Boolean variables A and B at time 95 and held stable until time 200, then the circuit node denoted by out should be equal to the value res from at least time 180 until time 200.

The functional specification expressed by *CmpBitLevel* and the timing conditions expressed by *timing* are combined in the top level COSMOS specification: (*timing* (*CmpBitLevel n A B*));.

The COSMOS system is able to derive the following theorem which states that the above specification is a logical consequence of the finite state machine derived from the extracted netlist of the circuit shown in Fig. 2.

$$\Psi \models (timing \ (CmpBitLevel \ 16 \ A \ B))$$

We now wish to derive a more abstract correctness result which expresses correctness at the arithmetic level. Currently, we hand-translate the COSMOS specifications into higher-order logic. Eventually, when the interface language is semantically embedded in higher-order logic, this translation will be a series of expansion steps governed by the inference rules of higher-order logic.

To formally establish a relationship between a bit level correctness result and a higher level correctness result expressed in terms of natural number arithmetic, we need to formally define a relationship between bit vectors and natural numbers. This is expressed by a definition called *BitsToNum* which is a data abstraction function that maps bit vectors to natural numbers. We also define the function *CmpNumLevel* which is the arithmetic level specification of the function we want the circuit in Fig. 2 to compute.

The HOL system can now be used to prove that $\forall n \ A \ B$:

$$(CmpBitLevel \ n \ A \ B) \equiv (CmpNumLevel \ (BitsToNum \ n \ A)(BitsToNum \ n \ B)).$$

Having established this equivalence, we can then derive a generalized correctness result which relates the bit level specification of the compare circuit to an arithmetic level specification for any value of n, i.e., we can show that $\forall n$:

$$(timing \ (CmpBitLevel \ n \ A \ B))$$
$$\implies (timing \ (CmpNumLevel \ (BitsToNum \ n \ A)(BitsToNum \ n \ B)))$$

Finally, we instantiate this generalized result for $n = 16$ to obtain,

$$(timing \ (CmpBitLevel \ 16 \ A \ B))$$
$$\implies (timing \ (CmpNumLevel \ (BitsToNum \ 16 \ A)(BitsToNum \ 16 \ B)))$$

which, together with the symbolic simulation result above constitutes a statement of correctness for the circuit in Fig. 2.

6 Conclusions

Different methods of formal verification involve tradeoffs between automation, flexibility, expressibility, and accuracy. We conclude that a promising balance of these tradeoffs can be achieved by using theorem-proving at higher levels and symbolic simulation at lower levels. By embedding the "high-level" specification logic used by COSMOS into HOL, we are able to efficiently verify systems from a very detailed electrical and timing domain up to a very abstract behavioral domain.

We think that this two-level approach will be particularly useful in the case of circuits where there is tight coupling between functional and temporal properties of the circuit level and high level abstractions, e.g., when a gate level or RTL abstraction is not available as an intermediate level. This is especially true in the case of high performance designs. Also, by integrating these two methods, we open up the possibility of verifying mixed software/hardware systems[1, 15].

We are currently in the process of formalizing the interface logic and implementing a compiler for this language in the COSMOS system. This involves not only modifying the existing, informal, compiler in COSMOS, but also to define the precise semantics of the language and proving the correctness of the compilation method.

References

[1] W. Bevier, W. Hunt, J Moore, and W. Young, "An Approach to Systems Verification", *Journal of Automated Reasoning*, Vol. 5, No. 4, November 1989.

[2] R. Boulton, M. Gordon, J. Herbert and J. Van Tassel, "The HOL Verification of ELLA Designs", in: P. Subrahmanyam, ed., *Proceedings of a Workshop on Formal Methods in VLSI Design*, 9-11 January 1991, Miami, Florida.

[3] R. S. Boyer and J.S. Moore, *A Computational Logic Handbook*, Academic Press, 1988.

[4] R.E. Bryant, "A Switch-Level Model and Simulator for MOS Digital Systems," *IEEE Trans. on Computers* Vol. C-33, No. 2, February, 1984, pp. 160–177.

[5] R.E. Bryant, "Symbolic Verification of MOS Circuits", *1985 Chapel Hill Conference on VLSI*, May, 1985, pp. 419-438.

[6] R.E. Bryant, and C-J. Seger, "Formal Verification of Digital Circuits Using Symbolic Ternary System Models", *DIMAC Workshop on Computer-Aided Verification*, Rutgers, New Jersey, June 18-20, 1990 (to appear in Springer Verlag's Lecture Notes in Computer Science).

[7] Albert John Camilleri, "Mechanizing CSP Trace Theory in Higher Order Logic", *IEEE Transactions on Software Engineering*, Vol. SE-16, No. 9, September 1990, pp. 993-1104.

[8] Paolo Camurati and Paolo Prinetto, "Formal Verification of Hardware Correctness", *IEEE Computer*, Vol. 21, No. 7, July 1988, pp. 8-19.

[9] M. J. C. Gordon, "Why Higher-Order Logic is a Good Formalism for Specifying and Verifying Hardware", in: G. Milne and P. Subrahmanyam, eds., *Formal Aspects of VLSI Design*, Proceedings of the 1985 Edinburgh Conference on VLSI, North-Holland, 1986, pp. 153-177.

[10] Michael J. C. Gordon, "Mechanizing Programming Logics in Higher Order Logic", in: G. Birtwistle and P. Subrahmanyam, eds., *Current Trends in Hardware Verification and Automated Theorem Proving*, Springer-Verlag, 1989, pp. 387-439. Also Report No. 145, Computer Laboratory, Cambridge University, September 1988.

[11] Roger W. S. Hale, *Programming in Temporal Logic*, Ph.D. Thesis, Report No. 173, Computer Laboratory, Cambridge University, July 1989.

[12] Warren A. Hunt, *FM8501, A Verified Microprocessor*, Ph.D. Thesis, Report No. 47, Institute for Computing Science, University of Texas, Austin, December 1985.

[13] Jeffrey J. Joyce, "A Verified Compiler for a Verified Microprocessor", Report No. 167, Computer Laboratory, Cambridge University, March 1989.

[14] Jeffrey J. Joyce, "More Reasons Why Higher-Order Logic is a Good Formalism for Specifying and Verifying Hardware", in: P. Subrahmanyam, ed., *Proceedings of a Workshop on Formal Methods in VLSI Design*, 9-11 January 1991, Miami, Florida.

[15] Jeffrey J. Joyce, "Totally Verified Systems: Linking Verified Software to Verified Hardware", in: *Specification, Verification and Synthesis: Mathematical Aspects*, Proceedings of a Workshop, 5-7 July 1989, M. Leeser and G. Brown, eds., Ithaca, N.Y., Springer-Verlag, 1989.

[16] Michael J. C. Gordon et al., *The HOL System Description*, Cambridge Research Centre, SRI International, Suite 23, Miller's Yard, Cambridge CB2 1RQ, England.

Efficient Algorithms for Verification of Equivalences for Probabilistic Processes

Linda Christoff   Ivan Christoff

Department of Computer Systems
Uppsala University
S-75120 Uppsala, Sweden

Abstract

We present algorithms for automatic verification of equivalences between probabilistic processes. The equivalences we shall verify are testing type equivalences, based on probabilities for probabilistic processes to perform strings of observable events when interacting with different environments (or tests). Our algorithms are based on a recent polynomial-time algorithm for establishing language equivalence of probabilistic automata by Tzeng. We show that the time complexity of our algorithms is polynomial with respect to the number of states in the compared processes.

1 Introduction

During the last decade several theories for specifying and analysing the behavior of concurrent processes have emerged (e.g. CCS by Milner [Mi 89], CSP by Hoare [Ho 85], and ACP by Bergstra and Klop [BK 84]). These theories, commonly referred to as *process algebras*, include different notions of equivalence between processes. Several verification methods for establishing equivalences between processes have been developed, and implemented in tools (e.g. see [GLZ 89, CPS 90, Ch 90a]).

In the past couple of years, probabilistic models for specifying and analysing behavior of concurrent processes have been introduced, e.g. see [LS 89, Ch 90b, GJS 90, HJ 90]. For these models, two types of equivalences have been defined: bisimulation type equivalences [LS 89, HJ 90], and equivalences based on probabilities for processes to perform strings of events [Ch 90b, JS 90].

The work presented in this paper is based on the probabilistic process model described in [Ch 90b, Ch 90c]. We shall present efficient algorithms for verification of three equivalences for probabilistic processes: probabilistic trace equivalence ($=_{tr}$), probabilistic failure equivalence ($=_{fe}$), and strong probabilistic test equivalence ($=_{ste}$).

The equivalences we shall consider are based on probabilities for processes to perform strings of observable events, when interacting with different types of tests. Verification of an equivalence between two processes involves showing that these probabilities are equal for all strings of observable events and all tests. For recursive processes, verification requires that an infinite number of probabilities are examined. The verification algorithms presented in this paper are based on finding *finite* subsets of probabilities for the compared processes, whose equality implies equivalence of all probabilities. To find such finite subsets efficiently, we adopt ideas from an algorithm for establishing language equivalence of probabilistic automata by Tzeng [Tz].

The paper is organized as follows: In section 2 we define the probabilistic process model and the equivalences. The verification algorithms are presented in section 3. The complexity of these algorithms is examined in section 4. In section 5 we summarize the results.

2 Process Model and Equivalences

In this section we shall define the probabilistic process model and the equivalences.

2.1 Probabilistic Processes

The operational behavior of probabilistic processes is modeled in [Ch 90b, Ch 90c], using Plotkin's notion of transition systems [Pl 81], extended with probabilities.

Definition 2.1.1 A finite labeled *probabilistic transition system* (PTS) is a triple, (S, E, π), where:

- S is a finite *set of states*, ranged over by s, s', $s1$, $s2$, etc.
- $E = L \cup \{\tau\}$, where $\tau \notin L$, is a finite *set of events* (ranged over by e, e', etc.), L is a finite *set of observable events* (ranged over by a, a', etc.), and τ is an *unobservable event*.
- $\pi : S \times E \times S \to [0,1]$, is a *transition probability function*. A requirement for π is:

$$\forall s \in S: \quad \sum_{e \in E, s' \in S} \pi(s,e,s') = \begin{cases} 1 & \text{if } \exists s': \pi(s,e,s') > 0 \\ 0 & \text{if } \neg \exists s': \pi(s,e,s') > 0 \end{cases}$$

Intuitively, $\pi(s,e,s')$ is the probability for performing event e at state s, and moving to state s'. We shall use L^* to denote the *set of strings of observable events* (ranged over by σ, σ', etc.), ε to denote the *empty string* and:

$$s \xrightarrow{e}_p s' \qquad \text{to denote that } \pi(s,e,s') = p$$
$$s \xrightarrow{e} s' \qquad \text{to denote that } \pi(s,e,s') > 0$$
$$s \xrightarrow{e} \qquad \text{to denote that } \exists s': \pi(s,e,s') > 0$$
$$s \xrightarrow{\tau^n} s' \qquad \text{to denote } s \xrightarrow{\tau} s_1 \xrightarrow{\tau} \dots\ s_{n-1} \xrightarrow{\tau} s' \text{ (where } n \geq 0)$$
$$s \xrightarrow{\tau^n a} \qquad \text{to denote } s \xrightarrow{\tau^n} s' \xrightarrow{a}$$

Definition 2.1.2 Let (S, E, π) be a PTS. A function that computes the states reached in a PTS after performing a string of observable events, $\mathcal{A}fter : 2^S \times L^* \to 2^S$, is defined for all $S' \subseteq S$, $a \in L$ and $\sigma \in L^*$, as:

$$1) \quad \mathcal{A}fter(S',\varepsilon) = \{s' \in S \mid \exists s \in S'. s \xrightarrow{\tau^n} s'\}$$
$$2) \quad \mathcal{A}fter(S',a\sigma) = \mathcal{A}fter(\{s' \in S \mid \exists s \in S'. s \xrightarrow{\tau^n a} s'\},\sigma)$$

Intuitively, $\mathcal{A}fter(\{s\},\sigma)$ defines the set of states reachable by any number of τ's, from the states reached after σ is performed from s.

Definition 2.1.3 (Probabilistic process) Let (S, E, π) be a PTS. We interpret each $s \in S$ as a *probabilistic process*, defined by (S_s, E, π_s), where:

- s is the initial state
- $S_s = \{s' \in S \mid \exists \sigma \in L^*.s' \in \mathcal{A}fter(\{s\},\sigma)\}$ defines the states reachable from s
- $\pi_s: S_s \times E \times S_s \to [0,1]$, is defined for all $s',s'' \in S_s$ and $e \in E$ as
  $$\pi_s(s',e,s'') = \pi(s',e,s'')$$

Figure 2.1.1 gives a graphical representation of probabilistic processes. The processes are displayed in a tree-like style in which 'loops' are represented by a reference to a node. For example, the process $s1$ has two 'loops' for which the corresponding transitions are $(s1,a,s1)$ and $(s1',a,s1')$.

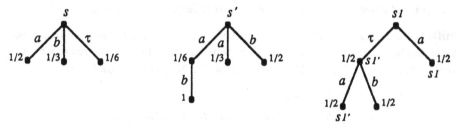

Figure 2.1.1 Probabilistic processes.

2.2 Equivalences

In this subsection we define three equivalences for probabilistic processes, based on probabilities for processes to perform strings of observable events when interacting with different types of environments.

First we shall discuss the role of the environment on the transition probabilities in a probabilistic process. When setting the probabilities for the transitions of a process at a state s, we assume that all the observable events that can be performed at s are offered by the environment (we also assume that the process can perform τ's regardless of which events are offered by the environment). If only a subset of the observable events at s are offered, we normalize the probabilities for the possible transitions at s, so that the sum of these probabilities is 1. The normalization is done in such a manner, so that the relative probabilities between the transitions that can be performed remains the same, as if all observable events were offered. For example, for process s in figure 2.1.1, if only a is offered by the environment, the normalized probabilities for a and τ would be 3/4 and 1/4, respectively.

Formally, we shall regard the environment of a probabilistic process as a string of sets of observable events, with which the process can interact.

Definition 2.2.1 (Offerings) Let L be a set of observable events. The *set of offerings* for L is defined as: $O=2^L - \{\{\}\}$.

To range over O we use L', L'', etc. O^* is used to denote the *set of strings of offerings* (ranged over by o, o', etc.), and λ to denote the *empty string*.

Our equivalences are based on probabilities for processes to perform strings of observable events, when offered strings of offerings. As an example, consider $s1$ in figure 2.1.1. We wish to compute the probability for process $s1$ to perform the string of observable events ab, when $\{a,b\}\{b\}$ is offered. Since τ's are unobservable there can be an arbitrary number of τ's interleaved in the string (e.g. $\tau^n a \tau^m b$, where $n{\geq}0$ and $m{\geq}0$). First we compute the probabilities for performing all $\tau^n a$ strings when $\{a,b\}$ is offered ($1/2$ for a and $1/4$ for τa), and from the states reached immediately after a and τa ($s1$ and $s1'$), we compute the probabilities for performing all $\tau^m b$ strings when $\{b\}$ is offered (1 for both τb and b). We then multiply our results to obtain the probabilities for performing τab and $a\tau b$, and sum these probabilities to obtain the probability for performing the string of observable events ab: $(1/2){\cdot}1 + (1/4){\cdot}1 = 3/4$.

To define a function which computes such string probabilities, we need to formalize the notion of 'states reached immediately after a string of observable events is performed'.

Definition 2.2.2 (Just-after states) Let $(S, L \cup \{\tau\}, \pi)$ be a PTS. A function for computing the states reached in a probabilistic process immediately after a string of observable events is performed, $\textit{Just-after}: 2^S \times L^* \to 2^S$, is defined for all $S' {\subseteq} S$, $a {\in} L$ and $\sigma {\in} L^*$, as:

    1) $\textit{Just-after}(S', \varepsilon) = S'$

    2) $\textit{Just-after}(S', a\sigma) = \textit{Just-after}(\{s' {\in} S \mid \exists s {\in} S'. s \xrightarrow{\tau^n a} s'\}, \sigma)$

We can now define a function which computes *specific* string probabilities (e.g. for process $s1$ in figure 2.1.1, the probability for $s1 \xrightarrow{\tau^n a} s1'$ when only $\{a\}$ is offered).

Definition 2.2.3 Let $(S, L \cup \{\tau\}, \pi)$ be a PTS. A function that computes probabilities for performing specific strings of events in probabilistic processes restricted by strings of offerings, $Q': S \times O^* \times L^* \times S \to [0,1]$, is defined for all $s, s' {\in} S$, $L' {\in} O$, $o {\in} O^*$, $a {\in} L$ and $\sigma {\in} L^*$, inductively as:

    1) $Q'(s, \lambda, a, s') = 0$

    2) $Q'(s, o, \varepsilon, s') = \begin{cases} 1 & \text{if } s'{=}s \\ 0 & \text{if } s'{\neq}s \end{cases}$

    3) $Q'(s, L', a, s') = $ if $(a {\notin} L')$ or $(s' {\notin} \textit{Just-after}(\{s\}, a))$ then 0

                    else $\pi_{L'}(s, a, s') + \sum_{s'' {\in} \textit{Stat}(s)} \pi_{L'}(s, \tau, s'') {\cdot} Q'(s'', L', a, s')$

    4) $Q'(s, L'o, a\sigma, s') = \sum_{s'' {\in} \textit{Just-after}(\{s\}, a)} Q'(s, L', a, s'') {\cdot} Q'(s'', o, \sigma, s')$

where $\textit{Stat}(s) = \{s' {\in} S \mid s \xrightarrow{\tau} s'\}$ and $\pi_{L'}(s, e, s') = \dfrac{\pi(s, e, s')}{\sum_{e' {\in} L' \cup \{\tau\}, s'' {\in} S} \pi(s, e', s'')}$

Note that $\pi_{L'}$ reflects the normalization procedure (note in particular that due to the conditions in rule 3, $\sum_{e' {\in} L' \cup \{\tau\}, s'' {\in} S} \pi(s, e', s'') \neq 0$). For any probabilistic process s, we use Q' to compute the probability for performing a string σ (when offered a string of offerings o), starting at s and terminating at a state s' in the set $\textit{Just-after}(\{s\}, \sigma)$.

Definition 2.2.4 (String probability) Let $(S, L \cup \{\tau\}, \pi)$ be a PTS. A function that computes probabilities for performing strings of events in probabilistic processes restricted by strings of offerings, $Q : S \times O^* \times L^* \to [0,1]$, is defined for all $s \in S$, $o \in O^*$ and $\sigma \in L^*$, as:

$$Q(s,o,\sigma) = \sum_{s' \in \textit{Just-after}(\{s\},\sigma)} Q(s,o,\sigma,s')$$

For two of the equivalences we shall define a function, with which environments that restrict processes to only performing a specific string of events can be defined.

Definition 2.2.5 We define a function that transforms a string of events to a string of offerings, $\textit{Sets} : L^* \to O^*$, for all $\sigma \in L^*$, as: 1) $\textit{Sets}(\varepsilon) = \lambda$ and 2) $\textit{Sets}(a\sigma) = \{a\} \textit{Sets}(\sigma)$.

We can now define three equivalences which distinguish processes by probabilities for performing strings of observable events when interacting with: environments that restrict the processes to performing specific strings of events ($=_{tr}$), environments that restrict the processes to performing specific strings of events followed by any set of events ($=_{fe}$), and any environment ($=_{ste}$). We regard these equivalences as *test equivalences*, since an environment (i.e. an offering string) can be interpreted as a test.

Definition 2.2.6 (Equivalences) Let $(S, L \cup \{\tau\}, \pi)$ be a PTS. We define, *probabilistic trace equivalence* ($=_{tr}$), *probabilistic failure equivalence* ($=_{fe}$) and *strong probabilistic test equivalence* ($=_{ste}$), for all $s, s' \in S$, as:

$$s =_{tr} s' \iff \forall \sigma \in L^* : \qquad\qquad Q(s, \textit{Sets}(\sigma), \sigma) = Q(s', \textit{Sets}(\sigma), \sigma)$$

$$s =_{fe} s' \iff \forall L' \in O, \sigma \in L^* : \quad \sum_{a \in L'} Q(s, \textit{Sets}(\sigma)L', \sigma a) = \sum_{a \in L'} Q(s', \textit{Sets}(\sigma)L', \sigma a)$$

$$s =_{ste} s' \iff \forall o \in O^*, \sigma \in L^* : \qquad\qquad Q(s, o, \sigma) = Q(s', o, \sigma)$$

A set of offering-event string pairs, which characterizes $=_{ste}$, is defined below.

Definition 2.2.7 (Set of pairs of offering-event strings of equal length) Let L be a non-empty set of observable events, and O the corresponding set of offerings. We define the *set of pairs of offering-event strings of equal length*, as: $Eq = \{(o,\sigma) \in O^* \times L^* \mid |o| = |\sigma|\}$.

Proposition 2.2.1 Let $(S, L \cup \{\tau\}, \pi)$ be a PTS. For any two probabilistic processes $s, s' \in S$:

$$s =_{ste} s' \iff \forall (o, \sigma) \in Eq : \quad Q(s, o, \sigma) = Q(s', o, \sigma)$$

Proof See [Ch 91].

3 Verification Algorithms

In this section we introduce a matrix representation for the Q' values associated with a probabilistic process, adopted from probabilistic automata [Pa 71]. Using this matrix representation we define algorithms for verification of the equivalences presented in section 2. Our algorithms are based on an algorithm for establishing language equivalence of probabilistic automata by Tzeng [Tz]. The main idea behind the algorithms is, for any two processes, to find a finite set of Q values whose equivalence implies equivalence of *all* Q values.

3.1 Preliminaries

In this subsection we shall define matrices and vectors associated with a probabilistic process, which can be used to compute Q values. The matrices we shall define contain the Q' values for a process. Since by the definition of Q', a Q' value greater than 0 is only possible for the states in a process reached just-after a string of events is performed, it is convenient to have a special notion for these 'just-after states'.

Definition 3.1.1 (Just-after states of a process) Let $(S, L \cup \{\tau\}, \pi)$ be a PTS. For any $s \in S$, we define the finite set $Jas(s) \subseteq S$, as:

$$Jas(s) = \{s' \in S \mid \exists \sigma \in L^* . s' \in Just\text{-}after(\{s\}, \sigma)\}$$

For notational convenience we shall assume that the states in $Jas(s)$ are renamed as $s_1, s_2, \ldots, s_n$ with $s_1 = s$ and $n = |Jas(s)|$.

We shall now define a matrix which contains the Q' values for a probabilistic process for a specific offering-event pair.

Definition 3.1.2 (Matrix of probabilities for an offering-event pair) Let $(S, L \cup \{\tau\}, \pi)$ be a PTS. For all $s \in S$, $L' \in O$ and $a \in L$ we define the matrix:

$$\mathbf{M}^s(L', a) = [\mathbf{m}^s_{ij}(L', a)] = [Q'(s_i, L', a, s_j)]$$

$\mathbf{M}^s(L', a)$ is a *square matrix* of order $|Jas(s)|$, indexed by the states in $Jas(s)$.

We use definition 3.1.2 to define a matrix of probabilities for a pair of offering-event strings.

Definition 3.1.3 (Matrix of probabilities for a pair of offering-event strings) Let $(S, L \cup \{\tau\}, \pi)$ be a PTS. We define a *matrix of probabilities for a pair of offering-event strings*, $\mathbf{M}^s(o, \sigma)$, for all $s \in S$ and $(L', a), (o, \sigma) \in Eq$, as: (1) $\mathbf{M}^s(\lambda, \varepsilon) = \mathbf{I}$ (i.e. $\mathbf{M}^s(\lambda, \varepsilon)$ is a square *unit matrix* of order $|Jas(s)|$) and (2) $\mathbf{M}^s(L'o, a\sigma) = \mathbf{M}^s(L', a) \cdot \mathbf{M}^s(o, \sigma)$.

Proposition 3.1.1 Let $(S, L \cup \{\tau\}, \pi)$ be a PTS. For all $s \in S$ and $(o, \sigma) \in Eq$:

$$\mathbf{m}^s_{ij}(o, \sigma) = Q'(s_i, o, \sigma, s_j)$$

Proof By induction on the length of o and σ (see [Ch 91]).

In order to express the Q values for a process in terms of the previously defined matrices, we need to define two vectors.

Definition 3.1.4 (Final vector). Let $(S, L \cup \{\tau\}, \pi)$ be a PTS. For any $s \in S$, we define a *final vector*, η^s, as a column vector, with all entries equal to 1 and $|\eta^s| = |Jas(s)|$.

The ith row of $\mathbf{M}^s(o, \sigma)$ contains the probabilities for performing σ when o is offered, starting at s_i and moving to a state s_j in $Jas(s)$. Since the ith entry of the vector $\mathbf{M}^s(o, \sigma) \cdot \eta^s$ is the sum of the entries in the ith row of $\mathbf{M}^s(o, \sigma)$, it represents the probability for performing σ when o is offered, starting at s_i and moving to *any* state in $Jas(s)$. By definition 3.1.1 we know that $s = s_1$. Consequently, $Q(s, o, \sigma)$ is the first entry in the vector $\mathbf{M}^s(o, \sigma) \cdot \eta^s$. In order to select individual entries from $\mathbf{M}^s(o, \sigma) \cdot \eta^s$ we shall define one more vector.

Definition 3.1.5 (Initial distribution vector). Let $(S, L \cup \{\tau\}, \pi)$ be a PTS. We define the *initial distribution vector*, ψ^s, for any $s \in S$, as: $\psi^s = (1, 0, ..., 0)$, with $|\psi^s| = |Jas(s)|$.

Proposition 3.1.2 Let $(S, L \cup \{\tau\}, \pi)$ be a PTS. For all $s \in S$ and $(o, \sigma) \in Eq$:

$$Q(s, o, \sigma) = \psi^s \cdot M^s(o, \sigma) \cdot \eta^s$$

Proof The proof uses the definitions of Q, ψ^s, η^s and proposition 3.1.1 (see [Ch 91]).

3.2 Algorithms for Verification of $=_{ste}$ and $=_{tr}$

In this subsection we shall define $=_{ste}$ and $=_{tr}$ in terms of ψ, M and η. Using these definitions, we develop verification algorithms for the equivalences. We shall begin with $=_{ste}$.

Proposition 3.2.1 Let $(S, L \cup \{\tau\}, \pi)$ be a PTS. For any $s, s' \in S$:

$$s =_{ste} s' \quad \Leftrightarrow \quad \forall (o, \sigma) \in Eq: \quad \psi^s \cdot M^s(o, \sigma) \cdot \eta^s = \psi^{s'} \cdot M^{s'}(o, \sigma) \cdot \eta^{s'}$$

Proof Follows directly from propositions 2.2.1 and 3.1.2.

From proposition 3.2.1 follows that we can verify $=_{ste}$ between two probabilistic processes s and s', by comparing if: $\psi^s \cdot M^s(o, \sigma) \cdot \eta^s = \psi^{s'} \cdot M^{s'}(o, \sigma) \cdot \eta^{s'}$, for all $(o, \sigma) \in Eq$. If s and s' are recursive processes, there are an infinite number of values to compare. Our objective is to find a *finite* set of such values, whose equivalence implies that $s =_{ste} s'$. In order to do this we adopt a notion of summation for matrices of probabilities from [Pa 71].

Definition 3.2.1 (Direct sum) Let $(S, L \cup \{\tau\}, \pi)$ be a PTS. For all $s, s' \in S$ and $(o, \sigma) \in Eq$, we define *the direct sum* of $M^s(o, \sigma)$ and $M^{s'}(o, \sigma)$, as:

$$M^{s+s'}(o, \sigma) = \begin{bmatrix} M^s(o, \sigma) & 0 \\ 0 & M^{s'}(o, \sigma) \end{bmatrix}$$

Note that $M^{s+s'}(o, \sigma)$ is a square matrix of order $|Jas(s)| + |Jas(s')|$, and that direct sum has the following property: $M^{s+s'}(oL', \sigma a) = M^{s+s'}(o, \sigma) \cdot M^{s+s'}(L', a)$.

We shall express $=_{ste}$ using the direct sum construct.

Proposition 3.2.2 Let $(S, L \cup \{\tau\}, \pi)$ be a PTS. For any $s, s' \in S$:

$$s =_{ste} s' \quad \Leftrightarrow \quad \forall (o, \sigma) \in Eq: \quad [\psi^s, \psi^{s'}] \cdot M^{s+s'}(o, \sigma) \cdot \begin{bmatrix} \eta^s \\ -\eta^{s'} \end{bmatrix} = 0 \qquad (1)$$

Proof The proof uses the definition of $M^{s+s'}$ and proposition 3.2.1 (see [Ch 91]).

In (1), $[\psi^s, \psi^{s'}] \cdot M^{s+s'}(o, \sigma)$, defines a row vector. We shall use the set of all such vectors, $\bigcup_{(o, \sigma) \in Eq} \{[\psi^s, \psi^{s'}] \cdot M^{s+s'}(o, \sigma)\}$, in the algorithm for verification of $=_{ste}$.

Definition 3.2.2 Let $(S, L \cup \{\tau\}, \pi)$ be a PTS. We define the $(=_{ste})$-*linear space* for any two processes $s, s' \in S$, as: $L_{ste} = span(\bigcup_{(o, \sigma) \in Eq} \{[\psi^s, \psi^{s'}] \cdot M^{s+s'}(o, \sigma)\})$, where *span* is a function, which for a set of vectors U, generates all the linear combinations of the vectors in U.

Since each $[\psi^s,\psi^{s'}] \cdot \mathbf{M}^{s+s'}(o,\sigma)$ is a row vector with $|\mathcal{J}as(s)| + |\mathcal{J}as(s')|$ elements, a basis for L_{ste} has at most $|\mathcal{J}as(s)| + |\mathcal{J}as(s')|$ vectors. We define $=_{ste}$ in terms of such a basis.

Lemma 3.2.1 Let $(S,L \cup \{\tau\},\pi)$ be a PTS. For any two processes $s,s' \in S$, if $\mathbf{U}$ is a basis for L_{ste}:

$$s =_{ste} s' \quad \Leftrightarrow \quad \forall \mathbf{U}_i \in \mathbf{U}: \quad \mathbf{U}_i \cdot \begin{bmatrix} \eta^s \\ -\eta^{s'} \end{bmatrix} = 0 \tag{2}$$

Proof The proof uses the fact that $\mathbf{U}$ is a basis for L_{ste}, and proposition 3.2.2 (see [Ch 91]).

In order to prove $s =_{ste} s'$ one can: (i) find $\mathbf{U}$, a basis for L_{ste}, and (ii) if (2) holds for $\mathbf{U}$ then $s=_{ste}s'$, otherwise $s \neq_{ste} s'$. We shall now give an algorithm which verifies $=_{ste}$ in this manner.

Algorithm 1 Let $(S,L \cup \{\tau\},\pi)$ be a PTS. For any $s,s' \in S$, we define an algorithm for verification of $=_{ste}$ as:

(1) $\mathbf{U} \leftarrow \{\}$;

(2)   *queue* $\leftarrow$ *vertex*(λ,ε);

(3)   **while** *queue* is not empty **do**

(4)   **begin**

(5)   Take an element *vertex*(o,σ) from *queue*;

(6)   Compute $[\psi^s,\psi^{s'}] \cdot \mathbf{M}^{s+s'}(o,\sigma)$;

(7)   **if** $[\psi^s,\psi^{s'}] \cdot \mathbf{M}^{s+s'}(o,\sigma) \notin span(\mathbf{U})$ **then**

(8)   **begin**

(9)   For all $L' \in O$ and $a \in L'$, add *vertex*$(oL',\sigma a)$ to *queue*;

(10) $\mathbf{U} \leftarrow \mathbf{U} \cup \{[\psi^s,\psi^{s'}] \cdot \mathbf{M}^{s+s'}(o,\sigma)\}$;

(11)   **end**;

(12)   **end**;

(13)   **if** for all $\mathbf{U} \in \mathbf{U}$, $\mathbf{U} \cdot \begin{bmatrix} \eta^s \\ -\eta^{s'} \end{bmatrix} = 0$ then return(yes) **else** return(no);

Algorithm 1 generates a rooted tree. Each vertex in the tree, *vertex*(o,σ), corresponds to a vector $[\psi^s,\psi^{s'}] \cdot \mathbf{M}^{s+s'}(o,\sigma)$ in L_{ste}. The root of the tree corresponds to the vector $[\psi^s,\psi^{s'}] \cdot \mathbf{M}^{s+s'}(\lambda,\varepsilon)$ (i.e. $[\psi^s,\psi^{s'}]$). As the tree grows, a basis for L_{ste} is constructed in $\mathbf{U}$. A *queue* is used to keep track of the vertices of the tree that have been created but not 'handled'.

The algorithm works as follows. Initially $\mathbf{U}$ is empty, and *vertex*(λ,ε) is the only element in the *queue*. A vertex, *vertex*(o,σ), is taken from the queue. If the vector corresponding to *vertex*(o,σ), $[\psi^s,\psi^{s'}] \cdot \mathbf{M}^{s+s'}(o,\sigma)$, is linearly independent w.r.t. the vectors in $\mathbf{U}$, it is added to $\mathbf{U}$. The tree is expanded from *vertex*(o,σ), with the vertices *vertex*$(oL',\sigma a)$, for all $L' \in O$ and $a \in L'$. These vertices are added to the queue. If the vector corresponding to *vertex*(o,σ) is linearly dependent on the vectors in $\mathbf{U}$, the tree is not expanded from this vertex, i.e. *vertex*(o,σ) becomes a *leaf* of the tree. The algorithm continues until the tree can not be expanded, i.e. *queue* is empty.

Theorem 3.2.1 Let $(S,L \cup \{\tau\},\pi)$ be a PTS. For all probabilistic processes $s,s' \in S$, algorithm 1 determines if $s =_{ste} s'$.

Proof See [Ch 91].

Since the approach for verification of $=_{tr}$ is the same as the one used for verification of $=_{ste}$, we shall only indicate the necessary modifications. In analogy to the definition of $\mathcal{L}_{ste}$, we define a $(=_{tr})$-*linear space*, $\mathcal{L}_{tr}$, as:

$$\mathcal{L}_{tr} = span(\bigcup_{\sigma \in L^*} \{[\psi^s, \psi^{s'}] \cdot M^{s+s'}(Sets(\sigma), \sigma)\}),$$

and if U is a basis for $\mathcal{L}_{tr}$, then analogously to lemma 3.2.1 we have that:

$$s =_{tr} s' \quad \Leftrightarrow \quad \forall v_i \in U: \quad v_i \cdot \begin{bmatrix} \eta^s \\ -\eta^{s'} \end{bmatrix} = 0$$

Algorithm 1 can be easily changed to find a basis for $\mathcal{L}_{tr}$ by changing line (9) to:

(9) For all $a \in L$, add $vertex(o\{a\}, \sigma a)$ to $queue$;

The revised algorithm is given in full in [Ch 91].

3.3 An Algorithm for Verification of $=_{fe}$

In this subsection we shall define $=_{fe}$ in terms of the direct sum construct. Using this definition, we develop a verification algorithm for $=_{fe}$.

Proposition 3.3.1 Let $(S, L \cup \{\tau\}, \pi)$ be a PTS. For any $s, s' \in S$:

$$s =_{fe} s'$$

$$\Leftrightarrow$$

$$\forall L' \in O, \sigma \in L^*: \quad [\psi^s, \psi^{s'}] \cdot M^{s+s'}(Sets(\sigma), \sigma) \cdot \sum_{a \in L} M^{s+s'}(L', a) \cdot \begin{bmatrix} \eta^s \\ -\eta^{s'} \end{bmatrix} = 0 \tag{3}$$

Proof The proof uses proposition 3.1.2, and the definition of $M^{s+s'}$ (see [Ch 91]).

Definition 3.3.1 Let $(S, L \cup \{\tau\}, \pi)$ be a PTS. We define the $(=_{fe})$-*linear space* for any two processes $s, s' \in S$, as:

$$\mathcal{L}_{fe} = span(\bigcup_{\sigma \in L^*, L' \in O} \{[\psi^s, \psi^{s'}] \cdot M^{s+s'}(Sets(\sigma), \sigma) \cdot \sum_{a \in L} M^{s+s'}(L', a)\})$$

Since each $[\psi^s, \psi^{s'}] \cdot M^{s+s'}(Sets(\sigma), \sigma) \cdot \sum_{a \in L} M^{s+s'}(L', a)$ is a row vector with $|\mathcal{J}as(s)| + |\mathcal{J}as(s')|$ elements, we know that a basis for $\mathcal{L}_{fe}$ has at most $|\mathcal{J}as(s)| + |\mathcal{J}as(s')|$ vectors. We shall now define $=_{fe}$ in terms of such a basis.

Lemma 3.3.1 Let $(S, L \cup \{\tau\}, \pi)$ be a PTS. For any two processes $s, s' \in S$, if U is a basis for $\mathcal{L}_{fe}$:

$$s =_{fe} s' \quad \Leftrightarrow \quad \forall v_i \in U: \quad v_i \cdot \begin{bmatrix} \eta^s \\ -\eta^{s'} \end{bmatrix} = 0 \tag{4}$$

Proof The proof uses the fact that U is a basis for $\mathcal{L}_{fe}$, and proposition 3.3.1 (see [Ch 91]).

In order to prove $s =_{fe} s'$ one can find U, a basis for $\mathcal{L}_{fe}$, and if (4) holds for U then $s =_{fe} s'$, otherwise $s \neq_{fe} s'$. We shall now give an algorithm which verifies $=_{fe}$ in this manner. Consider algorithm 2.

Algorithm 2 Let $(S, L \cup \{\tau\}, \pi)$ be a PTS. For any $s, s' \in S$, we define an algorithm for verification of $=_{fe}$ as:

(1) $\mathbb{U} \leftarrow \{\}$;

(2) $\mathbb{U}' \leftarrow \{\}$;

(3)   For all $L' \in O$, let $queue \leftarrow vertex(L')$;

(4)   **while** $queue$ is not empty **do**

(5)   **begin**

(6)   Take an element $vertex(Sets(\sigma)L')$ from $queue$;

(7)   Compute $[\psi^s, \psi^{s'}] \cdot \mathbf{M}^{s+s'}(Sets(\sigma), \sigma) \cdot \sum_{a \in L'} \mathbf{M}^{s+s'}(L', a)$;

(8)   **if** $[\psi^s, \psi^{s'}] \cdot \mathbf{M}^{s+s'}(Sets(\sigma), \sigma) \cdot \sum_{a \in L'} \mathbf{M}^{s+s'}(L', a) \notin span(\mathbb{U})$ **then**

(9)   **begin**

(10)   **if** for some $a \in L, \ L' = \{a\}$ **then**

(11)   **begin**

(12) $\mathbb{U} \leftarrow \mathbb{U} \cup \{ [\psi^s, \psi^{s'}] \cdot \mathbf{M}^{s+s'}(Sets(\sigma), \sigma) \cdot \mathbf{M}^{s+s'}(\{a\}, a) \}$;

(13)   For all $L'' \in O$, add $vertex(Sets(\sigma a)L'')$ to $queue$;

(14)   **end**;

(15)   **else** $\mathbb{U}' \leftarrow \mathbb{U}' \cup \{ [\psi^s, \psi^{s'}] \cdot \mathbf{M}^{s+s'}(Sets(\sigma), \sigma) \cdot \sum_{a \in L'} \mathbf{M}^{s+s'}(L', a) \}$;

(16)   **end**;

(17)   **end**;

(18)   **if** for all $\mathbb{U} \in \mathbb{U} \cup \mathbb{U}'$, $\mathbb{U} \cdot \begin{bmatrix} \eta^s \\ -\eta^{s'} \end{bmatrix} = 0$ **then** return(yes) **else** return(no);

Algorithm 2 produces several trees. The root of each tree is a vertex, i.e. $vertex(L')$ for some $L' \in O$. Each vertex in the trees, $vertex(Sets(\sigma)L')$, is associated with a vector

$$[\psi^s, \psi^{s'}] \cdot \mathbf{M}^{s+s'}(Sets(\sigma), \sigma) \cdot \sum_{a \in L'} \mathbf{M}^{s+s'}(L', a),$$

for some $\sigma \in L^*$ and $L' \in O$. As the trees grow, two sets of vectors, $\mathbb{U}$ and $\mathbb{U}'$, are constructed. In the correctness proof for the algorithm (see [Ch 91]), we show that a basis for $\mathcal{L}_{fe}$ can be constructed from the union of these two sets of vectors. A $queue$ is used to keep track of the vertices in all trees that have been created but not 'handled'.

The algorithm works as follows. Initially $\mathbb{U}$ and $\mathbb{U}'$ are empty, and for all $L' \in O$, $vertex(L')$ are the only elements in the $queue$. A vertex, $vertex(Sets(\sigma)L')$, is taken from the queue. If the vector corresponding to $vertex(Sets(\sigma)L')$ is linearly independent to the vectors in $\mathbb{U}$ and $|L'| = 1$ (i.e. $L' = \{a\}$ for some $a \in L$), the vector is added to $\mathbb{U}$. The tree containing $vertex(Sets(\sigma)\{a\})$ is expanded by adding the vertices $vertex(Sets(\sigma a)L'')$, for all $L'' \in O$, to the $queue$. If the vector corresponding to $vertex(Sets(\sigma)L')$ is linearly independent to the vectors in $\mathbb{U}$ and $|L'| > 1$, the vector is added to $\mathbb{U}'$. The tree containing $vertex(Sets(\sigma)L')$ is not expanded from this vertex, i.e. $vertex(Sets(\sigma)L')$ becomes a *leaf*. If the vector corresponding to $vertex(Sets(\sigma)L')$ is linearly dependent on the vectors in $\mathbb{U}$, the tree containing $vertex(Sets(\sigma)L')$ is not expanded from this vertex. The algorithm continues until no tree can be expanded, i.e. $queue$ is empty.

Theorem 3.3.1 Let $(S, L \cup \{\tau\}, \pi)$ be a PTS. For all probabilistic processes $s, s' \in S$, algorithm 2 determines if $s =_{fe} s'$.

Proof See [Ch 91].

4 Complexity Analysis

To determine the complexity of verifying $=_i$ (for $i \in \{tr, fe, ste\}$), we need to consider: i) the complexity of constructing the matrices required for the verification algorithm for $=_i$ and ii) the complexity of the verification algorithm for $=_i$.

The complexity of constructing matrices is defined by the number of matrices required times the complexity of constructing each matrix. The number of matrices required (per process) for verification of $=_{tr}$ is $|L|$, and for verification of $=_{fe}$ and $=_{ste}$, $(2^{|L|} - 1) \cdot |L|$. Constructing each matrix for a process s involves solving a system of $|S_s|$ linear equations for each column in the matrix. This can be done in $O(|S_s|^{2.81})$ time [AHU 74]. Since there are $|\mathcal{J}as(s)|$ columns in each matrix, any matrix can be constructed in $|\mathcal{J}as(s)| \cdot O(|S_s|^{2.81})$ time. Assuming $|L|$ is constant, and observing that $|\mathcal{J}as(s)| \leq |S_s|$, the complexity of constructing the matrices required for verification of any of the equivalences for any two processes s and s' is: $O(|S_s|^{3.81} + |S_{s'}|^{3.81})$.

The verification algorithm for $=_{ste}$ constructs a tree with at most $|\mathcal{J}as(s)| + |\mathcal{J}as(s')|$ internal nodes (i.e. *non-leaf* nodes), and $(|L| \cdot (2^{|L|} - 1) - 1) \cdot (|\mathcal{J}as(s)| + |\mathcal{J}as(s')|) + 1$ leaves [Kn 68]. For each node we must: a) compute the vector associated with the node, and b) determine if it is linearly dependent on the vectors in $\mathbf{U}$.

    a) The vector associated with each node can be calculated by multiplying the $(|\mathcal{J}as(s)| + |\mathcal{J}as(s')|)$-dimensional vector associated with the father of the node with a $\mathbf{M}^{s+s'}(L',a)$ matrix, of order $|\mathcal{J}as(s)| + |\mathcal{J}as(s')|$. This can be computed in $O((|\mathcal{J}as(s)| + |\mathcal{J}as(s')|)^2)$ time [Kn 69].

    b) Determining linear dependence requires $O((|\mathcal{J}as(s)| + |\mathcal{J}as(s')|)^3)$ time [Kn 69].

The complexity for the verification algorithm for $=_{ste}$ is consequently:

$$\left(|\mathcal{J}as(s)| + |\mathcal{J}as(s')| + ((|L| \cdot (2^{|L|} - 1) - 1) \cdot (|\mathcal{J}as(s)| + |\mathcal{J}as(s')|) + 1)\right) \cdot O((|\mathcal{J}as(s)| + |\mathcal{J}as(s')|)^3)$$

Assuming that $|L|$ is constant, this becomes: $O((|\mathcal{J}as(s)| + |\mathcal{J}as(s')|)^4)$.

The verification algorithms for $=_{tr}$ and $=_{fe}$ have the same 'cost' of handling each node as the verification algorithm for $=_{ste}$. The number of nodes that need to be handled for each of these algorithms is: $(|L| - 1) \cdot (|\mathcal{J}as(s)| + |\mathcal{J}as(s')|) + 1$, for $=_{tr}$, and $(2^{|L|} - 2) \cdot (|\mathcal{J}as(s)| + |\mathcal{J}as(s')|)$, for $=_{fe}$. If $|L|$ is assumed constant, the complexity of both algorithms becomes: $O((|\mathcal{J}as(s)| + |\mathcal{J}as(s')|)^4)$.

If we take into consideration that $|\mathcal{J}as(s)| + |\mathcal{J}as(s')| \leq |S_s| + |S_{s'}|$, the complexity of the verification algorithms for $=_{tr}$, $=_{fe}$ and $=_{ste}$ becomes: $O((|S_s| + |S_{s'}|)^4)$.

5 Summary of Results

We have presented algorithms for automatic verification of three equivalences for probabilistic processes. The verification algorithms are based on a matrix representation from probabilistic automata [Pa 71], and a polynomial-time algorithm for establishing language equivalence of probabilistic automata by Tzeng [Tz].

The time complexity of the verification algorithms is shown to be $O((|S_s| + |S_{s'}|)^4)$, where $|S_s|$ and $|S_{s'}|$ represent the number of states for the compared processes. It should be noted that the algorithms for verification of the $=_{tr}$ and $=_{fe}$ equivalences for probabilistic processes, stand in contrast to the computationally much harder algorithms for verifying the 'corresponding' equivalences for non-probabilistic processes. For example, for non-deterministic finite state automata, the problems of verifying trace and failure equivalence are known to be PSPACE-complete [KS 90].

Acknowledgements

We are grateful to Scott Smolka for drawing our attention to Tzeng's results, to Wen-Guey Tzeng for providing us with [Tz], and to the CAV'91 referees for their helpful comments. This work was in part supported by the Swedish National Board for Technical Development (STU).

References

[AHU 74]   A.V. AHO, J.E. HOPCROFT, J.D. ULLMAN. *The Design and Analysis of Computer Algorithms*, Addison-Wesley, 1974.

[BK 84]   J.A. BERGSTRA, J.W. KLOP. Process algebra for synchronous communication. *Information and Control* **60**, pp 109-137, 1984.

[Ch 90a]   I. CHRISTOFF. A method for verification of trace and test equivalence. In *Proc. Intl. Workshop on Automatic Verification Methods for Finite State Systems*, *LNCS* **407**, pp 81-88, Springer-Verlag, 1990.

[Ch 90b]   I. CHRISTOFF. Testing equivalences and fully abstract models for probabilistic processes. In *Proc. CONCUR '90*, *LNCS* **458**, pp 126-140, Springer-Verlag, 1990.

[Ch 90c]   I. CHRISTOFF. Testing Equivalences for Probabilistic Processes. PhD thesis, DoCS 90/22, Dept. of Computer Systems, Uppsala University, Sweden, 1990.

[Ch 91]   L. CHRISTOFF. Efficient Algorithms for Verification of Equivalences for Probabilistic Processes. Technical report, DoCS 91/28, Dept. of Computer Systems, Uppsala University, Sweden, 1991.

[CPS 90]   R. CLEAVELAND, J. PARROW, B. STEFFEN. The concurrency workbench. In *Proc. Intl. Workshop on Automatic Verification Methods for Finite State Systems*, *LNCS* **407**, pp 24-37, Springer-Verlag, 1990.

[GJS 90]   A. GIACALONE, C.-C. JOU, S.A. SMOLKA. Algebraic reasoning for probabilistic concurrent systems. In *Proc. Working Conf. on Programming Concepts and Methods*, Sea of Galilee, Israel, 1990.

[GLZ 89]   J.C. GODSKESEN, K.G. LARSEN, M. ZEEBERG. TAV Users Manual. Technical Report R 89-19, Dept. of Mathematics and Computer Science, University of Aalborg, Denmark, 1989.

[HJ 90]   H. HANSSON, B. JONSSON. A calculus for communicating systems with time and probabilities. In *Proc. 11th IEEE Real-Time Systems Symposium*, Orlando, Florida, 1990.

[Ho 85]   C.A.R. HOARE. *Communicating Sequential Processes*. Prentice Hall, 1985.

[JS 90]   C.-C. JOU, S.A. SMOLKA. Equivalences, congruences, and complete axiomatizations for probabilistic processes. In *Proc. CONCUR '90*, *LNCS* **458**, pp 367-383, Springer-Verlag, 1990.

[KS 90]   P.C. KANELLAKIS, S.A. SMOLKA. CCS expressions, finite state processes, and three problems of equivalence. *Information and Computation* 86:1, pp 43-68, 1990.

[Kn 68]   D.E. KNUTH. *Fundamental Algorithms*, Addison-Wesley, 1968.

[Kn 69]   D.E. KNUTH. *Seminumerical Algorithms*, Addison-Wesley, 1969.

[LS 89]   K.G. LARSEN, A. SKOU. Bisimulation through probabilistic testing. In *Proc. 16th ACM Symp. on Principles of Programming Languages*, pp 344-352, 1989.

[Mi 89]   R. MILNER. *Communication and Concurrency*. Prentice Hall, 1989.

[Pa 71]   A. PAZ. *Introduction to Probabilistic Automata*, Academic Press, 1971.

[Pl 81]   G. PLOTKIN. A Structural Approach to Operational Semantics. Technical Report DAIMI FN-19, Computer Science Department, Aarhus University, Aarhus, Denmark, 1981.

[Tz]   W.-G. TZENG. A polynomial-time algorithm for the equivalence of probabilistic automata. *SIAM Journal on Computing*. To appear.

PARTIAL-ORDER MODEL CHECKING:
A GUIDE FOR THE PERPLEXED

David K. Probst and Hon F. Li
Department of Computer Science
Concordia University
1455 de Maisonneuve West
Montreal, Quebec H3G 1M8

ABSTRACT

Practicing verifiers of finite-state concurrent systems should be able to adapt our partial-order methods for verifying delay-insensitive systems to other verification problems. We answer the question, is it possible to control state explosion arising from various sources during automatic verification (model checking) of delay-insensitive systems? State explosion due to concurrency is handled by introducing a partial-order representation for processes, and defining system correctness as a simple relation between two partial orders on the same set of system events. State explosion due to nondeterminism is handled when the system to be verified has a compact, finite recurrence structure. Backwards branching through representations is a further optimization. In system verification, we start with models of system components that explicitly distinguish concurrency, choice and recurrence structure; during model checking, this a priori structure of components allows us to construct a compact, finite representation of the specification-constrained implementation -- without prior composition of system components. The fully-implemented POM verification system has polynomial space and time performance on traditional asynchronous-circuit benchmarks that are exponential in space and time for other verification systems; in general, the cost of running our verification algorithm is proportional to the size of the constructed system representation.

Keywords delay-insensitive system, model checking, state explosion, partial-order representation, recurrence structure, state encoding.

1. Introduction

Delay-insensitive systems are motivated inter alia by difficulties with clock distribution and component composition in clocked systems [1,2,6,11]. In a delay-insensitive system, modules may be interconnected to form systems in such a way that system correctness does not depend on delays in either modules or interconnection media. An important question is, what restrictions must be placed on finite-state concurrent systems in order that efficient model-checking algorithms are possible? Among concurrent systems, delay-insensitive systems have the particularity of containing regular patterns of handshakes between input and output events. Our work on delay-insensitive model checking can be adapted to handle delay-constrained reactive systems where inputs enable outputs, and outputs enable inputs [10]. Delay insensitivity has a natural link to controlling state explosion during automatic verification; the simple enabling relations in delay-insensitive systems make it easy to discover a solution to the state-explosion problem based on causality checking. To build an efficient automatic verifier based on causality checking, you need the following items for each system component: (i) an expressive finite partial-order representation that explicitly distinguishes concurrency, choice and recurrence, and (ii) a "goal-directed" state encoding that is both causality comprehensive (includes all causality) and state minimal (has fewest states). Given this, you can combine the best features of automata- and partial-order-based methods, and obtain a verification algorithm whose cost in space and time is proportional to the size of the constructed system representation. This size is often polynomial in the number of system components.

The automata we use to represent processes are called behavior automata, which can be unrolled to produce infinite event structures called pomtrees. The latter are essentially sets of partially-ordered computations where the branching structure due to conflict resolution has been made explicit [6-10]. Partial orders and schedule/automaton duality are covered in [3-4]. Restrictions on behavior automata trade off between expressiveness and processability (e.g., the efficiency of verification algorithms).

This research was supported by the Natural Sciences and Engineering Research Council of Canada under grants A3363, A0921 and MEF0040121. Email: probst@crim.ca.

The following method allows us to keep the termination table small. We provide a behavior automaton that distinguishes concurrency, choice and recurrence structure for each implementation component and for specification P. We label arrows in behavior automata to encode the process state corresponding to an arbitrary partial execution. System correctness is defined as a simple relation on an "enriched" system pomtree S that contains both causal and noncausal partial orders. This pomtree represents the imaginary closed system (also called S) produced by linking the mirror mP of specification P to the implementation network *Net*. During model checking, we use the a priori information about component structure to define a small set of loop cutpoints in a finite representation of system pomtree S, implicitly constructing a behavior automaton for the specification-constrained implementation. The explicit structure allows a convention to be followed during model checking that makes the mapping from P states to S states one-to-few rather than one-to-many, leading to a small termination table. Intuitively, when we cycle in P, we can arrange to cycle in S. Results obtained since [8] include: (i) simpler views of correctness and state, (ii) backwards branching in behavior automata, and (iii) a clear statement of algorithm complexity.

2.   Abstract specification of asynchronous processes

Our specifications define externally-visible computational behaviors of processes; in partial-order representations, they specify precedence constraints [5,6]. A process P has a set of input ports and a set of output ports; a process action is a (port, token) pair, where the token represents a control or data value. Each performance of an action is a separate event. Processes are modelled by pomtrees, which are identical to computation trees except that their arcs are finite posets, and their vertices are input or output choice points. A process behavior $p \in P$ is a maximal conflict-free set of events of P, i.e., some full use of P by P's environment. If P is a process, then P's input actions are under the control of P's environment, while P's output actions are under the control of P. A requirements specification of a reactive process with asymmetry of control for input and output need not be equivalent to an ω-regular language containment problem of the traditional kind.

Safety properties (in DI systems, precedence properties) constrain both the process and its environment. A safety violation is the performance of an input or output action that is not enabled. A process receiving unsafe input logically fails ("explodes"). Liveness properties (in DI systems, response properties) constrain only the process. A liveness (progress) violation is the nonperformance of a required process output action. Fairness properties also constrain only the process; they assert fairness of conflict resolution in repeated process choice among output alternatives. Such fairness is the default assumption in all our specifications. Behavior automata allow integrated specification of safety and liveness properties, but fairness properties must be provided as a supplementary condition.

2.1.   Pomsets

A labelled partial order (lpo) is a 4-tuple (V, Σ, Γ, μ) consisting of (i) a countable set V of events in a computational behavior, (ii) a finite set Σ of process actions, (iii) a partial order Γ on V that expresses the necessary temporal precedences among the events in V, and (iv) a labelling function μ : V $\rightarrow$ Σ mapping each event $v \in V$ to the process action $\sigma \in \Sigma$ it performs [3]. The successor relation Ω is the transitive reduction of Γ. A pomset is an isomorphism class of lpo's. Process behavior $p \in P$ is an infinite pomset. Process P is an infinite pomtree. Each behavior segment (pomtree arc) of process P is a finite poset. $\pi(p)$ is the set of finite prefixes of p. $p - \alpha$ is the suffix in p of $\alpha \in \pi(p)$. $^\circ p$ is the set of action labels of initial events of p. In a determinate (single-behavior) process, $^\circ(p - \alpha)$ is the set of actions concurrently performable after α. If α is a choice point in a nondeterminate (multiple-behavior) process, then there are sets of actions concurrently enabled after α, but not concurrently performable [6,9].

2.2.   Behavior automata

Behavior automata are constructed in three phases. First, there is a deterministic finite-state machine (stick figure) D that expresses both conflict resolution (choice) and recurrence structure. D is a "small" automaton relative to the transition system dual to the pomtree [4]. Second, there is an expansion of dfsm transitions (sticks) into finite posets, with additional machinery (sockets) to specify nonsequential concatenation of posets. Third, there is an iterative process of labelling successor arrows in posets, which terminates with an appropriate state encoding.

We sketch the formal definition of behavior automaton. Given the disjoint alphabets Act (the set of process actions), Arr (the set of successor arrow labels), Com (the set of dfsm D transitions) and Soc (the set of sockets), first define Pos as the set of finite labelled posets over Act ∪ Soc. Each member of Pos is a labelled poset (B, Γ, ν), where (i) Γ is a partial order over $B \subseteq$ Act ∪ Soc, and (ii) $\nu: \Omega \rightarrow$ Arr assigns a label to each element in the successor relation Ω (the transitive reduction of Γ). A <u>behavior</u> <u>automaton</u> is a 3-tuple (D, ϵ, ψ), where (i) D is a dfsm over Com, (ii) ϵ: Com → Pos maps dfsm transitions to labelled posets, and (iii) ψ: Soc → powerset(Act) maps sockets to sets of process actions. Map ψ defines which process actions can "plug in" to an empty socket when a poset command is concatenated to a sequence of earlier poset commands as defined by dfsm D. There is also an imaginary reset action •.

A Petri net is uniquely characterized by the presets and postsets of its transitions. Similarly, sockets can be removed from a behavior automaton by concatenating commands, and considering predecessor and successor arrows of individual actions. A process action consumes its predecessor arrows (removes them from the old state), and produces its successor arrows (adds them to the new state). Behavior automata are typeset by writing the poset transitions separately, and using "digit colons" to identify dfsm vertices. These vertices are not state encodings. Commands are also called productions.

Fig. 1 shows a behavior automaton for a C-element. Each arrow in the production is assigned a distinct label. The semantics is straightforward. For example, action a^+ is enabled in any state containing arrow 1; when it is performed, arrow 1 is removed from the state and arrow 3 is added. Similarly, action c^+ is enabled and required (because of the bracket) in any state containing arrows 3 and 4. When it is performed, arrows 3 and 4 are removed from the state and arrows 5 and 6 are added. Since $\psi(\circ) = \{\bullet, c^-\}$, action c^- has its preset and postset given by: $\{7, 8\}\ \underline{c}^-\ \{1, 2\}$. The postset follows from the labels on arrows leaving $\circ$. For program convenience, behavior automata are decomposed into atoms of the form {predecessor arrows, action, successor arrows}, retaining the stick figure D as a structuring device.

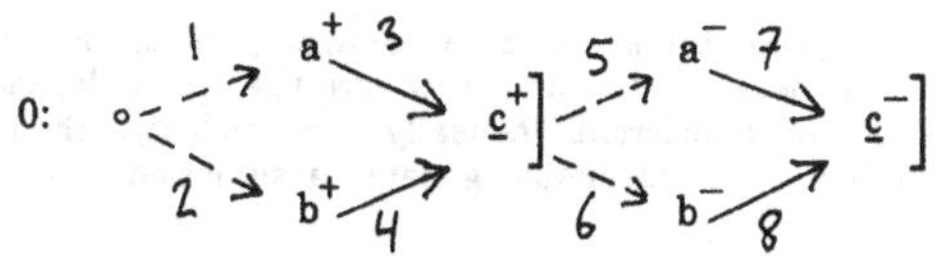

Fig. 1 Behavior automaton for a C-element.

The use of dashed and solid arrows is a reminder that a process specification includes both an <u>interprocess</u> protocol (given by the dashed arrows) and an <u>intraprocess</u> protocol (given by the solid arrows). Since the state is encoded as the set of arrows crossing a consistent cut, using fewer arrow labels would alter the enabling relation of the C-element; hence, this state encoding (arrow labelling) is fixed up to isomorphism.

Fig. 2 shows a behavior automaton for a delay-insensitive arbiter. Clients follow a four-cycle protocol. $\langle A \rangle = \underline{c}^+\ \big]\ \xrightarrow{2}\ a^-$ and $\langle B \rangle = \underline{d}^+\ \big]\ \xrightarrow{6}\ b^-$ are the two critical sections. The $\circ$ in command 1 is filled only by •, i.e., $\psi(\circ) = \{\bullet\}$. The top $\circ$ in command 2 is filled only by a^+, i.e., $\psi(\circ) = \{a^+\}$. The bottom $\circ$ in command 3 is filled only by b^+, i.e., $\psi(\circ) = \{b^+\}$. The middle $\circ$'s in commands 2 and 3 can be filled by •, a^- or b^-, i.e., $\psi(\circ) = \{\bullet, a^-, b^-\}$.

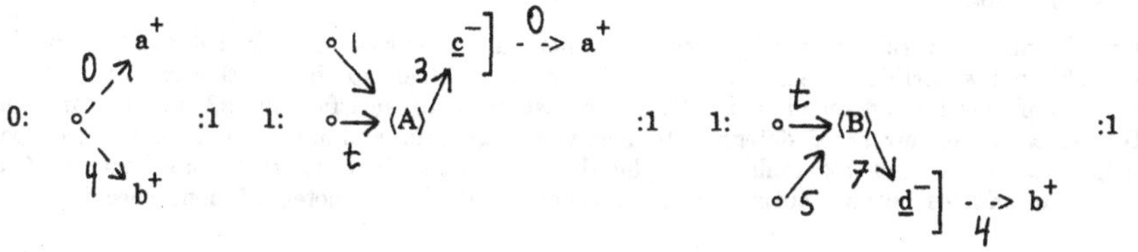

Fig. 2 Behavior automaton for a delay-insensitive arbiter.

When sockets have been removed, this set of actions generates the transition system of the fifteen-state arbiter dfsm [0]. However, care must be taken to keep the state encoding causality comprehensive. Arrow 1 in the C-element is two arrows in disguise ($\bullet - -> a^+$, $\underline{c}^- - -> a^+$); this is not a problem because of the special nature of $\bullet$. Arrows 0 and 4 in the arbiter are similar, but arrow t is $\underline{six}$ arrows in disguise (three sources, two sinks). Consider performing action $\underline{c}^+$ in state $\{1, 5, t\}$. Checking arrow t requires backing up in the behavior automaton to both process-action sources of t, viz., a^- and b^-. Again, $\bullet$ is not a problem. These are distinct causality arrows that must be checked separately. An arrow with multiple process-action sources is called an $\underline{equivalenced}$ arrow; all its sources are recorded in a table. In state $\{1, 5, t\}$, $\underline{c}^+$ and $\underline{d}^+$ are concurrently enabled but conflicting actions; hence, causality checking in this state requires both forwards and backwards branching through the behavior automaton.

2.3. Restrictions on processes

Which finite-state concurrent systems can be model checked efficiently? The efficiency gains in our algorithms stem from two sources: (i) making causality checking the primary activity, and (ii) recording as few system states as possible. Delay insensitivity $\underline{per}$ $\underline{se}$ is not a precondition for causality checking. However, well-behavedness conditions do restrict the class of event structures on which our programs operate. Among these are rules that allow processes to be used as components of delay-insensitive systems [6,11]. Each rule is a genuine restriction on concurrent systems. It is an important $\underline{metarule}$ that branching and recurrence structure be made explicit.

General rules

Rule a1 There is no autoconcurrency. Formally, any two events at the same port in $p \in P$ are ordered by Γ. (A good general rule).

Rule a2 Processes are finite state. Formally, there is an upper bound on the number of Ω arrows crossing a consistent cut of any $p \in P$. (Arrow labels can then be used to encode the process state).

Rule a3 A process has a representation with a compact, finite recurrence structure as defined by its dfsm D. Given finiteness, it is enough to require the independence of concurrent choices. Formally, if two choices are concurrent (causally independent), then neither can affect the existence or outcome of the other. (A reasonable general assumption).

Delay-insensitivity rules

Rule b1 There is handshaking between any two successive events at the same port. Formally, any two events at the same port in $p \in P$ are separated in Ω by at least one event at some other port. (A DI-specific rule related to zero buffering).

Rule b2 There is no specified successor relationship between two input events or two output events. Formally, each line in $p \in P$ consists of an infinite sequence of strictly alternating input and output events. (Simplifies causality checking by introducing a simple notion of preset).

Rule b3 If a set of enabled output actions can be performed concurrently, then they, or some conflicting set of concurrently performable output actions, must be performed. Formally, if $p \in P$, then all output events in p are bracketed. (A reasonable assumption in hardware systems).

One might ask if requiring concurrent choices to be independent is similar to requiring that Petri nets be free choice; the answer is no (arbiters are not free choice). In partial-order representations, finding a reasonable restriction on the generality with which conflicts can occur is the key issue in trading off between decision power and modelling power. Behavior machines are "free choice" only at the level of dfsm D, which explicitly distinguishes conflict resolution and recurrence structure.

Our algorithms verify systems efficiently when all processes satisfy rules a1 through b3. Rule a1 eliminates artificial examples. Rule a2 is central to finite checkability. Rule a3 eliminates nonphysical nondeterminism. The simplest way to satisfy rule a3 is to start with a dfsm D composed exclusively of determinate behavior segments and input or output choice points. In principle, rules b1 and b2 could be replaced -- provided there is still some notion of cross enabling (input enables output, output enables input). Rule b3 promotes efficient checking.

2.4. Semantics of behaviors

Fig. 3 shows an unlabelled behavior automaton for a determinate process. Action labels are pure names, but output actions are underlined. The partial order in this behavior is the transitive closure of a <u>successor</u> relation $\Omega = N \cup \Xi$, where N is a relation from input events to output events, and Ξ is a relation from output events to input events. Because of control asymmetry, we say that N is a <u>causal</u> relation and Ξ is a <u>noncausal</u> relation. Each output (input) action has a causal (noncausal) preset defined by the sources of its incoming solid (dashed) arrows. A process may perform an output action when the causal preset has occurred. An environment may perform an input action when the noncausal preset has occurred.

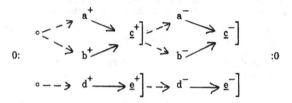

Fig. 3   Unlabelled behavior automaton (determinate process).

2.5. States in partial-order representations

The reduced finite-state machine for a delay-insensitive arbiter has fifteen states [0]; one of them is a choice state where the arbiter can give the token to either client. Reduction of the fsm means there is no record in the state of who returned the token. In the arbiter behavior automaton, either (i) we use different labels for different token arrows, or (ii) we use the same label (namely, t). Different labels distinguish the states resulting from the return of the token by different clients. Reduced fsms correspond to using equivalenced arrows. Verification by causality checking is <u>complete</u> when each distinct instance of causality has been checked. In particular, arrows leaving different critical sections must be checked separately. Nonreduced transition systems can be used to support completeness arguments for verification algorithms based on causality checking. This is the motivation for the distinction between <u>execution</u> state and <u>behavior</u> state [8]. In causality checking, behavior states can be used either explicitly (if equivalenced arrows are renamed to identify their sources) or implicitly (if tables of sources are kept). Conceptually, we explore all the distinct ways each process action can be enabled. Our current preference is to use equivalenced arrows and tables of sources; we perform "state-based" causality checking: an enabled action has its causality checked, not with respect to a particular past, but rather with respect to any past that would have resulted in the same state; in general, this requires backwards branching through systems of behavior automata.

3.   Correctness as a graph predicate

We define correctness in a causality-based scheme by using the mirror mP of specification P as a conceptual implementation tester [1]. We form an imaginary closed system S by linking the mirror mP of specification P to the implementation network of processes *Net*. This produces an "enriched" pomtree of system events with two partial orders; system correctness is defined as a simple, easily-checked relation between the two orders. The intuitive notion of correctness is as follows, given that implementations may be input liberal and output conservative [6,9]. Is there a failure somewhere, causing system S to become undefined? Does the system just stop, violating fundamental liveness? Is some progress requirement of P violated? Is there (program-detectable) nondeterminate livelock in S so that an appeal to fairness of system components is necessary to assert progress? Is some conflict corresponding to output choice in P resolved unfairly?

Mirror mP is formed by inverting the type of P's actions and the causal/noncausal interpretation of P's successor arrows, turning P's dashed arrows into solid arrows and vice versa. Brackets are preserved unchanged. Every action that can be performed in S is a linked (output action, input action) pair. As a result, we can check whether intraprocess protocols support interprocess protocols in closed system S.

We bootstrap the dashed (noncausal, interprocess protocol) and solid (causal, intraprocess protocol) relations from process actions to system actions, defining an event structure called an "enriched" pomtree, with a noncausal enabling relation on top of the usual causal enabling one. For example, a noncausal predecessor of system action σ is found by locating the embedded process input action, stepping back along a dashed process arrow, and returning to the system alphabet. This defines the <u>noncausal preset</u> of a system action. Essentially, the safety correctness relation is: whenever a dashed arrow links two system actions, a chain of solid arrows must also link the two actions.

Let σ be a system action that is causally enabled in S. There is a safety violation at σ unless (i) its noncausal preset is causally enabled in S, and (ii) each member of its noncausal preset is a causal ancestor of σ. The causal preset of σ is defined only when σ is a bracketed system action: it is the set of nearest performances of linked mP output actions on any causal chain coming into σ. In order that a bracketed σ in S is neither a safety nor a progress violation, it is necessary that the causal and noncausal presets of σ match exactly. When backwards branching is used to resolve multiple sources of equivalenced arrows, conditions for either safety or safety/progress must hold in each distinct past (backwards branch).

Fig. 4 is a simple illustration of correctness with only external events; solid arrows cover up dashed arrows in the system figure (covered dashed arrows are trivially supported). The dashed arrow from a to c in S is supported by a chain of solid arrows, so there is no safety violation at c. However, the noncausal preset of c, viz., {a}, does not match the causal preset, viz., {d}, so there is a progress violation at c.

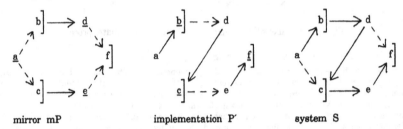

mirror mP   implementation P′   system S

Fig. 4 Partial orders and total correctness of an open system as a graph predicate.

Fig. 5 shows a second illustration. Every dashed arrow is supported by a chain of solid arrows, and all causal and noncausal presets of bracketed system actions match exactly. The implementation is correct. Although safety correctness is containment of the causal language in the noncausal language, this is not implementation language in the specification language. Since S represents the specification-constrained implementation, coupled system processes can prune each other's branching structure; this is the problem with traditional language containment.

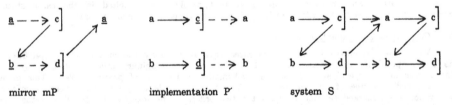

mirror mP   implementation P′   system S

Fig. 5 Partial orders and total correctness of an open system as a graph predicate, bis.

4. Model checking

The algorithm is also straightforward. We enumerate system actions and visit one system cut per action. We consider each enabled action in the context of a state we have reached. First, we repeatedly step back across single dashed arrows to compute the action's noncausal preset. Second, we repeatedly (finitely) chain back across multiple solid arrows to compute the action's partial causal ancestor set, or causal preset if the action is bracketed. When equivalenced arrows are encountered, we branch backwards to check each possible source. The speedup is due to two factors: (i) we effectively check cuts (through the generated past) we have not visited, and (ii) for equivalenced arrows, we effectively check cuts in pasts we have not generated. This kills state explosion due to concurrency and nondeterminism. We traverse each determinate segment (stick) of the implicitly constructed system behavior automaton (stick figure) precisely once. Backwards branching catches all causality that would have arisen had we traversed the system stick figure in some other way.

We keep the termination table small by making the mapping from P states to S states one-to-few rather than one-to-many. This is possible when all behavior automata have visible branching and recurrence structure. Hence, when we cycle in P, we can arrange to cycle in S. The top level of the algorithm visits system actions and tries to complete P sticks. The lower level of the algorithm does arrow checking.

The following algorithm assumes there is additional machinery to detect determinate livelock, or that such detection is not a problem. Logically, checkpoints are taken at system states corresponding to specification loop cutpoints. But _which_ system states correspond to specification states, given that any number of internal system actions can be performed without performing any external system action? A branching loop cutpoint in P corresponds to some number of causal branch points in S. A nonbranching loop cutpoint in P can be made to correspond to one nonbranching loop cutpoint in S. For each loop cutpoint in P, we identify a small number of system states we can consistently come back to. For this purpose, checkpoints are taken at (i) unique system states corresponding to nonbranching loop cutpoints in P, and (ii) causal branch points in S. We make each specification loop cutpoint, whether determinate (green problem) or nondeterminate (red problem), correspond to as few system states as possible, to minimize the number of entries in the termination table. Execution continues until no new checkpoints are found.

During model checking, we identify maximal determinate behavior segments of system pomtree S (the red problem). We do this by recognizing causal choice actions σ in closed system S. Each initial action of a P_i production leaving an output branch point, and each initial action of a P production leaving an input branch point, is marked with a red dot. Each causal choice action σ in system S is marked with a red dot. To ensure termination, we must also identify maximal path prefixes $\beta \in \pi(S)$ that correspond to determinate loop cutpoints in P's behavior automaton (the green problem). When we return to a P dfsm vertex, we want to return to as few system states as possible. Each initial action of a P production leaving a determinate loop cutpoint is marked with a green dot. Since P productions are the highest level of control for the performance of S actions, each initial system action σ of an S production leaving a determinate or nondeterminate loop cutpoint in S's (constructed) behavior automaton is now marked with a red or green dot.

We move forward cleanly to a branch point of S by not performing any red action as long as there are nonred actions still enabled. Branch points of S are scheduled for expansion in the usual way. Similarly, we move forward cleanly to a system path prefix $\beta \in \pi(S)$ that corresponds to a determinate loop cutpoint in P by not performing any green action as long as there are nongreen actions still enabled. Whenever (constructed) system determinate loop cutpoints or system causal branch points are encountered, the system state -- the vector of $(mP, P_1, ..., P_n)$ states -- is entered into the termination table, using the chosen process-state encoding. If the system state is already in the table, then system path prefix β is not extended further.

During verification, we perform actions that are causally enabled in the closed system, starting from initialization. When we perform a system action, we update the state of both processes to which the action is attributed. We perform these actions in arbitrary order, subject only to the constraint that unmarked actions are performed before marked actions. As we perform actions, we check the graph predicate of the previous section. Occasionally, we discover a safety violation immediately, i.e., without any graph searching: a system action is causally enabled, but the corresponding input action is noncausally not enabled, i.e., forbidden. This is the only discovery mode in model checking based on sequence enumeration. More typically, we compute the noncausal preset of the system action (from the behavior automaton of the process that owns the input action) and search backwards in the system computation to determine whether each member of the noncausal preset is a causal ancestor of the system action.

When a bracketed system action is causally enabled (and is not an immediate safety violation), it is more efficient to do combined safety/liveness checking. The noncausal preset is computed as in the previous paragraph. From the semantics of brackets, an mP dashed arrow can only be supported by a chain of solid arrows not containing an mP solid arrow. Using this, we search backwards in the system computation along each causal chain to find the first performance of an mP output action, thereby computing the causal preset. In order that there not be a safety/liveness violation, the two presets must be equal. Exploration of a system segment that begins with marked actions may cause a new specification production to be loaded. Failure to complete this production, once loaded, indicates the presence of progress violations not detectable by combined safety/liveness arrow checking; this special kind of progress violation occurs when actions performed in S form a noncausal preset of an mP input action, but do not causally enable the linked output action. The moving algorithm completes system sticks (modulo violations of fundamental liveness), and tries to complete P sticks, once they have been loaded. Two ideas make this algorithm work: (i) maintain the asymmetry of mP within S; use the special semantics of bracketed system actions, and use P productions as templates to schedule the performance of system actions, and (ii) construct a refinement mapping from P states of P dfsm vertices to system states in which the image sets are as small as possible. State-based causality checking (backwards branching in behavior automata) is a further optimization.

5. Empirical results

Benchmarks are a double-edged sword; your program may work well only when it happens to work well. To some extent, this state of affairs can be remedied by a theory of the causes of state explosion that defines the class of concurrent systems that can be verified efficiently. A more concrete result is that the cost in space and time of our verification algorithm is proportional to the size of the constructed system representation; when this is polynomial, our verification algorithm is polynomial. Our two primary benchmarks (ring of DME's, n-place buffer) were chosen because both producer/consumer and mutual-exclusion solutions are fundamental building blocks of concurrent systems. Since the polynomial cost functions are clearly benchmark sensitive, there is a clear need for a suite of benchmarks.

A complete verification package has been written by Lin Jensen in the Trilogy programming language running on an IBM PC. The POM system has polynomial space and time performance on benchmarks that are exponential in space and time for other verification systems. Consider the ring of DME elements benchmark. The runtime for verification of both safety and liveness properties is quadratic in n, the number of DME elements. The number of system states grows exponentially with n. For example, when n = 9, the time is 180 s (roughly 10^9 states); when n = 10, the time is 220 s (roughly 10^{10} states). The space requirements for these problems do not exceed 64K bytes, i.e., one IBM PC data segment. What are the asymptotic space requirements? One must store the input; this is linear. One must store the termination table; this is quadratic. Given reasonable garbage collection, the working storage to do backwards chaining in a system computation is linear, because we construct and compare simple presets. The asymptotically limiting resource is the quadratic space for the termination table. With 64K bytes, we never enter the asymptotic region; the linear space term predominates. Fig. 6 illustrates the algorithm's complexity on this benchmark more graphically. The size of the termination table is the number of vertices (•'s) times the size of a system state, which is $\Theta(n)$; this gives $\Theta(n^2)$ for space. The runtime is the time taken to traverse each stick of the system stick figure precisely once. The number of sticks grows linearly, and the time to traverse a variable-size stick is $\Theta(n)$; this gives $\Theta(n^2)$ for time.

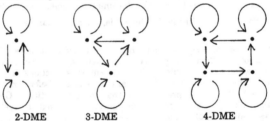

2-DME   3-DME   4-DME

Fig. 6   System stick figures for the n-DME verification problem.

6. Conclusion

For a given benchmark, the state encoding strategy is the primary determinant of the number of system sticks that must be examined. Heap exhaustion (within the compiler-imposed bound of 64K bytes) obviously limits the size of problems we can verify. To facilitate distribution and further experimentation, we will rewrite the POM system in a more widely-used programming language such as LISP or C. It is easy to explain why rings of DME's cause such problems for traditional sequence-based verification algorithms, but not for ours; given a system stick figure, it is clear that it can be traversed efficiently, and that successful termination implies total correctness of the implementation. The nontrivial part of our approach is the predefined strategy for constructing a set of system vertices, which are not given beforehand. This strategy is explained in section 4, and may be essential in any efficient partial-order algorithm for network verification. If branching and recurrence structure are not provided for components, then we lose

330

the one-to-few mapping from P states to S states. We would then need a replacement strategy for constructing a "small" automaton for S (this allows recording few system states). Other partial-order approaches to model checking, based in part on pruning pomset languages prior to checking language containment, appear to be less powerful in controlling state explosion. In any case, they address the problem of checking safety and liveness properties of (presumably large) precomposed closed systems, while we check the safety and liveness properties of (presumably large) open networks of processes.

Space is generally considered to be the critical resource in automatic verification. The asymptotic space complexity depends on the number of vertices in the constructed system behavior automaton. The asymptotic time complexity depends on the number and search complexity of individual sticks. Are there system behavior automata whose size is exponential in the number of system components? A simple-minded application of our techniques to show that there is no deadlock in a system of n dining philosophers with a circulating poison pill (or appetite suppressant) would examine a choice state in which n − 2 forks choose, producing as many branches as there are subsets of an (n − 2)-set. A priori, none of them could result in deadlock, so there is no point in generating exponentially-many branches. The space complexity is not a problem because there is only one choice state. The time complexity could conceivably be a problem if one were forced to explore every branch. A suite of nontrivial benchmarks for dining philosophers problems (something less symmetrical than deadlock detection) might allow meaningful comparison of different partial-order approaches. Combinatorial explosion of system behavior automata is a fruitful topic for future study.

References

[0] D.L. Black, "On the existence of delay-insensitive fair arbiters", Distributed Computing, Vol. 1, No. 4, October 1986, pp. 205-225.

[1] D.L. Dill, "Trace theory for automatic hierarchical verification of speed-independent circuits", Ph. D. Thesis, Department of Computer Science, Carnegie Mellon University, Report CMU-CS-88-119, February 1988. Also MIT Press, 1989.

[2] A.J. Martin, "Compiling communicating processes into delay-insensitive VLSI circuits", Distributed Computing, Vol. 1, No. 4, October 1986, pp. 226-234.

[3] V.R. Pratt, "Modelling concurrency with partial orders", Int. J. of Parallel Prog., Vol. 15, No. 1, February 1986, pp. 33-71.

[4] V.R. Pratt, "Modelling concurrency with geometry", Proc. 18th Ann. ACM Symposium on Principles of Programming Languages, January 1991, pp. 311-322.

[5] D.K. Probst and H.F. Li, "Abstract specification of synchronous data types for VLSI and proving the correctness of systolic network implementations", IEEE Trans. on Computers, Vol. C-37, No. 6, June 1988, pp. 710-720.

[6] D.K. Probst and H.F. Li, "Abstract specification, composition and proof of correctness of delay-insensitive circuits and systems", Technical Report, Department of Computer Science, Concordia University, CS-VLSI-88-2, April 1988 (Revised March 1989).

[7] D.K. Probst and H.F. Li, "Partial-order model checking of delay-insensitive systems". In R. Hobson et al. (Eds.), Canadian Conference on VLSI 1989, Proceedings, Vancouver, BC, October 1989, pp. 73-80.

[8] D.K. Probst and H.F. Li, "Using partial-order semantics to avoid the state explosion problem in asynchronous systems". In E.M. Clarke and R.P. Kurshan, (Eds.), Workshop on Computer-Aided Verification '90, June 1990, DIMACS Series, Vol. 3, 1991, pp. 15-24. Also Lect. Notes in Comput. Sci., Springer Verlag, forthcoming.

[9] D.K. Probst and H.F. Li, "Modelling reactive processes using partial orders". In M. Kwiatkowska et al. (Eds.), Semantics for Concurrency, Leicester 1990, Leicester, UK, July 1990, Workshops in Computing, Springer Verlag, 1990, pp. 324-343.

[10] D.K. Probst and L.C. Jensen, "Controlling state explosion during automatic verification of delay-insensitive and delay-constrained VLSI systems using the POM verifier". In S. Whitaker, (Ed.), Third NASA Symposium on VLSI Design, Moscow, ID, October 1991, Proceedings, pp. 8.2.1-8.2.8.

[11] J.v.d. Snepscheut, "Trace theory and VLSI design", Lect. Notes in Comput. Sci. 200, Springer Verlag, 1985.

[12] J.T. Udding, "A formal model for defining and classifying delay-insensitive circuits", Distributed Computing, Vol. 1, No. 4, October 1986, pp. 197-204.

TABLE I	TABLE II
Time to verify an n-arbiter implemented by a ring of n DME's (n system states in the table)	Time to verify an n-buffer implemented by n 1-buffers (one system state in the table)

n	seconds		n	seconds
2	20.60		2	6.32
3	32.08		3	8.08
4	47.13		4	9.83
5	65.63		5	11.43
6	87.77		6	13.13
7	114.03		7	14.89
8	144.51		8	16.59
9	179.60		9	18.35
10	220.03		10	20.05
			11	21.92
			12	23.67
			13	25.49
			14	27.30
			15	28.84
			16	30.70
			17	32.57
			18	34.44
			19	36.37
			20	38.28
			21	39.21
			22	41.36
			23	43.39

Using Partial Orders for the Efficient Verification of Deadlock Freedom and Safety Properties*

Patrice Godefroid   Pierre Wolper
Université de Liège
Institut Montefiore, B28
4000 Liège Sart-Tilman, Belgium
Email: {god,pw}@montefiore.ulg.ac.be

Abstract

This paper presents an algorithm for detecting deadlocks in concurrent finite-state systems without incurring most of the state explosion due to the modeling of concurrency by interleaving. For systems that have a high level of concurrency our algorithm can be much more efficient than the classical exploration of the whole state space. Finally, we show that our algorithm can also be used for verifying arbitrary safety properties.

1 Introduction

When reasoning assertionally about concurrent programs, separating safety and liveness properties is a well established paradigm [MP84, OL82]. Indeed, the proof techniques used for these two types of properties are quite different: safety properties are mostly established with invariance arguments whereas liveness properties require the use of well-founded orders.

Surprisingly, this distinction can often be ignored in model-checking [CES86, LP85, QS81, VW86]. Indeed, model checking can handle arbitrary temporal formulas which can represent both safety and liveness properties. Nevertheless, it has been noticed that restricting model-checking like techniques to safety properties can lead to better verification algorithms [BFG+91, BFH90, JJ89]. Intuitively, this can be understood by the fact that safety properties can be checked by only considering the finite behaviors of a system whereas liveness properties are only meaningful for infinite behaviors. Representing infinite behaviors requires the use of concepts such as automata on infinite words or trees [Büc62, Rab69] which are significantly harder to manipulate than their finite word or tree counterparts [Saf88, SVW87].

In this paper, we explore whether partial-order model-checking techniques such as those of [GW91, Val90] also benefit from being restricted to safety properties. The motivation for partial-order verification methods is that representing concurrency by interleaving is usually semantically adequate but quite often extremely wasteful. This wastefulness plagues model checking as well as other finite-state verification techniques since it creeps in when constructing the global state graph corresponding to a concurrent program. In [God90, PL90, Val89] among others, it is shown that most of the state explosion due to the modeling of concurrency by

---

*This research is supported by the European Community ESPRIT BRA project SPEC (3096).

interleaving can be avoided. For instance, the method used in [God90] is to build a state-graph where usually only one (rather than all) interleaving of the execution of concurrent events is represented. This reduced state-graph can then still be viewed as correctly representing the concurrent program by giving it an interpretation based on Mazurkiewicz's trace theory [Maz86].

We first turn to the grand-father of finite-state verification problems: deadlock detection. We show that for this problem, the algorithm of [God90] can be strongly simplified and improved. The main idea of the simplification is that since we are seeking deadlocks, one can generate a global representation of the program that chooses amongst independent events in a completely arbitrary way. The choices can even be completely "unfair" since, if there is a deadlock, favored processes will anyway eventually be blocked and the deadlock will be detected. This simplification leads to an algorithm that can be more easily and efficiently implemented than the one of [God90] and that often generates substantially fewer states.

Our next step is to turn to the verification of general safety properties. The approach we use here is that of "on the fly verification" [VW86, CVWY90, JJ89, HPOG89, FM91, JJ91]. Namely, we represent the safety property (or rather its complement) by an automaton on finite words and we check that the accepting states of this automaton are not accessible in its product with the automata representing the program. We thus reduce the problem of verifying safety properties to a state accessibility problem. This problem is in turn reduced by a simple transformation of the program and of the specification to a deadlock detection problem to which we apply our new algorithm.

The paper ends with a comparison between our contributions and related work.

2   A Representation of Concurrent Systems

We consider a concurrent program P composed of n concurrent processes P_i. Each process is described by a finite automaton A_i on finite words over an alphabet Σ_i. Formally, an automaton is a tuple $A = (\Sigma, S, \Delta, s_0)$, where Σ is an alphabet, S is a finite set of states, $\Delta \subseteq S \times \Sigma \times S$ is a transition relation, and $s_0 \in S$ is the starting state.

We consider automata without acceptance conditions. Thus a word $w = a_0 a_1 \ldots a_{n-1}$ is accepted by an automaton A if there is a sequence of states $\sigma = s_0 \ldots s_n$ such that s_0 is the starting state of A and, for all $0 \leq i \leq n-1$, $(s_i, a_i, s_{i+1}) \in \Delta$. We call such a sequence σ an execution of A on w. A state s is reachable from s_0 (notation $s_0 \overset{w}{\Rightarrow} s$) if there is some word $w = a_0 a_1 \ldots a_{n-1}$ and some execution $\sigma = s_0 \ldots s_n$ of A on w such that $s = s_n$.

An automaton A_G representing the joint global behavior of the processes P_i can be computed by taking the product of the automata describing each process. Actions that appear in several processes are synchronized, others are interleaved. Formally, the product ($\times$) of two (generalization to the product of n automata is immediate) automata $A_1 = (\Sigma_1, S_1, \Delta_1, s_{01})$ and $A_2 = (\Sigma_2, S_2, \Delta_2, s_{02})$ is the automaton $A = (\Sigma, S, \Delta, s_0)$ defined by

- $\Sigma = \Sigma_1 \cup \Sigma_2$,

- $S = S_1 \times S_2$, $s_0 = (s_{01}, s_{02})$,

- $((s,t), a, (u,v)) \in \Delta$ when

    - $a \in \Sigma_1 \cap \Sigma_2$ and $(s,a,u) \in \Delta_1$ and $(t,a,v) \in \Delta_2$,

$-$ $a \in \Sigma_1 \setminus \Sigma_2$ and $(s, a, u) \in \Delta_1$ and $v = t$,

$-$ $a \in \Sigma_2 \setminus \Sigma_1$ and $u = s$ and $(t, a, v) \in \Delta_2$.

Let $\Delta \subseteq S \times \Sigma \times S$ denote the transition relation of the product A_G of the n automata A_i. For each transition $t = (\mathbf{s}, a, \mathbf{s}') \in \Delta$ with $\mathbf{s} = (s_1, s_2, \ldots, s_n)$ and $\mathbf{s}' = (s'_1, s'_2, \ldots, s'_n)$, the sets (by extension, we consider the states of A_G as sets in the following definitions)

- ${}^{\bullet}t = \{s_i \in \mathbf{s} : (s_i, a, s'_i) \in \Delta_i\}$,

- $t^{\bullet} = \{s'_i \in \mathbf{s}' : (s_i, a, s'_i) \in \Delta_i\}$ and

- ${}^{\bullet}t^{\bullet} = {}^{\bullet}t \cup t^{\bullet}$

are called respectively the *preset*, the *postset* and the *proximity* of the transition t. Intuitively, the *preset*, resp. the *postset*, of a transition $t = (\mathbf{s}, a, \mathbf{s}')$ of A_G represents the states of the A_i's that synchronize together on a, respectively *before* and *after* this transition. We say that the A_i's with a nonempty preset and postset for a transition t are *active* for this transition.

Two transitions $t_1 = (\mathbf{s}_1, a_1, \mathbf{s}'_1)$, $t_2 = (\mathbf{s}_2, a_2, \mathbf{s}'_2) \in \Delta$ are said to be equivalent (notation $\equiv$) iff

$$ {}^{\bullet}t_1 = {}^{\bullet}t_2 \wedge t_1^{\bullet} = t_2^{\bullet} \wedge a_1 = a_2. $$

Intuitively, two equivalent transitions represent the same transition but correspond to distinct occurrences of this transition. These occurrences can only differ by the states of the A_i's that are not active for the transition. We denote by T the set of equivalence classes defined over Δ by $\equiv$.

3 Efficiently Detecting Deadlocks

A deadlock in a system composed of n concurrent processes P_i is defined as a reachable state of the system in which all processes P_i are blocked, i.e. where no transition is executable. Detecting deadlocks is usually performed by an exhaustive enumeration of all reachable states of the automaton A_G corresponding to the product of the n automata A_i. This enumeration amounts to exploring all possible transition sequences the system is able to perform and storing all intermediate states reached during this exploration. In concurrent systems, the number of reachable states can be very large: this is the well-known "state explosion" phenomenon. This combinatorial explosion limits both the applicability and the efficiency of the classical method.

In this section, we present a new simple method for detecting deadlocks without computing and storing all reachable states of the concurrent system. The basic idea is to describe the behavior of the system by means of partial orders rather than by sequences. More precisely, we use Mazurkiewicz's traces [Maz86] as a semantic model.

Traces are defined as equivalence classes of sequences. A trace represents a set of sequences defined over an alphabet Σ that only differ by the order of adjacent symbols which are independent according to a dependency relation D. For instance, if a and b are two symbols of Σ which are independent according to D, the trace $[ab]_{(\Sigma, D)}$ represents the two sequences ab and ba. A trace corresponds to a partial ordering of symbols and represents all linearizations of this partial order. If two independent symbols occur next to each other in a sequence of a trace, the order

```
1. Initialize: Stack is empty; H is empty;
             enter s₀ in H;
             push (s₀,∅) onto Stack;
2. Loop: while Stack ≠ ∅ do {
             pop (s,Sleep) from Stack;
             T = select_transitions(s,Sleep);
             if T = ∅ ∧ Sleep = ∅ then print "Deadlock!"
             for all t ∈ T do {
                 s' = (s \ •t) ∪ t•;
                 if s' is NOT already in H then {
                     enter s' in H;
                     push (s',sleep_attached_with(t)) onto Stack;
                 }
             }
       }
```

Figure 1: Deadlock Detection Algorithm

of their occurrence is irrelevant since they occur concurrently in the partial order corresponding to that trace.

To describe the behavior of the concurrent system represented by A_G in terms of traces, we define the *dependency* in A_G as the relation $D_{A_G} \subseteq T \times T$ such that

$$(t_1, t_2) \in D_{A_G} \text{ iff } {}^\bullet t_1^\bullet \cap {}^\bullet t_2^\bullet \neq \emptyset.$$

The complement of D_{A_G} is called the *independency* in A_G. Given an alphabet and a dependency relation, a trace is fully characterized by only one of its linearizations (sequences). Thus, *given the set of transitions T and the dependency relation D_{A_G} defined above, the behavior of A_G is fully investigated by exploring only one sequence (interleaving) for each possible trace (partial ordering) the system is able to perform.*

Note that *all* deadlocks of A_G will be detected during this exploration. Indeed, for each deadlock, there exists at least one transition sequence w leading to this deadlock from the starting state. Moreover, all other sequences belonging to the same equivalence class $[w]_{(T,D_{A_G})}$ also lead to the same deadlock. Thus, for detecting this deadlock, it is sufficient to explore only one of these sequences which can be chosen arbitrarily. This deadlock-preserving property of partial-order semantics was already pointed out in [Gai88, Val88] among others.

Figure 1 presents an algorithm for performing this exploration. The main data structures used are a *Stack* to hold the states from which the behavior of the system remains to be investigated, and a hash table H to store the states from which the behavior of the system has already been investigated. This algorithm looks like a classical exploration of all possible transition sequences. The difference is that, instead of executing systematically *all* transitions enabled in a state, we choose *only some* of these transitions to be executed. The basic idea for selecting amongst the enabled transitions those that have to be executed is the following. Whenever several independent transitions are enabled at a given state, we execute only one of these transitions. This will ensure that we generate only one interleaving of these independent transitions. When enabled transitions are dependent, their executions lead to different traces corresponding to different nondeterministic choices which can be made by the system. We then have to execute all these transitions in order to consider all possible traces the system is able to perform. The function **select_transitions** described in Figure 2 performs this selection.

To select amongst the enabled transitions those that have to be executed, the function **select_transitions** uses the notion of *sleep set*. A sleep set is a set of transitions. One sleep set is associated with each state s reached during the search. It is stored onto the stack with s. The sleep set associated with s is a set of transitions that are *enabled* in s but *will not be executed* from s. The sleep set associated with the initial state s_0 is the empty set. The function **select_transitions** uses the sleep set associated to the current state and returns a set of transitions that have to be executed. To each transition t of this set, it "attaches" the sleep set which will be associated to the state $s' = (s \setminus {}^\bullet t) \cup t^\bullet$ reached after the execution of t.

In what follows, two transitions t_1, t_2 are referred to as being in *conflict* iff $({}^\bullet t_1 \cap {}^\bullet t_2) \neq \emptyset$. Checking if two enabled transitions are dependent can be done by checking if they are in conflict. Two transitions t, t' are in *indirect conflict* iff $\exists t_1, \ldots, t_n : ({}^\bullet t \cap {}^\bullet t_1) \neq \emptyset \wedge ({}^\bullet t_1 \cap {}^\bullet t_2) \neq \emptyset \wedge \ldots \wedge ({}^\bullet t_{n-1} \cap {}^\bullet t_n) \neq \emptyset \wedge ({}^\bullet t_n \cap {}^\bullet t') \neq \emptyset$.

The function **select_transitions** performs two distinct tasks: it selects the transitions to be executed and it computes the sleep sets to be passed along with these transitions. We first describe the selection of transitions. Thereafter, we will describe the role of sleep sets and how they are computed. The selection of transitions starts with the enabled transitions that are not in the sleep set associated to the current state. Two cases can occur.

1. There is a transition that is only in conflict or indirect conflict with enabled transitions. Then, this transition and all the transitions that are in conflict or indirect conflict with it are selected. Indeed, these transitions are independent with respect to the rest of the system and their occurrence can not be influenced by it. An interesting special case is that of an enabled transition that is not in conflict with any other transition. In this situation, this transition alone is selected.

2. There is no transition that is only in conflict or indirect conflict with enabled transitions, i.e. each transition is in conflict or indirect conflict with at least one nonenabled transition. In this case all enabled transitions have to be explored. Indeed, let t be an enabled transition that is in conflict with a transition x that is not enabled in the current state (this is a situation of *confusion* [Rei85]). It is possible that x will become enabled later because of the execution of some other transitions independent with t. At that time, the execution of t could be replaced by the execution of x. Thus when we select t, we also have to check if the execution of t could be replaced by the execution of x after the execution of some other enabled transitions independent with t (i.e. to check if the confusion actually leads to a "conflict"): we thus have to select all enabled transitions that are dependent (as usual) and independent with t, i.e. all enabled transitions. Note that, if a confusion does not lead to a "conflict", several sequences corresponding to prefixes of several interleavings of a single trace will be explored.

The selection procedure we have given can lead to *independent* transitions simultaneously being selected. This can cause the wasteful exploration of several interleavings of these transitions. "Sleep sets" are introduced to control this wastefulness. Imagine, for instance, that

```
select_transitions(s,Sleep) {
    T = enabled(s)\Sleep;
    if ∃t ∈ T :conflict(t)⊆ enabled(s) then selection= {t} ∪ (conflict(t)∩T);
    else selection= T;
    result= ∅;
    while selection ≠ ∅ {
        t =one_element_of(selection);
        result=result ∪ attach(t, Sleep);
        Sleep = Sleep ∪ {t};
        selection=selection \{t};
    }
    return(result);
}
```

Figure 2: Selection Amongst Enabled Transitions

we have a situation of "confusion" with two enabled *independent* transitions a and b, and that a is in conflict with only one nonenabled transition c. We have to explore both the result of transition a and of transition b. Choosing transition a amounts to choosing one interleaving of a and b to be explored. The purpose of exploring the result of transition b is to check if it will eventually enable the transition c with which a is in conflict. So, when doing this, there is no point in exploring the result of transition a. Thus a is introduced in the sleep set that will be associated to the state reached after the execution of transition b. In the remainder of the search starting at that state, a will be only removed from the sleep set when a transition which is in conflict (i.e. *dependent*) with it is selected.

More generally, when independent transitions are selected, the computation of the sleep sets is as follows. One transition is selected first. This transition (let us call it t_1) is the first step in the exploration of *one* interleaving of the transitions. Its sleep set is the current sleep set unmodified except for the elimination of transitions that are dependent with it. When the next transition (t_2) is selected, t_1 is added to its sleep set as long as it is not dependent with it. One then proceeds in a similar way with the remaining transitions. Specifically, when a transition t_i is selected, its sleep set is augmented with all previous transitions (t_j with $j < i$) that are not dependent with it. Note that if only one transition is selected, the sleep set is passed on unmodified.

Let us now see how the procedure we have described is implemented in the algorithm of Figure 2. The function conflict(t) returns the transitions that are in conflict and in indirect conflict with t. The function enabled(s) returns all enabled transitions in state s. The first step is to ignore the transitions that are in the sleep set associated with the current state. If there is a transition t among the remaining enabled transitions such that all transitions in conflict(t) are enabled, then t and the transitions of conflict(t) that are not in the current sleep set are selected (in practice, if there are several such enabled transitions, one chooses one that minimizes the number of transitions in the selection set). The other remaining possibility is that of a case of "confusion" in which all enabled transitions that are not in the sleep set are selected.

The "while" loop then computes the sleep sets that have to be attached to the selected tran-

	Classical Algorithm			New Algorithm		
	Total Run Time (sec)	States	Trans.	Total Run Time (sec)	States	Trans.
rr4	0.7	144	368	0.1	20	24
rr5	1.6	360	1100	0.2	25	30
rr6	4.6	864	3072	0.3	30	36
rr7	12.7	2016	8176	0.3	35	42

Table 1: Analysis of the Round Robin Access Protocol

sitions. For doing this, we use the procedure **attach**(t,*Sleep*) which attaches to the transition t the transitions of *Sleep* that are independent with t, i.e. the set $\{t' \in Sleep : (^\bullet t \cap {}^\bullet t') = \emptyset\}$. The first transition to be selected in the "while" loop thus simply inherits the current sleep set minus the transitions that are dependent with it. The sleep set of the following transitions is then constructed from the inherited sleep set augmented with the already selected transitions.

All this ensures that *at least one* interleaving for each trace of the system is explored while still avoiding the construction of all possible interleavings of enabled independent transitions. The practical advantage of the algorithm presented here is that, by construction, the state-graph G' explored by this algorithm is a "sub-graph" of the usual state-graph G representing all possible transition sequences of the system. (By sub-graph, we mean that the states of G' are states of G and the transitions of G' are transitions of G.) Moreover, the function **select_transitions** required for constructing G' can be implemented in such a way that the order of its time complexity is the same as the one of the function **enabled** that is used to construct G. Thus our algorithm never uses more resources than (i.e. has the same worst-case asymptotic complexity as) the classical state space exploration algorithm and is often much more efficient in practice. Of course, if no simultaneous enabled independent transitions are encountered during the search, our method becomes equivalent to the classical one.

Table 1 compares the performance of a classical depth-first search algorithm against the deadlock detection algorithm presented in this section for analyzing the Round Robin Access Protocol described in [GS90] for a ring of 4 (rr4) to 7 (rr7) participants. One clearly sees that our method is much more efficient, *both in time and memory*, than the classical one. With our method, the number of states and transitions grows in a linear way with the number of participants in the protocol.

The algorithm presented in this paper is a simplified and improved version of the one presented in [God90] that was designed to generate at least one interleaving for each possible trace of a concurrent program. The simplification comes essentially from the fact that, when looking for deadlocks, if the algorithm detects that one of the concurrent processes can loop in the current trace being explored, the exploration of this trace can stop without generating the remainder of this trace as it had to be done in [God90]. Hence, the number of explored states and transitions with the new algorithm presented here is always less than or equal to the number explored with the algorithm described in [God90]. Moreover, in the present version, it is no longer necessary to store explicitly the transitions of the state-graph and the additional information that was required in the algorithm of [God90]. Hence the present version always requires less resources.

4 Verifying Safety Properties

In this section, we show how the reachability of a global state, the reachability of a local state, and finally the verification of a safety property can be reduced to deadlock detection. Note that we cannot directly use the algorithm of Section 3 to determine reachability since it usually does not generate all reachable states.

The algorithm presented in the previous section can easily be used to check if a given *global* state $s = (s_1, s_2, \ldots, s_n)$ of a concurrent program P is reachable. This is done by adding to all A_i's a transition $(s_i, \delta, stop_i)$ for $s_i \in s$. We call the modified system P_M. Then, the state $s' = (stop_1, stop_2, \ldots, stop_n)$ is a deadlock of P_M iff the state s is reachable. Indeed, the synchronization of all processes on the transition δ leading to s' in P_M is possible only if the global state s is reachable. Hence checking the reachability of s amounts to checking if s' is a deadlock of the modified system P_M.

Let us now turn to the problem of checking the reachability of a given *local* state ℓ. A local state is defined as an incompletely specified global state. In other words, it is a tuple of states of some (but not all) processes. For convenience, we define a local state ℓ as a subset of $\bigcup_i S_i$ such that, for each $1 \leq i \leq n$, $|\ell \cap S_i| \leq 1$. Checking for the reachability of a local state ℓ means checking for the reachability of *some* global state $s = (s_1, s_2, \ldots, s_n)$ such that $\ell \subset s$. One can reduce the problem of checking the reachability of a local state ℓ to that of checking the reachability of global states (and hence to deadlock detection) by enumerating all global states s such that $\ell \subset s$ and checking if at least one of these is reachable. Unfortunately, this approach is not practical since the number of states s such that $\ell \subset s$ can be very large.

We need a more direct reduction. A first step is to apply the construction we used above for transforming global reachability to deadlock detection. Specifically, we add to each automaton A_i that has a state $s_i \in \ell$ a transition $(s_i, \delta, stop_i)$. Let the modified system be P_M. Unfortunately, the reachability of ℓ does not induce a deadlock in P_M since processes that do no have a state in ℓ can still be active. We thus have a form of *livelock*. To simplify the following discussion, we denote by P_ℓ the processes that have a state in ℓ and by $P_{\neg \ell}$ those that do not have such a state.

The next step is to transform the system P_M in such a way that a deadlock rather than a livelock is reached if ℓ is reachable. The idea is to ensure that the processes in $P_{\neg \ell}$ can be blocked whenever the livelock of P_M corresponding to ℓ is reached. For each process $P_i \in P_{\neg \ell}$, we add a transition $(s_i, \delta_i, stop_i)$ to one state s_i of each cycle occurring in the graph A_i of P_i. Also, for each process $P_i \in P_\ell$, we add the transition $(stop_i, \delta_j, stop_i)$ for each j such that $P_j \in P_{\neg \ell}$. Let $P_{M'}$ denote the result of this transformation. It is easy to convince oneself that this transformation does not modify the reachability of ℓ.

The following theorem ensures that the reachability of ℓ can be determined by using our deadlock detection algorithm.

Theorem 4.1 *A local state ℓ of a system P is reachable iff there exists a deadlock s' in $P_{M'}$ such that $stop_i \in s'$ for all i corresponding to a process in P_ℓ.*

Sketch of the Proof: First we use the fact that if ℓ is reachable in P it is reachable in $P_{M'}$. Now, if ℓ is reachable in $P_{M'}$, there exists a global state s such that $\ell \subset s$ and s is reachable.

When the system reaches the state s, the processes in P_ℓ can execute the transition δ and reach their state $stop_i$. The other processes may still have the opportunity to evolve. Even if there are processes P_j in $P_{\neg l}$ that are able to remain active, by construction, we know that there exists at least one execution for each of these P_j that will eventually lead to a state where a transition δ_j is possible. This transition is synchronized with the processes in P_ℓ and can occur since the processes in P_ℓ are in their state $stop_i$ where they are ready to synchronize on any transition δ_j. After this synchronization, the process P_j reaches its state $stop_j$ and is blocked for ever. The same will happen for all other processes P_j in $P_{\neg l}$. Hence we reach a global state where all processes are in their state $stop_i$. This is a deadlock state. Indeed, in that state only the processes in P_ℓ have possible transitions in this state and these are synchronized with the processes in $P_{\neg \ell}$ which are blocked.

The other direction of the theorem is immediate to establish. ∎

One may wonder if adding the states $stop_i$ could increase the number of reachable states of the system. An analysis of our reduction shows that this is not the case if we stop the search as soon as a state s such that $\ell \subset s$ is reached.

We can now turn to the verification of safety properties. Safety properties can be represented by prefix closed finite automata on finite words [AS87, BFG+91]. We assume such a representation A_S and proceed as follows:

1. Build the automaton $A_{\neg S}$ corresponding to the complement of A_S. Since A_S is prefix closed, $A_{\neg S}$ is naturally an automaton with only one accepting state (denoted X).

2. Check if the local state X is reachable in the concurrent system composed of the automata A_i, $1 \leq i \leq n$, and of the automaton $A_{\neg S}$.

Note that this framework is still applicable for safety properties represented by more than one communicating automaton.

5 Comparison with Other Work and Conclusions

We have presented a new algorithm for detecting deadlocks. We have shown that this algorithm never uses more resources and can be much more efficient than the classical exploration of the whole state space of the system being checked. This algorithm is a simplified and improved version of the one presented in [God90]. The basic idea of the simplification is close to the one used in [Val88] where Valmari's stubborn set method is adapted to deadlock detection for Petri nets. The advantages of our method are that it can be very easily implemented and that its cost per state explored is comparable to the one incurred when doing an exhaustive exploration of the state space. Our method is also applicable to Petri nets as well as to communicating Petri nets. Finally, our approach to verifying general safety properties by using a deadlock detection algorithm is new.

Our method has the advantages of "on the fly verification", i.e. we compose the program and the property without ever building an automaton representing the global behavior of the program. Maybe surprisingly, this automaton is often smaller than the automaton for the program alone because the property acts as a constraint on the behavior of the program. Our method thus has a head start over methods that require an explicit representation for the global behavior of the program to be built. Note that our method is fully compatible with techniques for compactly representing the state space as described in [Hol88, CVWY90].

The main principles of our verification technique can also be profitably used for some applications in the field of Artificial Intelligence. In [GK91], it is shown that the algorithm presented here can be used as a search method suitable for planning the reactions of an agent operating in a highly unpredictable environment.

Acknowledgements

We wish to thank Costas Courcoubetis, Froduald Kabanza, Antti Valmari, Mihalis Yannakakis and anonymous referees for helpful comments on this paper.

References

[AS87]　B. Alpern and F. B. Schneider. Recognizing safety and liveness. *Distributed Computing*, 2:117–126, 1987.

[BFG+91]　A. Bouajjani, J.-C. Fernandez, S. Graf, C. Rodriguez, and J. Sifakis. Safety for branching semantics. In *Proc. 12th Int. Colloquium on Automata, Languages and Programming*. Lecture Notes in Computer Science, Springer-Verlag, July 1991.

[BFH90]　A. Bouajjani, J. C. Fernandez, and N. Halbwachs. On the verification of safety properties. Technical Report SPECTRE L12, IMAG, Grenoble, March 1990.

[Büc62]　J.R. Büchi. On a decision method in restricted second order arithmetic. In *Proc. Internat. Congr. Logic, Method and Philos. Sci. 1960*, pages 1–12, Stanford, 1962. Stanford University Press.

[CES86]　E.M. Clarke, E.A. Emerson, and A.P. Sistla. Automatic verification of finite-state concurrent systems using temporal logic specifications. *ACM Transactions on Programming Languages and Systems*, 8(2):244–263, January 1986.

[CVWY90]　C. Courcoubetis, M. Vardi, P. Wolper, and M. Yannakakis. Memory efficient algorithms for the verification of temporal properties. In *Proc. Workshop on Computer Aided Verification*, Rutgers, June 1990.

[FM91]　J.C. Fernandez and L. Mounier. On the fly verification of behavioural equivalences and preorders. In *Proc. Workshop on Computer Aided Verification*, Aalborg, July 1991.

[Gai88]　H. Gaifman. Modeling concurrency by partial orders and nonlinear transition systems. In *Linear Time, Branching Time and Partial Order in Logics and Models for Concurrency*, volume 354 of *Lecture Notes in Computer Science*, pages 467–488, 1988.

[GK91]　P. Godefroid and F. Kabanza. An efficient reactive planner for synthesizing reactive plans. In *Proceedings of AAAI-91*, volume 2, pages 640–645, Anaheim, July 1991.

[God90]　P. Godefroid. Using partial orders to improve automatic verification methods. In *Proc. Workshop on Computer Aided Verification*, Rutgers, June 1990.

[GS90]　S. Graf and B. Steffen. Using interface specifications for compositional reduction. In *Proc. Workshop on Computer Aided Verification*, Rutgers, June 1990.

[GW91]　P. Godefroid and P. Wolper. A partial approach to model checking. In *Proceedings of the 6th IEEE Symposium on Logic in Computer Science*, pages 406–415, Amsterdam, July 1991.

[Hol88]   G. Holzmann. An improved protocol reachability analysis technique. *Software Practice and Experience*, pages 137–161, February 1988.

[HPOG89]   N. Halbwachs, D. Pilaud, F. Ouabdesselam, and A.C. Glory. Specifying, programming and verifying real-time systems, using a synchronous declarative language. In *Workshop on automatic verification methods for finite state systems*, volume 407 of *Lecture Notes in Computer Science*, pages 213–231, Grenoble, June 1989.

[JJ89]   C. Jard and T. Jeron. On-line model-checking for finite linear temporal logic specifications. In *Workshop on automatic verification methods for finite state systems*, volume 407 of *Lecture Notes in Computer Science*, pages 189–196, Grenoble, June 1989.

[JJ91]   C. Jard and T. Jeron. Bounded-memory algorithms for verification on the fly. In *Proc. Workshop on Computer Aided Verification*, Aalborg, July 1991.

[LP85]   O. Lichtenstein and A. Pnueli. Checking that finite state concurrent programs satisfy their linear specification. In *Proceedings of the Twelfth ACM Symposium on Principles of Programming Languages*, pages 97–107, New Orleans, January 1985.

[Maz86]   A. Mazurkiewicz. Trace theory. In *Petri Nets: Applications and Relationships to Other Models of Concurrency, Advances in Petri Nets 1986, Part II; Proceedings of an Advanced Course*, volume 255 of *Lecture Notes in Computer Science*, pages 279–324, 1986.

[MP84]   Z. Manna and A. Pnueli. Adequate proof principles for invariance and liveness properties of concurrent programs. *Science of Computer Programming*, 4:257–289, 1984.

[OL82]   S. Owicki and L. Lamport. Proving liveness properties of concurrent programs. *ACM Transactions on Programming Languages and Systems*, 4(3):455–495, July 1982.

[PL90]   D. K. Probst and H. F. Li. Using partial-order semantics to avoid the state explosion problem in asynchronous systems. In *Proc. Workshop on Computer Aided Verification*, Rutgers, June 1990.

[QS81]   J.P. Quielle and J. Sifakis. Specification and verification of concurrent systems in cesar. In *Proc. 5th Int'l Symp. on Programming*, volume 137 of *Lecture Notes in Computer Science*, pages 337–351, 1981.

[Rab69]   M.O. Rabin. Decidability of second order theories and automata on infinite trees. *Transaction of the AMS*, 141:1–35, 1969.

[Saf88]   Shmuel Safra. On the complexity of omega-automata. In *Proceedings of the 29th IEEE Symposium on Foundations of Computer Science*, White Plains, oct 1988.

[SVW87]   A.P. Sistla, M.Y. Vardi, and P. Wolper. The complementation problem for Büchi automata with applications to temporal logic. *Theoretical Computer Science*, 49:217–237, 1987.

[Val88]   A. Valmari. Error detection by reduced reachability graph generation. In *Proc. 9th International Conference on Application and Theory of Petri Nets*, pages 95–112, Venice, 1988.

[Val89]   A. Valmari. Stubborn sets for reduced state space generation. In *Proc. 10th International Conference on Application and Theory of Petri Nets*, volume 2, pages 1–22, Bonn, 1989.

[Val90]   A. Valmari. A stubborn attack on state explosion. In *Proc. Workshop on Computer Aided Verification*, Rutgers, June 1990.

[VW86]   M.Y. Vardi and P. Wolper. An automata-theoretic approach to automatic program verification. In *Proc. Symp. on Logic in Computer Science*, pages 322–331, Cambridge, june 1986.

Complexity Results for POMSET Languages

Extended Abstract – CAV '91 proceedings[1]

Joan Feigenbaum	Jeremy A. Kahn	Carsten Lund
AT&T Bell Laboratories	Math Department	AT&T Bell Laboratories
600 Mountain Avenue	University of California	600 Mountain Avenue
Murray Hill, NJ 07974	Berkeley, CA 97420	Murray Hill, NJ 07974

Abstract

Pratt [13] introduced POMSETs (partially ordered multisets) in order to describe and analyze concurrent systems. A POMSET P gives a set of temporal constraints that any correct execution of a given concurrent system must satisfy. Let $L(P)$ (the *language of* P) denote the set of all system executions that satisfy the constraints given by P. We show the following for finite POMSETs P, Q, and system execution x.

- The POMSET Language Membership Problem (given x and P, is $x \in L(P)$?) is NP-complete.

- The POMSET Language Containment Problem (given P and Q, is $L(P) \subseteq L(Q)$?) is Π_2^P-complete.

- The POMSET Language Equality Problem (given P and Q, is $L(P) = L(Q)$?) is at least as hard as the graph-isomorphism problem.

- The POMSET Language Size Problem (given P, how many x are in $L(P)$?) is span-P-complete.

1   Introduction

Verification of concurrent systems has been studied as a formal language-containment problem for a number of years [1, 15, 5]. In this formulation, one is given a model M represented by a finite transition structure such as a finite state machine, automaton or Petri net (sometimes termed an *implementation*), together with an abstraction A of the model, represented by an automaton or logic formula (sometimes termed a *specification*, defining a property to be proved about the model M). The verification problem consists of testing whether $L(M) \subseteq L(A)$, where $L(X)$ is the formal language associated with X. Typically, M is large and therefore defined implicitly in terms of components. An inherent difficulty in this approach is the computational complexity of the language containment test as a function of the size of the representation of M in terms of components. For example, if M is defined in terms of coordinating state machines, then the size of M grows geometrically with the number of components defining it, and the language containment

---

[1]Because of space limitations, some of the results in this extended abstract are stated without proof. All proofs are given in the journal version of the paper, which is available in preprint form from the first author.

problem is PSPACE-complete [6, AL6, page 266]. This computational complexity issue has been addressed by a number of heuristics, notably homomorphic reduction [11, 10], inductive methods [2, 12], binary decision diagrams [4, 3, 16], and partial orders [7, 14].

In this paper, we consider the language containment problem for POMSETs (partially ordered multisets), which were introduced by Pratt [13]. Both the implementation and the specification of a system can be represented by POMSETs as follows. Let Σ denote a finite set of *actions* that the system can perform. So actions are things like "send 0 to processor p," "receive message m from processor q," and "wait." Each *vertex* v in the POMSET P corresponds to a distinct *event*. Intuitively, an event is a logical "step" taken by the system. The *label* $l(v)$ is an element of Σ, and distinct vertices may have the same label; this corresponds to the fact that a given action (say "send 0 to processor p") may be performed several times by the system during any execution. Each *arc* (v, w) in P represents a *constraint* of the form "event v must occur before event w in any execution of the system." For example, if $l(v)$ is "receive message m from processor p," and $l(w)$ is "if the value of register r is equal to m then signal processor q_1, else signal processor q_2," then the arc (v, w) has the obvious interpretation. The *language* of P is simply the set of all correct executions of the system.

The following example motivates the use of POMSETs. The language $L = \{ab_{i_1}b_{i_2} \cdots b_{i_n}a\}$, where $i_1 i_2 \cdots i_n$ is a permutation of $12 \cdots n$ and all of the b_i's are distinct, arises often in the description of concurrent processes. Its meaning is "perform action a, then perform each of the actions b_1 through b_n in any order, then perform action a again." An NFA that accepts L must have at least 2^n states. POMSETs, however, offer a much more compact representation: The $(n + 2)$-node POMSET of Figure 1 represents L.

Formally, the problem of interest is: Given POMSETs P and Q, is the language of P a subset of the language of Q? We call this the PLC problem, for POMSET Language Containment.

The POMSET P represents the implementation and Q the specification. We show that the PLC problem is Π_2^p-complete.

Note that P and Q are both finite POMSETs. Thus the languages in question are finite, and the strings in them are of finite length. If we were presenting an algorithm for PLC, this finiteness restriction would render the algorithm impractical, because real concurrent systems produce infinite sets of infinite sequences. However, we are giving a lower bound on the complexity of PLC, and hence the finiteness restriction makes our result all the more meaningful: Even in this restricted case, the problem appears to be intractable.

We also give an NP-completeness result for the following simpler problem: Given a

POMSET P and a string x, is x in the language of P? This is called the PLM problem, for POMSET Language Membership.

Once again, the finiteness restriction only strengthens our result, because we are providing a lower bound rather than an algorithm.

In the journal version of this paper, we also consider the following two problems. The POMSET Language Equality problem (PLE) is: Given two POMSETs P and Q, is the language of P equal to the language of Q? The POMSET Language Size problem (PLS) is: Give a POMSET P, what is the number of strings in the language of P? We show that PLE is at least as hard as the graph isomorphism problem and that PLS is complete for the complexity class span-P (cf. Köbler, Schöning, and Toran [9]).

2   Definitions and Notation

Throughout this paper, P and Q denote (finite) POMSETs, and x denotes a (finite) string. We now fix these ideas precisely.

Definition 2.1 *A POMSET P is a triple (V, A, l). The **vertex set** $V(P)$ consists of a finite number n of distinct elements $\{v_1, \ldots, v_n\}$, called the **events**. The **arc set** $A(P)$ consists of a set of ordered pairs (v, w), where v and w are distinct elements of V, called the **constraints**. The directed graph $(V(P), A(P))$ is acyclic. The mapping $l : V \to \Sigma$ assigns an **action** to each event in V, and $l(v)$ is called the **label** of vertex v.*

Recall that a linear ordering on $V = \{v_1, \ldots, v_n\}$ *extends* a partial ordering of V if, for all pairs v_i, v_j of distinct elements in V, $v_i < v_j$ in the partial ordering implies that $v_i < v_j$ in the linear ordering. Technically, a DAG (directed acyclic graph) may not be a partial ordering, because it may not be transitively closed. When we say that a linear ordering on V extends the DAG (V, A), we mean that it extends the transitive closure of the DAG.

Definition 2.2 *The **language** $L(P)$ of a POMSET $P = (V, A, l)$ is a subset of Σ^n, where $n = |V(P)|$. The string $\sigma_1 \cdots \sigma_n$ is in $L(P)$ if there is a linear ordering $v_{i_1} \cdots v_{i_n}$ of the vertex set V that extends the DAG (V, A) and satisfies $l(v_{i_j}) = \sigma_j$, for $1 \leq j \leq n$.*

3 PLC is Π_2^p-Complete

Theorem 3.1 *The PLC problem is* Π_2^p-complete.

Proof: First note that it is obvious that PLC is in Π_2^p. Suppose that we wish to know whether $L(P)$ is contained in $L(Q)$, where $V(P) = \{v_1, \ldots, v_n\}$ and $V(Q) = \{w_1, \ldots, w_n\}$. The following is a Π_2^p expression for $L(P) \subseteq L(Q)$: For all linear orderings $v_{i_1} \cdots v_{i_n}$, there exists a linear ordering $w_{j_1} \cdots w_{j_n}$ such that if $v_{i_1} \cdots v_{i_n}$ extends $A(P)$, then $w_{j_1} \cdots w_{j_n}$ extends $A(Q)$ and $l(v_{i_k}) = l(w_{j_k})$ for $1 \le k \le n$. The hypothesis "if $v_{i_1} \cdots v_{i_n}$ extends $A(P)$" is equivalent to "if $l(v_{i_1}) \cdots l(v_{i_n}) \in L(P)$," and the conclusion "then $w_{j_1} \cdots w_{j_n}$ extends $A(Q)$ and $l(v_{i_k}) = l(w_{j_k})$ for $1 \le k \le n$" is equivalent to "$l(w_{i_1}) \cdots l(w_{i_n}) \in L(Q)$ and is equal to $l(v_{i_1}) \cdots l(v_{i_n})$."

It is also obvious that PLC is NP-hard, because PLM is the special case of PLC in which $L(P)$ contains just one string, and PLM is NP-complete (see Section 4 below).

We show Π_2^p-completeness by reduction from the following Π_2^p-complete problem (cf. [6, page 166]).

Normalized B_2^c:

<u>Input</u> : Two sets $\{w_1, \ldots, w_m\}$ and $\{y_1, \ldots, y_n\}$ of boolean variables and a set $\{c_1, \ldots, c_k\}$ of clauses. Each clause is of the form $a \Rightarrow b \vee c \vee d$, where a is either w_i or $\overline{w_i}$ for some i and each of b, c, and d is y_j or $\overline{y_j}$ for some j.

<u>Question</u> : Is it the case that, for every truth assignment to the w_i's, there exists some truth assignment to the y_j's such that every c_l is satisfied?

Given an instance $(W = \{w_1, \ldots, w_m\}, Y = \{y_1, \ldots, y_n\}, C = \{c_1, \ldots, c_k\})$ of normalized B_2^c, we construct an instance (P, Q) of PLC as follows.

In $V(P)$, there are three disjoint sets of vertices. The first group contains n vertices, labeled y_1 through y_n. The second group in $V(P)$ contains $2m+k$ vertices. For $1 \le i \le m$, there are two vertices in this group labeled w_i; we refer to them as "the positive w_i vertex" and "the negative w_i vertex." For $1 \le l \le k$, there is one vertex in the second group labeled c_l. The third group of vertices in $V(P)$ is of size $n + 3k$. There is one vertex in this group labeled y_j, for $1 \le j \le n$, and there are three vertices in the third group labeled c_l, for $1 \le l \le k$. For every clause c_l in which w_i appears on the left side of the implication, there is an arc in $A(P)$ from the positive w_i vertex to the second-group vertex labeled c_l; for every c_l in which $\overline{w_i}$ appears on the left side of the implication, there is an arc in $A(P)$ from the negative w_i vertex to the second-group vertex labeled c_l. Every w vertex in the second group is joined by an arc to every c vertex in the third group. The rest of the arcs that make up $A(P)$ can be seen in Figure 2, where an example of this construction is given. The subscripts are omitted from the labels of some clause vertices in order to reduce clutter.

In $V(Q)$, there are two vertices labeled y_j, for $1 \leq j \leq n$, and two vertices labeled w_i, for $1 \leq i \leq m$. These are referred to as "the positive y_j (resp. w_i) vertex" and "the negative y_j (resp. w_i) vertex." $V(Q)$ also contains four vertices labeled c_l, for $1 \leq l \leq k$. One group of these c vertices is associated with the y vertices; each c vertex in this group has in-degree 1. For each clause c_l in which the literal y_j appears on the right side of the implication, there is an arc from the positive y_j vertex to a c_l vertex. Similarly, for each clause c_l in which the literal $\overline{y_j}$ appears on the right side of the implication, there is an arc from the negative y_j vertex to a c_l vertex. Note that each label c_l appears three times in this group, once for each literal in the clause. The second group of c vertices is associated with the w vertices; each c vertex in this group has in-degree 2. If w_i or $\overline{w_i}$ appears on the left side of the implication in clause c_l, then there are arcs from both the positive w_i vertex and the negative w_i vertex to the c_l vertex in the second group. See Figure 3 for an example of this construction. Once again, subscripts are omitted from some clause vertices to reduce clutter.

Suppose that (P, Q) is a yes-instance of PLC; so $L(P)$ is contained in $L(Q)$. We must show that (W, Y, C) is a yes-instance of B_3^c. Choose an assignment of truth values to the variables in W. We will construct an assignment of truth values to the variables in Y that, together with the initial assignment to those in W, satisfies all the clauses in C.

Consider the string

$$x = y_1 \cdots y_n w_1 \cdots w_m c_{q_1} \cdots c_{q_t} y_1 \cdots y_n w_1 \cdots w_m c_{q_{t+1}} \cdots c_{4k}$$

in $L(P)$ that is formed as follows. The prefix $y_1 \cdots y_n$ comes from the first group of vertices in $V(P)$. In the first substring $w_1 \cdots w_m$, each w_i represents a choice between the positive w_i vertex and the negative w_i vertex within the second group in $V(P)$. The substring $c_{q_1} \cdots c_{q_t}$ corresponds exactly to the clauses that are nontrivial to satisfy: If a clause vertex v in the second group in $V(P)$ is adjacent to the positive w_i vertex and w_i is TRUE in the initial assignment, then $l(v)$ goes into the substring $c_{q_1} \cdots c_{q_t}$; similiarly, if v is adjacent to the negative w_i vertex and w_i is FALSE in the initial assignment, then $l(v)$ goes into the substring $c_{q_1} \cdots c_{q_t}$. The rest of the string x is constructed in any way that is consistent with the constraints in $A(P)$, subject to y's, then w's, then c's.

Note that x is always in $L(P)$. Because (P, Q) is assumed to be a yes-instance of PLC, x is also in $L(Q)$. Consider the vertices $v(c_{q_1}), \ldots, v(c_{q_t})$ in $V(Q)$ that give rise to the substring $c_{q_1} \cdots c_{q_t}$ of x. These vertices must all be in the first group of c vertices in Q – that is, they must be in the group whose incoming arcs start with y's. This is because none of $c_{q_1}, \ldots, c_{q_t}$ is preceded in x by two occurrences of w_i, for any i. If $v(c_{q_1})$

is connected to the positive (resp. negative) y_j vertex, then assign the variable y_j the value TRUE (resp. FALSE). Assign arbitrary values to any remaining y variables. Note that no conflicts arise in making this assignment – that is, each y_j is assigned one value. This is because each y_j symbol appears once in the prefix of x, and hence only one of the two y_j vertices is used; if the y_j vertex that's used is adjacent to two vertices $v(c_{q_{l_1}})$ and $v(c_{q_{l_2}})$, then either y_j appears in both $c_{q_{l_1}}$ and $c_{q_{l_2}}$ or $\overline{y_j}$ appears in both $c_{q_{l_1}}$ and $c_{q_{l_2}}$. This assignment, together with the initial assignment to the w variables, satisfies all of the clauses in C. Because the initial assignment to the w variables was arbitrary, this shows that (W, Y, C) is a yes-instance.

Now suppose that (W, Y, C) is a yes-instance of normalized B_2^c. Let x be an arbitrary element of $L(P)$ in the corresponding instance of PLC. We must show that x is also in $L(Q)$.

We construct a truth assignment that corresponds to x as follow. Each symbol in x comes from a vertex in a linear ordering of $V(P)$ that extends $A(P)$. Take the first occurrence of w_i in x, and see whether it corresponds to the positive w_i vertex or the negative w_i vertex. If positive, assign the variable w_i the value TRUE and, if negative, assign it FALSE. Because (W, Y, C) is a yes-instance, there must be an assignment of truth values to the y variables that, together with the assignment to the w's, satisfies every clause in C. This assignment to the y's corresponds to the prefix $y_1 \cdots y_n$ of x in a way that will become clear below. Denote by A the full assignment to y's and w's.

Call a y vertex or w vertex in $V(Q)$ "active" if it corresponds to the truth assignment A – e.g., the positive y_j vertex is active if and only if the variable y_j is TRUE in A. Now Q is the disjoint union of subPOMSETs Q_1 and Q_2, where Q_1 contains exactly the active y vertices and the c vertices that are connected by arcs from active y vertices, and Q_2 contains exactly the active w vertices and the c vertices that are connected by arcs from active w vertices.

The only nontrivial task involved in finding a linear ordering of $V(Q)$ that extends $A(Q)$ and gives rise to x is this: Suppose that clause c_l contains the variable w_i and that the first occurrence of the symbol c_l in x falls between the two occurrences of the symbol w_i; what is the vertex in $V(Q)$ that gives rise to this first occurrence of c_l? By construction, this vertex can be found in $V(Q_1)$ – that is, the active y vertices correspond to the prefix $y_1 \cdots y_n$ of x. Thus x is in the shuffle of $L(Q_1)$ and $L(Q_2)$, which is $L(Q)$.

There are some special cases of PLC that are easily solved in polynomial time. For example, if each element of Σ occurs at most once as a label in each POMSET, then there is at most one bijection ϕ from $V(Q)$ to $V(P)$, given by the labels. If no such ϕ

exists, $L(P) \not\subseteq L(Q)$. Otherwise, let $T(P)$ (resp. $T(Q)$) be the transitive closure of $A(P)$ (resp. $A(Q)$). It is easily seen that $L(P)$ is contained in $L(Q)$ if and only if, for every arc (v, w) in $T(Q)$, the arc $(\phi(v), \phi(w))$ is in $T(P)$. We call this the *unique-label case* of PLC.

Similarly, the *no-autoconcurrence case* of PLC is solvable in polynomial time. "No autoconcurrence" means that, if v and w are in $V(P)$ (resp. $V(Q)$), and $l(v) = l(w)$, then either (v, w) or (w, v) is in $A(P)$ (resp. $A(Q)$). The no-autoconcurrence case can be reduced to the unique-label case as follows: For each $a \in \Sigma$, let $v_1, \ldots, v_m$ be all of the vertices of POMSET P with label a. These vertices must be linearly ordered in $A(P)$, or else there would be autoconcurrence. If the linear order is $v_{i1} < \cdots < v_{im}$, then relabel these vertices $l(v_{i1}) = a_{i1}, \ldots, l(v_{im}) = a_{im}$, where the a_{ij}'s are not in Σ. Do the same for all of the vertices with label a in Q, once again using the labels $a_{i1}, \ldots, a_{im}$.

4   PLM is NP-Complete

Theorem 4.1 *The* PLM *problem is* NP-complete.

Proof: Once again, it is obvious that PLM is in NP. To verify that $x = \sigma_1 \cdots \sigma_n$ is in $P = (V, A)$, where $V = \{v_1, \ldots, v_n\}$, simply guess a linear ordering $v_{i_1} \ldots v_{i_n}$ of V, and check that each arc in A joins a pair of vertices $v_{i_{j_1}}, v_{i_{j_2}}$ with $j_1 < j_2$ and that $l(v_i) = \sigma_i$ for each i.

We show completeness by reduction from the archetypal NP-complete problem 3SAT. Recall the statement of this problem.

Three Satisfiability (3SAT):

<u>Input</u> : Clauses c_1, ..., c_n on boolean variables y_1, ..., y_m. Each c_j is of the form $c_{j_1} \vee c_{j_2} \vee cj_3$, where each c_{j_k} is either y_i or $\overline{y_i}$ for some i.

<u>Question</u> : Is there an assignment of truth values to the variables y_1, ..., y_m that satisfies all of the clauses c_1, ..., c_n simultaneously?

Given an instance $(C = \{c_1, \ldots, c_n\}, Y = \{y_1, \ldots, y_m\})$ of 3SAT, we construct an equivalent instance (x, P) of PLM as follows. The vertex set V of P contains two vertices, say v_{i_1} and v_{i_2}, for each variable y_i and three vertices, say w_{j_1}, w_{j_2}, and w_{j_3}, for each clause c_j. Vertices v_{i_1} and v_{i_2} have label y_i, and vertices w_{j_1}, w_{j_2}, and w_{j_3} all have label c_j. For each clause c_j, consider the variables (say y_r, y_s, and y_t) that occur in c_j. Put in exactly one of arcs (v_{r_1}, w_{j_1}) and (v_{r_2}, w_{j_1}) (resp. $[(v_{s_1}, w_{j_2})$ and $(v_{s_2}, w_{j_2})]$ and $[(v_{t_1}, w_{j_3})$

and $(v_{t_2}, w_{j_3})]$), by choosing the first if y_r (resp. y_s and y_t) occurs in c_j and the second if $\overline{y_r}$ (resp. $\overline{y_s}$ and $\overline{y_t}$) occurs in c_j. The string in the PLM instance is

$$x = y_1 \cdots y_m c_1 \cdots c_n y_1 \cdots y_m c_1 c_1 c_2 c_2 \cdots c_n c_n.$$

See Figure 4 for an example of this construction.

It is easily seen that (x, P) is a yes-instance of PLM if and only if (C, A) is a yes-instance of 3SAT. The key point is that the choice of vertices that map to the prefix $y_1 \cdots y_m$ of x corresponds exactly to the choice of truth values in the satisfying assignment and that this choice "covers" the first occurrence of each c_j symbol in x. ∎

An alternative proof of Theorem 4.1, based on a reduction from the CLIQUE problem, was subsequently given by Kilian [8].

In the journal version of this paper, we show that the special case of PLM in which each label in Σ occurs at most twice is solvable in polynomial time.

5   Results on PLE and PLS

Proofs of the following two theorems are given in the journal version.

Theorem 5.1 *The PLE problem is as hard as graph isomorphism.*

Theorem 5.2 *The PLS problem is* span-P-*complete.*

6   Discussion

A natural next step to take is to identify interesting special cases of PLC and to develop algorithms for these cases. For these algorithms to be practical, they would have to test containment of infinite languages of infinite sequences. It is unclear how to represent such languages by POMSETs so as to facilitate language-containment testing. Some candidate representations are suggested in Pratt's original paper and in Probst-Li [14].

We propose the following notation. Each language is represented by a deterministic Büchi automaton A and a collection $P_1, \ldots, P_k$ of POMSETs. Assume that each P_i exhibits no autoconcurrency. Each transition of A is labeled by a POMSET P_i. The language given by $(A, P_1, \ldots, P_k)$ consists of all sequences $w_{i_1} w_{i_2} \cdots$, where $P_{i_1} P_{i_2} \cdots$ is in $L(A)$ and w_{i_j} is in $L(P_{i_j})$.

Suppose that $(A, P_1, \ldots, P_k)$ and $(B, Q_1, \ldots, Q_k)$ are two such representations. Note that an implicit one-to-one correspondence between the two collections of POMSETs is given by their subscripts. Form an automaton B' by starting with B and substituting for each transition label Q_i the corresponding label P_i. Then a sufficient, but not necessary, condition for the language given by $(A, P_1, \ldots, P_k)$ to be contained in the language given by $(B, Q_1, \ldots, Q_k)$ is: $L(A) \subseteq L(B')$ and, for each i, $L(P_i) \subseteq L(Q_i)$.

This test can be performed in polynomial time. We hope to investigate its applicability in future work.

Finally, there is a large gap between the known upper and lower bounds for PLE: We know that the problem is at least as hard as graph isomorphism and that it is in Π_2^p. It would be interesting to determine its exact complexity.

References

[1] S. Aggarwal, R. P. Kurshan, and K. K. Sabnani. *Protocol Specification, Testing and Verification III* (1983), 19–34.

[2] M. C. Brown, E. M. Clarke, and O. Grumberg. *Inf. and Comput.* 81:13–31, 1989.

[3] J. R. Burch, E. M. Clarke, K. L. McMillan, D. L. Dill, and J. Hwang. LICS '90, 428–439.

[4] O. Coudert, C. Berthet, and J. C. Madre. Springer Verlag LNCS 407, 1989, 365–373.

[5] D. L. Dill. Springer Verlag LNCS 407, 1989, 197–212.

[6] M. R. Garey and D. S. Johnson. *Computers and Intractability: A Guide to the Theory of NP-Completeness*, Freeman, San Francisco, 1979.

[7] P. Godefroid. DIMACS Series, vol. 3, 1991, 321–340.

[8] J. Kilian. Private communication.

[9] J. Köbler, U. Schöning, and J. Toran. *Acta Informatica* 26:363–379, 1989.

[10] R. P. Kurshan. Springer Verlag LNCS 430, 1990, 414-453.

[11] R. P. Kurshan. Springer Verlag LNCIS 103, 1987, 19–39.

[12] R. P. Kurshan and K. L. McMillan. PODC '89, 239–247.

[13] V. Pratt. *Intl. J. Parallel Programming* 15(1):33–71, 1986.

[14] D. Probst and H. Li. DIMACS Series, vol. 3, 1991, 15–24.

[15] A. P. Sistla, M. Y. Vardi, and P. Wolper. *Theor. Comput. Sci.* 49:217–237, 1987.

[16] H. J. Touati, R. K. Brayton, and R. P. Kurshan. Testing Language Containment for ω-Automata using BDD's, *Formal Methods in VLSI Design* (1991), ACM, to appear.

[17] L. Valiant. *Theor. Comput. Sci.* 8:189–201, 1979.

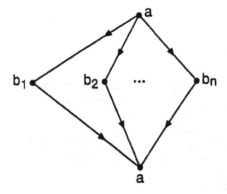

Figure 1

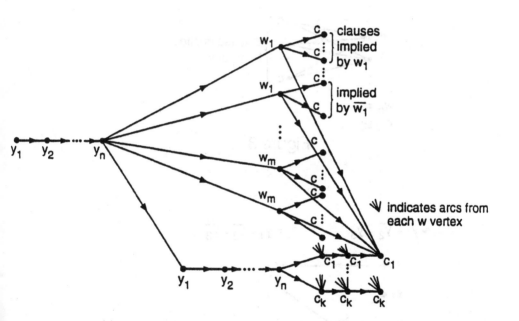

Figure 2

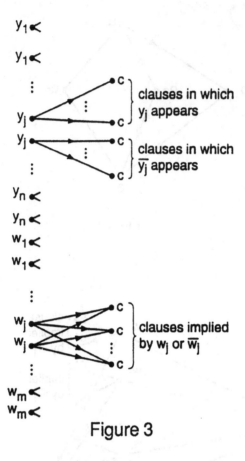

Figure 3

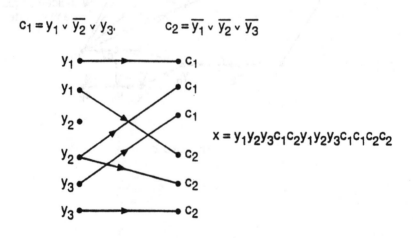

Figure 4

Mechanically Verifying Safety and Liveness Properties of Delay Insensitive Circuits

David M. Goldschlag

Computational Logic, Inc.
1717 West Sixth Street, Suite 290
Austin, Texas 78703-4776
U.S.A.
Telephone: (512) 322-9951
e-mail: dmg@cli.com

Abstract This paper describes, by means of an example, how one may mechanically verify delay insensitive circuits on an automated theorem prover. It presents the verification of both the safety and liveness properties of an n-node delay insensitive fifo circuit [8]. The proof system used is a mechanized implementation of Unity [2] on the Boyer-Moore prover [1], described in [5].

This paper describes the circuit formally in the Boyer-Moore logic and presents the mechanically verified correctness theorems. The formal description also captures the protocol that the circuit expects its environment to obey and specifies a class of suitable initial states.

This paper demonstrates how a general purpose automated proof system for concurrent programs may be used to mechanically verify both the safety and liveness properties of arbitrary sized delay insensitive circuits.

1. Introduction

General purpose theorem provers may be used to verify both safety and liveness properties of delay insensitive circuits. Although such mechanized proofs are not automatic, correctness properties may be both non-propositional and describe circuits of arbitrary size. Mechanical verification increases the trustworthiness of a proof. This paper describes the verification of an n-node first in first out (FIFO) queue.

The proof system used here is a version of a mechanized implementation of Unity [2, 5] on the Boyer-Moore prover [1]. The Unity logic is suitable for reasoning about programs under the interleaved model of concurrency. In this model, statements in a program run sequentially, but in an unknown order. Correctness properties are true only if they hold for all possible orderings.

Many researchers have used the interleaved model of concurrency as a basis for modeling delay insensitive circuits [8, 10, 2]. By restricting the power of program statements and assuming a non-deterministic yet weakly fair scheduling paradigm, interleaving adequately models circuit behavior. This paper does not propose criteria for determining whether a circuit is truly delay insensitive. Rather, given a delay insensitive circuit, it describes how to verify its correctness properties under the interleaved model of concurrency. The example here formalizes an n-node (FIFO) queue and presents the verification of its safety and the liveness properties. The basic element in this circuit is described in [8].

This paper is organized in the following way. Section 2 briefly describes the Boyer-Moore logic, its prover, and the mechanized implementation of Unity. Section 3 defines the FIFO circuit. Section 4 presents the correctness theorems, which are proved in section 5. Section 6 discusses related work and offers concluding remarks.

2. The Proof System

Mechanized Unity is implemented in the Nqthm version of the Boyer-Moore logic [1] enhanced with a facility for defining fully quantified definitions and the Kaufmann proof checker [7]. Nqthm is a quantifier-free first order logic with a prefix syntax and semantics similar to pure Lisp. Quantifiers are necessary for defining predicates describing properties of infinite sequences. The Kaufmann proof checker permits the user to guide the theorem prover at a low level, while still allowing calls to the entire automated system; this permits both efficient proof discovery and easy use of rewrite rules that have free variables in their hypotheses.

Mechanized Unity defines most of its specification predicates with respect to an operational semantics characterizing an arbitrary fair execution of a concurrent program. A fair execution is an infinite sequence of states, obtained from some initial state by the sequential application of program statements. The only restriction on the scheduling of statements is weak fairness: every statement must be scheduled infinitely often. Since specifications are defined with respect to an arbitrary fair execution, proved specifications are true for all fair executions. Consequently, specifications neither assume nor guarantee any particular timing characteristics of the program.

Specifications in this logic are proved by the use of proof rules that have been adapted from the Unity logic. These proof rules permit concise non-operational correetness proofs. The proof rules are sound because they are theorems of the operational semantics of concurrency described earlier.

We now illustrate terms in the logic by introducing the proof system's specification predicates. Assuming the term (INITIAL-CONDITION IC PRG) implies that IC holds on the initial state of any execution of the program PRG. In a similar way, the predicates for safety and liveness properties are defined:

- The term (INVARIANT P PRG) means that P holds on every state in the execution of PRG. To prove this, one may have to make assumptions about the initial state.

- The term (LEADS-TO P Q PRG) means that every P state in an execution of PRG is eventually followed by a Q state (Q may hold true immediately).

The Boyer-Moore Logic defines many other functions, including the logical operators AND, OR, NOT, and IMPLIES, which have the obvious meaning. One may extend the logic by adding recursive definitions, providing termination is proved.

A program in Mechanized Unity is a list of statements, where each statement has the form '(LIST FUNCTION-NAME ARG-1 ... ARG-N). The arguments may be wire names, if one wishes to use the same function in several statements. For example, the statement representing a NOR gate may be (LIST 'NOR-GATE A B C), where A and B are understood to be input wires and C is the output wire. The literal 'NOR-GATE refers to the function NOR-GATE which will be defined later.

Each function implementing a statement takes two arguments in addition to the ones specified in the statement. These two arguments represent the states before and after the execution of the statement. The function returns TRUE only if the NEW state is a possible successor state to the OLD state. It is useful for statements to be defined by functions that have access to both the previous and next states, since this permits non-deterministic transitions. Non-determinism simplifies modeling a circuit's environment, for example.

3. The FIFO Circuit

This FIFO circuit is composed of a producer and a consumer which *push* values upon and *pop* values from the internal nodes of the queue. The internal nodes are a sequence of similar nodes, each differing from the other by an index. Each node contains at most one bit; it may be TRUE, FALSE, or empty. A node attains its predecessor's value once it determines that its value has been copied to its successor. A node does not become empty simply because its value is copied to its successor. Therefore, in order for this circuit to operate correctly, the producer must push an empty value upon the queue between pushes of non-empty values. Furthermore, a popped value is considered non-empty only if it is non-empty and the previous popped value was empty. Intuitively, a value propagates along the queue leaving a trail of identical values. These copies are cleaned up by the empty value that is pushed upon the queue to delimit the next non-empty value.

An N node queue has N-1 internal nodes, indexed N-1, ..., 1. The I'th internal node in the FIFO circuit has the following components:

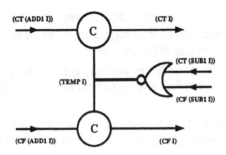

The labels on the wires are wire names; notice that each of the output wires from the C-elements [9] actually fork; one branch connects to the input of the successor node's corresponding C-element; the other connects to the predecessor's NOR gate. We take these forks to be isochronic [8] (assume that the signal propagates simultaneously to the gates at the end of each fork).

Each node behaves in the following way: A bit is encoded by double-rail coding. **TRUE** is represented by the C-element [9] **CT** being **TRUE**, and the other C-element **CF** being **FALSE**. **FALSE** is represented by the opposite configuration. If the node is empty, both C-elements are **FALSE**; never will both C-elements be **TRUE** simultaneously. This is because this circuit requires (and maintains) that if two adjacent nodes are non-empty, they must also represent the same value.

A node copies a new value from its predecessor when its successor differs from its predecessor. For example, assume that the successor is empty, and the predecessor is non-empty. Therefore, the incoming **TEMP** becomes **TRUE** and permits the other C-elements to become true, if their other inputs are **TRUE**.

In Mechanized Unity, this node is described by three statements corresponding to the two C-elements and single NOR gate components. The NOR gate is represented by the following function:

Definition: Nor-Gate

```
(NOR-GATE OLD NEW A B C)
  =
(AND (IFF (VALUE NEW C)
          (NOT (OR (VALUE OLD A)
                   (VALUE OLD B))))
     (CHANGED OLD NEW (LIST C)))
```

The term **(VALUE OLD A)** looks up the value of the variable named **A** in state **OLD**. **(CHANGED OLD NEW (LIST C))** states that only the variable **C** may change between states **OLD** and **NEW**. This function says that the value of **C** in state **NEW** becomes the *nor* of the values of **A** and **B** in state **OLD**. **OLD** and **NEW** represent successive states in the execution of the program. The statement for the NOR gate in the **I**'th node of the queue must instantiate **A**, **B**, and **C** to be the appropriate wire names. The statement is:

```
(LIST 'NOR-GATE  (CT (SUB1 I)) (CF (SUB1 I)) (TEMP I))
```

A statement is a list; the first element is the name of the function representing the VLSI component, remaining elements are the names of the input and output wires of that component. Since wire names are indexed, the functions CT, CF and TEMP take arguments.

Similarly, the C-element is described by the following function:

Definition: C-Element

```
(C-ELEMENT OLD NEW A B C)
  =
(IF (IFF (VALUE OLD A)
         (VALUE OLD B))
    (AND (IFF (VALUE NEW C) (VALUE OLD A))
         (CHANGED OLD NEW (LIST C)))
  (CHANGED OLD NEW NIL))
```

This function states that C in state NEW becomes equal to the inputs, if both inputs A and B are equivalent in state OLD; otherwise, all variables remain unchanged (NIL is the empty list). This function is used in the following two statements, each representing a single C-element:

```
(LIST 'C-ELEMENT (CT (ADD1 I)) (TEMP I) (CT I))
(LIST 'C-ELEMENT (CF (ADD1 I)) (TEMP I) (CF I))
```

A single node of the FIFO circuit is a collection of the two statements representing the two C-elements and the single statement representing the NOR gate. We define the term (FIFO-NODE I) to collect the three statements in node I.

The TEMP wire is truly an isochronic fork because (TEMP I) is the output of the NOR gate, and is an input to two C-elements. Adding a function that copies TEMP to another wire would add complexity to the verification without changing the overall behavior of the circuit. The output of each C-element is also an isochronic fork.

The internal nodes in our n-node queue will have indices (N-1, ..., 1). Nodes N and 0 will be, respectively, producer and consumer nodes. These nodes must obey the four-phase signalling that this queue expects, and keep track of the *pushed* and *popped* values. The producer node is defined as follows:

Definition: In-Node

```
(IN-NODE OLD NEW I)
  =
(IF (IFF (VALUE OLD (TEMP I))
         (EMPTY-NODE OLD I))
    (IF (EMPTY-NODE OLD I)
        (OR (CHANGED OLD NEW NIL)
            (AND (OR (TRUE-NODE NEW I)
                     (FALSE-NODE NEW I))
                 (EQUAL (VALUE NEW 'INPUT)
                        (CONS (TRUE-NODE NEW I)
                              (VALUE OLD 'INPUT)))
                 (CHANGED OLD NEW (LIST (CT I) (CF I) 'INPUT))))
        (OR (CHANGED OLD NEW NIL)
            (AND (EMPTY-NODE NEW I)
                 (CHANGED OLD NEW (LIST (CT I) (CF I))))))
  (CHANGED OLD NEW NIL))
```

The term **(EMPTY-NODE OLD I)** tests whether this **I**'th node is empty in state **OLD**. (Neither C-element in node **I** is **TRUE**.) Terms **(TRUE-NODE NEW I)** and **(FALSE-NODE NEW I)** test whether the **I**'th node in state **NEW** contains a **TRUE** or **FALSE** bit, respectively. In our example, the producer node will have index **N**. Its behavior is as follows: If the value of the tail of the queue (node **N**) has already been copied into node **N-1** (as indicated by the value of **(TEMP N)**) and the tail of the queue is empty, then a new value *may* be placed upon the tail of the queue. If the new value is **TRUE** or **FALSE**, then the variable **INPUT** is updated to reflect the newly pushed value. If the tail of the queue is not empty, yet has already been copied, then an empty value may be placed upon the tail of the queue. If the tail of the queue has not yet been copied, no change occurs.

The producer node is non-deterministic, since it never need push a new value. That is, this statement may execute repeatedly without ever changing any values. Therefore, the environment may stop.

The consumer node is defined as follows:

Definition: Out-Node

```
(OUT-NODE OLD NEW)
  =
(AND (IFF (VALUE NEW (CT 0))
          (VALUE OLD (CT 1)))
     (IFF (VALUE NEW (CF 0))
          (VALUE OLD (CF 1)))
     (IF (AND (EMPTY-NODE OLD 0)
              (NOT (EMPTY-NODE NEW 0)))
         (EQUAL (VALUE NEW 'OUTPUT)
                (CONS (TRUE-NODE NEW 0)
                      (VALUE OLD 'OUTPUT)))
         (EQUAL (VALUE NEW 'OUTPUT) (VALUE OLD 'OUTPUT)))
     (CHANGED OLD NEW (LIST (CT 0) (CF 0) 'OUTPUT)))
```

The consumer node's index is **0**. Node **1** is copied into the head of the queue. If the head of the queue is thereby changed from empty to non-empty, then the variable **OUTPUT** representing popped values is updated appropriately. Since the schedule of statements is unknown, the internal nodes in the queue cannot depend upon the rate at which values are popped.

The entire queue, consisting of a consumer, the internal nodes, and a producer (with the extra **(TEMP N)** line), is represented using the following three functions. The first collects the internal nodes:

Definition: Internal-Nodes

```
(INTERNAL-NODES N)
  =
(IF (ZEROP N)
    NIL
    (APPEND (FIFO-NODE N)
            (INTERNAL-NODES (SUB1 N))))
```

The next function collect the statements describing the external nodes:

Definition: External-Nodes

```
(EXTERNAL-NODES N)
  =
(LIST (LIST 'IN-NODE N)
      (LIST 'OUT-NODE)
      (LIST 'NOR-GATE   (CT (SUB1 N)) (CF (SUB1 N)) (TEMP N)))
```

Finally, the entire circuit is captured by the term (FIFO-QUEUE N):

Definition: Fifo-Queue

```
(FIFO-QUEUE N)
  =
(APPEND (EXTERNAL-NODES N)
        (INTERNAL-NODES (SUB1 N)))
```

In the correctness specifications, we use the term (FIFO-QUEUE N) denoting a FIFO queue of length N. As with all variables, N is universally quantified, so the theorems are true for queues of any length. (A hypothesis in these theorems requires that N exceed 1, implying the existence of at least one internal node.)

4. The Correctness Specifications

The important correctness properties, that pushed values are not lost, and that pushed values are eventually popped, both depend upon a invariant that characterizes legal states. Recall that the correct operation of the circuit depends upon adjacent non-empty nodes being equivalent. In addition, if a node differs from its successor, then its incoming TEMP wire must be up-to-date. These requirements are formalized in the following way:

Definition: Proper-Node

```
(PROPER-NODE STATE I)
  =
(AND (IMPLIES (AND (NOT (EMPTY-NODE STATE I))
                   (EMPTY-NODE STATE (SUB1 I)))
              (VALUE STATE (TEMP I)))
     (IMPLIES (AND (EMPTY-NODE STATE I)
                   (NOT (EMPTY-NODE STATE (SUB1 I))))
              (NOT (VALUE STATE (TEMP I))))
     (OR (TRUE-NODE STATE I)
         (FALSE-NODE STATE I)
         (EMPTY-NODE STATE I))
     (IMPLIES (NOT (EMPTY-NODE STATE I))
              (OR (EMPTY-NODE STATE (SUB1 I))
                  (IF (TRUE-NODE STATE I)
                      (TRUE-NODE STATE (SUB1 I))
                      (FALSE-NODE STATE (SUB1 I)))))))
```

The term (PROPER-NODES STATE N) checks whether nodes (N, ..., 1) are proper. The invariance property is stated as follows:

Theorem: Proper-Nodes-Invariant

```
(IMPLIES (AND (LESSP 1 N)
              (INITIAL-CONDITION '(PROPER-NODES STATE
                                                (QUOTE ,N))
                                 (FIFO-QUEUE N)))
         (INVARIANT '(PROPER-NODES STATE (QUOTE ,N))
                    (FIFO-QUEUE N)))
```

This theorem states that if the initial state is legal, then all subsequent states are legal. The legal state predicate is encoded as a backquoted term, in the following way: The first element of the term is the function symbol **PROPER-NODES**, so **PROPER-NODES** is the function that is invariant. The second element is **STATE**, which is a dummy literal: upon evaluating the backquoted term in the context of some state in the execution, **STATE** is bound to that state. The third element is **(QUOTE ,N)** which is a shorthand for introducing a variable into the formula. That is, the **N** in the hypothesis is the same **N** that is in the conclusion, and is the same universally quantified **N** specifying the size of the queue that we are describing via the function **(FIFO-QUEUE N)**.

The next invariant states that values are consumed in the order in which they are produced. To specify this, we define the term **(QUEUE-VALUES STATE N)** that returns a list of the values in the queue:

Definition: Queue-Values

```
(QUEUE-VALUES STATE N)
  =
(IF (ZEROP N)
    NIL
  (IF (AND (NOT (EMPTY-NODE STATE N))
           (EMPTY-NODE STATE (SUB1 N)))
      (CONS (TRUE-NODE STATE N)
            (QUEUE-VALUES STATE (SUB1 N)))
      (QUEUE-VALUES STATE (SUB1 N))))
```

Specifically, a node only *counts* if it is non-empty and its successor is empty. The invariant depends upon the queue being in a legal configuration and is specified in the following way:

Theorem: Queue-Values-Invariant

```
(IMPLIES (AND (INITIAL-CONDITION
               `(AND (PROPER-NODES STATE (QUOTE ,N))
                     (EQUAL (VALUE STATE (QUOTE INPUT))
                            (APPEND (QUEUE-VALUES STATE
                                                  (QUOTE ,N))
                                    (VALUE STATE
                                           (QUOTE OUTPUT))))))
              (FIFO-QUEUE N))
         (LESSP 1 N))
    (INVARIANT `(EQUAL (VALUE STATE (QUOTE INPUT))
                       (APPEND (QUEUE-VALUES STATE
                                             (QUOTE ,N))
                               (VALUE STATE
                                      (QUOTE OUTPUT))))
               (FIFO-QUEUE N)))
```

This invariant states that the produced values always equal the concatenation of the values in the queue and the consumed values. Interestingly, this invariant can be satisfied by an incorrect program: we must also prove that the variables **INPUT** and **OUTPUT** only grow. These statements have been proved also.

The liveness condition requires that values be passed through the queue. Without tagging queue values, this must be stated in the following way: if the queue is non-empty, then eventually the number of consumed values increases. This is expressed in the following **LEADS-TO** property:

Theorem: Output-Grows

```
(IMPLIES (AND (INITIAL-CONDITION '(PROPER-NODES STATE N)
                                 (FIFO-QUEUE N))
              (LESSP 1 N))
         (LEADS-TO '(AND (LISTP (QUEUE-VALUES STATE N))
                         (EQUAL (LENGTH (VALUE STATE
                                               (QUOTE OUTPUT)))
                                (QUOTE ,K)))
                   '(LESSP (QUOTE ,K)
                           (LENGTH (VALUE STATE
                                          (QUOTE OUTPUT))))
                   (FIFO-QUEUE N)))
```

These correctness properties have been mechanically verified on the Boyer-Moore prover, using many intermediate theorems.

5. The Correctness Proof

The proof of the invariance theorems proceeded by case analysis on the various statements in the program. Since the functions specifying both legal states and queue values are defined recursively, the proofs of these theorems were inductive and required that generalizations of the invariance theorems be proved first. It is unfortunate that the legal state invariant cannot be decomposed: although, the invariant is really three conjuncts, the stability of each depends upon all three.

The liveness property is a more interesting proof. We wish to prove that non-empty values on the queue are eventually popped off the queue; this was formalized by stating that the length of the history variable **OUTPUT** recording popped values eventually increases. We prove this by demonstrating a decreasing measure: non-empty values move forward in the queue; when one reaches node **1**, it is popped and the length of **OUTPUT** grows. We prove the decreasing measure in a restricted sense: if a queue value is non-empty and the entire subqueue ahead of it is empty, then that queue value moves forward. It is obvious that any non-empty queue also has a most forward element, so it is sufficient to prove this theorem.

6. Conclusion

This paper demonstrates how techniques for reasoning about concurrent programs may be applied to delay insensitive circuits. In this case, a proof system mechanizing Unity has been used to specify and verify both safety and liveness properties for an n-node FIFO circuit. This specification of the queue formalizes the assumptions about its environment. Mechanized Unity permits the mechanically verified proof of circuits of arbitrary size.

This work is similar to Synchronized Transitions [10] which was mechanized on the Larch Prover. Synchronized Transitions uses a syntax similar to Unity for specifying hardware. It can only be used, however, to prove invariance properties. The invariance property of a high level specification of a FIFO circuit was mechanically verified in [10]. **Synchronized Transitions** does provide a nice composition mechanism for hierarchical circuit design.

The Boyer-Moore prover has been used to verify parameterized clocked hardware as well. [6] verified a microprocessor; its ALU was verified for arbitrary register sizes. [4] verified several combinational designs as well. The circuits discussed there are synchronous and depend upon a clock. Ideally, one would like to merge verification techniques, in order to be able to reason about asynchronous collections of synchronous hardware.

Other research has produced promising techniques for fully automatic verification of certain safety [3] and liveness properties using trace theory and model checking. These systems check whether a finite state machine satisfies a formula by, essentially, completely simulating the machine. If the machine does not satisfy the formula, the system can return an offending trace; this facility is useful for debugging. Such systems may be more useful than semi-automatic techniques for verifying fixed size circuit components, since invariants specifying legal states become very complicated. However, these systems cannot reason about arbitrary sized components or about non-propositional correctness properties. Also one must still determine the circuit's suitable initial states, which, in the general case, is similar to determining invariants. A useful system (which does not yet exist) might combine automatic techniques for verifying fixed sized circuit components with semi-automatic techniques for combining these components.

Martin proposes synthesis, where VLSI components are specified as production rules in a non-deterministic program, and are obtained by correct refinements from higher level specifications [8].

There are two assumptions underlying this work. The first is that the behavior of delay insensitive circuits is accurately modeled by the interleaved model of concurrency. This assumption permits one to ignore isochronic forks and use the same wire in several inputs. The second is that the circuit being verified is truly delay insensitive. Several criteria have been proposed to test delay insensitivity: Martin checks whether his production rules map to VLSI components and the rules' preconditions are mutually exclusive. Straunstrup et. al, propose the two conditions of consumed values and correspondence, while Chandy and Misra suggest stability of preconditions. Since these conditions sometimes conflict, characterizing delay insensitive circuits remains an incompletely answered question. In this paper, an arbitrary sized circuit known to be delay insensitive was verified under the interleaved model of concurrency.

Acknowledgments

This work was supported in part at Computational Logic, Inc., by the Defense Advanced Research Projects Agency, ARPA Order 7406, and ONR Contract N00014-88-C-0454. The views and conclusions contained in this document are those of the author and should not be interpreted as representing the official policies, either expressed or implied, of

Computational Logic, Inc., the Defense Advanced Research Projects Agency, the Office of Naval Research, or the U.S. Government.

References

[1]   R. S. Boyer and J S. Moore.
       A Computational Logic Handbook.
       Academic Press, Boston, 1988.

[2]   K. Mani Chandy and Jayadev Misra.
       Parallel Program Design: A Foundation.
       Addison Wesley, Massachusetts, 1988.

[3]   David L. Dill.
       *Trace Theory for Automatic Hierarchical Verification of Speed-Independent
           Circuits.*   •
       The MIT Press, Cambridge, Massachusetts, 1988.

[4]   Steven M. German and Yu Wang.
       Formal Verification of Parameterized Hardware Designs.
       *Proceedings of the IEEE International Conference on Computer Design: VLSI in
           Computers* :549-552, 1985.

[5]   David M. Goldschlag.
       Mechanizing Unity.
       In M. Broy and C. B. Jones (editors), *Programming Concepts and Methods.* North
           Holland, Amsterdam, 1990.

[6]   Warren A. Hunt, Jr.
       Microprocessor Design Verification.
       Journal of Automated Reasoning 5(4):429-460, December, 1989.

[7]   Matt Kaufmann.
       *DEFN-SK: An Extension of the Boyer-Moore Theorem Prover to Handle First-
           Order Quantifiers.*
       Technical Report 43, Computational Logic, Inc., May, 1989.
       Draft.

[8]   Alain J. Martin.
       Self-Timed FIFO: An Exercise in Compiling Programs into VLSI Circuits.
       In *From HDL Descriptions to Guaranteed Correct Circuit Designs*, pages 133-153.
           North-Holland, Amsterdam, 1987.

[9]   R. E. Miller.
       Switching Theory.
       Wiley, 1965.

[10]   Jorgen Staunstrup, Stephen J. Garland, and John V. Guttag.
       Localized Verification of Circuit Descriptions.
       In J. Sifakis (editors), *Automatic Verification Methods for Finite State Systems*,
           pages 348-364. Springer-Verlag, 1990.

Automating Most Parts of Hardware Proofs in HOL

Klaus Schneider, Ramayya Kumar and Thomas Kropf

University of Karlsruhe, Institute of Computer Design and Fault Tolerance (Prof. D. Schmid)

P.O. Box 6980, 7500 Karlsruhe, Germany

1 INTRODUCTION

In safety critical applications it is mandatory to fabricate chips which are design error free. With the increasing complexity of designs this goal is hard to satisfy without methods specially dedicated to this task. Hence formal verification methods are gaining more and more importance.

To verify a today's ASIC, containing some 100,000 transistors, methods are needed which are capable of managing hierarchical and modular designs, as well as large and complex proof tasks. Moreover, it turns out that the underlying formalism must be powerful enough to allow natural descriptions which closely reflect the informal specification [1], [2].

Successful approaches in this regard are mostly based on higher-order logic [3], [4]. This formalism is ideally suited to compactly describe circuits, where input and output signals are represented as functions of time. In addition, it is easily possible to use parameterized modules, which are recursively definable, e.g. n-bit regular structures like adders and registers [5], [1]. However, higher-order logic is undecidable and automated theorem proving tools are not available. Hence, most of these approaches are based on interactive proof assistants like HOL, which grounds on natural deduction [1]. It provides a set of inference rules and theorems which may be combined by user-definable tactics to automate small portions of the proving process. Based on these approaches, parts of the processor VIPER and the complete TAMARACK have been successfully verified [6], [7], [8].

Although extensive research has been performed on hardware verification, it is still far away from being available to and accepted by normal designers as a standard tool like simulation. This is due to the fact, that up to now full automation is only achieved in the context of finite state verification and propositional temporal logic, both suited to verify only small and medium sized circuits [9], [10] [11]. On the other hand, the interactive approach as described above requires a fundamental knowledge of logic and theorem proving, so that any initial enthusiasm of a typical circuit designer, on hearing about the capabilities of verification, is instantly throttled. Hence the requirements for verification as an adequate design tool are automation (at least as much as possible) and guidance for the remaining interactive verification, so that the designer's creativity may be exercised without a sophisticated knowledge of formal logic.

This paper focuses on possibilities for automation which can be achieved in a twofold way. Our experiences in interactive hardware verification with HOL and LAMBDA [12] have shown, that most proofs follow a specific sequence of steps. This observation can be used to structure the hardware verification process and to find automatic decomposition methods (similar to a manually performed proof) to transform the original goal into smaller pieces. This kind of automation is implemented in MEPHISTO (Managing Exhaustive Proofs of Hardware for Integrated circuit designers by Structuring Theorem proving Operations), elaborated in more detail in the next section.

A large number of subgoals emerge from the decomposition process. The manual proof is cumbersome and takes a lot of time, although most of these subgoals are quite simple to prove since they are first-order-like with only few higher-order constructs. Automating the proof of these subgoals is also possible by integrating an automated theorem proving tool in HOL. It is based on $\mathcal{RSEQ}$, a modified form of the known sequent calculus $\mathcal{SEQ}$. $\mathcal{RSEQ}$ overcomes the inefficiencies of the standard sequent calculus approach. In section 3 $\mathcal{RSEQ}$ is described. The implementation of the prover FAUST (First-order Automation using Unification in a Sequent calculus Technique), which is based on $\mathcal{RSEQ}$ is explained in chapter 4. Experimental results are reported in section 5 and section 6 concludes the paper.

2 STRUCTURE OF HARDWARE PROOFS

In this section a brief overview of the structure of hardware proofs is given. A more elaborate version of MEPHISTO – the hardware oriented proof tool – is found in [13].

A thorough study of various reports on hardware verification [6], [7], [8] as well as our own investigations have shown, that it is possible to structure and classify the steps in interactive hardware verification as follows:

Step 1: Describe the specification and implementation of the circuit to be verified, and set the goal to be proved.

Step 2: Expand the definitions of the specification and the implementation, to obtain formulae at the desired level of abstraction.

Step 3: Simplify the goal into subgoals by applying induction rules and/or domain specific rules, e.g. theorems about n-bit values, natural numbers etc.

After this step several subgoals may be obtained, which are all proved using steps 4 and 5.

Step 4: Simplify each subgoal.

Step 5: Prove all the subgoals.

We illustrate the above-mentioned five steps by means of the parity example used in [14]. An informal specification of the synchronous even parity circuit is as follows:

Initially the output (out) is set to "T" (true). At every $n+1^{th}$ clock, the output is T iff there have been an even number of T's on the input line (in).

A sample formal specification is stated below and figure 1 shows a possible implementation:

$$\forall \text{ in, out. PARITY\_SPEC(in, out)} := \forall t . ((\text{out } 0 \leftrightarrow T) \wedge$$
$$(\text{out (suc t)} \leftrightarrow \text{EVEN (in,out)})$$

where the predicate EVEN is defined as:

$$\forall \text{ in, out. EVEN(in, out)} := \forall t . (\text{in (suc t)} \leftrightarrow \neg \text{ out t})$$

The predicate EVEN, encodes the informal specification — *at all time instants, EVEN is true, iff "in t+1" is equivalent to the complement of "out t"*.

Step 1:

The specification and implementation of the circuit are defined as predicates at the desired level of abstraction. They correspond to the behavior and the structure of the circuit, respectively and are described in the usual manner using higher-order logic [5]. The implementation can be automatically derived as a conjunction of predicates, each of which corresponds to the specification of some previously verified components. The formal implementation of the parity circuit is given in figure 2.

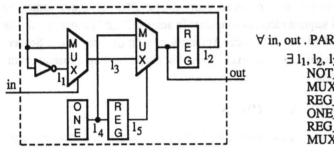

$\forall$ in, out . PARITY_IMP(in,out) :=

$\exists l_1, l_2, l_3, l_4, l_5. \forall t$.
  NOT_SPEC(l_2 t, l_1 t) $\wedge$
  MUX_SPEC(in t, l_1 t, l_2 t, l_3 t) $\wedge$
  REG_SPEC(out, l_2) $\wedge$
  ONE_SPEC(l_4 t) $\wedge$
  REG_SPEC(l_4, l_5) $\wedge$
  MUX_SPEC(l_5 t, l_3 t, l_4 t, out t)

Figure 1: Parity Implementation   Figure 2: Formal Description

The goal to be verified can now be specified as:

$$\forall \text{ in, out. PARITY\_IMP(in, out)} \leftrightarrow \text{PARITY\_SPEC(in, out)}$$

It is evident from the description of the goal, specification and implementation that a hierarchical verification is being performed. In the implementation specified above, a library containing the behavioral and structural descriptions of the used gates and their corresponding correctness theorems has been used (Table 1).

Table 1: Formal specifications of the library components

Component	Definition
NOT_SPEC (in,out)	$\forall$ in,out. (out $\leftrightarrow \neg$ in)
ONE_SPEC (out)	$\forall$ out. (out $\leftrightarrow$ T)
MUX_SPEC (sel,in$_1$,in$_2$,out)	$\forall$ sel, in$_1$, in$_2$, out. (out $\leftrightarrow$ ((sel $\rightarrow$ in$_1$) $\wedge$ ($\neg$sel $\rightarrow$ in$_2$)))
REG_SPEC (in,out)	$\forall$ in, out. ($\forall$ t. ((out 0 $\leftrightarrow$ F) $\wedge$ (out (suc t) $\leftrightarrow$ in t)))

Step 2:

The specification and the implementation are now expanded using the definitions in Table 1. The datatypes used, are also refined into their functional relationships at the next level of abstraction, e.g. natural numbers to bit-vectors. Applying this step on the parity example generates the formula:

$\forall$ in, out .
$\quad \exists\, l_1, l_2, l_3, l_4, l_5.\ \forall\, t\,.\ (l_1\, t \leftrightarrow \neg\, l_2\, t)\, \wedge$
$\qquad\qquad\qquad\qquad (l_3\, t \leftrightarrow ((\text{in}\ t \rightarrow l_1\, t) \wedge (\neg\ \text{in}\ t \rightarrow l_2\, t)))\, \wedge$
$\qquad\qquad\qquad\qquad (\forall\ t_1.\ \ (l_2\, 0 \leftrightarrow F)\, \wedge$
$\qquad\qquad\qquad\qquad\qquad (l_2\ (\text{suc}\ t_1) \leftrightarrow \text{out}\ t_1))\, \wedge$
$\qquad\qquad\qquad\qquad (l_4\, t \leftrightarrow T)\, \wedge$
$\qquad\qquad\qquad\qquad (\forall\ t_2.\ \ (l_5\, 0 \leftrightarrow F)\, \wedge$
$\qquad\qquad\qquad\qquad\qquad (l_5\ (\text{suc}\ t_2) \leftrightarrow l_4\, t_2))\, \wedge$
$\qquad\qquad\qquad\qquad (\text{out}\ t \leftrightarrow ((l_5\, t \rightarrow l_3\, t) \wedge (\neg\ l_5\, t \rightarrow l_4\, t)))$
$\quad \leftrightarrow$
$\quad \forall\, t\,.\ ((\text{out}\ 0 \leftrightarrow T)\, \wedge$
$\qquad\quad (\text{out}\ (\text{suc}\ t) \leftrightarrow (\text{in}\ (\text{suc}\ t) \leftrightarrow \neg\ \text{out}\ t))$

Step 3:

This is the creative step, where the user has to use his knowledge in breaking up the goal into subgoals, apply induction and the lemmas needed. Many design specific heuristics can be built in to aid the user here. However, due to the very nature of the problem, automating this step is often impossible. In the simple parity example, this step can be skipped.

Step 4:

Having broken up the original goal into subgoals, the subgoals can then be automatically simplified. This is performed by eliminating internal lines. This step, also called the unwind step, is performed by first converting the formula into a prenex form [15]. Afterwards, different rewrite rules are applied to eliminate internal lines, e.g. by replacing an output of a combinational element in terms of its inputs. Then further logical simplifications are performed.

Applying the unwind step to the parity example results in the following description -

$\quad \forall$ in, out .
$\qquad \forall\, t\,.\ ((\text{out}\ 0 \leftrightarrow T)\, \wedge$
$\qquad\qquad (\text{out}\ (\text{suc}\ t) \leftrightarrow ((\text{in}\ (\text{suc}\ t) \rightarrow \neg\ \text{out}\ t) \wedge (\neg\ \text{in}\ (\text{suc}\ t) \rightarrow \text{out}\ t))))$
$\qquad \leftrightarrow$
$\qquad \forall\, t\,.\ ((\text{out}\ 0 \leftrightarrow T)\, \wedge$
$\qquad\qquad (\text{out}\ (\text{suc}\ t) \leftrightarrow (\text{in}\ (\text{suc}\ t) \leftrightarrow \neg\ \text{out}\ t)))$

Step 5:

Our automated prover FAUST can now be used to prove automatically each of the subgoals generated in step 4.

3 THE THEORY UNDERLYING FAUST

FAUST is based on a modified form of sequent calculus ($\mathcal{SEQ}$) called "Restricted Sequent Calculus" or $\mathcal{RSEQ}$, which lends itself to efficient implementation. We shall first give a brief description of $\mathcal{SEQ}$ and a few basic definitions before the reasons for its inefficiency are outlined.

3.1 Sequent Calculus

<u>Definition 3.1</u>: A *sequent* is a pair (Γ, Δ) of finite (possibly empty) sets of formulae $\Gamma := \{\phi_1, ..., \phi_m\}$, $\Delta := \{\psi_1, ..., \psi_n\}$. The pair (Γ, Δ) will be henceforth written as "$\Gamma \vdash \Delta$". Γ is called the *antecedent* and Δ is called the *succedent*.

Detailed semantics of sequents can be found in various textbooks on logic [16, 15] and are omitted here. Intuitively, a sequent is valid, if the formula $(\phi_1 \wedge \ldots \wedge \phi_m) \rightarrow (\psi_1 \vee \ldots \vee \psi_n)$ is valid.

The calculus based on such sequents contains several rules which reflect the semantics of the various operators (including quantifiers), and a single axiom or rather an axiom scheme which is a sequent "$\Gamma \vdash \Delta$", such that, Γ and Δ contain some common proposition $(\Gamma \cap \Delta \neq \{\})$. An informal semantic for the axiom scheme corresponds to the sequent "$\Phi \vdash \Phi$". Proving the correctness of any statement within SEQ then corresponds to iterative rule applications which decompose the original sequent into simpler sequents, so that finally axioms are obtained. This process can be visualized as a proof tree $\mathcal{P}$ (Fig. 3) and a closed proof tree is one which has an axiom at each leaf node.

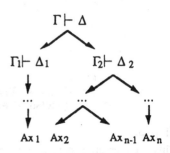

Figure 3: A closed proof tree

The rules can be classified into four types — α, β, δ and γ (cf. section 3.3). The former three rules are uncritical as they can be applied deterministically i.e. each application simplifies the sequent by eliminating the operator or quantifier. This implies that these rules can be applied only once on each operator (quantifier). The γ-rule on the other hand can be applied indefinitely (does not eliminate the quantifier) and the choice of the best term used for the quantifier substitution is unknown at the time of rule application. This choice greatly influences the depth of the proof tree. It is this rule which poses a major hurdle in the efficient implementation of SEQ. The problems with critical rule application also appears in the implementation of tableaux-based, first-order provers like HARP [17] which overcome these problems by using good heuristics in guessing the right term for substitution. We on the other hand, use an exact approach which plugs in a place-holder called a *metavariable* (not a part of the universe of terms) during the γ-rule application, and thereby postpone the choice of the exact term to a later appropriate time. When the proof tree construction process is ripened, we then use first-order unification for computing the terms that instantiate the introduced metavariable. This concept can be thought of as being similar to lazy evaluation within functional language implementations. The introduction of the metavariable and its consequences are the subject of the next sub-section.

3.2 Modifications to SEQ

The introduction of metavariables during the γ-rule application introduces problems as far as the δ-rules are concerned. An application of the δ-rule requires that the variable that is substituted for the quantified variable is new [15], i.e. it does not appear in the quantified formula. Since the choice of terms for the metavariables appearing in the formula is unknown at this point of time, we have to introduce *restrictions* on the terms that the metavariables can take, so that the terms to be computed in future do not contain the currently introduced constant. The use of such restrictions led us to christen our calculus as $RSEQ$ or "restricted sequent calculus".

In the definitions to follow, the following notations are used:

<u>Notations</u>:

$\mathcal{F}$	set of all first-order formulae	$\mathcal{T}$	the set of all first-order terms
$\mathcal{V}$	the set of all variables	$\mathcal{V}_M$	the set of all metavariables
$[\,]_x^t$	substitution of a variable x by the term $t \in \mathcal{T}$		

<u>Definition 3.2</u>: A *forbidden set* $fs_m \subseteq \mathcal{T}$ is defined for each metavariable $m \in \mathcal{V}_M$, such that fs_m contains all the variables introduced by δ-rule applications after the introduction of the metavariable m.

<u>Definition 3.3</u>: A *restricted sequent* is a modified sequent which has the form $\Gamma \vdash \Delta \parallel \mathcal{R}$, where $\Gamma, \Delta \subseteq \mathcal{F}$; $\mathcal{R} \subseteq \mathcal{V}_M \times 2^{\mathcal{V}}$, i.e. $(m, fs_m) \in \mathcal{R}$, and "$\parallel$" binds the restriction to the sequent.

<u>Definition 3.4</u>: A substitution σ applied on a restricted sequent is defined as
$$\sigma(\Gamma \vdash \Delta \parallel \mathcal{R}) := \sigma(\Gamma) \vdash \sigma(\Delta) \parallel \mathcal{R}$$

<u>Definition 3.5</u>: An *allowed substitution* σ of a restricted sequent is a substitution such that, for each $(m, fs_m) \in \mathcal{R}$, the terms occurring in σ do not contain the forbidden variables or in other words: $\forall \tau \in fs_m$. τ does not occur in $\sigma(m)$ for each (m, fs_m)

<u>Definition 3.6</u>: An allowed substitution is said to *close* a restricted sequent if
$$\sigma(\Gamma) \cap \sigma(\Delta) \neq \{\}.$$

The substitution σ (metaunifier) can be found by modifying the normal Robinson's first-order unification algorithm [18] in such a manner that only metavariables are considered as substitutable sub-terms. This leads to the concept of metaunification where metaunifiers are found. Given $\Gamma = \{\phi_1, ..., \phi_n\}$ and $\Delta = \{\psi_1, ..., \psi_m\}$, metaunifiers σ_{ij} can then be computed for each pair (ϕ_i, ψ_j), if ϕ_i and ψ_j are unifiable. The most general unifiers that are useful are allowed substitutions which do not violate the restrictions. The remaining unifiers are removed from the set of computed unifiers. Each of these substitutions are candidates for closing the restricted sequent. It is additionally possible to refine these substitutions by composing them with additional substitutions η. The compound substitution ση continues to unify the pair (ϕ_i, ψ_j) since σ is more general than η. It is also possible that choosing an appropriate refinement results in the closure of further sequents in the overall proof tree. Such closed sequents are all valid in $\mathcal{SEQ}$ as they correspond to axioms by definition.

3.3 Rules of $\mathcal{RSEQ}$

In the rules given below, both the variable y and the metavariable m are new, i.e. they do not appear in the sequent until this point of time. The function $\rho_y(\mathcal{R})$ used for updating the restrictions of the existing metavariables is defined recursively as follows:

$$\rho_y(\mathcal{R}) := \begin{cases} \{\}, & \text{if } \mathcal{R} = \{\} \\ \{(m, \{y\} \cup fs_m)\} \cup \rho_y(\mathcal{R}_1), & \text{if } \mathcal{R} = \{(m, fs_m)\} \cup \mathcal{R}_1 \end{cases}$$

Given that Γ, Δ are all sets of formulae, ϕ and ψ are formulae, m is a metavariable and x and y are variables, the following are the rules of $\mathcal{RSEQ}$. We use the notation ϕ,Γ instead of $\{\phi\}\cup\Gamma$.

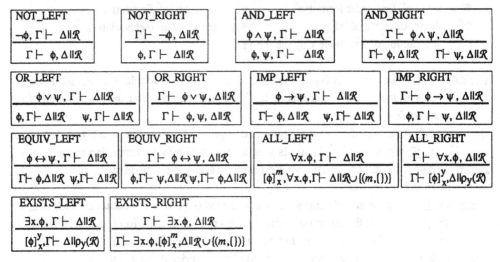

These rules can be classified into four types as stated earlier.

α-rule NOT_LEFT, NOT_RIGHT, AND_LEFT, OR_RIGHT, IMP_RIGHT

β-rule AND_RIGHT, OR_LEFT, IMP_LEFT, EQUIV_LEFT, EQUIV_RIGHT

δ-rule ALL_RIGHT, EXISTS_LEFT

γ-rule ALL_LEFT, EXISTS_RIGHT

In constructing proof trees the rules themselves are not as important as the types. Applying the different types of rules yields the following sequents:

$$\frac{\alpha}{\alpha_1} \qquad \frac{\beta}{\beta_1 \quad \beta_2} \qquad \frac{\delta}{\delta(y)} \qquad \frac{\gamma}{\gamma(m)}$$

Starting from the original sequent and recursively applying the rules the proof tree can be derived. An example illustrating the application of the rules is given below. It is to be noted that the formula appearing in the sequent obtained after the first δ-rule application "$\exists y \, \forall z \, . \, P \, c_1 \, z \to P \, c_1 \, y$", is abbreviated as Φ :

$\vdash \forall x \, \exists y \, \forall z . P \, xz \to P \, xy \parallel \{\}$
$\quad \downarrow \delta$ (ALL_RIGHT)
$\vdash \exists y \, \forall z . P \, c_1 z \to P \, c_1 y \parallel \{\}$
$\quad \downarrow \gamma$ (EXISTS_RIGHT)
$\vdash \Phi, \forall z . P \, c_1 z \to P \, c_1 m_1 \parallel \{(m_1, \{\})\}$
$\quad \downarrow \delta$ (ALL_RIGHT)
$\vdash \Phi, P \, c_1 c_2 \to P \, c_1 m_1 \parallel \{(m_1, \{c_2\})\}$
$\quad \downarrow \alpha$ (IMP_RIGHT)
$P \, c_1 c_2 \vdash \Phi, P \, c_1 m_1 \parallel \{(m_1, \{c_2\})\}$
$\downarrow$ UNIFY ($m_1 \leftarrow c_2$) possible, but forbidden
$P \, c_1 c_2 \vdash \Phi, P \, c_1 m_1 \parallel \{(m_1, \{c_2\})\}$

$\quad \downarrow \gamma$ (EXISTS_RIGHT)
$P \, c_1 c_2 \vdash \Phi, P \, c_1 m_1, \forall z , P \, c_1 z \to P \, c_1 m_2$
$\qquad\qquad \parallel \{(m_1, \{c_2\}), (m_2, \{\})\}$
$\quad \downarrow \delta$ (ALL_RIGHT)
$P \, c_1 c_2 \vdash \Phi, P \, c_1 m_1, P \, c_1 c_3 \to P \, c_1 m_2$
$\qquad\qquad \parallel \{(m_1, \{c_2,c_3\}),(m_2, \{c_3\})\}$
$\quad \downarrow \alpha$ (IMP_RIGHT)
$P \, c_1 c_2, P \, c_1 c_3 \vdash \Phi, P \, c_1 m_1, P \, c_1 m_2$
$\qquad\qquad \parallel \{(m_1, \{c_2,c_3\}),(m_2, \{c_3\})\}$
$\quad \downarrow$ UNIFY ($m_2 \leftarrow c_2$) possible
$P \, c_1 c_2, P \, c_1 c_3 \vdash \Phi, P \, c_1 m_1, P \, c_1 c_2$
$\qquad\qquad \parallel \{(m_1, \{c_2,c_3\}),(m_2, \{c_3\})\}$
$\qquad$ closed

The soundness and completeness proofs of $\mathcal{RSEQ}$ are given in [19] and [20].

4. IMPLEMENTATION OF $\mathcal{RSEQ}$ IN FAUST

An efficient implementation of $\mathcal{RSEQ}$ requires the clarification of certain concepts which are briefly given in this section.

4.1 Fairness of the rule application

In the course of the proof tree construction, it is possible that many different types of rules can be applied on the sequent, at any given time. A random application of the rules is dangerous as it could lead to an infinite growth of the proof tree. A trivial example of this would be to apply the γ-rule over and over again. Avoiding such pitfalls without the use of heuristics is achieved by giving an order of precedence for the rules $-\alpha \gg \delta \gg \beta \gg \gamma$.

Definition 4.1: An application of the rule is defined to be *fair* if no rule gets a continuing precedence over the others.

The uncritical rules (α, δ, β), can be applied only a finite number of times and hence they are fair among themselves. The γ-rules on the other hand, can be applied infinitely. Due to definition of the rule precedence, a γ-rule can be applied only when the uncritical rules are not applicable. Now it only remains to ascertain that the γ-rules are fair among themselves. This is achieved by introducing a queue local to each sequent containing the formulae belonging to the sequent, on which γ-rules have been applied. When a γ-rule is applied, the formula on which this rule has been applied is deleted from it and added to the end of the queue. This ensures the fairness among the γ-rules, as further γ-rule applications are done on quantified variables which have not been instantiated so far. If no further γ-rules can be applied and the sequent cannot be closed, then further γ-rule applications are done on the formulae stored in the queue, local to the sequent. A fair application of the rules on a valid first-order statement will always terminate and the proof of this statement is given in [19].

4.2 Depth-first construction of the Proof Tree

The unification algorithm produces the most general metaunifier σ of two formulae, i.e. σ satisfies the sufficiency conditions for being a unifier. Given that η is any substitution, the composition $\sigma\eta$ (also written as $\eta \cdot \sigma$) is still a unifier for the two original formulae, however no more the most general. This observation indicates that the substitutions needed for closing the proof-tree can be computed along with the construction of the proof-tree itself. A depth-first construction of the proof-tree incorporating the above-mentioned strategy is as follows:

1. The proof-tree $\mathcal{P}_0$ is initialized to $\Gamma \vdash \Delta \parallel \{\}$ and the substitution set Σ_0 to $\{id\}$, which is the identity substitution.

2. Given the proof-tree $\mathcal{P}_n$ after n rule applications and the substitution set Σ_n, we proceed with the left most node S which is not yet closed, in the following manner:

    (a) If an α rule is applicable, the path leading to S is extended by α_1 to generate $\mathcal{P}_{n+1}$ and $\Sigma_{n+1} := \Sigma_n$.

    (b) If a δ rule is applicable and no α rule is applicable, the path leading to S is extended by $\delta(y)$ to generate $\mathcal{P}_{n+1}$ and $\Sigma_{n+1} := \Sigma_n$. The variable y used is any new variable.

    (c) If a β rule is applicable and neither an α rule or a δ rule is applicable, the path leading to S is extended by two child nodes - β_1 and β_2 to generate $\mathcal{P}_{n+1}$ and $\Sigma_{n+1} := \Sigma_n$.

(d) Given that none of the uncritical rules are applicable but a γ rule is, the path leading to S is extended by $\gamma(m)$, to generate $\mathcal{P}_{n+1}$ and $\Sigma_{n+1} := \Sigma_n$, where m is a new metavariable. The queue local to the sequent S is updated as stated in 4.1.

(e) The steps a to d are repeated until they are not applicable any more directly on the sequent.

(f) $S := \Gamma \vdash \Delta \parallel \mathcal{R}$ now contains only atomic formulae and no more rules can be applied. Given $\Sigma_n = \{\sigma_1,...,\sigma_k\}$, we then try to unify the sequent $\sigma_i(\Gamma) \vdash \sigma_i(\Delta)$ for all i, where $1 \le i \le k$. This is achieved by unifying each formula in $\sigma_i(\Gamma)$ with each formula in $\sigma_i(\Delta)$ to obtain the set of unifiers for σ_i, represented as $\Pi_i = \{\pi_1^{(i)},..., \pi_{l_i}^{(i)}\}$. Now there are two possibilities, the first of which being that all Π_is are empty. In this case, the sequent S cannot be closed at this step and we proceed to step 2(g). On the other hand, even if one of the Π_is are not empty the substitution set Σ_{n+1} is calculated as follows:

$$\Sigma_{n+1} := \{\pi_j^{(i)} \bullet \sigma_i : \pi_j^{(i)} \in \Pi_i; \Pi_i \ne \{\}; i = 1,..., k; j = 1,..., l_i\}$$

It is to be noted that each unifier belonging to Σ_{n+1} continues to unify the sequent S. $\mathcal{P}_{n+1}$ is now obtained by declaring the sequent S as closed and step 2 of the proof construction is continued with the next left most node S' which is not closed. If all the sequents in $\mathcal{P}_{n+1}$ are closed, a proof of validity has been obtained.

(g) When no substitutions which close the leaf S are found in step 2(f), then there are two possibilities -

(i) The queue local to the sequent is empty. In this case the sequent is invalid and construction of the proof-tree is stopped with the message "Invalid Sequent ".

(ii) If the queue is not empty, a γ rule is applied to the head of the queue local to S. and the proof-tree construction proceeds from step 2(d).

We have also implemented a breadth-first algorithm and algorithms which perform skolemization within FAUST. Although the breadth-first algorithm is much slower than the depth-first algorithm, certain problems which are not solvable using a depth-first approach are provable using the breadth-first prover.

It can be observed that the above-mentioned depth-first algorithm generates a closed proof-tree in a fair manner. Furthermore due to the definition of the precedence rules and the proof of the completeness theorem, all valid sequents can be *theoretically* proved by the breadth-first prover after a finite number of rule applications, although this number may be very large. On the other hand, if the sequent to be proved is invalid then the proof construction process may diverge. Hence a definition of an upper bound on the number of rule applications is desirable, after which the proof construction is terminated with a message - "Goal too complex or invalid sequent".

Interaction with HOL has been achieved by introducing the proofs completed by FAUST as theorems using the "mk_thm" (make theorem) function in HOL. Since this can be dangerous, FAUST also generates a single HOL tactic which can then be used to *automatically* validate the automatic proofs within a normal HOL session [21].

5 EXPERIMENTAL RESULTS

The prover embedded in HOL was first tested for its correctness by using the propositional and first-order formulae in [22] and [23]. The runtimes of the more difficult Pelletier examples are found in Table 2. The ML-code has been incorporated in the public domain version of HOL, which runs on top of Common-Lisp on a SUN 4/65. The problem called Andrew's challenge was solved by generating 86 subgoals as compared to 1600 subgoals generated by resolution provers. Additionally, we have observed that specialized HOL tactics can be developed for difficult problems such as Uruquart's problems, which was then solved in linear time.

Having gained confidence about the correctness of our prover we have looked at some combinational circuits which also required a matter of seconds. At present we have proved the correctness of only small sequential circuits such as parity, serial adder, flipflops, and minmax. Thy did not require any interaction and were proved in a few seconds.

Table 2:Runtimes of Benchmark-Formulae (* indicates times taken by the breadth-first version)

Formula	Time	Formula	Time	Formula	Time	Formula	Time
P_{24}	1.4	P_{36}	1.8	P_{40}	9.9	P_{44}	1.2
P_{26}	1.0	P_{37}	1.8	P_{41}	3.0	P_{45}	6.2
P_{34}	19.1	P_{38}	14.4	P_{43}	– / 147.5*	P_{46}	182.1 / 9.9*

6 CONCLUSIONS AND FUTURE WORK

In this paper it has been shown that most hardware proofs can be broken into easily solvable subgoals by following the sequence of steps given in section 2. The creative steps involved in proving the correctness are few in number and most of the other steps can be automated. This part of the proof process has been implemented in MEPHISTO [13]. Furthermore we have elucidated that, although one needs higher order for specifying hardware, it is a restricted form which can be handled by first-order proving techniques. For this purpose, a modified form of sequent calculus has been proposed. An efficient implementation of the prover FAUST has been presented.We are also working on embedding our approach within the CADENCE framework, so that verification proceeds hand in hand with design.

Even if full automation in the context of complex hardware proofs is not reached with our approach, at least HOL-based verification is freed from a significant part of tedious interactive proof drudgery.

REFERENCES

1 M. J. C. Gordon: Why High-Order Logic is a good Formalism for Specifying and Verifying Hardware; Milne/Subrahmanyam (Eds.), Formal Aspects of VLSI Design, Proc. Edinburgh Workshop on VLSI 1985, North-Holland 1986, pp. 153-178.

2 J. Joyce: More Reasons Why Higher-Order Logic is a Good Formalism for Specifiying and Verifying Hardware; Proc. International Workshop on Formal Methods in VLSI Design, Miami, January 1991.

3 A. Camilleri, M. J. C. Gordon, T. Melham: Hardware Verification using Higher-Order Logic; Borrione (Ed.), Proc. IFIP Workshop on "From H.D.L. Descriptions to Guaranteed Correct Circuit Design", Grenoble 1986, North-Holland, pp.43-67.

4 S. Finn, M. Fourman, M. Francis, B. Harris: Formal System Design - Interactive Synthesis based on Computer Assisted Formal Reasoning; Proc. Intl. Workshop on Applied Formal Methods for Correct VLSI Design, Leuven, Nov. 1989.

5 F.K. Hanna, N. Daeche: Specification and Verification of Digital Systems Using Higher-Order Predicate Logic; IEE Proc. Pt. E, Vol. 133, No. 3, September 1986, pp. 242-254.

6 A. Cohn: Correctness Properties of the Viper Block Model: The Second Level; Current Trends in Hardware Verification and Automated Theorem Proving, Springer Verlag, 1988.

7 W.J. Cullyer: Implementing Safety Critical Systems: The VIPER Microprocessor; VLSI Specification, Verification and Synthesis, Eds. Birwistle G. and Subrahmanyam P.A., Kluwer, 1988.

8 J. Joyce: Formal Verification and Implementation of a Microprocessor; VLSI Specification, Verification and Synthesis, Eds. Birwistle G. and Subrahmanyam P.A., Kluwer, 1988.

9 J.R. Burch, E.M. Clarke, K.L. McMillan, D.L. Dill: Sequential Circuit Verification Using Symbolic Model Checking; Proc. 27th Design Automation Conference (DAC 90), 1990, pp. 46-51.

10 O. Coudert, C. Berthet, J.C. Madre: Verification of Synchronous Sequential Machines Based on Symbolic Execution; Proc. Workshop on Automatic Verification Methods for Finite State Systems, Grenoble, June 1989.

11 T. Kropf, H.-J. Wunderlich: A Common Approach to Hardware Verification and Test Generation Based on Temporal Logic; Proc. International Test Conference (ITC 91), Nashville, 1991.

12 Abstract Hardware Limited: LAMBDA - Logic and Mathematics behind Design Automation; User and Reference Manuals, Version 3.1, 1990.

13 K. Schneider, R. Kumar, T. Kropf: Structuring Hardware Proofs: First Steps towards Automation in a Higher-Order Environment; Proc. VLSI '91, Edinburgh, P.B. Denyer, A. Halaas (Eds.), North-Holland, 1991.

14 M. Gordon: A Proof Generating System for Higher-Order Logic; VLSI Specification, Verification and Synthesis, Eds. Birwistle G. and Subrahmanyam P.A., Kluwer, 1988.

15 M. Fitting: First-Order Logic and Automated Theorem Proving; Springer Verlag, 1990.

16 J.H. Gallier: Logic for Computer Science: Foundations of Automatic Theorem Proving; Harper & Row Computer Science and Technology Series No. 5, Harper & Row Publishers,New York, 1986.

17 Oppacher E., Suen: HARP: A Tableaux-based Theorem Prover, Journal of Automated Reasoning; Vol. 4, 1988, pp.69-100.

18 J.A. Robinson: A Machine-oriented logic based on the resolution principle; Journal of the ACM, Vol.12, pp.23-41, 1965.

19 K. Schneider: Ein Sequenzenkalkül für die Hardware-Verifikation in HOL; Diploma Thesis, Institute of Computer Design and Fault-Tolerance, University of Karlsruhe, 1991.

20 Schneider K., Kumar R., Kropf T.: Technical Report, Dept. of Comp. Sc. Univ. of Karlsruhe, 1991, (to appear).

21 R. Kumar, T. Kropf, K. Schneider: Integrating a First-Order Automatic Prover in the HOL Environment; Proc. 1991 International Tutorial and Workshop on the HOL Theorem Proving System and its Applications, Davis, California, Aug. 1991.

22 D. Kalish, R. Montague: Logic: Techniques of Formal Reasoning; World, Harcourt & Brace, 1964.

23 F.J. Pelletier: Seventy-Five Problems for Testing Automatic Theorem Provers; Journal of Automated Reasoning, Vol.2, pp.191-216, 1986.

24 Proceedings of the Third HOL Users Meeting; Aarhus University, Oct. 1990.

An Overview and Synthesis
on Timed Process Algebras*

Xavier Nicollin   Joseph Sifakis

Laboratoire de Génie Informatique
IMAG-Campus   B.P. 53X
38041 Grenoble Cedex – FRANCE

Abstract. We present an overview and synthesis of existing results about process algebras for the specification and analysis of timed systems. The motivation is double: present an overview of some relevant and representative approaches and suggest a unifying framework for them.

After presenting fundamental assumptions about timed systems and the nature of abstract time, we propose a general model for them: transition systems whose labels are either elements of a vocabulary of actions or elements of a *time domain*. Many properties of this model are studied concerning their impact on description capabilities and on realisability issues.

An overview of the language features of the process algebras considered is presented, by focusing on constructs used to express time constraints. The presentation is organised as an exercise of building a timed process algebra from a standard process algebra for untimed systems. The overview is completed by a discussion about description capabilities according to semantic and pragmatic criteria.

Keywords: real-time, specification of timed systems, process algebras

Contents

1 **Introduction**

2 **The models**

3 **The Languages — How to Cook your own Timed Process Algebra**

4 **Discussion**

1 Introduction

The paper presents an overview and synthesis of existing results about process algebras for the specification and analysis of timed systems. It has been motivated both by the

---

*Work supported by the ESPRIT BRA SPEC

drastically increasing number of contributions in the area and by the authors' conviction that most of the existing work admits a unifying common framework. Thus, the motivation is double: first, the presentation of an overview of some relevant and representative approaches in the area and second, the proposal of a framework for these approaches. The paper presents the rather incomplete and eventually biased authors' point of view than a survey of existing work in the area.

Although emphasis is put on algebraic behavioural specification formalisms, we believe that most of the ideas presented here have a more general applicability scope, as they are independent of the features and the nature of the description formalism considered. For instance, general ideas about the nature of time and the underlying model of timed systems may be used when designing logical specification languages; the results on process algebras can be easily transposed on other behavioural specification formalisms like automata, timed graphs, timed transition systems, etc.

A timed system is usually considered to be a system with a global parameter (state variable) called time, used to constrain the occurrences of the actions. Introducing time requires consistent assumptions about its progress with respect to the evolution of the system: correspondence between instants (domain of definition of the time parameter) and action occurrences, duration of the actions.

Most of the existing description formalisms for timed systems adopt implicitly the following view concerning their functioning:

- A timed system is the composition of cooperating sequential components (processes). Each component has a state variable defined on an appropriate time domain D with a binary operation + which has essentially the properties of addition on non negative numbers. A component may modify its state either by executing some (atomic) action or by increasing its time variable (letting time progress).

- System time progresses synchronously in all processes, i.e., from a given global state, time increases by a quantity d if all the components accept to do so.

- An execution sequence is a sequence of two-phase steps: In the first phase φ_1 of a step, components may execute, either independently or in cooperation, a finite though arbitrarily long sequence of actions. In the second phase φ_2, components coordinate to let time progress by some finite or infinite amount. A new step begins when the second phase terminates. Figure 1 illustrates this principle for two interacting processes.

The functioning described combines both synchronous and asynchronous cooperation in two alternating phases: one where all the components agree for the time to progress, and an eventually terminating asynchronous computation phase during which the progress of time is blocked.

Most modes of cooperation of concurrent systems can be obtained by simplifying this functioning scheme. In fact, in the so called asynchronous cooperation only the action execution phase exists. In synchronous languages like Lustre [CHPP87], Esterel [BC85]

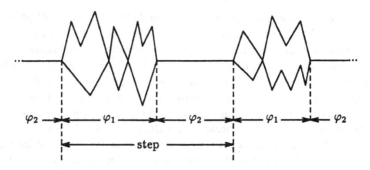

Figure 1: two-phase functioning schema

and the StateCharts [Har87], a step corresponds implicitly to one time unit and only the final state reached at the end of an asynchronous computation phase can be observed. This state is obtained by composing the effects of the actions (microsteps in the current terminology) and its computation raises some well-known causality problems. The so called synchronous cooperation, encountered in process algebras like SCCS [Mil83], CIRCAL [Mil91] and Meije [AB84], corresponds to a particular case of this functioning, where in addition, a process cannot perform more than one action in a step.

Such a mode of two-phase functioning is quite appropriate and natural for modelling reactive systems. For instance, the functioning of hardware and of systems for real-time control ideally follows this principle: a phase of asynchronous evolution is followed by a phase in which conceptually time progresses.

In a recent paper [NSY91], it is proposed a model for hybrid systems which adopts such a two-phase functioning principle. The phase where actions — "instantaneous" discrete changes of the state space — are executed is followed by a phase where state is transformed according to a law depending on time progress.

Considering such a mode of functioning allows to correlate the speeds of a system's components, as the flow of asynchronous computation can be cut by time progress phases in some appropriate manner. Furthermore, it introduces a concept of duration for an execution step and allows to assign durations to sequences of actions.

One might object that this two phase functioning assumption cannot faithfully model real systems where actions always take some non-zero time. In fact, direct consequences of this assumption are the following:

- Atomic actions take no time. This simplifies theoretical development and does not go against generality as non atomic actions can be modelled by sequences of atomic ones. It has been advantageously adopted by programming languages like Esterel [BC85].

- The time considered is *abstract* in the sense that it is used as a parameter to express constraints about instants of occurrences of actions. The implementability of such constraints taking into account speeds and execution times of processors, is a separate though not independent issue. This distinction between abstract and concrete or physical time is an important one. It allows simplifications that are convenient at conceptual level as it leads to simpler and more tractable models. For instance, the assumption that an action may take zero time, though not realistic for physical time, is quite convenient for abstract time. Of course, such an abstraction should take into account realisability issues by integrating requirements for safe implementations. For instance, eventual termination of the asynchronous computation phase is such a requirement; for a correct implementation it should be possible to determine the clock period as the upper bound of step durations computed so as to take into account execution time of sequences of ideally zero time actions.

It has been often argued that models where any action takes some non zero time — its execution time — allow more faithful descriptions. In fact such an assumption destroys abstractness of time as specifications depend on specific implementation choices. It will be shown that the zero duration assumption for atomic actions is more general and leads to much simpler theories.

The overview is carried out by considering successively the choices for a designer of a timed process algebra, at model level and at language level.

The choice of the model determines the semantics and thus the intrinsic expressivity of a process algebra. As various types of semantics have been used for the algebras considered, we take operational semantics — strong bisimulation semantics — as a basis of the comparison. The reason is that most algebras have been given such semantics or some operational semantics can be deduced in most of cases. In our comparison we take into account features allowing abstraction (silent actions, hiding) only as long as they enhance expressivity.

The languages used for timed process algebras can be viewed as extensions of the languages used for untimed process algebras by adding some specific constructs or by assuming that in some cases prefixing by an action may delay. Some criteria for the comparison of the languages considered are the minimality of the set of the operators and their appropriateness for a natural and direct description.

The paper is organised as follows:

- Section 2 is devoted to the presentation of a general model for timed systems defined for an arbitrary time domain. The model is transition systems labelled with either action names from an arbitrary action alphabet or by elements of an appropriate time domain D. Some general properties of this model are discussed as well as their importance concerning the capability to characterise time constraints of various types.

- In section 3, we present a comparison of the expressive capabilities of the following timed process algebras (presented in alphabetic order):

  - ACP_ρ (Real Time ACP) of J.C.M. Baeten and J.A. Bergstra [BB90,Klu91].

- ATP (Algebra of Timed Processes) of the authors [NRSV90,NS90]. We sometimes make reference to a variant of ATP presented in [NSY91].
- TCSP (Timed CSP) of G.M. Reed and A.W. Roscoe [RR88,DS89,Sch91].
- TeCCS (Temporal CCS, or TCCS) of F. Moller and C. Tofts [MT90].
- TiCCS (Timed CCS, or TCCS) of Wang Yi [Wan90,Wan91].
- TPCCS (Timed Probabilistic CCS) of H. Hansson and B. Jonsson. We focus only on features relative to time.
- TPL (Temporal Process Language) of M. Hennessy and T. Regan [HR90, HR91].
- U-LOTOS (Urgent LOTOS) of T. Bolognesi and F. Lucidi [BL91].

We especially focus on constructs used to describe time constraints and their semantics. The presentation is organised as an exercise for building a timed process algebra from a standard process algebra for untimed systems.

2 The models

In this section, we present a general model for timed systems. We consider labelled transition systems whose states are process expressions, and whose labels are either elements a of a *vocabulary of actions* A or elements d of a *time domain* D. A may contain non-visible (internal) actions denoted by τ; visible actions are denoted by α.

$P \xrightarrow{a} Q$ means that the process P may perform the atomic and timeless action a and then it behaves as Q.

$P \xrightarrow{d} Q$ means that the process P may *idle* for d time units after which it behaves as Q.

Before discussing the properties of such models, we propose a general definition of time domains.

2.1 Time domain

Definition: A *time domain* is a commutative monoid $(D, +, 0)$ satisfying the following requirements.

- $d + d' = d \Leftrightarrow d' = 0$

- the preorder $\leq$ defined by $d \leq d' \Leftrightarrow \exists d'' : d + d'' = d'$ is a total order

The following properties can be easily proved.

- 0 is the least element of D

- for any d, d', if $d \leq d'$, then the element d'' such that $d + d'' = d'$ is unique. It is denoted by $d' - d$

We denote $D - \{0\}$ by D_*. We also write $d < d'$ instead of $d \leq d' \wedge d \neq d'$.

D is called *dense* if $\forall d, d' : d < d' \Rightarrow \exists d'' : d < d'' < d'$

D is called *discrete* if $\forall d \exists d' : d < d' \wedge \forall d'' : d < d'' \Rightarrow d' \leq d''$. Since the order is total, d' is unique and is called the *successor* of d, denoted by $\mathrm{succ}(d)$. An important property of a discrete domain is that for any d, $\mathrm{succ}(d) = d + \mathrm{succ}(0)$. That is, any element of D can be obtained from 0 by adding as many $\mathrm{succ}(0)$ as necessary.

Examples of time domains are $\mathbb{N}$ (discrete), $\mathbb{Q}^+$ and $\mathbb{R}^+$ (dense), or even the singleton $\{0\}$.

In the transition relation defined in the beginning of this section, we do not allow 0 to be a label, that is, labels are elements of $A \cup D_*$.

2.2 The time domain in the algebras considered

TCSP and ACP$_\rho$ are explicitly defined over a dense time domain.

For TiCCS, TeCCS and U-LOTOS, the choice of a discrete or dense time domain is important neither for the syntax nor for the semantics. However, the axiomatisation strongly depends on this choice, especially for that of parallel composition. In TeCCS a complete set of axioms is provided in the discrete case. In [Wan91], Wang explains how an expansion theorem can be given in the dense case. This is possible only if we have a way of recording and use the instant when an action is performed.

TPCCS, TPL and ATP are defined over a discrete time domain. Extending them to a dense time domain requires some modification of the syntax. In [NSY91], a generalisation of ATP, parametrised by an arbitrary time domain, has been proposed.

2.3 Model properties

In this section we give an overview of the most important model properties and their importance for the characterisation of features of timed systems.

2.3.1 Time determinism

It is usually admitted that when a process P is idle (does not perform any action) for some duration d, then the resulting behaviour is completely determined from P and d. In other words, the progress of time should be deterministic. This property, satisfied by the models of all the algebras, we consider, can be expressed by

$$\forall P, P', P'', d : P \xrightarrow{d} P' \wedge P \xrightarrow{d} P'' \Rightarrow P' = P''$$

where $=$ is the syntactic equality.

2.3.2 Time additivity

In order to ensure the soundness of the notion of time, it is usually required that

- a process which can idle for $d + d'$ time units, can idle for d and then for d' time units, and vice-versa

- in both cases, the resulting behaviour is the same

We call this property *time additivity* (*time continuity* in [Wan90]). It is present in all the algebras and it is formally defined by

$$\forall P, P', d, d' : (\exists P'' : P \xrightarrow{d} P'' \wedge P'' \xrightarrow{d'} P') \Leftrightarrow P \xrightarrow{d + d'} P'$$

2.3.3 Deadlock-freeness

In untimed systems, a blocked or terminated process is represented by a deadlock in the model, since it cannot perform any action. For timed systems, it is natural to demand that, a terminated process does not block time, because of the strong synchrony hypothesis concerning time progress. If no distinction is made between termination and deadlock, this implies that there is no sink state in the model, which can be written as

$$\forall P \, \exists l \in A \cup D_* \, \exists P' : P \xrightarrow{l} P'$$

In algebras like TeCCS, U-LOTOS and ACP$_\rho$, there exist processes whose models do not satisfy this property, and thus they can block the progress of time Such *time-locks* may be used to detect some timing inconsistencies in specifications.

2.3.4 Action urgency

In all the considered algebras, there are processes which *must* perform an action without letting time pass, that is,

$$\exists P, a, P' : P \xrightarrow{a} P' \wedge \forall d : P \xrightarrow{d}\!\!\!\!/$$

This defines a notion of urgency for actions, as a process may block the progress of time and enforce the execution of an action before some delay.

However, in TPCCS, TPL, TCSP and TiCCS, urgency is possible — and is enforced — for invisible actions only; this can be expressed by

$$\forall P, P', d, Q : P \xrightarrow{\tau} P' \Rightarrow P \not\xrightarrow{d} Q$$

This property is called *minimal delay, maximal progress* or *tau-urgency*. In CCS-based algebras, it is strongly related to the communication mechanism. Indeed, a communication in CCS yields a tau action; thus, this property allows to ensure that two processes communicate as soon as they are ready to do so.

In models without the general action urgency, it is not possible, for instance, to characterise the situation where a process sends a message at most 3 time units after it has been requested to do so.

2.3.5 Persistency

In some algebras (TiCCS, U-LOTOS and TCSP), the progress of time cannot suppress the ability to perform an action. This property, called persistency, is expressed by

$$\forall P, Q, P', d, a : P \xrightarrow{a} P' \wedge P \xrightarrow{d} Q \Rightarrow \exists P'' : Q \xrightarrow{a} P''$$

This property is not satisfied by ATP, TPL, TPCCS, TeCCS and ACP_ρ. In the latter two, it is even possible, for instance, to specify a process which may perform an action a at time $\frac{1}{2}$ or an action b at time $\frac{5}{7}$. In TPCCS, TPL and ATP, such a behaviour does not exist. In the generic version of ATP presented in [NSY91], where the time domain may be dense, the models satisfy a weaker requirement than persistency, which we call *interval persistency*. This property asserts that if a process may let time progress, then any action it can perform remains possible during some time interval. This is expressed by

$$\forall P \exists d > 0 \forall d' \in]0, d[, \forall Q, P', a : P \xrightarrow{d'} Q \wedge P \xrightarrow{a} P' \Rightarrow \exists P'' : Q \xrightarrow{a} P''$$

Notice that this property is always true for a discrete time domain. Like ATP, TPL and TPCCS could be easily adapted to a dense domain, in which case their models would also have the interval persistency property.

2.3.6 Finite variability and bounded variability

A process has the *finite variability* (*non-Zenoness, well-timedness*) property if it can perform only finitely many actions in a finite time interval. The only algebra for which every process satisfy this requirement is TCSP. This is achieved by enforcing a *system-delay* between two actions of a sequential process. This assumption seems in fact to be the only solution to ensure finite variability, but it yields a complicated theory, and destroys abstractness of time.

To define formally this property, consider the family of relations $\overset{(a,d)}{\Longrightarrow}$ for $(a,d) \in A \times D_*$ on processes, defined by

$$P \stackrel{(a,\,d)}{\Longrightarrow} R \Leftrightarrow P \stackrel{d}{\longrightarrow} Q \wedge Q \stackrel{a}{\longrightarrow} R$$

A *time trace* of a process P is a maximal sequence $(a_0, d_0)\,(a_1, d_1)\ldots(a_i, d_i)\ldots$ such that

$$\exists P_1, P_2, \ldots, P_i, \ldots \; : \; P \stackrel{(a_0, d_0)}{\Longrightarrow} P_1 \stackrel{(a_1, d_1)}{\Longrightarrow} P_2 \ldots \stackrel{(a_i, d_i)}{\Longrightarrow} P_i \ldots$$

We represent by $T(P)$ the set of traces of P.

P satisfies the finite variability property if and only if

$$\forall d \; \forall \sigma = (a_0, d_0)\,(a_1, d_1)\ldots \in T(P) \; :$$
$$\left(i < j \leq \text{length}(\sigma) \wedge \sum_{k=i+1}^{j} d_k \leq d \right) \Rightarrow j - i < \infty$$

A stronger requirement should be satisfied by models in order that they represent implementable behaviours — we consider a behaviour to be *implementable* if it can be executed on a processor where the measure of time is provided by a discrete clock. We call this requirement *bounded variability*; it demands that for any duration d, there is an upper bound n of the number of actions performed within any time interval of length d.

This can be stated formally, for a given process P, by

$$\forall d \; \exists n \; \forall \sigma = (a_0, d_0)\,(a_1, d_1)\ldots \; \forall i, j \; :$$
$$\left(i < j \leq \text{length}(\sigma) \wedge \sum_{k=i+1}^{j} d_k \leq d \right) \Rightarrow j - i \leq n$$

This property guarantees implementability in the sense that one can establish a correspondence between model time d and a clock period for safe implementations. From this definition, for model time d one can take a clock period greater than or equal to $n.d_0$ where d_0 is an upper bound of atomic action durations. Bounded variability is satisfied by none of the considered algebras.

2.3.7 Bounded control

If we consider again realisability issues, for the same reasons as above, the set of initial actions of a process should not change too fast in a given time interval.

Given a process P, represent by $init(P)$ the set of the actions it can perform, i.e.,

$$init(P) = \{a \,|\, \exists P' \; : \; P \stackrel{a}{\longrightarrow} P'\}$$

A model has the bounded control property if there exists d such that for all states P and P' in the model, if $P \stackrel{d_1}{\longrightarrow} P'$ and $init(P) \neq init(P')$, then $d_1 \geq d$. In fact, the modification of

385

the initial actions corresponds to a change of the "control state" of the process. Bounded control expresses the fact that for any d, there is a bounded number of such changes in any time interval of duration d, and it means that it is possible to find a clock period which allows to handle these changes.

The bounded control property is satisfied for models defined over a discrete time domain, and for models of TCSP.

2.4 Discussion

An important question is which properties are essential and how their presence or absence influences description capabilities.

Most of the existing work adopt time determinism and additivity. Deadlock-freeness is not in our opinion an essential model property. Time-lock is of course an abnormal situation but in some theories it can correspond to non-realisable specifications.

A property like persistency seems to be a strong requirement which is very often adopted without justification. Saying that time progress does not change system's capabilities to perform actions seems to be counterintuitive as time is often used precisely as a parameter to control action executability (as in timeouts). This property, often combined with urgency with respect to τ only, allows to express the fact that some action *may* be executed during some time interval, but cannot guarantee *obligation* of execution. This corresponds, we believe, to a major distinction concerning description capabilities of formalisms.

Implementability properties prevent from having an unbounded number of state changes within finite time, which is an essential requirement for discrete machines. Both bounded variability and bounded control properties allow to establish a relationship connecting abstract (model) time with a processor's discrete clock period.

In the sequel, we consider models that are time deterministic and additive. As D is usually infinite, the models are generally infinitely branching transition systems. Figure 2 represents the model of the process "P timeout(3) Q" which behaves as P before time 3 or as Q at time 3, for $D = \mathbb{N}$, $D = \{0, 0.5, 1, 1.5, ...\}$ and D dense.

3 The Languages — How to Cook your own Timed Process Algebra

In this section we present an overview of the language features of the process algebras considered. We especially focus on constructs used to describe time constraints, their semantics, and the extension of the semantics of standard operators for timed transitions.

The presentation is organised as an exercise of building a timed process algebra TPA from a standard process algebra for untimed systems. Given such an untimed process algebra UPA we review the different ways of extending it encountered in the literature.

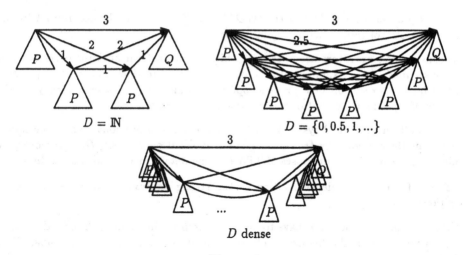

$D = \mathbb{N}$

$D = \{0, 0.5, 1, ...\}$

D dense

Figure 2

To make the comparison as concrete as possible, we define the meaning of constructs in terms of the common reference model presented in the previous section. The interpretation of the original semantics into this common framework required some simplifications that, we hope, do not bias the comparisons.

3.1 General principles

3.1.1 Process algebra

A process algebra PA is defined as a quadruple $(OP, L, R_L^{OP}, \sim)$ where

- OP is a set of operators defining the language of PA

- L is a set of transition labels

- R_L^{OP} is a set of structural operational semantics rules à la Plotkin [Plo81] associating with a term of PA a transition system labelled on L (a model)

- $\sim \subseteq$ PA × PA is a behavioural equivalence defined over the models. It it usually required that this equivalence be a congruence, since a compositional semantics is an crucial issue for a language

3.2 Timed process algebra

We consider here an *untimed process algebra* UPA $= (OP, A, R_A^{OP}, \sim)$, where A is a vocabulary of actions and $\sim$ is the strong equivalence relation [Mil80,Mil83].

The *timed process algebra* TPA $= (OP \cup OP', L, R_L^{OP \cup OP'}, \overset{T}{\sim})$ is defined from UPA by adding a set OP' of *time-constraining* operators.

Time-constraining operators are operators which can transform untimed processes into *time-constrained* ones. Examples of such operators are: time-lock constructs, operators which delay the execution of a process, operators which impose some urgency on the execution of a process, timeout operators, watchdog operators.

Processes of TPA are timed systems. Following the ideas in previous section, we decide to represent their models by transition systems labelled on $L = A \cup D_*$. Moreover, we require that the models of processes of TPA be time-deterministic and time-additive.

We choose for the equivalence relation $\overset{T}{\sim}$ the strong equivalence with respect to L-transitions.

In UPA, time progress does not have to be represented in the models, since by definition, it has no influence on the behaviour of an untimed process. In order to embed UPA in TPA, we have to choose the timed model corresponding to an untimed process (its time-equivalent). This must take into account the following requirements.

Semantics conservation: the untimed process and its time-equivalent should have the same behaviour as long as we observe execution of actions only. This imposes that the rules R_A^{OP} of UPA remain valid in TPA, *as far as they are applied on terms of UPA*.

Isomorphism: we also require that for any terms P, Q of UPA $P \sim Q$ if and only if $P \overset{T}{\sim} Q$. This requirement guarantees that the theory of processes of UPA is isomorphic to that of the restriction of TPA to operators of UPA. Thus, any theoretical development in UPA about an untimed process remains valid in TPA, and conversely.

In the sequel we consider a standard process algebra UPA and apply these principles.

3.3   Syntax and semantics of UPA

The language of terms of UPA is described by the following syntax, where Nil is is a constant, a and α are elements of A, $\alpha \neq \tau$, and X is an element of a set of process variables $\mathcal{X}$.

$$P ::= Nil \ | \ X \ | \ aP \ | \ P + Q \ | \ P \| Q \ | \ P \backslash \alpha \ | \ \mathbf{rec} X \cdot P$$

All the operators except $\|$ are taken from CCS [Mil80]. We choose prefixing instead of sequential composition to simplify the presentation, since it usually yields a simpler theory. The restriction operator $P \backslash \alpha$ prevents P from performing the visible action α.

We do not impose any choice of parallel composition operator, which can be CCS-like, ACP-like (in which case we must define a communication function for actions), or CSP or LOTOS-like (it should then be parametrised by sets of actions).

For such a language, we suppose that a standard operational semantics is defined, in terms of transition systems labelled by element of A (actions), by the following axiom and rules

$$aP \xrightarrow{a} P \qquad \frac{P \xrightarrow{a} P'}{P + Q \xrightarrow{a} P'} \qquad \frac{Q \xrightarrow{a} Q'}{P + Q \xrightarrow{a} Q'}$$

$$\frac{P \xrightarrow{b} P', b \neq \alpha}{P \backslash \alpha \xrightarrow{b} P' \backslash \alpha} \qquad \frac{P[(recX \cdot P)/X] \xrightarrow{a} P'}{recX \cdot P \xrightarrow{a} P'}$$

We do not provide the semantic rules for the parallel composition operator; we only demand that it has an interleaving semantics, as we take the models to be transition systems labelled on A.

3.4 Embedding UPA in a TPA

We first have to define how to add time to an untimed process, taking into account the requirements presented in 3.2.

Isomorphism. A simple answer to the isomorphism requirement is obtained by considering that time progress is possible without effect at any point of the execution of an untimed process. We obtain then the timed model of a term P of UPA by adding loops of the form $P \xrightarrow{d} P$ for any d of D_*. Another possibility is to allow P to idle if and only if it cannot perform any action u of some subset U of *urgent actions* of A. For instance, U may be the subset of internal actions of A. This induces urgency in the models for states with a u among their initial actions. We can express this solution by the rule

$$\frac{\forall u \in U, P \xrightarrow{u} \!\!\!\!\!\!/}{P \xrightarrow{d} P}$$

The latter principle is implicitly adopted in TiCCS, TPL and TPCCS with $U = \{\tau\}$, whereas the former one is adopted in U-LOTOS, ACP$_\rho$, TeCCS and ATP. We can consider the first solution as a particular case of the second one, with $U = \emptyset$.

In TCSP, the solution adopted (adding a system delay after execution of an action in a sequential process and before each recursive call) does not satisfy the requirement. For instance, the process $recX \cdot aX$ is not equivalent to the process $a\,recX \cdot aX$ in TCSP while they are equivalent in untimed CSP. Hence, the laws of CSP are no longer valid in TCSP.

Notice that the correspondence between operators of UPA and their equivalent in TPA is not immediate in ACP$_\rho$, TeCCS and ATP.

- In basic ACP_ρ, some of the operators of ACP are not present, but may be derived (for instance the atomic action constants).

- In TeCCS and ATP, the timed process $a\,P$ does not correspond to the untimed process $a\,P$. In fact, the latter corresponds, in TeCCS to $\delta\,a\,P$, and in ATP to $\lfloor a\,P \rfloor^\omega$. Similarly, in TeCCS, Nil does not correspond to 0, but to $\delta 0$. The confusion for prefixing may be removed if we denote it differently in the timed algebra.

In the sequel, we consider the general solution to the isomorphism requirement, with a set of urgent actions U.

Semantics conservation. The other requirement demands that the operational semantics rules for time-equivalent of untimed processes of UPA remain valid in TPA. For instance, in TPA, there should be a rule

$$\frac{P, P', Q \in \text{UPA}\ , P \xrightarrow{a} P'}{P + Q \xrightarrow{a} P'}$$

Since it is syntactically possible to determine whether a term of TPA is built using operators of UPA only, we can define a predicate $\text{InUPA}(P)$, whose value is true if P is in UPA. The rule may then be rewritten in

$$\frac{\text{InUPA}(P), \text{InUPA}(P'), \text{InUPA}(Q),\ P \xrightarrow{a} P'}{P + Q \xrightarrow{a} P'}$$

However, if we want to obtain a compositional semantics of TPA, the premise $P, P', Q \in \text{UPA}$ is not enough; it should be replaced by

$$\exists P_1, P'_1, Q'_1\ :\ \text{InUPA}(P_1),\ \text{InUPA}(P'_1),\ \text{InUPA}(Q_1),\ P \overset{T}{\sim} P_1,\ P' \overset{T}{\sim} P'_1,\ Q \overset{T}{\sim} Q_1$$

This kind of premise is clearly not acceptable in a structural operational semantics rule, since it is not based on a syntactic predicate, but on an semantic one: indeed, it means that we have to decide operationally whether some process of TPA has a model equivalent to a process of UPA.

We have thus to admit that this rule, and all the other rules of R_A^{OP} in UPA, are also valid in TPA.

3.4.1 Timed transitions of UPA operators

Concerning the definition of timed transitions, the semantics of OP in TPA must be defined so that

$$\frac{\forall u \in U, \; P \xrightarrow{u} \!\!\!\!\not\;\;}{P \xrightarrow{d} P}$$

for any P where only elements of OP occur.

Of course, such a rule should not be applicable to any TPA process. It can be checked that the semantic rules for TPA below satisfy the following properties.

- Their restriction to time-equivalents of UPA gives the same derivations as the above rule,

- They preserve time determinism and additivity,

Moreover, they are perfectly acceptable for TPA processes.

$$Nil \xrightarrow{d} Nil \qquad \frac{a \notin U}{aP \xrightarrow{d} aP} \qquad \frac{P \xrightarrow{d} P', \; Q \xrightarrow{d} Q'}{P + Q \xrightarrow{d} P' + Q'}$$

$$\frac{P \xrightarrow{d} P', \; Q \xrightarrow{d} Q', \; \forall u \in U : \left(P \| Q \xrightarrow{u} \!\!\!\!\not\;\; \wedge \; \forall d' < d \, \forall P' : P \| Q \xrightarrow{d'} P' \Rightarrow P' \xrightarrow{u} \!\!\!\!\not\;\; \right)}{P \| Q \xrightarrow{d} P' \| Q'}$$

$$\frac{P \xrightarrow{d} P'}{P \backslash \alpha \xrightarrow{d} P' \backslash \alpha} \qquad \frac{P[(\mathbf{rec}X \cdot P)/X] \xrightarrow{d} P'}{\mathbf{rec}X \cdot P \xrightarrow{d} P'}$$

The rule for parallel composition means that the composition of P and Q can idle for d if both can do so, and moreover, if the composition cannot perform an urgent action before d.

The rules for $+$, $\|$ and restriction apply when the operands of the operators have d-transitions. However, in TPS, there may be processes without such transitions. We have to decide what is the effect of these operators in this case.

- For parallel composition, it is not possible to add a rule without violating the strong synchrony hypothesis.

- In $P \backslash \alpha$, if α is in U and is the only urgent action that P may perform, then the rules for restriction yield a state which is, either a sink state, or a state where non-urgent actions are made urgent. If we do not want such behaviours, we have to add the following rule.

$$\frac{\forall u \in U : P \xrightarrow{u} \Rightarrow u = \alpha}{P \backslash \alpha \xrightarrow{d} P \backslash \alpha}$$

- For the alternative choice, we may decide that if P may idle, but not Q, then $P + Q$ may idle, by adding the rule

$$\frac{P \xrightarrow{d} P', Q \xrightarrow{d} \!\!\!\!\!\! /}{P + Q \xrightarrow{d} P'}$$

and its symmetric.

This semantics for + is adopted in ACP$_\rho$. In TeCCS, two alternative choice operators are defined: the *weak choice* operator, for which the latter rules are added, and the *strong choice* one, where they are not. The other algebras propose the strong choice operator (we only consider the external choice of TCSP, which is strong).

3.5 Time-constraining operators

We present time-constraining operators used in the process algebras considered. The aim of the presentation is a classification and comparison without caring about minimality. We also emphasise the effect of the operators on the properties of the models.

3.5.1 Time-lock

It is a constant 0 representing the process performing no transition. It is a basic operator of TeCCS, and it can be derived in U-LOTOS. In ACP$_\rho$, the process $\delta(d)$ is a time-lock at time d.

Naturally, a time-lock process may be present only if the deadlock-freeness property is not required.

3.5.2 Delay operators

Operators for delaying processes are the most common ones in process algebras. Their effect consists in postponing the execution of a process by a parameter d. We can classify them into three groups.

Finite idling is defined with various syntaxes as a basic operator in TiCCS, TeCCS, TPL, U-LOTOS and TCSP. We denote it by a prefixing operator (d). where $d > 0$. $(d)P$ behaves as P after exactly d time units. Its semantics is given by the following rules.

$$\frac{d' < d}{(d)P \xrightarrow{d'} (d - d')P} \qquad (d)P \xrightarrow{d} P$$

Finite idling may be modelised in ATP, TPCCS and ACP_ρ, though its definition is not trivial in the latter, especially in the absolute time version.

Time-stamped actions. In ACP_ρ, the basic construct of the algebra is obtained by imposing a *time-stamp* to actions. Two versions are presented, with absolute or relative time-stamps. In the absolute case $a(d)$ performs a at time d since the beginning of the process, whereas in the relative case, $a[d]$ performs a d time units after the previous action has been performed. In the latter case, and if we consider it as a prefixing operator, its semantics may be described by

$$\frac{d' \leq d}{a[d] \xrightarrow{d'} a[d - d']P} \qquad a[0]P \xrightarrow{a} P$$

Time-stamped actions induce the general urgency property in the models. It can be modelled only in algebras where this property is allowed. In ACP_ρ, due to the choice for the semantics of alternative choice, it suppresses also any kind of persistency in the transition systems.

Unbounded idling is defined in algebras where there may be urgent actions, like TeCCS and ATP. Its purpose is to suppress this urgency. However, it has a different semantics in these two algebras:

- in TeCCS, the unary operator δ has the following semantics:

$$\frac{P \xrightarrow{a} P'}{\delta P \xrightarrow{a} P'} \qquad \delta P \xrightarrow{d} \delta P$$

- in ATP, the operator $\lfloor \ \rfloor^\omega$ has the following semantics:

$$\frac{P \xrightarrow{a} P'}{\lfloor P \rfloor^\omega \xrightarrow{a} \lfloor P' \rfloor^\omega} \qquad \frac{P \xrightarrow{d} P'}{\lfloor P \rfloor^\omega \xrightarrow{d} \lfloor P' \rfloor^\omega} \qquad \frac{\forall d', P \xrightarrow{d'}\!\!\!\!/}{\lfloor P \rfloor^\omega \xrightarrow{d} \lfloor P \rfloor^\omega}$$

The difference is that in TeCCS, if P cannot execute immediately an action, then the process δP may only idle forever, whereas in ATP, the process P is allowed to let time progress.

Such operators are trivially definable in the other algebras, with the restriction that in those where τ is urgent, it is not possible to delay it.

Integral. In ACP_ρ, the integral operator $\int_{v\in V} P(v)$ for a process P parametrised by a time variable v behaves as P where v may be replaced by any value of the subset V of D. A simple use of this operator is $\int_{v\in I} a[v]$, where I is an interval. This process may perform an a at any time in I. Thus, it delays the execution of a by some value v in I. It can be described in TeCCS and ATP, provided the interval is right-closed.

Notice that in TiCCS, prefixing $a@v\, P$ is equivalent to an integral, where the interval I is the whole domain. The value v may be used in delay values in P. Such a construct is useful to provide an expansion theorem for parallel composition when the time domain is dense.

3.5.3 Urgency operators

Immediate actions. In TeCCS and ATP, prefixing by an action (aP) impose that this action be performed immediately. To avoid confusion with the prefixing operator of UPA, we denote this urgent prefixing by $\dot{a}P$. Its semantics is given by the unique axiom $\dot{a}P \xrightarrow{a} P$. It is also expressible in the algebras where urgency of actions are allowed, that is in U-LOTOS and ACP_ρ, if in the latter we allow the time-stamp 0. Conversely, it has no equivalent in the other algebras considered.

Time-stamped actions (ACP_ρ). They have been presented above. They have the double effect of delaying and imposing urgency once the delay has expired. We could call them a *punctuality* feature.

As soon as possible. In U-LOTOS, the primitive operator **asap** enforces the urgency of a set of actions in the whole execution of a process. For sake of simplicity, we only present its semantics in the case where this set of actions is reduced to a singleton.

$$\frac{P \xrightarrow{a'} P'}{\mathsf{asap}_a \text{ in } P \xrightarrow{a'} \mathsf{asap}_a \text{ in } P'} \qquad \frac{P \xcancel{\xrightarrow{a}}\ ,\ P \xrightarrow{d} P',\ \forall d'<d\,\forall Q,\ P \xrightarrow{d'} Q \Rightarrow Q \xcancel{\xrightarrow{a}}}{\mathsf{asap}_a \text{ in } P \xrightarrow{d} \mathsf{asap}_a \text{ in } P'}$$

The second rule means that the asap_a in P can idle for d if P can do so, and cannot perform an a before d.

This very powerful operator is expressible in ACP_ρ, ATP and TeCCS, and clearly not in the other algebras.

3.5.4 Timeout operators

A timeout is an operator with two arguments P and Q and a parameter $d \in D_*$. We call P the body and Q the exception of the timeout.

A timeout for P, Q and d behaves as P if an initial action of P is performed within time d, otherwise it behaves as Q, after time d.

Depending on the interpretation of "initial action" and "within time d", several variants of timeout operators have been proposed.

a) $P \overset{d}{\triangleright} Q$ in ATP_D ([NSY91]) with the following semantics.

$$\frac{P \xrightarrow{a} P'}{P \overset{d}{\triangleright} Q \xrightarrow{a} P'} \qquad \frac{P \xrightarrow{d'} P', \, d' < d}{P \overset{d}{\triangleright} Q \xrightarrow{d'} P' \overset{d-d'}{\triangleright} Q}$$

$$\frac{P \xrightarrow{d} P'}{P \overset{d}{\triangleright} Q \xrightarrow{d} Q} \qquad \frac{P \xrightarrow{d} P', \, Q \xrightarrow{d'} Q'}{P \overset{d}{\triangleright} Q \xrightarrow{d+d'} Q'}$$

The last rule is necessary to preserve time additivity.

With this operator an action that P may perform after some time is also interpreted as an "initial action" of P. "Within time d" is interpreted as "before time d"; we call timeouts with such a interpretation *strong timeouts*.

b) $\lfloor P \rfloor^d(Q)$ in ATP (start-delay operator) with the following semantics.

$$\frac{P \xrightarrow{a} P'}{\lfloor P \rfloor^d(Q) \xrightarrow{a} P'} \qquad \frac{P \xrightarrow{d'} P', \, d' < d}{\lfloor P \rfloor^d(Q) \xrightarrow{d'} \lfloor P' \rfloor^{d-d'}(Q)} \qquad \frac{\forall d' \, P \not\xrightarrow{d'}, \, d'' < d}{\lfloor P \rfloor^d(Q) \xrightarrow{d''} \lfloor P \rfloor^{d-d''}(Q)}$$

$$\lfloor P \rfloor^d(Q) \xrightarrow{d} Q \qquad \frac{Q \xrightarrow{d'} Q'}{\lfloor P \rfloor^d(Q) \xrightarrow{d+d'} Q'}$$

This operator differs from the previous one in that it also allows to postpone the urgent actions P may perform. It is a strong timeout too.

c) $P \triangleright_d Q$ in TPCCS is a strong timeout with a strict interpretation of initial actions:

$$\frac{P \xrightarrow{a} P'}{P \triangleright_d Q \xrightarrow{a} P'} \qquad \frac{d' < d}{P \triangleright_d Q \xrightarrow{d'} P \triangleright_{d-d'} Q}$$

$$P \triangleright_d Q \xrightarrow{d} Q \qquad \frac{Q \xrightarrow{d'} Q'}{P \triangleright_d Q \xrightarrow{d+d'} Q'}$$

d) The timeout of TCSP is a weak one, in the sense that at time d both the body and the exception can be executed; that is, P may start in the interval $[0,d]$, and Q may be chosen at d. The weak timeout preserves persistency in the models. The interpretation of initial actions is the same as in case a. In the semantics, an urgent internal action τ is used to enforce a choice between P and Q at time d. The weak timeout can be expressed in terms of the strong one, but the converse is not true.

3.5.5 Watchdog operators

A watchdog is an operator with two arguments P (body) and Q (exception) and a parameter d in D_*.

It behaves as P until time d. At time d, P is "aborted" and Q is started.

Such operators are proposed in ATP (execution delay) and TCSP (time interrupt). As for the timeouts, the watchdog is strong in ATP, and weak in TCSP (in the latter, P may still perform some action at time d, which is not the case in ATP).

In TCSP, if P terminates successfully, the watchdog is cancelled. In ATP, there is no operational notion of termination. However, the watchdog may be cancelled if P performs a special action ξ, called *cancel*. We present hereafter the semantics of the watchdog of ATP.

$$\frac{P \xrightarrow{a} P', a \neq \xi}{\lceil P\rceil^d(Q) \xrightarrow{a} \lceil P'\rceil^d(Q)} \qquad \frac{P \xrightarrow{\xi} P'}{\lceil P\rceil^d(Q) \xrightarrow{\tau} P'}$$

$$\frac{P \xrightarrow{d'} P', d' < d}{\lceil P\rceil^d(Q) \xrightarrow{d'} \lceil P'\rceil^{d-d'}(Q)} \qquad \frac{P \xrightarrow{d} P'}{\lceil P\rceil^d(Q) \xrightarrow{d} Q} \qquad \frac{P \xrightarrow{d} P', Q \xrightarrow{d'} Q'}{\lceil P\rceil^d(Q) \xrightarrow{d+d'} Q'}$$

4 Discussion

The paper is an overview and synthesis of existing results about timed process algebras. It hopefully contributes to the clarification of the following three different problems, designers of timed specification languages should in principle address.

1. **What are the underlying principles of functioning of timed systems?** In the introduction, we formulate some assumptions about the two-phase mode of functioning and provide pragmatic justifications. This functioning corresponds to some abstraction of the reality which has the advantage of clearly separating the actions from the time progress issue. It is argued that adopting such an "orthogonality" principle between actions and timed transitions is more paying than other approaches

imposing some non-zero durations to actions. In the latter, time is not abstract, i.e., independent of implementation choices.

2. What is a general model for timed systems, and what are its most relevant properties? Following assumptions about the functioning of timed systems, we take as models transition systems whose labels are either elements of an action vocabulary or elements of an appropriately chosen time domain.

   Concerning the properties studied, they can be classified as follows.

   - time determinism and additivity characterise fundamental properties of time.
   - properties characterising the expressivity of the model, like presence of time-locks and the different types of persistency or urgency.
   - realisability properties.

   The choice of a particular class of models should be determined for a given time domain as a compromise between realisability and expressivity.

3. How an untimed specification language can be consistently extended so as to obtain a timed specification language? We suggest a principle which has been more or less followed in several cases of consistent extensions (except for TCSP). Concerning the description capabilities of the language, it is difficult to make a precise comparison due to the differences of the semantic framework adopted. However, an important distinction appears concerning the expression of urgency.

This is a first partial synthesis of results in the area, which hopefully contributes to structuring them and suggests an approach for tackling the problem of introducing time in process algebras.

References

[AB84]   D. Austry and G. Boudol. Algèbre de processus et synchronisation. *Theoretical Computer Science*, 30, 1984.

[BB90]   J.C.M. Baeten and J.A. Bergstra. *Real Time Process Algebra*. Technical Report CS-R9053, Centre for Mathematics and Computer Science, Amsterdam, the Netherlands, 1990.

[BC85]   G. Berry and L. Cosserat. The ESTEREL synchronous programming language and its mathematical semantics. In *LNCS 197: Proceedings CMU Seminar on Concurrency*, Springer-Verlag, 1985.

[BL91]   T. Bolognesi and F. Lucidi. LOTOS-like process algebra with urgent or timed interactions. In *Proceedings of REX Workshop "Real-Time: Theory in Practice"*. Mook, the Netherlands, June 1991.

[CHPP87] P. Caspi, N. Halbwachs, D. Pilaud, and J. Plaice. LUSTRE: a declarative language for programming synchronous systems. In *14th Symposium on Principles of Programming Languages*, Munich, January 1987.

[DS89] J. Davies and S. Schneider. *An Introduction to Timed CSP*. Technical Report PRG-75, Oxford University Computing Laboratory, UK, August 1989.

[Har87] D. Harel. StateCharts : a visual approach to complex systems. *Science of Computer Programming*, 8–3:231–275, 1987.

[HR90] M. Hennessy and T. Regan. *A Temporal Process Algebra*. Technical Report 2/90, University of Sussex, UK, April 1990.

[HR91] M. Hennessy and T. Regan. *A Process Algebra for Timed Systems*. Technical Report 5/91, University of Sussex, UK, April 1991.

[Klu91] A.S. Klusener. *Completeness in Real Time Process Algebra*. Technical Report CS-R9106, Centre for Mathematics and Computer Science, Amsterdam, the Netherlands, January 1991.

[Mil80] R. Milner. A Calculus of Communicating Systems. In *LNCS 92*, Springer Verlag, 1980.

[Mil83] R. Milner. Calculi for Synchrony and Asynchrony. *Theoretical Computer Science*, 25, 1983.

[Mil91] G. J. Milne. The Formal Description and Verification of Hardware Timing. *IEEE Transactions on Computers*, 40 (7), July 1991.

[MT90] F. Moller and C. Tofts. A Temporal Calculus of Communicating Processes. In J.C.M. Baeten and J.W. Klop, editors, *LNCS 458. Proceedings of CONCUR '90 (Theories of Concurrency: Unification and Extension)*, Amsterdam, the Netherlands, pages 401–415, Springer-Verlag, August 1990.

[NRSV90] X. Nicollin, J.-L. Richier, J. Sifakis, and J. Voiron. ATP: an Algebra for Timed Processes. In *Proceedings of the IFIP TC 2 Working Conference on Programming Concepts and Methods*, Sea of Gallilee, Israel, April 1990.

[NS90] X. Nicollin and J. Sifakis. *The algebra of timed processes ATP: theory and application*. Technical Report RT-C26, LGI-IMAG, Grenoble, France, December 1990.

[NSY91] X. Nicollin, J. Sifakis, and S. Yovine. From ATP to Timed Graphs and Hybrid Systems. In *Proceedings of REX Workshop "Real-Time: Theory in Practice"*. Mook, the Netherlands, June 1991.

[Plo81] G.D. Plotkin. *A Structural Approach to Operational Semantics*. Technical Report DAIMI FN-19, Århus University. Computer Science Department, Århus, Denmark, 1981.

[RR88]   G.M. Reed and A.W. Roscoe. A timed model for Communicating Sequential Processes. *Theoretical Computer Science*, 58 (pp 249–261), 1988.

[Sch91]   S. Schneider. *An Operational Semantics for Timed CSP*. Programming Research Group, Oxford University, UK, February 1991.

[Wan90]   Wang Yi. Real-time behaviour of asynchronous agents. In J.C.M. Baeten and J.W. Klop, editors, *LNCS 458. Proceedings of CONCUR '90 (Theories of Concurrency: Unification and Extension), Amsterdam, the Netherlands*, pages 502–520, Springer-Verlag, August 1990.

[Wan91]   Wang Yi. CCS + Time = an Interleaving Model for Real Time Systems. In *Proceedings of ICALP '91, Madrid, Spain*, July 1991.

MINIMUM AND MAXIMUM DELAY PROBLEMS IN REAL-TIME SYSTEMS

Costas Courcoubetis [*]

Computer Science Institute, FORTH
and
Computer Science Dept.
University of Crete

Mihalis Yannakakis

AT&T Bell Laboratories
Murray Hill, NJ 07974

ABSTRACT

We consider a finite state system with a finite number of clocks, where the transitions may depend on the values of the clocks, and may reset some of the clocks. We address the complexity and provide algorithms for the following problems. Suppose that the system starts from a given current state with a given assignment of values to the clocks. Can a given target state ever appear in the history of the system? What is the earliest time it can appear? What is the latest time it can appear?

1. Introduction

The use of computers to control and interact with physical processes is rapidly growing as computing becomes faster and cheaper. An important characteristic which distinguishes such applications from traditional ones, is their real-time aspect. Real-time programs such as airplane controllers, real-time operating systems, switching software and process controllers in manufacturing plants are inherently reactive, and their interaction with the environment must occur in real-time. The correct operation of such systems is more than logical consistency in terms of event sequences, and extends to the satisfaction of "hard" real-time constraints: for example, it is not enough for the flight control to eventually react to an obstacle in the course of the plane, it must do this *on time*! Other systems in which the explicit notion of time plays an important role is communication systems and particularly communication protocols; the performance of such systems vitally depends on the value of timers, which control message retransmission. If the setting of these timers is incorrect and does not take into account the range of the round-trip message delay, the performance of the system will degrade due to unnecessary retransmissions. We should also mention the case of digital circuits, where the timing in the interaction of their components is crucial for their correct operation.

[*] Work partially supported by the BRA ESPRIT project SPEC

It is intuitively obvious that correctness of real-time systems is more subtle and harder than for traditional systems. One reason for this is that the parameter time is not discrete, does not range over a finite domain, and has its own dynamics beyond the control of the programs. This makes the verification of such systems a challenging and sometimes impossible task. Although for discrete time systems there has been extensive progress in the area of automatic verification, only recently there has been progress in the case of their real-time counterpart. There have been a number of models and logics to reason about real-time systems proposed in [AD90], [ACD90], [Di89], [Le90], [AH89]. Algorithms for the automatic verification of such systems have been proposed in [ACD90], [ACD91]. Correctness was defined in terms of the histories of a real-time system satisfying certain properties which explicitly depend on time. An important issue these papers did not address concerns the derivation of bounds for the time at which different events can occur. For example, although there are algorithms to check that "a message can arrive before time t", the problem of determining the maximum (or minimum) such time was still open. This is the type of problem we solve in this paper.

Our model of a real-time system is a *timed graph*, as introduced in [ACD90]. These graphs model "finite-state" real-time systems. Such a system has a finite set of states and a finite set of real-valued clocks. A clock can be reset simultaneously with any transition of the system. At any instant, the value of a clock is equal to the time elapsed since the last time this clock was reset. The real-time information is given in terms of enabling conditions of the edges; a transition is enabled if the values of the clocks satisfy a certain predicate. Formally, a timed graph is a tuple (S, E, C, π, τ), where S is a finite set of states, $E \subset S \times S$ is the set of edges, C is a finite set of clocks, $\pi : E \to 2^C$ tells which clocks should be reset with each transition, and τ is a function labeling each transition with an enabling condition built using the boolean connectives over the atomic formulas of the form $x \leq d$ and $d \leq x$, where $x \in C$, and $d \in N$ (N denotes the non-negative integers). We could generalize our approach to include enabling conditions of the form $x - y \leq d$ and $d \leq x - y$, where $x, y \in C$, and $d \in N$; we will not do that for keeping the presentation simple. Note also that comparing the value of the clocks with integers is as powerful as comparing them to rationals, since we could always define a unit of time sufficiently small with respect to which the rational constraints will turn into integer ones. An example of a timed graph can be found in figure 1.

Although the semantics of this model will be formally described in the following section, we can describe them intuitively as follows. The system starts in some initial state s_0 with some initial clock assignment. The values of the clocks increase uniformly with time. At any point in time, the system can make a transition if the associated condition is enabled by the current values of the clocks. The transitions are instantaneous. With each transition e, the clocks in $\pi(e)$ get reset to 0 and start counting time with respect to the time the transition occurred. At any point in time, the complete configuration of the system is described by specifying the current state and the values of the clocks. Clearly, such a system has uncountably many configurations. A *real-time trajectory* is a function giving the value of the complete configuration of this system as a function of time.

We will examine the following problems in the context of timed graphs.

The Timed Graph Reachability Problem: Given a timed graph G, some initial state s_0, some initial clock assignment v, and some final state s_f, determine if s_f appears in some real-time trajectory of G starting from configuration s_0, v. A variant of this problem is when we are not given an initial clock assignment, but we want to determine whether we can reach s_f starting from s_0 for *some* initial clock assignment v.

The Minimum Delay Problem in Timed Graphs: Given a timed graph G, some initial state s_0, some initial clock assignment v, and some reachable final state s_f, how fast can we reach s_f starting from the configuration s_0, v? Technically, there may be no "best" path; i.e., it is possible that every path can be shortened by an infinitesimal amount, so to be precise, we seek the greatest lower bound on the time t that it takes for all real-time trajectories starting from s_0, v to reach (some configuration with) state s_f.

The Maximum Delay Problem in Timed Graphs: Given a timed graph G, some initial state s_0, some initial clock assignment v, and some final state s_f, find the least upper bound on the time t at which any real-time trajectory of the system visits a configuration with state s_f. In both the maximum and the minimum delay problems we are also interested in the variants where we are not given an initial clock assignment v, but rather we wish to optimize over all possible v.

The example in figure 1 illustrates these problems. One can easily see that state s_4 is not reachable, that state s_3 can only appear during the open interval $(2, 3)$, and that state s_2 can appear at any time larger than 2.

The reachability problem can be solved using the techniques of [ACD90]. From a timed graph G, they show how to construct an ordinary graph, called the *region graph*, which provides a finitary representation of the system preserving the reachability properties of interest. The region graph has size polynomial in the number of states and edges of the timed graph, but exponential in (1) the number of clocks, and (2) the (binary) length of the constants that appear in the enabling conditions of the timed graph. We show that the reachability problem is PSPACE-complete. Furthermore, this holds even if the constants are small but there are many clocks, or there are few clocks but the constants are large, which indicates that both exponential dependencies are unavoidable. Our main positive results are efficient algorithms for the minimum and the maximum delay problems. We show that both problems can be solved in time that is essentially linear in the size of the region graph and the length of the initial clock assignment v. *

The paper is organized as follows. In Section 2 we give definitions and notation and review the concept of the region graph from [ACD90]. In Section 3 we prove the lower bounds for the simple reachability problem. In Sections 4 and 5 respectively we address the minimum and the maximum delay problems. Finally in Section 6 we offer some concluding remarks and address the remaining open problems.

2. Preliminaries

Let $G = (S, E, C, \pi, \tau)$ be a timed graph. We let $\Gamma(G)$ denote the set of *time assignments* for the clocks of G, i.e., the set of mappings from the set C of clocks to the set of non-negative reals. We represent a configuration of the system by the tuple $<s, v>$, where $s \in S$ and $v \in \Gamma(G)$. In what follows, we will use the above notation and the terminology "configuration of G" to refer to a configuration of the real-time system modelled by G. Also we denote by v_x the value of the clock x in the clock assignment v. Let $v \in \Gamma(G)$ and $t \in R$. Then $v + t$ denotes the time assignment for the clocks which assigns to each $y \in C$ the value $v_y + t$, and $[x \rightarrow t]v$ denotes the time assignment for the clocks in C which assigns t to the clock x and agrees with v on the values of the rest of the clocks.

---

* Assumming that v is rational. Our algorithms work also in the case that the initial clock assignment v is real, in the usual model of infinite precision real arithmetic.

A *real-time trajectory* of G starting from the configuration $<s_0, v_0>$ is a sequence of triplets $(s(i), v(i), t(i))$, $i = 0, 1, \cdots$, where $s(i) \in S$ is a state of the timed graph, $v(i) \in \Gamma(G)$ is a time assignment to the clocks, $t(i) \in R$ is a real time satisfying the following conditions:

(a) $s(0) = s_0$, $v(0) = v_0$, $t(0) = 0$,

(b)   the time of the $i+1$th transition is greater or equal to the time of the ith transition, $t(i+1) \geq t(i)$, $i = 0, 1, \cdots$,

(c) $e_i = (s(i), s(i+1))$ is an edge in E, and the time assignment $(v(i) + t(i+1) - t(i))$ satisfies the enabling condition $\tau(e_i)$,

(d)   the time assignment $v(i+1)$ at time $t(i+1)$ equals $[\pi(e_i) \to 0](v(i) + t(i+1) - t(i))$.

(e)   Every time is eventually reached; i.e., for every $t \in R$ there is an i such that $t(i) > t$.

From this definition, such a trajectory gives us all the information we need in order to construct a complete evolution of our system as a function of continuous time. We can think of a trajectory to be the embedding of a system continuous time behaviour at the times at which a transition occurs. Note that this definition allows more than one transitions to occur in the same time. That is, the time of the clocks is stopped, and the system can perform instantaneously several transitions which are enabled one after the other; each transition is enabled by the clock assignment which the previous one produced. Our results hold also in the model where this is not allowed; i.e., if the inequality in condition (b) is strict.

From the above discussion it follows that we can think of trajectories as being defined over continuous time. Let $<s(t), v(t)>$, $t \geq 0$, be such a continuous time version of a trajectory $(s(i), v(i), t(i))$, $i = 0, 1, \cdots$. If $t(i) < t(i+1) = \cdots = t(i+k) = t < t(i+k+1)$, we define $s(t)$ to be the list $s(i+1), \ldots, s(i+k)$, we let $v(t)$ be the list $v(i+1), \ldots, v(i+k)$, and define the function *last* such that $last(a_1, \ldots, a_k) = a_k$. Then if $t(j) \leq t < t(j+1)$ we define $s(t) = last(s(j))$ and $v(t) = last(v(j)) + t$. In the rest of the paper we will use both versions to represent trajectories, depending from the context. We will say that the trajectory $<s(t), v(t)>$ *hits* at time t_1 some configuration $<s, v>$ if $s(t_1) = s$ and $v(t_1) = v$, or s and v are corresponding elements of the lists $s(t_1)$ and $v(t_1)$ in case the trajectory makes several transitions at time t_1.

For each clock $x \in C$ we let c_x be the largest constant to which x is compared in any enabling condition of a transition of G. If t is a real number, we use $fract(t)$ to denote its fractional part. Given two clock assignments $v, v' \in \Gamma(G)$, we say that they are *equivalent* ($v \approx v'$) if the following two conditions are met:

(a)   For each $x \in C$, either the integral part of v_x and v'_x are the same, or both v_x and v'_x are greater than c_x.

(b)   For every $x, y \in C$ such that $v_x \leq c_x$ and $v_y \leq c_y$, we have that $fract(v_x) \leq fract(v_y)$ iff $fract(v'_x) \leq fract(v'_y)$, and that $fract(v_x) = 0$ iff $fract(v'_x) = 0$.

We denote by $[v]$ the equivalence class of $\Gamma(G)$ to which v belongs. Consider the following example for a timed graph G with $c_x = 2$ and $c_y = 1$. The equivalence classes are shown in figure 2. They correspond to corner points (e.g. $(1,1)$), open line segments (e.g. $\{(x,y) \mid 0 < x < 1 \text{ and } x = y\}$, $\{(x,1) \mid x > 2\}$), and open regions (e.g. $\{(x,y) \mid 0 < x < y < 1\}$, $\{(x,y) \mid 1 < x < 2 \text{ and } y > 1\}$).

We call an equivalence class α a *boundary class* if it lies on a hyperplane $v_i = d$; thus, for any $v \in \alpha$ and any $t > 0$, v and $v + t$ are not equivalent. An equivalence class is *open* if it is not a boundary class. For an equivalence class α we define its *successor* class $succ(\alpha)$ to be the equivalence class β with the following property. Consider the clocks starting at some arbitrary assignment $v \in \alpha$ at time 0. As time elapses, the value of the clocks $v(t) = v + t$ will eventually switch from α to a different equivalence class β. Then $\beta = succ(\alpha)$. Note that $succ$ is defined and is unique for all classes except the *end class*, the equivalence class satisfying $x > c_x$ for all clocks $x \in C$, that does not have a successor.

The following property concerning equivalent clock assignments is proved in [ACD90]. If $v \approx v'$, then for any trajectory starting from a configuration $<s, v>$ there is another trajectory starting from $<s, v'>$ going through the same sequence of states and equivalent clock assignments, and with its transitions times occurring "almost" at the same time with the corresponding transitions of the first trajectory. This motivates the definition of the region graphs.

We define a *region* as a pair $<s, [v]>$, where $s \in S$, and $[v]$ is an equivalence class of clock assignments. We also call a region $<s, [v]>$ a *boundary (open)* region if $[v]$ is a boundary (open) equivalence class. We can think of the region as denoting a set of system configurations; they all have the same state component, and their clock assignment is in the corresponding equivalence class. The *region graph* $R(G)$ corresponding to a timed graph G is a graph (V, M) defined over the set V of all possible regions, and its edge set M consists of two types of edges:

(a) Edges representing the passage of time ("time edges"); each vertex $<s, [v]>$ such that $[v]$ is not an end class, has an edge to $<s, succ([v])>$.

(b) Edges representing the transitions of G ("transition edges"); each vertex $<s, [v]>$ has for each edge $e = (s, s') \in E$ an edge to $<s', [[\pi(e) \to 0]v]>$, provided that v satisfies the enabling condition $\tau(e)$.

One can easily see that the number of equivalence classes of $\Gamma(G)$ induced by the above equivalence relation $\approx$ is bounded above by $|C|! \, 2^{|C|} \prod_{y \in C}(2c_y + 2)$. From this and the construction of $R(G)$ it follows that $|V| = O(|S| \, |C|! \prod_{y \in C} c_y)$, and $|M| = O((|S| + |E|) \, |C|! \prod_{y \in C} c_y)$.

The following lemma states the basic relation between trajectories of G and paths of $R(G)$ [ACD90].

Lemma 1: (1) For every trajectory $(s(i), v(i), t(i))$, $i = 0, 1, \cdots$ of the timed graph G, the corresponding sequence $<s(i), [v(i)]>$, $i = 0, 1, \cdots$, is a path in the region graph $R(G)$. (2) For every path in the region graph $R(i) = <s(i), \alpha(i)>$, $i = 0, 1, \cdots$ and for every configuration $<s(0), v(0)>$ in $R(0)$, there is a trajectory $(s'(i), v(i), t(i))$, $i = 0, 1, \cdots$, in G starting from that configuration, such that $s'(i) = s(i)$, and $[v(i)] = \alpha(i)$ for all $i = 0, 1, \cdots$.

3. The Timed Graph Reachability Problem

This problem reduces to an ordinary reachability problem in the corresponding region graph.

Proposition 1: There is a trajectory of the timed graph G starting from a configuration $<s_0, v>$ that hits the state s_f if and only if in the region graph $R(G)$ there is a path from the node $<s_0, [v]>$, to a node with first component s_f.

Proof: It is a direct consequence of Lemma 1.

$\square$

Thus, we can determine whether a configuration $<s_0, v>$ of G can reach a state s_f by computing the set of nodes of the region graph that are reachable from the node $<s_0, [v]>$. If we are not given an initial clock assignment v, then we just add a new node u to the region graph, add arcs to all the nodes with first component s_0, and compute the nodes reachable from u.

Corollary 1: The timed graph reachability problem can be solved in time linear in the size of the region graph, thus in time $O(|E| \, |C| ! \prod_{y \in C} c_y)$.

Alur, Courcoubetis and Dill used the region graph to derive an algorithm for model checking for a timed CTL logic [ACD90]. They also proved that model checking for general (complicated) formulas in this logic is PSPACE-complete. We show that even the basic reachability problem is hard. The following two theorems indicate that both sources of the exponential complexity in Corollary 1, namely, many clocks and large constants c_y, are apparently inherent.

Theorem 1: The timed graph reachability problem, restricted to instances with "small" constants (say, the constants are given in unary), is PSPACE-complete.

Sketch: The reduction is from the LBA acceptance problem. Given an LBA (Linear Bounded Automaton) M, and an input x, we construct a timed graph G with two distinguished states s_0 and s_f such that M accepts x iff there is a trajectory that reaches s_f starting from s_0 with the all zero clock assignment, iff there is a such a trajectory with an arbitrary initial clock assignment. The constants that appear in the enabling conditions of the transitions are 1 and 2. The states of G record the state and the head position of the LBA. There is one timer x_i for every cell of M. Assume without loss of generality that the tape alphabet of M is $\{1,2\}$. A move of the LBA is simulated by the following cycle. At the beginning each timer x_i has value 1 or 2 equal to the symbol in the ith cell. Reset "almost" all the 2's in zero time (by a sequence of instantaneous transitions); after one time unit, reset again "almost" all the 2's in zero time; let one time unit pass to complete the cycle and start the new cycle. By "almost all", we mean all except possibly the timer x_i corresponding to the cell where the tape head is, which is reset as follows: if the new symbol written in the ith tape cell is 2, then we reset the timer x_i in the first phase but not the second; if the new symbol is 1 then we reset x_i in the second phase. (A similar construction works if we cannot perform more than one instantaneous transitions one after the other, by using constants smaller than n.)
□

Theorem 2: The reachability problem for timed graphs with three timers is PSPACE-complete.

Sketch: We reduce again from the LBA acceptance problem. Assume a tape alphabet of $\{0,1\}$, and view a tape as a binary number. A move of the LBA is simulated by a cycle at the beginning of which a certain timer x_1 has value equal to the value of the tape. There is a part of the construction that decodes the appropriate bit of x_1 that corresponds to the current head position in order to determine the next move and update the state and the contents accordingly. The main problem is that this has to be done while time is running and the timer is changing. The two auxiliary timers are used to pass the value back and forth so that we do not lose track of the tape contents. We defer the details to the full paper.
□

4. The Minimum Delay Problem

We are given a timed graph G with set of clocks $C = \{x_1, \ldots, x_k\}$, a initial clock assignment $v_0 = t_1, \ldots, t_k$, an initial state s_0, and a final state s_f. Let F be the set of times at which the system can be in state s_f; that is, F is the set of times w such that there is a trajectory $<s(t), v(t)>$, starting from $s(0) = s_0$, $v(0) = v_0$, such that $s(w) = s_f$. We would like to compute $T_{min} = infimum(F)$. We solve this problem by solving the more general problem, where instead of specifying a state s_f one specifies an arbitrary region R. Clearly if we solve this more general problem for all regions containing the state s_f (there are finitely many of them), then the minimum of these solutions will be the solution of the original problem.

We solve this more general minimum time problem by reducing it to a shortest path problem in a ordinary weighted graph G'. Then, for efficiency reasons, we will transform it further to another graph G''. We proceed as follows.

Construction of G': The states V' consist of the regions in $R(G)$ with the addition of a source state R_s corresponding to the initial configuration $<s_0, v_0>$. Let R_0 be the region that contains the initial configuration $<s_0, v_0>$. The edges of G' are constructed as follows.

1. Every transition edge $R \rightarrow R'$ of the region graph is present in G' with length 0. Also we have an edge from R_s to the region R_0.

2. A time edge $R \rightarrow R'$ of the region graph is present in G' iff R is a boundary region (hence R' must be an open region); the edge has length $\varepsilon \ll 1$, which we treat as a symbol standing for an arbitrarily small positive number.

3. If R and R' are both boundary regions with the same timer, say x_i, equal to a constant c in R and c' in R', where $c' > c$, and if there is a path in the region graph from R to R' which does not reset the clock x_i, then we include an edge $R \rightarrow R'$ in G' with length $c' - c$. (It suffices actually to include these only for the case $c' = c + 1$.) Also, if the clock x_i does not have constant value over the region R_0, and there is a path in the region graph from R_0 to R' that does not reset the clock x_i, then we include an edge in G' from R_s to R' with length $c' - t_i$. (Again, it suffices to include these edges only if c' is equal to the integral part of t_i plus one.)

Let F_R denote the set of times that must elapse in order for the system to hit some configuration in the region R, starting from state $<s_0, v_0>$. Let $d(R, \varepsilon)$ denote the minimum distance in G' from R_s to R (a function of ε), and let $d(R)$ be the above minimum distance with ε set to 0 in G'. Then the following holds.

Proposition 2: The infimum of F_R is $d(R)$. Furthermore, the infimum is achieved, i.e., there exist a trajectory which reaches R in exactly $d(R)$ time units, if and only if $d(R, \varepsilon)$ does not depend on ε (and thus, is equal to $d(R)$).

Proof: Omitted.
□

We can compute the minimum delay T_{min} to reach a specified state s_f by adding a new node R_f with zero length arcs from all regions with first component s_f, and computing the shortest path from R_s to R_f. The case where an initial clock assignment is not specified, can be solved by a similar simple modification.

Proposition 2 leads to a (possibly) quadratic algorithm in the size of the region graph. The reason is that even though the region graph is "sparse" (all nodes have small degree), the graph G' may be dense due to the edges that are included by part 3 of the construction; also determining these edges involves some form of transitive closure computation.

We can modify G' as follows to obtain a graph G''. We include again one node for each region and the source node R_s. In addition, for every region R and clock i that is not constant in R we include a node (R,i). We include the edges of parts 1 and 2 in the construction of G'. Instead of the edges of part 3, we have the following edges:

a. $R \rightarrow (R',i)$ of length 1 if x_i is constant in R and $R' = succ(R)$;

b. $(R,i) \rightarrow (R',i)$ of length 0 if $R \rightarrow R'$ is an edge of the region graph that does not reset timer i;

c. $(R,i) \rightarrow R'$ of length 0 if x_i is constant in R' and $R' = succ(R)$.

d. $R_s \rightarrow (R_0,i)$ if x_i is not constant in the region R_0; the edge has length $1-fract(t_i)$.

Proposition 3: For every region R, the distance from the source node R_s to R in the graph G' is the same as the distance in the graph G''.

Sketch: The edges of parts a-d in the construction of G'' simulate the edges of part 3 in the construction of G'.

$\Box$

If the number of clocks is k, and the region graph has V nodes and M edges, then G'' has roughly kV nodes and kM edges; note that k is in general much smaller than V and M (at most logarithmic). The best general bound for computing single source shortest paths on such a graph has complexity $O(kM + kV logV)$. However, except for the edges coming out of R_s all other edges have length 0, 1, or ε. We can take advantage of this to obtain linear time in the size of G''.

Theorem 3: Let k be the number of clocks and M the size of the region graph. Then the minimum delay problem can be solved in time $O(kM)$.

5. The Maximum Delay Problem

The formulation is similar to the one for the minimum delay problem: We are given again a timed graph G with set of clocks $C = \{x_1,\ldots,x_k\}$, a initial clock assignment $v_0 = t_1,\ldots,t_k$, an initial state s_0, and a final state s_f. Let F be the set of times at which the system can be in state s_f. We want to compute T_{max}, the least upper bound of F. Again, we will solve the more general problem of determining the supremum of this set for the case of a target region instead of a state. We will again reduce this problem to a longest path problem in a different graph G'. We do this as follows.

Construction of G': The states V' consist of the regions in $R(G)$ with the addition of a source state R_s corresponding to the initial configuration $<s_0, v_0>$. We denote by R_0 the region that contains the initial configuration $<s_0, v_0>$. The edges of G' are constructed as follows.

1. Every transition edge $R \rightarrow R'$ of the region graph is present in G' with length 0.

2. If R and R' are both boundary regions with the same counter, say x_i, equal to a constant c in R and c' in R', where $c' > c$, and if there is a path in the region graph from R to R', then we include an edge $R \rightarrow R'$ in G' with length $c' - c$. (It suffices actually to include these only for the case $c' = c + 1$, and only if there is a path in the region graph from R to R' which does not reset clock x_i.) Also, if there is a path in the region graph from R_0 to R' and $c' > t_i$, then we include an edge in G' from R_s to R' with length $c' - t_i$.

3. If R' is an open region whose successor in time is region R'' that has $x_i = c'$, and R is a boundary region with $x_i = c$, where $c < c'$, and there is a path in the region graph from

R to R', then we include the edge $R \rightarrow R'$ with weight $c' - c - \varepsilon$. Also, if there is a path in the region graph from R_0 to R', we include the arc $R_s \rightarrow R'$ with weight $c' - t_i - \varepsilon$. If R' is an end region (has no successor in time, and hence all clocks can become arbitrarily large), then add the edges of the region graph that go into R', and add a self-loop edge $R' \rightarrow R'$ with weight equal to infinity (or we can treat these regions as special).

Let F_R denote again the set of times that must elapse in order for the system to hit some configuration in the region R, starting from state $<s_0, v_0>$. Let $D(R, \varepsilon)$ denote the maximum length of a path in G' from R_s to R (a function of ε); this may be ∞, either because it uses an edge of length ∞, or because it can become arbitrarily large. Let $D(R) = D(R, 0)$ be the above distance with $\varepsilon = 0$. Then the following holds.

Proposition 4: The supremum of F_R is $D(R)$. Furthermore, there exists a trajectory which reaches R in exactly $D(R)$ time units if and only if $D(R, \varepsilon)$ is finite and does not depend on ε.

Proof: Omitted.

$\square$

For the above graph G' we compute the maximum distance to a region R, $D(R, \varepsilon)$, as follows. We find the strong components (that are reachable from R_s), and we set $D(R, \varepsilon)$ to infinity if and only if there is a strong component B that is reachable from R_s and can reach R, which contains an edge of nonzero weight. After determining these regions, we remove them from the graph, we shrink all remaining strong components (their edges have 0 weight) to get an acyclic graph. Then we compute the longest path from the source R_s to every remaining node in a standard way processing the nodes in reverse topological order.

As in the previous section, simple modifications suffice to compute the version of the problem where the destination is a state of the timed graph instead of a region, and/or no initial clock assignment is specified. We can also transform the problem to a second graph G'' that is "almost" unweighted and sparse, and is more suitable for efficiency purposes.

Theorem 4: Let k be the number of clocks and M the size of the region graph. Then the maximum delay problem can be solved in time $O(kM)$.

6. Conclusions

There is another similar problem which we did not discuss, concerning the maximum time that a state can be visited for the first time. In other words: find the smallest time t (if it exists) such that if a trajectory starting from configuration $<s_0, v_0>$ has not visited state s_f by time t, then it will never visit it in the future. This problem can also be solved by a simple variant of the construction for the case of the maximum delay problem. We postpone the details to the full paper.

An important observation is that in the case that the initial clock assignment consists of rational numbers, one can always first refine the time scale of the system so that this configuration becomes a boundary region, and then there is a way of reducing the problem to a standard reachability problem by adding an extra clock. Although this is possible and is conceptually simple, the complexity of doing this grows much more rapidly since we have to refine our time scale and hence increase the constants c_x, $x \in C$. As a result, this approach would lead to an algorithm that is quadratic in the region graph and exponential (instead of linear) in the length of the given initial clock assignment. We avoid doing so in our approach.

A remaining open problem is the variant of the problems we considered in this paper in which the target is not a region (or a set of regions) but a configuration of the form $<s_f, v_f>$, for some arbitrary clock assignment v_f.

Acknowledgment: We would like to thank R. Alur and D. Dill for many helpful discussions.

References

[ACD90]   R. Alur, C. Courcoubetis, D. Dill, "Model-Checking for Real-Time Systems", 5th IEEE LICS, 1990.

[ACD91]   R. Alur, C. Courcoubetis, D. Dill, "Probabilistic Model Checking of Real-Time Systems", to appear in 18th ICALP, 1991.

[AD90]   R. Alur, D. Dill, "Automata for Modelling Real-Time Systems", 17th ICALP, 1990.

[AH89]   R. Alur, T. Henzinger, "A Really Temporal Logic", 30th IEEE FOCS, 1989.

[AK83]   S. Aggarwal, R. Kurshan, "Modelling Elapsed Time in Protocol Specification", *Protocol Specification, Testing and Verification*, III, 1983.

[Di89]   D. Dill, "Timing Assumptions and Verification of Finite-State Concurrent Systems", *Automatic Verification Methods for Finite-State Systems, LNCS* 407, 1989.

[Le90]   H. Lewis, "A Logic of Concrete Time Intervals", 5th IEEE LICS, 1990.

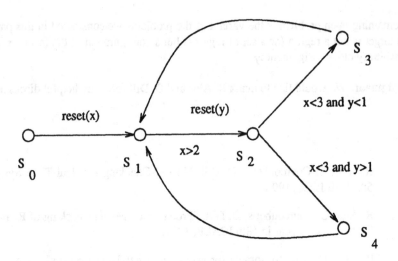

A timed graph

Figure 1

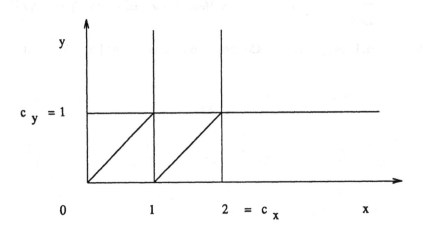

The time regions for $c_x = 2$, $c_y = 1$

Figure 2

Formal Verification of Speed-Dependent Asynchronous Circuits Using Symbolic Model Checking of Branching Time Regular Temporal Logic [1]

Kiyoharu HAMAGUCHI[†], Hiromi HIRAISHI[‡] and Shuzo YAJIMA[†]
† Department of Information Science, Faculty of Engineering,
Kyoto University, Kyoto, 606, JAPAN.
(E-mail: hama@kuis.kyoto-u.ac.jp)
‡ Department of Information & Communication Sciences,
Kyoto Sangyo University, Kita-ku, Kyoto, 603, JAPAN.

Abstract Firstly, we show how to deal with bounded *uncertain delays* of (speed-dependent) asynchronous circuits for symbolic model checking based on temporal logic. We adopt discrete-time model. In the modeling of uncertain delays, we consider two models, i.e. static delay and dynamic delay. These models are interpreted as parameterized sequential machines and nondeterministic sequential machines respecitively.

Secondly, we show a *symbolic model checking* algorithm for the above sequential machines. As a specification description language, a temporal logic named Branching Time Regular Temporal Logic (BRTL) is employed.

A prototype of verification system based on the proposed method has been implemented and some experimental results are reported.

1 Introduction

Asynchronous parts in a logic system tend to be small, because of its difficulty in design. Their timing verification, however, has to be strict and rigorous, because subtle timing errors cause wrong behavior of the whole system.

As one of rigorous verification methods, model checking approach based on temporal logics has been widely studied and applied to verify finite state machines such as protocols or sequential circuits[1, 2]. Relating to asynchronous circuits, formal verification techniques of speed-independent/dependent circuits have been researched[3, 4].

Recently, for the purpose of verifying real-time systems, various timing models have been researched and model checking methods based on the models have been established[5, 7, 8]. The models can treat uncertain delay rigorously. In [7, 6], model checking algorithms based on *continuous-time* model have been proposed and its complexity has also been shown. Although continuous-time model is the most general, its model checking is hard to execute because of its high complexity.

---

[1]This research is partially supported by Japan-USA cooperative research sponsored by JSPS and NSF.

In this report, we adopt discrete-time model and introduce uncertainty of delays to the framework of model checking. Indeed, discrete-time model is not as rigorous as continuous one, but it will help circuit designers find many errors.

We deal with two types of delay models, i.e, *(uncertain) static delay* and *dynamic delay*. In the static delay model, the delay of a gate is an uncertain integer between a bounded interval, but the delay does not fluctuate at each time unit. The key idea to treat this type of delay is to regard each gate as a *parameterized sequential machine*. For example, a sequential machine $M[d]$ parameterized by a variable d over $\{2,3,4\}$ is used to model a gate with a delay value $d = 2, 3$ or 4, where $M[i]$ ($i = 1, 2, 3$) corresponds to the gate with the delay value i. A parameterized sequential machine corresponding to a whole circuit can be constructed from a set of sequential machines associated with gates in the circuit.

In the other model, i.e., dynamic delay model, the delay for each gate can fluctuate at each time unit. Each gate of this type is regarded as a nondeterministic sequential machine. Assume that a delay fluctuates in the range of $\{3,4,5\}$. Then the gate is represented by a consecutive five one-bit registers. The next value for a register is chosen nondeterministically, depending on which delay value is chosen at the time unit.

The size of the sequential machine representing the whole circuits increases exponentially in the number of elements. Symbolic model checking using BDD (Binary Decision Diagram) is a recently developed model checking method and has succeeded in verifying large sequential circuits[2, 9]. In this report, a symbolic model checking algorithm for Branching Time Regular Temporal Logic (BRTL) [10] is shown.

BRTL has, as its temporal operators, deterministic finite automata whose edges are labeled by BRTL formulas. Its expressive power has been proved stronger than CTL.

When we apply model checking to parameterized sequential machines, what is obtained as a result is all value assignments to parameters such that the given specification is satisfied. This means that, in the static delay model we handle here, we can obtain all the possible combinations of delay values such that the specification is satisfied.

Furthermore, BRTL is also extended to express ambiguity of temporal properties by *parameterizing* its temporal operators. This extension means that we can describe a specification with some ambiguity.

In the following, Section 2 explains modeling of static delay and dynamic delay, and overviews formal verification of asynchronous circuits. Section 3 shows definitions of BRTL and symbolic model checking for BRTL. Section 4 reports some experimental results.

2 Verification of Asynchronous Circuits: Overview

2.1 Modeling of Static Delays

A parameterized sequential machine is regarded as a function $M : I \rightarrow \mathcal{M}$, where I is a finite interval of integers and $\mathcal{M}$ is a set of all sequential machines, i.e. $M[c]$ ($c \in I$) represents a sequential machine. Parameterized sequential machines with two or more parameters are defined similarly.

Since symbolic model checking based on manipulation of logic functions is introduced in Section 3, we describe parameterized sequential machines by transition relation functions, which represent sets of its transition edges, where a distinguished Boolean vector is assigned to each of $c \in I$.

In the following, Boolean variables $s_1, s_2, \cdots$ and $s'_1, s'_2, \cdots$ are used to express initial nodes and terminal nodes of transition edges respectively. i is an input variable.

$$d[1,4]$$

Figure 1: Delay Element

Static delay model is used in [11][2] and it has been shown that the model achieves higher accuracy in logic simulation, comparing with *ambiguous delay model* [12]. Let us consider a delay element shown in Figure 1. $d[1,4]$ means that its delay value is either of 1,2,3 or 4. In this model, it is assumed that the delay value does not change at each time unit, that is, the delay value of a gate is uncertain in its domain but it does not fluctuate.

The transition relation function of the element in Figure 1 is the conjunction of the following logic functions (1) – (4) . By introducing Boolean variables d_1 and d_0, we associate $d = 1, 2, 3$ and 4 with $\neg d_1 \wedge \neg d_0$, $\neg d_1 \wedge d_0$, $d_1 \wedge \neg d_0$ and $d_1 \wedge d_0$ respectively,

(1) $(\neg d_1 \wedge \neg d_0 \wedge (s'_4 \equiv i)) \vee (\neg d_1 \wedge d_0 \wedge (s'_4 \equiv s_1)) \vee (d_1 \wedge \neg d_0 \wedge (s'_4 \equiv s_2)) \vee (d_1 \wedge d_0 \wedge (s'_4 \equiv s_3))$,

(2) $s'_3 \equiv s_2$, (3) $s'_2 \equiv s_1$, (4) $s'_1 \equiv i$.

If $d = 2$, i.e. $d_1 = 0$ and $d_0 = 1$, then the above function represents an element with delay value 2.

The output function of the element is s_4 for $d = 1, 2, 3$ or 4.

2.2 Modeling of Dynamic Delays

Dynamic delay model is another modeling of delays bounded by minimum and maximum values. In this model, $d[1,3]$ means that the delay value can fluctuate over $\{1, 2, 3\}$. This model contains a complicated problem observed in rise/fall delay model[12] as well. Assume that a pulse $0 \to 1 \to 0$ of width 2 arrives at the input of the delay element. If delay value 3 is chosen at the first transition of the signals and delay value 1 is chosen at the second transition, a signal change at the output which is caused by the first transition has to be suppressed.

$d[1,3]$ is modeled by the following function.

$$
\begin{aligned}
&((s'_3 \equiv i) \wedge (s'_2 \equiv i) \wedge (s'_1 \equiv i)) &\vee \\
&((s'_3 \equiv s_2) \wedge ((s'_2 \equiv i) \wedge (s'_1 \equiv i)) &\vee \\
&((s'_3 \equiv s_2) \wedge (s'_2 \equiv s_1) \wedge (s'_1 \equiv i))
\end{aligned}
$$

The first term $((s'_3 \equiv i) \wedge (s'_2 \equiv i) \wedge (s'_1 \equiv i))$ corresponds to the case that the delay value is chosen to be 1. $(s'_2 \equiv i) \wedge (s'_1 \equiv i)$ means that the values stored previously in s'_1 and s'_2 are suppressed by i.

2.3 Specification in BRTL

BRTL is a branching time temporal logic which has deterministic ω finite automata as its temporal operators. Its formal definitions are described in the next section. In this section, an example of BRTL description is shown.

---

[2] In [11], this type of delay is referred to as *uncertain delay*.

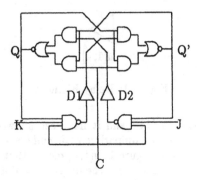

Figure 2: JK flip-flop

Figure 2 shows a design of JK flip-flop. A partial specification for the circuit is shown in Figure 3 (a). *Spec* is a BRTL formula which contains deterministic ω finite automata shown in Figure 3 (b), which are called automata connectives in the next section.

The automata accept infinite sequences composed from assignments of *true* or *false* to atomic propositions. Single circles and double circles mean rejecting states and accepting states respectively. (In BRTL, distribution of accepting or rejecting states are restricted as shown in Section 3.) If an input sequence hits some accepting states infinitely often, the sequence is accepted. Otherwise, it is rejected.

In the specification shown here, signal names in the circuit are also used as atomic propositions of BRTL. "Signal j = 1" corresponds to "j is true". Pulse(x) of Figure 3 expresses that x is true during the first four time units and x stays false after the fifth time unit. Always(x) expresses that x is always true and Fall(x) expresses that after the interval of length greater than or equal to 0 where x is true, x stays false permanently. Intuitively, *Spec* expresses the timing chart shown in Figure 4.

2.4 Verification

In this section, an overview of verification procedure for a logic circuit is shown.

Firstly a parameterized Kripke structure is constructed from the circuit. Kripke structure is defined formally in Section 3. We can perform this step *symbolically*, i.e. through manipulation of logic functions. More precisely, the conjunction of transition relation functions corresponding to gates in the circuit comes to represent the Kripke structure reflecting the behavior of the circuit.

Secondly model checking is performed for the Kripke structure and a given BRTL formula. If some parameters are used in the model, we can obtain all of the assignments of integers to the parameters such that the given specification is satisfied. That is, we can obtain all combinations of delay values such that the circuit works properly. If no variable is introduced for parameterization, then the result of model checking is yes/no.

A symbolic model checking algorithm for this step is shown in Section 3.

BRTL of this paper can also express ambiguity in specification by parameterizing automata in its formulas with variables. For example, Pulse[d](x) in Figure 5 means that d is the length of the first interval where x is true. The domain of d is a bounded interval of integers $\{3, 4, 5, 6\}$. The result of model checking for this specification contains the information about d such that the specification is satisfied.

$$Spec = \forall((Pulse(c) \land Always(\neg j \land k)) \Rightarrow Fall(q)$$

(a) Specification

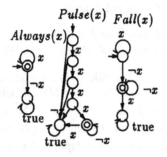

(b) Automata connectives

Figure 3: Specification for JK flip-flop (1)

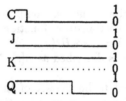

Figure 4: Timing Chart for JK flip-flop

$$Spec = \forall((Pulse[d](c) \land Always(\neg j \land k)) \Rightarrow Fall(q)$$

(a) Specification

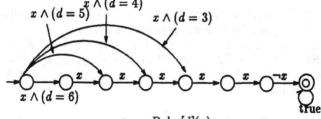

Pulse[d](x)

(b) Automaton connective

Figure 5: Specification for JK flip-flop (2)

3 Branching Time Regular Temporal Logic and Its Symbolic Model Checking

3.1 Branching Time Regular Temporal Logic

The definition of BRTL in this report is different from that of [10]. Firstly, it is *parameterized* and, secondly, Boolean operations of automata connectives in the scope of a path quantifier are allowed.

$I_i = \{a_{i1}, a_{i2}, \cdots, a_{in_i}\}$ $(i = 1, 2, \cdots, w)$ is called a finite interval, where a_{ij} are integers and $a_{ij+1} = a_{ij} + 1$. $D = (d_1, \cdots, d_w)$ is called a variable list, where d_i $(i = 1, 2, \cdots, w)$ is a variable over I_i. D is fixed in the following section. $I \stackrel{\text{def}}{=} I_1 \times I_2 \times \cdots \times I_w$ is the domain of D. $c \in I$ is called an *environment*. V_T represents *tautology*.

Definition 1 *A deterministic ω finite automaton type 1 (dfa-1)*

$A[D] = (Q, P, Br, q_0, F)$ is defined as follows.

Q is a set of finite number of states and $P = \{p_1, \cdots, p_n\}$ is a set of propositional variables. q_0 is the initial state. F is a set of accepting states and the elements of $Q - F$ are called rejecting states. Let BF be a set of all propositional formulas constructed from the elements of P. $Br : Q \times Q \times I \to BF$ is a partial function which satisfies the following three conditions.

Consider $Br(q, Q, c) = \{f | \exists q'. Br(q, q', c) = f\}$, for $q \in Q$ and $c \in I$.

(1) $f_1 \wedge f_2 = V_F$, for any $f_1, f_2 \in Br(q, Q, c)$.

(2) $\bigvee_{f \in Br(q,Q,c)} f = V_T$.

$A[D]$ accepts or rejects infinite sequences composed from the elements of $\Delta = 2^P$ under a given environment c. The transition function of $A[D]$ under c is defined to be $\delta_c : Q \times \Delta \to Q$ such that $\delta_c(q, v) = q' \Leftrightarrow Br(q, q', c)(v) = T$, where $v \in \Delta$

$A[D]$ under an environment c is described as $A[c]$. In $A[c]$, the third argument of Br is fixed to c.

For $\sigma \in \Sigma^\omega$, $\text{Inf}(\sigma)$ is defined to be the set of the states through which $A[c]$ goes infinitely often. Then the set of words accepted by $A[c]$ is $\{\sigma | \text{Inf}(\sigma) \cap F$ is not empty $\}$ and is described by $\langle A \rangle_c$.

(3) Under any environment c, there exists no path from a rejecting state q_r to q_r itself via some accepting state q_a. □

Lemma 1 For a dfa-1 $A[D] = (Q, P, Br, q_0, F)$, a dfa-1 $\overline{A[D]}$ which accepts $\Sigma^\omega - \langle A \rangle_c$ for each environment c is obtained by exchanging accepting states and rejecting states of $A[D]$.

Lemma 2 For dfa-1's $A_i[D] = (Q_i, \Sigma, P, Br_i, \delta_i, q_{i0}, F_i)$ $(i = 1, 2)$, a dfa-1 $A_1[D] | A_2[D]$ which accepts $\langle A_1 \rangle_c \cup \langle A_2 \rangle_c$ for each c is obtained as follows:

$Q = Q_1 \times Q_2 = \{(q_1, q_2) | q_1 \in Q_1 , q_2 \in Q_2\}$, $q_0 = (q_{10}, q_{20})$ and $F = \{(q_1, q_2) | q_1 \in F_1$ or $q_2 \in F_2\}$. $Br : Q \times Q \to BF$ is defined by $Br((q_1, q_2), (q'_1, q'_2), c) = Br_1(q_1, q'_1, c) \wedge Br_1(q_2, q'_2, c)$, where $q_i, q'_i \in Q_i$ $(i = 1, 2)$ and $c = c(D)$, and both of $Br_1(q_1, q'_1, c)$ and $Br_1(q_2, q'_2, c)$ are defined. □

Definition 2 $S[D] = \langle \Sigma, \text{As}, R, \Sigma_0 \rangle$ is called a Kripke structure, where Σ is a set of nodes, $\text{As} : \Sigma \to 2^{AP}$ is an assignment function, $R \subseteq \Sigma \times \Sigma \times I$ is a *total* relation for each $c \in I$, i.e, there exists $s' \in \Sigma$ such $(s, s', c) \in R$ for any $s \in \Sigma$. $\Sigma_0 \subseteq \Sigma$ is a set of initial states.

$S[D]$ under an environment c, denoted by $S[c]$, is a Kripke structure such that R is fixed by c. □

Definition 3 Syntax and Semantics

The syntax of BRTL is as follows:

<u>BRTL formulas:</u>

Let p be an atomic proposition in AP, ψ and ϕ be BRTL formulas, and B be an automaton connective. Then p, $\neg\psi$ and $\psi \vee \phi$ and $\exists B$ are BRTL formulas.

<u>Automata connectives</u>

Let $A[D]$ be a dfa-1 and B, B_1, B_2 be automata connectives. Then $A[D](\psi_1, \psi_2, \cdots, \psi_n)$, $\neg B$ and $B_1 \vee B_2$ are also automata connectives.

$A[D](\psi_1, \psi_2, \cdots, \psi_n)$ is obtained by replacing each atomic proposition $p_i \in P$ ($1 \leq i \leq n$) with $\psi_i \subseteq BF$ corresponding to p_i simultaneously.

The semantics of BRTL is defined on a Kripke structure $S[D] = \langle \Sigma, I, R, \Sigma_0 \rangle$ under a given environment c. $S[D], s \models_c f$ means that the BRTL formula f holds at the state s on $S[D]$ under c. In the following, $p \in AP$, ψ and ϕ are BRTL formulas and $A[D]$ is a dfa-1 and B is an automaton connective. $\mathrm{Trans}(B)$ represents an automaton connective obtained by applying Lemma 1 and 2 to B until all of $\neg$ and $\vee$ in B are deleted.

- $S[D], s \models_c p$ iff $p \in As(s)$

- $S[D], s \models_c \psi \vee \phi$ iff $S[D], s \models_c \psi$ or $S[D], s \models_c \phi$

- $S[D], s \models_c \neg\psi$ iff $S[D], s \not\models_c \psi$

- $S[D], s \models_c \exists A[D](\psi_1, \psi_2, \cdots, \psi_n)$ iff there exists an infinite sequence $\sigma = s_0 s_1 s_2 \cdots$ starting from s on $S[c]$ and a run (a sequence of states) $q_0 q_1 q_2 \cdots$ in Q such that, $S[D], s_i \models_c Br(q_i, q_{i+1}, c)$ holds and at least one state $q \in Q$ which appears infinitely in the run is in F.

- $S[D], s \models_c \exists B$ iff $S[D], s \models_c \exists(\mathrm{Trans}(B))$

If $\forall s \in \Sigma_0. S[D], s \models_c f$, then we describe $S[D] \models_c f$. □

The Boolean operators $\wedge$, $\equiv$ and $\Rightarrow$ are also used. Besides we define $\forall B \stackrel{\text{def}}{=} \neg\exists\neg B$ and $\forall\neg B \stackrel{\text{def}}{=} \neg\exists B$.

3.2 Symbolic Model Checking of BRTL

The symbolic model checking technique shown in this section is an extension of the methods found in [2]. The difference is that parameters have to be handled.

Definition 4 Model checking problem

Given a Kripke structure $S[D]$ and a BRTL formula ψ, model checking problem is to obtain a set of environments c under which $S[D] \models_c \psi$ holds. □

In the following, a unique code composed from $B = \{0, 1\}$ is assigned to each node on the Kripke structure. For a node s, $\mathrm{cd}(s)$ represents the code assigned to s. Assume that n bit of vector is required to represent $s \in \Sigma$. $\vec{s} = s_1, s_2, \cdots, s_n$ and $\vec{s'} = s'_1, s'_2, \cdots, s'_n$ are defined to be variable vectors over B^n.

Each $c \in I$ is also encoded by B. For each $c_i \in I_i$, $\mathrm{cd}(c_i)$ represents the code assigned to c_i and $\mathrm{cd}(c)$ is the concatenation from $\mathrm{cd}(c_1)$ to $\mathrm{cd}(c_w)$. If n_i bit is required to encode c_i, then $\vec{c_i}$ is a variable vector over B^{n_i} and $\vec{c}$ is a variable vector over $B^{\Sigma_i n_i}$.

The Kripke structure is represented by logic functions:

1. Transition relation: $f_S(\mathrm{cd}(s), \mathrm{cd}(s'), \mathrm{cd}(c)) = 1$ iff $(s, s', c) \in R$.

2. Assignment of atomic propositions: $f_p(\mathrm{cd}(s)) = 1$ iff $p \in As(s)$.

3. Initial states: $f_{init}(cd(s)) = 1$ iff $s \in \Sigma_0$

Besides the above vector variables, $\vec{q_j}$ and $\vec{q'_j}$ are used for each dfa-1 $A_j[D]$ in the BRTL formula ψ. The code for a state q_j in $A_j[D]$ is represented by $cd(q_j)$.

Algorithm 1 model checking algorithm

- Input: BRTL formula ψ and the above f_S, f_p and f_{init}.
- Output: The logic function $f_{env}(\vec{c})$ such that $f_{env}(cd(c)) = 1$ iff $S[D] \models_c \psi$.
- Method: Shown below.

1. For each dfa-1 $A_j[D]$ in ψ, the following logic functions are constructed:

    - For each $(q_j, q'_j, c) \in Q_j \times Q_j \times I$, $f_{E_j(\psi_k)}(cd(q_j), cd(q'_j), cd(c)) = 1$
      $\Leftrightarrow Br(q_j, q'_j, c) = \psi_k$.
    - q_j is an accepting state of $A_j \Leftrightarrow f_{F_j}(cd(q_j)) = 1$

2. For each subformula ϕ_i of ψ, a logic function $f_{\phi_i}(\vec{s}, \vec{c})$ which represents $S[D], s \models_c \phi_i$ is constructed in bottom up manner. Let $\theta, \theta_1, \theta_2$ are BRTL formulas.

    (a) If ϕ_i is an atomic proposition, f_{ϕ_i} is returned.
    (b) If ϕ_i is $\theta_1 \vee \theta_2$ or $\neg\theta$, then $f_{\theta_1 \vee \theta_2} = f_{\theta_1} \vee f_{\theta_2}$ and $f_{\neg\theta} = \neg f_\theta$ are returned.
    (c) If ϕ_i is $\exists B$, then the following i.– vi. are performed.

        i. For each $A_j[D](\psi_{j_1}, \psi_{j_2}, \cdots, \psi_{j_{n_j}})$ $(j = 1, 2, \cdots, m)$, vectors of variables representing the states of A_j, $\vec{q_j}$ and $\vec{q'_j}$ are introduced. Let $\vec{q} = \vec{q_1}\#\vec{q_2}\# \cdots \#\vec{q_m}$ and $\vec{q'} = \vec{q'_1}\#\vec{q'_2}\# \cdots \#\vec{q'_m}$, where $\#$ means concatenation of vectors. Let Q be defined as $Q_1 \times Q_2 \times \cdots Q_m$. $\vec{v} \overset{def}{=} \vec{s}\#\vec{q}$ and $\vec{v'} \overset{def}{=} \vec{s'}\#\vec{q'}$.

        ii. A logic function $f_E(\vec{v}, \vec{v'}, \vec{c})$ is constructed, which represents a set of edges of the graph G consisted of the nodes $\Sigma \times Q$.
        $$f_E(\vec{v}, \vec{v'}, \vec{c}) \overset{def}{=} \bigwedge_{j=1,2,\cdots,m} \{ \bigvee_{k=1,2,\cdots,n_j} (f_{E_j(\psi_{jk})}(\vec{q_j}, \vec{q'_j}, \vec{c}) \wedge f_{\psi_{jk}}(\vec{s}, \vec{c})) \} \wedge f_S(\vec{s}, \vec{s'}, \vec{c})$$

        iii. A logic function $f_{F_B}(\vec{q})$ is constructed, which represents the set of accepting states of $\text{Trans}(B)$. It is calculated recursively as follows:
            - If $B = A_j[D](\psi_{j_1}, \psi_{j_2}, \cdots, \psi_{j_{n_j}})$, then $f_{F_B}(\vec{q}) \overset{def}{=} f_{F_j}(\vec{q_j})$.
            - If $B = \neg B_1$, then $f_{F_B}(\vec{q}) \overset{def}{=} \neg f_{F_{B_1}}(\vec{q})$.
            - If $B = B_1 \vee B_2$, then $f_{F_B}(\vec{q}) \overset{def}{=} f_{F_{B_1}}(\vec{q}) \vee f_{F_{B_2}}(\vec{q})$.

        iv. Let V' be a set of nodes $\{(s, q) | f_{F_B}(cd(q)) = 1\}$ and G' be a restriction of G to V'. A logic function $f_{C'}(\vec{v}, \vec{c})$ is constructed, which represents the set of nodes which are in strongly connected components of G' or are reachable to the strongly connected components.
        $$f_{E'}(\vec{v}, \vec{v'}, \vec{c}) \overset{def}{=} f_{F_B}(\vec{q}) \wedge f_{F_B}(\vec{q'}) \wedge f_E(\vec{v}, \vec{v'}, \vec{c})$$
        Set $f^0_{C'}(\vec{v}, \vec{c}) \overset{def}{=} f_{F_B}(\vec{q}, \vec{c})$. $f^1_{C'}, \cdots f^k_{C'}$ are calculated until $f^{k+1}_{C'} \equiv f^k_{C'}$ holds.
        $$f^{i+1}_{C'}(\vec{v}, \vec{c}) \overset{def}{=} (\exists \vec{v'}.(f_{E'}(\vec{v}, \vec{v'}, \vec{c}) \wedge f^i_{C'}(\vec{v'}, \vec{c}))) \wedge f^i_{C'}(\vec{v}, \vec{c})$$
        $$f_{C'}(\vec{v}, \vec{c}) \overset{def}{=} f^k_{C'}(\vec{v}, \vec{c})$$

        v. A logic function f_R is constructed, which represents the set of nodes which are in G and reachable to $V_{C'}$. Set $f^0_R(\vec{v}, \vec{c}) \overset{def}{=} f_{C'}(\vec{v}, \vec{c})$. $f^1_R, f^2_R, \cdots f^k_R$ are calculated until $f^{k+1}_R \equiv f^k_R$ holds.

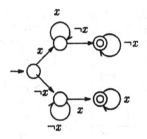

Figure 6: Automaton connective: Change(x)

$$f_R^{i+1}(\vec{v}, \vec{c}) \stackrel{\text{def}}{=} (\exists \vec{v'}.(f_E(\vec{v}, \vec{v'}, \vec{c}) \wedge f_R^i(\vec{v'}, \vec{c}))) \vee f_R^i(\vec{v}, \vec{c})$$
$$f_R(\vec{v}, \vec{c}) \stackrel{\text{def}}{=} f_R^k(\vec{v}, \vec{c})$$

vi. $f_{\psi_i}(\vec{s}, \vec{c}) \stackrel{\text{def}}{=} \exists \vec{q}.(f_R(\vec{s}, \vec{q}, \vec{c}) \wedge f_I(\vec{q}))$, where $f_I(\vec{q})$ represents the initial state of B.

(d) $(\vee_{c \in I} f_{cd}(c)) \wedge \forall \vec{s}.(f_{init}(\vec{s}) \Rightarrow f_{\psi}(\vec{s}, \vec{c}))$ is returned, where $f_{cd}(c)$ represents a logic formula (minterm) representing $cd(c)$.

4 Experimental Results

A prototype verifier based on the above methods was implemented. The verifier is written in language C and runs on a SPARC 1+ workstation. This program utilizes the Boolean function manipulator developed by Minato et.al. [13], which uses SBDD (Shared Binary Decision Diagram) representation as its internal representation. SBDD is an improvement of the binary decision diagram[14], which shares all possible subgraphs among multiple functions. There are many advantages besides those of the BDD. For example, equivalence of two functions can be checked only by comparing the pointers.

For the purpose of efficient manipulation of SBDD, the whole transition relation functions are not generated. Each of logic functions corresponding to the gates in the circuits is handled separately as shown in [15].

Each element in the circuit is initialized to an arbitrary stable value, that is, the set of all stable states of the circuits is used as the set of initial states for the verifier. The verified conditions are f_1 for sjk4, sjk5, mjk1, mjk2 and mjk3, and f_2 for the others. ($Change(x)$ is shown in Figure 6.) The length of the consecutive x in $Pulse(C)$ is adjusted for each example. For all the examples, SBDD size is limited to 500,000.

$$f_1 = \forall((Pulse(C) \wedge Always(\neg J \wedge K)) \Rightarrow (Fall(Q))) \tag{1}$$
$$f_2 = \forall((Pulse(C) \wedge Always(\neg J \wedge K)) \Rightarrow (Fall(Q) \wedge Fall(\neg q'))) \wedge$$
$$\forall((Pulse(C) \wedge Always(J \wedge K)) \Rightarrow (Change(Q) \wedge Change(Q'))) \tag{2}$$

The verification results for the circuits in Figure5 are shown in Table 1. Several combinations of the delay values were checked.

Static delay model was used for sjk's and dynamic delay model for djk's. mjk's mean that, for example, the delays [4, 12] for D1 and D2 were divided into eight dynamic delays $[4, 5], [5, 6], \cdots, [11, 12]$, and each of the delays was associated with a Boolean vector. By introducing Boolean variables for them, the verifier checked which fluctuation among $[4, 5], [5, 6], \cdots, [11, 12]$ satisfies the given condition.

The meaning of each column is also shown in Table 1. For example, the row sjk1

Table 1: Experimental Results

	#OP	time	#var	dl1	dl2	v/i
sjk1	34	62	21	[1,5]	[1,1]	○
sjk1*	36	64	21	[1,5]	[1,1]	○
sjk2	42	828	33	[7,8]	[2,2]	○
sjk3	34	1784	27	[0,0]	[1,3]	×
sjk4	15	2118	33	[1,7]	[1,2]	○
sjk5	23	—	43	[1,8]	[1,3]	—
djk1	34	34	19	[1,5]	[1,1]	×
djk1+	38	179	24	[9,10]	[1,1]	○
djk2	42	907	43	[11,12]	[1,2]	○
djk3	58	5658	59	[15,16]	[2,3]	×
mjk1	17	584	43	⟨4, 12)	[1,2]	○
mjk2	22	8777	59	⟨8, 16)	[2,3]	×
mjk3	26	—	67	⟨17, 20)	[2,3]	—

#OP: Number of states in BRTL automata connectives

time CPU time (seconds)

#var: Number of input and internal Boolean variables

dl1: Delays for $D1$ and $D2$

dl2: Delays for the rest of gates

v/i: ○ (resp., ×) means that the verifier found a (resp., no) combination such that the given condition is satisfied. If there is no parameters, ○ (resp., ×) means yes (resp., no).

means that static delays d1[1,5] and d2[1,5] were assigned to the delay elements $D1$ and $D2$. The delays of the rest of the gates were fixed to 1. '—' in the column means that the verifier failed to finish verification under the limit of SBDD size.

In sjk1*, the length of the consecutive x in $Pulse(x)$ was parameterized. The result shows that at least four 1's is necessary for the required behavior.

The results for djk1 and djk1+ show that, under dynamic delay model, the delays of $D1$ and $D2$ have to be longer than under static delay model.

The experimental results show that the cost of verification is very sensitive to the increase of the delay values. Especially for static delay model, it is hard to handle a large amount of uncertainty, though in sjk4, $7^2 \times 2^8$ possible combinations were checked.

5 Conclusion

In this report, we have considered formal verification method of speed-dependent asynchronous circuits which have, in particular, gates with uncertain delays. We have shown how to represent delays of gates by parameterized sequential machines or by nondeterministic sequential machines. When we use parameters, we can obtain all the assignments to parameters such that a given specification is satisfied. By using symbolic model checking method, some experimental results were shown.

One of interesting future works is to extend the timing model to treat continuous quality. In [7, 6], it has been shown that the model checking for TCTL on continuous-time model can be solved decidably and the problem can be reduced to a certain problem over finite graphs. This suggests that it would be possible to handle the continuous-time model by symbolic model checking. When we try to use BDD for the verification based on continuous-time model, however, much more efficient methods will be required.

Acknowledgements
The authors would like to thank anonymous referees for helpful comments.

References

[1] E. M. Clarke, E. A. Emerson, and A. P. Sistla. Automatic Verification of Finite State Concurrent Systems Using Temporal Logic Specifications: A Practical Approach. In *10th ACM Symposium on Principles of Programming Languages*, pages 117–126, January 1983.

[2] J. R. Burch, E. M. Clarke, K. L. McMillan, D. L. Dill, and J. Hwang. Symbolic Model Checking: 10^{20} States and Beyond. In *Proceedings of 5th IEEE Symposium on Logic in Computer Science*, June 1990.

[3] M. C. Browne, E. M. Clarke, D. L. Dill, and B. Mishra. Automatic Verification of Sequential Circuits Using Temporal Logic. *IEEE Transactions on Computers*, C-35(12):1035–1044, December 1986.

[4] D. L. Dill and E. M. Clarke. Automatic Verification of Asynchronous Circuits Using Temporal Logic. *IEE Proceedings*, 133:276–282, September 1986.

[5] R. Alur and D. Dill. Automata for Modeling Real-Time Systems. In *Proceedings of ICALP 90'*, 1990.

[6] R. Alur, C. Courcoubetis, and D. Dill. Model-Checking for Real-Time Systems. In *Proceedings of 5th IEEE Symposium on Logic in Computer Science*, pages 414–425, June 1990.

[7] H. R. Lewis. A Logic of Concrete Time Intervals. In *Proceedings of 5th IEEE Symposium on Logic in Computer Science*, pages 380–389, 1990.

[8] J.S. Ostroff. Automated Verification of Timed Transition Models. *Automated Verification Methods for Finite State Systems*, pages 247–256, 1989.

[9] O. Coudert, C. Berthet, and J-C. Madre. Verification of Sequential Machines Using Functional Vectors. *Proceedings of IMEC-IFIP International Workshop on Applied Formal Methods for Correct VLSI Design*, pages 111–128, November 1989.

[10] K. Hamaguchi and H. Hiraishi and S. Yajima. Branching Time Regular Temporal Logic for Model Checking with Linear Time Complexity. *Workshop on Computer-Aided Verification*, June 1990.

[11] Nagisa Ishiura, Yutaka Deguchi, and Shuzo Yajima. Coded Time-Symbolic Simulation Using Shared Binary Decision Diagram. *Proceedings of 27th Design Automation Conference*, pages 130–135, 1990.

[12] M. Abramovici, M. A. Breuer, and A. D. Freidman. *Digital Systems Testing and Testable Design*. Computer Science Press, 1990.

[13] Shin ichi Minato, Nagisa Ishiura, and Shuzo Yajima. Shared Binary Decision Diagram with Attributed Edges for Efficient Boolean Function Manipulation. *Proceedings of 27th Design Automation Conference*, pages 52–57, 1990.

[14] R. E. Bryant. Graph-Based Algorithms for Boolean Function Manipulation. *IEEE Transactions on Computers*, C-35(8):677–691, August 1986.

[15] J. R. Burch, E. M. Clarke, and D. E. Long. Representing Circuits More Efficiently in Symbolic Model Checking. *Proceedings of 28th Design Automation Conference*, June 1991.

Verifying Properties of HMS Machine Specifications of Real-Time Systems*

A. Gabrielian and R. Iyer

Thomson-CSF, Inc.

Palo Alto, CA

U.S.A.

Abstract

A "hierarchical multi-state (HMS) machine" is an automaton in which multiple states may be true, multiple transitions may fire simultaneously, a state may be expanded into a lower-level HMS machine, and in which the transitions are "controlled" by predicates in a temporal interval logic called TIL. HMS machines provide a compact formalism for specifying and verifying the behavior of concurrent hard real-time systems. Two approaches to verification of properties of non-recursive HMS machines are presented: (1) an extension of tableau-based theorem proving that utilizes the logic TIL and the execution semantics of machines to verify safety properties, and (2) a variation of model checking that uses "interacting" parametric "computation graphs." The first verification approach avoids the construction of a complete computation graph and the second approach permits the analysis of behavior of certain types of HMS machines using multiple, relatively simple computation graphs.

1   Introduction

A variety of formalisms have been studied during the recent past for the specification and verification of real-time systems. Variations of finite-state automata, such as Büchi automata [AS89], temporal extensions of Petri nets [GM89], or modifications of standard temporal logic have been the key representation languages for many of these studies. The concept of "hierarchical multi-state (HMS) machine" is obtained by integrating hierarchical and parallel or "multi-state" automata with a temporal interval logic called TIL, resulting in a compact formalism for specifying concurrent hard real-time systems, in which complex temporal dependencies can be defined conveniently [GF88, FG89, GF90, GI91, Ga91].

In an HMS machine, multiple states may be true at a moment of time, multiple transitions may fire simultaneously, states may be expanded (recursively) into lower-level HMS machines, and transition enablement is defined by predicates in a temporal interval logic called TIL. The following are some of the key characteristics of HMS machines:

- Each transition in an HMS machine is specifically designated to be either *deterministic* or *nondeterministic*. At a particular moment of time, all enabled deterministic transitions and any subset of enabled nondeterministic transitions may fire. Thus, in contrast to Petri nets, multiple transitions from a single boolean state may fire simultaneously.

---

*This work was supported in part by the Office of Naval Research under Contract N00014-89-C-0022.

- The use of TIL predicates for defining conditions under which transitions are enabled provides a much richer language for controlling transitions than timed Petri nets [GM89] and time-based extensions of state models (see, e.g., [HMP91]). These TIL predicates may contain as a literal any state of the machine, thus allowing complex causal dependencies among states to be modeled quite naturally. The logic TIL allows a uniform treatment of time for the past, the present and the future, subsuming most of the common interval-based logics defined in the literature [DM88, Me88, PH88].

- A "multi-level specification" approach can be used to give a combination of axiomatic and executable specification of a system at multiple levels of abstraction that reduces the effort in specification and offers a high degree of reusability and modularity [GF90].

In [FG89] a method for verifying safety properties of HMS machines was presented that was based on the following scheme: (1) Given an HMS machine H and a safety property $\Box p$, an "extended" state Q for H is created that becomes true if and only if the safety property is violated. Thus, to prove that H satisfies $\Box p$, it is sufficient to show that Q is unreachable. (2) A set of correctness-preserving transformations are applied to H that modify the structure of H, without changing its behavior, such that the state Q becomes isolated (and unreachable) if the safety property is indeed satisfied by H. In [GI91], a branching time version of TIL called BTIL was defined and preliminary results on a model checking approach to verification of HMS machine properties were presented.

In this paper, two approaches to verification of real-time properties of HMS machines are presented. In the first approach, an extension of tableau-based theorem proving [Ab87, Fi90] is used to verify safety properties. The extension involves (1) the use of the interval-based TIL instead of standard temporal logic, and (2) the consideration of execution semantics of HMS machines, as well as logical alternatives, to derive facts about states and transitions. As in the correctness-preserving transformation technique [FG89], safety properties are represented as extended states and the refutation proceeds in a heuristic fashion. In the second approach, a variation of model checking is used on "interacting" parametric "computation graphs" to verify properties of HMS machines. This is possible when the associated machine can be partitioned into a set of components, such that separate but interacting computation graphs can be constructed for each component. The interactions are defined in terms of parametric delays that characterize the execution of nondeterministic transitions. Such a partitioning can reduce the size of a computation graph significantly and the use of parameters allows a simple encoding of nondeterministic behavior. The two verification techniques are illustrated for a railroad crossing example with nondeterministic transitions and real-time constraints.

In Section 2 we present an overview of HMS machines. We ignore multi-level specification and limit the discussion to non-recursive hierarchies. Formal definitions of multi-level specification and recursive hierarchies can be found in [GF90] and [GI91, Ga91], respectively. In Sections 3 and 4 we present our two verification approaches and in Section 5 we present a brief summary and the conclusions.

2   Overview of Hierarchical Multi-State (HMS) Machines

As indicated earlier, an HMS machine consists of a parallel or multi-state (hierarchical) automaton in which predicates in a temporal interval logic called TIL determine the conditions under which transitions are enabled. We assume that we are given a set S of "states" and we define a "marking" of S at the relative time t to be a mapping $M_t : S \rightarrow \{F, T\}$, where F and T represent false and true, respectively.

In addition, we call a sequence $\ldots, M_{-1}, M_0, M_1, \ldots$ of markings on a set S a "marking sequence." We consider a discrete model of time with 0 denoting the "current moment."

We now introduce the logic TIL, which is obtained by augmenting standard propositional logic with four temporal operators. In the sequel, given a marking M and a formula ψ, we denote the satisfiability of ψ in M by $M \models \psi$.

$O(t')$ At relative time t'
$$M_t \models O(t')\psi \Leftrightarrow M_{t+t'} \models \psi$$

$[t_1, t_2]$ Always between t_1 and t_2
$$M_t \models [t_1, t_2]\psi \Leftrightarrow \forall t' \; t_1 \leq t' \leq t_2 \text{ implies } M_t \models O(t')\psi$$

$<t_1, t_2>$ Sometime between t_1 and t_2
$$M_t \models <t_1, t_2> \psi \Leftrightarrow \exists t' \text{ such that } t_1 \leq t' \leq t_2 \wedge M_t \models O(t')\psi$$

$<t_1, t_2>!$ Sometime-change between t_1 and t_2
$$M_t \models <t_1, t_2>!\psi \Leftrightarrow \exists t' \text{ such that } ((t_1 - 1) \leq t' < t_2) \wedge (M_t \models O(t')\neg\psi) \wedge (M_t \models <t'+1, t_2> \psi).$$

We note that standard temporal operators, including finite versions [DM88, PH88] are special cases of TIL operators. Thus, $\square = [0, \infty]$, $\Diamond = <0, \infty>$, and $[t] = [0, t]$. The sometime-change operator $<>!$ is not normally defined in standard temporal logics. It plays an important role in the theorem proving technique to be introduced in Section 3.

We now turn to the definition of HMS machines and we introduce our visual notation for representing such machines. In this paper, we do not address recursive hierarchies [GI91, Ga91] and we assume that non-recursive hierarchies are expanded (or flattened) to yield a machine in which all transitions are between "primitive" states only. This involves no loss of generality in the absence of recursion.

Definition 2 An HMS machine is a triple $H = (S, \Gamma_D, \Gamma_N)$ such that

(a) S is a set of "states." If $\{A, B, \ldots\}$ a subset of S, we denote it by $(A, B, \ldots)$

(b) Γ_D and Γ_N consist, respectively, of "deterministic" and "nondeterministic" transitions of the form

$$\text{(PRIMARIES) (CONTROL)} \rightarrow \text{(CONSEQUENTS)},$$

where PRIMARIES $\subseteq S$, CONSEQUENTS $\subseteq S$ and CONTROL is a predicate in TIL with literals from the set S. For a particular transition $\gamma = (A, B, \ldots) (P) \rightarrow (E, F, \ldots)$ in $\Gamma_D \cup \Gamma_N$, we write PRIMS$(\gamma) = (A, B, \ldots)$, CNTRL$(\gamma)=P$, and CNSQS$(\gamma)=(E, F, \ldots)$.

Figure 2.1 presents the specification of a railroad crossing HMS machine example using our visual notation. Rectangles represent states, dark arrows denote transitions with nondeterminism indicated by an asterisk, and the short vertical bars connected to the transitions t_5 and t_7 denote infinite resources that are always true. TIL controls are indicated by a combination of VLSI notation and temporal operators next to the symbol ⓣ . Thus, for example, for the deterministic transition t_4 and the nondeterministic transition t_5 in the figure, we have

PRIMS$(t_4) = (UP)$, CNTRL$(t_4) = LG \wedge [-20, 0]UP$, and CNSQS$(t_4)=DN$

PRIMS$(t_5) = (\;)$, CNTRL$(t_5) = [-10, 0]\neg TS$, and CNSQS$(t_5)=TS$.

Intuitively, the transition t_4 fires if its primary state UP is true and the following control condition holds: the state LG is true and UP has been true from -20 moments to the present (i.e., $[-20, 0]UP$). When the transition fires, UP becomes false and DN becomes true. Similarly, t_5 may fire in which case TS will become true (a new train starts), if $[-10, 0]\neg TS$ is true.

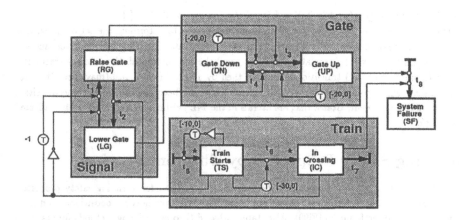

Figure 2.1. HMS Machine Specification of a Railroad Crossing

We note two major differences between the notion of nondeterminism in HMS machines and nondeterminism in traditional automata and Petri nets. In an HMS machine, a transition is explicitly designated as deterministic or nondeterministic. The firing of a nondeterministic transition is independent of the firing of all other transitions. In contrast, for traditional automata and Petri nets, nondeterminism is imposed by structural considerations. In addition, only one transition out of a set of related transitions may fire.

In this railroad crossing, the nondeterministic behavior of train arrivals is defined by the hierarchy Train, the signaling for raising and lowering the gate is defined by Signal, and the gate behavior is defined by Gate. The state SF is an "extended" state that defines the following "safety property" for the system: $\Box\neg(IC \wedge UP)$. This represents the requirement that the train should never be in the crossing when the gate is up. We verify this requirement in Sections 3 and 4 using two different verification techniques.

We consider next the semantics of execution for HMS machines. For a non-operational definition see [Ga91]. Here, we give an operational and logical definition of execution. For a transition u, by abuse of notation, we let (1) PRIMS(u)$= s_1 \wedge \ldots \wedge s_n$, where $\{s_1,\ldots,s_n\}$ is the set of primary states of u, and (2) CNSQS(u)$= q_1 \wedge \ldots \wedge q_m$, where $\{q_1,\ldots,q_m\}$ is the set of consequents of u. Also, we denote by $\Gamma_{in}(s)$ and $\Gamma_{out}(s)$ the sets of transitions into and out of s, respectively, and we use the symbol $\Rightarrow^*$ to represent a non-standard "nondeterministic implication," so that a formula $\lambda \Rightarrow^* \theta$ is interpreted as follows: if λ is true, θ may be true.

Definition 3 Given an HMS machine $H = (S, \Gamma_D, \Gamma_N)$, the set of transitions that will fire at the next moment is defined by the following two "Transition Firing" rules:

(TF-1)   PRIMS(u) $\wedge$ CNTRL(u) $\Rightarrow$ O(1)u, where u is deterministic
(TF-2)   PRIMS(u) $\wedge$ CNTRL(u) $\Rightarrow^*$ O(1)u, where u is nondeterministic.

The updating of values of states is defined by the following "State Updating" rule:

(SU) $O(1)s \Leftrightarrow (s \wedge (\bigwedge_{u\in\Gamma_{out}(s)} O(1)\neg u)) \vee (\bigvee_{v\in\Gamma_{in}(s)} O(1)v),$

where for a function ψ $\bigwedge_{x \in X} \psi(x) = T$ if $X = \{\}$ and $\bigvee_{x \in X} \psi(x) = F$ if $X = \{\}$.

At a moment of time, we first apply the Transition Firing rules to determine the set of transitions that will fire at the next moment ($t = 1$). We then apply the State Updating rule to determine the states of the machine that will be true at $t = 1$. If at $t = 0$ the control and all the primary states of a deterministic (nondeterministic) transition u are true then by TF-1 (TF-2) u will (may) fire. If u fires its consequent state will become true and a primary state s of u will become false unless some transition fires into s at the same moment. States that are literals in the TIL predicate CNTRL(u) are not affected by the firing of u.

3   Verifying Safety Properties by Theorem Proving

In this section, we introduce a tableau-based theorem proving method for verifying safety properties of HMS machines. A classical treatment of tableau-based theorem proving for propositional and first-order standard logic can be found in [Fi90]. Also, tableau-based theorem proving methods for standard temporal logic with the next operator (O) and mu-calculus appear in [Ab87] and [SW89], respectively.

The tableau method presented here is adapted from [Fi90] with the following two extensions: (1) facts are stated in the interval-based temporal logic TIL rather than propositional logic, and (2) rules based on the execution semantics of HMS machines are used to deduce additional facts during the theorem proving process. We limit our discussion to HMS machines with finite number of states and finite "past" controls which are inherently decidable. We note, however, that the state reachability problem for such machines has been shown to be NP-complete [FG89].

In Definition 3 of Section 2, we defined the semantics of execution of HMS machines in terms of two Transition Firing rules and a State Updating rule. We now introduce two additional sets of rules that are particularly useful in our theorem proving method.

Derived Execution Rules
The following three rules, which capture the key characterisitics of execution of HMS machines, are derived from a combination of the Transition Firing and State Updating rules of Section 2.

(DE-1) $<t_1, t_2>!\neg s \Rightarrow <t_1, t_2> (\bigvee_{u \in \Gamma_{out}(s)} u)$

(DE-2) $<t_1, t_2>!s \Rightarrow <t_1, t_2> (\bigvee_{v \in \Gamma_{in}(s)} v)$

(DE-3) $O(t)u \Rightarrow O(t-1)(PRIMS(u) \wedge CNTRL(u)) \wedge O(t)CNSQS(u)$

Intuitively, rule DE-1 (DE-2) formalizes the following observation: if a state s becomes false (true) in an interval of time, then one or more transitions fire from (into) s in that interval. The rule DE-3 states that if a transition u fires at t, then its primary states and control were true at $t-1$ and its consequent states are true at t.

TIL Inference Rules
Let φ and ψ be TIL formulae, and let T stand for true. The following rules can then be derived using the definitions of TIL operators and propositional logic.

$$(O(t)\varphi \wedge (\varphi \Rightarrow \psi)) \Rightarrow O(t)\psi$$
$$<t_1, t_2>!\varphi \Rightarrow <t_1, t_2> \varphi$$
$$T \Rightarrow (<t_1, t_2> \varphi \vee [t_1, t_2]\neg\varphi)$$
$$[t_1, t_2]\varphi \Rightarrow (O(t_1)\varphi \wedge \ldots \wedge O(t_2)\varphi)$$
$$<t_1, t_2> \varphi \Rightarrow (O(t_1)\varphi \vee \ldots \vee O(t_2)\varphi)$$

$$O(t)[t_1,t_2]\varphi \Rightarrow [t_1+t,t_2+t]\varphi$$
$$O(t)<t_1,t_2>\varphi \Rightarrow <t_1+t,t_2+t>\varphi$$

Given an HMS machine H, let $\Box p$ be a safety property of H where p is a "past" TIL formula (cf. [MP89]). Following the procedure introduced in [FG89], we represent this safety property by adding a deterministic transition w to H with an empty set of primary states (always true), an extended state Q as its consequent, and $\neg p$ as its TIL control ($Q = SF$ in Figure 2.1). It can be shown that any safety property about H can be represented in this manner. The proof that $\Box p$ holds for H in the theorem proving method to be introduced next is by refutation and is based on heuristics rather than exhaustive enumeration techniques. The refutation is accomplished by demonstrating that if Q has been false for a certain period of time, it can never become true.

Tableau-Based Theorem Proving Method

1. Define a "tableau" containing an "initial node" labeled with the formula $[-m,0]\neg Q \wedge O(1)Q$, which states the following assumption: machine H has been safe for $m+1$ moments and becomes unsafe at the next moment. The choice of m depends on the HMS machine considered and assumptions about the initial conditions. The initial node also defines a terminal node of a "path" to itself in the tableau.

2. For each terminal node N in the tableau, deduce a new fact φ using the Transition Firing, State Updating, Derived Execution and TIL Inference rules. For each disjunct φ_i, $i = 1,\ldots,k$ of φ extend the tableau by creating a branch i with a new terminal node N_i and label N_i with φ_i.

3. For each branch i, $i = 1,\ldots,k$ at N, define an "extension" of the path from the initial node to N that ends at the new node N_i. Remove N from the set of terminal nodes.

4. Repeat steps 2 and 3 until every path of the tableau is "closed." A path and all its extensions are "closed" if one of its nodes is labeled with F (false) or if one node is labeled with a TIL formula X while another one is labeled with $\neg X$. The process terminates with no conclusions about $\Box p$ if a formula of the form $O(-m')s$ is deduced, where s is a state in H and $m' > m$ (indicating inadequate assumptions about the initial conditions).

The choice of m in Step 1 plays an important role in closing a tableau. In practice, we initially choose $m = \infty$ and we attempt to close the tableau. Let m' be the largest value such that $O(-m')s$ is deduced in a closed tableau. Then, to complete the proof, we need to show by a simulation process that, starting from a desired initial set of markings, Q cannot be true for $m'+1$ moments, indicating that in Step 1 any finite m such that $m \geq m'$ is adequate. If the safety property is indeed true, this is usually relatively simple to verify, requiring only a fragment of steps necessary to prove safety by model checking (see, e.g., proof of Theorem 1 below). On the other hand, if the safety property is not true for H, then there exists some execution of length at most m' that will cause Q to be true.

As in traditional theorem proving, the choice of rules to be applied in Step 2 of our theorem proving method is not deterministic and the process is not guaranteed to terminate. Experience and heuristic guidelines are helpful in reducing the lengths of proofs. However, the method can be shown to be *complete* in the following sense: if a safety property is true about an HMS machine, there exists a tableau-based proof for it. This follows from the completeness of the transformational proof method of [FG89] since all the necessary transformations are derivable from the rules presented in this paper.

We now introduce a generic safety property that is often useful in closing the branches of a tableau in our theorem proving method. It is a variation of S-invariance for Petri nets [Re85].

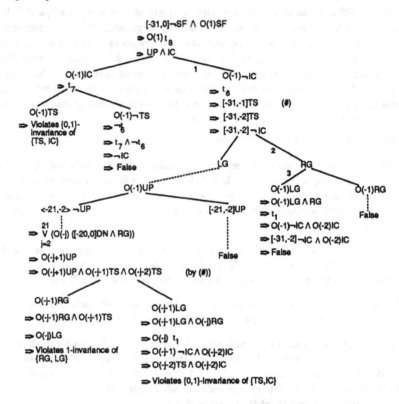

Figure 3.1. Partial Tableau for Theorem 1 (Safety of Railroad Crossing)

Definition 4 (K-invariance) Let K be a set of integers, S be a subset of states in an HMS machine H, and $\#T(S)$ be the number of states in S that are true. Then, S is said to be "K-invariant" if the following holds: If at anytime $\#T(S) \in K$, then $\square(\#T(S) \in K)$. When K is a singleton set $\{n\}$, we say a set S is "n-invariant" if it is $\{n\}$-invariant.

We demonstrate in Theorem 1 the use of our theorem proving method by verifying the safety of the railroad crossing example of Figure 2.1. The proof of the theorem uses the following lemma that can be derived by a straightforward application of our theorem proving method.

Lemma 1 $\{TS, IC\}$ is $\{0,1\}$-invariant and both $\{RG, LG\}$ and $\{UP, DN\}$ are 1-invariant.

It follows that in the railroad example of Figure 2.1 if initially $RG = UP = T$ and $TS = IC = DN = LG = F$, then at most one of the two states TS and IC can be true and RG (UP) is true if and only if LG (DN) is false.

Theorem 1 The HMS specification of the railroad crossing example is safe.

Sketch of Proof: A partial tableau for the proof is shown in Figure 3.1, where $m = -31$ indicating that the extended state SF is assumed to have been false for at least 31 moments. This can easily be verified by running the machine for 31 moments starting from any initial marking where $TS = IC = F$. Solid lines represent branches in the tableau, while broken lines indicate that a number of intermediate steps, possibly involving additional branches, have been skipped. As an illustration, we walk through branches 1, 2, and 3 of the tableau. We first create the initial node following step 1 of our method with the label $\neg SF \wedge \mathbf{O}(1)SF$. By Derived Execution rules DE-2 and DE-3 we deduce $UP \wedge IC$. The tautology $\mathbf{O}(-1)IC \vee \mathbf{O}(-1)\neg IC$ gives rise to the first pair of branches in the tableau. Along branch 1, we conclude that t_6 fires at $t = 0$ by Derived Execution rule DE-2 since $IC \wedge \mathbf{O}(-1)\neg IC$ holds. By Derived Execution rule DE-3 the control of t_6 was satisfied at $t = -1$, i.e., $[-31, -1]TS$ holds. Next, using the $\{0,1\}$-invariance of $\{TS, IC\}$ (Lemma 1), we conclude $[-31, -2]\neg IC$. At this point, we create two branches, with RG being true along branch 2. Along branch 3, we conclude that t_1 fires at $t = 0$ by Transition Firing rule TF-1 since $\mathbf{O}(-1)LG \wedge RG$ holds. By Derived Execution rule DE-3, the control of t_1 was satisfied at $t = -1$, i.e., $\mathbf{O}(-1)\neg IC \wedge \mathbf{O}(-2)IC$ holds. However, $\mathbf{O}(-1)\neg IC \wedge \mathbf{O}(-2)IC$ contradicts $[-31, -2]\neg IC$. This closes branch 3 of the tableau. Other branches can be closed in a similar manner. As indicated in Figure 3.1, the closing of certain branches involves the use of *parametric* TIL formulae containing the parameter j, for $j = 2, \ldots, 21$. In such cases, the refutation for an entire range of values of the parameters is accomplished in a single step.

The tableau-based theorem proving method presented here is particularly useful in proving safety properties of HMS machines with many *nondeterministic* transitions. Like the transformational approach of [FG89] and in contrast to traditional model checking approaches, it has the important advantage that the length of a proof does not directly depend on the size of the machine. The length of a proof depends only on the safety property being verified and the structure of the relevant portions of the associated machine.

4 Verifying Properties with Parametric Computation Graphs

In [GI91, Ga91] the basic ideas of a model checking approach for HMS machines were presented in which the set of all possible behaviors of a machine is represented in terms of a parametric "computation graph" and desirable behavior is defined in a branching time extension of TIL, called BTIL. In BTIL, the two additional operators $\exists$ (there exists an execution) and $\forall$ (for all executions) are used to characterize nondeterministic behavior for the past, the present and the future. Verification of a BTIL property is then achieved by the traversal of the associated computation graph.

In this section, we present some preliminary results on an approach to partitioning the computation graph of an HMS machine in terms of "interacting" parametric computation graphs that can be collectively much simpler than the computation graph of the entire machine. We limit our discussion to cases where the HMS machine consists of a "composition" [GI91, Ga91] of "cyclic" HMS machines, in which there is a partial order on controls between separate machines. As in the case of the "submachines" Signal, Gate, and Train in Figure 2.1, an HMS machine is cyclic if there is a circular path of transitions connecting all the states. In case of Train, the two infinite resources (vertical bars) are identified as a single state.

In more specific terms the HMS machines considered in this section can be characterized as follows: Given a machine $H = (S, \Gamma_D, \Gamma_N)$, S can be partitioned into disjoint subsets $S_1, \ldots, S_k$, such that for each $\gamma \in \Gamma_D \cup \Gamma_N$, there exists an $i \in \{1, \ldots, k\}$ with $\text{PRIMS}(\gamma) \cup \text{CNSQS}(\gamma) \in S_i$ and if s is a literal in $\text{CNTRL}(\gamma)$ then $s \in S_1 \cup \ldots \cup S_i$. Each partition S_i gives rise to an HMS cyclic submachine H_i such that the behavior of H_1 is independent of all the other submachines and the behavior of H_i for $i > 1$ depends only on $H_1, \ldots, H_{i-1}$. In our example of the railroad crossing of Figure 2.1, the HMS machine can be partitioned into the three submachines $H_1 =$ Train, $H_2 =$ Signal and $H_3 =$ Gate. Train is independent of Signal and Gate, Signal depends only on Train, and Gate depends on Signal.

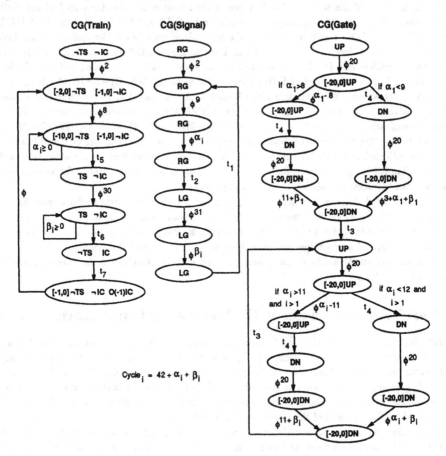

Figure 4.1. Interacting Parametric Computation Graphs for Railroad Crossing

The form of computation graph considered here consists of (1) nodes labeled with TIL formulae recording state marking histories, and (2) arcs between nodes labeled with sets of transitions or terms of the form ϕ^i. Here ϕ represents a "wait" or "no action" and i is either an integer constant or an integer variable with the interpretation that ϕ^i represents a parametric wait of i moments. Given a computation graph for an HMS machine H, assume that a node N_i is labeled with the set $\mu(N_i)$ of TIL formulae and an arc α_{ij} from node N_i to node N_j is labeled with $\gamma(\alpha_{ij})$. Then, if all the formulae $\mu(N_i)$ are true, the execution of $\gamma(\alpha_{ij})$ will make all the formulae in $\mu(N_j)$ true.

We note the following characteristics of our computation graphs: (1) nodes contain state histories defined in TIL for multiple states, (2) arcs record simultaneous firings of transitions or parametric waits, and (3) for each state a "maximum relevant history" [GI91, Ga91] can be defined that limits the length of history for the state that needs to be recorded. The key notion to be exploited in this section is the establishment of *interactions* among the computation graphs of submachines of an HMS machine in terms of the parametric waits. As a result, a significant reduction in the size of a computation graph can be achieved.

Figure 4.1 illustrates the concept of interacting parametric computation graphs for the railroad crossing HMS machine of Figure 2.1. We first construct the computation graph CG(Train) for the submachine Train which, as indicated earlier, does not depend on Signal or Gate. We begin with the assumption that TS and IC are both initially false so that after a wait of 10 moments $[-10, 0]\neg TS$ will be true. At this time, since t_5 is nondeterministic, it will fire after a parametric wait of α_1 moments for $\alpha_1 \geq 0$. The parameter α_i designates a similar wait during the ith traversal of CG(Train). Another arbitrary wait $\beta_i \geq 0$ occurs before the firing of the nondeterminisitic transition t_6. We then construct in sequence the computation graphs CG(Signal) and CG(Gate) for the submachines Signal and Gate, respectively. All three computation graphs turn out to have a cycle length of $42 + \alpha_i + \beta_i$ for the ith iteration. Note that the parametric waits α_i and β_i in CG(Train) determine uniquely the lengths of certain waits for certain branches of CG(Signal) and CG(Gate). In addition, for CG(Gate) alternative branches are chosen depending on the values of α_i and β_i.

The three relatively simple interacting computation graphs in Figure 4.1 permit a complete analysis of the behavior of our railroad crossing example. In contrast, a combined computation graph would have been quite complex, potentially involving the "cross product" of the individual computation graphs. As a result, the analysis of the behavior of the railroad crossing using the combined computation graph would have been much more difficult.

The proof of the safety property $\Box\neg(IC \land UP)$ of the railroad crossing can now be demonstrated analytically from the computation graphs of Figure 4.1 since $O(k)IC$ for $k = 42i + \Sigma(\alpha_i + \beta_i), i \geq 1$, from CG(Train) and $O(42i + \Sigma(\alpha_i + \beta_i)), i \geq 1$, from CG(Gate). Thus, whenever IC is true the gate is down (DN) and therefore UP is false by the 1-invariance of $\{DN, UP\}$.

5   Summary and Conclusions

The HMS machine concept provides a rich and compact formalism for the specification of systems with complex real-time constraints. Tableau-based theorem proving and interacting parametric computation graphs offer two complementary methods for verifying properties of HMS machine specifications. The former approach introduces the use of the interval-based temporal logic TIL and execution semantics of HMS machines into the theorem proving process. The latter approach simplifies the representation of computation graphs significantly. Current research is directed towards the generalization of the specification and verification techniques into an algebraic framework and the development of heuristic guidelines for the application of the verification methods discussed in this paper.

References

[Ab87]   Abadi, M., "Temporal-logic theorem proving," Dissertation, Stanford Univ., 1987.

[AS89]   Alpern, B., and F.B. Schneider, "Verifying temporal properties without temporal logic," *ACM Transactions on Programming Languages and Systems*, Vol. 11, No. 1, January 1989, pp. 147-167.

[DM88]   Da-Hai, L., and T.S.E. Maibaum, "Developing a high level specification formalism," in *Formal Methods: Theory and Practice*, P.N. Scharbach (Ed.), CRC Press, Boca Baton, FL, 1988.

[Fi90]   Fitting, M., *First-Order Logic and Automated Theorem Proving*, Springer-Verlag, 1990.

[FG89]   Franklin, M.K., and A. Gabrielian, "A transformational method for verifying safety properties in real-time systems," *Proc. 10th Real-Time Systems Symposium*, Santa Monica, CA, December 5-7, 1989, pp. 112-123.

[Ga91]   Gabrielian, A., "HMS machines: a unified framework for specification, verification and reasoning for real-time systems," *Foundations of Real-Time Computing: Formal Specifications and Methods*, A. van Tilborg (Ed.), Kluwer Academic Publishers, Norwell, Mass., 1991, to appear.

[GF88]   Gabrielian, A., and M. K. Franklin, "State-based specification of complex real-time systems," *Proc. IEEE Real-Time Systems Symposium*, 1988, pp. 2-11.

[GF90]   Gabrielian, A., and M.K. Franklin, "Multi-level specification and verification of real-time software," *12th Int. Conf. Software Engineering*, March 26-30, 1990, Nice, France, pp. 52-62. Revised version in *Communications of the ACM*, May 1991, pp. 50-60.

[GI91]   Gabrielian, A., and R. Iyer, "Integrating automata and temporal logic: a framework for specification of real-time systems and software," *The Unified Computation Laboratory*, Inst. of Math. and its Applications, Stirling, Scotland, Oxford University Press, 1991.

[GM89]   Ghezzi, C., D. Madrioli, et al., "A general way to put time in Petri nets," *Proc. Fifth Int. Workshop on Software Specif. and Design*, Pittsburgh, PA, May 1989, pp. 60-67.

[HMP91] Henzinger, T.A., Z. Manna, and A. Pneuli, "Temporal proof methodologies for real-time systems," *Proc. 18th Annual ACM Symposium on Principles of Programming Languages*, 1991.

[Me88]   Melliar-Smith, P.M., "A graphical representation of interval logic," in *Proc. Concurrency 88*, LNCS 335, Springer-Verlag, 1988, pp. 106-120.

[MP89]   Manna, Z., and Pnueli, A., "The anchored version of the temporal framework," *Proc. Linear Time, Branching Time and Partial Order in Logics and Models for Concurrency*, LNCS 354, Springer-Verlag, 1989, pp. 201-284.

[PH88]   Pnueli, A., and E. Harel, "Applications of temporal logic to the specification of real-time systems (extended abstract)," *Proc. Symp. Formal Techniques in Real-Time and Fault-Tolerant Systems*, LNCS 331, Springer-Verlag, 1988, pp. 84-98.

[Re85]   Reisig, W., *Petri Nets*, Springer-Verlag, 1985.

[SW89]   Stirling, C., and D. Walker, "CCS, liveness, and local model checking in the linear time mu-calculus," *Proc. Automatic Verification Methods for Finite State Systems*, Grenoble, 1989, LNCS 407, Springer-Verlag, 1990, pp. 166-178.

A linear time process algebra

Alan Jeffrey

ABSTRACT. This paper presents a variant of Milner's Calculus for Communicating Systems enriched with a notion of time. Time here is considered to be a totally ordered monoid rather than a particular numerical domain. A set of laws for the algebra are presented, as well as a transition system semantics. The laws are then shown to be consistent and complete.

1 Introduction

Milner's *Calculus for Communicating Systems* (CCS) [Mil80, Mil89] is a well developed theory of untimed concurrency. This has recently been extended to include a notion of time by Wang [Wan90, Wan91], Hennessy and Regan [HR90], and Moller and Tofts [MT90]. In addition, Bergstra and Klop's ACP [BW90] has been given timed variants by Baeten and Bergstra [BB91] and Nicollin and Sifakis [NS90]; and Hoare's CSP [Hoa85] has a timed model given by Reed and Roscoe [RR86].

Despite these models being developed independently, they have many features in common, one being that they are all *real time* models—the notion of time is assumed to be either **N** or $[0, \infty)$. In this paper we develop a generalization of Wang's Timed CCS, with three new concepts.

- Time is considered to be an *abstract* notion. We do not specify what the time domain should be, as long as it is a totally ordered monoid, with a few extra conditions. This means that Wang's calculus and Hennessy and Regan's calculus can be seen as examples of the model presented here. If we take the trivial time domain $\{0\}$ with only one time, we have a model isomorphic to Milner's untimed CCS.

- We can produce a *complete axiomatization*. Wang has a complete axiomatization for regular agents, that is ones built without parallelism, restriction, or alphabet transformation. However, due to the lack of an expansion theorem, he was unable to provide a complete axiomatization for parallelism. He has suggested [Wan91] a different prefixing operator $\alpha@t.P_t$ to alleviate this problem. Here, we suggest another prefix, $\alpha{:}P$, and show an expansion theorem using it.

- We explicitly allow *time-stop* processes. In many other calculi, time-stops are implicitly allowed through constructs like $\mu x.x$. Here, we are allowing them because of the interaction of *maximal progress* and *unbounded sum*. If we assume that $\tau{:}P$ will not allow time to pass, but insists on performing its τ action, then the process $\sum\{\varepsilon t{:}\tau{:}P \mid t \neq 0\}$ will not allow time to pass, but

Presented to Computer Aided Verification 1991.
Also available as Programming Methodology Group Technical Report 61.
Author's address: Department of Computer Sciences, S-412 55 Göteborg, Sweden.
E-mail: jeffrey@cs.chalmers.se.

cannot perform a τ action. Hence it is a time-stop. It might be possible to restrict ourselves to a language where such processes were not possible, but it turns out to be algebraically much simpler just to allow time-stops. We can regard these as the 'complex numbers' of this calculus—they do not correspond to anything we might have a computational intuition for, but they simplify the algebra.

Unfortunately, this paper is by no means complete.

- The language considered here only allows finite processes, and has no primitive for recursion. This should not be too difficult to rectify, although finding a complete set of laws to include recursion might be slightly tricky.

- The calculus includes an uncountable sum operator $\sum$. This is the operator that gives our calculus its expressive power, but with an obvious loss—equivalence is no longer decidable. It is an interesting question as to whether we can restrict ourselves to some notion of decidable sum. We still want to be able to make uncountable summations (such as in the definition of $\mu@t.P$) but we may be able to restrict ourselves so as to recover decidability. For example, if our time domain has a topological structure, we might be able to restrict ourselves to summation over closed sets.

This model is a *transition system* model, in the tradition of Milner [Mil80] and Plotkin [Plo81] so there is an implicit assumption that all history can be made linear. This is the reason we are limited to totally ordered time domains. In [Jef91], the author showed how timed process algebra could be applied to partially ordered time domains.

2 Assumptions

We are going to produce a timed variant of Milner's CCS, and so we will need the same notion of *name*.

ASSUMPTION 1. *There is a set $\mathcal{A}$ of names, ranged over by a, b and c.*

A *label* is either a name a or its complement $\overline{a}$.

DEFINITION 2. *The set $\mathcal{L}$ of labels is $\mathcal{A} \cup \overline{\mathcal{A}}$, where $\overline{\mathcal{A}} = \{\overline{a} \mid a \in \mathcal{A}\}$. $\mathcal{L}$ is ranged over by l. Let $\overline{\overline{a}} = a$.*

An *action* is either a label, the special silent action τ.

DEFINITION 3. *The set Act of actions is $\mathcal{L} \cup \{\tau\}$, ranged over by α and β.*

So far, we have followed Milner's untimed calculus. If we are going to produce a timed calculus, though, we will need some notion of time. In fact, we are never interested in *absolute* time (such as '9.26am on 24 January 1990') just *relative* time (such as 'five hours from now'). We can assume there is a zero time ('now') and any two times can be added together ('five hours from now' plus 'three hours from now' is 'eight hours from now'). So we assume time is a totally ordered monoid.

ASSUMPTION 4. *There is a monoid $(\mathcal{T}, +, 0)$ of times, ranged over by t, u and v, such that if $t + u = t + v$ then $u = v$.*

DEFINITION 5. *$t \leq v$ iff $\exists u \, . \, t + u = v$*

ASSUMPTION 6. $\leq$ *is a total order, with bottom 0, and every non-empty set T has a greatest lower bound* $\inf T$.

For example:

- $(\mathbb{N}, +, 0)$ gives a discrete timed model of CCS, similar to [HR90].
- $([0, \infty), +, 0)$ gives a continuous timed model, similar to [Wan91].
- $(\{0\}, +, 0)$ gives the untimed model of CCS.

The *events* we can use in our language are labels, τ actions or times.

DEFINITION 7. *The set Σ of events is $\mathcal{L} \cup \{\tau\} \cup \{\varepsilon t \mid t \in T\}$, ranged over by σ and ρ.*

A *prefix* is an action, or the special time-stop prefix δ. We are using a prefix to represent time-stop in the same way as ACP [BW90] uses δ to represent deadlock.

DEFINITION 8. *The set Pre of prefixes is $Act \cup \{\delta\}$, ranged over by μ and ν.*

Finally, for technical reasons, we need an upper bound on the nondeterminism our language allows.

ASSUMPTION 9. *There is a regular cardinal $\lambda > |T|$.*

3 Syntax

Let us consider *Linear Timed CCS*, based on Wang's Timed CCS, in turn based on Milner's CCS.

DEFINITION 10. *LTCCS is defined by*

$$P ::= \mu{:}P \mid \varepsilon t{:}P \mid \sum \mathcal{P} \mid P \mid P$$

where P, Q and R range over LTCCS and $\mathcal{P}$ and $\mathcal{Q}$ are subsets of LTCCS strictly smaller than λ.

This is the same as Milner's CCS, except that:

- $l{:}P$ can only do an l at time 0, otherwise it deadlocks.
- $\tau{:}P$ will not let time pass, but insists that the τ happens immediately. This is called *maximal progress* by Wang.
- $\delta{:}P$ will not let time pass at all.
- $\varepsilon t{:}P$ delays P by time t.

From these primitives, we can build the operators in Wang's calculus:

DEFINITION 11.

$$0 = \sum \emptyset$$
$$P + Q = \sum \{P, Q\}$$
$$\alpha@t.P_t = \sum \{\varepsilon t{:}\alpha{:}P_t \mid t \in T\}$$

We now give a set of laws for this language, and write $\vdash P = Q$ if we can prove P and Q are equal using them. To begin with, we inherit three properties from Wang's Timed CCS:

LAW 1 (TIME CONTINUITY). $\vdash \varepsilon t{:}\varepsilon u{:}P = \varepsilon(t + u){:}P$

LAW 2 (TIME DETERMINACY). $\vdash \varepsilon t{:}\sum \mathcal{P} = \sum\{\varepsilon t{:}P \mid P \in \mathcal{P}\}$

LAW 3 (ZERO DELAY). $\vdash \varepsilon 0{:}P = P$

and three new properties of $\delta{:}P$:

LAW 4 (MAXIMAL PROGRESS). $\vdash \tau{:}P = \tau{:}P + \delta{:}Q$

LAW 5 (TIME-STOP). *If* $t \neq 0$ *then* $\vdash \delta{:}P = \delta{:}P + \varepsilon t{:}Q$

LAW 6 (TIME-STOP CONTINUITY). *If* $I \neq \emptyset$ *then:*

$$\vdash \sum\{\varepsilon t_i{:}\delta{:}P_i \mid i \in I\} = \varepsilon(\inf\{t_i \mid i \in I\}){:}\delta{:}Q$$

as well as the standard rules for $\sum$ from CCS:

LAW 7 (SUM UNIT). $\vdash \sum\{P\} = P$

LAW 8 (SUM HOMOMORPHISM). $\vdash \sum\{\sum \mathcal{P}_i \mid i \in I\} = \sum \bigcup\{\mathcal{P}_i \mid i \in I\}$

and a continuity condition on summation:

LAW 9 (SUM CONTINUITY). *If* $\forall Q \in \mathcal{Q}.\ \vdash P = P + Q$ *then* $\vdash P = P + \sum \mathcal{Q}$.

Finally, we have a variant of the expansion theorem:

LAW 10 (EXPANSION THEOREM). *If:*

$$\begin{aligned} P &= \sum\{\varepsilon t_i{:}\mu_i{:}P_i \mid i \in I\} \\ Q &= \sum\{\varepsilon u_j{:}\nu_j{:}Q_j \mid j \in J\} \end{aligned}$$

then:

$$\begin{aligned} \vdash P \mid Q = \ &\sum\{\varepsilon t_i{:}\mu_i{:}(P_i \mid Q_{t_i}) \mid i \in I\} \\ &+ \sum\{\varepsilon u_j{:}\nu_j{:}(P_{u_j} \mid Q_j) \mid j \in J\} \\ &+ \sum\{\varepsilon t_i{:}\tau{:}(P_i \mid Q_j) \mid i \in I \wedge j \in J \wedge t_i = u_j \wedge \overline{\mu_i} = \nu_j\} \end{aligned}$$

where:

$$\begin{aligned} P_t &= \sum\{\varepsilon u{:}\mu_i{:}P_i \mid i \in I \wedge t + u = t_i\} \\ Q_t &= \sum\{\varepsilon u{:}\nu_j{:}Q_j \mid j \in J \wedge t + u = u_j\} \end{aligned}$$

This is just a variant on the standard expansion theorem, which says that when P is placed in parallel with Q, one of three things can happen:

- P delays by t_i, performs μ_i, and becomes P_i. In the mean time, Q must move on to time t_i and become Q_{t_i}.
- Q delays by u_j, performs ν_j, and becomes Q_j. In the mean time, P must move on to time u_j and become P_{u_j}.
- Both P and Q delay by time t_i, then P performs μ_i, Q performs $\overline{\mu_i}$, and the resulting system performs a τ action.

It turns out that these laws are the only ones we shall need to prove bisimulation of any agents.

4 Semantics

As with Wang's calculus, we shall give our syntax a *transition system* semantics, with arrows labeled by Σ.

- $P \xrightarrow{l} Q$ means P performs an l action, and becomes Q. This transition takes no time.
- $P \xrightarrow{\tau} Q$ means P performs a silent move, and becomes Q. This transition takes no time.
- $P \xrightarrow{\varepsilon t} Q$ means that P can idle for time t and become Q.

Furthermore, we can place some restrictions on which transition systems we will consider, taken from [Wan91].

AXIOM 1 (TIME CONTINUITY). *If* $P \xrightarrow{\varepsilon(t+u)} R$ *then* $\exists Q . P \xrightarrow{\varepsilon t} Q \xrightarrow{\varepsilon u} R$.

AXIOM 2 (MAXIMAL PROGRESS). *If* $P \xrightarrow{\tau} Q$ *and* $P \xrightarrow{\varepsilon t} R$ *then* $t = 0$.

AXIOM 3 (TIME DETERMINACY). *If* $P \xrightarrow{\varepsilon t} Q$ *and* $P \xrightarrow{\varepsilon t} R$ *then* $Q \equiv R$.

Note, however, that we do *not* have Wang's 'time persistency', because our prefixing primitive $l{:}P$ will offer an l at time 0, but not at any later time. We are allowing $P \xrightarrow{\varepsilon 0} Q$ as a transition, though, so we need an extra axiom.

AXIOM 4 (ZERO DELAY). $P \xrightarrow{\varepsilon 0} P$

This is a matter of style, and is used because it makes the transition rules simpler.

We can now give the transition rules for each of the operators. These semantics are the same as Wang's, with the exception of prefixing, and some technicalities to do with transitions of the form $P \xrightarrow{\varepsilon 0} P$.

To begin with, a prefix $\alpha{:}P$ can either do a α action immediately, or wait for no time. Also, the process $l{:}P$ can wait and become 0. Note that the only transition $\delta{:}P$ has is $\delta{:}P \xrightarrow{\varepsilon 0} \delta{:}P$.

$$\frac{}{\alpha{:}P \xrightarrow{\alpha} P} \qquad \frac{}{\mu{:}P \xrightarrow{\varepsilon 0} \mu{:}P} \qquad \frac{}{l{:}P \xrightarrow{\varepsilon t} 0}\,[t \neq 0]$$

Note that we insist $l{:}P \xrightarrow{\varepsilon t} 0$ rather than Wang's $l.P \xrightarrow{\varepsilon t} l.P$. It is this crucial difference that allows us to find a complete axiomatization for our language. The rules for delay are, however, similar to Wang's.

$$\frac{P \xrightarrow{\alpha} P'}{\varepsilon 0{:}P \xrightarrow{\alpha} P'} \qquad \frac{}{\varepsilon(t+u){:}P \xrightarrow{\varepsilon t} \varepsilon u{:}P} \qquad \frac{P \xrightarrow{\varepsilon u} P'}{\varepsilon t{:}P \xrightarrow{\varepsilon(t+u)} P'}$$

As is the rule for summation.

$$\frac{P \xrightarrow{\alpha} P'}{\sum \mathcal{P} \xrightarrow{\alpha} P'}\,[P \in \mathcal{P}] \qquad \frac{\mathcal{P} \xrightarrow{\varepsilon t} \mathcal{Q}}{\sum \mathcal{P} \xrightarrow{\varepsilon t} \sum \mathcal{Q}}$$

Here $\mathcal{P} \xrightarrow{\varepsilon t} \mathcal{Q}$ iff $\forall P \in \mathcal{P} . \exists Q \in \mathcal{Q} . P \xrightarrow{\varepsilon t} Q$ and $\forall Q \in \mathcal{Q} . \exists P \in \mathcal{P} . P \xrightarrow{\varepsilon t} Q$.

The only real problem, as in [Wan91] is how to deal with parallel composition. It is easy to give the rules for when each side can perform an action, as these are just Milner's rules from [Mil89].

$$\frac{P \xrightarrow{\alpha} P'}{P\,|\,Q \xrightarrow{\alpha} P'\,|\,Q} \qquad \frac{Q \xrightarrow{\alpha} Q'}{P\,|\,Q \xrightarrow{\alpha} P\,|\,Q'} \qquad \frac{P \xrightarrow{l} P' \quad Q \xrightarrow{\bar{l}} Q'}{P\,|\,Q \xrightarrow{\tau} P'\,|\,Q'}$$

The problem comes with delay. It is *not* true that if $P \xrightarrow{\epsilon t} P'$ and $Q \xrightarrow{\epsilon t} Q'$ then $P\,|\,Q \xrightarrow{\epsilon t} P'\,|\,Q'$. For example, $a{:}P\,|\,\bar{a}{:}Q$ can do a τ action, so by the assumption of maximal progress, it cannot do a time transition.

The solution, as in [Wan91] is to look at the *initial actions* that a process can do before time t. If no communication is possible, then we can allow a time t transition to take place.

Define *inits* P to be the initial actions of P together with the times they are available. If $(t, \alpha) \in$ *inits* P and P can wait for time t then P can do an α at time t.

DEFINITION 12.

$$\begin{aligned}
\text{inits } \alpha{:}P &= \{(0, \alpha)\} \\
\text{inits } \delta{:}P &= \emptyset \\
\text{inits } \epsilon t{:}P &= \{(t + u, \alpha) \mid (u, \alpha) \in \text{inits } P\} \\
\text{inits } \textstyle\sum P &= \bigcup\{\text{inits } P \mid P \in \mathcal{P}\} \\
\text{inits } P\,|\,Q &= \text{inits } P \cup \text{inits } Q \cup \{(t, \tau) \mid (t, l) \in \text{inits } P \wedge (t, \bar{l}) \in \text{inits } Q\}
\end{aligned}$$

Then we can say a process is *stable* until t if no τ action can happen before t.

DEFINITION 13. $P \downarrow t$ iff $\forall u < t \,.\, (u, \tau) \notin$ *inits* P.

So we can give a side-condition on the rule for parallelism to make sure that we are not breaking maximal progress.

$$\frac{P \xrightarrow{\epsilon t} P' \quad Q \xrightarrow{\epsilon t} Q'}{P\,|\,Q \xrightarrow{\epsilon t} P'\,|\,Q'} [P\,|\,Q \downarrow t]$$

We have now defined the transition system $(LTCCS, \Sigma, \longrightarrow)$. All we have to do now is ensure that it respects our axioms for timed transition systems.

LEMMA 14. *The transition system* $(LTCCS, \Sigma, \longrightarrow)$ *satisfies Axioms 1–4.*

PROOF. A variant of [Wan91], except for Axiom 4, which is an induction. □

5 Bisimulation

Following [Mil89] and [Wan91], we can define a *strong bisimulation* (from now on just *bisimulation*), which we shall use as our equivalence on *LTCCS*.

DEFINITION 15. *A relation* $\mathcal{R}$ *is a bisimulation iff, for every* $P \mathcal{R} Q$:

- if $P \xrightarrow{\sigma} P'$ then $\exists Q' \,.\, Q \xrightarrow{\sigma} Q'$ and $P' \mathcal{R} Q'$, and
- if $Q \xrightarrow{\sigma} Q'$ then $\exists P' \,.\, P \xrightarrow{\sigma} P'$ and $P' \mathcal{R} Q'$.

We shall then say P and Q are *bisimilar* iff there is a bisimulation which identifies them.

DEFINITION 16. $P \sim Q$ iff there is a bisimulation $\mathcal{R}$ such that $P \mathcal{R} Q$.

We then have to show that $\sim$ is a congruence.

LEMMA 17. $\sim$ is a congruence.

PROOF. A variant of the proof in [Wan91]. □

6 Consistency

We now have two notions of equivalence on $LTCCS$—the laws which prove $\vdash P = Q$, and the bisimulation equivalence $P \sim Q$. We would like to show that these are in fact the same thing, i.e. that they are *consistent* and *complete*. To begin with, we can see that our laws are consistent.

THEOREM 18. If $\vdash P = Q$ then $P \sim Q$.

PROOF. This is a matter of showing that all of our laws are sound. In each case we construct a relation $\mathcal{R}$ containing our law, and show that it must be a bisimulation. Again, most of our laws are contained in either [Mil89] or [Wan91], but we shall prove some of the more interesting ones here.

For sum continuity, assume that for every $Q \in \mathcal{Q}$ there is a bisimulation $\mathcal{R}_Q$ containing $(P, P + Q)$. Then define P_t and Q_t such that $P \xrightarrow{\varepsilon t} P_t$ and $Q \xrightarrow{\varepsilon t} Q_t$, and $\mathcal{Q}_t$ as $\{Q_t \mid Q \in \mathcal{Q}\}$. Then define $\mathcal{R}$ as:

$$\mathcal{R} = \bigcup\{\mathcal{R}_Q \mid Q \in \mathcal{Q}\} \cup \{(P_t, P_t + \textstyle\sum Q_t) \mid t \in T\}$$

By a simple case analysis, $\mathcal{R}$ is a bisimulation, and so since by zero delay and time determinacy, $P_0 \equiv P$ and $Q_0 \equiv Q$, we have shown sum continuity to be sound.

For the expansion law, assume:

$$P = \sum\{\varepsilon t_i{:}\mu_i{:}P_i \mid i \in I\}$$
$$Q = \sum\{\varepsilon u_j{:}\nu_j{:}Q_j \mid j \in J\}$$

and define:

$$P_t = \sum\{\varepsilon u{:}\mu_i{:}P_i \mid i \in I \wedge t + u = t_i\}$$
$$Q_t = \sum\{\varepsilon u{:}\nu_j{:}Q_j \mid j \in J \wedge t + u = u_j\}$$
$$R_t = \sum\{\varepsilon u{:}\mu_i{:}(P_i \mid Q_{t_i}) \mid i \in I \wedge t + u = t_i\}$$
$$+ \sum\{\varepsilon u{:}\nu_j{:}(P_{u_j} \mid Q_j) \mid j \in J \wedge t + u = u_j\}$$
$$+ \sum\{\varepsilon u{:}\tau{:}(P_i \mid Q_j) \mid i \in I \wedge j \in J \wedge t_i = u_j \wedge \overline{\mu_i} = \nu_j\}$$

It is a straightforward case analysis to show that $I \cup \{(P_t \mid Q_t, R_t) \mid t \in T\}$ is a bisimulation, and therefore $P_0 \mid Q_0 \sim R_0$. However, $P_0 \equiv P$, $Q_0 \equiv Q$, and R_0 is the rhs of the expansion law. □

7 Completeness

We can now turn to the meat of this paper—the proof that Laws 1–10 are *complete*, so if $P \sim Q$ then $\vdash P = Q$. As usual, we shall find a *normal form* which we can transform all of our agents into, and then show that any equivalent normal agents must be identical.

DEFINITION 19. *P is in summand form if it is of the form:*

$$P \equiv \sum\{\varepsilon t_i{:}\mu_i{:}P_i \mid i \in I\}$$

where each of the P_i are in summand form.

This is *not* a normal form, since $\sum\{\varepsilon 0{:}\tau{:}P\}$ and $\sum\{\varepsilon 0{:}\tau{:}P, \varepsilon 0{:}\delta{:}0\}$ are bisimilar, and both are in summand form. However, it is a step towards a normal form, and every agent can be transformed to one in summand form.

LEMMA 20. *If P and Q are in summand form, then there is an R in summand form such that $\vdash P \mid Q = R$.*

PROOF (BY INDUCTION ON P AND Q). Assume:

$$P \equiv \sum\{\varepsilon t_i{:}\mu_i{:}P_i \mid i \in I\}$$
$$Q \equiv \sum\{\varepsilon u_j{:}\nu_j{:}Q_j \mid j \in J\}$$

and define:

$$P_t \equiv \sum\{\varepsilon u{:}\mu_i{:}P_i \mid i \in I \wedge t + u = t_i\}$$
$$Q_t \equiv \sum\{\varepsilon u{:}\nu_j{:}Q_j \mid j \in J \wedge t + u = u_j\}$$

then by the expansion law:

$$\begin{aligned}
\vdash P \mid Q = {} & \sum\{\varepsilon t_i{:}\mu_i{:}(P_i \mid Q_{t_i}) \mid i \in I\} \\
& + \sum\{\varepsilon u_j{:}\nu_j{:}(P_{u_j} \mid Q_j) \mid j \in J\} \\
& + \sum\{\varepsilon t_i{:}\tau{:}(P_i \mid Q_j) \mid i \in I \wedge j \in J \wedge t_i = u_j \wedge \overline{\mu_i} = \nu_j\}
\end{aligned}$$

By induction, we can find summand forms for $P_i \mid Q_{t_i}$, $P_{u_j} \mid Q_j$ and $P_i \mid Q_j$, and so we are finished. □

LEMMA 21. *For any P, there is a Q in summand form such that $\vdash P = Q$.*

PROOF (BY INDUCTION ON P).

$P \equiv \mu{:}P'$ By induction, there is an Q' in summand form such that $\vdash P' = Q'$. By sum unit and zero delay, $\vdash P = \sum \varepsilon 0{:}\mu{:}Q'$, which is in summand form.

$P \equiv \varepsilon t{:}P'$ By induction, we can show $\vdash P' = \sum\{\varepsilon t_i{:}\mu_i{:}P_i \mid i \in I\}$ and so by time continuity and time determinacy, $\vdash P = \sum\{\varepsilon(t + t_i){:}\mu_i{:}P_i \mid i \in I\}$.

$P \equiv \sum\{P_i \mid i \in I\}$ By induction, for every $i \in I$ we can find a $\sum Q_i$ in summand form such that $\vdash P_i = \sum Q_i$. Then by sum homomorphism, $\vdash P = \sum \bigcup\{Q_i \mid i \in I\}$ which is in summand form.

$P \equiv P_1 \mid P_2$ By induction, P_1 and P_2 can be transformed into summand form, and so by Lemma 20, P can be transformed into summand form. □

We can now define the normal form we've been looking for.

DEFINITION 22. *P is in normal form if it is of the form:*

$$P \equiv \sum\{\varepsilon t_i{:}\mu_i{:}P_i \mid i \in I\}$$

where:

- each of the P_i are in normal form,

- if $\mu_i = \tau$ then $\exists j . t_i = t_j \wedge a_j = \delta$, and
- if $\mu_i = \delta$ then $\forall j . t_j \leq t_i$ and $P_i \equiv 0$.

This is the same as summand form, except we insist on maximal progress, remove any actions which happen after a time-stop, and insist that all time-stops are of the form $\delta{:}0$. For example $\sum\{\varepsilon0{:}\tau{:}P\}$ is not in normal form, but $\sum\{\varepsilon0{:}\tau{:}P, \varepsilon0{:}\delta{:}0\}$ is. We can now show that any agent in summand form can be converted to normal form.

LEMMA 23. *If P is in summand form, then there is a Q in normal form such that $\vdash P = Q$.*

PROOF. Assume:

$$P \equiv \sum\{\varepsilon t_i{:}\mu_i{:}P_i \mid i \in I\}$$

then by induction we can find Q_i in normal form such that $\vdash P_i = Q_i$. Define:

$$I_M = \{i \in I \mid \mu_i \in M\}$$

If $I_{\{\tau,\delta\}}$ is empty, then $P = \sum\{\varepsilon t_i{:}\mu_i{:}Q_i\}$, which is in normal form. Otherwise:

$$t_\delta = \inf\{t_i \mid i \in I_{\{\tau,\delta\}}\}$$
$$J = \{j \in I_{\mathcal{L} \cup \{\tau\}} \mid t_j \leq t_\delta\}$$
$$Q \equiv \sum(\{\varepsilon t_j{:}\mu_j{:}Q_j \mid j \in J\} \cup \{\varepsilon t_\delta{:}\delta{:}0\})$$

Then for any $i \in I \setminus J$, there are two possibilities. If $t_i \leq t_\delta$, then from the definition of J this is only possible if $t_i = t_\delta$ and $\mu_i = \delta$. Then:

$$
\begin{aligned}
\vdash Q &= Q + \sum\{\varepsilon t_\delta{:}\delta{:}0\} & \text{(sum laws)} \\
&= Q + \varepsilon(\inf\{t_\delta\}){:}\delta{:}Q_i & \text{(time-stop continuity)} \\
&= Q + \varepsilon t_\delta{:}\delta{:}Q_i & \text{(definition of inf)} \\
&= Q + \varepsilon t_i{:}\mu_i{:}Q_i & \text{(above)}
\end{aligned}
$$

Otherwise, if $t_\delta < t_i$, there is some $t \neq 0$ such that $t_\delta + t = t_i$. Then:

$$
\begin{aligned}
\vdash Q &= Q + \varepsilon t_\delta{:}\delta{:}0 & \text{(sum laws)} \\
&= Q + \varepsilon t_\delta{:}(\delta{:}0 + \varepsilon t{:}\mu_i{:}Q_i) & \text{(time-stop)} \\
&= Q + \varepsilon t_\delta{:}\delta{:}0 + \varepsilon t{:}_\delta \varepsilon t{:}\mu_i{:}Q_i & \text{(time determinacy)} \\
&= Q + \varepsilon t_\delta{:}\delta{:}0 + \varepsilon t{:}_i\mu_i{:}Q_i & \text{(time continuity)} \\
&= Q + \varepsilon t{:}_i\mu_i{:}Q_i & \text{(sum laws)}
\end{aligned}
$$

So:

$$
\begin{aligned}
\vdash Q &= Q + \sum\{\varepsilon t_i{:}\mu_i{:}Q_i \mid i \in I \setminus J\} & \text{(sum continuity)} \\
&= \sum\{\varepsilon t_i{:}\mu_i{:}Q_i \mid i \in I\} + \varepsilon t_\delta{:}\delta{:}0 & \text{(sum laws)} \\
&= \sum\{\varepsilon t_i{:}\mu_i{:}P_i \mid i \in I\} + \varepsilon t_\delta{:}\delta{:}0 & \text{(definition of } Q_i) \\
&= P + \varepsilon t_\delta{:}\delta{:}0 & \text{(definition of } P) \\
&= P + \varepsilon(\inf\{t_i \mid i \in I_{\{\tau,\delta\}}\}){:}\delta{:}0 & \text{(definition of } t_\delta) \\
&= P + \sum\{\varepsilon t_i{:}\delta{:}P_i \mid i \in I_{\{\tau,\delta\}}\} & \text{(time-stop continuity)}
\end{aligned}
$$

$$\begin{aligned}
&= P + \sum\{\varepsilon t_i{:}\delta{:}P_i \mid i \in I_{\{\delta\}}\} + \sum\{\varepsilon t_i{:}\delta{:}P_i \mid i \in I_{\{\tau\}}\} && \text{(sum laws)}\\
&= P + \sum\{\varepsilon t_i{:}\delta{:}P_i \mid i \in I_{\{\tau\}}\} && \text{(definition of } I_{\{\delta\}})\\
&= P + \sum\{\varepsilon t_i{:}\tau{:}P_i \mid i \in I_{\{\tau\}}\} + \sum\{\varepsilon t_i{:}\delta{:}P_i \mid i \in I_{\{\tau\}}\} && \text{(definition of } I_{\{\tau\}})\\
&= P + \sum\{\varepsilon t_i{:}\tau{:}P_i \mid i \in I_{\{\tau\}}\} && \text{(maximal progress)}\\
&= P && \text{(definition of } I_{\{\tau\}})
\end{aligned}$$

So $\vdash P = Q$, and Q is in normal form. $\qquad\square$

COROLLARY 24. *For any P, there is a Q in normal form such that $\vdash P = Q$.*

Finally, all we have to do is show that our normal form is indeed normalizing.

LEMMA 25. *If $P \sim Q$ are in normal form, then $P \equiv Q$.*

PROOF (BY INDUCTION ON P AND Q). Assume:

$$\begin{aligned}
P &\equiv \textstyle\sum \mathcal{P}\\
\mathcal{P} &\equiv \{\varepsilon t_i{:}\mu_i{:}P_i \mid i \in I\}\\
Q &\equiv \textstyle\sum \mathcal{Q}\\
\mathcal{Q} &\equiv \{\varepsilon u_j{:}\nu_j{:}Q_j \mid j \in J\}
\end{aligned}$$

If $\varepsilon t{:}\delta{:}0 \in \mathcal{P}$, then $P \xrightarrow{\varepsilon u}$ iff $u \le t$, so $Q \xrightarrow{\varepsilon u}$ iff $u \le t$, so $\varepsilon t{:}\delta{:}0 \in \mathcal{Q}$. If $\varepsilon t{:}\tau{:}P_i \in \mathcal{P}$, then $P \xrightarrow{\varepsilon t}\xrightarrow{\tau} P_i$, so $Q \xrightarrow{\varepsilon t}\xrightarrow{\tau} Q_j$ and $P_i \sim Q_j$, so by induction $P_i \equiv Q_j$, so $\varepsilon t{:}\tau{:}P_i \in \mathcal{Q}$. If $\varepsilon t{:}l{:}P_i \in \mathcal{P}$, then $P \xrightarrow{\varepsilon t}\xrightarrow{l} P_i$, so $Q \xrightarrow{\varepsilon t}\xrightarrow{l} Q_j$ and $P_i \sim Q_j$, so by induction $P_i \equiv Q_j$, so $\varepsilon t{:}P{:}_i \in \mathcal{Q}$. So $\mathcal{P} \subseteq \mathcal{Q}$, and similarly $\mathcal{Q} \subseteq \mathcal{P}$, so $P \equiv Q$. $\qquad\square$

This means we can now show the main result of this paper.

THEOREM 26. *If $P \sim Q$ then $\vdash P = Q$.*

PROOF. By Corollary 24, we can show $\vdash P = P'$ and $\vdash Q = Q'$ where P' and Q' are in normal form. Then by Lemma 25, $P' \equiv Q'$, so $\vdash P = Q$. $\qquad\square$

References

[BB91] J. C. M. Baeten and J. A. Bergstra. Real time process algebra. *Formal Aspects Comp. Sci.*, 3:142–188, 1991.

[BW90] J. C. M. Baeten and W. P. Weijland. *Process Algebra*. Cambridge University Press, 1990.

[Hoa85] C. A. R. Hoare. *Communicating Sequential Processes*. Prentice-Hall, 1985.

[HR90] M. Hennessy and T. Regan. A temporal process algebra. Technical Report 2/90, CSAI, University of Sussex, 1990.

[Jef91] Alan Jeffrey. *Observation Spaces and Timed Processes*. D.Phil. thesis, Oxford University, 1991.

[Mil80] Robin Milner. *A Calculus of Communicating Systems*. Springer-Verlag, 1980. LNCS 92.

[Mil89] Robin Milner. *Communication and Concurrency*. Prentice-Hall, 1989.

[MT90] F. Moller and C. Tofts. A temporal calculus of communicating systems. In *Proc. Concur 90*, pages 401–415. Springer-Verlag, 1990. LNCS 458.

[NS90] X. Nicollin and J. Sifakis. The algebra of timed processes ATP: Theory and application. Technical Report RT-C26, Laboratoire de Génie Informatique de Grenoble, 1990.

[Plo81] Gordon Plotkin. A structural approach to operational semantics. Technical Report DAIMI-FN-19, Computer Science Dept., Århus University, 1981.

[RR86]   G. M. Reed and A. W. Roscoe. A timed model for communicating sequential processes. In *Proc. ICALP 86*, pages 314–323. Springer-Verlag, 1986. LNCS 226.

[Wan90] Wang Yi. Real-time behaviour of asynchronous agents. In *Proc. Concur 90*, pages 502–520. Springer-Verlag, 1990. LNCS 458.

[Wan91] Wang Yi. CCS + time = an interleaving model for real time systems. In J. Leach Albert, B. Monien, and M. Rodríguez, editors, *Proc. ICALP 91*, pages 217–228. Springer-Verlag, 1991. LNCS 510.

Deciding Properties of Regular Real Timed Processes

Uno Holmer *   Kim Larsen [†]   Wang Yi *

Abstract

We discuss the *decidability* problem associated with verifying properties of processes expressed in the real time process calculus TCCS of [W90]. A regular subcalculus TC of TCCS is considered. Two operational semantics, and associated timed notions of bisimulation, are given: a standard infinite semantics, and a symbolic finite semantics. The consistency between the two semantics is proved. We show that both the equivalences are decidable for regular processes relative to comparisons between real numbers.

As an alternative specification formalism, we present a timed modal logic. It turns out that this logic characterises timed bisimulation equivalence in the sense that equivalent processes enjoy exactly the same properties expressed within the logic. Moreover, we prove that the problem of deciding whether a given regular real timed process satisfies a given property of the logic is decidable, relative to first order assertions about real numbers. Two interpretations of the modal logic are offered, based on the standard and symbolic operational semantics of TC respectively and the consistency between these interpretations is proved.

1 Motivation

Recently, numerous models within the frameworks for timed processes based on process calculi and temporal logic have been developed [ACD90, AD90, HR90, MT90, RR86, S90, W90]. In this paper, we discuss the *decidability* problem associated with verifying properties of processes expressed in the real time process calculus TCCS of Wang [W90].

As the specification language for expressing such properties one may choose to use the timed calculus itself, with the notion of correctness given in terms of some time–sensitive abstracting equivalence (a timed version of bisimulation equivalence, say). In a discrete timed model such as [S90, HR90], only one unique time event is introduced into the untimed model of CCS [M89] to deal with timing information, which represents a clock tick. In these models the addition of time does not contribute to the *infiniteness* of the labelled transition system in terms of which the the operational semantics of processes is given. As a consequence one may readily apply the existing standard decision algorithm for bisimulation equivalences [CPS89, PT87] to decide the correctness of an implementation P with respect to a specification S (i.e. whether they are equivalent). However, in a dense timed model such as [W90], it is not obvious that bisimulation equivalence is decidable: for each time instant, a process will have a corresponding state; consequently the state–space of any process will certainly be infinite (in fact there will be a continuum of states). Let us specify a coffee machine in timed CCS [W90].

$$S_0 = coin.S_1$$
$$S_1 = coffee.S_0 + \epsilon(30).\tau.S_0$$

Note that we have used the delay construct $\epsilon(d).P$ of timed CCS [W90], which means "waits for d seconds and then behaves like P". The τ models a time-out event.

Informally, the machine waits for the user to insert a coin after which it is willing to offer a cup of coffee. If the user takes the drink within 30 seconds, it returns to the initial state. After 30 seconds, the

---

*Address: Department of Computer Sciences, Chalmers University of Technology, S–412 96 Göteborg, Sweden. E–mail: holmer@cs.chalmers.se, yi@cs.chalmers.se

[†]Address: Department of Mathematics and Computer Science, Aalborg University, Fredrik Bajersvej 7, 9220 Aalborg, Denmark. E–mail: kgl@iesd.auc.dk

machine will time-out and return autonomously to its initial state to collect another coin. According to the operational semantics of [W90], we have a continuum of time-transitions for S_1,

$$S_1 \xrightarrow{\epsilon(d)} coffee.S_0 + \epsilon(30 - d).\tau.S_0$$

for all $d \in]0, 30]$. For instance,

$$S_1 \xrightarrow{\epsilon(0.5)} coffee.S_0 + \epsilon(29.5).\tau.S_0$$

That is, the machine has a dense and infinite state space. Hence, given a process M we cannot directly use the existing algorithmic techniques such as [CPS89, PT87] to decide whether $M \sim S_0$.

In this paper, we shall consider the *regular real timed processes* of [W90] which are the regular part of CCS plus a delay construct $\epsilon(d).P$ where $d \in \mathcal{R}^+$. We formally define a notion of timed bisimulation equivalence, and show that this equivalence is decidable for regular processes relative to comparisons between real numbers.

As an alternative (logical) specification formalism, we present a timed modal logic. This logic allows one to specify properties such as: "After a coin has been inserted, coffee will be continuously available for 30 seconds". It turns out that this logic characterises (timed) bisimulation equivalence in the sense that equivalent processes enjoy exactly the same properties expressed within the logic. Moreover, we prove that the problem of deciding whether a given regular real time process satisfies a given property of the logic is decidable (relative to first order assertions about real numbers).

The outline of the paper is as follows: In section 2 we introduce the calculus TC of regular real time processes. Two operational semantics (and associated timed notions of bisimulation) are given: the standard (infinite) semantics of [W90] and a (finite) symbolic semantics. The consistency between the two semantics provides the key to our decidability results. In section 3 we introduce the timed modal logic TML. Again two interpretations are offered, based on the standard and symbolic operational semantics of TC respectively. The consistency between these interpretations again leads to our decidability results. In section 4 we state our conclusions and directions for future work.

2 A Timed Calculus

In this section we present a subcalculus TC of [W90]. Assume a set of action names Δ ranged over by $a, b, \ldots$ and a special action $\tau \notin \Delta$. Let $Act = \Delta \cup \{\tau\}$ and $\mu, \nu, \ldots$ range over Act. Let $A = Act \cup \{\epsilon(c) \mid c \in \mathcal{R}^+\}$ where $\mathcal{R}^+$ are the positive real numbers, and let σ range over A. Assume a set of process variables V ranged over by $x, y, \ldots$. The regular process expressions are given by the following abstract syntax:

$$E ::= NIL \mid x \mid \sigma.E \mid E + E \mid rec\, x : E$$

Closed process expressions will be denoted by the letters $P, Q, \ldots$ We will restrict all processes to be *action guarded* in the following sense:

Definition 2.1 x *is action guarded in* E *iff every free occurrence of* x *in* E *is within a subexpression (a guard) of the form* $\mu.F$ *in* E. E *is action guarded iff every free variable in* E *is action guarded in* E, *and for every subexpression of the form* $rec\, x : F$ *in* E, x *is action guarded in* F. $\square$

We denote by Pr the set of all closed and action guarded process expressions.

Example 2.2 $a.NIL$ and $\tau.(rec\, y : x + b.y)$ are action guarded whereas $rec\, x : x + b.x$ and $rec\, x : \epsilon(c).x + a.x$ are not. The latter is not action guarded because $\epsilon(c).x$ is not a guard. $\square$

2.1 Standard Operational Semantics

The standard semantics is given by the transition system $\langle Pr, A, \longrightarrow \rangle$ where $\longrightarrow$ is the least relation generated by the rules in table 1.

Inaction	$$NIL \xrightarrow{\epsilon(c)} NIL$$	
Prefix	$$\overline{\mu.P \xrightarrow{\mu} P}$$	$$\overline{a.P \xrightarrow{\epsilon(c)} a.P}$$
	$$\overline{\epsilon(c).P \xrightarrow{\epsilon(c)} P} \quad \dfrac{P \xrightarrow{\epsilon(c)} P'}{\epsilon(d).P \xrightarrow{\epsilon(c+d)} P'}$$	$$\overline{\epsilon(c+d).P \xrightarrow{\epsilon(c)} \epsilon(d).P}$$
Summation	$$\dfrac{P \xrightarrow{\mu} P'}{P+Q \xrightarrow{\mu} P'} \quad \dfrac{Q \xrightarrow{\mu} Q'}{P+Q \xrightarrow{\mu} Q'}$$	$$\dfrac{P \xrightarrow{\epsilon(c)} P' \quad Q \xrightarrow{\epsilon(c)} Q'}{P+Q \xrightarrow{\epsilon(c)} P'+Q'}$$
Recursion	$$\dfrac{E\{rec\ x : E/x\} \xrightarrow{\sigma} P}{rec\ x : E \xrightarrow{\sigma} P}$$	

Table 1: Standard operational semantics for TC.

For most processes P, the state space and/or the set of transitions which can be generated from P, via $\longrightarrow$, is (wildly) infinite. The most immediate example is NIL for which we can derive $NIL \xrightarrow{\epsilon(c)} NIL$ for any positive real number c. Thus the transition relation is infinite although the state space is not in this case.

Another example is $\epsilon(c).NIL$ which has the ϵ-derivatives $\epsilon(c-d).NIL$ for any $d < c$. Here both the state space and the transition relation are infinite.

The most discouraging consequence of this is that we cannot apply existing techniques for deciding *bisimulation equivalence* based on the standard semantics. Another serious defect is that we cannot draw transition diagrams for simple behaviours such as the coffee machine.

The following lemma gives some crucial properties of the semantics:

Lemma 2.3

i) $P \xrightarrow{\tau} \Rightarrow P \xnrightarrow{\epsilon(c)}$ (maximal progress)

ii) $P \xrightarrow{\tau} \vee P \xrightarrow{\epsilon(c)}$ (transition liveness)

iii) $P \xrightarrow{\epsilon(c)} P' \wedge P \xrightarrow{\epsilon(c)} P'' \Rightarrow P' \equiv P''$ (time determinacy)

iv) $\forall c, d > 0.P \xrightarrow{\epsilon(c+d)} P'' \Leftrightarrow \exists P'.P \xrightarrow{\epsilon(c)} P' \wedge P' \xrightarrow{\epsilon(d)} P''$ (time continuity)

v) $P \xrightarrow{\epsilon(d)} P' \wedge P \xrightarrow{a} Q \Rightarrow P' \xrightarrow{a} Q$ (persistency)

where $\equiv$ in *iii* is syntactical identity and $P \xrightarrow{\sigma}$ means $\exists P'.P \xrightarrow{\sigma} P'$.   □

From the standard operational semantics we define *timed bisimulation equivalence* as usual.

Definition 2.4 *Let $\mathcal{F}(R)$ be the set of all (P,Q) satisfying*

i) *Whenever $P \xrightarrow{\sigma} P'$ then $Q \xrightarrow{\sigma} Q'$ with $(P',Q') \in R$ for some Q'*

ii) *Whenever $Q \xrightarrow{\sigma} Q'$ then $P \xrightarrow{\sigma} P'$ with $(P',Q') \in R$ for some P'*

Then R is a timed bisimulation if $R \subseteq \mathcal{F}(R)$ and timed bisimulation equivalence, written $\sim$, is defined to be the greatest fixpoint of $\mathcal{F}$.   □

2.2 Symbolic Operational Semantics

In this section we give an alternative operational semantics which turns out to be equivalent to the standard operational semantics—up to bisimulation equivalence. It is called "symbolic" because now every process will only give rise to a finite state space and a finite transition relation and we may draw a graph to represent it. The intuition behind the symbolic interpretation is based on the persistency property. Due to this property the behaviour of a process may be completely inferred from the first time-instant at which a transition is enabled.

First we define the *maximal life-time* of a process to be the (unique) time-instant at which a τ-action is enabled. If no τ-action is ever possible, the maximal life-time is ∞.

Example 2.5 *The process $a.P + \epsilon(3).\tau.Q$ remains stable for at most 3 time units. If the environment has not offered a up to time 3 then the process will autonomously become Q at time 3. The process $a.P + \epsilon(3).b.Q$ on the other hand, remains stable forever if the environment never offers a or b.* □

Definition 2.6 *For a process expression E we define the maximal-life-time function $M(E) : (\mathcal{V} \to [0, \infty]) \to [0, \infty]$ inductively as follows:*

$$
\begin{array}{llll}
M(NIL)\rho & = \infty & M(E+F)\rho & = min(M(E)\rho, M(F)\rho) \\
M(a.E)\rho & = \infty & M(x)\rho & = \rho(x) \\
M(\tau.E)\rho & = 0 & M(rec\ x : E)\rho & = \mu t.M(E)\rho[x \mapsto t] \\
M(\epsilon(c).E)\rho & = c + M(E)\rho &&
\end{array}
$$

where $\mu t.f(t)$ denotes the least fixpoint of f. For closed process expressions we define $M(P) = M(P)\rho_0$ where ρ_0 is the time environment mapping any process variable to 0. □

The following lemma relates M with the standard semantics.

Lemma 2.7

i) $\forall c \in]0, M(P)] - \{\infty\}.P \xrightarrow{\epsilon(c)}$
ii) $P \xrightarrow{\tau} \Leftrightarrow M(P) = 0$
iii) $P \xrightarrow{\epsilon(c)} P' \Rightarrow M(P') = M(P) - c$

iv) $P \xrightarrow{\epsilon(c)} \Rightarrow M(P) \geq c$
v) $P \xrightarrow{\epsilon(c)} P' \xrightarrow{\tau} \Rightarrow M(P) = c$
vi) $P{\sim}Q \Rightarrow M(P) = M(Q)$

□

The new semantics is defined by the transition system

$$\langle Pr, Act \times [0, \infty[, \to^* \rangle$$

where $\to^*$ is generated by the rules in table 2. We use the notation $P \xrightarrow{\mu}{}^*_c P'$ for $(P, (\mu, c), P') \in \to^*$, which may be interpreted as "the transition $P \xrightarrow{\mu} P'$ is enabled at time c".

The most important property of the symbolic semantics is that the state space as well as the set of transitions of a process will now be *finite*. We can draw circles to represent states and let numbers inside the circles denote the maximal life-times of the corresponding states. The transitions are drawn in the obvious way.

Example 2.8 *The coffee machine example from the motivation may be expressed in TC as rec x : coin.(coffee.x + $\epsilon(30).\tau.x$). The symbolic transition system for the coffee machine can then be drawn as follows:*

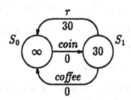

where $S_0 = rec\ x : coin.(coffee.x + \epsilon(30).\tau.x)$ and $S_1 = coffee.S_0 + \epsilon(30).\tau.S_0$. □

Prefix	$$\overline{\mu.P \xrightarrow{\mu}{}^{\bullet}_0 P}$$	$$\frac{P \xrightarrow{\mu}{}^{\bullet}_c P'}{\epsilon(d).P \xrightarrow{\mu}{}^{\bullet}_{c+d} P'}$$
Summation	$$\frac{P \xrightarrow{\mu}{}^{\bullet}_c P'}{P+Q \xrightarrow{\mu}{}^{\bullet}_c P'} \ [M(Q) \geq c]$$	$$\frac{Q \xrightarrow{\mu}{}^{\bullet}_c Q'}{P+Q \xrightarrow{\mu}{}^{\bullet}_c Q'} \ [M(P) \geq c]$$
Recursion	$$\frac{E\{rec\ x : E/x\} \xrightarrow{\mu}{}^{\bullet}_c P}{rec\ x : E \xrightarrow{\mu}{}^{\bullet}_c P}$$	

Table 2: Symbolic operational semantics for TC.

Definition 2.9 *Let derivatives(P) be the least set of processes satisfying the following:*

$$P \in derivatives(P)$$
$$Q \in derivatives(P) \wedge Q \xrightarrow{\mu}{}^{\bullet}_c R \Rightarrow R \in derivatives(P)$$

and let

$$labels(P) = \{(\mu, c) \mid \exists Q, R \in derivatives(P).Q \xrightarrow{\mu}{}^{\bullet}_c R\}$$
$$\to^{\bullet}(P) = (derivatives(P) \times labels(P) \times derivatives(P)) \cap \to^{\bullet}$$

□

Proposition 2.10 *For every action guarded process P, derivatives(P) and labels(P) are finite.* □

Thus every $P \in Pr$ generates a finite *local transition system* given by

$$\langle derivatives(P), labels(P), \to^{\bullet}(P)\rangle$$

This property of the symbolic semantics is crucial for the decidability results which follow later.

Starting from the symbolic semantics instead of the standard one we define *symbolic timed bisimulation*. A symbolic timed bisimulation is a much coarser relation than an ordinary timed bisimulation in that it only contains the "important" states. As before, when matching two processes against each other, every transition of one of them must be matched by a corresponding transition of the other—and vice versa—and leading to equivalent states. However, the requirement on the matching transition is now relaxed: its enabling time may *precede* the enabling time of the other transition.

Example 2.11 *Consider the following processes:*

$$P = \epsilon(1).a.P_1 + \epsilon(2).a.P_2 \quad \text{and} \quad Q = \epsilon(1).a.Q_1 + \epsilon(3).a.Q_2$$

A symbolic bisimulation containing (P,Q) must also contain (P_1, Q_1), (P_2, Q_1) and either (P_1, Q_2) or (P_2, Q_2). □

We define symbolic timed equivalence as follows:

Definition 2.12 *Let $\mathcal{F}^{\bullet}(R)$ be the set of all (P,Q) satisfying*

i) *Whenever $P \xrightarrow{\mu}{}^{\bullet}_c P'$ then $Q \xrightarrow{\mu}{}^{\bullet}_d Q'$ with $(P',Q') \in R$ for some Q' and $d \leq c$*

ii) *Whenever $Q \xrightarrow{\mu}{}^{\bullet}_c Q'$ then $P \xrightarrow{\mu}{}^{\bullet}_d P'$ with $(P',Q') \in R$ for some P' and $d \leq c$*

Then R is a symbolic timed bisimulation if $R \subseteq \mathcal{F}^{\bullet}(R)$ and symbolic timed equivalence, written $\sim^{\bullet}$, is defined to be the greatest fixpoint of $\mathcal{F}^{\bullet}$. □

We are now ready for our first main theorem:

Theorem 2.13 *Symbolic timed equivalence between action guarded TC processes is decidable relative to inequations between positive real numbers.* □

2.3 Relating the two Semantics

The following relationships between the two transition relations will turn out to be useful:

Lemma 2.14

i) $P \xrightarrow{\mu}_0^* Q \Leftrightarrow P \xrightarrow{\mu} Q$
   iii) $P \xrightarrow{\epsilon(c)} Q \xrightarrow{\mu} R \Rightarrow \exists d \leq c.P \xrightarrow{\mu}_d^* R$

ii) $c > 0 \wedge P \xrightarrow{\mu}_c^* Q \Rightarrow \exists P'.P \xrightarrow{\epsilon(c)} P' \xrightarrow{\mu} Q$
   iv) $P \xrightarrow{\mu}_c^* Q \wedge P \xrightarrow{\epsilon(d)} Q' \Rightarrow Q' \xrightarrow{\mu}_{c\ominus d}^* Q$

Where $x \ominus y$ equals $x - y$ if $x \geq y$ and 0 otherwise. □

As one would expect, symbolic bisimilar processes have equal life-times.

Lemma 2.15 *Using lemmas 2.7 and 2.14(i–iii) we can prove that* $P \sim^* Q \Rightarrow M(P) = M(Q)$. □

Our second main theorem reveals the fact that timed bisimulation equivalence and symbolic timed equivalence coincide on action guarded TC processes:

Theorem 2.16 $\sim \; = \; \sim^*$ □

Corollary 2.17 *Timed bisimulation equivalence* ($\sim$) *between TC processes is decidable relative to inequations between positive real numbers.* □

3 A Timed Modal Logic

We introduce a logic which allows constraints on the timed behaviour of processes to be expressed explicitly. The logic TML is an extension of the well known Hennessy–Milner Logic [HM85], and the formulae of the logic are given by the following abstract syntax:

$$F ::= tt \mid \neg F \mid F \wedge G \mid \langle \mu \rangle_{\forall \phi} F \mid \langle \mu \rangle_{\exists \phi} F$$

where μ is an action and ϕ is a time-set, i.e. $\phi \subseteq \mathcal{R}_0^+$.[1]

Intuitively, for a process to satisfy $\langle \mu \rangle_{\forall \phi} F$ any state reached after time–delays within the set ϕ must have a μ–derivative satisfying F. Thus, $\langle \mu \rangle_{\forall \phi} F$ specifies a property which holds invariantly for all time–delays in ϕ. Similarly, to satisfy $\langle \mu \rangle_{\exists \phi} F$ the process must after *some* time–delay within the set ϕ reach a state with a μ–derivative satisfying F. Thus, $\langle \mu \rangle_{\exists \phi} F$ specifies a property which holds eventually for some time–delay in ϕ.

3.1 Standard Interpretation

Below we give an interpretation of TML with respect to the standard semantics of the calculus TC:

Definition 3.1 $\models$ *is the (satisfaction) relation between TC and TML defined inductively as[2]:*

   i) $P \models tt \Leftrightarrow true$
   ii) $P \models \neg F \Leftrightarrow not\ (P \models F)$
   iii) $P \models F \wedge G \Leftrightarrow P \models F$ and $P \models G$
   iv) $P \models \langle \mu \rangle_{\forall \phi} F \Leftrightarrow \forall d \in \phi. \exists P' \exists P''. P \xrightarrow{\epsilon(d)} P' \xrightarrow{\mu} P'' \wedge P'' \models F$
   v) $P \models \langle \mu \rangle_{\exists \phi} F \Leftrightarrow \exists d \in \phi. \exists P' \exists P''. P \xrightarrow{\epsilon(d)} P' \xrightarrow{\mu} P'' \wedge P'' \models F$

   □

---

[1] We use $\mathcal{R}_0^+$ as abbreviation for $\mathcal{R}^+ \cup \{0\}$

[2] Here we apply the convention that $P \xrightarrow{\epsilon(0)} P'$ if and only if $P = P'$.

Note that $\langle\mu\rangle_{\forall\phi}F$ requires that the process can delay for any time–instant of ϕ. We shall often use the following derived operators:

$$i)\ \mathit{ff} = \neg tt, \quad ii)\ F \vee G = \neg(\neg F \wedge \neg G), \quad iii)\ [\mu]_{\exists\phi}F = \neg\langle\mu\rangle_{\forall\phi}\neg F, \quad iv)\ [\mu]_{\forall\phi}F = \neg\langle\mu\rangle_{\exists\phi}\neg F$$

Intuitively $[\mu]_{\exists\phi}F$ specifies a process which after some time–delay within ϕ may reach a state where all μ–derivatives satisfy F. Similarly, $[\mu]_{\forall\phi}F$ specifies the processes for which all μ–derivatives of states reachable by time–delays within ϕ satisfy F.

Obviously we have the following two equivalences[3]:

$$\langle\mu\rangle_{\forall\phi}F \equiv tt \qquad\qquad \langle\mu\rangle_{\exists\phi}F \equiv \mathit{ff}$$

Also, whenever $\phi \subseteq \psi$ then it is easy to see that the following implications hold[4]:

$$\langle\mu\rangle_{\forall\phi}F \Leftarrow \langle\mu\rangle_{\forall\psi}F \qquad\qquad \langle\mu\rangle_{\exists\phi}F \Rightarrow \langle\mu\rangle_{\exists\psi}F$$

Now, for $\phi \subseteq \mathcal{R}_0^+$ define the closure set $\phi{\downarrow}$ as follows:

$$\phi{\downarrow} = \{t \in \mathcal{R}_0^+ \mid \exists c \in \phi. t \leq c\}$$

Then as $\phi \subseteq \phi{\downarrow}$ it follows that:

$$\langle\mu\rangle_{\exists\phi}F \Rightarrow \langle\mu\rangle_{\exists\phi{\downarrow}}F \tag{1}$$

Note, that (1) is not an equivalence in general for the simple reason that $\langle\mu\rangle_{\exists\phi}F$ requires the life time of a process to exceed some time–instant of ϕ, and hence imposes a lower bound on the life time. In contrast the formula $\langle\mu\rangle_{\exists\phi{\downarrow}}F$ makes no such requirements.

Recall that the lifetime of a TC process P is the infimum over time–instants $t \in \mathcal{R}_0^+$ such that:

$$P \xrightarrow{\epsilon(t)} P' \xrightarrow{\tau} P''$$

for some P' and P''. To express that d is a lower bound for the life time of a process one may thus use the following formula:

$$\neg(\langle\tau\rangle_{\exists\{t \mid t \leq d\}}tt)$$

For ϕ a dense set[5] we are now able to turn the implication (1) into an equivalence by adding the required lower bound on life time:

$$\langle\mu\rangle_{\exists\phi}F \equiv \langle\mu\rangle_{\exists\phi{\downarrow}}F \wedge \neg(\langle\tau\rangle_{\exists S(\phi)}tt)$$

where $S(\phi) = \{d \in \mathcal{R}_0^+ \mid \forall c \in \phi. d < c\}$. Note that for any set ϕ, both $\phi{\downarrow}$ and $S(\phi)$ are simple intervals either of the form $[0, t[$ for $t \in \mathcal{R}_0^+ \cup \{\infty\}$ or of the form $[0, t]$ for $t \in \mathcal{R}_0^+$.

Furthermore, it is also possible to show that the universal modality $\langle\mu\rangle_{\forall\phi}$ is indeed a derived operator. In fact the following equivalence holds:

$$\langle\mu\rangle_{\forall\phi}F \equiv \langle\mu\rangle_{\exists B(\phi)}F \wedge \neg(\langle\tau\rangle_{\exists E(\phi)}tt)$$

where $B(\phi) = \{t \in \mathcal{R}_0^+ \mid \forall c \in \phi. t \leq c\}$ and $E(\phi) = \{t \in \mathcal{R}_0^+ \mid \exists c \in \phi. t < c\}$. Here the first conjunct expresses that a process satisfying $\langle\mu\rangle_{\forall\phi}F$ must have an F–satisfying μ–derivative being enabled before the time–instants of ϕ. Due to the persistency property this μ–derivative will exist for all future time–instants of the process (including those of ϕ). The second conjunct ensures that the life time is greater than or equal to any time–instant of ϕ (in accordance with the semantic definition of $\langle\mu\rangle_{\forall\phi}F$).

Now consider the sublogic TML of TML which only permits *existential* quantification. Then from the above discussion we may state the following expressiveness result:

---

[3] Here $F \equiv G$ means that F and G are satisfied by the same TC processes.

[4] Here $F \Rightarrow G$ means that any TC process satisfying the formula F also satisfies the formula G.

[5] A set $\phi \subseteq \mathcal{R}_0^+$ is *dense* if whenever $c, d \in \phi$ then also $[c, d], [d, c] \subseteq \phi$

Theorem 3.2 *For any TML formula F there exists an equivalent TML formula G.* □

From the results of the next subsection it will furthermore follow that TML (and hence TML) provides an alternative characterisation of timed bisimulation equivalence between TC processes.

Theorem 3.3 *Let P and Q be TC processes. Then $P \sim Q$ holds if and only P and Q satisfy the same TML formulae.* □

3.2 Symbolic Interpretation

In order to provide an effective means for determining whether or not a TC process satisfies a given TML formula we offer in this section what turns out to be an equivalent interpretation of TML based on the symbolic operational semantics of TC (see section 2.2). First, for $\bowtie$ a binary relation on $[0, \infty]$, we make the obvious extension to sets. That is, for $\phi, \psi \subseteq [0, \infty]$:

$$\phi \bowtie \psi \Leftrightarrow \forall c \in \phi \forall d \in \psi . c \bowtie d$$

Also, we shall make no distinction between an element $d \in [0, \infty]$ and the singleton set $\{d\}$.

Definition 3.4 $\models$ *is the (satisfaction) relation between TC and TML defined inductively as:*

i) $P \models tt \Leftrightarrow true$

ii) $P \models \neg F \Leftrightarrow not\,(P \models F)$

iii) $P \models F \wedge G \Leftrightarrow P \models F$ and $P \models G$

iv) $P \models \langle \mu \rangle_{\vee \phi} F \Leftrightarrow (\phi \leq M(P)) \wedge \exists d \exists P'. d \leq \phi \wedge P \xrightarrow{\mu}_d^* P' \wedge P' \models F$

v) $P \models \langle \mu \rangle_{\exists \phi} F \Leftrightarrow \exists d \exists c \in \phi . \exists P'. d \leq c \leq M(P) \wedge P \xrightarrow{\mu}_d^* P' \wedge P' \models F$

□

First we verify that $\models$ is indeed equivalent to $\models$.

Theorem 3.5 *Let P be a TC process and let F be a TML formula. Then $P \models F$ if and only if $P \models F$.* □

Example 3.6 *Consider the coffee machine from example 2.8. We want to show that after a coin has been inserted, coffee is continuously available for 30 seconds. This property may be expressed in TML as:*

$$[coin]_{\vee[0,\infty[} \langle coffee \rangle_{\vee[0,30]} tt$$

As $S_0 \xrightarrow{coin}_0^* S_1$ is the only symbolic coin–transition of S_0 and $M(S_0) = \infty$, S_0 will satisfy the above property just in case:

$$S_1 \models \langle coffee \rangle_{\vee[0,30]} tt$$

which is true as $S_1 \xrightarrow{coffee}_0^* S_0$ with $0 \leq [0, 30]$ and $[0, 30] \leq M(S_1) = 30$.

The property that after any coin–insertion, there will be no coffee available after 30 seconds can be expressed in TML as:

$$[coin]_{\vee[0,\infty[} \neg \langle coffee \rangle_{\exists]30,\infty[} tt$$

To demonstrate that S_0 satisfies this property reduces to demonstrating $S_1 \not\models \langle coffee \rangle_{\exists]30,\infty[} tt$. However, this is obvious as the life time of S_1 is exactly 30. □

We are now able to show that TML does indeed characterise timed bisimulation between TC processes. We first consider the symbolic interpretation case.

Theorem 3.7 *Let P and Q be TC processes. Then the following equivalence holds:*

$$P \sim^{\bullet} Q \quad \text{if and only if} \quad \forall F.\, P \models F \Leftrightarrow Q \models F$$

$\square$

Corollary 3.8 *Let P and Q be TC processes. Then the following equivalence holds:*

$$P \sim Q \quad \text{if and only if} \quad \forall F.\, P \models F \Leftrightarrow Q \models F$$

$\square$

Example 3.9 *Consider the following processes:*

$$P = a.\epsilon(1).b.NIL + a.\epsilon(2).b.NIL \quad \text{and} \quad Q = a.(\epsilon(1).b.NIL + \epsilon(2).b.NIL)$$

Then clearly $P \not\sim^{\bullet} Q$: the only possible match for the transition $P \xrightarrow{a}_0^* \epsilon(2).b.NIL$ is $Q \xrightarrow{a}_0^* \epsilon(1).b.NIL + \epsilon(2).b.NIL$. However, this is clearly not an acceptable match as $\epsilon(1).b.NIL + \epsilon(2).b.NIL \xrightarrow{b}_1^* NIL$, whereas $\epsilon(2).b.NIL \xrightarrow{b}_d^*$ for no $d \le 1$. A property satisfied by Q but not by P is:

$$[a]_{\forall [0,\infty[} \langle b \rangle_{\exists [1,2[} tt$$

$\square$

An important consequence of the equivalence between the standard and symbolic interpretation of TML is that the associated satisfaction problem becomes (relative) decidable.

Theorem 3.10 *The problem of satisfaction $P \models F$ for a given TC process P and a given TML formula F is decidable relative to first–order assertions about sets and elements of $\mathcal{R}_0^+$.* $\square$

Moreover, it can easily be seen that the above satisfaction problem becomes decidable for TML when the intervals $]0, t[$, $]0, t]$, $[0, t[$ and $[0, t]$ are restricted to rational time–instants t.

3.3 Extended Timed Modal Logic

In this section we introduce an extension of TML where the quantification over action–transitions and time–transitions has been separated. The formulae of the logic is given by the following abstract syntax:

$$F ::= tt \mid \neg F \mid F \wedge G \mid \langle \mu \rangle F \mid \exists \phi.F$$

where $\phi \subseteq \mathcal{R}_0^+$. Below we give an interpretation of ETML with respect to the standard semantics of the calculus TC:

Definition 3.11 $\models$ *is the (satisfaction) relation between TC and ETML defined inductively as:*

$$
\begin{aligned}
i) \quad & P \models tt \Leftrightarrow \text{true} \\
ii) \quad & P \models \neg F \Leftrightarrow \text{not}\,(P \models F) \\
iii) \quad & P \models F \wedge G \Leftrightarrow P \models F \text{ and } P \models G \\
iv) \quad & P \models \langle \mu \rangle F \Leftrightarrow \exists P'.\, P \xrightarrow{\mu} P' \wedge P' \models F \\
v) \quad & P \models \exists \phi.F \Leftrightarrow \exists d \in \phi. \exists P'.\, P \xrightarrow{\epsilon(d)} P' \wedge P' \models F
\end{aligned}
$$

$\square$

It is easy to see that ETML is an extension of TML in the sense that for any formula of TML there exists an equivalent formula of ETML. In particular we note the following equivalence:

$$\langle \mu \rangle_{\exists \phi} F \equiv \exists \phi.\langle \mu \rangle F$$

Example 3.12 *Consider the coffee machine from example 2.8 extended with a choice for tea. The new machine behaves a little strange—for some reason—tea will not be available until after five minutes after a coin insertion.[6] It can be expressed in TC as $rec\ x : coin.(coffee.x + \epsilon(5).tea.x + \epsilon(6).\tau.x)$ and its symbolic transition system can then be drawn as follows*

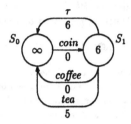

where $S_0 = rec\ x : coin.(coffee.x + \epsilon(5).tea.x + \epsilon(6).\tau.x)$ and $S_1 = coffee.S_0 + \epsilon(5).tea.S_0 + \epsilon(6).\tau.S_0$. The state S_1 obviously satisfies the properties: "sometimes coffee is available but no tea" and "whenever tea is available, then so is coffee" which can be expressed in ETML as:

$$\exists[0,\infty[.((coffee)tt \wedge \neg(tea)tt) \qquad\qquad \forall[0,\infty[.((tea)tt \supset (coffee)tt)$$

where $\forall\phi.F = \neg\exists\phi.\neg F$ and $F \supset G = \neg F \vee G$. These properties cannot be expressed in TML since $\exists$ does not in general distribute over $\wedge$. However, there are restricted forms of $\exists$-distributivity (see the lemma below). ☐

Lemma 3.13 *The basic properties of TC processes given in lemma 2.3 correspond to the following laws of ETML:*

$$
\begin{array}{lll}
i) & \langle\tau\rangle tt \Rightarrow \neg\exists]0,\infty[.tt & \text{(maximal progress)} \\
ii) & \neg\langle\tau\rangle tt \Rightarrow \exists]0,\infty[.tt & \text{(transition liveness)} \\
iiia) & \exists\{c\}.(F \wedge G) \equiv \exists\{c\}.F \wedge \exists\{c\}.G & \text{(time determinacy)} \\
iiib) & \exists\phi.(\langle\mu\rangle F \wedge \langle\nu\rangle G) \equiv \exists\phi.\langle\mu\rangle F \wedge \exists\phi.\langle\nu\rangle G & \text{(time convergence)} \\
iv) & \exists\phi.\exists\psi.F \equiv \exists(\phi+\psi).F & \text{(time continuity)} \\
v) & (\exists\phi.tt \wedge \langle a\rangle G) \Rightarrow \exists\phi.\langle a\rangle G & \text{(persistency)}
\end{array}
$$

where $\phi + \psi = \{c + d \mid c \in \phi \wedge d \in \psi\}$. ☐

Unfortunately, we do not know whether it is possible to provide ETML with an equivalent semantic interpretation based on the *symbolic* semantics of TC. Thus whether the satisfaction problem for ETML is (relative) decidable is left as an interesting open problem that we hope to settle in near future.

4 Conclusion and Future Work

In this paper, we have shown that the timed bisimulation equivalence for the regular real time processes of [W90] is decidable relative to comparisons between positive real numbers. Moreover, a timed modal logic has been presented, which characterises the equivalence. Model checking with respect to this logic has been shown to be decidable relative to the first-order assertions about the positive reals.

The key behind our decidability results is the introduction of a symbolic transition system, which provides a *finite* representation for each regular real time process. The symbolic semantics turns out to be consistent with the standard operational semantics of [W90] for the regular processes — for all P and Q, we have $P \sim Q$ iff $P \sim^* Q$. An open problem is how to extend the present method to deal

---

[6] *The machine maybe uses instant coffee powder and tea bags which must draw for five minutes.*

with parallel composition. It is not obvious whether we can give a symbolic semantics for the parallel operator, while at the same time preserving the consistency with the standard one of [W90].

In [W91] a timed action prefix $\mu@t.P$ has been introduced to achieve an expansion theorem for parallel composition, where t is a time variable and P may depend on t. Intuitively, $\mu@t.P$ denotes a process which may perform μ and become $P\{d/t\}$ where d is the time delay before μ is actually performed. The regular processes of [W91] are generated by the grammar:

$$E ::= NIL \mid x \mid \mu@t.E \mid \epsilon(e).E \mid E + F \mid rec\ x : E$$

where e ranges over the time expressions built out of the positive reals, time variables and the binary operators $+$ and $\ominus$. An exciting challenge is to develop a symbolic semantics for this set of regular processes, which is equivalent to the standard semantics. Then, by the expansion theorem, a composite process can be transformed to a regular one and we may achieve a finite graphical representation even for a composite process. This would permit the decidability results presented in this paper to be extended to composite processes. Certainly, this will be one line of research that we intend to pursue in the future.

The decidability question for model checking with respect to the extended timed modal logic also provides an interesting subject for future work.

References

[AD90]   R. Alur and D.Dill, *Automata for Modelling Real-Time Systems*, LNCS 443, 1990.

[ACD90] R. Alur, C.Courcoubetis and D.Dill, *Model-Checking for Real-Time Systems*, Proceedings from LICS'90 pp. 414-425, 1990.

[CPS89] R. Cleaveland, J. Parrow and B. Steffen, *The Concurrency Workbench*, LNCS 407, 1989.

[HM85]   M. Hennessy and R. Milner, *Algebraic Laws for Nondeterminism and Concurrency*, JACM, Vol. 32, pp. 137-161, 1985.

[HR90]   M. Hennessy and T. Regan, *A Temporal Process Algebra*, Technical Report 2/90, University of Sussex, 1990.

[M89]   R. Milner, *Communication and Concurrency*, Prentice Hall International Series in Computer Science, 1989.

[MT90]   F. Moller and C. Tofts, *A Temporal Calculus of Communicating Systems*, LNCS 458, 1990.

[PT87]   R. Page and R.T. Tarjan, *Three Partition Refinement Algorithms*, SIAM Journal of Computing, Vol 16, no 6 Dec. 1987.

[RR86]   G.M. Reed and A.W. Roscoe, *A Timed Model for Communicating Sequential Processes*, LNCS 226, 1986.

[S90]   J. Sifakis etc. *ATP: an Algebra for Timed Processes*, Laboratoire de Genie Informatique, IMAG-Campus, B.P.53X, 38041 Grenoble Cedex, France, 1990.

[W90]   Y. Wang, *Real Time Behaviour of Asynchronous Agents*, LNCS 458, 1990.

[W91]   Y. Wang, *CCS + Time = an Interleaving Model for Real Time Systems*, ICALP'91, Madrid, 1991.

An Algebra of Boolean Processes *

Costas Courcoubetis
Department of Computer Science
University of Crete
Heraklion, Greece

Susanne Graf   Joseph Sifakis
IMAG-LGI
BP 53X
F-38041 Grenoble

Abstract

This work has been motivated by the study of the S/R models which allow to represent systems as a set of communicating state machines cooperating through a shared memory.

We show that S/R models can be expressed in terms of a process algebra called Boolean SCCS which is a special case of Milner's SCCS, in the sense that the actions are elements of some boolean algebra. We define for Boolean SCCS an operational and a symbolic semantics modulo strong bisimulation equivalence. A complete axiomatisation of bisimulation and simulation equivalences on this algebra is proposed.

Furthermore, we propose a very general *renaming* operator, and show by means of examples that it allows the definition of *abstractions*.

1 Introduction

Most existing algebraic specification languages for concurrent systems such as process algebras, are based on the communicating processes model. They suppose that a system is composed of a set of components with disjoint state spaces, interacting by exchanging messages. Although of equal importance, models relying upon shared memory communication mechanisms did not attract so much the attention of researchers. A reason might be that the communicating processes model is sufficiently general to represent them. On the other hand, the use of shared memory formalisms leads to compact specifications due to the use of powerful communication mechanisms. By allowing processes to be labelled with complex boolean formulas instead of simple actions, we obtain processes with fewer states since a transition label can represent a set of atomic actions.

Besides obtaining compact specifications, there are other issues which make such formalisms very interesting. They have to do with the possibility of doing reductions at the symbolic level, and in general, the possibility to perform a large part of the verification process at the same level. In order to achieve that, one can use the symbolic manipulation mechanisms provided by the boolean calculus. It is important to note that any reduction at the symbolic level will greatly enhance the applicability of the verification procedures by diminuishing the state explosion effects. This paper attempts to define the notions of *symbolic bisimulation* and *abstraction* for such shared memory communicating processes. It also shows that the process algebra paradigm can be directly applied to shared memory models. Interestingly enough, abstraction and renaming in the above models are richer concepts than abstraction and renaming in the traditional communicating processes models.

In order to motivate the reader for using such shared memory formalisms, we start in Section 2 by describing the example of such a formalism which has been successfully used for specifying and verifying large concurrent systems. This is the Selection/Resolution model by R. Kurshan. In Section 3, we give the general definition of boolean transition systems, that is, transition systems whose labels are elements of a boolean algebra, and which is our model of the shared memory communicating processes.

---

*This work has been partially supported by ESPRIT Basic Research Action 'Spec'

Section 4 presents an algebra of boolean processes, for which two different semantics in terms of boolean transition systems modulo bisimulation are defined: an *'operational'* one, whose models are usual action-labelled transition systems, and a *'symbolic'* one, whose models are transition systems whose labels are boolean expressions. We give notions of strong bisimulation for both semantics and show that they coincide on terms. Furthermore, we propose a complete axiomatisation of bisimulation on terms, showing that our algebra is a particular case of $SCCS$ with boolean actions. In this section, we give also some results on renaming functions and illustrate their use for the definition of abstractions by an example. In Section 5, we define notions of simulation preorder and equivalence.

2 The Selection/Resolution Model

2.1 Informal presentation

The *selection/resolution* (S/R) model [AKS83a,AC85,GK80,Ku90,ABM86a] provides a method of describing a system as a set of coordinating finite state machines. Experience has shown that complex systems can be specified by using this model, and there are currently tools which automatically verify properties of the behaviours of such formal specifications, managing systems with millions of reachable states [Ku90]. An important feature is the fact that the coupling between machines is described in terms of predicates. This helps in many cases to obtain concise and understandable specifications.

A system is decomposed into a set of simple components; each component or *process* is an edge labelled directed graph (see Figure 1). The vertices of this graph are *states* of the process; each directed edge describes a transition corresponding to one computation step. In each state, a process can nondeterministically choose from a set of *selections*, which are essentially values of a shared memory used for synchronization. In fact, there is a shared memory in the system consisting of a finite number of variables ranging over a finite domain. With each process is associated a subset of *selection variables* which are distinct for each process. A process can read all variables, whereas it can update only its own selection variables (selections are enclosed in braces next to the states in Figure 1, an example in which the selection functions are all deterministic).

A computation step of the system consists of a selection followed by a resolution phase. The *selection* of a process consists in choosing a value for each one of its selection variables. The *resolution* is done by calculating the *global selection*, i.e., the vector of all the current selections of the processes. Each process checks which transitions are consistent with the current selections of all processes, and then chooses one of these enabled transitions.

2.2 The S/R-processes

Notation 2.1 B *is a boolean algebra with* $\lor$, $\land$, $\bar{\ }$, $\Rightarrow$ *denoting respectively disjunction, conjunction, complementation and implication. By convention, 0 and 1 represent respectively the bottom and the top element of* B *and* $atoms(B)$ *is the set of atoms of* B.

Definition 2.2 *($S/R-process$)*
An $S/R-process$ *on a boolean algebra* B *is a triplet* $SR = (Q, \delta, \sigma)$, *where*

- Q *is a set of* states,
- $\delta : Q \times Q \mapsto B$ *is a transition function,*
- $\sigma : Q \mapsto B$ *is a selector function.*

An $S/R-process$ can be represented by a state- and edge-labelled directed graph whose vertices are the states. There is an edge from state q to q' labelled by ℓ iff $\delta(q, q') = \ell$ and $\ell \neq 0$.

Definition 2.3 *(parallel composition on* $S/R-processes$)
Let $SR_i = (Q_i, \delta_i, \sigma_i)$ *for* $i = 1, 2$ *be two* $S/R-processes$ *on* B. *The parallel composition of* SR_1 *and* SR_2 *is the* $S/R-process$ $SR_1 \times SR_2 = (Q, \delta, \sigma)$ *where,*

- $Q = Q_1 \times Q_2$,
- $\sigma(q_1, q_2) = \sigma_1(q_1) \wedge \sigma_2(q_2)$
- $\delta((q_1, q_2), (q_1', q_2')) = \delta_1(q_1, q_1') \wedge \delta_2(q_2, q_2')$

Example We demonstrate the use of the S/R model for the description of a simple modulo 8 counter whose output (the integers between 0 and 7) is represented by 3 boolean variables y_0, y_1, y_2. Its input, the signal incrementing the counter, is represented by a boolean variable x.

The counter is modelled as the parallel composition of three S/R-processes SR_0, SR_1, SR_2 with selection variables respectively y_0, y_1 and y_2 (Figure 1).

Such specifications can be treated by tools such as COSPAN and SPANNER and prove properties of the infinite sequences of the global memory assignments (see [ABM86a,b], [ACW90], [KK86]).

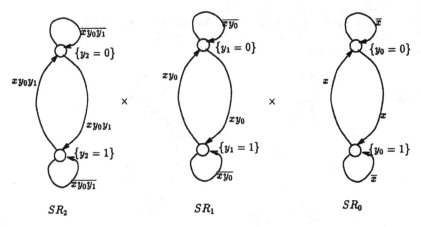

Figure 1: A modulo 8 counter

3 Boolean Transition Systems

In this section, we define *boolean transition systems*, which are transition systems labelled by elements of a boolean algebra $\mathcal{B}$. They differ from S/R−processes only by the fact that they have no labels on states. We show the relationship between these two models.

3.1 S/R−processes as boolean transition systems ($\mathcal{B}TS$)

Definition 3.1 *(Boolean transition systems)*
A boolean transition system on a boolean algebra $\mathcal{B}$ is a pair $S = (Q, \rightarrow)$, where

- Q *is a set of states,*
- $\rightarrow \subseteq Q \times (\mathcal{B}-\{0\}) \times Q$ *is the transition relation, where we write $q \xrightarrow{\ell} q'$ for $(q, \ell, q') \in \rightarrow$.*

Definition 3.2 *With an S/R−process $SR = (Q, \delta, \sigma)$ on $\mathcal{B}$, we associate a $\mathcal{B}TS$, $Bts(SR) = (Q, \rightarrow)$, where $\rightarrow$ is defined as the least relation, subset of $Q \times (\mathcal{B}-\{0\}) \times Q$, such that:*

$$(\delta(q, q') = \ell \text{ and } \ell \wedge \sigma(q) \neq 0) \text{ implies } q \xrightarrow{\ell \wedge \sigma(q)} q'.$$

The parallel composition on S/R−processes can easily be translated into the parallel composition of boolean transition systems:

Definition 3.3 *(parallel composition on BTS)*
Let $S_i = (Q_i, \rightarrow_i)$ for $i = 1, 2$ be two BTSs. The parallel composition of S_1 and S_2 is the BTS, $S = S_1 \times S_2 = (Q, \rightarrow)$ where,

- $Q = Q_1 \times Q_2$,
- $(q_1, q_2) \xrightarrow{\ell} (q_1', q_2')$ iff $(\ell \neq 0$ and $\exists \ell_1, \ell_2.(\ell = \ell_1 \wedge \ell_2$ and $q_i \xrightarrow{\ell_i} q_i'$ for $i = 1, 2))$.

In fact, we obtain in a straight forward manner the following proposition:

Proposition 3.4 *For any S/R−processes SR_1, SR_2,*
$$Bts(SR_1 \times SR_2) = Bts(SR_1) \times Bts(SR_2).$$

Example: translation of an S/R-process into a BTS
Consider again the counter of Figure 1 given as an S/R model. The corresponding BTS, $Bts(SR_0 \times SR_1 \times SR_2)$ is obtained by calculating the parallel composition $Bts(SR_0) \times Bts(SR_1) \times Bts(SR_2)$ as shown in Figure 2.

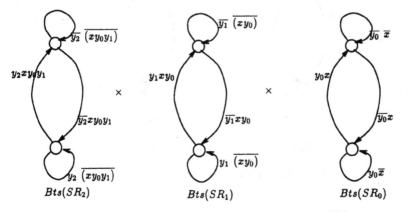

Figure 2: The modulo 8 counter as BTS

We introduce hereafter some useful notations for boolean transition systems.

Definition 3.5 *Let $S = (Q, \rightarrow)$ be a BTS and $q \in Q$. Then,*

1. *The enabling condition of a state q, $enable(q)$ is the boolean expression*
$$enable(q) = \bigvee_{\exists q'.q \xrightarrow{\ell_i} q'} \ell_i.$$

2. *q is called finitely branching iff*
   $\forall \ell \in B$ there is a finite number of labels ℓ' such that $(q \xrightarrow{\ell}$ and $\ell \Rightarrow \ell')$.

3. *q is called deterministic iff*
   $\forall \ell_1, \ell_2 \ q \xrightarrow{\ell_1} q_1$ and $q \xrightarrow{\ell_2} q_2$ implies $(\ell_1 = \ell_2$ and $q_1 = q_2)$ or $\ell_1 \wedge \ell_2 = 0$.

4. *q is called complete iff $enable(q) = 1$*

5. *q is called canonical iff $\forall q'(q \xrightarrow{\ell} q'$ implies $\ell \in atoms(B))$.*

S is respectively called finitely branching, deterministic, complete or canonical if all its states have the corresponding property.

4 Boolean SCCS, an algebra for boolean transition systems

In this section, we define a process algebra that can be considered as a particular case of SCCS [Mi83], i.e., a process algebra with a synchronous parallel operator. Its action operators are the elements of some boolean algebra $\mathcal{B}$. Processes of this algebra have boolean transition systems as underlying models. We study in particular bisimulation semantics for this algebra.

Notation 4.1 *(renaming function)*
Let $\mathcal{B}$ be a boolean algebra. Any mapping $\phi : \mathcal{B} \mapsto \mathcal{B}$ satisfying $\phi(0) = 0$ and which is distributive over disjunction $(\forall \ell_1, \ell_2 \in \mathcal{B} . \phi(\ell_1 \vee \ell_2) = \phi(\ell_1) \vee \phi(\ell_2))$ is called a renaming function on $\mathcal{B}$.

Definition 4.2 *(Syntax of $\mathcal{B}SCCS$)*
Let $\mathcal{B}$ be a boolean algebra, ϕ a renaming function and Z a set of variables. Represent by ℓ and z respectively, elements of $\mathcal{B}$ and Z. Consider the term language defined by the following grammar:

$$t_s ::= \emptyset \,|\, z \,|\, \ell t_s \,|\, t_s + t_s \,|\, recz.t_s,$$
$$t ::= t_s \,|\, t \times t \,|\, t[\phi] \,|\, \ell t \,|\, t + t$$

We call $\mathcal{B}SCCS$ the sub-algebra of the closed terms, named also processes. As usually, a term is called guarded if in any subterm of the form $recz.t$ all occurrences of z in t are in the scope of an action-operator ℓ.

Notice that a term of $\mathcal{B}SCCS$ has no occurrences of $\times$ within the scope of a recursion operator as we want to restrict ourselves to regular processes.

4.1 Operational semantics

Definition 4.3 *(operational semantics)*
For $\ell \in \mathcal{B}, a, a' \in atoms(\mathcal{B}), t_1, t_2, t \in \mathcal{B}SCCS$, ϕ a renaming function and z a process variable, the transition relation $\leadsto$ on $\mathcal{B}SCCS$ is defined as the smallest relation specified by the following rules.

1. $\ell t \overset{a}{\leadsto} t$ iff $a \Rightarrow \ell$
2. $t_1 \overset{a}{\leadsto} t_1'$ implies $t_1 + t_2 \overset{a}{\leadsto} t_1'$ and $t_2 \overset{a}{\leadsto} t_2'$ implies $t_1 + t_2 \overset{a}{\leadsto} t_2'$
3. $t_1 \overset{a}{\leadsto} t_1' \wedge t_2 \overset{a}{\leadsto} t_2'$ implies $t_1 \times t_2 \overset{a}{\leadsto} t_1' \times t_2'$
4. $t \overset{a}{\leadsto} t' \wedge a' \Rightarrow \phi(a)$ implies $t[\phi] \overset{a'}{\leadsto} t'[\phi]$
5. $t \overset{a}{\leadsto} t'$ implies $recz.t \overset{a}{\leadsto} t'[recz.t/z]$

These rules associate with any term of Boolean SCCS a canonical $\mathcal{B}TS$ by defining for any operator an operator on $\mathcal{B}TSs$. The set of atoms can also be considered as the set of labels of a usual labelled transition system.

Remarks:

- If the boolean algebra $\mathcal{B}$ is generated by a set of boolean variables, then atoms can also be considered as valuations, i.e. functions associating boolean values with the boolean variables generating the algebra,

- The renaming operator $[\phi]$ plays the role of both an abstraction and a restriction operator, depending on the nature of ϕ. If ϕ associates 0 with some atoms, and leaves the others unchanged, then it corresponds to a restriction operator. The use of renaming as an abstraction operator will be illustrated later (see Section 4.5).

We are interested in strong bisimulation semantics on $\mathcal{B}TS$.

Notation 4.4 *(strong bisimulation ~)*

- *We denote by ~ the strong bisimulation relation induced by the transition relation ⤳.*
- *We denote as usual by $\sim_i$ the bisimulation up to depth i. We have $\sim = \bigcap_{i=1}^{\infty} \sim_i$ as even for infinite B any term has only a finite number of 'a-derivations' for any $a \in atoms(B)$.*

As in [Mi83], we obtain the following proposition. For the renaming operator to preserve bisimulation it is necessary that the renaming functions are strict and distributive over disjunction.

Proposition 4.5 *~ is a congruence on $BSCCS$.*

4.2 Symbolic semantics for Boolean SCCS

In this section, we give a different operational semantics associating an arbitrary BTS with a term of Boolean SCCS. We define a *symbolic bisimulation* which is proven to coincide with strong bisimulation on $BSCCS$.

Definition 4.6 *(symbolic semantics)*
For $\ell_1, \ell_2, \ell \in B$, $t_1, t_2, t \in BSCCS$ and z a process variable, let $\to$ be the transition relation, defined as the smallest relation specified by the following rules.

1. $\ell t \xrightarrow{\ell} t$ iff $\ell \neq 0$

2. $t_1 \xrightarrow{\ell} t_1'$ implies $t_1 + t_2 \xrightarrow{\ell} t_1'$ and $t_2 \xrightarrow{\ell} t_2'$ implies $t_1 + t_2 \xrightarrow{\ell} t_2'$

3. $t_1 \xrightarrow{\ell_1} t_1' \wedge t_2 \xrightarrow{\ell_2} t_2' \wedge (\ell_1 \wedge \ell_2 \neq 0)$ implies $t_1 \times t_2 \xrightarrow{\ell_1 \wedge \ell_2} t_1' \times t_2'$

4. $t \xrightarrow{\ell} t' \wedge \phi(\ell) \neq 0$ implies $t[\phi] \xrightarrow{\phi(\ell)} t'[\phi]$

5. $t \xrightarrow{\ell} t'$ implies $recz.t \xrightarrow{\ell} t'[recz.t/z]$

Remarks:

- As for the operational semantics, these rules allow to associate in an obvious manner with any term of Boolean SCCS a BTS (not necessarily a canonical one) by defining for any operator an operator on $BTSs$.

- Conversely, with any finite BTS can be associated a process in an obvious manner. Thus, in the sequel we identify a term of Boolean SCCS with its corresponding boolean transition system.

- Therefore, the notations of Definition 3.5 can be applied to terms. We say for a term t, $enable(t)=\ell$, t is respectively *finitely branching, deterministic, complete* or *canonical* if and only if this is the case for the BTS associated via its symbolic semantics.

Definition 4.7 *(symbolic bisimulation)*
Let be $t_1, t_2 \in BSCCS$. Then, $\simeq$ is defined as the largest symmetric relation, solution of $\Phi(\mathcal{R}) = \mathcal{R}$, where
$(t_1, t_2) \in \Phi(\mathcal{R})$ iff
$\forall \ell \in B \ \forall t_1 \in BSCCS \ (t_1 \xrightarrow{\ell} t_1'$ implies $\exists I.((\ell \Rightarrow \bigvee_{i \in I} \ell_i)$ and $\forall i \in I \ \exists t_{2i}.(t_2 \xrightarrow{\ell_i} t_{2i}$ and $(t_1', t_{2i}) \in \mathcal{R})))$

As usually, we write $t_1 \simeq t_2$ instead of $(t_1, t_2) \in \simeq$ and we say that t_1 *symbolically bisimulates* t_2.

Remarks:

- $t_1 \simeq t_2$ implies $enable(t_1) = enable(t_2)$.

- Any complete term symbolically bisimulates the process $\mathbb{1}$, defined as $\mathbb{1} = recz.1z$.

The characterization of bisimulation as the intersection of bisimulations up to depth i can also be shown for symbolic bisimulation.

Proposition 4.8 $\simeq = \bigcap_{i=1}^{\infty} \simeq_i$, where

- $\simeq_0 = BSCCS \times BSCCS$
- $\simeq_{i+1} = \Phi(\simeq_i)$ $\forall i \in I\!N, i > 0$

This result can be used to compute $\simeq$, and thus to reduce processes, and also finite BTSs. In Figure 3, we give two symbolically bisimilar BTSs. The small one is the quotient modulo $\simeq$ of the other.

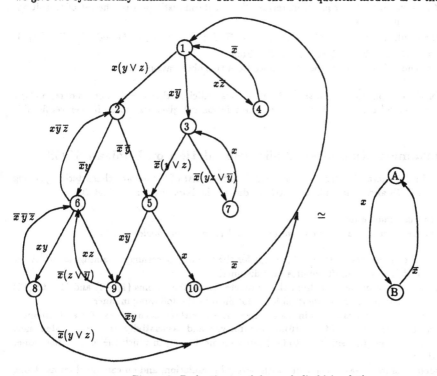

Figure 3: Reduction modulo symbolic bisimulation

Proposition 4.9 *Symbolic and strong bisimulation agree on Boolean SCCS, i.e.* $\simeq = \sim$.

Proof: We prove that for any i, $\sim_i = \simeq_i$ by induction. The proof is easy if we use the observation that $\forall a \in atoms(B)$ $t \overset{a}{\leadsto} t'$ iff $\exists \ell \in B.(a \Rightarrow \ell$ and $t \overset{\ell}{\longrightarrow} t')$ $\square$

Proposition 4.10 $\simeq$ *is a congruence on BSCCS.*

Proof: Direct from the proposition above and the fact that $\sim$ is a congruence on BSCCS. $\square$

4.3 Results for deterministic processes

For deterministic processes the definition of $\simeq$ can be simplified in the following manner:

Definition 4.11 Let $\simeq^d$ be the largest symmetric relation on $\mathcal{BSCCS}$, solution of $\Phi_1(\mathcal{R}) = \mathcal{R}$, where $(t_1, t_2) \in \Phi_1(\mathcal{R})$ iff

- $enable(t_1) = enable(t_2)$
- $t_1 \overset{\ell}{\longrightarrow} t_1'$ implies $\forall \ell', t_2'((\ell \wedge \ell' \neq 0$ and $t_2 \overset{\ell'}{\longrightarrow} t_2')$ implies $(t_1', t_2') \in \mathcal{R})$

Proposition 4.12 *(characterization of $\simeq$ on deterministic processes)*
For $t_1, t_2 \in \mathcal{BSCCS}, t_1, t_2$ *nondeterministic* $(t_1 \simeq t_2$ iff $t_1 \simeq^d t_2)$.

Proof: We have already noticed that $t_1 \simeq t_2$ implies $enable(t_1) = enable(t_2)$. Furthermore, the definition of $\simeq$ says that for any ℓ-transition of t_1 leading to t_1', there exists a set of transitions from t_2 whose labels cover ℓ and which lead to equivalent terms. For a deterministic process the set of transitions whose labels cover ℓ is unique.
In this case the condition in the definition of $\simeq$, $\forall \ell \in B \,\exists I, \{t_i\}.((\bigvee_{i \in I} \ell_i \Rightarrow \ell)$ and $\forall i \in I \; t \overset{\ell_i}{\longrightarrow} t_i)$ is equivalent to $\forall \ell \in B(\exists \ell' \in B, t' \in \mathcal{BSCCS}.(\ell \wedge \ell' \neq 0$ and $t \overset{\ell'}{\longrightarrow} t'))$.
The fact that $\simeq$ and $\simeq^d$ coincide, is easy to deduce from this observation. $\quad\square$

Notice that for the comparison of two terms t and t', it is sufficient that one of them is deterministic in order that $\simeq$ and $\simeq^d$ coincide. Furthermore, the relation $\simeq^d$ gives rise to a simpler verification algorithm.

4.4 An axiomatisation of symbolic bisimulation on Boolean SCCS

The axioms and rules characterizing $\simeq$ on Boolean SCCS consist of the axioms characterizing strong bisimulation on SCCS and some additional axioms due to the laws of the action set B.

Theorem 4.13 *(axiomatization)*
The axiomatization given in Table 1 is sound and complete for $\simeq$ on Boolean SCCS.

Proof: The proof of soundness is standard, except for the axioms concerning renaming, for which we need the fact that ϕ is strict and distributes over disjunction.
The completeness can be deduced from the completeness of the axioms (1), (2) and (11) to (13) for strong bisimulation on terms in canonical form obtained in the following manner.
In a first step, a term is transformed into an equivalent one without occurrences of $\times$ and renaming operators by means of the axioms (4) to (10), commutativity and associativity. In a second step, such a term can be transformed by using (14) to (16) into canonical form, in which the only action names are atoms of B.
We have already shown that $\simeq$ coincides with strong bisimulation, and on canonical terms strong bisimulation can be characterized by the axioms and rules (1),(2) and (11) to (13) [Mi84]. $\quad\square$

4.5 Some results on renaming

In the following propositions we give some sufficient conditions on functions ϕ in order that the corresponding renaming operators $[\phi]$ preserve particular properties of terms.

Proposition 4.14 Let ϕ be a renaming function on B.
$\forall t_1, t_2 \in \mathcal{BSCCS} \; (t_1 \times t_2)[\phi] = t_1[\phi] \times t_2[\phi]$, i.e., $[\phi]$ distributes over $\times$, iff
$\forall \ell_1, \ell_2 \in B \; \phi(\ell_1 \wedge \ell_2) = \phi(\ell_1) \wedge \phi(\ell_2)$, i.e. ϕ distributes over conjunction.

(1) Axioms of SCCS:

1. + is commutative, associative and idempotent,

2. $t + \oslash = t$

3. $\times$ is commutative and associative

4. $t \times \oslash = \oslash$

5. $t \times (t_1 + t_2) = (t \times t_1) + (t \times t_2)$

6. $\ell_1 t_1 \times \ell_2 t_2 = (\ell_1 \wedge \ell_2)(t_1 \times t_2)$

7. $\mathbb{1} \times t = t$

8. $\oslash[\phi] = \oslash$

9. $(at)[\phi] = a(t[\phi])$

10. $(t_1 + t_2)[\phi] = t_1[\phi] + t_2[\phi]$

11. $recz.(z + t') = recz.t'$

12. $recz.t = t[recz.t/z]$

13. $t' = t[t'/z]$ implies $t' = recz.t$ provided that t' is guarded

(2) Axioms and rules specific to $\mathcal{B}$SCCS:

14. $0t = \oslash$

15. $\ell_1 t + \ell_2 t = (\ell_1 \vee \ell_2)t$

16. $\ell_1 \equiv \ell_2$ implies $\ell_1 t = \ell_2 t$

Table 1: Axiomatisation of $\simeq$ on $\mathcal{B}$SCCS

Notice that distributivity over conjunction is a very strong requirement for a renaming function, and the renaming functions used for abstraction of our example given at the end of the section do not have this property.

Proposition 4.15 *Let ϕ be a renaming function on $\mathcal{B}$ and t a term of Boolean SCCS.*

1. *If ϕ is increasing, i.e. $\forall \ell \in \mathcal{B}(\ell \Rightarrow \phi(\ell))$, then
   $[\phi]$ preserves completeness of t, i.e. if t is complete then $t[\phi]$ is also complete.*
2. *If ϕ is such that $(\forall \ell_1, \ell_2 \in \mathcal{B} \ \ell_1 \wedge \ell_2 = 0$ implies $\phi(\ell_1) \wedge \phi(\ell_2) = 0)$ then
   $[\phi]$ preserves determinism of t, i.e. if t is deterministic then $t[\phi]$ is also deterministic.*
3. *If ϕ maps atoms to atoms, i.e. $\phi : atoms(\mathcal{B}) \mapsto atoms(\mathcal{B})$, then
   $[\phi]$ preserves canonicity of t, i.e. if t is canonical then $t[\phi]$ is also canonical.*

Notice that the condition of (3) implies the condition of (2).

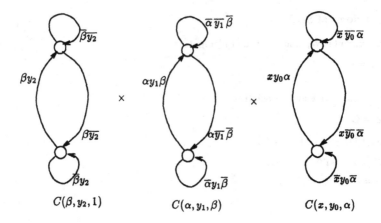

$$C(\beta, y_2, 1) \qquad C(\alpha, y_1, \beta) \qquad C(x, y_0, \alpha)$$

Figure 4: C_8, a modulo 8 counter

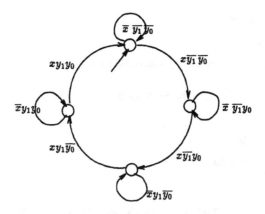

Figure 5: The reduced $\mathcal{B}$TS of $C_8[\phi_1][\phi_2]$

An Example: modulo 8 counter (see [Ma91])

In this example, we illustrate the use of renaming functions to obtain abstractions. Consider again a modulo 8 counter, defined in a slightly different manner than in Section 3. C_8 is defined as the parallel composition $C_8 = C(\beta, y_2, 1) \times C(\alpha, y_1, \beta) \times C(x, y_0, \alpha)$ where the subterms $C(v_1, v_2, v_3)$, defined in Figure 4, represent modulo 2 counters changing their state on input signal v_1 with state variable v_2 and output variable v_3, representing the overflow bit. The observable variables of the modulo 8 counter are the global input x and the state variables y_2, y_1, y_0 whereas α and β are only used for synchronization. The renaming function ϕ_1 defined by

$$\phi_1(\ell(x, y_2, y_1, y_0, \alpha, \beta)) = \exists \alpha \beta \; \ell(x, y_2, y_1, y_0, \alpha, \beta) \equiv$$
$$\ell(x, y_2, y_1, y_0, 0, 0) \vee \ell(x, y_2, y_1, y_0, 0, 1) \vee \ell(x, y_2, y_1, y_0, 1, 0) \vee \ell(x, y_2, y_1, y_0, 1, 1)$$

allows to make abstraction from the overflow variables α and β.
The $\mathcal{B}$TS corresponding to $C_8[\phi_1]$ has 8 states and cannot be reduced modulo symbolic bisimulation, but its boolean expressions are simpler than that of the $\mathcal{B}$TS of C_8.

Consider the renaming function ϕ_2

$$\phi_2(\ell(x, y_2, y_1, y_0)) = \exists y_2\ \ell(x, y_2, y_1, y_0) \equiv \ell(x, 0, y_1, y_0) \vee \ell(x, 1, y_1, y_0)$$

which applied to $C_8[\phi_1]$ allows to abstract from y_2.

The boolean transition system corresponding to the process $C_8[\phi_1][\phi_2]$ can be reduced to the one presented in Figure 5 and corresponds clearly to a counter modulo 4.

5 Simulation preorders and equivalences on $\mathcal{B}$SCCS

Bisimulation is a strong equivalence, and if we are interested in verifying safety properties much weaker equivalences are interesting [BGFRS90]. In this section, we study simulation preorders and the equivalences they introduce on Boolean SCCS.

Definition 5.1 *(simulation preorder $\sqsubseteq^\bullet$)*
$\forall t_1, t_2 \in BSCCS\ \ t_1 \sqsubseteq^\bullet t_2$
$\quad t_1 \xrightarrow{\ell} t_1'$ *implies* $\exists I.((\ell \Rightarrow \bigvee_{i \in I} \ell_i)$ *and* $\forall i \in I\ \exists t_{2i}.(t_2 \xrightarrow{\ell_i} t_{2i}$ *and* $t_1' \sqsubseteq^\bullet t_{2i}))$
The simulation equivalence induced by $\sqsubseteq^\bullet$ is denoted by $\simeq^\bullet$.

Remark: As in the case of bisimulation, it can be shown that the above defined simulation preorder coincides on canonical $\mathcal{B}$TS with the usual simulation preorder.

Proposition 5.2 *(characterization of $\sqsubseteq^\bullet$)*
$\forall t \in BSCCS\ \ \{t' \in BSCCS\,|\,t' \sqsubseteq^\bullet t\} = \{t'\,|\,\exists t'' \in BSCCS.t' \simeq^\bullet t'' \times t\}$

1. All axioms of Table 1, where each equation $t_1 = t_2$ stands

   for two equations $t_1 \leq t_2$ and $t_2 \leq t_1$

2. $\oslash \leq t$

3. $t_1 \leq t_2[t_1/z]$ implies $t_1 \leq recz.t_2$ provided z guarded in t_2

4. $t_2[t_1/z] \leq t_1$ implies $recz.t_2 \leq t_1$ provided z guarded in t_2

5. $\ell_1 \Rightarrow \ell_2$ implies $\ell_1 t \leq \ell_2 t$

Table 2: Axiomatisation of $\simeq^\bullet$ on Boolean SCCS

Proposition 5.3 *(Axiomatization of $\sqsubseteq^\bullet$)*
The axiomatization given in Table 2 is sound and complete for $\sqsubseteq^\bullet$ on Boolean SCCS.

Proof: The soundness of this axiomatisation is easy to check. The completeness proof is very similar to the one of Theorem 4.13. As before, each term can be transformed into one in canonical form. In [BGFRS90] it has been shown for a term algebra isomorphic to the subalgebra of canonical terms that the above axiomatization (without rule (5) and based on the axioms of SCCS only) characterizes completely the usual simulation preorder. $\Box$

6 Conclusion

This work establishes a connection between the S/R model and process algebras. For this, we introduce boolean transition systems, an extension of ordinary transition systems.

We believe that the Boolean Process Algebra and its underlying model deserve a further study as such, independently of the S/R model. In fact, they seem to be fairly appropriate formalisms to describe hardware and in general finite systems where data are coded by boolean variables.

Furthermore, symbolic bisimulation allows compare descriptions given by state transition models where labels represent sets of actions. The two given semantics show that boolean processes are more abstract.

It would be interesting to introduce weaker equivalences, such as stuttering equivalence on these models. Another interesting question would be to characterize the renaming functions introducing interesting abstraction criteria.

References

[ABM86a] S. Aggarwal, D. Barbara, K. Z. Meth. "SPANNER - A Tool for the Specification, Analysis, and Evaluation of Protocols," IEEE Trans. on Software Engineering (to appear).

[AC85] S. Aggarwal, C. Courcoubetis. "Distributed Implementation of a Model of Communication and Computation," Proceedings of the Int. Conf. on System Sciences, January, 1985.

[AKS83a] S. Aggarwal, R. P. Kurshan, K. K. Sabnani. "A Calculus for Protocol Specification and Validation," in Protocol Specification, Testing and Verification III, North-Holland, 1983.

[Ku90] R. Kurshan, "Analysis of Discrete Event Coordination". LNCS 430 (1990).

[ACW90] S. Aggarwal, C. Courcoubetis, P. Wolper. "Adding Liveness Properties to Coupled Finite-State Machines", ACM TOPLAS, Vol. 12, No 2, April 1990.

[GK80] B. Gopinath, B. Kurshan. "The Selection/Resolution Model for Coordinating Concurrent Processes", AT&T Bell Laboratories Technical Report.

[KK86] J. Katzenelson, B. Kurshan, "S/R: A Language for Specifying Protocols and other Coordinating Processes", Proc. 5th Ann. Int'l Phoenix Conf. Comput. Commun., IEEE, 1986.

[BGFRS90] A. Bouajjani, J.-C. Fernandez, S. Graf, C. Rodriguez, J. Sifakis. *Safety for Branching Semantics*, ICALP 91, Madrid, LNCS Vol. 510, 1991.

[Ma91] F. Maraninchi. *Argos: a graphical synchronous language for the description of reactive systems*, Report Spectre C-29, Grenoble, March 91, submitted to SCP

[Mi80] R. Milner. *A Calculus for Communicating Systems*, LNCS 92, 1980

[Mi83] R. Milner. *Calculi for Synchrony and Asynchrony*, Theoret. Comp. Sci. 25, 1983.

[Mi84] R. Milner. *A Complete Inference System for a Class of Regular Behaviours*, Journal of Comp. and Syst. Sci. Vol. 28, 1984

[Mi89] R. Milner. *Communication and Concurrency*, Prentice Hall, 1989

Comparing Generic State Machines[*]

M. Langevin   E. Cerny

Département d'Informatique et de Recherche Opérationnelle
Université de Montréal, C.P. 6128, Succ. A
Montréal, Québec, CANADA, H3C 3J7

e-mail: {langevin, cerny}@iro.umontreal.ca, FAX: (514) 343-5834

Abstract

This paper presents a technique for comparing generic state machines (i.e., machines where the size of manipulated data is not yet specified). The machine behavior is modeled using transfer formulas, a special kind of first order logic formulas. The technique is a mix of theorem proving methods with an automata comparison algorithm, in which first order logic terms are used to represent the values of the inputs, states and outputs of the machines.

1 Introduction

Attractive algorithms [5,7,8,9] have been proposed to compare finite state machines (synchronous circuit). In the case of circuits composed of a control part and data part, verification can be reduced to comparing only the control parts if a mapping is established between the data parts. If this mapping is not known, a complete comparison has to be performed, but this can be intractable due to the state explosion resulting from the data width. This is unfortunate especially when the data width is meaningless as far as the circuit behavior is concerned. Moreover, when the data width is not yet specified, i.e. generic circuits, this kind of comparison is impossible because such circuits are not finite state machines anymore.

This paper is concerned with the verification of generic state machines. The comparison of this kind of circuits can be tractable if the data nodes are considered as symbols representing bit vectors (terms), instead of sets of Boolean variables. Unfortunately, propositional logic is no more sufficient for modeling and comparing such synchronous circuits, and predicate calculus has to be used. Systems such as HOL [11] or Boyer-Moore [2] are not ideal for comparing generic state machines, however. HOL is too powerful and this implies that no decision procedure is available for proofs, while Boyer-Moore which is efficient for inductive proofs is not well adapted for substitution [18] that is required in state exploration of the product machine.

In this paper we present a formalism sufficiently powerful for modeling the behavior of generic state machines; it is a subset of predicate calculus. The language HOP is a different formalism specialized to model generic state machines [10]; even if an efficient algorithm is proposed to compose two such descriptions, nothing has been proposed to compare them. We then give an algorithm for comparing such

---

[*] Partially supported by NSERC Canada Grant No MEF0040113, and by the equipment loan of the CMC

machines; it is a mix of theorem proving methods with an automata comparison algorithm, in which first order logic terms are used to represent the values of the inputs, states, and outputs of the machines. In Section 2, we introduce the formalism and give an example. The comparison algorithm is presented in Section 3, including a partial solution to the difficult problem of detecting already visited states of generic machines. Finally, possible improvements of our approach are discussed in Section 4.

2   Modeling Generic State Machines

A generic state machine (or a generic synchronous circuit) is a machine where the width of some data paths is not yet numerically specified. This section introduces a formalism for modeling generic state machines, and presents how this model can be extracted from the register transfer level (RTL) description of a synchronous circuit.

2.1 Formalism

The objects **variable** and **operator** are used to represent the bit vector value of the input, output, and memory nodes. All objects possess an attribute which is the width of the bit vector represented by the object. A variable x representing a bit vector of width w is noted x:w. An operator is a function transforming a set (possibly empty) of bit vectors (the parameters) into a bit vector of a fixed width, e.g., predefined operators used in some HDL [1]. An operator OP representing a bit vector of width w, and taking p formal parameters $x_1,...,x_p$ such that the ith parameter represents a bit vector of width w_i, is noted $OP(x_1:w_1,...,x_p:w_p):w$. The operators of arity zero, i.e., taking no parameters, are **operator-constants**.

A **bit-constant** of width w is a bit vector $(b_{w-1},...,b_1,b_0)$ where $b_i = 0$ or 1 is the ith bit of the constant. The truth values TRUE and FALSE are represented respectively with the one-bit constants (1) and (0). Also, a special symbol DC is used to represent don't care values; its width corresponds to the width of the node to which it is affected. Each DC symbol is considered a distinct variable symbol, and it is used to represent the initial value of certain memory nodes. Moreover, the DC symbols are used for behavioral modeling of incompletely specified machines.

The values that a circuit node can hold are represented with a **term** (a symbolic value). A term is defined recursively as:

i)   A constant is a term,
ii) A variable is a term, and
iii) If $OP(x_1:w_1,...,x_p:w_p):w$ is an operator and $T_1,...,T_p$ are terms such that the width of T_i is w_i then $OP(T_1,...,T_p)$ is a term.

We consider that the operators have well defined semantics, modeled with a set of rewriting rules which forms a complete reduction system (noetherian and confluent) [4]. This means that two terms are equivalent iff their reduced forms are syntactically equal. One such set of operators and rewriting rules is presented in [16]. Moreover, known techniques can be used to assure that the set of rewriting rules is complete [4].

The 1-bit wide terms are **predicates**. An **assignment** is a homomorphic mapping v from the set of terms into the set of constants [4]. The value of a term T at v, noted $v(T)$, is the constant resulting of the evaluation of T where each of its variable symbols is replaced by a constant specified by v. For example, let ADD(x:2,y:2):2 be an operator; if T = ADD(DC,DC) is a term and v = {first DC = (0,1), second DC = (1,0)} is an assignment then $v(T) = (1,1)$. As mentioned earlier, the DC symbols are considered as distinct symbols.

The **alphabet** (image) of a term T of width w, noted $\alpha(T)$, is the set of constants represented by T: $\alpha(T) = \{y = (b_{w-1},...,b_0) \mid \exists$ an assignment $v \ni y = v(T)\}$. For example, using the same operator as above and the variable symbols a:2 and b:2, $\alpha(ADD(a,b)) = \{(0,0), (0,1), (1,0), (1,1)\}$ and $\alpha(ADD(a,a)) = \{(0,0), (1,0)\}$. The alphabet of a set $X = \{x_1:w_1,...,x_n:w_n\}$ of n distinct variables, denoted $\alpha(X)$, is $\{0,1\}^w$ where $w = \Sigma\, w_i$. A **generic state machine** is a 6-tuple (X,Y,Z,I,δ,λ) where

$X = \{x_1:u_1,...,x_n:u_n\}$ is the set of input variables,

$Y = \{y_1:v_1,...,y_r:v_r\}$ is the set of state variables,

$Z = \{z_1:w_1,...,z_m:w_m\}$ is the set of output variables,

I is the initial symbolic state,

$\delta:\alpha(X) \times \alpha(Y) \rightarrow \alpha(Y)$ is the next state function, and

$\lambda:\alpha(X) \times \alpha(Y) \rightarrow \alpha(Z)$ is the output function.

In the output and the next state functions, the input, state, and output variables are used to represent the value of the input, memory, and output nodes of the circuit. Generic nodes of the machine are those which have their width unspecified. A symbolic state of the machine is a tuple $(T_1,...,T_r)$ where T_i, a term of width v_i, represents the value of y_i. Since the values of the input, output, and state variables are modeled with terms, the next state and output functions can be described using formulas of predicate calculus [17]. In our case, however, only a special kind of formulas is used, called **transfer formula** (TF). A TF for a non-constant term T of width w describes the possible values which correspond to T. The general form of a TF is: (similar to the VHDL case statement [21])

$$cond_1 \wedge EQU(T,T_1) \vee cond_2 \wedge EQU(T,T_2) \vee ... \vee cond_k \wedge EQU(T,T_k) \text{ where}$$

i) EQU is a **data transfer predicate** (DTP) representing the transferred values,

ii) T_i's are **transferred terms**, the width of T_i is also w and T does not appear in T_i,

iii) the conditions $cond_i$ are formulas generated from a set $P_1,...,P_h$ of predicates (the **control terms**), using only the connectives $\wedge$, $\vee$, and — (logical not),

iv) for all $i \neq j$, $cond_i \wedge cond_j$ = False, and

v) $\bigvee_{i=1}^{n} cond_i$ = True.

For any conditions, the TF represents one and only one transferred term T_i. Let $Var(f)$ be the set of non-DC variables appearing in the control and transferred terms of the TF f. For describing the output function λ, a TF f is defined for each output variable of the machine, such that each variable in $Var(f)$ is an input or a state variable. Similarly, for the next state function δ, a TF f is defined for each next state variable (i.e., primed state variable), such that each variable of $Var(f)$ is an input or state variable. It was shown in [14] that TFs can be efficiently represented and manipulated using directed acyclic graph similar to BDDs [3], in which the internal nodes are labeled by the control terms and the leaf nodes contain the transferred terms.

Example: Consider a 3-word deep stack where each word consists of n bits. The inputs of the machine are the controls *nop* and *pop*, and the n-bit vector *in*, while the outputs are the error flag *err* and the n-bit vector *out*. The state variable of the machine are the stack pointer *sp* and the stack memory *sm*. If the control input *nop* is true then nothing happens, otherwise a pop (if the input *pop* is true) or a push (if the input *pop* is false) is performed. The output *err* is True if a pop is attempted when the stack is empty.($sp = (1,1)$), or a push when the stack is full ($sp = (0,0)$). The output *out* is the value of the top of the stack at any time (when the stack is empty *out* is zero, otherwise, it is the word of *sm* pointed by *sp*). The stack memory *sm* contains 3 words. The operator $Mem(v_0:n,v_1:n,v_2:n):3*n$ symbolizes a memory containing 3 words of n bits, indexed from 0 to 2 inclusively. In fact, this operator represents an array where the operators Read and Write (defined below) are used to consult and update the array. The other operators used for describing the behavior of the stack are:

$Zero():n$	represents the n-bit vector zero,
$EquZ(x:2):1$	return true iff x is zero,
$Not(x:2):2$	complements all bits of x,
$Inc(x:2):2$	increments x modulo 4,
$Dec(x:2):2$	decrements x modulo 4,
$Read(m:3*n,a:2):n$	read memory m at address a, and
$Write(m:3*n,a:2,d:n):3*n$	write data d in memory m at address a.

The machine description is Stack-Spec = $(X_S,Y_S,Z_S,I_S,\delta_S,\lambda_S)$ where

$X_S = \{in:n,nop:1,pop:1\}$,
$Y_S = \{sp:2,sm:3*n\}$,
$Z_S = \{out:n,err:1\}$,
$I_S = ((1,1), Mem(DC,DC,DC))$,
δ_S is represented using the following TFs, one for each of the next state variables,

$(nop \vee pop \wedge EquZ(Not(sp)) \vee \overline{pop} \wedge EquZ(sp)) \wedge EQU(sp',sp) \vee$

$\overline{nop} \wedge pop \wedge \overline{EquZ(Not(sp))} \wedge EQU(sp',Inc(sp)) \vee \overline{nop} \wedge \overline{pop} \wedge \overline{EquZ(sp)} \wedge EQU(sp',Dec(sp))$

$(\text{nop} \vee \text{pop} \vee \overline{\text{pop}} \wedge \text{EquZ(sp)}) \wedge \mathbf{EQU}(\text{sm'},\text{sm}) \quad \vee$

$\overline{\text{nop}} \wedge \overline{\text{pop}} \wedge \overline{\text{EquZ(sp)}} \wedge \mathbf{EQU}(\text{sm'},\text{Write}(\text{sm},\text{Dec}(\text{sp}),\text{in}))$

λ_S is described using the following TFs, one for each of the output variables.

$\text{EquZ}(\text{Not}(\text{sp})) \wedge \mathbf{EQU}(\text{out},\text{Zero}) \quad \vee \quad \overline{\text{EquZ}(\text{Not}(\text{sp}))} \wedge \mathbf{EQU}(\text{out},\text{Read}(\text{sm},\text{sp}))$

$(\text{nop} \vee \text{pop} \wedge \overline{\text{EquZ}(\text{Not}(\text{sp}))} \vee \overline{\text{pop}} \wedge \overline{\text{EquZ(sp)}}) \wedge \mathbf{EQU}(\text{err},(0)) \quad \vee$

$\overline{\text{nop}} \wedge (\text{pop} \wedge \text{EquZ}(\text{Not}(\text{sp})) \vee \overline{\text{pop}} \wedge \text{EquZ(sp)}) \wedge \mathbf{EQU}(\text{err},(1))$

The first TF of the next state function of this machine describes the next value of the node *sp*; it is incremented if a pop has occurred, decremented if a push has occurred, or unchanged if no operation has occurred. The other TFs can be interpreted in a similar way.

2.2 Composition

Since TFs can be used for describing RTL components of synchronous circuits, the generic state machine description can be easily extracted from an implementation defined in terms of interconnected components. The designer specifies its interface, i.e., its set of input and output variables. Also, the initial state is specified or can be computed (e.g., reset signal). The state variables of the circuit are the state variables appearing in the component models. The interconnections are the internal nodes of the circuit, they carry no state information. Every loop in the circuit must contain clocked memory elements. In order to obtain the generic state machine description, the next state and output functions are extracted from the circuit implementation by a composition operation.

The extraction algorithm is similar to [14] for comparing two synchronous circuits having the same set of registers; the idea is to transform all TFs into an **observable** form. A TF f is observable iff each variable of Var(f) is an input or a state variable. In order to compute the output function, the TF for a particular output variable is found in one component model of the circuit implementation, and it suffices to transform this TF into its observable form. This is achieved by substituting all internal variables appearing in the TF by their corresponding observable TF, and by applying rewriting rules to the operators appearing in the TF [14,15]. The extraction of the next state function proceeds in a similar fashion. In fact, the machine description is the conjunction of all component models in which predicate calculus rules are applied to abstract internal nodes.

Figure 1 shows a possible implementation of Stack-Spec, named Stack-Impl (the clock signal is implicit). The stack is constructed using shift registers, instead of a memory bank. We assume that the counter is reset at power on (this initial state should be verified, e.g. [19]). The extracted generic state machine is Stack-Impl = $(X_I, Y_I, Z_I, I_I, \delta_I, \lambda_I)$ where:

$X_I = \{\text{in}:n, \text{nop}:1, \text{pop}:1\},$

$Y_I = \{c{:}2, r_1{:}n, r_2{:}n, r_3{:}n\}$,
$Z_I = \{out{:}n, err{:}1\}$,
$I_I = ((0,0), DC, DC, DC)$,

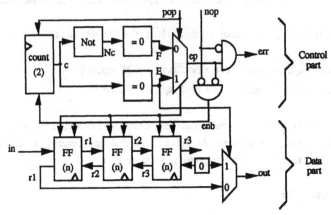

Figure 1: Implementation of the stack

δ_I is described with the following TFs:

Derived observable TF for c

$(nop \lor pop \land EquZ(c) \lor \overline{pop} \land EquZ(Not(c))) \land \mathbf{EQU}(c',c) \lor$

$\overline{nop} \land pop \land \overline{EquZ(c)} \land \mathbf{EQU}(c',Dec(c)) \lor \overline{nop} \land \overline{pop} \land \overline{EquZ(Not(c))} \land \mathbf{EQU}(c',Inc(c))$

Derived observable TF for r_1

$(nop \lor pop \land EquZ(c) \lor \overline{pop} \land EquZ(Not(c))) \land \mathbf{EQU}(r_1',r_1) \lor$

$\overline{nop} \land pop \land \overline{EquZ(c)} \land \mathbf{EQU}(r_1',r_2) \lor \overline{nop} \land \overline{pop} \land \overline{EquZ(Not(c))} \land \mathbf{EQU}(r_1',in)$

Derived observable TF for r_2

$(nop \lor pop \land EquZ(c) \lor \overline{pop} \land EquZ(Not(c))) \land \mathbf{EQU}(r_2',r_2) \lor$

$\overline{nop} \land pop \land \overline{EquZ(c)} \land \mathbf{EQU}(r_2',r_3) \lor \overline{nop} \land \overline{pop} \land \overline{EquZ(Not(c))} \land \mathbf{EQU}(r_2',r_1)$

Derived observable TF for r_3

$(nop \lor pop \land EquZ(c) \lor \overline{pop} \land EquZ(Not(c))) \land \mathbf{EQU}(r_3',r_3) \lor$

$\overline{nop} \land pop \land \overline{EquZ(c)} \land \mathbf{EQU}(r_3',Zero) \lor \overline{nop} \land \overline{pop} \land \overline{EquZ(Not(c))} \land \mathbf{EQU}(r_3',r_2)$

λ_I is described with the following TFs:

Derived observable TF for out

$EquZ(c) \land \mathbf{EQU}(out,Zero) \lor \overline{EquZ(c)} \land \mathbf{EQU}(out,r_1)$

Derived observable TF for err

$(nop \vee pop \wedge \overline{EquZ(c)} \vee \overline{pop} \wedge \overline{EquZ(Not(c))}) \wedge EQU(err,(0)) \vee$

$\overline{nop} \wedge (pop \wedge EquZ(c) \vee \overline{pop} \wedge EquZ(Not(c))) \wedge EQU(err,(1))$

3 Comparison Algorithm

This section presents a comparison algorithm for verifying the equivalence of two generic state machines. The skeleton of the algorithm is presented in the Section 3.1, while some critical parts of the algorithm are detailed in the subsequent sections: Comparison of the output values, and computation of the new reached states of the product automaton.

3.1 Algorithm Skeleton

The goal of the comparison is to verify if two generic state machines have the same observable behavior. First, the two machines must have the same interface. Let $M_1 = (X,Y_1,Z,I_1,\delta_1,\lambda_1)$ and $M_2 = (X,Y_2,Z,I_2,\delta_2,\lambda_2)$ be the generic state machines to be compared, where $Y_1 = \{y_{11},...,y_{1q}\}$ and $Y_2 = \{y_{21},...,y_{2r}\}$. As in [8], the idea is to explore the reachable state space of the product machine $M_1 \times M_2$, without constructing it explicitly. A total symbolic state of the product machine is the concatenation of symbolic states of M_1 and M_2. In particular, the total initial state I_T is the concatenation of I_1 and I_2. The next state and output functions of the product machine are defined as usual [13]. Our algorithm is a compromise between the breadth first traversal [8] and the depth first traversal [9]. Symbolic input values are fed to the machine during the traversal, but symbolic states are visited one at the time. The algorithm consists in enumerating the symbolic states of the product machine reachable from the total initial state. Since a symbolic state in fact represents a set of numeric states of the machine, the algorithm does not degenerate into state enumeration. The algorithm is presented at Figure 2.

```
PROCEDURE Compare-GSM(M₁, M₂);
   Var     Reach, From, New: Set-Of-Total-States;
           S: Total-State;                            # Concatenation of Y₁ and Y₂
           X: Input;
   BEGIN
   Reach := From := {I_T};
   WHILE (From ≠ ∅) DO
       BEGIN
       S := An-Element-Of(From);
       From := From - {S};
       X := New-Input();
       Compare-Ouput-Values(M₁, M₂, X, S);
       New := Generate-New-Reached-States(M₁, M₂, X, S, Reach);
       From := From ∪ New;
       Reach := Reach ∪ New;
       END;
   END;
```

Figure 2: Comparison algorithm

The set *Reach* is used to keep track of the symbolic states reached during the exploration, while the set *From*, a subset of *Reach*, contains the reached states not already visited. The set *New* computed from a particular state S using the procedure *Generate-New-Reached-States* (to be described in Section 3.3) contains all the states reachable from Y but not included in the *Reach* set. The procedure *New-Input* generates new symbolic variable(s) representing the value of the input(s). The traversal of the state space proceeds in a depth first or breadth first manner depending on the state sequence returned by the procedure *An-Element-Of*.

3.2 Comparison of Output Values

The comparison of the output values at a particular symbolic total state S under a symbolic input vector X is performed by the *Compare-Output-Value* procedure. For each output z two TFs TF_1 and TF_2 are computed using λ_1 and λ_2, respectively, based on the values of X and S. The sets $Var(TF_1)$ and $Var(TF_2)$ contain only the symbolic inputs of the product machine. If these TFs are equivalent for each output then the two machines have the same observable behavior in state S.

Since the system of rewriting rules is complete and the TFs are represented as BDDs, two TFs are equivalent iff their reduced forms are syntactically equal [14,15]. For example, during the comparison of Stack-Spec and Stack-Impl, the total initial state I_T of the state node (sp, sm, c, r_1, r_2, r_3) is ((1,1), Mem(DC,DC,DC), (0,0), DC, DC, DC); in this state the following TFs are computed for *out* and *err*, for both the Stack-Spec and Stack-Impl, given the symbolic input (in_1,nop_1,pop_1):

EQU(out,Zero)

$(nop_1 \vee \overline{pop_1}) \wedge EQU(err,(0)) \vee \overline{nop_1} \wedge pop_1 \wedge EQU(err,(1))$

Consequently, the two machines are equivalent in the initial state. As will be seen in the next section, the total state S_1 = ((1,0), Mem(DC,DC,in_1), (0,1), in_1, DC, DC) is reachable from I_T. Again, the machines are equivalent in the state S_1 since the following TFs are computed for *out* and *err*, for both the Stack-Spec and Stack-Impl, given the symbolic input (in_2,nop_2,pop_2):

EQU(out,in1)

EQU(err,(0))

3.3 Computation of New Reached States

This section is concerned with the computation of the states reachable from a symbolic state S under the symbolic input X, and the detection of states reached previously. This is performed by the *Generate-New-Reached-States* procedure. First, the computation of the reachable states is explained. The TF for the next state tuple $(y_{11}',...,y_{1q}',y_{21}',...,y_{2r}')$ can be computed from the next state function δ_1 and δ_2, based on the value of X and S. Let f be the TF resulting from the conjunction of the TFs for the next state variables.

Here again, the only non-DC variables that can appear in f, i.e., Var(f), are the symbolic inputs of the product machine. The reachable states are the data transferred by f, i.e., the transferred terms in the leaves of the BDD graph representation of f. For example, the possible next state values of the product machine Stack-Spec×Stack-Impl reachable directly from the initial state are described by the following TFs, one for each next state variable:

$(\text{nop}_1 \vee \text{pop}_1) \wedge \mathbf{EQU}(\text{sp'},(1,1)) \ \vee \ \overline{\text{nop}_1} \wedge \overline{\text{pop}_1} \wedge \mathbf{EQU}(\text{sp'},(1,0))$

$(\text{nop}_1 \vee \text{pop}_1) \wedge \mathbf{EQU}(\text{sm'},\text{Mem(DC,DC,DC)}) \ \vee \ \overline{\text{nop}_1} \wedge \overline{\text{pop}_1} \wedge \mathbf{EQU}(\text{sm'},\text{Mem(DC,DC,in}_1))$

$(\text{nop}_1 \vee \text{pop}_1) \wedge \mathbf{EQU}(\text{c'},(0,0)) \ \vee \ \overline{\text{nop}_1} \wedge \overline{\text{pop}_1} \wedge \mathbf{EQU}(\text{c'},(0,1))$

$(\text{nop}_1 \vee \text{pop}_1) \wedge \mathbf{EQU}(\text{r}_1',\text{DC}) \ \vee \ \overline{\text{nop}_1} \wedge \overline{\text{pop}_1} \wedge \mathbf{EQU}(\text{r}_1',\text{in}_1)$

$\mathbf{EQU}(\text{r}_2',\text{DC})$

$\mathbf{EQU}(\text{r}_3',\text{DC})$

The transferred terms of the conjunction of the above TFs represent the two following states:

((1,1), Mem(DC,DC,DC), (0,0), DC, DC, DC),
((1,0), Mem(DC,DC,in$_1$), (0,1), in$_1$, DC, DC).

We can notice that the first state has been reached earlier (it is the initial state), while the second state is new. The detection of already reached states is performed by comparing the reachable states with the set of reached states: If the set of numeric states represented by a reachable symbolic state S is included in the set represented by a reached symbolic state then we can conclude that the state S has been reached previously. As will be seen below, this is just a sufficient condition, not a necessary one. In the following, we suppose that each DC symbol is renamed using an unique variable symbol. As for terms, the set of numeric states represented by a symbolic state S is the alphabet α(S) of S. Let $S = (T_1:w_1,...,T_k:w_k)$ be a symbolic state, then $\alpha(S) = \{(c_1,...,c_k)$ where c_i is a w_i-bit constant $| \exists$ an assignment $v \ni c_i = v(T_i)\}$.

A **substitution** is a homomorphic mapping σ from terms into terms (states into states), associating terms to some variables appearing in a term (state) [12]. A term (state) S is an **instance** of a term (state) T iff there exist a substitution σ such that $S = \sigma(T)$. For example, the state ((1,1), Mem(DC$_6$,DC$_7$,in$_1$), (0,0), DC$_8$, DC$_9$, Zero), reached after a push and a pop from I_T, is an instance of the initial state ((1,1), Mem(DC$_0$,DC$_1$,DC$_2$), (0,0), DC$_3$, DC$_4$, DC$_5$) since the following substitution can be used: $\sigma = \{$DC$_0 \leftarrow$ DC$_6$, DC$_1 \leftarrow$ DC$_7$, DC$_2 \leftarrow$ in$_1$, DC$_3 \leftarrow$ DC$_8$, DC$_4 \leftarrow$ DC$_9$, DC$_5 \leftarrow$ Zero$\}$. This is an important result:

Theorem: For all symbolic terms (states) T and substitution σ: $\alpha(T) \supseteq \alpha(\sigma(T))$.

The proof is based on the fact that all occurrences of each variable of T are replaced by the same term. This can only reduce the possible numeric values represented by the occurrences of the variable in T, and thus also the numeric values represented by T, i.e., $\alpha(T)$. Using this theorem, we can conclude that a state S has been reached previously if there exists a state S_i in *Reach* such that S is an instance of S_i. Of course, this is a sufficient condition, but not a necessary one. There could be two state S_i and S_j such that $\alpha(S_i) \cup \alpha(S_j) \supseteq \alpha(S)$ where S is neither an instance of S_i nor of S_j, but this is a harder condition to detect. To determine if a term is an instance of another one, a simple adaptation of the unification algorithm can be used [12].

In order to improve the detection process, the set *Reach* should be in a reduced form, i.e., no state in the set is an instance of another state of the set. Using this algorithm, the comparison of the two stack machines is performed by exploring the following four symbolic states:

$$((1,1), Mem(DC,DC,DC), (0,0), DC, DC, DC),$$
$$((1,0), Mem(DC,DC,in_1), (0,1), in_1, DC, DC),$$
$$((0,1), Mem(DC,in_2,in_1), (1,0), in_2, in_1, DC),$$
$$((0,0), Mem(in_3,in_2,in_1), (1,1), in_3, in_2, in_1).$$

However, what can we say about the finite termination of the exploration? The sequence of new total states $S_1,S_2,\ldots$ reachable from the initial state must be bounded. We know that the generic nodes of the machine can take an unbounded number of values since their sizes are unspecified. However, we remark that in the traversal of the product machine of Stack-Spec and Stack-Impl, the generic constant value (i.e., Zero) never appears as a parameter of an operator in a reduced term. In a case like this, an infinite sequence of symbolic states where each one is not the instance of another one is impossible, hence finite exploration is assured. This result can be generalized: We know that a term can be represented as a tree where the leaf nodes are variable or constant symbols, and the internal nodes are operator symbols [4]. The **depth** of a node (subterm) in a term is its distance from the root. If the depth of generic constants is always finite in all reduced terms computed during the comparison of machines then a finite exploration is assured. This result holds because an infinite number of terms where each term is not an instance of another one cannot be computed. In the case where the finite depth condition on the generic constants is not verified, finite exploration is not assured. It could be interesting to determine conditions that imply infinite exploration, but this may be undecidable in general.

4 Conclusion

This paper has presented a technique for comparing generic state machines described at the RT level of abstraction. The originality of the technique is in the combination of theorem proving methods and an automata equivalence algorithm, in which first order logic terms are used to represent the values of the inputs, states and outputs of the machines.

A prototype of our system is under construction, as an evolution of [14,15], however, a number of problems still must be resolved: The possible state space explorable during the comparison of two machines must be studied in more depth to assure a finite search. Also, a complete system of rewriting rules must be computed (statically or dynamically), because it is required for comparing formulas.

Further research is required to see if states could be represented symbolically using characteristic functions [8,20] and if the incremental technique based on cross-controllability calculation [6] could be used in the case of generic machines.

References

[1] M. R. Barbacci, "A Comparison of Register Transfer Languages for Describing Computers and Digital Systems", IEEE Trans. on Comp., Vol. C-24, No. 2, February 1975.

[2] R. S. Boyer, J. S. Moore, "A Computational Logic", ACM Monograph Series, Academic Press Inc., 1979.

[3] R. E. Bryant, "Graph-Based Algorithms for Boolean Function Manipulation", IEEE Trans. on Comp., Vol. C-35, No. 8, August 1986.

[4] B, Buchberger, R. Loos, "Algebraic Simplification", in Buchberger and al. eds., Computer Algebra: Symbolic and Algebraic Computation, Springer, 1982.

[5] J. R. Burch, E. M. Clarke, K. L. McMillan, D. L. Dill, L. J. Hwang, "Symbolic Model Checking: 10^{20} States and Beyond", in Proc. of the Int. Work. on Formal Methods in VLSI Design, Miami, January 1991.

[6] E. Cerny, C. Mauras, "Tautology Checking using Cross-Controllability and Cross-Observability Relations", ICCAD, Santa Clara, November 1990.

[7] O. Coudert, C. Berthet, J. C. Madre, "Verification of Synchronous Sequential Machines Using Symbolic Execution", in Proc. of the Work. on Automatic Verification Methods for Finite State Systems, Grenoble, June 1989.

[8] O. Coudert, C. Berthet, J. C. Madre, "Verification of Sequential Machines Using Boolean Functional Vectors", in L. Claesen, editor, Proc. of the int. Work. on Applied Formal Methods for Correct VLSI Design, Leuven, November 1989.

[9] S. Devadas, H.-K. T. Ma, A. R. Newton, "On the Verification of Sequential Machines at Different Levels of Abstraction", IEEE Transaction on CAD, Vol. 6, No. 7, June 1988.

[10] G. C. Gopalakrishnan, R. M. Fujimoto, V. Akella, N. S. Mani, "HOP: A Process Model for Synchronous Hardware; Semantics and Experiments in Process Composition", Integration: The VLSI Journal, August 1989.

[11] M. Gordon, "Why Higher-Order Logic is a Good Formalism for Specifying and Verifying Hardware", in Formal Aspects of VLSI Design, 1986.

[12] K. Knight, "Unification: A Multidisciplinary Survey", ACM Computing Surveys, Vol. 21, No. 1, 1989.

[13] S. Kohavi, "Switching and Finite Automata Theory", McGraw-Hill, New-York, 1978.

[14] M. Langevin, "Automated RTL Verification Based on Predicate Calculus", in Proc. of the Work. on Computer Aided Verification, Rutgers, June 1990.

[15] M. Langevin, E. Cerny, "Verification of Processor-Like Circuit", in Proc. of the Advanced Research Workshop on Correct Hardware Design Methodologies, Turin, June 1991.

[16] T. Larsson, "Hardware Verification Based on Algebraic Manipulation and Partial Evaluation", in Proc. of the Int. Working Conf. on the Fusion of Hardware Design and Verification, Glasgow, July 1988.

[17] Z. Manna, "Mathematical Theory of Computation", McGraw-Hill, 1974.

[18] L. Pierre, "The Formal Proof of the Min-Max Sequential Benchmark Described in CASCADE Using the Boyer-Moore Theorem Prover", in L. Claesen, editor, Proc. of the int. Work. on Applied Formal Methods for Correct VLSI Design, Leuven, November 1989.

[19] C. Pixley, G. Beihl, "Quotient and Isomorphism Theorems of a Theory of Sequential Hadrware Equivalence", in Proc. of the Int. Work. on Formal Methods in VLSI Design, Miami, January 1991.

[20] H. J. Touati, H. Savoj, B. Lin, R. K. Brayton, A. Sangiovanni-Vincentelli, "Implicit State Enumeration of Finite State Machines Using BDDs", ICCAD, Santa Clara, November 1990.

[21] VHDL Language Reference Manual, Intermetrics Inc., 1987.

An Automata Theoretic Approach to Temporal Logic

Gjalt G. de Jong *

Eindhoven University of Technology
Department of Electrical Engineering
P.O. Box 513, 5600 MB Eindhoven, The Netherlands
Tel. +31 40 473345, Fax: +31 40 464527
Email: gjalt@es.ele.tue.nl

Abstract

A syntax directed mapping is presented from Propositional Temporal Logic (PTL) formu-lae to Müller type finite automata. This is a direct and much more elegant and easier to implement approach than previously described methods. Most of these methods are based on tableau methods for satisfiability checking, and after that a Büchi type of automaton is extracted. Büchi and Müller automata are equally expressive. However, Müller automata have nicer properties than Büchi automata, for instance deterministic Müller automata are expressive as non-deterministic ones, while this is not true for Büchi automata. Also deterministic Büchi automata are not closed under complement. This transformation is the first step in a decision procedure, since the resulting Müller automaton represents the models of the temporal logic formula, and on which further verification and analysis can be performed.

1. Introduction

Temporal logic has proven to be a well suited formalism for program verification [1] as well as hardware specification and verification [2, 3]. The theory of finite automata is also very well-known and a very suitable formalism to describe and analyze systems in. Since the semantics of temporal logic is based on a state transition graph, these two formalisms can be linked together. It is shown in [4, 5] that propositional temporal logic is contained in the class of ω-regular expressions. This is based on a tableau kind decision procedure from which then a Büchi automaton is extracted. From then on, papers have appeared to show how certain properties, described as temporal logic formulae, can be stated as Büchi automata, for instance [6, 7]. However, transformations from temporal logic formulae

---

* This research is part of the ASCIS project sponsored by the European Community under contract BRA 3281.

onto Büchi automata all suffer from the drawback that deterministic Büchi automata are not closed under complementation [8], which then gives a burden on the complexity [9].

This approach gives us alternative ways to check satisfiability and tautology, but also allows us to mix freely temporal logic and state-transition based formalisms for specification, verification [3] as well as manipulation.

This paper is organized as follows. First we will discuss temporal logic and give its semantics. In the next chapter we will give a short overview of finite automata, and two types of accepting conditions for automata accepting languages of infinitary-length words: Büchi and Müller acceptance condition. After that, we will present a syntax directed transformation of temporal logic formulae onto Müller automata, which describe the models of the temporal logic formulae.

2. Temporal Logic

Temporal logic is the natural extension of propositional logic to include time related information. Whereas propositional logic can be said to express facts to be true or false at a certain moment, or state, temporal logic allows one to express the relation between such facts at several moments or states. Each state then announces particular atomic propositions to be true and others to be false. The language of propositional temporal logic (PTL) may be regarded as a superset of the language of propositional logic adding the operators $\square$ (*always*), $\lozenge$ (*sometime*), U (*until*) and O (*next*). Of intuitively means that f is true in the **next** state; $\square f$ that f is true in **all** future states; $\lozenge f$ that f is true in **some** future state; fUg that f is true for all states until g becomes valid in a state.

Formally, the semantics of a temporal logic formula (with a set P of propositional variables) is defined with respect to a triple $M = (S, N, p_i)$, where S is a finite set of states, $N : S \rightarrow S$ a total successor function giving for each state a unique next state and $p_i : S \times P \rightarrow \{True, False\}$ a truth-assignment giving a truth value to each propositional variable in each state.

The truth of a PTL formula is inductively defined relative to a structure M and a state s by:

$$<M, s>|= p \text{ iff } p_i(s,p) = True, \; p \in P$$

$$<M, s>|= \neg f \text{ iff not } <M, s>|= f$$

$$<M, s>|= f \vee g \text{ iff } <M, s>|= f \text{ or } <M, s>|= g$$

$$<M, s>|= f \wedge g \text{ iff } <M, s>|= f \text{ and } <M, s>|= g$$

$$<M, s>|= Of \text{ iff } <M, N(s)>|= f \tag{1}$$

$$<M, s> \models \Diamond f \text{ iff } \exists_{i \geq 0} <M, N^i(s)> \models f$$

$$<M, s> \models \Box f \text{ iff } \forall_{i \geq 0} <M, N^i(s)> \models f$$

$$<M, s> \models fUg \text{ iff } \exists_{i \geq 0} (<M, N^i(s)> \models g \text{ and } \forall_{0 \leq j < i} <M, N^j(s)> \models f)$$

where $N^i(s)$ denotes the ith successor of s.

An interpretation or model for a PTL formula consists of a structure M with a designated set of states S, truth-assignment p_i, successor function N and an initial state s_0.

Because the set of states S is finite and the successor relation is a total function, any infinite sequence of occurrences of states, may be represented in a finite way by a ω-regular string over the alphabet S, i.e. it consists of a certain possible empty prefix sequence followed by an endless repetition of a cycle of 1 or more states.

A PTL formula is satisfiable, i.e. can be made true, if we can find a model $<M, s_0>$ such that $<M, s_0> \models f$ holds. If a formula is true in a model we also say that the model, or sequence of states with associated truth-assignment satisfies the formula.

A formula is said to be valid, or is a tautology, iff it is true in every appropriate model, notation: $\models f$. A formula that cannot be satisfied by any model is a contradiction. Two formulas f and g are said to be equivalent, notated $f = g$, when $\models (f \leftrightarrow g)$ holds. Note that a formula is unsatisfiable if and only if its negation is a tautology and conversely a formula is valid iff its negation is unsatisfiable.

3. Finite Automata

A finite automaton M is a five tuple $(\Sigma, Q, \delta, I, F)$, where Σ is an alphabet of symbols, Q a finite set of states, δ a mapping $Q \times \Sigma \rightarrow 2^Q$ that represent the state transitions labeled by a symbol, $I \subset Q$ a set of initial states and $F \subset Q$ a set of final states. An automaton M accepts a word $w = \sigma_1..\sigma_n$ ($\in \Sigma*$) whenever there exists a sequence $q_0 ... q_n$ ($q_i \in Q$) such that $q_0 \in I$, $q_i \in \delta(q_{i-1}, \sigma_i)$ and $q_n \in F$. The language that an automaton M accepts is the set of all words that are accepted by the automaton. The class of languages which can be accepted by finite automata is the class of regular languages.

δ can be extended in the natural way to a mapping of $Q \times \Sigma* \rightarrow 2^Q$. The symbol $\varepsilon \notin \Sigma$ denotes the empty word. An automaton M is called deterministic, when it has only one initial state, and δ is a mapping $Q \times \Sigma \rightarrow Q$. Non-deterministic automata can be converted to deterministic automata by the subset method [10].

Finite automata can also be used to accept the class of ω-regular languages, which is a class of languages consisting of infinitary-length words. A language is ω-regular if it can be written as UV^ω where U and V are regular languages. Two major types of finite automata exist which are equally expressive, both able to recognize the class of ω-regular languages: Müller and Büchi automata. These automata differ only in their accepting condition.

A Büchi automaton is a five tuple $(\Sigma, Q, \delta, I, F)$ as above. However, an infinitary length word w is accepted by a Büchi automaton if $INF(w) \cap F \neq \emptyset$, where $INF(w)$ is defined as the set of states that are 'visited' infinitely many times.

A Müller automaton is a five tuple $(\Sigma, Q, \delta, I, A)$ with Σ, Q, δ and I as before. But the accepting condition is defined by $A \subset 2^Q$. A word w is accepted by a Müller automaton if $INF(w) \in A$. More intuitively: if in the long run, a word stays in a particular subset of the state space.

The class of Müller and Büchi automata is closed under union, intersection. Both types of automata are also closed under the operation of prefixing with normal finite automata. Only deterministic Müller automata are closed under complementation. These operations are defined for Müller automata as: (where $fa_i = (\Sigma, Q_i, \delta_i, I_i, A_i)$ and dfa is a deterministic automaton.)

$$Union(fa_1, fa_2) = (\Sigma, Q_1 \cup Q_2, \delta_1 \cup \delta_2, I_1 \cup I_2, A_1 \cup A_2)$$

$$Complementation(dfa) = (\Sigma, Q, \delta, I, 2^Q - A)$$

By DeMorgan, intersection, or product, is then also defined. But this may also be written as:

$$Intersection(fa_1, fa_2) = (\Sigma, Q_1 \times Q_2, \delta, I_1 \times I_2, A_1 \times A_2)$$
where $(q_i \times q_{i'}, \sigma, q_j \times q_{j'}) \in \delta$ if $(q_i, \sigma, q_j) \in \delta_1$ and $(q_{i'}, \sigma, q_{j'}) \in \delta_2$.

$$Concatenation(fa_1, fa_2) = (\Sigma, Q_1 \cup Q_2, \delta_1 \cup \delta_2 \cup \delta_{fi}, I_1, A_2),$$
where fa_1 is a normal finite automaton $(\Sigma, Q_1, \delta_1, F)$, and
$\delta_{fi} = \{(q_{f_1}, \varepsilon, q_{i_j}) | q_{f_1} \in F_1 \wedge q_{i_j} \in I_2\}$

These operations are similar in the case of Büchi automata, except for the complement operation.

Determinization of Müller automata can also be done by the subset method, however it is then necessary that there does **not** exist a path going out of an accepting component. So it may be necessary to duplicate state sets, and its transitions. Duplication of an accepting set $A_k \in A$ is defined as:

$$M' = (\Sigma, Q', \delta', I, A') \tag{2}$$
where
$Q' = Q \cup \{q'_i | q_i \in A_k\}$
$\delta' = \delta \cup \{(q_i, \sigma, q'_j) | (q_i, \sigma, q_j) \in \delta \wedge q_i \in A_k \wedge q_j \in A_k\}$

$$\cup \{(q'_i, \sigma, q'_j) | (q_i, \sigma, q_j) \in \delta \wedge q_i \in A_k \wedge q_j \in A_k\}$$
$$A' = \{A'_k\}, A'_k = \{q'_i | q_i \in A_k\}$$

The accepting sets of the deterministic automaton after the subset method are:
$$A' = \{A_k\}, A_k = \{q \in P(Q) | \exists A_k \in A : q \subset A_k \neq \varnothing\} \tag{3}$$
Note that only those sets that are strongly connected contribute to accepting paths.

In Fig. 1 and Fig. 2 it is illustrated that duplication of states is indeed necessary.

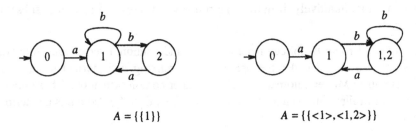

$$A = \{\{1\}\} \qquad\qquad A = \{\{<1>, <1,2>\}\}$$

Figure 1. Incorrect determinization with the subset method

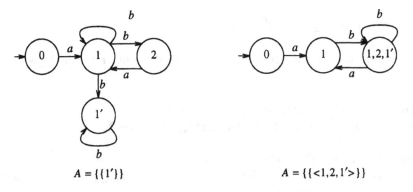

$$A = \{\{1'\}\} \qquad\qquad A = \{\{<1,2,1'>\}\}$$

Figure 2. Determinization with the subset method after duplication of accepting sets

Theorem 1: Duplication of accepting sets of a Müller automaton $M = (\Sigma, Q, \delta, I, A)$ automaton results in an equivalent Müller automaton M' according to (2).

Proof: Since Müller automata are closed under union, let, without loss of generality, $A = \{a\}$. Let ρ be a run for an ω-word accepted by M. Since there are no transitions removed, every path in M also exists in M'. At some instant, ρ on M enters a (at state q_0) and from then on it will stay in a. The corresponding ρ' on M' also enters a (at the same state q_0) on M'. The next move on M will be from one state in a to a next state q_1 in a. M' can make the corresponding move to state q'_1 in a', because for every move from a state $q_0 \in a$ towards $q_1 \in a$ a transition is made from $q_0 \in a$ towards $q_1 \in a'$. All subsequent moves on M within a have corresponding moves on M' within a'. Thus $L(M) \subset L(M')$.

The converse is analogous. Let ρ' be a run for an ω-word accepted by M'. At some time, ρ' moves on M' from a state $q_0 \notin a'$ to a state $q_1 \in a'$. Because every transition towards a state $q' \in a'$ on M' corresponds to a transition towards $q \in a$ on M, it is clear, that M can enter its accepting set too. The only possible subsequent transitions on M' are all within a' and because of the duplication, all these transitions have corresponding transitions within a on M. Thus $L(M') \subset L(M)$.

From Fig. 1 and Fig. 2 it is clear that the subset method does not result in a correct automaton when transitions exist between states of accepting sets as defined in (3) and there does not exist a corresponding transition, i.e. with the same label, within the original accepting set. In the following it is proven that such transitions do not exist in the deterministic automaton when all the accepting sets are duplicated according to (2).

Theorem 2: The subset method applied to a nondeterministic Müller automaton $M = (\Sigma, Q, \delta, I, A)$ with each accepting state set A_k duplicated according to (2) yields an equivalent Müller automaton M' with A' according to (3).

Proof: We only need to show that no illegal transition exist, i.e. that no transitions exist between accepting states if does not exist an corresponding transition within the accepting set of the NFA after duplication.

Because Müller automata are closed under union, let, without loss of generality, $M = (\Sigma, Q, \delta, I, A)$ be the NFA, where A is the singleton $\{a\}$ which is the result of duplication.

Let $M' = (\Sigma, Q', \delta', I', A')$ the DFA, constructed via the subset-construction out of M. Now take any $(Q_1, \sigma, Q_2) \in \delta'$, with $Q_1 \in a'$ and $Q_2 \in a'$. Q_1 is the 'super'state of M' consisting of states in Q, which are all reachable in M from some state, by the same word. If $Q_1 \cap a = \varnothing$, then $Q_1 \notin A'$ and this implies a contradiction. Thus it follows $Q_i \cap a \neq \varnothing$. If $\exists q_0 \in Q_1 \cap a : \delta(q_0, \sigma) \neq \varnothing$ then of course $Q_2 \in A'$ and the transition is legal, because it has its corresponding transition within the accepting set of M. Else $\forall q_0 \in Q_1 \cap a : \delta(q_0, \sigma) = \varnothing$. In that case, if $\forall q \in Q_1 : \delta(q, \sigma) \cap a = \varnothing$, then $Q_2 \notin A'$, again a contradiction. Now take $q_1 \in Q_1$ and $q_1 \notin a$ and $(q_1, \sigma, q_2) \in \delta$, with $q_2 \in a$. This implies, that this transition will occur in the accepting set a' of the DFA M', while it was not in the accepting set a of the NFA M. However, the duplication ensures, that the only transitions pointing towards a state $q_2 \in a$ must come from a state $q_1 \in a$ (contradiction) or else, an equivalent transition will exist within the accepting set, i.e. $\exists q_3 \in a : (q_3, \sigma, q_2) \in \delta$ and this q_3 exists because it is the duplication of q_1. It also follows from the duplication, that q_1 and q_3 are reachable from the initial states of M, by the same word. That however would finally imply, that there is a corresponding transition for (Q_1, σ, Q_2) within the original accepting set a. This completes the proof, that there can be no 'new' transition introduced in the accepting set of the DFA, when the duplication method is used, before the subset-construction.

It is proven that Büchi and Müller automata are equally expressive, since they both define the class of ω-regular languages [11]. It is also proven that deterministic and nondeterministic Müller automata are equally expressive, while deterministic Büchi automata are less expressive [8]. Since also the complementation operation on Müller automata is much more efficient that on Büchi automata [9], we find the type Müller automata more convenient for our purposes.

4. Temporal Logic to Müller automata

For temporal logic, the above described types of automata are extended to be able to model propositional logic formulae as the labels on the transitions, instead of symbols out of an alphabet Σ. So a Müller type of automaton is then described by the five tuple: (P, Q, δ, I, A) with P the set of propositional variables, and δ is a mapping $Q \times PL \rightarrow 2^Q$ where PL is a propositional logic formula which can be seen as element of 2^P. All previous defined operations can be extended in the natural way on this type of automaton. Note that in fact a boolean algebra on P is defined of which the conventional type of transitions is a special case.

In fact, such an automaton can be seen as a compact representation of all the models $<M, s>$ with respect to which a PTL formula f is defined. Only the states and transitions have changed roles, because in a model for a PTL formula f each state has a set of propositions which are valid in that state. In our case, these sets of valid propositions are on the transitions. But these two types of state transition graphs are each others dual and can therefore be transformed into each other.

Now a transformation of a PTL formula f to a Müller automaton M is given, for which the set of all *accepting* paths t are all the models m of f where

$$M = (P, Q, \delta, I, A) \tag{4}$$

$t = <s_0, s_1, \dots >$ with $s_0 \in I$ and $(s_i, p, s_{i+1}) \in \delta$

$m = <s'_0, s'_1, \dots >$ with $p_i(s_i) = p$, $(s_i, p, s_{i+1}) \in \delta$

This transformation $FA:PTL \rightarrow MFA$, where MFA is the type of Müller automata, is defined inductively as:

— Case $f = p \in P$:
$$FA(f) = (P, \{q_0, q_1\}, \{(q_0, p, q_1)(q_1, True, q_1)\}, \{q_0\}, \{\{q_1\}\}$$

— Case $f = \neg f_1$:
$$FA(f) = Complement(FA(f_1))$$

— Case $f = f_1 \wedge f_2$:
$$FA(f) = Intersection(FA(f_1), FA(f_2))$$

— Case $f = f_1 \vee f_2$:
$$FA(f) = Union(FA(f_1), FA(f_2))$$

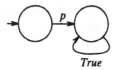

Figure 3. Automaton of a propositional formula p

— Case $f = \bigcirc f_1$:
$$FA(f) = Concatenation(FA_\bigcirc, FA(f_1))$$
where
$$FA_\bigcirc = (P, \{q_0, q_1\}, \{(q_0, True, q_1)\}, \{q_0\}, \{q_1\})$$
This is illustrated in Fig. 4.

Figure 4. Automaton of $\bigcirc f$

— Case $f = \Diamond f_1$:
$$FA(f) = Concatenation(FA_\Diamond, FA(f_1))$$
where
$$FA_\Diamond = (P, \{q_0\}, \{(q_0, True, q_0)\}, \{q_0\}, \{q_0\})$$
This is illustrated in Fig. 5.

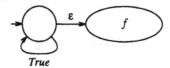

Figure 5. Automaton of $\Diamond f$

— Case $f = \Box f_1$:
Since $\Box f = \neg \Diamond \neg f$, the automaton for $\Box f$ can be constructed with the previous operations.

— Case $f = f_1 \ U \ f_2$:
Since $f \ U \ g = \Diamond g \wedge (g \vee (f \wedge (f \ U \ g)))$, the automaton for $f \ U \ g$ can be constructed as the automaton for $\Diamond g \wedge \Box(X = g \vee (f \wedge \bigcirc X))$, so by introducing an auxiliary variable which can be hided later.

Now we proof that the above transformation results in a Müller automaton M for a PTL formula f which accepts the same language as the PTL formula f, or equivalently represents all models of f as defined in (4). The proof is based on language equivalence. So we first define the following two functions L and M:
$$L: MFA \rightarrow R^\omega \tag{5}$$

where R^ω is the type of ω-regular languages. The alphabet may be seen as the set of propositional variables P which have the value *True* assigned. This function is the classical mapping of automata to (ω-)regular languages.

$$M:PTL \to R^\omega \tag{6}$$

M is the mapping of models to ω-regular strings as defined in section 2.

Theorem 3: $L(FA(f)) = M(f)$, or equivalently: the models of f are just the accepting paths of M as defined in (4).

Proof: The proof is by induction on the length of PTL formula f.

— Case $f = p \in P$:
   The models for this formula are the sequences $<s_0, s_1, s_2, ...>$ in which $p_i(s_0) = p$ and $p_i(s_i) = True$ for all $i > 0$. It is trivial to check that this is equivalent with $FA(f)$.

— Case $f = \neg f_1$:
   According to (1), $M(f) = \Sigma^\omega - M(f_1)$. By induction, $L(FA(f_1)) = M(f_1)$. Also $L(FA(f)) = L(FA(\neg f_1)) = \Sigma^\omega - L(FA(f_1))$. So $L(FA(f)) = M(f)$.

— Case $f = f_1 \vee f_2$:
   According to (1), $M(f) = M(f_1) \cup M(f_2)$. By induction, $L(FA(f_i)) = M(f_i)$. Also $L(FA(f)) = L(FA(f_1 \vee f_2)) = L(FA(f_1)) \cup L(FA(f_2))$. So $L(FA(f)) = M(f)$.

— Case $f = f_1 \wedge f_2$:
   According to (1), $M(f) = M(f_1) \cap M(f_2)$. By induction, $L(FA(f_i)) = M(f_i)$. Also $L(FA(f)) = L(FA(f_1 \wedge f_2)) = L(FA(f_1)) \cap L(FA(f_2))$. So $L(FA(f)) = M(f)$.

— Case $f = \bigcirc f_1$:
   According to (1), $M(f) = True \cdot M(f_1)$, which again is trivial to check that this is equivalent with $L(FA(f))$.

— Case $f = \Diamond f_1$:
   According to (1), models for f consists of a prefix in which any truth assignment is satisfactory, prefixed to models of f_1. So $M(f) = True * \cdot M(f_1)$ to which $L(FA(f))$ is equivalent.

— The cases $f = \Box f_1$ and $f = f_1 U f_2$ are a composition of the other cases.

The subset method to make automata deterministic may cause an exponential blow-up in the number of states. When implementing this transformation, it is clear that this approach is only practical when determinizations of Müller automata have to be done as few times as possible. Also the enumeration of the accepting sets in case of complementation may cause an exponential blow-up.

Complement and intersection are determinism preserving operations, only the union operation is not determinism preserving. Note that also the construction of arbitrary propositional formulae is determinism preserving. This is even the case for PTL formulae with only the ◯ as temporal operator. So these type of formulae can be dealt with as special simple cases. Examination of the transformation function *FA* even shows that the other temporal cases can also be simplified when one or both arguments is a propositional variable, or a PTL formula with only ◯ operators.

The resulting automaton can be used as a model for the PTL formula, and on which other verifications and analyses can be performed. For example, a test on satisfiability, or model checking [12]. It is clear that satisfiability checking will become a trivial decision procedure, because when the PTL formula is satisfiable, it will result in a Müller automaton which accepts a non-empty 'language'. And an unsatisfiable PTL formula, i.e. a contradiction, results in an empty automaton.

Acknowledgements

I would like to thank the anonymous reviewers for their helpful and stimulating remarks. Also I wish to thank my colleague Geert-Leon Janssen with whom I had innumerable discussions on temporal logic and the various ways for finite and efficient representations of models.

The transformation method presented in this paper has been implemented on top of a finite automaton manipulation package. Interested readers are invited to write to the author to obtain a copy of the program and the finite automaton package.

References

[1]   PNUELI, A., "Applications of Temporal Logic to the Specification and Verification of Reactive Systems: A Survey of Current Trends," *Current Trends in Concurrency: Overviews and Tutorials*, ed. J. W. de Bakker, W.-P. de Roever and G. Rozenberg, Lecture Notes in Computer Science 224, Springer Verlag, Berlin, pp. 510-584.

[2]   V. BOCHMANN, G., "Hardware Specification with Temporal Logic: An Example," *IEEE Trans. on Computers*, vol. C-31, no. 3, March 1982, pp. 223-231.

[3]   JANSSEN, G. L. J. M., "Hardware verification using Temporal Logic: A Practical View," *Formal VLSI Correctness Verification, VLSI Design Methods-II, Proc. of the IMEC-IFIP WG10.2 WG 10.5 International Workshop on Applied Formal Methods for Correct VLSI Design*, ed. L. J. M. Claesen, North-Holland, 1990, pp. 159-168.

[4]   WOLPER, P., "Temporal Logic Can Be More Expressive," *Information and Control*, vol. 56, 1983, pp. 72-99.

[5]   WOLPER, P., M. Y. VARDI, AND A. P. SISTLA, "Reasoning about Infinite Compu-
      tation Paths," *Proc. 24th Ann. Symp. on Foundations of Computer Science*, Tucson,
      AZ, November 7-9,1983, pp. 185-193.

[6]   MANNA, Z. AND A. PNUELI, "Specification and Verification of Concurrent Pro-
      grams by ∀-Automata," *Proc. 14th ACM Symp. on Principles of Programming
      Languages*, Munich, January 21-23, 1987, pp. 1-12.

[7]   ALPERN, B. AND F. B. SCHNEIDER, "Verifying Temporal Properties without Tem-
      poral Logic," *ACM Trans. on Programming Languages and Systems*, vol. 11, no. 1,
      January 1989, pp. 147-167.

[8]   CHOUEKA, Y., "Theories of Automata on ω-Tapes: a Simplified Approach," *J.
      Comput. System Sci.*, vol. 8, 1974, pp. 117-141.

[9]   SISTLA, A. P., M. Y. VARDI, AND P. WOLPER, "The Complementation Problems
      for Büchi Automata with Applications to Temporal Logic," *Proc. 12th Int. Collo-
      quium on Automata, Languages and Programming (ICALP'85)*, Lecture Notes in
      Computer Science 194, Springer Verlag, Berlin, Napflion, Greece, July 1985, pp.
      465-474.

[10] RABIN, M. O. AND D. SCOTT, "Finite Automata and their Decision Problems,"
      IBM J. Res. Develop., vol. 3, 1959, pp. 114-125.

[11] MCNAUGHTON, R., "Testing an Generating Infinite Sequences by a Finite Automa-
      ton," *Information and Control*, vol. 9, 1966, pp. 521-530.

[12] LICHTENSTEIN, O. AND A. PNUELI, "Checking That Finite State Concurrent Pro-
      grams Satisfy Their Linear Specification," *Proc. 12th ACM Symp. on Principles of
      Programming Languages*, New Orleans, January 14-16, 1985, pp. 97-107.

Lecture Notes in Computer Science

For information about Vols. 1–504
please contact your bookseller or Springer-Verlag

Vol. 505: E. H. L. Aarts, J. van Leeuwen, M. Rem (Eds.), PARLE '91. Parallel Architectures and Languages Europe, Volume I. Proceedings, 1991. XV, 423 pages. 1991.

Vol. 506: E. H. L. Aarts, J. van Leeuwen, M. Rem (Eds.), PARLE '91. Parallel Architectures and Languages Europe, Volume II. Proceedings, 1991. XV, 489 pages. 1991.

Vol. 507: N. A. Sherwani, E. de Doncker, J. A. Kapenga (Eds.), Computing in the 90's. Proceedings, 1989. XIII, 441 pages. 1991.

Vol. 508: S. Sakata (Ed.), Applied Algebra, Algebraic Algorithms and Error-Correcting Codes. Proceedings, 1990. IX, 390 pages. 1991.

Vol. 509: A. Endres, H. Weber (Eds.), Software Development Environments and CASE Technology. Proceedings, 1991. VIII, 286 pages. 1991.

Vol. 510: J. Leach Albert, B. Monien, M. Rodríguez (Eds.), Automata, Languages and Programming. Proceedings, 1991. XII, 763 pages. 1991.

Vol. 511: A. C. F. Colchester, D.J. Hawkes (Eds.), Information Processing in Medical Imaging. Proceedings, 1991. XI, 512

Vol. 512: P. America (Ed.), ECOOP '91. European Conference on Object-Oriented Programming. Proceedings, 1991. X, 396 pages. 1991.

Vol. 513: N. M. Mattos, An Approach to Knowledge Base Management. IX, 247 pages. 1991. (Subseries LNAI).

Vol. 514: G. Cohen, P. Charpin (Eds.), EUROCODE '90. Proceedings, 1990. XI, 392 pages. 1991.

Vol. 515: J. P. Martins, M. Reinfrank (Eds.), Truth Maintenance Systems. Proceedings, 1990. VII, 177 pages. 1991. (Subseries LNAI).

Vol. 516: S. Kaplan, M. Okada (Eds.), Conditional and Typed Rewriting Systems. Proceedings, 1990. IX, 461 pages. 1991.

Vol. 517: K. Nökel, Temporally Distributed Symptoms in Technical Diagnosis. IX, 164 pages. 1991. (Subseries LNAI).

Vol. 518: J. G. Williams, Instantiation Theory. VIII, 133 pages. 1991. (Subseries LNAI).

Vol. 519: F. Dehne, J.-R. Sack, N. Santoro (Eds.), Algorithms and Data Structures. Proceedings, 1991. X, 496 pages. 1991.

Vol. 520: A. Tarlecki (Ed.), Mathematical Foundations of Computer Science 1991. Proceedings, 1991. XI, 435 pages. 1991.

Vol. 521: B. Bouchon-Meunier, R. R. Yager, L. A. Zadek (Eds.), Uncertainty in Knowledge-Bases. Proceedings, 1990. X, 609 pages. 1991.

Vol. 522: J. Hertzberg (Ed.), European Workshop on Planning. Proceedings, 1991. VII, 121 pages. 1991. (Subseries LNAI).

Vol. 523: J. Hughes (Ed.), Functional Programming Languages and Computer Architecture. Proceedings, 1991. VIII, 666 pages. 1991.

Vol. 524: G. Rozenberg (Ed.), Advances in Petri Nets 1991. VIII, 572 pages. 1991. pages. 1991.

Vol. 525: O. Günther, H.-J. Schek (Eds.), Advances in Spatial Databases. Proceedings, 1991. XI, 471 pages. 1991.

Vol. 526: T. Ito, A. R. Meyer (Eds.), Theoretical Aspects of Computer Software. Proceedings, 1991. X, 772 pages. 1991.

Vol. 527: J.C.M. Baeten, J. F. Groote (Eds.), CONCUR '91. Proceedings, 1991. VIII, 541 pages. 1991.

Vol. 528: J. Maluszynski, M. Wirsing (Eds.), Programming Language Implementation and Logic Programming. Proceedings, 1991. XI, 433 pages. 1991.

Vol. 529: L. Budach (Ed.), Fundamentals of Computation Theory. Proceedings, 1991. XII, 426 pages. 1991.

Vol. 530: D. H. Pitt, P.-L. Curien, S. Abramsky, A. M. Pitts, A. Poigné, D. E. Rydeheard (Eds.), Category Theory and Computer Science. Proceedings, 1991. VII, 301 pages. 1991.

Vol. 531: E. M. Clarke, R. P. Kurshan (Eds.), Computer-Aided Verification. Proceedings, 1990. XIII, 372 pages. 1991.

Vol. 532: H. Ehrig, H.-J. Kreowski, G. Rozenberg (Eds.), Graph Grammars and Their Application to Computer Science. Proceedings, 1990. X, 703 pages. 1991.

Vol. 533: E. Börger, H. Kleine Büning, M. M. Richter, W. Schönfeld (Eds.), Computer Science Logic. Proceedings, 1990. VIII, 399 pages. 1991.

Vol. 534: H. Ehrig, K. P. Jantke, F. Orejas, H. Reichel (Eds.), Recent Trends in Data Type Specification. Proceedings, 1990. VIII, 379 pages. 1991.

Vol. 535: P. Jorrand, J. Kelemen (Eds.), Fundamentals of Artificial Intelligence Research. Proceedings, 1991. VIII, 255 pages. 1991. (Subseries LNAI).

Vol. 536: J. E. Tomayko, Software Engineering Education. Proceedings, 1991. VIII, 296 pages. 1991.

Vol. 537: A. J. Menezes, S. A. Vanstone (Eds.), Advances in Cryptology – CRYPTO '90. Proceedings. XIII, 644 pages. 1991.

Vol. 538: M. Kojima, N. Megiddo, T. Noma, A. Yoshise, A Unified Approach to Interior Point Algorithms for Linear Complementarity Problems. VIII, 108 pages. 1991.

Vol. 539: H. F. Mattson, T. Mora, T. R. N. Rao (Eds.), Applied Algebra, Algebraic Algorithms and Error-Correcting Codes. Proceedings, 1991. XI, 489 pages. 1991.

Vol. 540: A. Prieto (Ed.), Artificial Neural Networks. Proceedings, 1991. XIII, 476 pages. 1991.

Vol. 541: P. Barahona, L. Moniz Pereira, A. Porto (Eds.), EPIA '91. Proceedings, 1991. VIII, 292 pages. 1991. (Subseries LNAI).

Vol. 542: Z. W. Ras, M. Zemankova (Eds.), Methodologies for Intelligent Systems. Proceedings, 1991. X, 644 pages. 1991. (Subseries LNAI).

Vol. 543: J. Dix, K. P. Jantke, P. H. Schmitt (Eds.), Nonmonotonic and Inductive Logic. Proceedings, 1990. X, 243 pages. 1991. (Subseries LNAI).

Vol. 544: M. Broy, M. Wirsing (Eds.), Methods of Programming. XII, 268 pages. 1991.

Vol. 545: H. Alblas, B. Melichar (Eds.), Attribute Grammars, Applications and Systems. Proceedings, 1991. IX, 513 pages. 1991.

Vol. 546: O. Herzog, C.-R. Rollinger (Eds.), Text Understanding in LILOG. XI, 738 pages. 1991. (Subseries LNAI).

Vol. 547: D. W. Davies (Ed.), Advances in Cryptology – EUROCRYPT '91. Proceedings, 1991. XII, 556 pages. 1991.

Vol. 548: R. Kruse, P. Siegel (Eds.), Symbolic and Quantitative Approaches to Uncertainty. Proceedings, 1991. XI, 362 pages. 1991.

Vol. 549: E. Ardizzone, S. Gaglio, F. Sorbello (Eds.), Trends in Artificial Intelligence. Proceedings, 1991. XIV, 479 pages. 1991. (Subseries LNAI).

Vol. 550: A. van Lamsweerde, A. Fugetta (Eds.), ESEC '91. Proceedings, 1991. XII, 515 pages. 1991.

Vol. 551: S. Prehn, W. J. Toetenel (Eds.), VDM '91. Formal Software Development Methods. Volume 1. Proceedings, 1991. XIII, 699 pages. 1991.

Vol. 552: S. Prehn, W. J. Toetenel (Eds.), VDM '91. Formal Software Development Methods. Volume 2. Proceedings, 1991. XIV, 430 pages. 1991.

Vol. 553: H. Bieri, H. Noltemeier (Eds.), Computational Geometry - Methods, Algorithms and Applications '91. Proceedings, 1991. VIII, 320 pages. 1991.

Vol. 554: G. Grahne, The Problem of Incomplete Information in Relational Databases. VIII, 156 pages. 1991.

Vol. 555: H. Maurer (Ed.), New Results and New Trends in Computer Science. Proceedings, 1991. VIII, 403 pages. 1991.

Vol. 556: J.-M. Jacquet, Conclog: A Methodological Approach to Concurrent Logic Programming. XII, 781 pages. 1991.

Vol. 557: W. L. Hsu, R. C. T. Lee (Eds.), ISA '91 Algorithms. Proceedings, 1991. X, 396 pages. 1991.

Vol. 558: J. Hooman, Specification and Compositional Verification of Real-Time Systems. VIII, 235 pages. 1991.

Vol. 559: G. Butler, Fundamental Algorithms for Permutation Groups. XII, 238 pages. 1991.

Vol. 560: S. Biswas, K. V. Nori (Eds.), Foundations of Software Technology and Theoretical Computer Science. Proceedings, 1991. X, 420 pages. 1991.

Vol. 561: C. Ding, G. Xiao, W. Shan, The Stability Theory of Stream Ciphers. IX, 187 pages. 1991.

Vol. 562: R. Breu, Algebraic Specification Techniques in Object Oriented Programming Environments. XI, 228 pages. 1991.

Vol. 563: A. Karshmer, J. Nehmer (Eds.), Operating Systems of the 90s and Beyond. Proceedings, 1991. X, 285 pages. 1991.

Vol. 564: I. Herman, The Use of Projective Geometry in Computer Graphics. VIII, 146 pages. 1992.

Vol. 565: J. D. Becker, I. Eisele, F. W. Mündemann (Eds.), Parallelism, Learning, Evolution. Proceedings, 1989. VIII, 525 pages. 1991. (Subseries LNAI).

Vol. 566: C. Delobel, M. Kifer, Y. Masunaga (Eds.), Deductive and Object-Oriented Databases. Proceedings, 1991. XV, 581 pages. 1991.

Vol. 567: H. Boley, M. M. Richter (Eds.), Processing Declarative Kowledge. Proceedings, 1991. XII, 427 pages. 1991. (Subseries LNAI).

Vol. 568: H.-J. Bürckert, A Resolution Principle for a Logic with Restricted Quantifiers. X, 116 pages. 1991. (Subseries LNAI).

Vol. 569: A. Beaumont, G. Gupta (Eds.), Parallel Execution of Logic Programs. Proceedings, 1991. VII, 195 pages. 1991.

Vol. 570: R. Berghammer, G. Schmidt (Eds.), Graph-Theoretic Concepts in Computer Science. Proceedings, 1991. VIII, 253 pages. 1992.

Vol. 571: J. Vytopil (Ed.), Formal Techniques in Real-Time and Fault-Tolerant Systems. Proceedings, 1992. IX, 620 pages. 1991.

Vol. 572: K. U. Schulz (Ed.), Word Equations and Related Topics. Proceedings, 1990. VII, 256 pages. 1992.

Vol. 573: G. Cohen, S. N. Litsyn, A. Lobstein, G. Zémor (Eds.), Algebraic Coding. Proceedings, 1991. X, 158 pages. 1992.

Vol. 574: J. P. Banâtre, D. Le Métayer (Eds.), Research Directions in High-Level Parallel Programming Languages. Proceedings, 1991. VIII, 387 pages. 1992.

Vol. 575: K. G. Larsen, A. Skou (Eds.), Computer Aided Verification. Proceedings, 1991. X, 487 pages. 1992.